During the early 20th century, and even
during the late 19th, many more people – not
just the very wealthy – began to travel abroad.
The photographs of Venice (this page),
Florence and Palermo (following pages) show
how these cites would have looked to travelers
of that era. Venice's island of San Giorgio
Maggiore, with its elegant domed church and
tall campanile, was once a free port, as is
indicated by its two lighthouse towers.

In Florence the waters of the Arno were once so clean that laundresses (like the ones seen above, near the Santa Trinità Bridge) washed clothes in the river. On the Ponte Vecchio (right) goldsmiths and silversmiths displayed their wares in *madielle* (small stalls). The main picture on this page shows the Palazzo Vecchio, on the magnificent Piazza della Signoria, in the 1890's.

The most adventurous travelers, especially the British, journeyed the entire length of Italy and on to Sicily, attracted by the island's beauty. The photograph above shows Palazzo Bonagia, one of Palermo's most sumptuous residences. Below, two Gothic arches, spanning Via Matteo Bonello, join the façade of the cathedral to the bell tower (*c.*1890's).

EVERYMAN GUIDES
PUBLISHED BY DAVID CAMPBELL PUBLISHERS LTD, LONDON

ITALY – ISBN 1-85715-843-1

© 1998 David Campbell Publishers Ltd

Originally published in Italy by Touring Club Italiano. Copyright © 1997
by Touring Editore s.r.l. Milan, 1997. Architecture and nature sections
copyright © Éditions Nouveaux-Loisirs, Paris, 1997

First published 1998

NUMEROUS SPECIALISTS AND ACADEMICS HAVE
CONTRIBUTED TO THIS GUIDE.

ITALY:
EDITORS: Fabio Pelliccia *with the assistance of*
Luca Giannini and Alda Venturi
GRAPHICS: Silvia Pecora *with the assistance of*
Marta Del Zanna and Marina Forlizzi
PICTURE RESEARCH: Irvana Malabarba and
Pupa Bologna *with the assistance of*
Rocco Testa
NATURE: Mario Chiodetti
HISTORY: Gianni Bagioli
ARTS AND TRADITIONS: Italo Sordi
FOOD: Marco Guarnaschelli Gotti
ARCHITECTURE: Flavio Conti
ITALY AS SEEN BY PAINTERS: Silvia Mascheroni
ITALY AS SEEN BY WRITERS: Lucinda Gane

ITINERARIES:
TURIN: Gian Michele Tortolone
GENOA: Roberto Peretta
MILAN: Roberto Peretta
VENICE: Roberto Peretta
BOLOGNA: Roberto Peretta
FLORENCE: Luca Giannini
PERUGIA: Luca Carra
ROME: Carla Compostella and Luca Giannini
NAPLES: Roberto Peretta
BARI: Adriano Bon
PALERMO: Franco Barbagallo and Adriano
Bon
CAGLIARI: Luca Carro

TECHNICAL COORDINATION: Giovanni Schiona

MAPS:
Servizio cartografico Touring Editore s.r.l.
(endpaper maps), L'Atelier, Modena (map of
the city), Éditions Gallimard (regional maps)

TRANSLATED BY LORNA MACFARLANE, JENNIFER MACKINLAY,
ROGER O'KEEFE AND SUE ROSE.
EDITED AND TYPESET BY BOOK CREATION SERVICES, LONDON.
PRINTED IN ITALY BY EDITORIALE LIBRARIA.

EVERYMAN GUIDES
79 Berwick Street
London W1V 3PF

ITALY

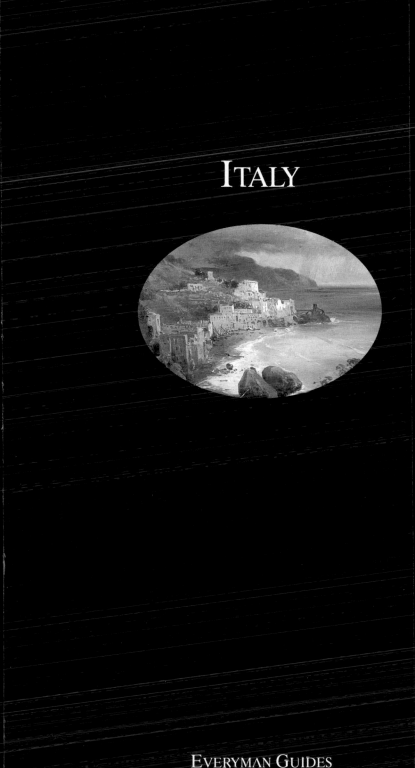

EVERYMAN GUIDES

Contents

HOW TO USE THIS GUIDE

The symbols at the top of each page refer to the different parts of the guide:

■ NATURAL ENVIRONMENT

● KEYS TO UNDERSTANDING

▲ ITINERARIES

◆ PRACTICAL INFORMATION

The mini-map locates the particular itinerary within the wider area covered by the guide.

The itinerary map shows the main points of interest along the way and is intended to help you find your bearings.

● ▲ ■ ◆
The symbols alongside a title or within the text itself provide cross-references to a theme or place dealt with elsewhere in the guide.

★ The star symbol signifies that a particular site has been singled out by the publishers for its special beauty, atmosphere or cultural interest.

CROSSING BACK OVER THE ARNO

Variety is the keynote in the part of the city between the Palazzo Pitti and San Frediano: the stately architecture of Via Maggio is little more than a stone's throw away from the lovely medieval buildings on Borgo San Jacopo, while not far from the elegant palaces

Nature

THE ITALIAN LANDSCAPE

MONTE ROSA
This group of peaks in the Alps has over 2,500 glaciers. It is an important source for Italy's river systems.

Although it is not a particularly large country, Italy enjoys great variety in its landscape, due in part to its geological history. In the Cenozoic era, around 65 million years ago, the collision of the African and European plates formed Italy's two great mountain ranges, the Alps and the Apennines. Surrounding these were deep depressions, which were later covered partly by detritus, becoming plains or hills, and partly by the sea. Over the past million years the alternation of warm and glacial periods has determined the form of the terrain, creating a landscape of great beauty and variety. If you travel the length of Italy (a distance of less than 1,000 miles), you will pass from a subtropical climate in Sicily to year-round snow in parts of the Alps.

The birthplace of ancient civilizations, Sardinia couples splendid coasts with a mountainous interior.

The Tuscan archipelago, made up of Elba and other smaller islands, lies between Tuscany and Corsica.

Sicily, with a total area of just under 1,000 square miles, is not only Italy's largest island but also the largest in the whole of the Mediterranean.

LAKE TRASIMENE
The lakeside landscapes of Italy are among the most interesting and varied, ranging from the majesty of the great lakes of the north to the tranquil beauty of those further south, like Lake Trasimene in Umbria.

SANDY COASTLINES
The Italian coastline is nearly 5,000 miles long, with numerous sandy beaches, like the sands of Tindari (above), and dunes.

ROCKY COASTLINES
The rocky Sardinian coast is home to many species of animal, including the increasingly rare monk seal.

THE PO VALLEY
Surrounded by the Alps, the Apennines and the Adriatic Sea, the Po valley is one of the most densely populated areas of Italy. In places, there are over 1,000 inhabitants per 0.4 square miles.

THE APENNINES
Geologically older than the Alps, the Apennines have lower, more rounded peaks. They are divided into the Northern, Abruzzan, Umbro-Marchan and Southern Apennines (*Appennino settentrionale, abruzzese, umbro-marchigiano, meridionale*).

The Po river, stretching 405 miles from Monviso in Piedmont to the Adriatic Sea, is Italy's longest river.

The curve of the Alps, which extends from Piedmont and the Valle d'Aosta to Friuli-Venezia Giulia, divides Italy from the neighboring countries: France, Switzerland, Austria and Slovenia.

The Apennine ridge runs the length of the Italian peninsula and contributes to the variety of Italy's climate and natural environments.

The volcanically formed lakes of central Italy are a reminder of the turbulent geological history of this area.

Widespread from Liguria to Puglia and encouraged by the Mediterranean climate, olive growing represents not only a major economic factor in Italian society, but also an important cultural one.

THE MEDITERRANEAN CLIMATE
The sea has a beneficial influence on the climate of the south and its islands, raising the mean annual temperature to 63°F.

THE ALPINE CLIMATE
The Alps have a fixed climate, characterized by cold winters with frequent snowfalls and hard frosts, even at low altitudes.

The Sciliar is a
dolomitic massif in south Tyrol/Alto
Adige which overlooks the vast plateaux of the Swiss Alps.
In 1974 the Sciliar Natural Park (*Parco Naturale dello Sciliar*)
was established by the provincial authorities of Bolzano. It is
characterized on one side by the rock faces, steep peaks and
ledges that typify the wilder aspects of the Alpine climate. On
the other side are the pastures of the Swiss Alps, a lightly farmed
landscape transformed by human enterprise in harmony with

nature. The compact shape of
the Sciliar results from the layers
of loam covering the central
block of the Dolomites. Such is
the geological importance of this
mountain range that the rock
of which it is composed is known
as Sciliar dolomite.

CHAMOIS *Rupicapra rupicapra*
During the summer months chamois live at
high altitudes, but in winter they move down
to the valleys and woods in search of food.

MARMOT *Marmota marmota*
This rodent lives in small family groups and
digs deep, complex underground burrows. Its
whistle can often be heard in the mountains,
emitted as an alarm signal or to assemble the
other marmots.

GOLDEN EAGLE
Aquila chrysaëtos
Eagles fly low over the slopes and above the fringes of woods, hunting for small mammals such as marmots.

THE WOODS
The woods are chiefly composed of spruce, with smaller numbers of Scots pine, silver fir, larch, ash, silver birch and rowan. On hillsides more than 6,000 feet above sea level, these are replaced by the thickets of mountain pine typical of the Dolomites.

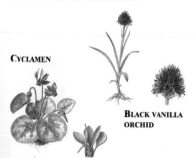

CYCLAMEN

BLACK VANILLA ORCHID

FLORA
Thanks to the diverse nature of the soil and rocks, and the lack of glacier cover during the Pleistocene epoch, the Sciliar possesses a great variety of vegetation. Shown above are cyclamen (*Cyclamen europaeum*) and the black vanilla orchid (*Nigritella nigra*).

MOUNTAIN PINE *Pinus mugo*
An evergreen shrub or tree that favors rocky habitats up to 9,000 feet above sea level. It can grow to as much as 60 feet tall.

19

An ancient gulf which gradually filled with fluvial deposits, the Po valley covers around a sixth of the total area of Italy. There are distinct variations in the landscape: hills alternate with cultivated fields, reclaimed land and canals. This region can be divided into two parts, the high and the low plains. The high plain is more arid, with zones of moorland and sparse trees; here cultivation has always been difficult, and today it is home to a variety of industrial complexes. In contrast, the low plain is well watered, which allows for intense agricultural exploitation. This has changed the natural landscape, transforming it into paddies and rice fields, crossed by a dense network of man-made channels.

EDIBLE FROG
Rana esculenta
Once extremely common in the rice fields, frogs have suffered a drastic

GREAT DIVING BEETLE
Dytiscus marginalis
This carnivorous aquatic beetle is a strong swimmer, and even preys on fish and small amphibians.

THE RICE FIELD
At one time these paddies supported a rich ecosystem. Today egrets and night herons are still commonly found here.

reduction in numbers as a result of the use of pesticides.

POPLAR TREES
Poplars have been planted among the rice paddies, fields and meadows. The two characteristic species are the white poplar (*Populus alba*) and the black poplar (*Populus nigra*).

1 Harvest mouse
(*Micromys minutus*)
2 Rabbit
(*Oryctolagus cuniculus*)
3 Mole
(*Talpa europaea*)

MOORHEN *Gallinula chloropus*
Lives in wet zones, such as ditches, streams, and ponds rich in vegetation.

BLACK-WINGED STILT
Himantopus himantopus
Eats insects on the surface of water and in shallow marshes.

PURPLE HERON *Ardea purpurea*
Lives in the reed beds, where it thrives on a diet of frogs and fish.

■ THE VENETIAN LAGOON

The geography of the Venetian lagoon is characterized by *velme* – muddy depths that emerge at low tide – and *barene*, grass-covered islets that are awash at high tide.

A lagoon is formed between the confines of land and sea by tidal movement and fresh water running from rivers. The flowing water carries alluvium, which forms thin stretches of sand, eventually enclosing a section of sea. The innermost part of the lagoon, which is known as the *laguna morte* ("dead lagoon"), contains small pools among bogs and marshy vegetation where the water has evaporated. The Venetian lagoon is the largest in Italy (136,000 acres). It is strewn with small islands that are subject to tidal activity, and encompasses a variety of ecosystems.

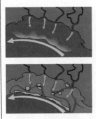

THE FORMATION OF LAGOONS
Silt and detritus carried by the river and molded by marine currents are deposited on the sea bed, creating an offshore sand bar, known as a barrier; eventually the water of the lagoon becomes completely enclosed. To prevent excessive build-up of sand, engineers often divert the course of the main rivers flowing into a lagoon. This modification of the landscape strikes a balance between the needs of man and those of nature.

SEDGE WARBLER
Acrocephalus schoenobaenus
Found in reed beds or vegetation bordering lakes and rivers. Often sings in flight.

GREAT REED WARBLER
Acrocephalus arundinaceus
Almost as big as a starling, it has a distinctive song with harsh, shrill notes.

WATER RAIL
Rallus aquaticus
Commonly found by ponds, this elusive bird is especially active at sunset.

REED BUNTING
Emberiza schoeniclus
Lives in reed beds and, in the winter, in cultivated fields. The male has a characteristic black "hood".

Mestre

Porto Marghera

Vittorio Emanuele Canal

Malamocco Marghera Canal

MALAMOCCO BASIN

CHIOGGIA BASIN

Sile

Iesolo

MAGGIORE
MARSH

Torcello

Mazzorbo

San Felice
Canal

Burano

LIDO
BASIN

urano

Treporti

Murano Canal

Treporti Canal

VENICE

Sant'Erasmo

Le Vignole

Porto di Lido

Giudecca
Canal

Lido

MEDITERRANEAN GULL
During the mating season the
head is chocolate brown.

San Michele

decca

Malamocco

WATERSHED

Porto di
Malamocco

San Pietro
in Volta

Pellestrina

1 Mantis shrimp   7 Sardines
2 Gray mullet   8 Anchovies
3 Bass   9 Sole
4 Orifrango   10 Gurnard
5 Red mullets   11 Eel
6 Gilthead   12 Cuttlefish

Porto di
Chioggia

Chioggia

Sottomarina

Brenta

**FISHING
IN THE LAGOON**
The local fishermen
have developed a
number of techniques
for catching fish,
including the use of
outriggers, baskets
tied to their boats,
fixed vertical nets,
and devices to steer
the fish into the nets.

23

Established in
1923, the Abruzzi National Park
(*Parco Nazionale d'Abruzzo*) extends
along the extreme southerly section
of the Abruzzan Apennines. Most of the
Abruzzi has a typical limestone landscape,
but there are dolomitic areas (some of them
calcareous) in the Camosciara, the Canneto valley
and Mount Godi, and loamy or sandy soils in the
lower-lying areas.

THE CAMOSCIARA
The Camosciara,
in the southern part
of the park, is a
protected reserve.
The chamois (which
give the region its
name) are easily
spotted and can be
approached, as they
are accustomed
to the presence of
tourists.

MARSICAN BROWN BEAR
Ursus arctos marsicanus
Intense hunting has threatened the survival
of this species, of which only about a hundred
animals remain. The park authorities now
guarantee compensation to farmers whose
crops or livestock are damaged by the bears,
and this has led to a reduction in poaching.
Recently, Marsican brown bears have also
been seen outside the park, in places such as
the Maiella massif.

WHITE-BACKED WOODPECKER
Dendrocopus lilfordi
Its strong laughing call is heard in spring.

ROCK THRUSH
Monticola saxatilis
Its song is very varied and melodic.

WALLCREEPER
Tichodroma muraria
Feeds on insects and spiders. During the winter it comes down from the woods and visits inhabited areas in the foothills, where it searches for food among castles, towers and ruins.

LADY'S SLIPPER
Cypripedium calceolus
Found throughout the park, especially in mixed woods of broadleaved trees and conifers. One of the most beautiful wild orchids, it is a protected plant.

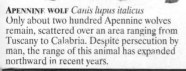

APENNINE WOLF *Canis lupus italicus*
Only about two hundred Apennine wolves remain, scattered over an area ranging from Tuscany to Calabria. Despite persecution by man, the range of this animal has expanded northward in recent years.

ORSINI'S VIPER *Vipera ursinii*
This is the smallest and least poisonous of the Italian vipers. It lives in grassy meadows around 6,500 feet above sea level.

THE MAREMMA NATIONAL PARK AND THE TRAPPOLA MARSHES

The Uccellina coast.

Maremma ("swampland") is an apt description for the flat land along the Tuscan coast, made marshy by frequent river floods. The Maremma National Park is perhaps the last stretch of this distinctive coastline preserved in its original state. The park encompasses the Trappola marshes, the mouth of the Ombrone river and the Uccellina mountains. The Trappola marshes, between Principina a Mare and the mouth of the Ombrone, contain sparse vegetation intermingled with semi-dry meadows, thickets of maquis, and pines. During the migratory months they are host to a multitude of waterside birds. The northern part of the park is characterized by sandy coasts, while the southern part has rocky cliffs interrrupted by small inlets. The Maremma National Park (*Parco Nazionale della Maremma*) is situated south of Grosseto, between the Via Aurelia and the sea.

HOLM OAK
Quercus ilex
This species is found either as a bush in the maquis or as a tree up to 65 feet high.

STONE PINE *Pinus pinea*
Unmistakable because of its umbrella-like shape, the stone pine is typical of this coastline. It is cultivated for its pine nuts.

MYRTLE *Myrtus communis*
A highly aromatic evergreen shrub. The berries are used to make a perfumed liqueur, while the leaves yield an essential oil used in fragrances.

Flowers on the Maremma dunes. The plants that grow along the sandy shores of the Maremma have developed a tolerance to the salty environment – as well as an ability to flourish on beaches, in the unlikely medium of sand.

The Ombrone river at Trappola. These marshes were once typical of this damp area of Tuscan coastline. Waders and other wintering birds, as well a variety of mammals (foxes, badgers, coypu), are attracted by the abundance of food.

WILD BOAR *Sus scrofa*
Gathers in groups, formed exclusively of mothers with babies of various ages. Burrowing with its snout, it leaves deep furrows in the earth.

BLUE ROCK THRUSH
Monticola solitarius
The male has splendid slate-blue plumage. It nests among rocks or in old ruins.

SEA DAFFODIL
Pancratium maritimum
The large white flowers of this plant decorate the sand dunes.

PEREGRINE FALCON
Falco peregrinus
Nests on rocky cliffs. Extremely fast, it can prey on medium-sized birds, capturing them in mid flight with spectacular strikes.

PORCUPINE *Hystrix cristata*
This is one of the largest Italian rodents. It gathers in small groups, lives in deep dens and is a nocturnal creature.

POND TORTOISE *Emys orbicularis*
Usually to be found in still or slow-flowing waters. Often remains on the surface of the water.

■ VOLCANOS

A string of volcanos stretches from Tuscany to Sicily in the belt between the Tyrrhenian coast and the Apennines. In the north the volcanos are older and have been inactive longer, while the southern volcanos were formed more recently and are often still live. The most famous are Vesuvius and Etna, the largest active volcano in Europe. Its fascination lies not only in its grandiose eruptions and incandescent lava flows, but also in the unique environment surrounding it. The lower slopes are covered by typical Mediterranean vegetation, which gives way to endemic species as the altitude increases, until at 10,000 feet above sea level the lava desert finally begins.

BLACK REDSTART
Phoenicurus ochruros
This bird is often found along rocky shores and sings perched on walls and rooftops.

PAINTED LADY
Cynthia cardui
A handsome butterfly that completes long migrations from Sicily to the Sahara and back.

GREEN HAIRSTREAK
Callophrys rubi
Camouflages itself well against Etna's thick vegetation.

LEOPARD SNAKE *Elaphe situla*
A snake that favors rocky places exposed to the sun.

WILDCAT *Felis silvestris*
A mainly solitary nocturnal animal that silently stalks its prey before pouncing.

MOUNT ETNA BROOM *Ginestra aetnensis*
A thorny shrub with bright yellow flowers. This type of broom grows on the slopes of Etna and is an endemic species.

GARDEN DORMOUSE *Eliomys quercinus*
A capable climber, this dormouse builds its nest in holes in tree trunks or cracks in walls and among rocks.

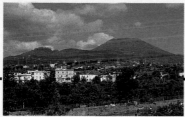

The slopes of Vesuvius are densely populated; consequently the volcano's caprices present a potential danger for the 700,000 people living within a 4-mile radius of the crater.

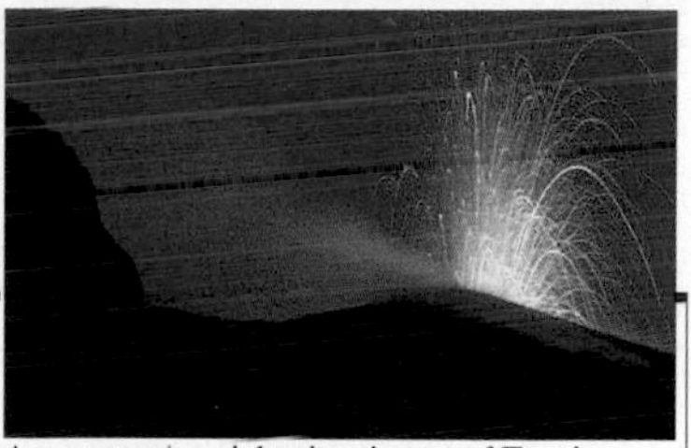

A spectacular night-time image of Etna's eruption in 1984. This major European volcano is surrounded by a regional park of the same name.

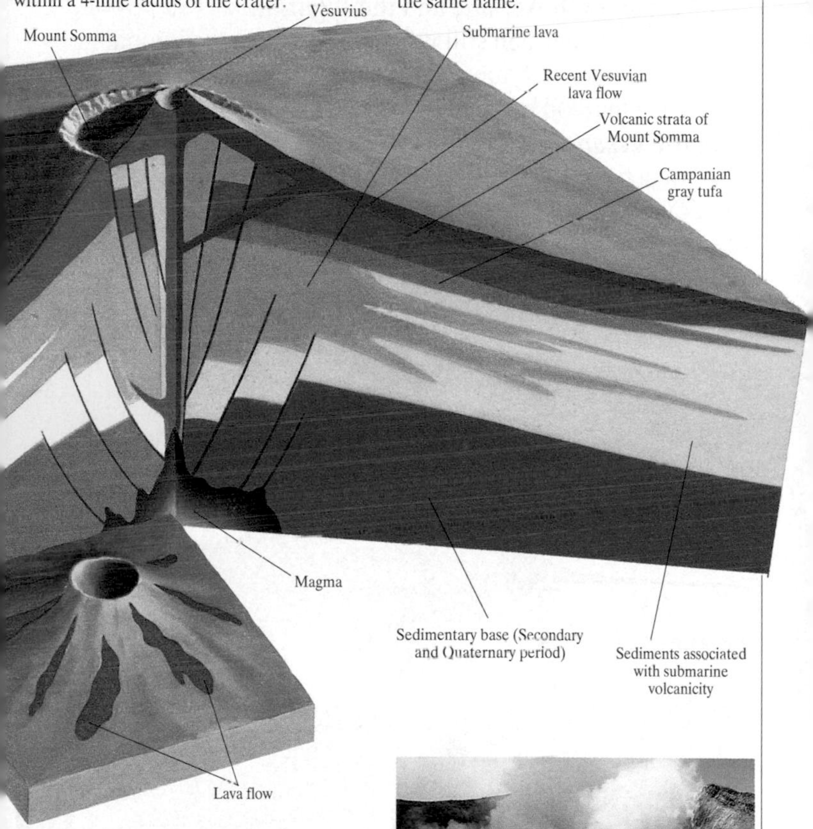

Vesuvius
Mount Somma
Submarine lava
Recent Vesuvian lava flow
Volcanic strata of Mount Somma
Campanian gray tufa
Magma
Sedimentary base (Secondary and Quaternary period)
Sediments associated with submarine volcanicity
Lava flow

THE VOLCANOS OF SOUTHERN ITALY

There are plenty of volcanos between Campania and Sicily. Some remain active, and all create fertile terrain and crumbly rock. Although the most famous volcano in Campania is Vesuvius, which is still active, the whole of the area around Pozzuoli and the Phlegrean Fields (between Naples and Cumae) is characterized by volcanic phenomena and frequent steam emissions.

VULSINI
SABATINI
ALBANI
ERNICI
ROCCAMONFINA
VULTURE
VESUVIO
STROMBOLI
USTICA
LIPARI
VULCANO
ETNA
PANTELLERIA

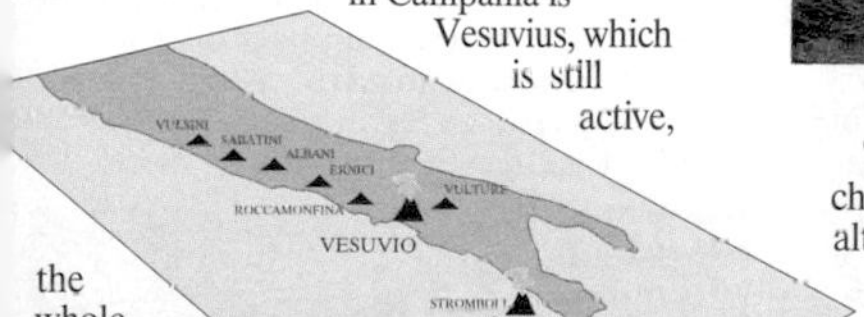

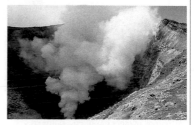

FLORA AND LAVA ON ETNA

The slopes of this Sicilian volcano are characterized by rich vegetation. At lower altitudes, as on the rest of the island, typical Mediterranean vegetation can be found. Higher up, the vegetation becomes increasingly enriched with endemic species (which originate from pre-existing forms adapted to the volcanic climate). Finally, in the zone above 10,000 feet one reaches the lava desert, with its extreme environmental conditions (pictured above). The top 2,000 feet of Etna are covered with snow for long periods.

■ FISHING IN THE MEDITERRANEAN

The *passerella*, a typical Messinan craft used for fishing for swordfish.

Although Italy has an extensive and varied coastline, there are relatively few places that support a typical seafaring way of life. The most notable examples are Sicily, Naples, the north Adriatic and the Ligurian Sea. Sicilian fishermen still use time-honored traditional methods. They catch the second largest quantity of fish in all Italy. One method is the *mattanza*, which involves killing tuna fish in *carnere della morte* ("death-chambers"). Another is to use a *passerella*, a special boat from Messina: from the top of its 100-foot central trellis mast, fishermen can spot shoals of swordfish in the depths.

TUNA *Thunnus thynnus*

SWORDFISH *Xiphias gladius*

Although tuna fishing is an ancient Sicilian tradition, nowadays it is practiced by a decreasing number of skilled fishermen. The photographs show: (**1**) the boats setting off for the *mattanza* at dawn; (**2** and **3**) the crucial moment in tuna fishing, accompanied by shouts and colors, mingling in a lively scene *da corrida* (here pictured on the island of Favignana in the Egadi archipelago); and finally (**4**) gutting the fish, back on shore.

History

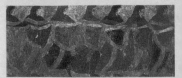

The peoples of pre-Roman Italy

1800 BC
Beginning of Nuraghic civilization in Sardinia

1000–800 BC
Peak of Villanovian culture

7TH–5TH CENTURY BC
Most magnificent period in Etruscan civilization

From the Paleolithic to the Iron Age. In the period 10,000–8000 BC the population of what is now Italy began to take on its unique characteristics. Around 5000 BC the expansion of agriculture allowed for the first stable settlements in the south, while in the north it was not until 3000 BC that the first lakeside and coastal settlements appeared. During the last few centuries of the second millennium BC and the opening centuries of the first, the regional map of Italian civilizations began to take shape: in the central and southern parts of the peninsula the so-called Italic peoples established themselves (Umbrians, Latins, Volscians, Samnites and others); the northeast

753 BC
Legendary date for founding of Rome

753–510 BC
Rome ruled by seven legendary kings

415 BC
Athenian offensive against Syracuse

312 BC
Via Appia opens from Rome to Capua

287 BC
Archimedes is born in Syracuse

was occupied by the Venetians and the northwest by the Ligurians, while the Sardinians and Sicilians inhabited the two major islands. This situation changed with the flowering of the first urban civilizations (Etruscan and Greek), from 800–700 BC, and with the arrival in what is now known as the Po valley of French tribes of Celtic descent (from the 6th to the 5th century BC).

The rise and fall of the Etruscans. By 900 BC the Etruscans had already established themselves in the region between the valleys of the Arno and the Tiber. There they built their most important cities, among them Arezzo, Chiusi, Cortona, Orvieto, Perugia, Populonia, Tarquinia and Volterra. Etruscan society was structured not as a single nation but around city-states headed by a priestly king called the *lucumone*. Their economic and cultural dominance over the peoples of central Italy remained unchallenged until the 5th century BC. The Etruscans' slow demise, already beginning in 400 BC, was accelerated by the military expansion of the Roman Empire – which from the 3rd century BC became increasingly aggressive and powerful, and was eventually responsible for the extinction of this fascinating civilization ▲ *326*.

> **"... Happy in the tawny pelt/ his nurse, the she-wolf, wears, young Romulus/ will take the leadership, build walls of Mars,/ and call by his own name his people, Romans."** Virgil, *The Aeniad*

THE GREEKS.

An important phenomenon of the period 800–500 BC was the migration that pushed tens of thousands of Greeks toward Sicily and southern Italy, into the area known as Magna Graecia. This included the Tyrrhenian and Ionian coasts in the south, where the cities of Paestum (in Campania) and Taranto (in Puglia) were built. In Sicily Greek colonizers encountered the Phoenicians, who had founded Mozia and Palermo on the west coast. The first wave of immigrants (735 BC) populated colonies on the Ionian coast, founding Naxos and Syracuse (the latter is of particular note, as it saw the flowering of the genius of Archimedes, Aeschylus and Pindar). Subsequently colonies were founded at Gela and Selinunte, then Agrigento and Taormina.

216 BC
Hannibal defeats the Romans at Cannae

31 BC
Octavian defeats Antony and Cleopatra at Actium

14 BC
Augustus dies and is succeeded by Tiberius

AD 79
Eruption of Vesuvius destroys Pompeii and Herculaneum

117–38
Hadrian is emperor

THE SUPREMACY OF ROME

ROMAN UNIFICATION. The first unification of Italy (the second came two thousand years later) was achieved by the Romans in just over two centuries, from 400–200 BC, although the extension of the Italian border as far as the Alps was only made official in 42 BC.

FROM MONARCHY TO REPUBLIC. When it was ruled by kings, from the 8th to the 6th century BC, Rome alternately fought against and allied itself with the Sabines and the Etruscans. After the establishment of the *lega latina* (Latin law) in 494 BC, Roman expansion was unstoppable. The Etruscans and Samnites were conquered, and the overthrow of Taranto brought the submission of the south, as well as Sicily and Sardinia. As for Alpine Gaul, the founding of Aquileia in 181 BC sealed its conquest. The Republic's final century saw the consolidation of Rome's grip on the Mediterranean, despite the rivalry of Marius and Sulla and that of Caesar and Pompey.

271–5
Construction of the Aurelian walls around Rome

293
Diocletian divides the Roman Empire in four

326
First basilica of St Peter's inaugurated in Rome

374
Saint Ambrose proclaimed Bishop of Milan

THE IMPERIAL AGE. The murder of Julius Caesar in 44 BC was followed by a turbulent transitional period for the Republic, culminating in 27 BC when Octavian became the first Roman emperor, choosing the title of Augustus. The empire lasted five centuries and left innumerable examples of its art and civilization all over Europe. On the political and administrative level it was already in crisis in the 3rd century AD, but it survived until the last emperor of the West, Romulus Augustulus, was deposed by Odoacer in Ravenna in 476.

402
Ravenna becomes capital of the Empire of the West

476
Odoacer deposes Romulus Augustulus

The "Augustus of Primaporta", in the Vatican Museums, one of the most famous masterpieces of Roman sculpture.

INVASIONS AND INCURSIONS

GOTHS AND BYZANTINES.

A people of Baltic origin, the Goths were historically divided into Visigoths (who ransacked Rome in AD 410, headed by Alaric ▲ *341*) and

Ostrogoths, whose chief Theodoric ruled Italy from Ravenna ▲ *267* between AD 493 and 526. After his death, Justinian instigated a war against the Goths in an attempt to bring Italy under the direct control of the Eastern (Byzantine) Empire. This war, which lasted from 535 to 553, devastated the entire Italian peninsula, resulting in the imposition of a harsh fiscal regime.

FROM THE LOMBARDS TO THE ARABS.

The Lombards were a people of Germanic descent who stormed Pavia in 572, making it the capital of their new kingdom and smashing the country's territorial unity. However, some of the provinces remained Byzantine, including Ravenna, Rome, Naples, Sicily and Sardinia. Spoleto and Benevento were among the longest

established of the Lombard duchies. Charlemagne, King of the Carolingian Franks, was invited into Italy by Pope Hadrian I and overthrew the Lombards in 774. The reign of the Franks was the most stable of the Roman-barbaric kingdoms. The coronation of Charlemagne as emperor in St Peter's in Rome, on Christmas Day, AD 800, signaled the birth of the Holy Roman Empire, which extended across western Europe. Nevertheless, by the mid 9th century the breakdown of the Franco-Carolingian empire had already commenced. The Arab conquest of Sicily (827–902) introduced new protagonists – though ironically this coincided with the first signs of weakening of the Islamic Empire, which stretched from the Iberian peninsula to India. The emirate of Palermo ▲ *446*, which lasted until the second half

of the 11th century, brought economic prosperity and a cultural renaissance to the island of Sicily.

THE NORMANS. After centuries of intermittent incursions from their native Scandinavia, the Normans – or Norsemen, meaning "men of the north" – settled in Normandy. And it was from here, during the 11th century, that they launched their conquests of both England and southern Italy. The leaders in the latter enterprise were the Hautevillians (from the small feudal domain of Hauteville-le-Guichard), who captured Byzantines and Arabs from Sicily and the south. Ruggero II unified the Norman territories during the first half of the 12th century, creating the Kingdom of Naples and Sicily, which

was destined to last, ruled by various dynasties, until 1860.

SWABIANS AND ANGEVINS. The sovereignty of the Swabians (or Hohenstaufens) over southern Italy and Sicily began with Holy Emperor Henry VI, who in 1194 inherited the crown of the last Norman king of Sicily, William the Good. He was succeeded by his son, Frederick II – whose own son Manfred was defeated at Benevento in 1266 by Charles of Anjou (son of King Louis VIII of France), summoned to Italy by Pope Urban IV to aid the papal cause. The last Hohenstaufen, Corradine, was decapitated in Naples aged sixteen, in 1268. The victory of Charles of Anjou signaled the decline of the Ghibelline estates in Italy. The new sovereign ruled the Norman and Swabian territories from Naples, but his successors had to surrender to

Sicily, where in 1282 the anti-Angevin rising ▲ 447 known as the Sicilian Vespers provoked Aragonese intervention. The Angevin dynasty survived in Italy until 1435. Seven years later, Sicily was reunited with the Kingdom of Naples under Alfonso of Aragon.

1030
Norman county of Aversa founded

1061
Norman Ruggero I storms Messina

1130–54
Ruggero II of Hauteville is crowned King of Sicily

1174
Founding of the Cathedral of Monreale

1186
Emperor Henry VI marries Constance of Hauteville

1197
Basilica of St Nicholas built in Bari

1229–49
Castel del Monte built in Puglia

1250
Frederick II dies

1266–85
Charles of Anjou crowned King of Naples and Sicily

1282–1302
War of the Sicilian Vespers

PAPACY, EMPIRE AND FREE TOWNS

962
Otto I unites the Italian crown with that of the Germanic Holy Roman Empire

1059
Reconsecration of the baptistery in Florence

1073–85
Papacy of Gregory VII

1088
Founding of the University of Bologna

1094
St Mark's Cathedral in Venice is consecrated

1099
The "Compagna Communis" is instituted in Genoa

1115
Countess Matilda of Canossa dies

1162
Milan capitulates after siege by Frederick Barbarossa

THE CONFLICT OVER INVESTITURE. The rivalry between the papacy and the Holy Roman Empire dominated Italian history for several centuries after AD 1000. The issue of investiture was taken up by the Roman pontiffs, who tried to undermine the so-called "Caesar's papism" introduced by Otto the Great in AD 962. These pontiffs endeavored to establish the *vescovi-conti* ("bishop counts"), and even gave the emperor power of veto over the nomination of the pope. This was extended to the power of direct selection under Henry III (1046) and Niccolò II (1059); and Gregory VII reacted with the *Dictatus Papae* of 1075. This schism gave rise to forty-seven years of counter-depositions and threatened excommunications. It was fear of excommunication that led Henry IV to make a humiliating supplication in Canossa (1077), where Gregory VII was the guest of the Countess Matilda. Eventually peace was agreed by Henry V and Callisto II in Worms in 1122, a compromise which enabled the political establishment of the free towns (*comuni*) that were appearing in central and northern Italy.

THE CONFLICT OVER INDEPENDENT GOVERNMENTS. The Holy Roman Emperor Frederick I, known as Frederick Barbarossa, or "Redbeard", strove to suppress the rise of the gentry – mostly merchants and artisans – in the *comuni* of Verona and Lombardy, but was defeated at Legnano in 1176 and forced to recognize the rights of the free towns. His grandson, Frederick II, continued Barbarossa's efforts to restore the power of the Holy Roman Empire but encountered stubborn resistance from Charles of Anjou, King of Naples and Sicily, who inflicted decisive defeats on Ghibelline forces at Benevento (1266) and Tagliacozzo (1268).

> **"ANYONE WHO WANTS TO SET UP A REPUBLIC IN A TERRITORY WHERE THERE ARE MANY *GENTILUOMINI*, CANNOT SUCCEED UNLESS HE FIRST WIPES THEM ALL OUT."**
>
> NICCOLÒ MACHIAVELLI, *DISCOURSES*

FROM FREE TOWNS TO DOMAINS

THE CULTURE OF THE "COMUNI".

The principal *comuni* (free towns) of central and northern Italy grew up in the 11th and 12th centuries, and gradually expanded as they gained political and economic control of the surrounding countryside and smaller towns; later, during the 13th and 14th centuries, the *comuni* gave way to the *signoria* (lordly domains). This fruitful epoch witnessed the establishment of the first universities and a wider accessibility to literature, which was now available to the emergent bourgeoisie as well as to courtiers. During this period Franciscan ethics inspired medieval religious dramas, and poetry moved on from the Florentine *"dolce stil nuovo"* ("sweet new style") and entered the great era of Dante. In architecture, the period of the *comuni* was typified by solemn Romanesque cathedrals and town halls and by the beginnings of Gothic art in Italy.

THE VARIOUS FORMS OF SIGNORIAL POWER.

The distinctive character of the *signorie* meant that the lords exercised personal power over them and then handed it down within their family or clan. Venice, Genoa and Pisa were exceptions to this rule: in these three cities the governing body consisted of an oligarchy drawn from the mercantile class. Siena also managed to maintain a balance between the representatives of the aristocracy and those of the populace. In Milan the Viscontis ▲ *184*, a Lombard family of feudal origin, took over control of the city and governed it from the end of the 13th century. In Florence it was the Medicis ▲ *275*, of merchant stock, who held power. Although they did not succeed in dismantling the Florentine republican institutions until the 15th century, they ruled the city for a good three centuries. Other long-standing domains were those of the Estes in Ferrara ▲ *265*, the Gonzagas in Mantua ▲ *263*, and the Montefeltros in Urbino ▲ *334*. The rule of the Scaligeri in Verona ▲ *237*, though short-lived, left a rich heritage of art that has survived.

1222
Founding of the
University of Padua

1252
Gold florins issued in
Florence

1267
Saint Thomas Aquinas
begins work on his
Summa Theologiae

1278
Otto Visconti declared
Lord of Milan

1284
Victory of the Genoese
fleet over the Pisan
fleet at Meloria

1295
Marco Polo returns to
Venice after twenty-five
years' absence

1299
The building of the
Palazzo Vecchio
in Florence begins

1303–5
Giotto paints frescos
in the Scrovegni
Chapel in Padua

1311
Duccio di
Buoninsegna's Maestà
altarpiece is erected in
Siena Cathedral

37

The cities of Amalfi, Genoa, Pisa and Venice were known as "the maritime republics", and their coats of arms appear on the flag of the Italian navy, reflecting their power during the most rapid phase of their commercial development (between the 11th and 13th centuries). In fact, these republics had very different, indeed often opposing, histories. Amalfi, already busy with trade in the 10th century, declined after being ransacked by the Pisans in 1135; Pisa, powerful and thriving in the 12th century, was ruined in 1284 when it was defeated by the Genoese at Meloria; Venice and Genoa, the most stable and longest established, fought each other repeatedly in the 13th and 14th centuries. In spite of this, these four Italian maritime republics played a significant role in advancing the culture and civilization of Europe through technological exchanges with the East.

The coats of arms of the four maritime republics. From the left: Amalfi, Genoa, Pisa and Venice.

PISA ▲ 298

Pisa reached its peak around 1165, when it owned the coastline between Portovenere and Civitavecchia, as well as the feudal domain of Sardinia and various rights over Naples, Salerno, Calabria and Sicily.

AMALFI ▲ 415 AND GENOA ▲ 160

Amalfi developed in Byzantine Italy as an independent port serving the inland area as far north as Rome. Genoa began to assert its power in the 11th century, along with Pisa, first in the alliance against the Saracens and then by defeating its pirate rivals.

VENICE ▲ 216

In the 10th century Venice was already one of the principal centers of commerce with the East and with central Europe. It thrived on the special privileges gained from its economic relations with the Byzantine Empire, and by AD 1000 controlled the entire Dalmatian coast. In 1202 the Fourth Crusade, against Constantinople, was actively backed by Venice. Venetians even reached the Far East: in 1275 Marco Polo (left) arrived in Peking after crossing Asia.

39

1418
Brunelleschi wins the competition to design a duomo or cupola for Florence Cathedral

STABILITY IN THE RENAISSANCE. The peace established at Lodi in 1454 ended the war over the succession of the Duchy of Milan and saw the start of forty years of peace between the Italian states, known as the period of "Renaissance stability". This was abruptly shattered (1494) by the French king, Charles VIII, who returned the kingdom of Naples, which had been "usurped" by the Aragonese in 1442, to Angevin rule ▲ *393*.

THE PAPAL STATE. Despite the rifts in the church caused by the move of the papal seat to Avignon (1309–77) and the "schism of the West" (1378–1417), it was between the 14th and 15th centuries that the Papal State strengthened its territorial assets and aligned itself, as a theocratic principality, with the major Italian states of the *ancien régime*.

1442
Alfonso of Aragon is crowned King of Naples and Sicily

The main protagonist of this reorganization was the Spanish cardinal Egidio Albornoz. At the behest of Pope Innocent VI, this unusual "warrior priest" reestablished order in Rome and Lazio and subjugated the local lords of Umbria, the Marche and Romagna.

1459
Mantegna arrives in Mantua

VENICE: "ST MARK'S REPUBLIC". Venice ("la Serenissima") had already confirmed its status as a powerful republic with an impressive naval performance in the Fourth Crusade (1202–4), followed by the storming of Constantinople – an event that had been long desired by the city of doges. The crisis of the Duchy of Milan that followed the death of Gian Galeazzo Visconti (1402) led the Venetian republic to look for new territory.

1469–92
Lorenzo de' Medici ("the Magnificent") is proclaimed Lord of Florence

1499–1500
The troops of King Louis XII of France overthrow the Duchy of Milan

Maclodio's victory over the Milanese (1427) added Brescia and Bergamo to the conquests of Vincenza, Padua, Verona and Udine; and the Treaty of Lodi (1454) established the Adda river as the western border of the Venetian state. However, French troops of the Cambrai league claimed a victory over St Mark's Republic at Aquadello in 1509, and this marked the beginning of Venice's long, resplendent decline.

Cardinal Albornoz is officially invested with the power of defending the Church.

ITALY AS A BATTLEFIELD. The policy of stability which had been long and diplomatically piloted in Florence by Lorenzo de' Medici was shattered by Charles VIII of France, who crossed the Alps in 1494 intent on conquering the Kingdom of Naples. This expedition triggered Spanish intervention, resulting in a Spanish victory being declared over the French, and the Treaty of Cateau-Cambrésis (1559). Charles V of Hapsburg inherited the crown in 1516 and in 1519 was declared Emperor. He had direct sovereignty over the Duchy of Milan and the Kingdom of Naples and Sicily, supplemented by power in the Medicean state of Tuscany and the Republic of Genoa. The French gained the Marquisate of Saluzzo, while the Papal State, the Venetian Republic and the Duchy of Savoy, together with various minor *signorie*, remained independent.

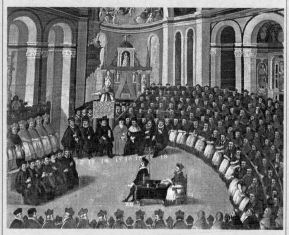

1509–17
Raphael paints frescos in the Vatican

1525
Spanish victory over French troops under François I at Pavia

1530
Charles V receives the Italian and imperial crowns in Bologna

1536–41
Michelangelo paints the Last Judgement *in the Sistine Chapel*

1545–63
Council of Trent formulates doctrines to combat Protestantism

1555
Siena captured by Florentine and imperial troops after an 18-month siege

1569
Cosimo I de' Medici becomes Grand Duke of Tuscany

1570
Palladio appointed Venice's architect

1571
Battle of Lepanto

THE HOUSE OF SAVOY. In 1563 Duke Emmanuele Filiberto transferred the capital of the House of Savoy from Chambray to Turin. The House of Savoy was a dynasty founded by Umberto Biancamano during the 11th-century. It had long been engaged in holding off French invasions from its stronghold in the western Alps, under leaders such as Amedeo VI "The Green Duke" (duke between 1343 and 83), Amedeo VII "The Red Duke" (1383–91), and Carlo II "The Good" (1504–53). Under Filiberto (who was known as "Testa di Ferro," or "Ironhead", 1553–80) and his successors, the House of Savoy successfully established itself in the Piedmontese region and entered the Italian political arena. By 1714 a Duke of Savoy – Vittorio Amedeo II – had acquired the title of King of Sicily, an island that was later to be exchanged in 1720 for the island of Sardinia ▲ *482*.

1603
The Accademia dei Lincei is founded in Rome

SPANISH PREDOMINANCE. Following the Treaty of Cateau-Cambrésis in 1559, the Spanish dominated Italy throughout the whole of the 17th century. The Spanish maintained direct control over the Kingdom of Sicily and Naples, the lands of the ex-Duke of Milan, and the Tuscan *Stato dei Presidi* ("State of the Garrison"). Various tutelages ensured a more subtle influence, and there was an implicit requirement for Madrid's approval of any new government policies. Spanish dominance coincided with a long phase of depression, which was partly due to the economic crisis affecting all of Europe and the shift in trade from the Mediterranean to the Atlantic, as well as incompetent government and a harsh fiscal regime. The Thirty Years' War (1618–48), which started as a religious

1610
Caravaggio dies near Porto Ercole

1630
Pikemen sack Mantua

1632
Galileo's Dialogue on the Great Systems is published in Florence

1647
Revolt and killing of Masaniello in Naples

1657–66
Bernini builds the colonnade in the piazza in front of St Peter's in Rome

1693
Southeastern Sicily is devastated by an earthquake

struggle and ended in a bitter clash over continental supremacy between the Bourbons and the Hapsburgs did not have a direct effect on Italy. However, Spain emerged from the war somewhat weaker and the balance of power was now in France's favor.

THE GRAND DUCHY OF TUSCANY. The Grand Duchy of Tuscany was established in 1569, when Pope Pius V granted the title of Grand Duke to Cosimo I de' Medici ▲ 275, who until then had been "the head of the government of the city of Florence and its dominions". The creation of the grand duchy accelerated the process of Florentine regional expansion that had been going on over the 13th and 14th centuries since its proclamation as a city by Cosimo il Vecchio ("the Old") and Lorenzo the Magnificent. Cosimo I

overthrew Florence's old rival, Siena, with the help of Charles V's imperial militias (1555). The grand duchy acquired considerable commercial significance by building the port of Livorno (Leghorn) in 1577, and during the 17th century was gradually to free itself from Spanish tutelage. The Medicis ruled the Tuscan Grand Duchy until 1737, when it was passed onto Francesco Stefano di Lorena, due to a lack of Medicean heirs.

THE LATER MODERN AGE

FROM THE SPANISH TO THE AUSTRIANS. The long stability in Italy after the Thirty Years' War was broken by the aftermath of the War of the Spanish Succession (1701–13). Philip V of Bourbon ascended the throne in Madrid, although the Milanese territories fell to the Austrian Hapsburgs, and the crown of Naples and Sicily was assigned to Charles of Bourbon following the War of the Polish Succession. The Treaty of Vienna gave Sardinia to Vittorio Amedeo II of Savoy, and installed the Hapsburg-Lorenas in the Grand Duchy of Tuscany. This intricate balance of power between the Hapsburgs, Savoys and Bourbons was carried through to the unification of Italy, without interruption apart from the Napoleonic Wars. The delicate complexity of this political situation favored a climate of reformism throughout the region, which also reflected trends in European enlightenment. The most impressive and lasting results of this political and cultural evolution were found in Lombardy, Piedmont, Tuscany and Naples.

1713
Peace of Utrecht marks end of Spanish supremacy in Italy

1720
The reign of the House of Savoy over Sardinia begins

1725
Giambattista Vico's Principles of a New Science *is published in Naples*

1748
The excavations at Pompeii are opened to the public

1764
Cesare Beccaria publishes his essay On Crimes and Punishments *in Milan*

1768
Genoa cedes Corsica to France

THE BOURBONS IN THE SOUTH. Under Charles of Bourbon (1734–59), son of the Spanish King Philip V and Elisabeth Farnese, the Kingdom of Naples underwent a number of reforms. Charles' successor, his son Ferdinand IV (1759–1825), married Maria Carolina of Hapsburg in 1768 and increasingly aligned the kingdom's foreign policies with Anglo-Austrian positions, moving away from the infuence of Spain.

"Yesterday our Leader did not go to breakfast with the King. He said that he'd already had breakfast. But then he ate bread and cheese while engaged in conversation under the portico of a little church, surrounded by his friends, sad, collected, resigned." So wrote Giuseppe Cesare Abba, one of Garibaldi's "Mille" ("Thousand Red Shirts"). That "yesterday" was October 26, 1860, the day on which the republican Giuseppe Garibaldi handed over the former Bourbon "Kingdom of the Two Sicilies" to Vittorio Emmanuele II in Teano. This occasion marked the end of one of the most astonishing military feats of the 19th century. It began on May 6, when the 1,150 voluntary soldiers, or Red Shirts, sailed from Quarto ▲ 173, near Genoa. They took Palermo on May 30 and Naples on September 7. The "Expedition of the Thousand" aroused interest and admiration abroad. Its leader, Garibaldi, was to achieve immense fame.

"FROM QUARTO TO GENOA [...] THERE WERE CROWDS EAGER TO SEE AND GREET US AND TO WISH OUR GREAT LEADER VICTORY IN THE NAME OF ITALY."

GIUSEPPE BANDI

THE LIBERATION OF THE SOUTH

Southern Italy had already been the scene of naval attacks, like the tragic ones made by Pisacane and the brothers Bandiera. This time, however, propaganda ensured that the expedition had popular support. Sicilian peasants hoped for agrarian reforms, and the bourgeoisie wanted a liberal constitution. The ranks of the "Mille" grew from victory to victory. In April they defeated the Bourbons at Catafimi and Milazzo, having first taken Palermo ▲ 446; by September Garibaldi was already at the gates of Naples ▲ 394.

COMMEMORATIVE MEDAL
A medal was presented to each of the volunteers who followed Garibaldi. Shown here are the face (left) and reverse (above) of the medal; pinned to the ribbon is the "Trinacria", the symbol of Sicily.

AN ICONOGRAPHY OF CELEBRATION
After the "Expedition of the Thousand" the markets were flooded with prints, postcards and books celebrating the first truly romantic Italian hero.

THE NAPOLEONIC DISASTER. On April 12, 1796 the twenty-seven-year-old Corsican Napoleon Bonaparte defeated the Austro-Piedmontese troops at Cairo Montenotte. The young general had been declared commander of the Italian Armed Forces by the Paris Directory, France's governing body in the post-Jacobin phase of the revolution. The years between this victory and October 13, 1815 – when Joachim Murat, King of Naples ▲ *394* since 1808, was executed by a firing squad, at Pizzo Calabro, on Napoleon's orders – were nineteen of the most convulsive in all Italian history. Not only was the political and territorial order overturned, but also the juridical and economic bases of the *ancien régime*. These nineteen years of profound, often contradictory change saw the growth of democratic and nationalistic unrest which culminated in the Risorgimento ("Resurgence") movement, despite the harsh controls of the restoration period following the fall of the Napoleonic Empire.

1769
The Uffizi Gallery in Florence is opened to the public

1786
Goethe visits Italy

1805
Napoleon is crowned King of Italy in Milan

THE RISORGIMENTO PERIOD

1814–15
Napoleon is confined on the island of Elba

THE RESTORATION. After the French Revolution and the fall of the Napoleonic Empire, the Congress of Vienna, after seven months of hard deliberation, established guidelines for the restoration of the ousted European monarchies. Austria gained direct sovereignty over the Lombard and Venetian

1818
Introduction of compulsory elementary education in the Lombardy-Veneto region

1831
Mazzini launches the Giovine Italia ("Young Italy") movement in Marseilles

The anti-Austrian "Cinque Giornate" ("Five Days") insurrection in Milan.

regions (the Venetian Republic having been eliminated) and imposed a military alliance over the Kingdom of the Two Sicilies, while assuming the role of policing the reinstated balance of power between the Hapsburgs, Savoys and Bourbons. The Kingdom of Sardinia incorporated the suppressed Republic of Genoa ▲ *161* into its territories. Completing the political geography of the peninsula were the Papal State, the Grand Duchy of Tuscany and the small duchies of Parma, Piacenza, Modena and Reggio, which were all subject in one form or other to Austria's iron control.

However, the absolutist system of the Viennese was to last no more than a few decades, undermined as it was by anachronistic regulations, as well as being repeatedly shaken by both nationalistic and liberal-democratic rebellions.

THE BACKGROUND OF THE RISORGIMENTO. The first phase

of the Risorgimento ("Resurgence") movement was marked by bouts of fragmentary conspiratorial activity and then, between 1820 and 1831, by insurrectional plots and riots, which were all harshly suppressed. This was followed by another phase, guided by the ideology of Giuseppe Mazzini, who argued for a unitarian and republican solution to "the Italian question". This phase came to an end in 1844 with the Bandiera brothers' tragic expedition to Calabria. Besides Mazzini, the outstanding figures in the democratic camp were the radical Filippo Buonarroti and the federalists Carlo Cattaneo and Giuseppe Ferrari. In the moderate camp were Vincenzo Gioberti (who advocated

a confederation of states presided over by the Pope), Cesare Balbo and Massimo d'Azeglio (who favored independence under the guidance of Piedmont). Although the

first War of Independence (1848-9) saw the defeat of Piedmont by the Austrians, there was more active popular participation in the insurrections of Venice, Milan, Parma, Modena, Rome and Brescia. The Piedmontese statesman Cavour patiently paved the way for the second War of Independence (1859), using diplomatic initiatives which ensured that the movement was firmly steered by the House of Savoy, to which Garibaldi's "Expedition of the Thousand" ▲ *44* and the *plebisciti* (who sought popular support for the nascent monarchic state) had recourse in order to embody their political ideals.

1837
Giacomo Leopardi dies in Naples

1839
The first Italian railroad is built, from Naples to Portici

1842
Alessandro Manzoni's The Betrothed *is published, in its final form, in Milan*

1852
Cavour becomes head of the Piedmontese government

1857
Carlo Pisacane's "Sapri Expedition" ends in failure

Camillo Benso, Count of Cavour, was a Torinese statesman and a principal figure in the Risorgimento. He advocated the monarchic solution, which he devised.

A UNIFIED ITALY

1887
Triumphant premiere of Verdi's opera Otello *at La Scala in Milan*

1913
First Italian election with universal vote for men

1922
Benito Mussolini forms Fascist government

THE KINGDOM. Proclaimed in Turin on March 14, 1861, the Kingdom of Italy found itself faced with the public debts of all the annexed states, the expenses of the war of 1859, and a need for a unified economic and administrative structure. Over the following decade a rigorous financial policy, coupled with massive investments (including 2,500 miles of railroad construction), constituted the first steps in Italy's struggle to modernize. Veneto and Friuli were reclaimed from Austria in 1866; and in 1870 Lazio and Rome, the new capital, were handed over by the Pope. The acquisition of the northeastern territories (the *"terre irredente"*, or unredeemed lands) was not achieved until the victorious conclusion of World War One in 1918, in which the young nation participated although still facing serious problems. The mood was one of restless social

conflict centered around the "southern question", mass emigration, the anti-liberal opposition of the Church, and agricultural and industrial development. In the postwar era the situation became even more extreme: the political crisis of the liberal state came with the fall of successive governments headed by Nitti, Bonomi and Facta, and with Giolitti's failed mediation between the old order and the new. All this contributed to the conditions which brought about the end of democracy and saw the advent of Fascist dictatorship. The 1920's and 1930's witnessed the evolution of a repressive, authoritarian state whose foreign policy was directed toward imperialistic expansion, as was clearly evident from Mussolini's invasion of Ethiopia in 1935.

1925
The first autostrada, from Milan to Laghi, is opened

1929
Signing of the Lateran Treaty, recognizing the sovereignty of the Vatican State and regulating the position of the Catholic Church in Italy

> **"BULLETS AND SHRAPNEL WHISTLE AND SHRIEK JUST INCHES AWAY FROM THE SHUTTERS, THEN BURY THEMSELVES IN THE OLD PLASTER FAÇADES."**
>
> GIACOMO DEBENEDETTI, *OCTOBER 16, 1943*

WAR AND RESISTANCE.

fuori i tedeschi

Following Nazi Germany's attack on Poland on September 1, 1939, Mussolini was convinced that the Germans were only a step away from complete victory. This led him to enter the war alongside the Third Reich, in June 1940. It was a risky decision – which, together with the failures in Greece (October 1940), Cyrenaica and Ethiopia, condemned a militarily unprepared Italy to a subordinate role beside its powerful ally. The events during the second half of 1943 – from the Allies landing in Sicily (July 9–10) to the deposition of Mussolini and his arrest on July 25, and from the armistice of September 8 (which created mayhem in an Italian army left without precise orders) to the birth of the Italian Socialist Republic – all bear witness to the dramatic consequences of such a hazardous decision. A redeeming contrast to this was the partisan resistance, which developed mainly in the north up until 1945, by which time World War Two had long been seen as a war against Fascism and Nazism. All of the anti-Fascist factions in Italy, coordinated by the Committees for National Liberation (CLN), took part in the struggle against the "new order" which Mussolini and Hitler had sought to impose. On April 24 the Allies crossed the Po; next day the CLN proclaimed insurrection. With the liberation of Bologna, Genoa, Milan, Venice and Turin, the war was over for Italy. Mussolini was captured in Dongo, while attempting to escape to Switzerland dressed as a German soldier, and on April 28 he was executed. The Duce's body, together with those of several other leading Fascists, was hung in Piazza Loreto in Milan, where during the previous year the Fascists had shot fifteen partisans.

1937
Writer Antonio Gramsci dies in Rome

1944
June 4: Allied troops enter Rome

1948
Attempt on the life of Palmiro Togliatti, the Communist Party secretary

1954
First television broadcast in Italy

1956
July 26: fifty five people die when the Andrea Doria *sinks in the Atlantic*

IL BESTIALE FASCISMO E VINTO!

Partisan formations parade in Milan's Piazza del Duomo in 1945.

1957
Treaty of Rome institutes the EEC

1963
Pope John XXIII issues the encyclical Pacem in Terris

1966
The flooding of the Arno

THE REPUBLIC. The history of the Italian Republic, which was instituted by a referendum held on June 2, 1946, is that of a country risen from the ravages of war with an extraordinary energy. This engendered a revitalizing economic boom, of which the Autostrada del Sole (Milan–Naples highway), built between 1956 and 1964, is a symbol. Despite the political divisions provoked by the Cold War and the organized crime, terrorism and killings that raged from 1969 until the early 1980's, Italy has never lost sight of its democratic purpose and has managed to establish a place for itself among the world's major economic powers, despite massive public debt. In view of the elections held in April 1994, which installed a center-right coalition in government, and those of April 1996, which installed a center-left coalition, it would appear that Italy has tacitly adopted a "bipolar" approach, directed toward political reconciliation, and has opted for a "democracy of change".

causes devastation in Florence

1968
Belice in Sicily is hit by an earthquake

1992
Magistrates Falcone and Borsellino are murdered in an ambush in Palermo

1993
Proportional representation is replaced by majority voting

TRADITIONS AND GASTRONOMY

TRADITIONS

GASTRONOMY

Popular religion is often expressed through the celebration of traditional religious festivals in which the element of performance is often foremost. Sometimes these celebrations can have disconcerting elements that hint at the survival of pagan rituals. Yet the traditionalists find no difficulty with the profane aspects of some religious festivals. Many religious celebrations in Italy include some test of skill or strength – for example, those in which troops of young men have to run while carrying huge, heavy symbolic structures, such as the *gigli* (lilies) of Nola or the *ceri* (huge candles) of Gubbio. Holy Week sees the most intense expression of popular religious feeling, with its penitentiary processions, rich in pomp and color yet inspired by a deep faith.

SACRED AND PROFANE
The profane aspects of religious celebrations often seem to prevail over elements of the Catholic liturgy. The photographs above show: (top) the *corsa* *dei ceri* in Gubbio ▲ *333*, and (bottom) the reenactment of the arrival in Bari of Saint Nicholas' relics from the Far East ▲ *429*. Left: a votive candle holder in Cagliari.

**THE ABRUZZAN "SERPARI"
(SNAKE CHARMERS)**
During the feast of San
Domenico (right and below) at
Cocullo (L'Aquila) and Pretoria
(Chieti), in early May, the
statue of the saint is paraded
through the streets – covered in
live snakes. According to
popular belief, the saint is
said to protect against
poisonous snake bites.

THE RITES OF HOLY WEEK
At Easter there is a series of processions
featuring representations of popular sacred
figures. Among
these are the
giant puppets
symbolizing the
apostles and the
Madonna (left),
in Calabria and
Sicily, and the
"masked Jews" of
San Fratello.

● POPULAR ART IN "EX VOTOS"

To the faithful, *ex votos* (votive offerings) are a tangible means of giving thanks for prayers answered or for grace received. They have been a part of Italian culture since pre-Roman times and have been adopted by the Catholic church. They are generally found in places claiming to be the site of some miraculous event. These votive objects can be representations of a part of the body healed by the Virgin Mary or a saint or, more typically, small paintings on wood by naive artists, depicting a miraculous event according to the witnesses' accounts. Exhibited for hundreds of years on church walls, *ex votos* depict their subjects being saved from many a horrible fate, often in a very lively fashion.

FOR GRACE RECEIVED
While votive offerings cast in wax or metal often have an impersonal character, painted tablets – almost always the work of anonymous artists, but often imbued with a lively sensibility – are more diverse and usually depict a specific event. In general, the supernatural figure of the miracle worker appears on a cloud in the top half of the painting.

Left: survivors rescued from a shipwreck. Above (from the top): a bear attacking two men; the healing of a sick child (1812); San Giovanni of Capistrano saving a person who has fallen from a ladder.

Painted votive offerings provide an extraordinary illustrated history of everyday life and popular beliefs, dating from the 16th century to the present day.

Left: the exorcism of a possessed woman. Below: the survivor of a bombing; an overturned carriage; the Virgin Mary saving a soldier whose rifle has exploded.

Carnival is the celebration of liberty and the overthrow of social conventions represented in scenes of comedy and fantasy through different media: from ancient rituals in Mamoiada and Ottana (Sardinia) and Schignano (Lombardy) to the elegant dances of Bagolino (Lombardy); from the processions of huge floats in Viareggio (Tuscany), satirizing current affairs, to the exquisite finery of Venetian masks.

COSTUMES

Costumes can reflect a taste for the comic or grotesque, as in Schignano and Como (above); or for pomp and elegance, like the ones of the dancers in Bagolino and Brescia (left and below left).

HISTORICAL REENACTMENTS

In Sampeyre (Cuneo) the splendid costumes (above) evoke the capture of the Saracens in a story of revolt against an oppressive power.

THE "BATTLE OF THE ORANGES"

As with other manifestations of carnival spirit, Ivrea is the setting for a ritual dispute. Here two teams (one on foot and the other in horse-drawn carriages) come face to face and try to hit each other with oranges.

ALLEGORIC FLOATS

Political and cultural satire sets the theme for the procession of floats, created by skilled local craftsmen, during the carnival in Viareggio.

MASKS

In Ottana the *boes* (above) don sheepskins and animal masks. The *mamuthones* of Mamoiada (below left) wear anthropomorphic masks, while the Venetian carnival (below) is noted for its fantastic creations.

A very appealing element of Italian popular theater is the puppet show, which is found in several different forms. Small portable puppet theaters are a typical sight in the piazza.

The puppeteer performs lively comedies, operating hand puppets by holding three fingers in the puppet to move the head and body. The performances usually end with a good fight emphasizing the victory of the "goodie" over the "baddie". Marionettes are manipulated by hanging strings. They perform incredibly realistic versions of classic dramas and comedies after the fashion of 19th- century theater.

Rod puppets are typical of Sicily: in a series of shows, held over several months, legendary tales of Charlemagne and his knights – victors of countless thunderous duels – are vividly related.

Puppets and marionettes can be viewed in various public collections, such as those at the Dramatic School of Art in Milan or the International Marionette Museum (*Museo Internazionale della Marionetta*) in Palermo ▲ 452.

MARIONETTES AND HAND PUPPETS
A grotesque hand puppet (above) contrasts with elegant marionettes. Left, an example from the 18th century; below, marionettes from Milan.

PUPPETEERS
Puppetry is sometimes a family affair: often the husband creates the characters and paints the sets, while the wife sews the costumes. Above: F. Napoli, a Catanian puppeteer.

SICILIAN ROD PUPPETS
The expression of an ancient and complex theatrical tradition, these are extremely heavy figures, manipulated by metal rods. Facial features and armor distinguish the different characters.

● RISOTTO PRIMAVERA

Cultivation of short-grain rice became widespread in northern Italy from the 15th century onward. It lends itself best to risotto dishes, which break down the starch to produce the creaminess characteristic of the risottos of northern Italy, subtly binding in flavors added to it. The recipe given here perfectly blends the flavors of spring vegetables from the Venetian lagoon.

1. Chop the onion and celery as finely as possible.

2. Dice the carrots, zucchini and artichoke hearts.

3. Blanch the tomatoes and asparagus tips.

4. Gently fry the onion and celery in 2 tablespoons of butter. Add the rice.

6. In the meantime, lightly fry the carrots, zucchini, peas and asparagus tips in some butter.

5. Stir the rice and pour in the white wine (allow it to evaporate). Add the hot stock a little at a time.

> **"THE VENETIAN CHARACTER CONTAINS A GREAT WELL OF JOY;
> THE PEOPLE'S CARDINAL SIN MAY BE GLUTTONY,
> BUT IT IS A LIFE-ENHANCING SORT OF GLUTTONY."**
>
> GEORGE SAND

INGREDIENTS
(to serve 4)
1½ cups of short-grain white rice; 4 pints of hot chicken stock (with the fat removed); 2 small carrots; 1½ cups of shelled peas; 4 artichoke hearts; 2 baby zucchini; 2 tomatoes; 1 cup of asparagus tips; 1 large scallion; 1 stalk of white celery; 1 glass of white wine; ¼ cup of grated Parmesan; ¼ cup of butter; basil; parsley.

7. Finely chop the parsley and basil.

8. About 5 minutes before the rice is fully cooked, add all the vegetables, stirring well.

9. Stir in the butter and Parmesan, turn off the cooker and leave the pan covered on the hob for a couple of minutes.

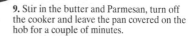

10. Before serving, sprinkle the rice with the chopped basil and parsley.

● SARDE A BECCAFICO

This dish incorporates some of the most delightful characteristics of Sicilian cuisine: the refinement to be found in simplicity; open-mindedness in the mixing of various flavors absorbed through the many cultures that have influenced the island – from Greeks to Romans, Byzantines to Arabs, Normans to Spaniards. Sardines (*sarde*) are perhaps the best-loved fish in Sicilian cooking, being also a key ingredient in *pasta cui sardi*, a delicious pasta dish flavored with wild fennel.

1. Soak half the breadcrumbs in the vinegar until you obtain a paste-like texture.

2. Add to this the pine nuts and sultanas (ensuring they are very well drained).

3. Amalgamate this mixture with the oil; make small balls from the soft mixture and place one inside each sardine.

4. Roll the sardines into little cylinders, with the stuffing inside them.

5. Place the sardines side by side in an ovenproof dish, wedging slices of onion in between. Add a few bay leaves.

6. Add some saffron and the spoonful of sugar to the remaining breadcrumbs.

> ## "THE DISCOVERY OF A NEW DISH IS MORE IMPORTANT [...] THAN THAT OF A NEW STAR."
>
> BRILLAT-SAVARIN

INGREDIENTS
(to serve 2)
6 or 7 filleted sardines; vinegar; pine nuts; sultanas soaked in warm water; 1 onion; saffron; oil; 1 tablespoon of sugar; bay leaves; 2 cups of breadcrumbs; salt; 1 orange.

8. Sprinkle with the remaining breadcrumbs, then place in a preheated oven and cook for 15 minutes at 350°F.

7. Drizzle some oil onto the sardines and season with salt.

9. Serve warm or cold, garnished with slices of orange.

● PASTA AND PIZZA

Pasta and pizza are considered truly Neapolitan because of their association with the classic Neapolitan tomato sauce, a tradition from the early 19th century.

Other than the fact that they are both made from flour and water, pasta (often simply called *maccheroni* in Italy) and pizza have something else in common: the mistaken idea that they are a Neapolitan invention. Instead they hail from Sicily, where they were introduced from Arabia. From Sicily they went on to conquer the palates of all Italians. Their original Arab name, *itrya*, is still used today in the form of "tria" in Sicily and Puglia. The classic pizza, consisting of a disc of dough topped with sauce then cooked in the oven, only arrived in Naples at the beginning of the 19th century. Before that there were only *pizzelle*, fritters cooked and sold by vendors on street corners.

To make a good pizza ▲ 402, kneading the dough properly and cooking it in a wood-burning pizza oven are essential. The three colors of the national flag decorate the real Neapolitan pizza, known as the *Margherita*, in honor of the queen of that name. Today all sorts of toppings are used – sometimes including the strangest ingredients – from mushrooms, mussels, ham and peppers to highly imaginative combinations on a *Capricciosa*. But the "classic" Italian toppings (tomato and oregano; *pecorino* (sheep's cheese) and onion; tomato,

anchovies and *mozzarella*), remain among the most popular. *Calzoni* ("stockings") are no less delicious; these are hot, oven-cooked pizzas folded over (hence the name) and filled, usually, with cheese and ham.

In Italy today three types of pasta are used: the "dry" type (for example, classic spaghetti ▲ 402), which is made from *grano duro* (durum wheat) flour and water; egg pasta (tagliatelle, fettucine); and filled pasta (ravioli, tortellini, cappelletti, cannelloni).

Various types of dried pasta (in Italy now all often called *maccheroni*, after the Neapolitan usage) have always been made by passing the dough through a bronze cutter, usually by professional pasta makers rather than at home. Natural drying methods required hot sun and so were best suited to the climate of southern and central Italy. Nowadays the drying process is artificial, and dried pasta is mostly produced by large factories in various parts of Italy. Nevertheless, the taste hasn't changed, the quality remains high, and *grano duro* (now almost entirely grown in America) is highly sought after.

Egg pasta and filled pasta are frequently made in the home, especially in Emilia and Piedmont. There are numerous shapes and fillings (ranging from meat or fish to *ricotta* cheese or vegetables) and countless ways of eating pasta: with meat sauces, in clear or rich broths, and even under a pie crust – the delicious *timballi in pastafrolla* (bottom right). Pasta must surely be the most universal Italian dish!

Bread and salami in Italy can just mean a quick snack – but trying the various types of bread with salami or *salumi* (cured-pork products) is an interesting way of getting to know Italy. From the north to the south, there are many different bread doughs and shapes, eaten with all manner of salami and *salumi*. These in turn are made from various types of pork, cured and flavored according to necessity, climate and type of animal. Thus from Sicily to Friuli, from the smoked *prosciuttini* of Sauris to sausages flavored with fennel, the countless varieties of salami reveal different farming and curing methods. Even though now often mass-produced, they have not lost their traditional character.

Unsalted breads, often made from unrefined flour, go well with hams from Tuscany and Umbria or salamis made with coarse-ground meat, like the Tuscan *finocchiona* and the Umbrian *corallina* or the flavorsome *ventriciana* from the Abruzzi.

PANE FERRARESE (FERRARAN BREAD)

PANE TOSCANO (TUSCAN BREAD)

ROSETTA OR MICHETTA (LOMBARDY)

MICCA (EMILIA)

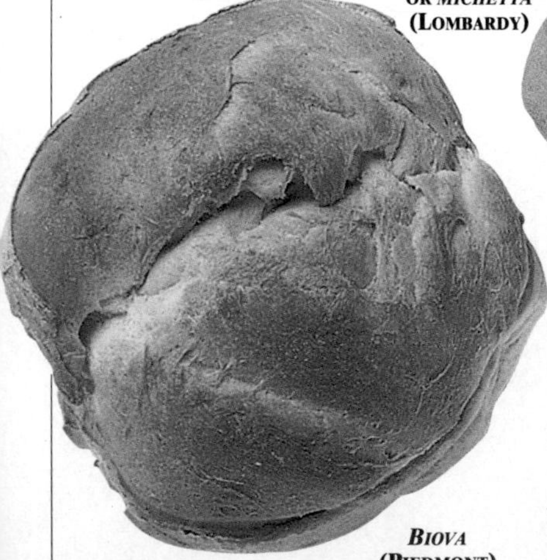

Breads made from refined flour with a crunchy crust and soft white inside (such as *biova*, *micca* and *michetta*) and biscuit-like breads such as *grissini* (bread sticks) or the Ferraran *manine* ("little hands") all go well with San Daniele and Parma hams, fragrant salamis from Felino, garlic salamis from Ferrara, or aromatic ones from Varzi. They also go well with delicate *cotti* and *prosciutti*, pork shoulders, and *mortadella* with pistachio (the pride of Bologna since medieval times).

BIOVA (PIEDMONT)

Combined baker's and butcher's store, from a fresco (15th–16th century) in the Castello di Issogne in the Valle d'Aosta.

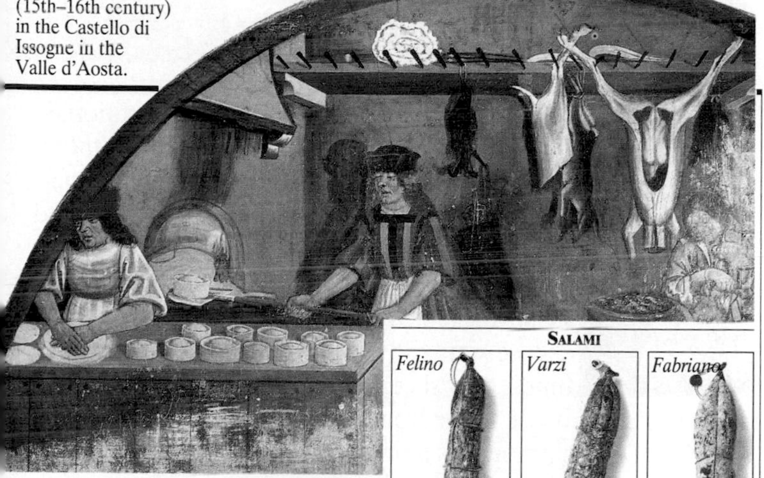

SALAMI

Felino

Varzi

Fabriano

Neapolitan dried sausage

PANE CON SESAMO
SESAME BREAD
(SICILY)

PROSCIUTTI (CURED HAMS)

San Daniele

Fiocco

Coppa

PROSCIUTTI COTTI (COOKED HAMS)

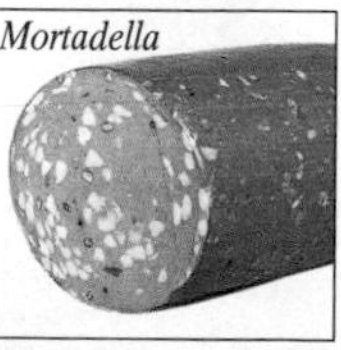

Mortadella

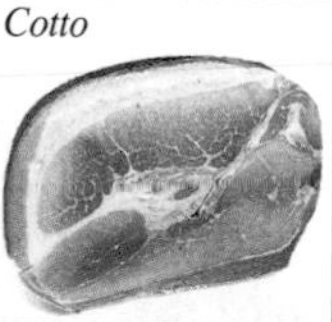

Cotto

Well-flavored breads, often made with *grano duro* (durum wheat), like those from Calabria and Puglia, make a delicious lunch eaten together with spicy local sausage.

E DI ALTAMURA
AMURAN BREAD
(PUGLIA)

SALUMI (CURED-PORK PRODUCTS)

Ventricina

Soppressata calabrese

Soppressata veneta

Ciauscolo

There are more than four hundred traditional Italian cheeses (and in addition to these, there are more recently manufactured products such as cheese spreads). Cheese is an important and old-established feature of Italian gastronomy. Columella, a Roman of the Augustan era, had strict rules for the production of a sheep's-milk cheese similar to Pecorino Romano. In ancient times, only sheep's-milk and goat's cheeses were eaten in Italy. Cheese made from cow's milk was produced from the Middle Ages onward as a result of the agricultural revolution, which created abundant pastures in the Italian plains. Well-known Italian cheeses, such as Parmesan, Fontina, Gorgonzola and Mozzarella are now exported. More recently, buffalo's-milk Mozzarella has also become popular abroad.

Fatty cheeses include Fontina, which is made exclusively in the Valle d'Aosta, and buffalo's-milk Mozzarella, originally made in the south (though nowadays not always) by rolling the cheese into a dough-like paste and then drawing it out like a ribbon. Other cheeses made in this way are Provolone, Scamorza and Caciocavallo.

There is a large family of *pecorini* (sheep's-milk cheeses) made all over Italy, though traditionally they are a product of Tuscany and the south of Italy, including Sicily and Sardinia. The different varieties are determined by the type of pasture grazed by the sheep, the ripening process and temperature. Goat's cheeses (*caprini*) are less popular.

Although there are few varieties, mostly from Piedmont and Lombardy, cheeses like Gorgonzola (known as *erboratini*) are very important.

Gorgonzola has streaks of green mold, which are produced by a special method.

Both mild and strong varieties are made (*dolce* and *piccante*).

Parmesan and Grana Padano have been written about by many famous authors. These medium-fat hard cheeses are cooked and then allowed to ripen for at least a year (preferably two). They are continually tested with hammers and borers, and vary according to production methods and the origin of the milk used. For Parmesan, the milk comes from Parma, Reggio, Modena, Mantua and Bologna; for Grana Padano, it comes from the Po valley. Both are widely used in cooking.

Italy produces more wine than any other country, and nowadays it is also renowned for the quality of its wines, following the huge improvements in the technology of wine-making everywhere. Much has been done over the past thirty years to improve quality: research has been undertaken on grape varieties, soil types and methods of production. Italian wine has thus reclaimed the good name it had during the Renaissance, when it was the only wine that Sante Lancerio, wine waiter to Pope Paul III Farnese, considered worthy of a nobleman's table; in a famous letter, written around 1550, he described the characteristics, virtues and defects of all Italian wines of that time. Today there are hundreds of Italian wines, yet certain grape varieties are still used for the most famous among them.

Two grape varieties produce the great Piedmontese wines ▲ 155. The first of these, Nebbiolo, is of medium yield and very delicate, but capable of producing excellent wines in a good year. The second, Barbera, is more consistent in quality but varies according to soil types. Among the grapes used for white wine, Moscato excels and is usually made into sparkling wine. Fine still white wines are made from Cortese and Arneis grapes.

MOSCATO

CORTESE

In order to appreciate its color and clarity, wine should be served in glasses made of thin, smooth, transparent, colorless glass or crystal. They should always be held by the stem, so as to avoid heating the wine with your hand.

PINOT NERO

PINOT BIANCO

Pinot (both white and black, used for making white wine), Riesling (both the Italian and German varieties) and, more recently, Chardonnay and Sauvignon are the principal grape

varieties that produce the huge and diverse range of white wines from the Lombardy, Veneto, Trentino and Friuli regions. The character of these wines vary according to the area which they

come from and the production process. They range from very dry and delicately perfumed whites to more full-bodied ones, some of which can be kept to mature for several years.

VERNACCIA

SCHIAVA

There are also a great variety of red wines from the same regions. Many are made from Cabernet and Merlot grapes, but Sciava, Pinot

Nero and Refoscoro are also used. They often have a strong herby bouquet, and in certain areas they are made with the body and depth of *grands*

vins. Recioto grapes also make impressive red and white wines. Throughout central Italy, the Sangiovese grape triumphs and is the base of many of the most famous wines – including Chianti ▲ *301* and Montepulciano and Brunello (Brunello and Morellino are both varieties of the Sangiovese grape). Trebbiano, Malvasia and Vernacca grapes are utilized in the production of some much loved, if less famous, white wines.

VERMENTINO

AGLIANICO

There is no lack of diversity in the grapes of southern Italy, especially the local varieties. The grape

varieties used for making red wines include: Negroamaro Primitivo and Aleatico in Puglia;

Piedirosso and Aglianico in Campania; Monica in Sardinia; and Nerello in Sicily. Fiano, Vermentino, Carricante, Ansonica, Bombino and Bianco d'Alessano produce dry, fruity white wines. In recent years there has been a resurgence in Marsala production. Today it is made with great attention to quality; not surprisingly, the results are often outstanding.

In wine production the nature and quality of the soil is of crucial importance, as each type of vine has its own preferred growing conditions.

CORATINA OLIVE

There are olive trees which according to botanists are more than three hundred years old, like the "witch's tree" in Magliano di Grosseto. Olives and olive oil have been a part of Mediterranean civilization from its origins, the cultivation of olive trees extending from Egypt to Greece. Italy has developed the most refined production methods. Even in Augustan Rome, the commodity market already recognized five categories, according to the ripeness and healthiness of the olives used. Today there are more than fifty recognized varieties of Italian olive oil, which differ according to the kind of olive used and the climate of its cultivation.

Olive oil described on its label as *extra vergine* (extra virgin) is the only type produced by traditional processes. Today quality-control laws also guarantee its origin, in a similar way to DOC wines.

The olive tree is long-lived, and its fruit is widely used. As well as being crushed to extract the oil, olives figure prominently in Italian cookery and are a tasty ingredient in many dishes.

The most common varieties of olive tree are: Taggiasca (Liguria), Frantoiana (Garda, Tuscany, Umbria), Leccina (Tuscany, Umbria), Callina, and Rosciola (Lazio and the Marche).

MORAIOLA OLIVE (TUSCANY AND UMBRIA)

Architecture

1   2   3

Italy is a land of cities. This tradition began to take root in the Roman era, when most of the major Italian cities were born. It was firmly established in medieval times, when almost all of the smaller city centers were founded or rebuilt, and in most cases the medieval layout remains to this day. It is no surprise that the most typical Italian houses – from the Roman *insula* (apartment block) to the medieval *casa-torre* (tower house) and Renaissance *palazzo* (palace) – are city dwellings. Or that modern town planning has its origins in the Renaissance, when the first studies of the form and organization of the city were undertaken.

THE "CASA-TORRE" (TOWER HOUSE)

In most parts of medieval Europe the upper classes were feudal landowners who lived in rural castles. In Italy, however, especially in the central and northern parts, most of the landowners were townsfolk, often of merchant stock. Their typical dwelling was the tower house, a kind of "vertical castle" which became a characteristic feature of the urban landscape. The Florentine towers of the Marsilians, the Castagnans and the Amideians are typical of the variations on this theme that evolved between the 11th and the 13th centuries. Later, many tower houses were incorporated into more complex structures, or else "clipped" (lowered). Eventually they were abandoned in favor of the palazzo.

THE "IDEAL CITY"
During the Renaissance Italian architects were inspired by the idea of the "ideal city" – that is, the harmonious arrangement of all the city structures, including monuments, piazzas, streets and fortifications. These studies laid the theoretical foundations for town planning. The illustrations show plans for ideal cities by Filarete (**1**), Francesco di Giorgio (**2**), Pietro Cataneo (**3**) and Vincenzo Scamozzi (**4**).

MEDIEVAL HOUSES
Courtyard houses, typically found in towns, vary in their proportions but always consist of a four-sided building constructed around a courtyard.

THE URBANIZATION OF THE LAND
The commune of Brescia effectively "colonized" the surrounding area by setting up "tax-free" townships. This way it persuaded more and more of its neighbors to become dependent on its central control.

THE WALLED CITY
Lucca ▲ *298* is still enclosed within its walls, which separate the city from the surrounding countryside. Lucca and other Italian cities and towns were typically seen as autonomous, self-contained societies, while the surrounding countryside was viewed as merely an empty space available for colonization by city dwellers. This tradition has its roots in the Latin world.

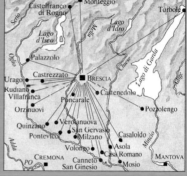

THE "INSULA"
The quintessential town dwelling created by the Romans was the *insula*. This was a communal habitation, a sort of multi-story apartment block, like the splendid ones that have been excavated in Ostia ▲ *378*. The pre-eminent role of the Italian city was a legacy of the Romans.

THE PALAZZO
The elegant Venetian Gothic forms of the Ca' d'Oro ▲ *229* make it a remarkable building, even in a city of outstanding architecture, yet it is just one example of the urban palazzo. These grand houses were mostly the residences of rich merchants or town-dwelling noblemen. From the 14th century, Italian cities were organized around palazzos.

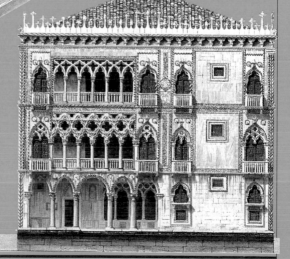

One of the most characteristic and significant creations in Italian architecture, the piazza was the axis around which civic and religious life gravitated. In Renaissance times monuments began to appear in the piazzas, dedicated to the most important men in the city. During the Baroque era fountains and obelisks took over as focal points. In many towns communal life spilled over from the piazza into colonnaded streets full of craftsmen and merchants' stores. It is this system of interlinked public spaces, constantly pulsating with activity and life, that gives Italian cities their unmistakable character.

TYPES OF PIAZZA
The piazzas of medieval Italian cities varied according to differing urban needs. Sometimes the seats of civic and religious power opened onto a single piazza, as in Pistoia (above, center). Other cities, such as Todi (above, top) and Bergamo (above, bottom), had two linked piazzas, the one reserved for civic and the other for religious functions. The most important cities often had three large piazzas, one in the center housing the main church, another for the market, and yet another for the civic center, overlooked by the offices of local government.

"EPHEMERAL ARCHITECTURE"

The crowded stalls of the small market in the Piazza delle Erbe in Verona ▲ 236 – here drawn by John Ruskin (1819–1900) – are a good example of "ephemeral architecture", a typical feature of Italian piazzas that are dedicated to commercial activity.

COLONNADES

Bologna is famous for its colonnades ▲ 256, which line a number of streets in the city center. Colonnades are a typical feature of many towns in central and northern Italy. They offer protection from both the burning summer sun and harsh winter weather, as well as being a vital setting for communal life.

PAVING DESIGN

An equestrian statue of Marcus Aurelius (replaced by a copy in 1997) is the centerpiece of the beautiful paving designed by Michelangelo for the Piazza del Campidoglio in Rome ▲ 347.

A THEATRICAL SPACE

Siena's Piazza del Campo ▲ 305 typifies the Italian view that the piazza is the town's stage. The Palazzo Pubblico and its huge tower, the Torre del Mangia, a symbol of the power of local government, face onto this large "auditorium". Here the townspeople gather on important occasions, such as the famous Palio race ▲ 306, an event which epitomizes the enthusiastic involvement of the Sienese in town life. The piazza is a unifying element where everyone meets, and a focal point for outlying districts.

Historically, the lack of political unity in Italy has always meant that cultural and civic life had many centers of control, a factor which has profoundly influenced Italian architecture: every medieval town had its town hall (*palazzo pubblico*), offices and symbols of communal life. Later, the aristocracy built palaces in almost every part of Italy. These evolved from family homes and the princely residences of the rulers of small states to Baroque palaces housing the heads of the larger kingdoms into which the land was subsequently reorganized. This may explain why Italy abounds in buildings of incredible richness, beauty and power, from every era and of every type.

THE "BROLETTO"
The life of medieval communes was developed around the town hall, or *broletto* as it was called in Lombardy (the illustration on the right shows the one in Milan). The design was always the same: a colonnaded area on the ground floor for the common assembly, and one or more rooms on the floor above for the judiciaries.

ROYAL PALACES OF THE RENAISSANCE: URBINO
The ducal Palace of Urbino ▲ *334* was built in the second half of the 15th century by Luciano Laurana and Francesco di Giorgio for Duke Federico da Montefeltro. It is the archetypal princely residence of Renaissance Italy. The rulers of the small states competed by endowing their capitals with palaces inspired by the fashionable new architecture, enriched with splendid works of art.

THE BASILICA, VINCENZA ▲ *236*
When, in the second half of the 16th century, Andrea Palladio added two levels of loggias to the 15th-century Palazzo della Ragione, he retained the overall design used for medieval town halls in northern Italy, even though it was no longer appropriate to the building's function.

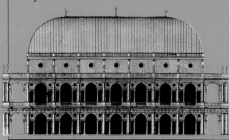

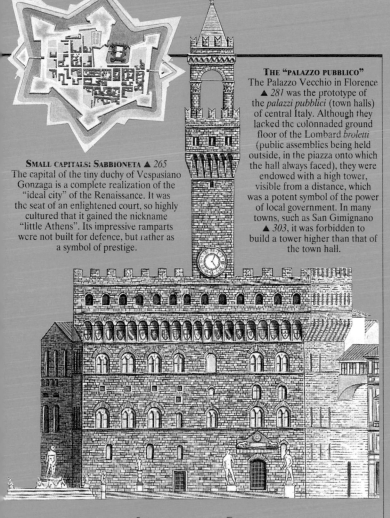

SMALL CAPITALS: SABBIONETA ▲ *265*
The capital of the tiny duchy of Vespasiano
Gonzaga is a complete realization of the
"ideal city" of the Renaissance. It was
the seat of an enlightened court, so highly
cultured that it gained the nickname
"little Athens". Its impressive ramparts
were not built for defence, but rather as
a symbol of prestige.

THE "PALAZZO PUBBLICO"
The Palazzo Vecchio in Florence
▲ *281* was the prototype of
the *palazzi pubblici* (town halls)
of central Italy. Although they
lacked the colonnaded ground
floor of the Lombard *broletti*
(public assemblies being held
outside, in the piazza onto which
the hall always faced), they were
endowed with a high tower,
visible from a distance, which
was a potent symbol of the power
of local government. In many
towns, such as San Gimignano
▲ *303*, it was forbidden to
build a tower higher than that of
the town hall.

LARGE ROYAL PALACES: TURIN
Between the 17th and 18th centuries the rulers of Italy, following the example of France's
"Sun King", Louis XIV, endowed their capitals with sumptuous royal palaces. Turin,
carefully developed by the Savoy family since the 16th century, was one of the first. The
entire city was planned around the Palazzo Reale ▲ *141* – from the formidable citadel to the
fortified ramparts at the perimeter, which enclosed the
various amplifications made
over the centuries.

● SHAPING THE LANDSCAPE

A NEW SCHEME
The Romans devised the *centuriato*: the division of the land into a grid system with equal-sized square plots, oriented in line with the cardinal points. The application of this system shaped much of the landscape of the Italian peninsula.

Much of the Italian landscape is man-made, even in areas where there is a striving for a "natural" effect. Ever since Roman times, when the plains of Italy were marked by *centuriazioni* (see above and below), there has been both a desire and a creative ability to mold the landscape artificially, a phenomenon which had an impact on Italian artists. During the Baroque era, *Sacri Monti* ("sacred mountains") were built through a blend of ardent religious faith and artistic sensibility for the landscape. During the Renaissance, the villa was reinvented, with its exquisitely architectural landscaped garden *all'italiana*.

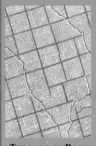

THE MARK OF ROME
The agricultural district of Villanova di Camposampiero in the province of Padua is still organized according to the *centuriazione* scheme – some two thousand years after the Romans divided the land up. The plot division is oriented in relation to the flow of the Brenta river, which runs parallel to canals for irrigation and drainage.

THE VILLA AND THE LANDSCAPED GARDEN
The lords of the Renaissance and their architects revived the Roman concept of the villa – that is, a country house for landed gentry. Villa design was adapted to suit the taste of the time, the landscaped garden *all'italiana* being one of the new features introduced. An architectural, geometric garden with paths and greenery became an invariable feature of the Renaissance villa.

ARTIFICIAL HILLS
A cross-section of the
Villa d'Este in Tivoli.
Architectural modeling
of hills can be found
in Baroque gardens and
in the *Sacri Monti*.

PALESTRINA
The temple of Fortuna Primigenia in
Palestrina is a huge construction of
terraces and steps, upon which the
great palace of the Barbieri
was built in the 17th century.
It is an excellent example
of this type of Italian
residence, built on an
artificial hill during
the era when that
was in fashion.

VILLA D'ESTE
The Villa
d'Este in Tivoli
has a vast scenic
garden of graduated
terraces, enlivened by
regularly spaced blocks of
vegetation and by fountains. It
is the most perfect execution of the
garden *all'italiana* in the country,
based on a completely artificial
architectural approach.

THE ISOLA BELLA
▲ *204*

The Isola Bella was
created during
the 17th century by
the Borromeo princes
on one of the three
Borromeo islands in
the middle of Lake
Maggiore. About 800
yards from Stresa,
it seems to float like a
fantastic tree-lined
ship, composed
of a large palace and
a terraced garden.
It is perhaps the
best-known and most
theatrical example
of architectural
landscape modeling
in the country.

81

● LOCAL AND RURAL ARCHITECTURE

Italy has a wide range of local and rural architecture: Alpine houses made from wood and stone, dairy farms linked to the rich agricultural heritage of the Po valley, the brightly painted houses of Ligurian fishermen, attractive Tuscan farmhouses, the *masserie* (large livestock farms) of the south, the *trulli* (see right) of Puglia, and so forth. These houses mirror the civilizations that built them, and are one of the most delightful features of the Italian countryside.

WALSER HOUSES
The Walser are a German-speaking people who during the Middle Ages migrated from their original home in Vallese (hence the name Walser) in Valle d'Aosta to Valsesia in Val d'Ossola, occupying the high land just beside the border. They took with them their typical architecture in wood and stone, which made use of the raw materials available in the mountainous environment of the Valle d'Aosta.

THE PAINTED HOUSES OF LIGURIA
In Liguria, especially on the Riviera di Levante, a particular type of house became prominent from the 16th to the 18th century. Many examples can still be seen in Camogli, Lavagna, Sestri Levante and further inland. These are tall, many-storied houses, with a smooth plaster façade enlivened by a magnificent, often exuberant, wash of color, or animated by trompe-l'œil painting, giving a distinctive character to the atmosphere of the local towns.

THE "TRULLO"

Originating in the Baroque era in the Valle d'Itria, the *trullo* is a type of farmhouse built from the soft local stone, readily available in large fragments that could be used for dry walling. These strange, unique dwellings were grouped together and are often embellished with pinnacles and symbolic painted signs.

THE "CASCINA"

A typical rural structure of the Po valley, the *cascina* was a complex, autonomous agricultural production center, and was the basis of northern Italy's agricultural development between the 18th and 19th centuries. A multi-functional building, it housed the owner's residence, the workers' quarters, cowsheds, pigsties and the dairy farm. In fact, the name *cascina* literally means a dairy farm, or dairy, and is derived from *caseus*, Latin for cheese.

THE "MASSERIA"

This typical southern farmhouse – most commonly found in Puglia, Calabria and Sicily – takes its name from the *massaro* (cattle farmer) who managed it. Often, it was fortified as a defense against the attacks from bandits and Saracens that frequently took place in those areas.

TUSCAN FARMHOUSE

A type of rural building seen frequently all over central Italy, the traditional Tuscan farmhouse (*fattoria*) consisted of a compact single building, used as house, hay barn and stables. Placed in the center of the farm, it was managed by the *fattore* (farmer).

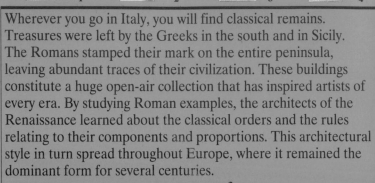

Wherever you go in Italy, you will find classical remains. Treasures were left by the Greeks in the south and in Sicily. The Romans stamped their mark on the entire peninsula, leaving abundant traces of their civilization. These buildings constitute a huge open-air collection that has inspired artists of every era. By studying Roman examples, the architects of the Renaissance learned about the classical orders and the rules relating to their components and proportions. This architectural style in turn spread throughout Europe, where it remained the dominant form for several centuries.

THE CLASSICAL ORDERS

The creation of architectural orders, which are most easily distinguished by the form of their capitals (top of page), was the basis of classical architecture.

The capitals can be Doric or Tuscan (**1**), Ionic (**2**), Corinthian (**3**) or Composite (**4**). These orders were applied to classical buildings according to rigorous rules.

Doric capital with ovolo decoration, an unusual variation (Doric capitals are normally plain).

PEDIMENT AND GABLE

The pediment – that is, the triangular part over the portico, corresponding to the roof – has a gable (the timpanum) enclosed between two raking (projecting) cornices. On the roof, the pediment was furnished with plinths (acroteria), masking the roof's ridge and gutters. The Romans used these plinths as pedestals for ornamental statues.
1. Timpanum.
2. Raking cornices.
3. Acroteria on the ridge and edges.

ENTABLATURE

4. Architrave. In the Doric order this was smooth; in the Ionic and Corinthian orders it was divided into three sections.
5. Frieze. Either smooth (**a**) or absent in the Ionic order; with metopes and triglyphs in the Doric order (**b**); and carved in the Corinthian (**c**).
6. Cornice.

COLUMNS

7. Doric: with a plain (Roman) or tapered (Greek) shaft.
8. Tuscan: with a smooth shaft.
9. Ionic: the capital has volutes (scrolls).
10. Corinthian: the capital is decorated with acanthus leaves.
11–12. Composite: with an Ionic capital superimposed above a Corinthian one.

BASE

The base of the building was modest in Greece, often being just a platform or plinth (**13**), and more developed in Rome, where it became a podium (**14**) that raised the building from the ground. Later, the columns were sometimes placed on pedestals (**15**).

THE GREEK LEGACY

The Greeks left a rich architectural heritage on Italian soil, in the form of large temples in the south, such as the Temple of Neptune at Paestum ▲ 417, in Campania. These were to influence Roman style.

"GROTESQUES"

Roman decorative motifs, often featuring flowers, birds or mythological figures (like the one above), became fashionable in Renaissance times.

TRIUMPHAL COLUMNS

These were tall, hollow columns with sculpted reliefs celebrating a military victory running round the shaft. They were frequently erected during the Roman Imperial Age.

LARGE-SCALE MONUMENTS

The skill achieved by Roman builders in casting huge arches made from concrete – a mix of inert material and water, bound with *pozzolana* (volcanic sand) – allowed them to construct very large monuments, a task that had been difficult with the Greeks' more limited techniques. The Pantheon ▲ 365 (below), erected by Agrippa during the Augustan era and later rebuilt, is one of the best examples.

"PARTITO ALLA ROMANA" (ROMAN DIVISION)

The use of interposed classical columns to relieve a series of arches was revived in the 16th century and became a common feature of European architecture.

THE USE OF THE ARCH

The Romans used arches on a grand architectural scale, allowing them to construct large public buildings – such as amphitheaters (like the one above), theaters and baths – that were far more complex than those of the Greeks. Following their example, all Western architecture from the Romanesque period onward began to make use of arched roofs at some point in its development.

Italy has a long tradition of large ecclesiastical buildings. Simple paleo-Christian basilicas exist side by side with churches intended for the use of the court or dignitaries. The Middle Ages saw a rich flourishing of baptisteries. The Romanesque phenomenon blossomed after AD 1000, and each Italian region or large city contributed its own version. During the Gothic era, the Franciscans and the Dominicans introduced a new type of church, suited to preaching to crowds in towns. Mosaic ornamentation was followed by the development of fresco painting, for didactic as well as decorative purposes.

BAPTISTERIES
The baptistery is another typical construction of the Middle Ages in Italy. The oldest examples date from the paleo-Christian era; the latest are the large Romanesque-Gothic baptisteries of central Italy like the San Giovanni baptistery in Florence (below). Usually designed on an octagonal floor plan, they were built alongside the principal churches.

THE EVOLUTION OF GROUND PLANS
The typical paleo-Christian basilica had three or five naves, like St Peter's in Rome (**1**) before the intervention of Bramante. In the Byzantine era circular churches appeared, like San Vitale in Ravenna (**2**). In Romanesque churches bays were often used to create a cruciform plan, as in San Michele in Pavia (**3**). The churches built by the holy orders generally had a single nave, like the Basilica of St Francis in Assisi (**4**).

CAMPANILES
Usually the bell tower was detached from the church itself (above, the bell tower designed by Giotto ▲ *278* for the Duomo in Florence). Pushed to great heights, bell towers became a prominent feature of Italian medieval architecture, symbolizing the city's sense of identity and civic pride.

MOSAICS
Techniques for creating mosaic decorations, derived from classical and Byzantine traditions, were exploited to dazzling effect in St Mark's in Venice and the baptistery in Florence, and in Norman churches in Sicily.

2

3

ROMANESQUE FAÇADES

Romanesque façades usually have a sloping roof (**1**) or broken gradients (**2** and **3**). Before the advent of rose windows, the façade was often decorated with small blind loggias.

GOTHIC FAÇADES

The cathedral at Orvieto (left) ▲ *329* has a typical Italian Gothic façade with pointed pediments and high pinnacles, corresponding to the plan of the naves.

SANT'AMBROGIO

The Basilica of Sant'Ambrogio in Milan ▲ *197* was rebuilt during the Romanesque era on the foundations of a paleo-Christian basilica, from which it derives its ample colonnaded atrium (**1**). The design is based on large bays with cross vaulting (**2**), which at each side of the central nave contain a series of smaller bays (**3**) and a gallery, known as a matroneum, reserved for women (**4**). These are in turn supported by external buttresses (**5**). It is the foremost example of Italian Romanesque. The splendid *tiburio* – the polygonal structure covering the cupola (**6**) – is typical of medieval Lombard architecture.

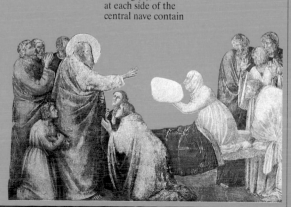

FRESCOS

Fresco painting, with didactic and narrative aims, is typical of Italian art and is found in many churches, Gothic as well as Romanesque. Its role was similar to that of the stained-glass windows of northern cathedrals.

Medieval fortifications are still a prominent feature of the Italian landscape. They can be grouped into three main categories: castles located in the countryside at the center of the feudal domain which they guarded; encircling city walls erected by the community to ensure their own safety; urban towers and safe houses built by merchants and noblemen for support during civic struggles or as a sign of rank. Between the 14th and 15th centuries *castelli-reggia* were added to this repertoire, fortified palaces constructed by urban aristocrats and rich landowners to display their power.

THE CASTLE
Sirmione Castle is a prime example of the castle at the height of its power. The various lines of defense – there is even a fortified wet dock – become progressively higher, culminating in the main tower of the massive keep at the center of the castle. The virtue of this arrangement is that the inner defenses overlook the outer ones, and could keep them under fire if they succumbed to an attack. The entrances to the complex were carefully protected by drawbridges guarded by armed sentries.

1. Keep
2. Corner turrets
3. Entrances
4. Fortified wet dock
5. Internal wall
6. External wall
7. Moat

THE WALLS OF THE COMMUNITY

Towns in medieval Italy had an importance as yet unknown to the rest of Europe, and they developed strong communities. In many Italian cities the old walls survive. Those of Montagnana (above) were erected between the 14th and the 15th century; they were defended by twenty-four bastions and had two castles at the points of entry.

A CHAIN OF CASTLES

The most important boroughs and domains of the peninsula developed a system of *scacchieri fortificati*, a network of castles protecting their territory. The Sforza and Visconti families made very effective use of this system.

GHIBELLINE	GUELPH

TYPES OF BATTLEMENTS

According to popular belief, "swallowtail" battlements mean that a castle was Ghibelline (belonging to the followers of the Emperor), whereas square-topped battlements indicate that its owners were Guelphs (supporters of the Pope). In fact the style was usually a result of regional variation and available materials.

CASTLE AND CITY

Castles with the dual function of garrison and lookout post are found in many parts of Italy. Castel Sant'Angelo (below) ▲ 373, built by the popes to guard the city of Rome, is well situated: on top of the ancient mausoleum of Hadrian. In response to the changing face of warfare, after being converted from medieval castle to 15th-century citadel with *torrioni* (massive embattled towers), it was converted into a 16th-century fortress with ramparts.

URBAN TOWERS

Tall, narrow towers, like the famous Asinelli Tower in Bologna (above), were built in towns by noble or wealthy families. A tower of this kind was used as a home as well as serving as a stronghold during the disturbances and family feuds that were a common feature of medieval life. It was also a proud emblem and visible reminder of its owner's power.

THE RENAISSANCE: REVIVING CLASSICAL FORMS

The Renaissance, the artistic expression of humanism, created new types of buildings and new esthetic ideals based on ancient forms. Palazzos were built in towns and villas in the suburbs, instead of castles and towers. Renaissance architects applied the classical system of architectural orders to their work, using it to render visible the mathematical schemes by which they proportioned their buildings. These were always based on a unified geometric plan and usually designed around a central point, giving their work a tremendously expressive force.

THE "IDEAL CITY"
During the Renaissance architecture began to be studied as a science based upon exact rules. For this reason, it involved intense theoretical research, not only on the structure of buildings but also on that of cities. Plans for "ideal cities", like the one devised by Cesare Cesarino (left), attempted to incorporate every aspect of town planning into an organic scheme.

THE BIRTH OF TREATISES
The architects of the Renaissance did not limit themselves to designs. They also wrote numerous tracts on the theory and practice of architecture, taking up the only example of this sort from antiquity: Vitruvius' treatise on architecture.

SANTA MARIA DEGLI ANGIOLI IN FLORENCE (BRUNELLESCHI)

CENTRAL PLANNING
The ground plans for Renaissance churches often featured a circular construction, around a fixed central point. This expressed the new concepts of perspective and the humanistic vision which saw man as "a measure of all things", to be placed in the center of every realization. Central planning was even applied to buildings such as villas, whose function might not have been expected to suggest a circular ground plan.

ST PETER'S IN ROME (BRAMANTE)

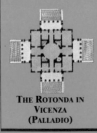

THE ROTONDA IN VICENZA (PALLADIO)

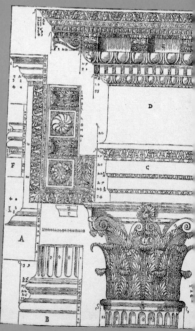

DELLA ROBBIA'S "TONDI"
The mathematical severity of Brunelleschi's Ospedale degli Innocenti in Florence is relieved by Andrea della Robbia's lively medallions decorating the portico.

PERSPECTIVE
The study of the rules of perspective was one of the great developments of the Renaissance. Devised to simulate three-dimensional reality on a single plane, they were frequently used to create a vista, or scenic "view". An oustanding example is Michelangelo's Piazza del Campidoglio.
▲ 347

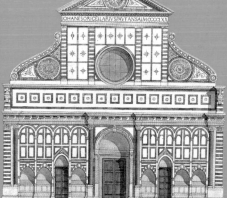

TRACED DIMENSIONS
Renaissance architecture is based on simple arithmetic and geometric rules. This is clearly illustrated by the façade of Santa Maria Novella (left and above) in Florence ▲ 289, which was redesigned by Leon Battista Alberti. The proportions of the various parts of a building were generally obtained by using traced-out dimensions rigidly correlated to create a harmonious unity in the structure.

THE PAZZI CHAPEL ▲ 293
The Pazzi Chapel by Filippo Brunelleschi (part of the Santa Croce complex in Florence) is a classic example of early Renaissance architecture. The ground plan and elevation are designed according to simple geometric relationships between the various parts. The traced proportions (see right) are rendered visible by the architectural framework, which consists of smooth stone that stands out against the white plaster of the walls, and on the ground by bands of colored stone that contrast with the rest of the floor.

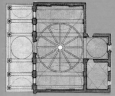

The geometric "rules" governing the design of the Pazzi Chapel are boldly expressed in Brunelleschi's architectural framework.

● THE BAROQUE

The Baroque was the artistic expression of the
Counter-Reformation. It was the evolution of
Renaissance style, from which it inherited the use
of classical forms. However, it introduced a series of new
elements, including a taste for movement, contradiction, more
complex mathematical forms, a cross-referencing of the various
artistic media (painting, sculpture, architecture), and a love of
strong contrasts of light and shadow. This created a radically new
artistic style, the aim of which
was to captivate its audience.

ARCHITECTURAL DRAMA
The Baroque was a
movement which
appealed to the senses
rather than the reason
of the spectator. For
this reason it favored
highly theatrical
designs like Bernini's
Ecstasy of Saint Teresa
in Santa Maria
della Vittoria
in Rome.

GEOMETRIC COMPLEXITY
Research into
complex relationships
between space and
light based on
elaborate geometric
patterns was typical
of the Baroque.
It found its strongest
expression in the
domes of Guarino
Guarini, such as that
of San Lorenzo ▲ *140*
in Turin (top of
page). This was
architecture of
genius, requiring
supreme
technical
mastery.

CONCAVE AND CONVEX CURVES
Movement, especially sinuous movement, is
perhaps the most idiosyncratic feature of
the Baroque. In particular, as can be seen in
Bernini's Sant'Andrea al Quirinale ▲ *369*
in Rome (right), the combination of concave
and convex curves was a favorite device.

SCENIC PLANNING
The theatrical taste
of the Baroque was
ideally suited to town
planning – as witness
the monumental
Trevi Fountain ▲ *369*
in Rome, situated at
the intersection of
two major roads and
dramatically backed
by the façade of
an aristocratic palace.

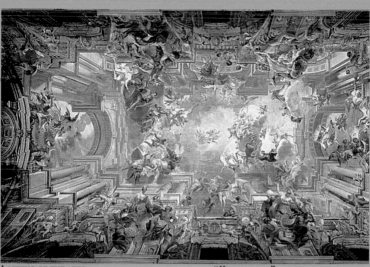

A MIXING OF THE ARTS

The Baroque taste for the theatrical extended to mixing artistic forms within a single work. It was thus that illusionistic pictures originated, like the one painted by Andrea Pozzo on the arched ceiling (above) of the Church of Sant'Ignazio ▲ 361 in Rome. The perspective used in painting this vault creates a continuation of the reality experienced by the spectator below.

"QUADRATURA"

Trompe-l'œil painted architecture, known as "quadratura", was based on the reproduction of architectural structures through the use of perspective on a flat or curved surface. The surface was subdivided into squares, the vertices of which were determined by lines converging on the vanishing point.

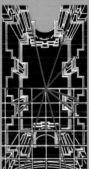

ARCHITECTURAL COMPLEXITY

The Church of Santa Maria della Salute in Venice ▲ 225 is a good example of the complex designs used by Baroque architects, while incorporating simple architectural solutions – here a series of triumphal arches inspired by ancient Rome, which are topped by an imposing cupola, embellished with gigantic volutes.

The Church of Santa Maria della Salute, designed in 1631 by Baldassare Longhena.

● NEOCLASSICISM, ECLECTICISM AND ART NOUVEAU

Neoclassical architecture in the late 18th and early 19th centuries left its mark on a number of cities, most notably Milan and Trieste. The Eclectic style of the 19th century, though not a great architectural success, nevertheless created some noteworthy urban architecture, such as the *gallerie* in Milan and Naples. However, toward the end of the century this decayed into Umbertine architecture (see below), of which a typical example is the gigantic "Vittoriano" in Rome. The Art Nouveau or "Liberty" era, although also short-lived (less than twenty years), shaped entire districts in Milan, Palermo and Turin.

ART NOUVEAU
Known as "Liberty" or "Floreale" in Italy, Art Nouveau was not a very widespread phenomenon in architectural terms. However, there are a few splendid examples surviving that bear witness to the flamboyant effects this style could achieve.

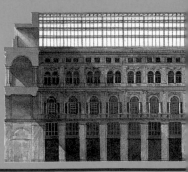

THE "VITTORIANO"
▲ 345
Built between 1885 and 1911, the "Vittoriano" or Vittorio Emanuele II Monument is a massive construction in glistening white marble, inspired by Hellenistic and Roman temples. It is the most impressive example of the ornate Umbertine architecture of the late 19th century.

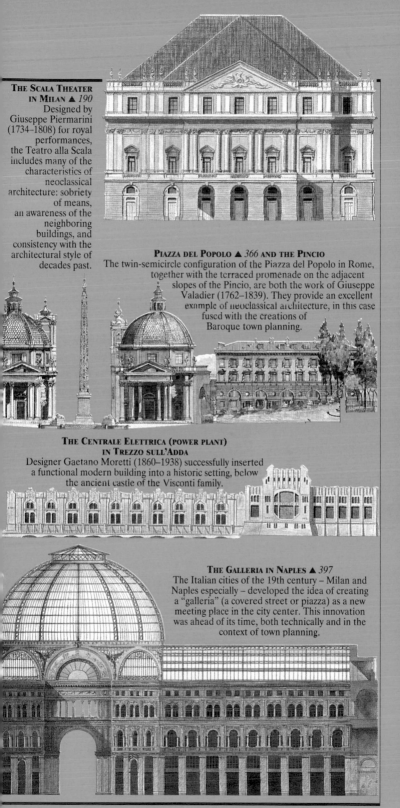

THE SCALA THEATER IN MILAN ▲ *190*
Designed by Giuseppe Piermarini (1734–1808) for royal performances, the Teatro alla Scala includes many of the characteristics of neoclassical architecture: sobriety of means, an awareness of the neighboring buildings, and consistency with the architectural style of decades past.

PIAZZA DEL POPOLO ▲ *366* **AND THE PINCIO**
The twin-semicircle configuration of the Piazza del Popolo in Rome, together with the terraced promenade on the adjacent slopes of the Pincio, are both the work of Giuseppe Valadier (1762–1839). They provide an excellent example of neoclassical architecture, in this case fused with the creations of Baroque town planning.

THE CENTRALE ELETTRICA (POWER PLANT) IN TREZZO SULL'ADDA
Designer Gaetano Moretti (1860–1938) successfully inserted a functional modern building into a historic setting, below the ancient castle of the Visconti family.

THE GALLERIA IN NAPLES ▲ *397*
The Italian cities of the 19th century – Milan and Naples especially – developed the idea of creating a "galleria" (a covered street or piazza) as a new meeting place in the city center. This innovation was ahead of its time, both technically and in the context of town planning.

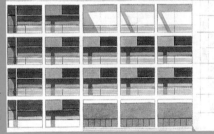

Italy was a late convert to modern architecture. It developed a style with certain typical traits, the most significant probably being the study of the expressive possibilities of structures made of reinforced concrete. Before long a number of movements arose that were inspired by the idea of combining the vocabulary of modern architecture with historic traditions. The "Neo-Liberty" of the 1950's and the Postmodernism of the 1980's are the most noteworthy examples. Of these, the former was exclusively Italian, while the latter was linked to an international movement.

THE CHURCH OF ST JOHN THE BAPTIST Giovanni Michelucci (1891–1990), the designer of the Church of San Giovanni Battista on the Milan-Naples highway, founded the "organic" wing of modern Italian architecture, influenced by Expressionism. Like many Italian architects, he explored in depth the demonstrative power of reinforced concrete.

THE CASA DEL FASCIO Giuseppe Terragni (1904-1943) was the greatest Italian architect of the first half of the 20th century. This building ▲ 205, in Como, typifies his concept of architecture, based on a careful geometric proportioning of parts.

THE PALAZZETTO DELLO SPORT IN ROME ▲ 378 Pierluigi Nervi (1891–1979), was the greatest exponent of the use of monumental structural forms in reinforced concrete. This multi-functional "palazzetto" with its prefabricated dome, built in just thirty days and placed on top of Y-shaped pillars, is a prime example of Nervi's design techniques, which were influenced by those of the great Baroque architects.

STAZIONE TERMINI IN ROME ▲ 371 Modern Italian architecture found a form of expression even during the Fascist era, in the construction of some important railway stations. This one, designed by a group of "rationalist" architects, was begun in 1938, although it was not completed until 1967. The design couples a rigidly geometric façade with plastic forms in the spacious interior.

ITALY AS SEEN BY PAINTERS

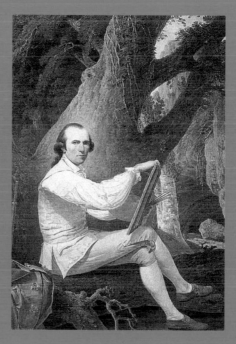

"WHEREVER YOU TURN YOUR EYES, EVERY KIND OF VISTA, NEAR AND DISTANT, CONFRONTS YOU [...] ALL OF THEM OFTEN SO CLOSE TOGETHER THAT THEY COULD BE SKETCHED ON A SINGLE SHEET OF PAPER."

JOHANN WOLFGANG GOETHE

From the 17th century onward, travel in Italy was an essential part of the Grand Tour, the obligatory journey around Europe enjoyed by privileged young European aristocrats intent on acquiring a cultural education. By the 18th century Italy was a popular destination for all kinds of visitors keen on learning, who regarded the country's artistic and cultural heritage as a vast "open museum". Their travels were well documented through diaries, essays, correspondence and memoirs; and the wealth of subjects for drawing and painting encouraged artists to create a detailed pictorial record, invaluable to scholars and fascinating for modern visitors to Italy. The paintings reproduced here are *View of Verona* (**1**) by GASPAR VAN WITTEL (c.1651–1736) and *View of the Valley of Ariccia with a Traveler Intent on Drawing* (**2**) by ABRAHAM-LOUIS DUCROS (1748–1810). Goethe was one of Italy's most famous foreign visitors.

During his first visit, in 1786, he spent almost all his time in Rome – the "capital of the world" – and was painted in the Roman countryside (**3**) by a friend, the German painter JOHANN WILHELM TISCHBEIN (1751–1829). Many artist-travelers stayed on in Italy. Ducros, for instance, lived in Rome for over thirty years; and for some it was the country where they chose to remain for the rest of their lives.

1

2

3

The hardships of crossing Calabria and the hazards of a sea crossing delayed the tourist invasion of Sicily until the 19th century. In 1787 PHILLIPP HACKERT (1737–1807) executed a series of paintings for Ferdinand IV entitled *Ports of the Kingdom of the Two Sicilies*, of which the views of Messina (**5**), Palermo and Syracuse have survived.

During the 17th and 18th centuries travelers generally followed the easier roads and stopped at post houses; the Montecenisio Pass and the Brenner Pass were the usual routes. In the first half of the 19th century the wild, uncultivated landscape of the Alps exercised a particular fascination for travelers, especially the British, despite the hazards inevitably encountered in climbing inhospitable mountains. The rugged Alpine scenery of northern Italy inspired some powerful images, such as the *St Gotthard Pass* (**4**) by J.M.W. TURNER (1775–1851). In 1839 the Naples to Portici railroad was inaugurated (**6**). The spread of train routes transformed traveling in Italy, and soon the country was no longer restricted solely to adventurous explorers.

4	**5**
6	

"ST PETER'S DOME STANDS OUT IN SILHOUETTE AGAINST THE PURE ORANGE DUSK, WHILE OVERHEAD THE OCCASIONAL STAR BEGINS TO SHINE THROUGH."

STENDHAL

Self-portrait by Giovanni Paolo Pannini.

"Today . . . I have seen an entire Roman city preserved underground with all its buildings" – so wrote Sir Horace Walpole in 1740. The excavations of Herculaneum ▲ 414 and Pompeii ▲ 414 allow direct contact with the distant, buried civilizations of the past, and the discovery of these antiquities was a revolutionary event. Paestum ▲ 417 was also a stop on the Grand Tour from the second half of the 18th century onward. This site acquired a particular significance as the meeting point of the vestiges of Greek history and Doric art; and its temples were captured in numerous drawings and paintings, such as *The Temple of Paestum* (**3**) by ANTON SMINCK PITLOO (1791–1837).

During the 18th century the genre of "*capriccio* with ruins" evolved, with fragments of ancient buildings in an imaginary landscape symbolically evoking an era long past. Single monuments were featured, as in the painting of *The Arch of Titus* (**2**), by JUAN BAUTISTA MARTÍNEZ DEL MAZO (1610/15–67), or architectural details such as the column (**4**) so carefully painted by NICOLAS POUSSIN (1594–1665). In *Imaginary Galleries with Views of Ancient Rome* (**1**) the artist, GIOVANNI PAOLO PANNINI (1691–1765), appears to have been consciously catering for the obsession with antiquity that was current among the commissioning aristocracy of the 18th century.

It was in the early 17th century, with the paintings of ANNIBALE CARRACCI (1560–1609) (**2**), that landscape painting became recognizable as a separate genre. The subtle contour of a boat slipping along the shimmering waters of a lake, the trees prominent in the foreground, the hazy outline of the mountains in the distance: each element in Carracci's painting is a component of an idealized and harmonious image of nature. The large number of drawings executed by Carracci indicate the immense interest and pleasure he gained from representing nature. In depicting the natural environment he did not always pursue the aim of faithful observation, in order to reproduce vegetation and landscape exactly; instead, he very often sought to bring out the emotions and sentiments experienced. In the age of Romanticism, the portrayal of nature frequently became a vibrant interpretation of the humor of the artist, a veritable "landscape of the soul" that reflected a particular atmosphere. A vivid example of this is the painting (**1**) by GIOVANNI CARNOVALI (1804–73, whose nickname was *Il Piccio*), where the effects of light and shade, transparency and color are subtly blended to convey the sensations of resting in a wood by a stream. The tradition of classical landscape painting had its main origin in the works of NICOLAS POUSSIN (1594–1665) and CLAUDE LORRAIN (1600–82). The work of both these artists is characterized by lyrical themes and an idealized vision

1
2

JEAN-BAPTISTE COROT (1796–1875), like Claude Lorrain, chose the Roman countryside as his favorite subject for landscape painting. The beauty of the Roman *campagna* was revealed to the artist on his first Italian journey, from 1825 to 1828 (he was to return in 1838 and 1843). Corot's approach to nature was an emotional one, combining realism with a study of light, as in the painting of the ancient-Roman bridge at Narni (**4**). Sometimes the themes of studies like this would be reworked and used in larger compositions. The paintings of Giovanni Carnovali ● *104* can be linked with those of the bohemian artists of Lombardy, such as TRANQUILLO CREMONA (1837–89) and DANIELE RANZONI (1843–89): their landscape work is characterized by a particular sensitivity and the use of transparent color washes. "I read from the great book of nature", wrote GIOVANNI FATTORI (1825–1908), who in landscapes such as *Beach with Clouds* (**5**) sought to convey "the impression of truth" through the forms and tonal values in his work. Fattori – along with the rest of the *macchiaioli* (members of the Impressionist movement in central Italy) – lived in Tuscany and drew inspiration for studies and paintings from the Tuscan landscape. The artists of the school of Rivara documented their aim to "study the countryside with love, with a free and frank impulse" (Giovanni Camerana, 1872) and to continue the tradition of landscape painting that found one of its most original interpreters in ANTONIO FONTANESI (1818–82). Modern Italian artists such as GIORGIO MORANDI (1890–1964) have tended to reconfigure and transform the realities of nature, as in *Green Landscape* (**3**), a pictorial synthesis of the Emilian countryside around Grizzana, where the painter had his retreat.

4

3

5

"[A FEELING OF] INEFFABLE JOY COMES OVER THE SOUL, AS YOU SAIL OVER THIS CALM SEA THAT GLISTENS IN THE EARLY MORNING SUN."

LEMONNIER, *MEMORIES OF ITALY*

The seascape was one of the most popular genres of the 17th century, and it remains a genre much loved by Italian painters to this day. In a lyrical vision of the Amalfi coast (**2**) GIACINTO GIGANTE (1806–76) – who in 1830, with Anton Pitloo ● *103*, gathered together the landscape painters of the Posillipo school – captured harmonies of light and freed his work from the traditional schemes of composition. Further north, MOSÈ BIANCHI (1840–1904) painted this scene at Chioggia (**3**): "Arrived in Chioggia and began with my paintbrushes even before sunrise", he noted in 1883. He also depicted aspects of daily life on the Venetian lagoon and along the *fondamenta* (paved streets) and canals of Venice, with a realistic touch. Children playing, a boat being pushed down to the sea and people enjoying their leisure, all rendered in pure, brilliant colors, characterize the *Beach at Alassio* (**1**) by EMILIO GOLA (1851–1923). Painted at the beginning of the 20th century, this is a "modern" image, the natural landscape of the bay and the stretch of sand being enlivened by a variety of figures involved in familiar activities.

1	2
3	

The piazza was the social, political and religious hub of all Italian towns. It was also a subject that was frequently chosen by painters. The result is a valuable historic and social record of many Italian towns in the days before photography. BERNARDO BELLOTTO (1720–80) painted *The Piazza San Martino in Lucca* (**2**) at a quiet moment during the course of an ordinary day. This painting is an historical document of considerable value, because it is one of the few images of Lucca executed during the 18th century that have survived. As well as being the customary place for meeting and gathering, the piazza was where the town's most important social rituals took place – a natural venue for traditional festivities and competitions, such as the horse race that is vividly depicted in *Race in the Old Piazza of Santa Maria Novella* (**1**) by ANTONIO CIOCI (1732–92). *St Mark's Square* (**3**), painted by GIOVANNI MIGLIARA (1785–1837), presents a truly striking image of Venice's most famous piazza – a scene which for many visitors to Italy offers the most poignant expression of the great richness and splendor of the Venetian civilization during the era of the doges.

1

2	3

> "EVERY TOWN SHOULD HAVE A SQUARE, RIGHT NEXT TO THE MAYOR'S RESIDENCE, WHERE THE PEOPLE CAN ASSEMBLE."
>
> *ITALY IN WORDS AND PICTURES*, 1838

At the end of the 19th century the Industrial Revolution transformed the physiognomy of some Italian cities, changing forever the familiar, recognizable features they had preserved for centuries. The new elements of this period were the stark emblems of modern architecture, such as railroads, gasworks, iron bridges, tower blocks, and construction sites. These structures reflected the essence of the Industrial Revolution. "I feel that I want to paint the new, the fruit of our industrial era", noted UMBERTO BOCCIONI (1882–1916) in Milan in 1907. In a painting called *The Rising City* (1910) Boccioni vividly captured the intense energy and vitality of the construction work involved in a growing, mutating city. *The Urban Landscape* (above) is a recurrent theme in the work of MARIO SIRONI (1885–1961); profiles and outlines of urban houses and blocks of apartments, factory chimneys, streets traversed by trams or flanked by railroads: these are constant elements in his work. It is the vision of a fragmented, silent city, where the total absence of human figures imparts a sense of solitude and alienation.

ITALY AS SEEN BY WRITERS

THE ADVENTURE OF TRAVEL

ACROSS THE ALPS

Benvenuto Cellini (1500–71) was a Florentine sculptor, a gold- and silversmith and an engraver. His patrons included two popes, Clement VII and Paul III, and King Francis I of France.

❝When we had crossed the mountains of the Simplon, we came to a river near a place called Indevedro. [Probably the Doveria in the Valdivedro.] It was broad and very deep, spanned by a long narrow bridge without ramparts. That morning a thick white frost had fallen; and when I reached the bridge, riding before the rest, I recognised how dangerous it was, and bade my servants and young men dismount and lead their horses. So I got across without accident, and rode on talking with one of the Frenchmen, whose condition was that of a gentleman. The other, who was a scrivener, lagged a little way behind, jeering the French gentleman and me because we had been so frightened by nothing at all as to give ourselves the trouble of walking. I turned round, and seeing him upon the middle of the bridge, begged him to come gently, since the place was very dangerous. The fellow, true to his French nature, cried out in French that I was a man of poor spirit, and that there was no danger whatsoever. While he spoke these words and urged his horse forward, the animal suddenly slipped over the bridge, and fell with legs in the air close to a huge rock there was there. Now God is very often merciful to madmen; so the two beasts, human and equine, plunged together into a deep wide pool, where both of them went down below the water. On seeing what had happened, I set off running at full speed, scrambled with much difficulty on to the rock, and dangling over from it, seized the skirt of the scrivener's gown and pulled him up, for he was still submerged beneath the surface. He had drunk his bellyful of water, and was within an ace of being drowned. I then, beholding him out of danger, congratulated the man upon my having been the means of rescuing his life. The fellow to this answered me in French, that I had done nothing; the important things to save were his writings, worth many scores of crowns; and these words he seemed to say in anger, dripping wet and spluttering the while. Thereupon, I turned round to our guides, and ordered them to help the brute, adding that I would see them paid. One of them with great address and trouble set himself to the business, and picked up all the fellow's writings, so that he lost not one of them; the other guide refused to trouble himself by rendering any assistance.❞

BENVENUTO CELLINI, *THE LIFE OF BENVENUTO CELLINI*,
TRANS. JOHN ADDINGTON SYMONS,
PUB. MACMILLAN, LONDON, 1925

APPROACH VIA THE SEA

The English novelist Charles Dickens (1812–70) made a tour of Italy in 1844, just after the completion of his book "Martin Chuzzlewit". He recorded his impressions of that visit in a collection entitled "Pictures from Italy".

❝We went down to the harbour, where sailors of all nations were discharging and taking in cargoes of all kinds: fruits, wines, oils, silks, stuffs, velvets, and every manner of merchandise. Taking one of a great number of lively little boats with gay-striped awnings, we rowed away, under the sterns of great ships, . . . against and among other boats, and very much too near the sides of vessels that were faint with oranges, to the Marie Antoinette, a handsome steamer bound for Genoa, lying near the mouth of the harbour. By-and-by, the carriage, that unwieldy 'trifle from the Pantechnicon', on a flat barge, bumping against everything, and giving occasion for a prodigious quantity of oaths and grimaces, came stupidly alongside; and by five o'clock we were steaming out in the open sea. The vessel was beautifully clean; the meals were served under an awning on deck; the night was calm and clear; the quiet beauty of the sea and sky unspeakable.

We were off Nice, early next morning, and coasted along, within a few miles of the Cornice road (of which more in its place) nearly all day. We could see Genoa before three; and watching it as it gradually developed its splendid amphitheatre, terrace rising upon terrace, garden upon garden, palace upon palace, height upon height, was ample occupation for us, till we ran into the stately harbour. Having been duly astonished, here, by the sight of a few Cappucini monks, who were watching the fair-weighing of some wood upon the wharf, we drove to Albaro, two miles distant, where we had engaged a house.

The way lay through the main streets, but not through the Strada Nuova, or the Stradi Balbi, which are the famous streets of palaces. I never in my life was so dismayed! The wonderful novelty of everything, the unusual smells, the unaccountable filth (though it is reckoned the cleanest of Italian towns), the disorderly jumbling of dirty houses, one upon the roof of another; the passages more squalid and more close than any in St. Giles's or old Paris; in and out of which, not vagabonds but well-dressed women, with white veils and great fans, were passing and repassing; the perfect absence of resemblance in any dwelling-house, or shop, or wall, or post, or pillar, to anything one had ever seen before; and the disheartening dirt, discomfort, and decay; perfectly confounded me. I fell into a dismal reverie. I am conscious of a feverish and bewildered vision of saints and virgins' shrines at the street corners – of great numbers of friars, monks, and soldiers – of vast red curtains, waving in the door-ways of the churches – of always going up hill, and yet seeing every other street and passage going higher up – of fruit-stalls, with fresh lemons and oranges hanging in garlands made of vine-leaves – of a guard-house, and a drawbridge – and some gateways – and vendors of iced water, sitting with little trays . . . – and this is all the consciousness I had, until I was set down in a rank, dull, weedy courtyard, attached to a kind of pink jail; and was told I lived there.

I little thought, that day, that I should ever come to have an attachment for the very stones in the streets of Genoa, and to look back on the city with affection as connected with many hours of happiness and quiet! But these are my first impressions honestly set down; and how they changed, I will set down too. At present, let us breathe after this long-winded journey.❞

CHARLES DICKENS,
PICTURES FROM ITALY,
PUB. CHAPMAN & HALL,
LONDON, 1846

On the way

A street in Milan

The whimsical and satirical American writer and essayist Washington Irving (1783–1859) lived in Europe for seventeen years.

❝The city of Milan bears more the appearance of a french town than any other that I have seen in Italy. There is a great bustle and vivacity in the looks and motions of the inhabitants that is not often found among the Italians. They have assumed considerable of the french character from their frequent intercourse with that nation. There are numerous places of amusement for the poorer classes who cannot afford the expence of the grand theatres; and for the honest mob there is always a variety of entertainments going on in the grand square. We amused ourselves with walking there yesterday after dinner – At one end of the square a juggler had drawn around him a numerous rabble whom he was entertaining with the trick of shaking eggs out of an apparently empty bag – the fellow went thro a variety of deceptions with admirable dexterity and tho I watched him for some moments with the strictest attention I could not detect one of them –The honest multitude took no pains to discover his impositions – contenting themselves with the old conclusion that he dealt with the devil. Not far from him another Juggler had attracted an audience equally numerous and respectable – he had displayed a great variety of apparatus which were arranged on the ground – and was performing a number of feats of dexterity in balancing swords platters tables &c. In another place punch & his family were holding forth from a little portable theatre and in a fifth a sturdy fellow was exhibiting his agility & graces on a little horse which he had learned a number of tricks & manouvres. These humble candidates for the favors of the multitude have no price for their performances but throw themselves upon the generosity of their audience who reccompence them with a few sous for their strenuous efforts to please. Some of these fellows are not deficient in humor & eloquence and I have heard them hold forth to the mob for some time with an energy and volubility that generally succeeded in drawing the pence from the pockets of their hearers.**❞**

WASHINGTON IRVING, *JOURNALS AND NOTEBOOKS, VOL. 1, 1803–06,* ED. *NATHALIA WRIGHT,* PUB. UNIVERSITY OF WISCONSIN PRESS, MADISON, 1969

Vesuvius

In September 1786 Johann Wolfgang Goethe (1749–1832), the German poet, novelist and dramatist, left Weimar to travel to Italy. The journal that he kept during this time later became the basis for his book "Italiensche Reise" ("Italian Journey").

❝*March 2*
Today I climbed Vesuvius, although the sky was overcast and the summit hidden in clouds. I

took a carriage to Resina, where I mounted a mule and rode up the mountain through vineyards. Then I walked across the lava flow of 1771 which was already covered with a fine but tenacious moss, and then upward along its edge. High up on my left I could see the hermit's hut. Climbing the ash cone, which was two-thirds hidden in clouds, was not easy. At last I reached the old crater, now blocked, and came to the fresh lava flows, one two months, one two weeks, and one only five days old. This last had been feeble amd had already cooled. I crossed it and climbed a hill of ashes which had been recently thrown up and was emitting fumes everywhere. As the smoke was drifting away . . . I decided to try and reach the crater. I had only taken fifty steps when the smoke became so dense that I could hardly see my shoes. The handkerchief I pressed over my mouth was no help. In addition, my guide had disappeared and my steps on the little lava chunks which the eruption had discharged became more and more unsteady. I thought it better, therefore, to turn back and wait for a day with less cloud and less smoke. At least I now know how difficult it is to breathe in such an atmosphere.

March 3

Today the sky is overcast and a sirocco is blowing – just the weather for writing letters. I won't say another word about the beauties of the city and its situation, which have been described and praised so often. As they say here, '*Vedi Napoli e poi muori!*' 'See Naples and die!' **99**

JOHANN WOLFGANG GOETHE, *ITALIAN JOURNEY*, TRANS. W.H. AUDEN AND ELIZABETH MAYER, PUB. COLLINS, LONDON, 1962

CARRARA

In the following extract Charles Dickens gives a vivid description of his journey to Carrara.

66 The Magra safely crossed in the Ferry Boat – the passage is not by any means agreeable, when the current is swollen and strong – we arrived at Carrara, within a few hours. In good time next morning, we got some ponies, and went out to see the marble quarries.

They are four or five great glens, running up into a range of lofty hills, until they can run no longer, and are stopped by being abruptly strangled by Nature. The quarries, 'or caves', as they call them there, are so many openings, high up in the hills, on either side of these passes, where they blast and excavate for marble: which may turn out good or bad: may make a man's fortune very quickly, or ruin him by the great expense of working what is worth nothing. Some of these caves were opened by the ancient Romans, and remain as they left them to this hour. Many others are being worked at this moment; others are to be begun to-morrow, next week, next month; others are unbought, unthought of; and marble enough for more ages than have passed since the place was resorted to, lies hidden everywhere: patiently waiting its time of discovery.

As you toil and clamber up one of these steep gorges (having left your pony soddening his girths in water, a mile or two lower down) you hear, every now and then, echoing among the hills, in a low tone, more silent than the previous silence, a melancholy warning bugle, – a signal to the miners to withdraw. Then, there is a thundering, and echoing from hill to hill, and perhaps a splashing up of great fragments of rock into the air; and on you toil again until some other bugle sounds, in a new direction, and you stop directly, lest you should come within the range of the new explosion.

There were numbers of men, working high up in these hills – on the sides clearing away, and sending down the broken masses of stone and earth, to make way for the blocks of marble that had been discovered. As these came rolling down from unseen hands into the narrow valley, I could not help thinking of the deep glen . . . where the Roc left Sinbad the Sailor; and where the merchants from the heights above, flung down great pieces of meat for the diamonds to stick to. There were no eagles here, to darken the sun in their swoop, and pounce on them; but it was as wild and fierce as if there had been hundreds.**"**

CHARLES DICKENS, *PICTURES FROM ITALY,*
PUB. CHAPMAN & HALL, LONDON, 1846

TURIN

John Ruskin (1819–1900) spent much of his life traveling in Europe and was particularly attached to northern Italy. His preference was for the landscapes, arts and architecture, rather than the people he found there.

"I shall not fail to send you a full account of Turin palace, though as it is fine weather just now, and the sun is precious in the gallery of paintings, I reserve the palace for a darker day. But you are right in guessing that Turin would look livelier; it seems in as high a state of prosperity as it is possible for an Italian town to be. It will take very long however before they can do anything great. I should say by the look of them – they were quite lost, but as they certainly do manage a railroad well, I don't see why other things should not come in time. But there is a look about the Italian women which is very hopeless. The French show quite as much attention to dress, but in the Italians one sees that this attention occupies the whole of their brains. A French woman dresses with care; then can think and talk of something else. The Italians look as if dressing were all they lived for, and this gives a particular vulgarity of prominence to the dress itself which makes every well dressed Italian one meets, look impudent. The fashion of bonnet, here quite caricatured from London & Paris, throwing forward faces in themselves sufficiently bold and powerful, adds much to this effect – a slight touch of the Borgia seems occasionally added where the features are very fine. It is said that the Italian gentlemen think of nothing else but amours; if this be so, the necessary result will be giving to the modestest and best conducted women a general air of defiance and resistance which, with these adjuncts of unfortunate fashion, will sufficiently account for the absence of all sweet and soft expression.**"**

JOHN RUSKIN, *JOHN RUSKIN – LETTERS FROM THE CONTINENT 1858,*
ED. JOHN HAYMAN, PUB. UNIVERSITY OF TORONTO PRESS,
TORONTO, 1982

CITIES IN THE MIRROR

MILAN

As well as novels, short stories, plays and essays, the American author Henry James (1843–1916) wrote several volumes of travel sketches.

❝I have been strolling about Milan all the morning, drinking in the delicious Italian sun, which fortunately shines, and giving myself up to the sweet sense of being once more – after an interval of several years – in the adorable country it illumines. It is Sunday and all the world is in the streets and squares . . . Churches and galleries have such a fatal chill that being sorethroatish and neuralgic I have had to keep out of them – but the Duomo lifts all its pinncales and statues into the far-away light, and looks across at the other white needles and spires of the Alps in the same bewildering cluster.❞

HENRY JAMES, *LETTERS, VOL. III*, ED. LEON EDEL, PUB. MACMILLAN, LONDON, 1981

THE CHARM OF MILAN

Rome, Naples, Florence and Milan were all dear to the French novelist Stendhal (pseudonym of Henri Beyle, 1783–1842). The following extract is taken from "Naples and Florence", the first book in which he used the pen name 'Stendhal'.

❝Nothing can be more mild, more amiable, more attractive than the manners of the Milanese women; they are the very opposite to the English manners; at Milan every lady has her *cavaliere* by her side, while mild jokes, lively disputes, laughs which come from the heart fly about, but never any airs or self-importance. When we are once accustomed to the charm of this sort of society, at Milan, we can never relish any other. Many a Frenchman, while this city was in its prosperity, has come hither to receive chains which he has carried with him to the tomb.

Milan has the handsomest streets and Course of any town in Europe; it contains four or five thousand columns of granite. The people present a combination of two things, which I have seldom seen united together in an equal degree, goodness and wisdom. . . .❞

STENDHAL, *ROME, NAPLES AND FLORENCE IN 1817*,
PUB. HENRY COLBURN, LONDON, 1818

A MORE CRITICAL VIEW

Washington Irving found the busy city of Milan to be decidedly lacking in appeal.

❝*April 30.* Milan is an extensive town and very populous. The streets are crowded by people who seem all busy – This together with the vast number of shops give it an air of great business. It appears to be by no means deficient in manufactures particularly in gold & silver work – such as gold & silver laces, embroideries – tinsel – gold and silver thread – also silk handkerchiefs – stockings – gloves – raw silk &c &c.

It is a kind of deposit for the merchandize that passes between Italy France Switzerland & part of Germany – and the goods passing thro the hands of the Milanese enrich them very much by commissions.

The streets are not by any means handsome nor does the city possess any squares of importance excepting the one in front of the cathedral – This is a singular building of vast size which has been building about four hundred years and is yet unfinished. Those who commenced it sat out on a scheme of grandeur and expence that they could not complete and their successors have contented themselves rather with repairing what was already built than compleating the edifice. Workmen are constantly employed on it, but as fast as they build up one part another gives way so that . . . the work does not seem to be nearer to completion at the end of the year than it was at the beginning . . .

As far as it is completed it affords a beautiful specimen of the Gothic style but strangely mingled in some parts with other styles of architecture. The whole outside of the church is covered with fine Carrara marble excepting the front, part of which still remains rough brick work.

The profusion of statues, reliefs and other carved ornaments with which the outside is decorated is astonishing. . . .

The grand steeple is very high and of superb Gothic architecture (180 feet high) and of white marble. This church was begun in 1386 and is after St Peters at Rome the largest church in Italy. From the . . . marble & carvings, it has already cost more than St Peters tho the latter is finished.**99**

WASHINGTON IRVING, *JOURNALS AND NOTEBOOKS, VOL. 1, 1803–06,* PUB. THE UNIVERSITY OF WISCONSIN PRESS, MADISON, MILWAUKEE, LONDON, 1969

VENICE

Anton Pavlovich Chekhov (1860–1904), Russian dramatist and short-story writer, was thrilled by everything Venice had to offer.

66*Venice, March 24, 1891.* One thing I can tell you – in all my life I have never seen any cities more remarkable than Venice. It is utter enchantment, brilliance, joy of life. In lieu of streets and alleys, canals; in lieu of cabbies, gondolas; the architecture is amazing, and there isn't the least spot that would fail to arouse historic or artistic interest. You float along in a gondola and see the palazzos of the doges, the house where Desdemona lived, the houses of famous artists, houses of worship. And in these houses of worship the sculpture and painting are such as we have never dreamed of . . .

All day from morning to evening. I loll in a gondola and float through the streets or ramble over the famous Piazza of St. Mark. This piazza is as even and clean as a parquet floor. Here one finds the Cathedral of St. Mark (something which is beyond description), the Palazzo of the Doges, and certain edifices which are to my sensations what scored notes are to singers. . . .

In the evening, being unaccustomed to it all, you could die. You are riding in a gondola – warmth, stillness, stars. . . . Gondolas darting all around.... Here's a gondola riding along, with little lanterns hung all over it. Seated in it are a double bass, violins, a guitar, a mandolin, a cornet, two or three ladies, several men – and you hear singing and instruments. They sing operatic arias. What voices! . . .

Venice, March 25, 1891. Ah, Signori e Signorine, what a wondrous city this Venice is! Picture to yourselves a city made up of . . . an inebriating architecture in which everything is as graceful, light, as the birdlike gondola . . . And everything . . . is inundated by sun.**99**

ANTON CHEKHOV, *LETTERS OF ANTON CHEKHOV,* SELECTED AND EDITED BY AVRAHM YARMOLINSKY, PUB. THE VIKING PRESS, NEW YORK, 1973

FLORENCE

The novels of the English writer E.M. Forster (1879–1970) are filled with shrewd observations of life and an attention to detail that allows to him create a vivid impression of the times in which he lived.

❝*Chapter II*
In Santa Croce with no Baedeker
It was pleasant to wake up in Florence, to open the eyes upon a bright bare room, with a floor of red tiles which look clean though they are not . . . It was pleasant, too, to fling wide the windows, pinching the fingers in unfamiliar fastenings, to lean out into the sunshine with beautiful hills and trees and marble churches opposite, and, close below, the Arno, gurgling against the embankment of the road.

Over the river men were at work with spades and sieves on the sandy foreshore, and on the river was a boat, also diligently employed for some mysterious end. An electric tram came rushing underneath the window. No one was inside it, except one tourist; but its platforms were overflowing with Italians, who preferred to stand. Children tried to hang on behind, and the conductor, with no malice, spat in their faces to make them let go.**❞**

E.M. FORSTER, *A ROOM WITH A VIEW,*
PUB. EDWARD ARNOLD & CO., LONDON, 1908

ROME

On this particular visit, Dame Freya Stark (1893–1993), British travel writer and photographer, chose to arrive in Rome in true Italian style.

❝Dearest Jock,
Such a lark, we have Vespa'd down to Rome from Perugia. Of course it has been icy ever since we left Asolo in a snowstorm to come south (that awful Mediterranean cold that cuts through you like a knife): the Vespa had to be fitted into the car to get her to Padova. . . . Then in Florence, rain, snow on the hills, huge cloudy skies, everyone said I was killing Stewart – so on to the train again, to Perugia. By this time we began to look on the Vespa with aversion as a holiday pet. We warmed to her after a fine day at Assisi, but then more rain came down and Stewart was all for waiting and doing the whole train business over again to Rome. But the little page boy of the hotel, who had become passionately interested in us and the Vespa, said the wind was in the right quarter (the North Pole it felt like), so there was no more dallying. We spent the afternoon going to Todi and slept in a primitive little set of rooms over the pawnshop – very cold, but Stewart was cheered by discovering a Roman forum and I would suffer a lot for a sight of the deserted piazza at night, those gaunt thirteenth-century palaces and churches staring at each other, with the wind swaying the electric lights, and puddles glittering below them. . .

Next day, yesterday, we came all the way to Rome – about eighty miles I suppose – along the beautiful ridges that slope down to Terni and then by a small despised

forgotten non-tarmac road that reaches up and down over small ranges to the Tiber in the south. . . We got here for tea and risked our lives across Rome where no one thinks of traffic rules but only gives a look to see whether the opposing vehicle is larger or smaller; of course the Vespa is fair game for anyone to run at!**99**

FREYA STARK, *OVER THE RIM OF THE WORLD, SELECTED LETTERS*
PUB. FABER & FABER, LONDON, 1975

WHEN IN ROME. . .
John Cheever (1912–82), American novelist and short-story writer, clearly has his own views on how best to experience living in Rome.

66I'm going out and buy a car this morning; I'm going out and try to buy a car. Then I will try to drive it for the traffic here is really murderous. When you first arrive and Fiats keep ripping the buttons off your suitcoat you think Ah yes, but no one ever gets killed. Then you see an old lady bowled over by a Vespa and rolled the breadth of the Piazza Rotounda like a beer keg and you begin to wonder. Then you're shown statistics and realize that more people are run over in a year than were ever killed in the gladitorial combats as you poke along the corso you think up moral judgements about life in Rome.**99**

JOHN CHEEVER, *THE LETTERS OF JOHN CHEEVER*,
PUB. SIMON & SCHUSTER, NEW YORK, 1988

A TOUR OF THE CITY
Judging by the following account, Rome failed to live up to the expectations of Irish writer James Joyce (1882–1941).

66I have seen S. Peter's, the Pincio, Forum, Colisseum [sic]. The Vatican is closed on Sundays, my only free day. S. Peter's did not seem to me much bigger than S. Paul's in London. The dome from inside does not give the same impression of height. S. Peter is buried in the middle of the church. The Pincio is a fine garden overlooking one gate of the city. I expected to hear great music at the mass in S. Peter's but it was nothing much. However it was a side-altar high mass. The church has about twenty altars. The neighbourhood of the Colisseum is like an old cemetary with broken columns of temples and slabs. You know the Colisseum from pictures. While we were in the middle of it, looking at it all round gravely from a sense of duty, I heard a voice from London on one of the lowest gallery [sic] say:

The first thing I look for in a city is the café. Rome has one café and that one is not as good as any of the best in Trieste. This is a damn bore for me. It has however countless little coffee-bars. I am forced to go to a little Greek restaurant, frequented by Amiel, Thackeray, Byron, Ibsen and Co...

Yesterday I went to see the Forum. I sat down on a stone bench overlooking the ruins. It was hot and sunny. Carriages were full of tourists, postcard sellers, medal sellers, photograph sellers. I was so moved that I almost fell asleep and had to rise brusquely. I looked at the stone bench ruefully but it was too hard and the grass near the Colosseum was too far. So I went home sadly. Rome reminds me of a man who lives by exhibiting to travellers his grandmother's corpse. On the way home from the Forum being very tired I went into a Dominican church where I found a comfortable straw chair. I watched two nuns at confession. Confession over confessor and penitents left the church in the direction of the cloister. But the nuns came back very shortly and knelt down beside me.**"**

JAMES JOYCE, *SELECTED LETTERS*, ED. RICHARD ELLMANN,
PUB. FABER & FABER, LONDON, 1975

CAGLIARI

The British writer D.H. Lawrence (1885–1930) was particularly fond of Italy and even made it his home for part of his life. His atmospheric descriptions of his travels are particularly impressive.

"After a really good meal we went out to see the town. It was after three o'clock and everywhere was shut up like an English Sunday. Cold, stony Cagliari: in summer you must be sizzling hot, Cagliari, like a kiln. The men stood about in groups, but without the intimate Italian watchfulness that never leaves a passer-by alone.

Strange, stony Cagliari. We climbed up a street like a corkscrew stairway. And we saw announcements of a children's fancy-dress ball. Cagliari is very steep. Half-way up there is a strange place called the bastions, a large level space like a drill ground with trees, curiously suspended over the town, and sending off a long shoot like a wide viaduct, across above the corkscrew street that comes climbing up. Above this bastion place the town still rises steeply to the Cathedral and the fort. What is so curious is that this terrace or bastion is so large, like some big recreation ground, that it is almost dreary, and one cannot understand its being suspended in mid-air. Down below is the little circle of the harbour. To the left a low, malarial-looking sea plain, with tufts of palm trees and Arab-looking houses. From this runs out the long spit of land towards that black-and-white watch-fort, the white road trailing forth. On the right, most curiously, a long strange spit of sand runs in a causeway far across the shallows of the bay, with the open sea on one hand, and vast end-of-the-world lagoons on the other. There are peaky, dark mountains beyond this – just as across the vast bay are gloomy hills. It is a strange, strange landscape: as if here the world left off.**"**

D.H. LAWRENCE, *SEA AND SARDINIA*,
PUB. WILLIAM HEINEMANN, LONDON, 1956

DISCOVERING HABITS AND CUSTOMS

A VISIT TO THE POPE

In his journal, Michel Eyquem de Montaigne (1533–92), the French moralist and essayist, describes people, as well as places, that he encountered during his travels.

❝On December 29th M. d'Abein, our ambassador, a learned gentleman and a longstanding friend of M. de Montaigne, advised him to go and kiss the feet of the Pope. M. de Montaigne and M. d'Estissac went in the coach of the ambassador, who, after he had been granted an audience, caused them to be called by the Pope's chamberlain. According to custom, only the ambassador was with the Pope, who had by his side a bell which he would ring when he might wish any one to be introduced. The ambassador was seated, uncovered, at his left hand; the Pope himself never uncovers before any one, nor can any ambassador remain covered in his presence. . . . After taking a step or two into the chamber, in a corner of which sits the Pope, the incomer, whoever he may be, kneels and waits for the Pope to give him benediction. This done, he will rise and advance to the middle of the room, but a stranger rarely approaches the Pope by going direct across the floor, the more ordinary practice being to turn to the left on entering, and then, after making a détour along the wall, to approach his chair. But when the stranger has gone half the distance he must kneel again on one knee, and, having received a second benediction, next advances as far as the thick carpet spread out some seven or eight feet in front of the Pope. Here he must kneel on both knees, while the ambassador who presents him kneels on one, and moves back the Popes's robe from his right foot, which is shod in a red shoe with a white cross thereupon. The kneeling stranger must keep himself in the same posture until he is close to the Pope's foot, and then bend down to kiss it. . . . They all kissed it one after the other, making room for each other after the ceremony was done. Then the ambassador covered the Pope's foot, and, having risen to his seat, said what seemed necessary on behalf of M. d'Estissac and M. de Montaigne. The Pope, with courteous expression of face, admonished M. d'Estissac to cultivate learning and virtue, and M. de Montaigne to maintain the devotion he had always exhibited towards the Church and the interests of the most Christian King: whatever service he could do them they might depend on, this being an Italian figure of speech. They said nothing, but, having been blessed again before rising as a sign of dismissal, they went back . . . Each one retreats as it seems best, but the ordinary custom is to go backward, or at least sideways, so as always to look the Pope in the face. As in entering, each one kneels half-way on one knee for another benediction, and again at the door for the last. ❞

MICHEL EYQUEM DE MONTAIGNE, *THE JOURNAL OF MONTAIGNE'S TRAVELS IN ITALY BY WAY OF SWITZERLAND AND GERMANY IN 1580 AND 1581*, TRANS. W.G. WATERS, PUB. JOHN MURRAY, LONDON, 1903

VENETIAN AMOURS

The poet Lord Byron (1788–1824) spent five years in Italy in total. He seemed very impressed with Venice in general and with Venetian women in particular.

❝[Venice] pleases me – I have found some pleasing society – & the romance of the situation – & it's extraordinary appearance – together with all the associations we are accustomed to connect with Venice – have always had a charm for me – even before I arrived here – and I have not been disappointed in what I have seen – I have fallen in love with a very pretty Venetian of two and twenty – with great black eyes – she is married – and so am I – which is very much to the purpose – we have found & sworn eternal attachment – which has already lasted a lunar month – & I am more in love than ever – & so is the lady – at least she says so – & seems so, – she does not plague me (which is a wonder –) and I verily believe we are one of the happiest – unlawful couples on this side of the Alps. – She is very handsome – very Italian or rather Venetian – with something more of the Oriental case of countenance; – accomplished & musical after the manner of her nation – her spouse is a very good kind of man who occupies himself elsewhere – and thus the world goes on here as elsewhere. – This adventure came very opportunely to console me – for I was beginning to be 'like Sam Jennings very *unappy*' but at present – at least for a month past – I have been very tranquil – very loving – & have not so much embarrassed myself with the tortures of the last two years.**❞**

LORD BYRON, *LORD BYRON – SELECTED LETTERS AND JOURNALS*, ED. LESLIE A. MARCHAND, PUB. JOHN MURRAY, LONDON, 1982

CARNIVAL IN ROME

The lively, colorful Italian carnivals were very different from any celebrations that Charles Dickens would have experienced in Victorian England.

❝But if the scene be bright, and gay, and crowded, on the last day but one, it attains, on the concluding day, to such a height of glittering colour, swarming life, and frolicsome uproar, that the bare recollection of it makes me giddy at this moment. The same diversions, greatly heightened and intensified in the ardour with which they are pursued, go on until the same hour. The race is repeated; the cannon are fired; the shouting and clapping of hands are renewed; the cannon are fired again; the race is over; and the prizes are won. But the carriages – ankle-deep with sugar-plums within, and so be-flowered and dusty without, as to be hardly recognisable for the same vehicles that they were, three hours ago: instead of scampering off in all directions, throng into the Corso, where they are soon wedged together in a scarcely moving mass. For the diversion of the Moccoletti, the last gay madness of the Carnival, is now at hand; and sellers of little tapers like what are called Christmas candles in England, are shouting lustily on every side, 'Moccoli, Moccoli! Ecco Moccoli!' – a new item in the tumult; quite abolishing that other item of 'Ecco Fióri! Ecco Fio – r – r!' which has been making itself audible over all the rest, at intervals, the whole day through.

As the bright hangings and dresses are all fading into one dull, heavy, uniform colour in the decline of the day, lights begin flashing . . in the windows, on the house-tops, in the balconies, in the carriages, in the hands of the foot-passengers: little by little . . . until the whole long street is one great glare and blaze of fire. Then, everybody present has but one engrossing object; that is, to extinguish other people's candles, and to keep his own alight; and everybody: man, woman, or child, gentleman or lady, prince or peasant, native or foreigner: yells and screams, and roars incessantly, as a taunt to the subdued, 'Senza Moccolo, Senza Moccolo!' (Without a light! Without a light!) until nothing is heard but a gigantic chorus of those two words, mingled with peals of laughter.

The spectacle, at this time, is one of the most extraordinary that can be imagined. Carriages coming slowly by, with everybody standing on the seats or on the box, holding up their lights at arms' length, for greater safety; some in paper shades; some with a bunch of undefended little tapers, kindled altogether; some with blazing torches; some with feeble little candles; men on foot, creeping along, among the wheels, watching their opportunity, to make a spring at some particular light, and dash it out; other people climbing up into carriages, to get hold of them by main force; others, chasing some unlucky wanderer, round and round his own coach, to blow out the light he has begged or stolen somewhere, before he can ascend to his own company, and enable them to light their extinguished tapers . . . other people at the windows, fishing for candles with lines and hooks, or letting down long willow-wands with handkerchiefs at the end, and flapping them out, dexterously, when the bearer is at the height of his triumph; others, biding their time in corners, with immense extinguishers like halberds, and suddenly coming down upon glorious torches . . . others, raining oranges and nosegays at an obdurate little lantern, or regularly storming a pyramid of men, holding up one man among them all, who carries one feeble little wick above his head, with which he defies them all! . . . Beautiful women, standing up in coaches, pointing in derision at extinguished lights, and clapping their hands, as they pass on, crying 'Senza Moccolo! Senza Moccolo!'; low balconies full of lovely faces and gay dresses, struggling with assailants in the streets; some repressing them as they climb up . . . graceful figures – glowing lights, fluttering dresses, Senza Moccolo, Senza Moccolo, Senza Moc-co-lo-o-o-o! – when in the wildest enthusiasm of the cry, and fullest ecstasy of the sport, the Ave Maria rings from the church steeples, and the Carnival is over in an instant – put out like a taper, with a breath!**99**

CHARLES DICKENS, *PICTURES FROM ITALY*,
PUB. CHAPMAN AND HALL, LONDON, 1846

ITALIAN FOOD AND CULTURE

Elizabeth David (1913–92) wrote about food and cookery in a style that was both passionate and poetic. She was interested in the culture of food and the country which produced it, and had a much greater interest in regional cooking than in haute cuisine.

66In Italy the best fish is actually to be eaten on the coast, the finest Parmesan cheese in and around Parma, the tenderest beef in Tuscany, where the cattle are raised. So the tourist, having arrived in Italy via Naples and there mistakenly ordered a beef steak which turns out to be a rather shrivelled slive of veal, will thereafter avoid *bistecca*, so that when he visits Florence he will miss that remarkable *bistecca alla Fiorentina*, a vast steak, grilled over a wood fire, which, tender and aromatic, is a dish worth going some way to eat. How many transatlantic travellers landing in Genoa have dined in some Grand Hotel or other and gone on their way without ever suspecting that Genoa possesses a cookery of a most highly individual nature, unique in Europe? Everyone has heard of the *mortadella* sausage of Bologna, but how

many hurrying motorists drive past the rose and ochre coloured arcades of Bologna quite unaware that behind modest doorways are some of the best restaurants in Italy? Alas for them, they will remain ignorant of those remarkable dishes consisting of a breast of chicken or turkey cooked in butter, smothered with fine slices of those white truffles which are one of the glories of Italian cooking. Every Italian restaurant abroad serves a dish of so called *tagliatelle Bolognese*; it is worth visiting Bologna to find out what this dish really tastes like, and to accompany it with a bottle of that odd but delicious Lambrusco wine which combines so well with the rich Bolognese cooking. In Venice, nursing aggrieved memories of wooly Mediterranean fish, the traveller will refuse sole on the grounds that it can be eaten only in London or Paris. He will miss a treat, for the soles of the Adriatic have a particularly fine flavour. In Parma he will scarcely fail to eat Parma ham; but if he is not sufficiently inquisitive he will not taste another first-class local speciality, the Felino *salame*, which is one of the most excellent sausages produced in Italy. There are still dishes which are made in certain seasons or for certain festivals and at no other time of the year. Heavy winter dishes such as the *polenta pasticciata* of Lombardy, the *lasagne verdi al forno* of Bologna and the brown bean soup of the Veneto give way after Easter to lighter dishes of *pasta in brodo*, or *antipasti* (hors d'œuvre) of raw vegetables, or little *crostini*, fried bread with cheese and anchovies. One of the summer dishes common to all Italy is *vitello tonnato*, cold veal with a tunny fish flavoured sauce (this sounds outlandish, but is, in fact, a most excellent combination).

The names of Italian dishes are to say the least, confusing, and vary immensely from region to region. Ravioli as we think of it in England is called ravioli only in Piedmont and Genoa, but it is never stuffed with the coarse mixture met with outside Italy and never smothered with an oily tomato sauce. In other districts there are endless varieties of ravioli called *tortellini, anolini, tortelli, cappelletti, malfatti, agnolotti*. The *pasta* which we should call noodles, is known variously as *fettuccine, tagliatelle, tagliarini, pappardelle;* there are thin, match-like strips of the same pasta called tagliolini in Florence, *trenette* in Genoa, *tonnarelli* in Rome. *Pasticciata* is a meat stew in Verona, a *polenta au gratin* in Milan. The names of fish are particularly hard to disentangle. The squid and cuttle-fish family are known as *seppie, totani, calamari, calamaretti, moscardini, fragole di mare, sepolini*, and several other names according to the local dialect. Mussels are *cozze* in Naples, *peoci* in Venice, *telline* in Florence: they are also known as *muscoli* and *mitili*, and *telline* are also clams, which are *vongole* in Rome and Naples, *capperozzoli* in Venice, *arselle* in Genoa and Sardinia.

Saltimbocca, bocconcini, quagliette di vitello, braciolette, uccelletti, scappati, gropetti, involtini, are all variations of the same little slices of veal with a piece of ham or some kind of stuffing inside; they may be rolled up or they may be flattened out, they may be fried or baked or grilled. *Fritelle* may indicate anything from a very small rissole of meat and herbs (also called *polpette*) to a huge rustic potato cake made with yeast. Its unpredictable nature adds the charm of surprise to the discovery of Italian cooking, a charm which will perhaps replace that operetta conception of romantic Italy in which the tourist lolled in eternal sunshine on a vine-hung terrace, drinking wine for a song, while the villagers in peasant costume danced and sang in the piazza below. 99

ELIZABETH DAVID,
ITALIAN FOOD, REVISED EDITION,
PUB. BARRIE & JENKINS LTD,
LONDON, 1987

BRESCIA
Here John Stanford describes the work of the famous Italian designer Ettore Bugatti (1878–1944).

❝Often called the 'Brescia', after its sweeping success in the *Grand Prix des Voiturettes* there in 1921, [the T22 Bugatti] was a sensational small car for its day. It was not until about 1922 that the 'Brescia' began to achieve fame as a production car, while by 1926 it was virtually obsolete; but for a few years it was the fastest small car on the market.

Bugatti designs have been the subject of numberless resounding *clichés* over the years, mostly concerned with the alleged Innate Artistry of their creator. It is easy to be misled by the undoubted aesthetic appeal of all Bugatti products into thinking that they embody unconventionality for its own sake. In fact, if unorthodox in execution, they are without exception founded on well-proven practice. Where their layout differs from that of other designers, it is for some good reason; only occasionally was accessibility or convenience placed after superficial elegance. Even so, the market for which Bugatti was catering was wealthy enough for this not to matter, and labour costs were low enough between the wars for technical finish to be carried to extremes on every car which left the factory. It would be impossible for this reason alone to produce a modern equivalent of these cars – each one of which was in effect a toolroom job – except at astronomical cost.❞

JOHN STANFORD, *THE SPORTS CAR – DEVELOPMENT AND DESIGN,* PUB. B.T. BATSFORD LTD., 1957

DRIVING THROUGH ITALY
John Ruskin (1819–1900) gives this vivid and poetic account of a journey through Italian countryside.

❝August 29th. BRESCIA. Left the Albergo Reale at ¼ past 9, Signor Bruschetti presenting us with a plate of large, fresh, sweet oranges for our journey. Eighteen miles of railroad between acacia trees, and soft, intense, dark blue Alps, mixed with the morning sky. Got into coupé of diligence at Treviglio; then monotonous driving on the wearisome, straight, broad, Italian level roads, with round headed stone posts at intervals of every twenty feet; and small mulberry trees, and maize, and acacias in continual succession, concealing the view without a single point of interest in themselves. No large trees, no châteaux nor cottages – perpetual maize and a little hay; hardly any vines. The towns and villages less picturesque than usual, the chief noticeable things in them being the great red watermelons sliced on little wooden tables at every door, and the immense quantities of unripe stone peaches. As we drove on the sky gathered into more distinct masses of silver grey cloud, with spaces of intense and tender blue; then the silver grey heaped itself into a cumuli of purer white, whose shadows deepened, and still deepened until, underneath, they gathered into one mass of thunder grey, through which, as we neared it, we saw the forked lightning play in thin, trickling, glittering, horizontal streams, like fine strips of tinsel shaken in the black air. It spent itself, however and we had only the shaking of the trees by the thunder wind around us, and the soft burning of a rainbow on the eastern hills.❞

JOHN RUSKIN, *THE DIARIES OF JOHN RUSKIN 1848–1873* SELECTED AND EDITED BY JOAN EVANS AND JOHN HOWARD WHITEHOUSE PUB. OXFORD UNIVERSITY PRESS, OXFORD, 1958

Itineraries

▲ Aeolian Archipelago.

▲ The rocky coast at Scopello in Sicily.

The Gulf of Orosei in Sardinia. ▼

▲ Capo Spulico in Calabria.

▲ Isola dei Conigli at Lampedusa.

The coastline at Iglesias in Sardinia. ▼

▲ The rice fields of Novara.

▲ Umbrian landscape.

Olive trees in Puglia. ▼

▲ The hills of Monferrato.

▲ Cypress trees in Tuscany.

Spring flowers in Umbria. ▼

▲ The snow fields of Mont Blanc.

Fall in Val Cordevole. ▼

▼ Alpine lake.

TURIN, PIEDMONT AND THE ALPS OF THE VALLE D'AOSTA

Turin, Piedmont and the Alps of the Valle d'Aosta

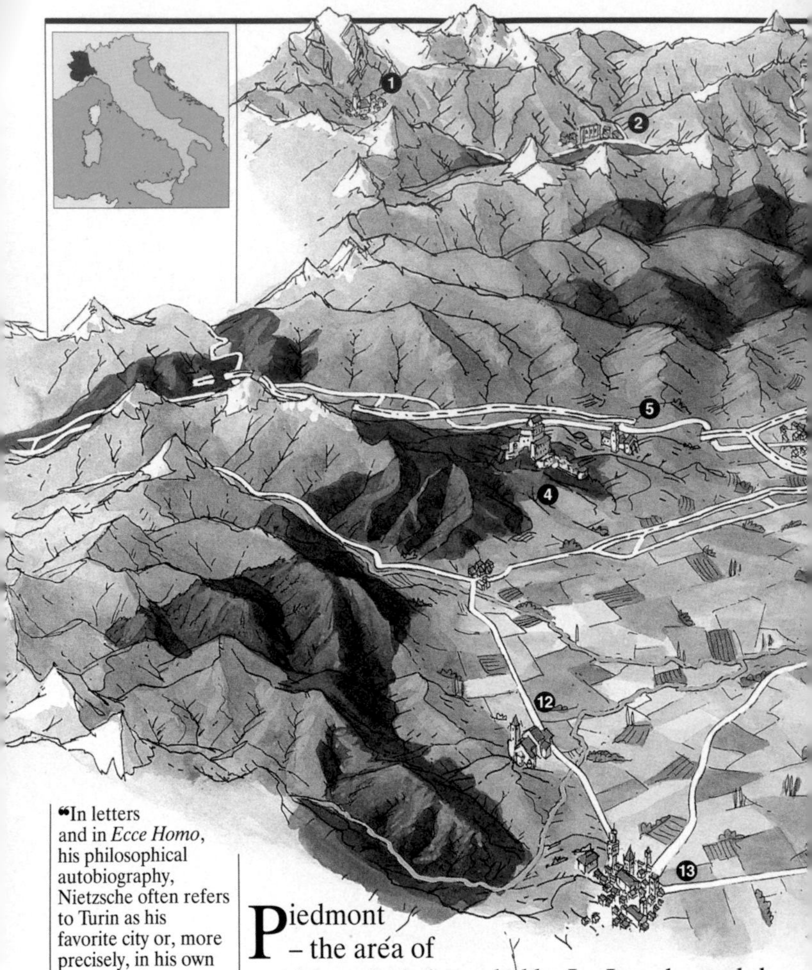

❝In letters and in *Ecce Homo*, his philosophical autobiography, Nietzsche often refers to Turin as his favorite city or, more precisely, in his own words, his 'heart's inspiration'. He chose it as his home, considering it to be the most charming, elegant and spacious town in Italy, with a 'wonderful climate', even in winter.❞

G.B. Angioletti, *I grandi ospiti* *(The grand hosts)*

Piedmont – the area of northwest Italy bounded by Le Langhe and the Alpine region of the Valle d'Aosta – has an impressive concentration of outstanding cultural attractions. In a book of this size it would be impossible to provide a detailed round-up of all the places of interest in the region, but the following pages include the key historical and artistic landmarks and the most important monuments and sites. Turin, the elegant capital of Piedmont, boasts a rich artistic and historical heritage. Not far from Turin, two of the region's most outstanding religious buildings – the majestic Sacra di San Michele (one of the most important fortified monasteries in Piedmont) and the Abbey of

1 Courmayeur
2 Aosta
3 Breuil-Cervinia
4 Sacra di San Michele
5 Sant'Antonio di Ranverso
6 Turin
7 Santa Maria di Vezzolano
8 San Secondo di Cortazzone
9 Santi Nazario e Celso di Montechiaro
10 Asti
11 Vercelli
12 Abbazia di Staffarda
13 Saluzzo

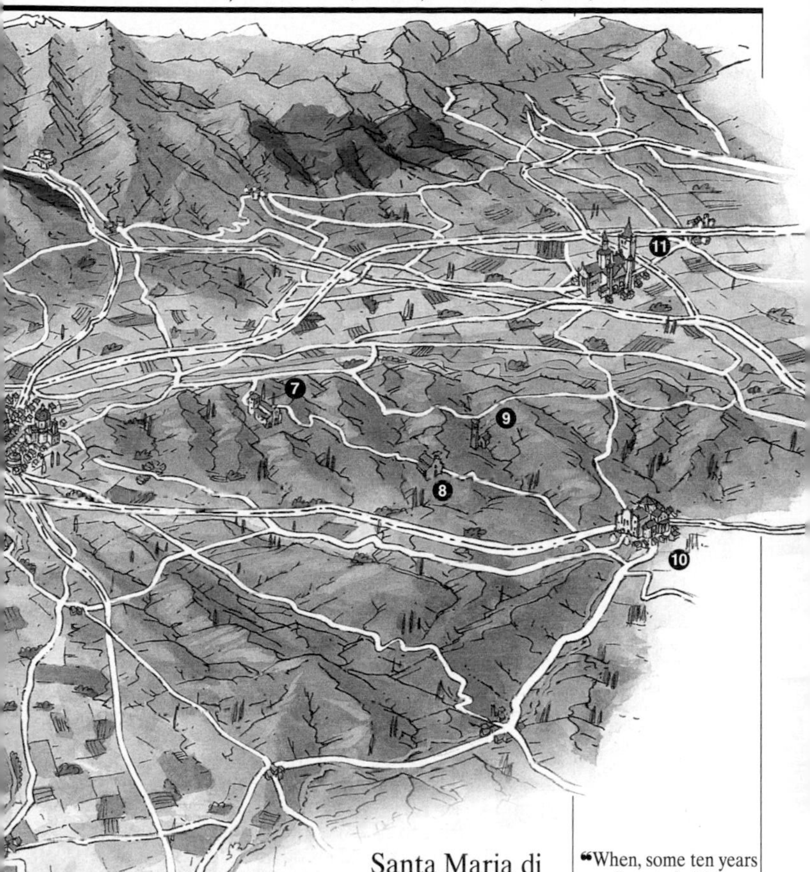

Santa Maria di Vezzolano – are well worth a visit. While touring central and southern Piedmont, be sure to visit Asti, a fascinating city of art only 32 miles from Turin yet within reach of the compelling landscapes of Le Langhe. Saluzzo and the remarkable medieval Abbey of Staffarda, nearby, should not be missed. Vercelli, the rice capital of Piedmont, which has the dazzling Basilica di Sant'Andrea, is also well worth a visit. The Valle d'Aosta provides a breathtaking setting for the second part of our itinerary. The town of Aosta, the region's capital (68 miles from Turin), boasts some outstanding Roman and medieval architecture. The Valle d'Aosta's best-known tourist resorts, Breuil-Cervinia and Courmayeur, were among the first mountain-climbing and skiing centers.

"When, some ten years ago, I started visiting Turin fairly regularly, I fell willing victim to its charms. It seemed to me, at the same time, a Pythagorean city, a North European city, a seventeenth-century city, a courtly city: it was spiced with the incense of an extinct ecclesiastical hierarchy, everything seemed noble, highly polished and yet at the same time contemporary. Turin could boast a recent intellectual history that was singularly prestigious. . . . It was a studious, book-loving city, a follower of the Enlightenment."
Giorgio Manganelli, *Lunario dell'orfano sannita (The Samnite Orphan's Almanac)*

VITTORIO AMEDEO I.

The lure of the old and the excitement of the new: fascinating vestiges of Turin's history chart the city's development from its ancient origins as the home of the Taurini and its colonization by the Romans, via the vicissitudes of the Middle Ages, to its designation as the capital first of the margravate and then of the kingdom. Not only is the city rich in architectural and artistic monuments, such as churches, palaces and museums, but it also boasts some impressive modern industrial architecture, the hallmark of a changing society.

FROM FOUNDATION TO DOMINION. The city owes its name to the tribe of the Taurisci or Taurini, who appear to have resulted from the amalgamation of a Tyrrhenian tribe from Asia Minor with a Ligurian tribe of Iberian origin. Allies of Rome, the Taurini were besieged by Hannibal in 218 BC and witnessed the destruction of their city. In the Roman Colonia Iulia, founded in the time of Julius Caesar, Octavian built a communications center, Augusta Taurinorum (28 BC), on the slopes of the Alps in the upper Po valley. In 568 the territory was invaded by the Lombards, who established a duchy lasting two centuries. In 773 the city became a Carolingian countship, under the margravate of Ivrea. After the Franks lost their dominion over the territory (888), it became an independent march until 1091. It then came under the control of the bishopric, until it effectively passed into the hands of the city seigniories in 1204.

THE ADVENT OF THE HOUSE OF SAVOY. In 1248 Tommaso II of Savoy first acquired the seigniory of Turin, which was gradually to become the chief town of the territory ruled by the House of Savoy. In 1404 the university was founded, and castles and palaces began to be built. In 1533, during the conflict between the king of France and the Hapsburgs, the French army occupied Piedmont; when Turin once again came under the rule of the Savoys with Emanuele Filiberto, it became their

"HAPPY AND FORTUNATE TURIN!
HOME OF THE ILLUSTRIOUS HERO [CARLO EMANUELE I];
TOWERING OVER ALL OTHER BEAUTIFUL CITIES."

GIAMBATTISTA MARINO

definitive capital in 1563. During the 17th century the Savoys were involved in various military tussles, and the city was once more occupied by the Spanish and the French. The 18th century saw the War of the Spanish Succession; after a long siege and the final defeat of the French (1706), Vittorio Amedeo II was made King of Sicily, a title that was later altered to King of Sardinia (1720).

A MODERN CITY IN THE MAKING. In 1796 Napoleon's victories brought him to power, and from 1802 Turin became the capital of a French *département*. The Savoys were forced into exile in Sardinia ▲ *482*. The House of Savoy returned to power in 1814, with Carlo Alberto di Savoia-Carignano, who became king in 1831, and this marked the beginning of the Risorgimento. The king set up the

THE CAPITAL MOVES FROM TURIN TO FLORENCE
In 1864 France requested and obtained the transfer of the Italian capital to Florence. The traditionally peace-loving people of Turin reacted *en masse*, organizing demonstrations in Piazza Castello and Piazza San Carlo. The protest resulted in a death toll of 187 and the resignation of the government. It then fell to Lamarmora to approve the transfer of the capital to Florence, which took place in 1865, seriously damaging Turin's economy.

State Council, reformed the civil code, founded the Art Gallery and the Technical College, and regulated the Academy; in 1847 he initiated an administrative reform program and in 1848 promulgated the Constitution. In 1849 Vittorio Emanuele II continued the wars that were to lead to Italy being proclaimed a united kingdom on March 14, 1861. Turin became the new country's capital, only to lose this title – and political influence with it – in 1865. The city then came to rely on its financial and industrial activities. The first cars appeared in Turin as early as 1895. Italy's first motor show took place there in 1900, and the Universal Exhibition in 1911.

TURIN TODAY. In the 1950's and 1960's Turin's level of production reached an all-time high. These years were characterized by large-scale immigration, industrial expansion and urban growth. In the 1970's the city suffered from the recession, which from 1976 hit the major industries very hard. Since then its economy has revived.

THE ITALIAN MOVIE CAPITAL
At the beginning of the 20th century a new industry took up residence in Turin with the construction of the Italian movie-production studios (1904). In 1914 the Turin company Itala Film produced the famous silent movie *Cabiria*, directed by Giovanni Pastrone and with subtitles written by Gabriele D'Annunzio.

139

PIAZZA CASTELLO

This piazza is the historical center of old Turin. At one time you could walk through the Palazzo Reale, the Armeria and the Library, which was connected to Palazzo Madama, to reach the former Secretariat of State, then continue through the Accademia Militare and finish up at the Regia Zecca. Internal corridors made it possible to move from one building to another without ever having to step outside, so ensuring the personal safety of the king and his officers. Over the centuries the city has expanded outward, as can be seen by the wide roads opening out from the square, which have helped determine the layout of the Piedmontese capital.

PALAZZO MADAMA ★. In the center of the Piazza Castello stands the quadrangular castle that gave the square its name. In the 13th century the Marquis of Monferrato erected a fortress behind two towers of the old Porta Pretoria. This then fell into the hands of the Savoys, who extended and fortified it, building two large towers at the back. When the court moved to Turin, the palace lost its defensive function and became a royal residence. But it was the two "madame reali" ▲ *138*, Maria Cristina (regent from 1637) and Maria Giovanna Battista of Savoia-Nemours (regent from 1675), who were responsible for its present splendor. Juvarra was given the task of embellishing the palace, which he did by adding a Baroque façade (1718–21) that incorporated two of the old towers, an imposing assembly hall and a sweeping double staircase. Since 1934 it has housed the MUSEO CIVICO D'ARTE ANTICA, which contains wooden sculptures (13th–14th century) from the Valle d'Aosta and some important paintings, including the *Portrait of an Unknown Man* (1476) by Antonello da Messina. There are also illuminated books, and collections of ceramics, enamel and glass.

SAN LORENZO. This church, which also stands on Piazza Castello (to the left of Piazzetta Reale), was commissioned by Emanuele Filiberto, but work on it was not begun until 1634

ITALIAN MOTOR PRODUCTION IN TURIN
On July 1, 1899 Fiat, the vehicle-making company, was born at the Burello Café, the brainchild of nine friends, among them Giovanni Agnelli.

Like Piaggio's Vespa, the Fiat soon became a common sight throughout Italy. The dream of producing a car with universal appeal was to reach its fullest expression with the legendary "Cinquecento" (Fiat 500), from 1957.

and it was only completed, by Guarini, in 1680. It has an octagonal dome ● *92*, ▲ *146*, with a lantern composed of intertwined arches, and a lavish high altar (1684, also by Guarini), while the stucco work and gilt details also display typical Baroque exuberance.

Palazzo Reale ● *79*. The official residence of the Savoy rulers until 1865, this palace, which looks out over the Piazzetta Reale, has a typical Baroque façade (1658) by Carlo Morello. A succession of different court architects were responsible for the additions and restructuring work, which continued until the 19th century. Climb the monumental staircase and cross the Sala degli Svizzeri, with its large painting of the *Battle of San Quintino* (1557, Palma Giovane),

A SWEET TRADITION
Butter, cocoa and hazelnuts are the main ingredients of *gianduiotti* – delicious chocolates that melt in your mouth. The name of these chocolates recalls Gianduia, the popular masked figure who, through his strength of purpose, generosity and political fervor, came to symbolize the deeply patriotic feelings of the people of Turin during the wars of independence.

141

VIA ROMA
One of the city's most elegant thoroughfares, the Via Roma, starts at Piazza Castello. Many of Turin's most luxurious shops can be found here, particularly under the double portico which surrounds Piazza San Carlo and extends as far as Porta Nuova.

to reach the reception rooms, including the Throne Room, which is one of the most sumptuous rooms in the palace, and the Audience Room. After passing through these rooms, you will come to the Appartamenti Reale (Royal Apartments), famous for their frescoed ceilings and vaults and their paintings and tapestries. The famous Scala delle Forbici (1720), an ingenious pincer-like structure by Juvarra, rises between the first and second floors. The back of the palace opens onto the GIARDINI REALI (Royal Gardens).

ARMERIA REALE. The royal armory is in the wing of the palace flanking the Piazzetta Reale on the left. Built by order of Carlo Alberto, it was opened in 1837. It houses equipment from the arsenals of Genoa and Turin, as well as subsequent acquisitions, displayed in three rooms, reached by a staircase designed by Benedetto Alfieri. The armory includes a collection of ancient and medieval arms, curios dating from the 15th to the 17th centuries, Savoy and Napoleonic mementos, and a variety of oriental collections. Continuing under the porticos of Piazza Castello, you will arrive at the new Teatro Regio. Built by Alfieri, between 1738 and 1740, it was destroyed by fire in 1936 and reopened in 1973.

TEATRO REGIO
In this theater, in February 1893, the premiere of Puccini's *Manon Lescaut* won him the fame that had hitherto been denied him. Three years later, despite scathing reviews, *La Bohème* kept the Regio's audiences enthralled for 23 days. The conductor in 1896 was the young Arturo Toscanini.

DUOMO. Dedicated to Giovanni Battista, the city's patron saint, the cathedral is the only surviving example of Renaissance architecture in Turin. The white marble façade is graced by a tympanum and three decorated portals. The interior has a nave and two aisles in the shape of a Latin cross. On either side of the presbytery there is a black marble staircase, with a tall portal, leading to the Chapel of the Holy Shroud.

CAPPELLA DELLA SACRA SINDONE ★. Designed by Guarino Guarini, who began its construction in 1668, the chapel ▲ *147*, with its lavish altar by Bertola (1694), once guarded the silver reliquary containing the Holy Shroud. The chapel walls are lined with black marble, and the whole is crowned by a beautifully proportioned conical dome. In April 1997 a fire that had started in a wing of the Palazzo Reale spread as far as the chapel, seriously damaging the dome.

The Holy Shroud, which miraculously escaped damage, was temporarily transferred to the archbishop's palace, which will probably remain its home.

PORTA PALATINA. Taking Via XX Settembre from Piazza San Giovanni, (the square where the cathedral stands), you will come to Porta Palazzo, the only surviving Roman gate of the four that once provided access to the city. Built of brick in the 1st century, it has two five-storied, sixteen-sided towers separated by a short expanse of wall; this section has two rows of arched windows and four arched openings, two carriage gateways and two pedestrian gateways. Continuing to the left, down Corso Regina Margherita, on the right (at no. 105) you pass the MUSEO DI ANTICHITÀ, opened in 1989. Eventually you come to the noted group of hospitals, schools and charitable institutions that includes the COTTOLENGO, named after its founder. Just beyond is the Istituto Salesiano.

THE HOLY SHROUD
According to tradition, the Holy Shroud was the sheet in which Jesus was wrapped when he was placed in the Holy Sepulcher. In the West documentation about this relic dates back to the 14th century. In 1453 it became the property of the House of Savoy and was kept at Chambéry. After the capital of the Duchy was moved to Turin, the shroud was also moved, in 1578, finding a resting place in Guarini's chapel a century later.

MUSEO DI ANTICHITÀ
This museum houses archeological finds that range from prehistory to the Barbarian invasions. Outstanding exhibits include the so-called "Marengo treasure", unearthed in 1928: one item is a bust (2nd century AD) of Emperor Lucius Verus.

CAFFÈ DEI FRATELLI FIORIO

INTELLECTUALS AND REACTIONARIES
Citizens of 19th-century Turin tended to favor one of two famous cafés: the Caffè Fiorio, in Via Po, whose regular clientele was made up of the "codini", or elderly conservatives, and the San Carlo, whose regulars, the intellectuals, turned the café into a stronghold of the Risorgimento. Today the two cafés seem unchanged, immersing visitors in a 19th-century atmosphere as they sit sipping hot chocolate with whipped cream.

THE MONUMENTAL BAROQUE CENTER

The area running from the Piazza San Carlo to the Mole Antonelliana, passing through Via Po, provides a fascinating trip down memory lane. The hub of the Risorgimento movement and the capital of the new kingdom, it still exudes the spirit of 19th-century Turin.

PIAZZA SAN CARLO. Regarded as the finest square in Turin, Piazza San Carlo was originally a drill ground, then became a marketplace. It was redesigned in the mid 17th century by Carlo di Castellamonte, who was responsible for the architectural backdrop of porticos and palaces. You can reach this well-proportioned square by taking the porticoed Via Roma, which leads from the Piazza Castello to the Porta Nuova station. The twin churches of Santa Cristina and San Carlo stand at the back of the square, which has a fine equestrian statue of Emanuele Filiberto (1838) by Carlo Marocchetti at its center. A variety of interesting and inviting cafés, which first opened their doors in the early 19th century, shelter under the porticos.

PALAZZO CARIGNANO. Crossing Via dell'Accademia delle Scienze, you come to this palace (1679–84) with a distinctive façade by Guarini that is one of the most original examples of Piedmontese Baroque. The curvilinear brick façade, with its elliptical central section, encloses the oval salon on which the entire structure is based. Since 1935 it has housed the MUSEO NAZIONALE DEL RISORGIMENTO, where 27 rooms chart the various stages of the unification of Italy.

ACCADEMIA DELLE SCIENZE. On the street of the same name (at no. 6) stands the Palazzo dell'Accademia. This severe, stately building with exposed brickwork was begun by Guarini in 1679 and completed by Garove in 1687. Formerly the Jesuit Collegio dei Nobili, in 1787 it became the home of the prestigious educational

institution founded in 1757 by Lagrange (mathematics), Cigna (medicine) and Saluzzo (chemistry). Since 1824 it has housed the Egyptian Museum and since 1865 the Galleria Sabauda, Turin's two most famous museums.

EGYPTIAN MUSEUM ★. The first of its kind, and one of the leading museums in the world due to the number and quality of its exhibits (more than 30,000), the Museo Egizio has benefitted from many additions to the original royal collection dating from the early 18th century. The museum's most famous exhibits include the Statue of Rameses II, the monolithic Colossus of Sethi II, the small Rock Temple of Ellessya, the Tomb of Khaiè and Meriè, the "Mine Papyrus" (the oldest topographical map in existence) and an exquisite *ostrakon* (potsherd) decorated with a dancing woman.

GALLERIA SABAUDA ★. Founded in 1832 by Carlo Alberto and installed in the Palazzo Madama, the gallery was donated to the State in 1860 and moved to its present location at the Accademia in 1865. It contains a fine collection of paintings by various Italian and Flemish artists.

VIA PO. Designed by Amedeo di Castellamonte, this thoroughfare was built in 1673, during the second phase of urban expansion. It runs from the Piazza Castello to the Piazza Vittorio Veneto – which was opened in 1825 to link the Baroque center of Turin with the village on the other side of the Po, via the Vittorio Emanuele I Bridge (1810–14), which leads finally to the neoclassical Church of Gran Madre di Dio ▲ *148*. The arcaded street, lined by old palaces, leads into the piazza. Beyond the piazza lies the river, which can be reached by descending the 19th-century MURAZZI.

TURIN'S PORTICOS. The continuous portico of Via Po is just one section of the city's 11 miles of porticos. Begun in the 16th century, their construction continued until well into the 20th century.

MOLE ANTONELLIANA ★. Turning from the Via Po into Via Montebello, you will come to one of Turin's most prominent landmarks. Begun by Alessandro Antonelli in 1862 as a Jewish synagogue, it then became municipal property and was completed in 1878, becoming the highest brick building in Europe (549 feet). In 1953 the spire was destroyed by a storm and was replaced with a metal structure. It functions as an exhibition hall and (since 1966) houses the MUSEO DEL CINEMA.

THE COLOSSUS OF SETHI
To move this exhibit from Genoa to Turin, a special transporter had to be made. It was mounted on gun carriages and drawn by sixteen horses.

A NETWORK OF PORTICOS
The streets and squares of the town center, lined with porticos sheltering a variety of stores and cafés of historical interest, are ideal for meeting up with friends or taking a leisurely stroll.

PIEDMONTESE BAROQUE

A TASTE FOR THE UNUSUAL
Baroque artists gave free rein to their inventive originality and theatrical inspiration in ornamental details, resulting in work that is sometimes reminiscent of Gothic art.

Turin was one of the principal capitals of Italian Baroque and certainly the one where, after Rome, it reached its creative zenith. Due to the work of a succession of fine engineers, the Savoy dynasty rivaled the architectural achievements of the great European monarchies. The work of Guarini, who attained heights of sheer virtuosity in his approach to structure and light, was particularly important, while Juvarra created an exultant and magnificent image of the new kingdom with his spectacular and grandiloquent style of architecture.

COURT LIFE
Following the example of the French court of Louis XIV, court buildings functioned as genuine "theaters of power", serving as backdrops for court ceremonies, such as hunts (as in this picture of Stupinigi), balls, carousels, stately thanksgiving ceremonies for victory in battle, and weddings.

DOMES
The different interpretations of Baroque style by Juvarra and Guarini can be clearly seen in their domes in Turin. The one by Juvarra for the Basilica di Superga (above) is classical and majestic in form, while Guarini's dome for the Church of San Lorenzo (right) is acrobatic and mathematically sophisticated.

DRAMATIC ARCHITECTURE
This relief model, designed by Filippo Juvarra, shows how the architect prepared his works. They were conceived as large-scale stage sets for the ruling powers, in which the parts of the actors were unwittingly played by the courtiers.

GEOMETRIC VIRTUOSITY
Guarino Guarini was a mathematician and physicist. This is apparent in his brilliantly inventive use of structure and light in his domes, which display a uniquely mathematical approach to Baroque style.

A SOARING PINNACLE
The dome of the Chapel of the Holy Shroud by Guarino Guarini was clearly influenced by the achievements of Francesco Borromini, but it strongly emphasized the fantastic and bizarre aspects of the latter's work, becoming a fairy-tale genre of architecture in its own right. This taste for soaring spires is typical of Piedmontese architecture and was also to reappear in the 19th century with the construction of the lofty Mole Antonelliana (visible in the background) – which, although completely different in form and content, reproduces the vertical thrust of Guarini's dome.

PUBLISHING IN TURIN
Various prominent names bear witness to the long tradition of Piedmontese enterprise in printing and book publishing. UTET, SEI, Einaudi, Bollati-Boringhieri, together with many smaller publishers, continue to uphold the prestige of a world-class publishing industry.

EMILIO SALGARI
Veronese adventure-story writer Emilio Salgari conjured up images of fabulous Indian landscapes and the distant shores of the Caribbean while strolling beside the Po and across the bridges of Turin, the city where he died in 1911.

BESIDE THE PO AND IN THE HILLS

Monte dei Cappuccini and Superga afford some breathtaking views of Turin against the backdrop of the Alps, especially on clear days in spring; and the Parco del Valentino, which lies beside the river, offers some equally attractive landscapes.

GRAN MADRE DI DIO. At the foot of the hill, facing Vittorio Emanuele I Bridge, this neoclassical temple was erected (1827–31) to celebrate the return of King Vittorio Emanuele I (1814) to Turin from Sardinia, after Napoleon's defeat.

MONTE DEI CAPPUCCINI. Climbing Viale Lanze, you will reach the summit where the convent of Santa Maria was built for Carlo Emanuele I by Ascanio Vitozzi (1584) on the remains of a 13th-century military garrison. After the Capuchins were driven out (1866), the monastery became municipal property (1871) and was subsequently acquired by the Club Alpino Italiano (1874). It houses the MUSEO NAZIONALE DELLA MONTAGNA, dedicated to Luigi di Savoia, Duke of Abruzzi (1873–1942), a famous climber and explorer.

VILLA DELLA REGINA. Perhaps the most famous of the four hundred villas scattered over the hills of Turin, this was the residence of Marie-Anne d'Orléans (1713). Formerly the home of Cardinal Maurizio, who commissioned it from Vitozzi (1615), it has been enlarged several times and includes additions by Filippo Juvarra. The villa stands in the street of the same name, leading from the Piazza Gran Madre.

IL VALENTINO. This comprises a medieval village, a castle and a large 19th-century park. The original nucleus was the CASTELLO, begun in the 16th century then enlarged (1630–60) by Carlo and Amedeo di Castellamonte. It was built as a riverside villa, but successive modifications extended it toward the city, with the addition of a main courtyard, side wings and quadrilateral towers. The PARK was designed in the mid 19th century by the French landscape designer Barillet-Deschamp. It extends from Umberto I Bridge to Isabella Bridge and contains the fascinating Botanical Garden founded by Vittorio Amedeo II in 1729. An outstanding attraction in the picturesque grounds bordering the Po is the BORGO MEDIEVALE (medieval village). Built in 1884, this was intended to provide a faithful reproduction of medieval architecture. Continuing uphill from the *borgo*, you will pass the monumental Fontana dei Mesi (1898) designed by Carlo Ceppi.

PALAZZO TORINO ESPOSIZIONI. This is a group of pavilions (1938–50) used for trade fairs, shows and exhibitions. Particularly interesting is the vaulted self-supporting structure of the CENTRAL HALL (1948–50), designed by Pier Luigi Nervi.

MOTOR MUSEUM ★. This museum was built in Corso Unità d'Italia in 1960. It traces the development of self-powered vehicles from the first pneumatic machines to present-day vehicles, including racing cars. It provides an overview ranging from pioneering vehicles, with systems of propulsion such as air and steam, to the automobiles of the late 19th and early 20th centuries.

PALAZZO DELLE MOSTRE. This exhibition hall made of glass and reinforced concrete, also on the Corso Unità d'Italia, stands out from the Italia '61 complex – built to celebrate the centenary of the unification of Italy – thanks to its hexagonal dome with three single points of support, which has earned it the nickname of *palazzo a vela* (literally "sailing building"). The PALAZZO DEL LAVORO was also built by Pier Luigi and Antonio Nervi in 1959, for the same occasion.

LINGOTTO. Nearby is the former Fiat factory (the entrance is in Via Nizza). Closed in 1983 and restored by Renzo Piano, it is now an exhibition and conference center, staging events such as the annual Turin Book Fair. The building has five floors, with spiral staircases (1926), and a rooftop test circuit more than half a mile long.

SUPERGA. This basilica can be reached either by car or by the rack railway, which replaced the old funicular in 1935 and takes only fifteen minutes to make the 1,375-foot ascent. The basilica (completed in 1731) was commissioned from Juvarra in 1717 by Vittorio Amedeo II to celebrate the defeat of the French in the siege of 1706.

ARCHITECTURAL "QUOTATIONS"
The medieval village, Il Valentino's main tourist attraction, was built specifically for an exhibition held in Turin in 1884. It draws its inspiration from the architectural features of various castles and churches in Piedmont and the Valle d'Aosta. The old-world charm of the craftsmen's shops will make you feel that you have stepped back in time.

THE TRAGEDY OF SUPERGA
A plaque behind the basilica marks the spot where a plane crashed in 1949, killing 31 people, including the entire Turin football team.

▲ TURIN

PIETRO MICCA
In 1706, during the night of August 29–30 French grenadiers managed to penetrate the tunnels under the Citadella. Pietro Micca, a young Italian sapper, became aware of the danger and succeeded in exploding a mine,

sacrificing his life in order to repel the invasion. In 1958 the site of the explosion was established, in a section of tunnel that can now be visited.

GIACOMO CASANOVA IN VIA DORAGROSSA
In 1791 Casanova was visiting Turin for the second time. In his *Memoirs* he wrote that in the city "the fair sex possess all the charms that love could desire, but the police are more troublesome than anywhere else." Consequently he had to avail himself of the services of shrewd procuresses. One of these was the owner of a dressmaking establishment in Via Doragrossa, and Casanova rented the quarters above her shop in order to enjoy the favors of countless seamstresses and shop assistants – before eventually being expelled from Turin.

WESTERN EXPANSION

There is plenty to admire in Via Garibaldi which, with its rich blend of past and present and sacred and profane, is one of the most attractive streets in Turin.

VIA GARIBALDI. This straight, narrow road, laid out in 1736, follows the route of the old Roman *decumanus maximus*, which led from Piazza Castello in the direction of the Valle di Susa and Via Francigena. This street was originally used as a market and became known as "Via Doragrossa" because of the channel, carrying water diverted from the Dora Riparia, that flowed down it. This channel, which replaced the old Roman sewerage system, was not covered over until the reign of Carlo Felice (1823).

CAPPELLA DEI BANCHIERI E MERCANTI. This chapel is all that remains of the charitable congregation that was formed in 1663; its entrance is through the "Casa dei Gesuiti". All the frescos, paintings and statues in this Baroque gem are centered around the theme of the Nativity, providing ample work for painters (Andrea Pozzo, Sebastiano Taricco), sculptors, wood carvers and craftsmen. This is where the Savoys used to attend mass on Epiphany.

SANTUARIO DELLA CONSOLATA. This church's entrance (a neoclassical pronaos) is on the piazza of the same name. Passing through the oval vestibule, you will reach the sanctuary proper, with its hexagonal votive chapel by Guarini and four elliptical chapels. The main point of focus inside is the lavish altar by Juvarra. The Romanesque campanile belonging to the demolished Church of Sant'Andrea stands adjacent to it.

CITTADELLA. Designed by Francesco Paciotto di Urbino, this pentagonal defensive building was erected in less than two years (1564–6). It covered an area of around 62 acres, with bastions and a moat, barracks and servants' quarters. The surviving buildings include the KEEP – restored in 1893 to house the NATIONAL HISTORICAL MUSEUM OF ARTILLERY – and some tunnel sections. In one of them Pietro Micca (see left) lost his life in the siege of 1706.

GALLERY OF MODERN AND CONTEMPORARY ART. Restored and reopened in 1993, this gallery provides a fascinating overview of 19th- and 20th-century art, with the focus on Italian painters. On the second floor, 20th-century artists include Grosso,

"STUPINIGI, DESIGNED WITH GREAT INVENTIVENESS, IF NOT GREAT SIMPLICITY, BY JUVARRA, AN ARCHITECT BORN TO BUILD HOMES FOR KINGS."

ITALY IN WORDS AND PICTURES, 1838

Carena, Bistolfi, Casorati, Boccioni, Balla, De Chirico, Sironi, Carrà, Savinio, De Pisis, Morandi and Manzù. The gallery also has works by Klee, Chagall, Picabia, Ernst and Modigliani. In the rooms dedicated to contemporary art, there are works by Burri, Fontana, Manzoni, examples of Arte Povera (Michelangelo Pistoletto), pop art (Andy Warhol), op art and various new movements. The third floor is devoted to 19th-century painting, including works by Mazzola, Reviglio, Canova, D'Andrade, Fontanesi, Camerana, Pellizza, Fattori, Renoir and Courbet.

THE OUTSKIRTS OF TURIN

To the west of the city, the interesting sites of Stupinigi and Rivoli are within easy reach.

STUPINIGI. Following Corso Unione Sovietica, you will come to the PALAZZINA DI CACCIA at the end of a broad, straight avenue. At the sides are the former farmsteads, stables and stores that belonged to this hunting lodge, which was used by the Savoys until 1919, when it became the property of the Mauritian Order. The residence was built by Filippo Juvarra in 1729 for Vittorio Amedeo II. The central pavilion has four wings in the shape of a cross, which were extended along the sides of the main courtyard. Subsequent additions were made in 1739, 1759 and 1779. The hunting lodge now houses the fascinating MUSEUM OF FURNITURE.

RIVOLI. Take the Corso Francia west from Turin to reach Rivoli, where the CASTELLO affords some magnificent views. It was built by the Savoys as an elegant royal palace (17th–18th century) on the site of a former medieval fortress. Restoration work began in 1979, and in 1984 it became the home of the MUSEO D'ARTE CONTEMPORANEA. Contemporary artistic trends are well represented in the rooms of this museum, where visitors can also admire the 17th- and 18th-century decorations.

FILIPPO JUVARRA (1678–1736)
The epitome of a royal architect, Juvarra left his mark on the sacred and secular architecture of the period. His hand can be seen both in the hunting lodge at Stupinigi and the Castello di Rivoli. Sicilian by origin, he started his career in Rome as an architect-designer in the service of Cardinal Ottoboni; he was then appointed court architect to Vittorio Amedeo II and began working for the House of Savoy. He also worked on the Basilica di Superga, Palazzo Madama and Palazzo Reale, on numerous churches and on the general layout of Turin.

From Turin the itinerary takes you to Valle di Susa and Asti, then to Saluzzo and Vercelli, and finally the Valle d'Aosta below the Mont Blanc.

From the Valle di Susa to Monferrato

Head west from Rivoli to Avigliana and then toward Susa to discover two artistic gems: Sant'Antonio di Ranverso and the Sacra di San Michele. In the opposite direction, toward Asti, the Abbazia di Vezzolano rises amid vineyards.

Sant'Antonio di Ranverso, a Gothic abbey. This abbey hospital was founded in 1188 by Umberto III, who gave it to the Hospitalers of St Anthony of Vienne (then in the French Dauphiné) to care for pilgrims and sufferers of "St Anthony's fire". Restored several times, it boasts some fine 15th-century frescos by Giacomo Jaquerio.

Sacra di San Michele, a mountain-top refuge. High on Mount Pirchiriano, this basilica was built on top of Romanesque remains dating from 998. It was a place of worship for the Lombards. The ruins of the three original chapels form the crypt of the main church, which was built in Gothic style (12th–13th century).

Santa Maria di Vezzolano ★, an ancient abbey. It is not known when this abbey, near Albugnano, was founded, but it reached the height of its glory between the 13th and 15th centuries. An interesting

feature inside is the bas-relief (1189) on the French-style rood screen (*jubé*) made of green stone.

Asti, city of towers and churches. The oldest and largest tower in Asti is the Torre Rossa. An extra floor was added to it in the Middle Ages, in red

Saint Michael
The imagery of the archangel fighting the dragon is taken from a passage in the *Apocalypse* (12,7). In the Christian liturgy, Michael accompanies the souls of the dead on their ascent to heaven. He was worshipped devoutly by the Lombards.

> **"ASTI, THE MOST CHARMING CITY IN MONFERRATO, SEEMS EMPTY: ITS MINOR NOBILITY PREFER TO KEEP THEMSELVES TO THEMSELVES."**
>
> JOHANN VOLKMANN, 1770

brick and white stone (the town's colors). Two of Asti's many churches are particularly well worth visiting. Starting from the elegant, porticoed Piazza Alfieri, take Corso Alfieri (to the left), which leads to SAN SECONDO in the piazza of the same name. The church has a Romanesque façade, a Lombard Gothic interior and a 10th-century crypt. From the Corso Alfieri, the Via Goltieri (to the right) leads to the CATHEDRAL, which has a Gothic exterior and a Baroque interior.

SAN SECONDO DI CORTAZZONE / SANTI NAZARIO E CELSO DI MONTECHIARO. San Secondo, dating from the Romanesque period (11th–12th century), has some fine, well-preserved bas-reliefs depicting medieval themes and allegories. Santi Nazario e Celso, which stands in an enchanting setting of woods and hills, is a Romanesque parish church with graceful ornamentation on the portal and windows and a campanile (in brick and tufa) with mullioned windows.

FROM THE UPPER PO VALLEY TO VERCELLI

To the south-west of Turin, against the backdrop of Monviso, Saluzzo is a city steeped in history and rich in art. On the opposite side of Turin, in the Po plain, Vercelli bears the stamp of an ancient culture.

SALUZZO, THE PROVINCIAL RENAISSANCE. Influential at the end of the 12th century, this marquisate became a center of cultural rebirth between the 15th and 16th centuries. The most striking medieval part is the PIAZZETTA DI SAN GIOVANNI, with its Torre Civica and Church of San Giovanni (14th century). Interesting features of the latter include Gothic choir stalls, the chapter-house (16th century) and the mausoleum of Galeazzo Cavassa, by Sammicheli. The CASTIGLIA (castle) was commissioned by Tommaso I in 1270; additions altered its appearance in 1491–5 and in the 19th century. The CASA CAVASSA, the royal residence from the 15th to the 16th century, still has its original 16th-century furnishings.

FRESCOS IN THE CASTELLO AT MANTA. Heading south from Saluzzo, you will reach the town of Manta with its castle, bought in 1984 by the Fondo per l'Ambiente Italiano. A 14th-century fortress, it was converted into a royal residence in the 16th century and boasts a series of well-preserved secular court frescos (1418–30).

ABBAZIA DI STAFFARDA, A CISTERCIAN GEM. Heading north from Saluzzo, you will come to this abbey featuring a church that is a fine example of the stylistic transition from Romanesque to Gothic.

VERCELLI AND ITS MASTERPIECES. The city's most famous monument, the BASILICA OF SANT'ANDREA, is a striking example of early Gothic, built between 1219 and 1227. The façade, in grayish-green marble from Varallo, has three huge arched portals of red Veronese stone. Vercelli's DUOMO (on Piazza Sant'Eusebio) was rebuilt in the 16th century, then modified in the 18th century by Benedetto Alfieri.

THE PALIO OF ASTI
In 1275, when the people of Asti were laying siege to Alba, they organized a tournament below the city walls. This gave rise to the Palio, which now takes place every year, in Piazza Alfieri, on the second Sunday in September. Almost a thousand people take part in the historic parade before the race. The winner is awarded the Palio (banner), while the jockey who comes last receives an anchovy.

THE "MANUALE TIPOGRAFICO"
This is the title of the work that marked the high point in the life and career of Giambattista Bodoni, who was born in Saluzzo in 1740. The son and grandson of printers, he learnt the rudiments of printing in his father's office and then moved to Rome where, while working as a compositor at Propaganda Fide, he perfected a new typeface which is still known as Bodoni (used on the cover of this guide). He passed the first edition of his manual (1788) for press in Parma. Subsequently his wife arranged for it to be reprinted, after his death in 1813.

153

"A vineyard climbing the crest of a hill to become etched against the sky is a familiar sight, and yet these curtains formed by the plain, dense rows resemble a magic door. Under the vines is the dark tilled land, the foliage conceals treasures and beyond the foliage is the sky." This description of the landscape comes from the pen of Cesare Pavese, who was born in Le Langhe and spent his life here. This part of southern Piedmont is bounded by the Tanaro and Bormida di Spigno rivers and by the provinces of Cuneo, Asti and Alessandria. An ancient region, it rose above sea level in the Miocene epoch of the Tertiary period. The extremely hilly terrain is at its most evocative in the fall, when the rugged landscape is shrouded in delicate blue clouds.

TRUFFLES

A traditional product of Le Langhe, white truffles have an aura of mystery. *Trifulau* (truffle sellers) hunt for them secretly at night, with small well-trained dogs, so that they do not give away all the good places. True truffles (*Tuber magnatum* – other species are not highly prized) grow between the roots of oak trees, lime, willows and poplars, and each has a subtly different smell. They are found in other parts of Italy too, but it is here that these mystical delicacies are used to best advantage.

White truffles are eaten raw (the black ones are sometimes cooked), thinly sliced over *risotto bianco*, *tagliolini* or exquisite Piedmontese meats. You can also eat them on top of fried eggs and, surprisingly, they are sometimes eaten layered between desalted anchovies.

Wine is the pride and glory of Le Langhe: a wide range of wines is available, as can be seen from the various labels and bottles.

Dolcetto

Barbera

FIRST-CLASS WINES
Barolo, Barbera and Barbaresco are well known outside Italy, but the Le Langhe area has hundreds of vineyards and boasts many other excellent wines, including four DOC wines (Alba Diano, Dogliani and Langhe Monregalesi) that are made from the Dolcetto grape.

Nebbiolo d'Alba is the grape used for most of the famous wines, but there are other pleasing grapes

Nebbiolo d'Alba

and wines, including muscatels, Grignolino and the Piedmontese *freise*. Discover the hidden delights of Le Langhe by visiting the cellars and castles that belonged to famous wine growers of the past, such as Cavour (Grinzane) and King Carlo Alberto (Verduno); or the cellars at Serralunga, the villa of "Bela Rosin", the mistress of King Vittorio Emanuele II.

FINE CHEESES
Both Robiola di Roccaverano (a soft cheese) and Toma di Murazzano are DOC cheeses made from cow's and sheep's milk; they possess the sharp, strong taste typical of Le Langhe cheese. Castelmagno, Bra and Raschera are more mature and

mellow DOC cheeses that come from the summer pastures in the Cuneo mountains. They make a splendid addition to the cheese platter, and can also be used in cooking. Sample the gnocchi and crêpes made with Castelmagno. Or try grated Bra sprinkled over *tajarin*.

Robiola di Roccaverano and Raschera d'alpeggio

Toma di Murazzano

GRAN PARADISO NATIONAL PARK
Established in 1922 by the trustees of the former hunting preserve of the House of Savoy, this park situated between the Valle d'Aosta and Piedmont was the forerunner of Italy's national parks. The vegetation is largely made up of copses of larch, fir and pine. The park's emblem is the ibex, which became a protected species in 1821, when it was reserved for hunting by the Savoys. There are currently some four thousand ibex, demonstrating the success of the park's commitment to environmental protection. There are also ten pairs of golden eagles, numerous chamois and marmots, and plans to reintroduce the lammergeier (a bird of prey).

THE VALLE D'AOSTA

Besides breathtaking landscapes and sites of natural beauty – including the protected GRAN PARADISO NATIONAL PARK, which the region shares with Piedmont – the Valle d'Aosta boasts more than 130 castles and royal residences, dating from the Middle Ages to the Renaissance. Most of them were built on rocky crags or hilltops, taking advantage of natural defensive positions. Over the years, the castles lost their defensive function and became royal residences. Some were modified and restored in the 19th century – such as FÉNIS CASTLE (1337), the present home of the Museo del Mobile Valdostano, and the one at ISSOGNE (1480), with its frescos depicting scenes from Renaissance life. The most attractive tourist centers in the Valle d'Aosta – which are also easily accessible from France through the Mont Blanc tunnel and the Great St Bernard Pass – include COURMAYEUR, lying at the foot of Mont Blanc, COGNE (in the valley of the same name) and BREUIL-CERVINIA, which nestles at the foot of the Matterhorn (Monte Cervino) and is connected to the Zermatt glaciers by cable car.

ROMAN AND MEDIEVAL ARCHITECTURE IN AOSTA. The town of Aosta boasts many Roman remains, including the ARCH OF AUGUSTUS, the PORTA PRETORIA, a section of city wall with two towers intact, an amphitheater and a theater. The TORRE BRAMAFAM, which was part of the castle of the Challants, is the most impressive of the medieval towers. One of the city's most striking churches is the COLLEGIATE CHURCH OF SANT'ORSO, which has a tall bell tower (1131) and a magnificent cloister with capitals decorated with biblical scenes and events linked to the life of the religious community. The CATHEDRAL has an important sequence of frescos (1030–40), restored in 1986–91. Its treasury contains a famous ivory diptych (406) dedicated to the Emperor Honorius.

GENOA,
THE ITALIAN RIVIERA
AND THE INLAND
LIGURIAN VALLEYS

GENOA, *160*

Genoa, which stretches for more than 19 miles at the apex of the wide gulf formed by the Ligurian sea, is the administrative and historical capital of the curved strip of coastal land that shelters in the lee of the Alpine-Apennine chain. This small region, which has played an active role in the history of Italy over the centuries, boasts a coastline of breathtaking beauty which has resulted in its rising popularity as an international tourist destination since the mid 19th century.

From Genoa – the "Proud Republic", which Petrarch described as a "royal city" and the "mistress of the sea" – visit first the Riviera di Ponente, then the Riviera di Levante to discover for yourself Liguria's many charms, both inland and on the coast. Make a stop at Noli, which still shows traces of its time as a small maritime republic; at ancient Albenga, where you will marvel at the impressive Roman remains in the town center; at Alassio, a fashionable seaside resort enjoyed by high society for over one hundred years; and at Cervo, an ancient village full of atmosphere, which looks out over the sea from its high vantage point. It is only 91 miles from Genoa

1 BALZI ROSSI 2 DOLCEACQUA 3 SAN REMO 4 TRIORA 5 TAGGIA 6 CERVO 7 ALASSIO 8 ALBENGA 9 NOLI 10 GENOA 11 MONTE DI PORTOFINO 12 GULF OF TIGULLIO 13 CINQUE TERRE 14 PORTOVENERE 15 LERICI

to San Remo, the indisputable queen of the Riviera di Ponente, with its medieval old town, known as "La Pigna", which still remains relatively undiscovered by tourists. Just before reaching San Remo, it is worth making a detour to the villages of Taggia and Triora, which are a testimony to the long historical past of the inland Ligurian valleys. Starting once again from Genoa, this time our itinerary heads in the direction of the Riviera di Levante. Our first destination – passing through Nervi, an elegant holiday resort and Recco, renowned for its gastronomy – is Camogli, the traditional gateway to the lovely Portofino peninsula and its popular tourist resorts: San Fruttuoso, Portofino itself and Santa Margherita Ligure. The next stop is the steep, rocky coastal strip, made up of five villages, which is known as the Cinque Terre – the first of which, Monterosso al Mare, is 61 miles from Genoa. The Cinque Terre forms an isolated region of Liguria which, with its fusion of maritime and rural cultures, has been little altered. Portovenere, the colorful village which marks the end of our itinerary, casts its reflections into the deep blue sea of the beautiful gulf of La Spezia and is one of the most atmospheric coastal villages in Liguria, full of character and life, a delightful blend of ancient and modern.

"A rocky, barren landscape, like the most rugged parts of Calabria, a refuge for fishermen and farmers who eked out a living on a strip of coast which, in certain places, narrowed virtually to a ledge, one of the most barren and primitive terrains in Italy. Monterosso, Vernazza and Corniglia, falcons' and gulls' nests, Manarola and Riomaggiore: these, moving west to east, are the small villages that form a barricade between the rocks and the sea."

Eugenio Montale,
Fuori di casa
(Out Of Doors)

"The gaze of the sea/ Seems so colorless at this hour/To the eyes (smudges of indigo, barely sky-blue)/Of the bathing-attendant as he beaches the boats.//
The last ray of the sun/ Falls like a gaffsail.// Of all that feminine laughter,/Only a sluggish white froth on the seaweed, and a cool salt wind on the face/Remain."

Giorgio Caproni,
Spiaggia di sera
(Evening Beach)

▲ GENOA

The city's coat of arms, a red cross on a white or silver field, was adopted during the crusades of the 11th century.

THE HILL FORTS
The Mura Nuove, begun in 1626, formed a protective 8-mile ring around Genoa along the crest of the amphitheater of hills. They now enclose almost 2,224 acres of parkland, which provides a marvelous setting for the Belvedere

del Righi ▲ *170* and numerous forts, all renovated in the 19th century by the Genio Militare Sardo. In the summer, Fort Sperone, the highest at 1,680 feet, stages a program of open-air performances in conjunction with the Teatro della Tosse ▲ *167*.

Mistress of the trade routes across the Mediterranean from the 13th to the 15th centuries, Genoa was the third most important Italian maritime republic after Amalfi and Pisa ● *38*. In the centuries that followed, it remained one of the main ports in Europe and, in the early 20th century, played an increasingly vital role in the industrialization of the whole of northern Italy. Even in the face of later difficulties resulting from its flagging industrial sector, Genoa firmly refused to admit defeat and, in the last few years, has launched an overall program to restore the city's magnificent historical heritage dating back to its golden age. "La Superba" or "Proud City", as Genoa is known, can congratulate itself on finally making a name for itself as a city of art.

THE APENNINES AND THE LANTERNA. Although seaward Genoa's horizon stretches as far as the eye can see, inland the city is bounded by the steep slopes of the Apennine foothills, where walkers can enjoy the breathtaking panoramic views and mild climate. Equally panoramic views can be had from the Lanterna, an elegant lighthouse built in the mid 16th century which stands out sharply against the backdrop of hills and is a distinctive shape on the city's skyline.

ORIGINS AND ACHIEVEMENTS. The Ligurians originally settled in the 6th century BC on the hill now known as the Collina di Castello. The village grew in Roman times, but it was not until the Middle Ages that Genoa started to become a force to be reckoned with. Crucial stages in the city's Mediterranean expansion were the conquest of Antioch in 1097, dominion over part of Constantinople in 1155, the acquisition of the monopoly of trade in the Black Sea in 1261, and the definitive defeat of its rival, Pisa ▲ *298*, at the battle of Meloria in 1284.

MARITIME REPUBLIC. From the end of the 11th century, the type of government chosen by the city was the *compagna communis*, derived from a secular association of sailors and merchants. This was consolidated in some ways in 1260, when the

> **"A** REGAL CITY, ALPINE HILLS AT HER BACK, PROUD OF HER MEN AND HER RAMPARTS – JUST BY LOOKING AT HER YOU CAN TELL SHE IS MISTRESS OF THE SEA.**"**

PETRARCH

city's first Capitano del Popolo, Guglielmo Boccanegra, ordered work to start on the building that was to confirm the official nature of his position. As a result, the future Palazzo Ducale became the city's headquarters in 1291. But, after initial signs that Genoa's maritime power was on the wane – such as the failure of its attempt to destroy Venice in 1381 and Ottoman domination of the Black Sea from 1453 – the government's sphere of influence shrank.

THE DORIA FAMILY. Genoa was saved from being conquered or crushed by the rivalry of the great powers by an alliance negotiated and concluded by Admiral Andrea Doria ▲ *164* with the Emperor Charles V in the early 16th century. This alliance enabled the Doria family, a dynasty which had been a prominent scion of the republic's mercantile and financial aristocracy for centuries, to consolidate their preeminent position with regard to other important local families, such as the Spinolas, the Grimaldis (who still reign in the principality of Monaco to this day) or the Fieschis. This gave rise to a new oligarchic republic – which remained undefeated until 1797, when it fell to the French revolutionary armies.

GENOA UNDER THE HOUSE OF SAVOY. At the end of the Napoleonic era Genoa was assigned to the Franco-Italian dynasty of the Savoys, who already reigned over Piedmont and who had coveted this important Ligurian port for some time. The city joined the new kingdom of Italy in 1861, as part of the kingdom of Piedmont, having contributed to the nation's rebirth by producing Giuseppe Mazzini, the noble republican regarded as the "father of the country".

CURRENT TIMES. Genoa's renewed importance as a port within the framework of monarchical Italy led to extensive urban growth (the population doubled during the 19th and 20th centuries) and to its becoming the vital maritime component in the "industrial triangle" with Turin and Milan. The city now has almost 700,000 inhabitants and is preparing to enter the third millennium on the back of the international exhibition which, in 1992, heralded its return to the international arena.

THE BOAT SHOW Every year, in October, Genoa brings together enthusiasts from all over Europe (and from further afield) for a massive boat show. The Fiera di

Genova provides a showcase for sailing boats, motor boats, canoes and the best that the Mediterranean shipbuilding industry can offer in terms of small tonnage.

EXPO 1992 Five centuries after Columbus' voyage, Genoa celebrated the anniversary of this event by organizing a major international exhibition that gave the city a major new attraction, with the revival of the Porto Vecchio ▲ *165* by Renzo Piano.

1 PALAZZO DORIA-PAMPHILI (DEL PRINCIPE)
2 CASTELLO D'ALBERTIS
3 PALAZZO REALE
4 SANTISSIMA ANNUNZIATA DEL VASTATO
5 PALAZZO BIANCO
6 PALAZZO ROSSO
7 PALAZZO TURSI (MUNICIPIO)
8 PALAZZO SPINOLA (NATIONAL GALLERY)
9 AQUARIUM
10 PORTA SIBERIA
11 PALAZZO SAN GIOR

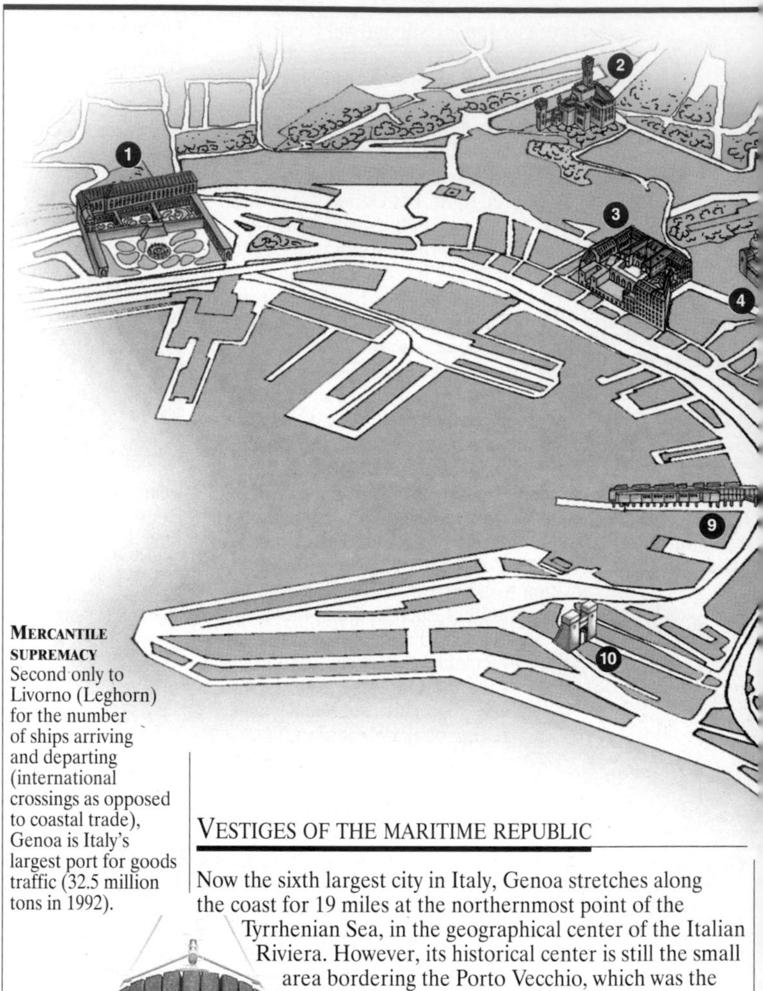

MERCANTILE SUPREMACY
Second only to Livorno (Leghorn) for the number of ships arriving and departing (international crossings as opposed to coastal trade), Genoa is Italy's largest port for goods traffic (32.5 million tons in 1992).

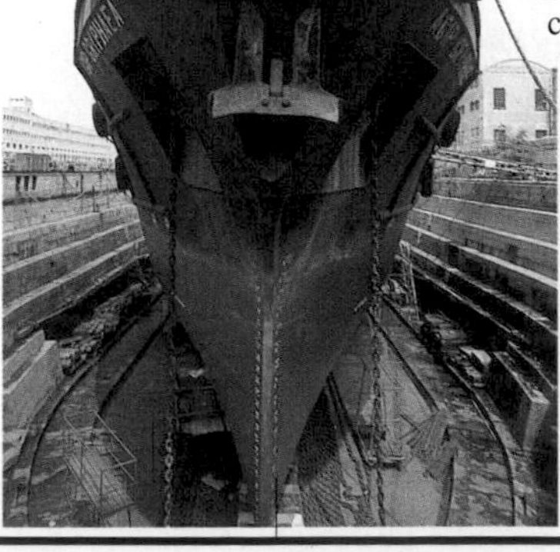

VESTIGES OF THE MARITIME REPUBLIC

Now the sixth largest city in Italy, Genoa stretches along the coast for 19 miles at the northernmost point of the Tyrrhenian Sea, in the geographical center of the Italian Riviera. However, its historical center is still the small area bordering the Porto Vecchio, which was the point of departure for the republic's galleys when the city was at the height of its glory.

PALAZZO DUCALE. Behind the monumental façade facing onto Piazza Matteoti, the historical seat of the government's law courts is a splendid 16th-century building with two colonnaded courtyards (the one on the right opens onto Piazza De Ferrari). Recently converted into the Palazzo della Cultura, it now regularly houses major art exhibitions, flower shows and antique fairs ▲ *169*.

PIAZZA SAN MATTEO. Narrow old streets connect the Palazzo Ducale with the square which takes its name from the CHURCH OF SAN MATTEO, founded in 1125 and renovated toward the end of the 13th century. The façade is decorated with alternating strips of white marble and dark stone, embellished with inscriptions and reliefs. The church faces the CASE DEI DORIA, which are almost as old (at one time, the whole area was owned by this important Genoese family).

THE ORIGINS OF A NAME

No real scholarly consensus has been reached about the origins of Genoa's name. In the early 13th century scholars argued that it was derived from the Latin word *ianua*, meaning "gate". This theory quickly gained popularity, being highly appropriate for a Mediterranean republic in the throws of expansion, a city that marked a point of transit between land and sea.

163

A carved capital from
the interior of
the Cathedral of
San Lorenzo.

**ANDREA DORIA'S
SPEECH**
In 1528, in Piazza San
Matteo, Andrea
Doria gave a speech
to convince the
townspeople of the
advantages of his
proposed alliance
with Charles V
▲ 161. In honor of
this event, the small
palace on the corner,
sporting mullioned
windows with several
lights and a Lombard
Gothic loggia, was
named after him by
the city senate.

SAN LORENZO ★. The right-hand flank of the cathedral stands
on Via San Lorenzo, which leads down from the Palazzo
Ducale. This spectacular building, with three early 13th-
century Norman Gothic portals and a 16th-century dome,
designed by Galeazzo Alessi, dates back to the 9th century.
However, the 12th-century portals on the north and south
sides are Romanesque. Inside, as well as 14th-century naves,
there is the Renaissance Chapel of St John the Baptist, which
has niches containing statues by
Matteo Civitali and Andrea
Sansovino. Other works, such
as the neo-Byzantine frescos
on the interior façade, the
17th-century frescos in the
apse, the 14th-century tomb
of Cardinal Luca Fieschi,
and the wooden choir
stalls (16th century), bear
witness to a rich artistic
heritage spanning many
centuries. The cathedral
museum, designed by
Franco Albini, in the
Treasury (see opposite),
is also well worth a visit.

> "**P**ARIS AND **L**ONDON ARE NOTHING COMPARED
> WITH THIS BEAUTIFUL CITY; THEY ARE JUST JUMBLES
> OF HOUSES AND STREETS."

RICHARD WAGNER

SAN LORENZO MUSEUM
The entrance to the Treasury of Genoa's cathedral, with its spectacular display of gold and silver work and ecclesiastical ornaments and vestments, is adjacent to the Chapel of St John the Baptist. The underground rooms housing this valuable collection, designed by Franco Albini, are worth a visit in their own right.

PIAZZA BANCHI. Via Canneto il Curto, one of the old roads leading off Via San Lorenzo below the cathedral, follows the curve once described by the oldest city walls and leads into the historical heart of the city. Until 150 years ago the small piazza that stands in front of the Church of San Pietro alla Porta was, with its shops, businesses and financial offices, the true hub of Genoa. Piazza Banchi still retains its late-16th-century appearance, with the LOGGIA DEI MERCANTI, which now houses exhibitions.

PIAZZA CARICAMENTO. This was once the site of the medieval harbor, converted in the mid 19th century into a goods yard, and is now a pedestrian thoroughfare, below the Sopraelevata (elevated highway) built in the 1970's to speed up the flow of traffic. At ground level, the spacious arcades of the PORTICI DI SOTTORIPA (or Porticato della Ripa), built in accordance with the consul's orders of 1133, bustle with life.

PALAZZO SAN GIORGIO ★. This building stands in the Piazza Caricamento. Between 1407 and 1904 it served as the headquarters of the Banco di San Giorgio, which for centuries handled the republic's finances. The oldest part of the building was begun in 1260 as the palace for the Capitani del Popolo, while the harborside extension dates from 1570. The entire building, has been substantially renovated.

PORTO VECCHIO. The historical harbor area was extensively revamped for Expo 1992 ▲ *161*. The work was coordinated by Renzo Piano, the acclaimed Genoese architect. Besides the AQUARIUM, IL BIGO and other new projects, the so-called PORTA SIBERIA or Porta del Molo Vecchio, a masterpiece by Galeazzo Alessi, dating from 1533, has become a focus of attention.

AQUARIUM
One of the new attractions that Expo 1992 gave Genoa was the Ponte Spinola Aquarium, the largest aquarium in Europe, with fifty tanks filled with species from the Mediterranean, the Amazon and the Atlantic Ocean.

MARGARET OF BRABANT
The most outstanding sculptural group in the Museo di Sant'Agostino is the sepulchral monument (detail below) commissioned by Emperor Henry VII of Luxembourg in honor of his wife, Margaret of Brabant, who died unexpectedly in Genoa in 1311. One of Giovanni Pisano's last works, it was found in a Franciscan church that is no longer standing.

CHRISTOPHER COLUMBUS
The most famous native of Genoa is Columbus, who in 1492 navigated the *Santa Maria* and two smaller Spanish caravels from Palos to what is now known as San Salvador Island, in the Bahamas. Very little information has survived about Columbus' physical appearance – all the known portraits of him are works of imagination.

BETWEEN THE COLLINA DI CASTELLO AND THE PORTA SOPRANA

On land, medieval Genoa's life was played out against the more intimate backdrop of the streets and palaces between Porto Vecchio ▲ *165* and the Collina di Castello, the nearest hill to the coast.

SANTA MARIA DI CASTELLO. The first large church dedicated by Genoa to the Madonna stands in a working-class neighborhood, with old houses and steeply sloping streets. Rebuilt in Romanesque style in the 12th century, it became the property of the Dominicans in the 15th century, to whom it still belongs. The Grimaldi family then financed the construction of the convent (now a small but fascinating museum), where the second 15th-century cloister contains a well-preserved fresco by Iustus de Alemania (Giusto di Ravensburg). In the church, which is not far from the TORRE DEGLI EMBRIACI, the chapel displays 16th- and 17th-century decorations.

SAN DONATO. Between Santa Maria di Castello and the Palazzo Ducale stands the beautiful octagonal bell tower of San Donato. This dates from the 12th century, although the row of mullioned windows is a 19th-century addition. The church incorporates Roman columns; and there is a *Madonna and Child* from the late 14th century, by Niccolò da Voltri, in the apse on the right.

SANT'AGOSTINO. The third largest church in the vicinity of the Collina di Castello was built after 1260; the interior, now deconsecrated, is used as an auditorium. The cloisters of the former church have been

**"As for paintings [Giovanni Carlo Doria]
has amassed a collection that . . . no other
private gentleman can rival."**

Andrea Scoto

converted into the Museum of
Ligurian Sculpture and
Architecture, which charts the key
stages in Genoa's history, with
exhibits dating from the Middle Ages
to the 18th century. The entrance to
these well-proportioned, elegant
rooms, which were designed (1977)
by Franco Albini and Franca Helg,
is in the nearby Piazza Sarzano. The
Teatro della Tosse stands opposite
the church.

Porta Soprana. Leaving Piazza
Sarzano and walking away from the
sea, you will come to this impressive
gate, which is the best-preserved
example of those that provided access
to the city through the 12th-century
walls. This famous landmark is also
known as Porta di Sant'Andrea.

Paganini's Violin
The instrument
played by violin
vituoso and composer
Niccolò Paganini
(1782–1840),
the most famous
Genoese in history
after Columbus,
is kept at the Palazzo
Tursi. There is also an
urn here which, since
1878, has contained
some of Christopher
Columbus' ashes.

Chiostro di Sant'Andrea. In the shadow of Porta Soprana,
in what is now known as Piazza Dante, carved columns and
capitals are all that survive of the old Benedictine Monastery
of Sant'Andrea, due to extensive demolition work in the 20th
century. Two 1930's skyscrapers (one designed by Marcello
Piacentini) tower above the so-called Casa di Cristoforo
Colombo, which is actually a 17th-century
reconstruction of a mid-15th-century
wool merchant's house.

16th- and 17th-century Genoa

Two streets in particular, the 16th-
century Strada Nuova – which in
1884 became Via Garibaldi – and
Via Balbi (laid out almost a century
later by the Balbi family) are
associated with the most glorious
period in the city's history.

Via Garibaldi ★. The magnificent
Strada Nuova was laid out in 1551
by the Genoese ruling family – who
demolished a working-class quarter
to do so and built some
elegant monumental
residences in its place. In
the space of some twelve
years a number of palaces
were built: Palazzo
Cambiaso (no. 1),
Spinola (nos. 2 and 5),
Carrega-Cataldi (no. 4),
Lercari (no. 3) ▲ *169*
and Doria (no. 6). A short
distance away, you will come to
Palazzo Cattaneo-Adorno (nos.
8–10) and Palazzo Tursi, built by one of
the Grimaldis but now Genoa's City Hall. It has
a magnificent staircase, loggias and hanging gardens.

Between the 16th and 17th centuries Genoa was at the height of its glory. The city was enriched by scores of new palaces and brightened by magnificent outdoor frescos, and its nobility was painted first by Rubens and then by his pupil, Van Dyck. The Emperor Charles V called this period – from 1528, when the new oligarchic government was formed, to the completion of the Mura Nuove in the mid 17th century – "the century of the Genoese". Improved architecture and impressive town planning projects, with their dramatic and effective treatment of steep slopes and narrow spaces, bear striking witness to the originality and elegance of the Genoese culture of the day. Individual works of particular note from the city's palaces and other buildings are spotlighted here to form a concise résumé of this important period.

"Gentleman" by Rubens
This painting (kept at the Palazzo Spinola) symbolizes, perhaps more clearly than any other, the international influence enjoyed by the Genoese aristocracy during its golden age. In this dramatic portrait, one of these notable citizens is depicted on horseback by Pieter Paul Rubens.

Albergo dei Poveri
This monumental poorhouse, erected shortly after "the century of the Genoese", was intended to highlight the strength and magnanimity of the oligarchic republic. Built for the benefit of the poor, it has an imposing façade.

The telamons of Palazzo Lercari

The residence of the Lercari family in Via Garibaldi (the former Strada Nuova) was completed in 1571, the year the Genoese fleet helped defeat the Turks at Lepanto. The telamons (male caryatids) on the façade of the family's palace are shown with their noses cut off, the same fate that one of the Lercaris had inflicted on his enemies after defeating them.

Patrician women

The paintings exhibited on the third floor of the Palazzo Rosso include these magnificent portraits of Geronima Sale, with her daughter, and of Paolina Adorno Brignole-Sale. They were painted by Anthony Van Dyck, who lived and worked in Genoa between 1621 and 1627.

The chapel of the Palazzo Ducale

Amid rooms in which the future fate of the republic was decided, the Doge had a small room decorated for use as a chapel. Its walls are completely covered with frescos painted by the Genoese artist Giovanni Battista Carlone, depicting scenes that link the fortunes of the city with those of Catholicism. In one of them Christopher Columbus is shown planting the Cross in the New World.

Accademia Ligustica di Belle Arti

This fascinating art gallery, on Piazza De Ferrari, is devoted to the Genoese school from the 16th to the 17th century. Outstanding works include the remarkable triptych of *Saint Erasmus* by Perin del Vaga (above) and two night scenes, *Virgin with Child in Swaddling Clothes* and *Christ Brought before Caiaphas*, by Luca Cambiaso.

THE RIGHI
FUNICULAR RAILWAY
Next to the Largo
della Zecca, and
just down from the
Palazzo Bianco,
is the station for the
funicular railway that
climbs some 990 feet
to Righi, stopping
off in places that
afford increasingly
panoramic views.

PALAZZO ROSSO GALLERY. The Palazzo Rosso (late 17th
century, owned by the Brignole-Sale family) and the Palazzo
Bianco (18th century, although largely rebuilt after World
War Two) stand almost opposite each other on Via
Garibaldi. At the PALAZZO ROSSO it is still possible
to see the former owners' magnificent art collection
– including works by Pisanello, Dürer, Veronese,
Van Dyck ▲ 169, Guido Reni and Guercino. The
gallery of the PALAZZO BIANCO is also well worth a
visit: it has works by Lippi, Caravaggio, Grechetto,
Rubens, Zurbarán and Murillo. Like the
cathedral's Treasury ▲ 165 and the museum at
Sant'Agostino ▲ 167, the Palazzo Bianco was
converted by Franco Albini. The station for RIGHI FUNICULAR
RAILWAY, which climbs to a panoramic viewpoint, is nearby.
GALLERIA NAZIONALE DI PALAZZO SPINOLA. Several streets
nearer to the sea (beside the bustling Via San Luca and
the Piazzette di Pelliceria), another aristocratic palace, which
belonged first to the Grimaldis and then to the Spinolas,
has been converted into an art gallery. As well as works
by Antonello da Messina, Van Dyck and Rubens, it contains
some fascinating period furniture and furnishings.
SANTISSIMA ANNUNZIATA DEL VASTATO. This sumptuous
16th-century church by Lomellini stands on the piazza that
leads into Via Balbi. The church still has altarpieces by the
Genoese artists Cambiaso, Strozzi and Assereto. The interior
boasts an outstanding work, *The Last Supper*, by Giulio

THE PRINCE AND
THE EMPEROR
The Palazzo del
Principe owes
its name to Prince
Giovanni Andrea
Doria, the nephew
of the more famous
Andrea. It was,
however, the latter
who built this palace,
where he entertained
Emperor Charles V
▲ 161, who was
keen to charter his
galleys.

Cesare Procaccini. Behind the church,
Via Brignole-De Ferrari leads to the
splendid ALBERGO DEI POVERI ▲ 168.
VIA BALBI. This road shares a similar
history to that of the Via Garibaldi, but
was built privately by the Balbi family.
Its construction led to the building of
Palazzo Durazzo-Pallavicini (at no. 1),
which dates from 1618, the Palazzo dell'
Università (at no. 5), dating from 1650,
and PALAZZO REALE, which was erected
in the late 17th century. The latter now
houses a gallery that provides a splendid
example of the lavish apartments of the
Genoese nobility in the 18th century.
The hanging gardens and the picture
gallery – which has works by Guercino,
Grechetto, Reni, Strozzi, Tintoretto,
and Van Dyck – are equally fascinating.
PALAZZO DORIA-PAMPHILI. Close to
today's town center, the Palazzo Doria-
Pamphili (or Palazzo del Principe) was

> **❝B**ELOVED GREAT GRAY CITY,
> YET SUCH A BRIGHT, CHEERFUL GRAY!**❞**

VALERY LARBAUD

built in the mid 16th century as a suburban villa for the prominent Genoese family. The rooms, which have decorations by Perin del Vaga, provide a good indication of Genoese Renaissance style, though perhaps less sophisticated here than in the Strada Nuova ▲ *167* (built soon after) or in the slightly later terraced gardens of this palace, which face seaward.

18TH-CENTURY GENOA

Under the Savoys – however much the city might initially have disliked them – Genoa became more than a trading and financial center and began to industrialize. It acquired a modern appearance with the building of straight roads, central piazzas and functional new residential buildings on the hillsides.
PIAZZA DE FERRARI ★. This is the largest and most famous piazza in the city center, situated between the fresco-covered flank of the Palazzo Ducale ▲ *162* and the new extension of the TEATRO CARLO FELICE. The square takes its name from Raffaele de Ferrari, Duke of Galliera, a leading financial backer of the port and of Genoese cultural life. The theater, dating from 1828, was almost entirely rebuilt in 1991. This piazza is also the home of the ACCADEMIA LIGUSTICA DI BELLE ARTI ▲ *169* and of the STOCK EXCHANGE (a mix of Art Nouveau and neo-Baroque).
VIA XX SETTEMBRE. This street, as spacious and impressive as the Piazza De Ferrari, which leads to it, is the busiest street in the city, with movie theaters and stores. It was laid out at the end of the 19th century as part of a successful urban planning

STAGLIENO CEMETERY
In the hills behind the historical center of Genoa, the huge green expanse of Staglieno cemetery is a fine example of Genoese middle-class self-glorification. This is a huge open-air exhibition of funeral vaults, mausoleums and statuary by 19th- and 20th-century

sculptors whose works display incredibly detailed realism or the sophisticated sensibility of Art Nouveau.

program, leaving the churchyard and Romanesque CHURCH OF SANTO STEFANO (founded nine centuries previously) perched high above it on top of a stylish portico. The church is noteworthy for its striped façade and its early 13th-century apse.

PIAZZA CORVETTO. The wide road leading off Via XX Settembre (level with Santo Stefano) will take you to this beautiful 19th-century piazza, a charming tree-lined ring that regulates traffic heading for the "Circonvallazione a monte".

CIRCONVALLAZIONE A MONTE. This is the longest tourist route in Genoa. The *circonvallazione* consists of a series of avenues, designed in the mid 19th century and built during the 1890's, that zigzag between Via Assarotti and Corso Ugo Bassi. They flank various parks – as well as fascinating buildings such as the Villa Grüber (which houses the MUSEO AMERICANISTICO FEDERICO LUNARDI), examples of Ligurian Art Nouveau, funicular railway stations and period kiosks.

CASTELLO D'ALBERTIS. The neo-Gothic villa at the western end of the "Circonvallazione a monte" was built in the late 19th century by Captain Enrico d'Albertis – a man who, among other things, founded the first Italian Yacht Club, in 1879. It contains exhibits of ethnographic material collected by the sailor on his travels.

FROM CARIGNANO TO ALBARO

In the direction of the Riviera di Ponente, Genoa is primarily industrial. But if you head the other way, toward the Riviera di Levante, the coastline becomes greener as the road leads toward Monte di Portofino ▲ *178*. This area's many cultural

MUSEO AMERICANISTICO FEDERICO LUNARDI
Since 1979 the Villa Grüber (16th–18th century) has housed a fine collection of pre-Columbian art. Located in the Corso Solferino (part of the "Circonvallazione a monte"), it is a legacy of the Savoys' town planning programs. All that remains of the 16th-century building is a square tower, evidence of the need for defence at a time when the residence was an outpost near the city wall. The Palladian-style double staircase dates from the 18th century.

MUSEO CHIOSSONE
This museum, on Piazza Corvetto, houses the sculptures, pictures and applied art collected in the Far East by Edoardo Chiossone during a period of more than twenty years. Due to the vast number of items in its keeping, the museum has to rotate the exhibits on display.

attractions include the Abbey of San Giuliano and historical monuments such as the one at Quarto dei Mille, the place where Garibaldi set sail for Sicily with his Red Shirts ● 44.

SANTA MARIA ASSUNTA IN CARIGNANO. The hill toward the Riviera di Levante, at the edge of the historical heart of the city, is called the Collina di Carignano. It is dominated by the bulk of a late-16th-century basilica designed by Galeazzo Alessi. In addition to having a breathtaking location, the church is outstanding for its majestic symmetry, its elegance and the interior of its dome.

PASSEGGIATA A MARE. Beyond Carignano, the Bisagno river used to flow down to the sea. Its course is now covered by what is today known as the Foce quarter. The Riviera di Levante seafront begins here and continues along CORSO MARCONI then CORSO ITALIA, winding a verdant course between the sea and the many villas in Eclectic or Art Nouveau style.

BOCCADASSE. A short distance further east from the Lido di Albaro (with its bathing establishments, cafés and seaside terraces), the fishing village of Boccadasse, with its brightly colored houses, has retained its traditional charm. It lies beyond the sprawling outskirts of the city.

VILLA GIUSTINIANI-CAMBIASO. Just behind Albaro, still well within the bounds of the city, extensive gardens surround the first suburban villa built in Liguria by Galeazzo Alessi. This villa, completed in 1548 and now the administrative seat of the university, had a profound influence on residential architecture in the region.

VILLA SALUZZO-BOMBRINI. This villa, like Villa Giustiniani-Cambiaso, is screened by the lush greenery along Via Albaro. It is a majestic 16th-century building by Andrea Vannone with an extremely beautiful Renaissance terraced garden and, inside, some 17th-century frescos. It is privately owned.

QUARTO DEI MILLE
In Quarto dei Mille, on the Ligurian coast beyond Albaro and Sturla, a monument (erected in 1915) marks the spot where the Expedition of the Thousand ("Mille"), led by Giuseppe Garibaldi, embarked for Sicily in 1860. This military expedition played a decisive part in bringing about Italian unification.

THE FLOWERS OF THE RIVIERA DI PONENTE Over the centuries, the flood waters of the Centa, the river near Albenga, have

ensured that this town is surrounded by particularly fertile soil, which has proved eminently suitable for growing flowers. The entire Riviera di Ponente, from here to San Remo – as the number of hothouses sparkling in the sunlight on the terraced ridges indicates – is famous for its flowers, which are exported to other regions of Italy and abroad.

Liguria is one of the smallest regions in Italy, although one of the most densely populated. This strip of land lies between the sea and the nearby peaks of the Apennines.

The Riviera di Ponente

The Riviera di Ponente is made up of the two provinces of Savona (an interesting city steeped in history, although now somewhat industrial in appearance) and Imperia (a provincial capital created in the 1920's by merging the port of Oneglia with the coastal village of Porto Maurizio). This area boasts a virtually unbroken string of well-known holiday resorts, right up to the border with France.

NOLI, A SMALL MARITIME REPUBLIC. Four maritime republics have their emblems on the flag of the Italian Navy. There could easily be five, if Noli's maritime past was acknowledged. The town – which, like Naples, was originally called Neapolis – stands on a small bay facing the Tyrrhenian Sea, some 9 miles to the southwest of Savona. Its lack of recognition is due to the fact that at the end of the 13th century Noli's independence was assured by the protection of Genoa, which soon overshadowed it. The well-preserved BORGO MEDIEVALE bears witness to Noli's past glories, with monuments like the 14th-century Palazzo del Comune, the ancient CATHEDRAL OF SAN PIETRO (13th century, but renovated in the Baroque period) and, most importantly, the Romanesque CHURCH OF SAN PARAGORIO, which still retains its original 8th-century structure, and a wooden crucifix and bishop's throne dating from the 12th and 13th centuries.

> **"THE CHURCHES OF LIGURIA,**
> **LIKE SHIPS ABOUT TO BE LAUNCHED…"**

VINCENZO CARDARELLI

ALBENGA, A WELL-PRESERVED HISTORICAL CENTER. The most interesting historical center in the entire Riviera di Ponente is Albenga, situated on an alluvial plain halfway between Noli and Imperia. The streets still reflect the grid system of the Romans, although the town's origins are even older, perhaps dating back to the 6th century BC. Piazza San Michele is at the center, together with the most important medieval monuments. The CATHEDRAL OF SAN MICHELE, founded in the 5th century, has Romanesque carvings and some original sections dating from the 11th and 12th centuries, as well as a late-Gothic campanile built at the end of the 14th century. Nearby, the 14th-century PALAZZO VECCHIO DEL COMUNE, with its 15th-century loggia, is the home of the Museo Ingauno, which has a collection of archeological artefacts. This stands in front of the 5th-century BAPTISTERY, the most celebrated paleo-Christian building in the whole of Liguria. Behind the church, three stone lions brought from Rome in the 16th century sit in the PIAZZA DEI LEONI, a narrow cobblestone square named after them. Also in Piazza San Michele, opposite the cathedral, the MUSEO NAVALE ROMANO in Palazzo Peloso-Cepolla exhibits the remains of a Roman vessel – salvaged in the 1950's from its resting place on the sea bed just offshore – together with its cargo of amphorae (wine jars).

LA GALLINARA
This small island off the coast of Alassio, once famous as a refuge for hermits and monks, can be reached by boat. La Gallinara, which is privately owned, now comes under the jurisdiction of the Parco Naturale Regionale, an organization which protects both the rare wild flowers growing there and the interesting sea caves that can be found on its shores.

ALASSIO, A TOURIST TRADITION. An ancient maritime center which for more than two hundred years (from the 14th to the 16th century) belonged to Albenga, Alassio was one of the first small towns to welcome the international tourist trade at the end of the 19th century. From that time onward, hotels and boarding houses have sprung up between the Via Aurelia and the sea – without, however, marring the period atmosphere of Via XX Settembre (known as the BUDELLO). A short distance away, the MURETTO (see below) has ceramic reproductions of the autographs of celebrities who visited the town in the 1970's. Historical monuments worth visiting include the CHURCH OF SANT'AMBROGIO, with its magnificent Renaissance slate portal, and SANTA CROCE, a Romanesque church, although subsequently restored.

This latter church enjoys panoramic views from its picturesque setting high up on the headland of the same name. From Alassio, it is only a short boat ride to the protected ISOLA DELLA GALLINARA, one of the small islands off the Ligurian Riviera.

SIGNATURES OF THE FAMOUS
Alassio's "Muretto" is an Italian version of Los Angeles' footprints of the stars on Sunset Boulevard, with the signatures, handprints and crests of the rich and famous preserved on ceramic plaques embedded in a wall. The wall forms an unusual testimony to the hoards of visiting celebrities who come to this traditionally friendly resort, a place where ordinary mortals are also made welcome.

▲ From the Riviera di Ponente to the Riviera di Levante

Cervo, the early middle ages above the sea. Cervo is a small ridge-top village, directly above the coast, some 6 miles to the northeast of Imperia. Its center boasts some lovely medieval lanes, flights of steps and terraces, as well as an interesting CASTELLO that now houses

Triora
The castles and walled gates of this village are a visible reminder that it was once a Genoese outpost in the Alps. The Collegiata dell'Assunta (which is partly Gothic and partly Romanesque) contains works by Luca Cambiaso and an extraordinary Sienese painting by Taddeo di Bartolo.

exhibitions on the history and culture of the region. Lower down, there are numerous Baroque buildings, including the CHURCH OF SAN GIOVANNI BATTISTA, begun in 1686. Its concave façade, which has a sweeping staircase, towers over the piazza, while the slender campanile, built in 1773, forms a distinctive shape on the village's skyline.

Taggia, the ancient culture of the hinterland. On the last stretch of the stream (the Argentina) that flows through the valley east of San Remo lies the village of Taggia. Its 16th-century walls enclose a host of palaces, towers, oratories and fountains built between the 15th and 17th centuries. The CHURCH OF SANTI GIACOMO E FILIPPO (late 17th century) was probably designed by Bernini; and, a little lower down, the waters of the stream flow beneath the sixteen arches of an impressive 16th-century bridge. On the other

Dolceacqua
This village is famous for its Rossese wine, and also for the ruins of the Castello dei Doria and the well-preserved medieval streets.

side of the walls, the CONVENT OF SAN DOMENICO (1460–90) was the leading cultural center of the Riviera di Ponente for three centuries. Its Gothic church contains numerous works by local artists – such as Francesco and Ludovico Brea – who formed a creative transition between Gothic and Renaissance styles at the end of the 15th century. Ascending the Valle Argentina (16 miles), you will come to TRIORA, a medieval village that was an important Genoese outpost.

San Remo, a blend of ancient and modern. The last major resort on the Riviera di Ponente before the frontier with France now enjoys a slightly frivolous reputation, thanks to the popularity of its Casino and its annual festival of Italian pop music. However, San Remo has its roots in a very different past, as witness the vestiges of its medieval origins, such as the CATHEDRAL OF SAN SIRO (a fascinating Gothic-Romanesque church enlarged during the 17th and 18th centuries) or the old town, LA PIGNA, with its tangle of lanes, flights of steps, little squares and

> **"MEAGER STRIP OF LAND BORDERING THE SEA LINING THE BARREN MOUNTAIN RIDGE."**
>
> CAMILLO SBARBARO

TRADITIONAL CUISINE
Ligurian cooking makes admirable use of plain ingredients. The key to many of the local dishes are traditional recipes such as *pesto* sauce, made from basil, oil, garlic, pine nuts, Sardinian Pecorino (sheep's-milk cheese) and Parmesan cheese, blended together, using a pestle and

mortar. The region is also noted for the *focaccia* from Recco, a special kind of loaf made from dough, salt and Ligurian *formaggetta*.

fountains and its Porta di San Giuseppe, built in the 12th century. The booming tourist trade of the new town is not a particularly recent development. It dates back to the late 19th and early 20th century, when international tourism first began in earnest. In 1910 the local Russian "colony" built their own church. Not far from San Remo, heading further inland in the direction of Ventimiglia, you will come to the well-preserved village of DOLCEACQUA. If, on the other hand, you head toward the French frontier, you can visit the BALZI ROSSI CAVES, which contain fascinating prehistoric cave paintings.

THE RIVIERA DI LEVANTE

La Spezia, the only major town on the coast to the east of Genoa, is deeply rooted in its industrial and military shipbuilding traditions. Between Genoa and La Spezia two areas of breathtaking natural beauty – Monte di Portofino and the Cinque Terre – enclose a stretch of coastline with a high number of internationally renowned tourist centers and resorts, such as Portofino, Santa Margherita Ligure, Chiavari, Sestri Levante and Rapallo.
FROM NERVI TO RECCO. The boundaries of the city of Genoa now include NERVI, with its magnificent municipal park – created in the 1920's by combining the parks of villas Serra, Gropallo and Grimaldi – and Art Nouveau hotels. The Via Aurelia winds past the campanile and the little beach of SORI (the Picasso family's place of origin), before reaching RECCO, the gastronomic capital of Liguria (flattened by bombing in 1943–4 and rebuilt in a somewhat anonymous style). CAMOGLI ▲ *178*, about one mile away, is the gateway to the MONTE DI PORTOFINO ▲ *178*.

BALZI ROSSI
These caves have yielded fossils that have played a vital role in reconstructing the climatic periods of Southern Europe. Traces of prehistoric civilization have also been found there.

The massive clear-cut bulk of Monte di Portofino on the Ligurian coast – between Camogli and Rapallo – is a magnificent ecological paradise. Once colonized by monks, it is now a regional park, with an interesting mix of broadleaved woodlands and Mediterranean maquis (*macchia*). Walking along the paths that cross the mountain, you will notice changes in vegetation. Were you to travel by boat, these would be seen as changing landscapes as you move from the brightly colored houses of Camogli to the small bay of San Fruttuoso, from the exclusive atmosphere of Portofino to the social merry-go-round of Santa Margherita Ligure. Everywhere you go, you will be captivated by the interplay of sky and sea, struck by the towering height of the cliffs (and the eye-catching colors caused by geological stratification around Punta Chiappa) and tempted by the many opportunities for bathing or scuba diving.

CAMOGLI

A row of tall period houses, in the traditional reds, ochers, yellows and greens, make Camogli the most picturesque ● *82* historical resort on the Riviera di Levante. The church and Dragonora castle, which houses the Tyrrhenian Aquarium, border the fishing smacks and boats of the small port. Along the promenade, overlooking the pebble beach, you can buy *focaccia* from the bakeries, rum-based specialties called *camogliesi* from the pastry shops and specialty ice creams called *pinguini*, dipped in hot chocolate.

SAN FRUTTUOSO

You can take a boat trip from either Camogli or Portofino to the isolated village of San Fruttuoso, which grew up around the former Benedictine abbey that was the mausoleum of the Doria family between the 12th and 13th centuries.

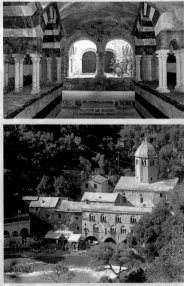

> **"I DON'T THINK I HAVE EVER FELT AS I DID WHEN I ENTERED THIS VERDANT BAY [PORTOFINO]."**
>
> GUY DE MAUPASSANT

PORTOFINO

Elegant shops, yachts riding at anchor and flights of steps climbing up into the woods provide a backdrop for the small port from which the mountain derives its name. Above the village, which is completely closed to traffic, you can stroll from the Church of San Giorgio to the Castello di San Giorgio, converted into a private residence in the 19th century. A short distance along the coast road from Santa Margherita Ligure, you come to the deep cove of Paraggi and its beach.

SANTA MARGHERITA LIGURE

This medieval village has now developed into a sizable town amid the woods of Monte di Portofino. It is a lively tourist resort with large, elegant hotels, a seaside promenade, a flourishing fishing trade and a bustling harbor. Above the town, the 16th-century Villa Durazzo-Centurione affords some breathtaking views along the coast from its fine public park.

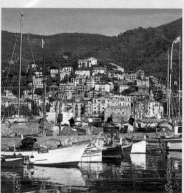

RAPALLO

The largest town in the area, Rapallo is at the center of the Gulf of Tigullio. Although its appearance was marred in the 1960's and 1970's by a rash of building, the interesting parish church, Santo Stefano, founded in the 11th century but rebuilt in the 17th century, still stands in the town's historical center. For a glimpse of society life, visit the cafés along the Vittorio Veneto promenade.

▲ Romantic Liguria: the Cinque Terre, Portovenere and Lerici

THE VIA DELL'AMORE
The Via dell'Amore ("Path of Love") between Riomaggiore and Manarola, is the most famous, as well as the most romantic, of the breathtaking coastal paths, high above the sea, that link the five villages of the Cinque Terre. Its start, which is well signposted, is just by Riomaggiore railroad station.

LORD BYRON
In the days of the Grand Tour, when well-bred Englishmen toured continental Europe to see the classical sights, two Romantic poets, who will be forever associated with the area, came to Liguria. In the early 19th century Lord Byron took up residence in a villa on the Gulf of Spezia. In 1822 Percy Bysshe Shelley drowned while attempting to sail to Lerici from Livorno. Byron attended the cremation of his unfortunate friend.

THE CINQUE TERRE. Perhaps the most famous tourist destination on the Riviera di Levante is the stretch of coastline which is home to a series of five ancient villages standing on the rocky cliffs amid Mediterranean vegetation. These villages are far more accessible by rail and by coastal paths than by the winding roads, which have deliberately not been improved in order to protect the environment.

The tiny village of VERNAZZA resembles some of the resorts on the French Riviera and has the Gothic church of Santa Margherita d'Antiocha; it is the second of the Cinque Terre from the north after MONTEROSSO AL MARE, the most popular of the five villages, which has a much visited beach. Less altered in recent times are picturesque CORNIGLIA (with its church of San Pietro), colorful MANAROLA (which has a magnificent rose window in the façade of its 14th-century church of San Lorenzo) and RIOMAGGIORE (with its parish church, San Giovanni Battista, which also dates from the 14th century). Of the last three, Corniglia is a farming and winegrowing village (amphorae from the Roman Cornelia were discovered at Pompeii), while the other two have earned a living from the sea for a thousand years.

PORTOVENERE AND LERICI, HISTORY AND ROMANCE.
The town once known as Portus Veneris, dedicated to the goddess of love, stands on the western slope of the Gulf of Spezia – virtually opposite LERICI and its famous castle, built in the 13th century by the Pisans. The Genoese took possession of PORTOVENERE at the end of the 12th century, fortifying the impressive castle in the 16th and 17th centuries. The village sprawls along the promontory, where the main buildings of note are the church of San Pietro (built at the tip of the promontory, on the site of an assortment of buildings from different periods) and the church of San Lorenzo – a Romanesque building, dating from 1130, although altered in the Gothic and Renaissance periods – which contains a 15th-century marble altarpiece by a sculptor, or sculptors, of the Florentine school.

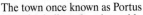

FROM MILAN TO THE TOWNS, LAKES AND RIVERS OF LOMBARDY

MILAN, *184*

The starting point of this itinerary is Milan, the administrative rather than geographical hub of a region that derives its name from the Longobards (Lombards). Milan may not be regarded as an artistic city, but it boasts a rich array of priceless works in its close-knit historical center that are equaled by few other cities. From Milan our itinerary will head out to the main tourist resorts within fairly easy reach of this city. We will then travel through northwest Lombardy – stopping at Castiglione Olona (a remarkable enclave of Tuscan art), the Parco del Ticino with its beautiful riverside walks, and Stresa and the lush Borromean Islands on Lake Maggiore in Piedmont – to the breathtaking scenery around Lake Como, an elegant and exclusive tourist center of long standing. Then onto the hilly region of La Brianza, dotted with small industries and

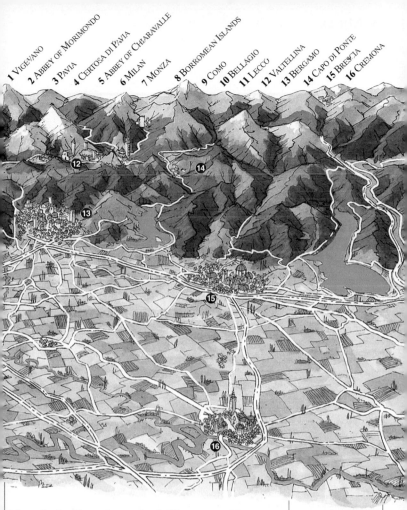

historical villas where the Milanese nobles used to spend their vacations. We travel from the ancient and modern town of Monza to the Alpine landscapes that form a ring around San Pietro al Monte, a magnificent and isolated example of early Lombard Romanesque. The plain of Lower Lombardy is scattered with farms, and affords some fine examples of medieval and Renaissance civilization: the Milanese Abbey of Chiaravalle, the Certosa di Pavia of the Visconti, and the piazzas of Vigevano (Renaissance) and Cremona (medieval). The final part of the itinerary, "Venetian" Lombardy, beyond the Adda river, offers the enchanting walled city of Bergamo Alta and Brescia with its spectacular monuments that range from Roman to neoclassical in style.

> "The workers who polished the cast iron by hand would arrive every morning at six in sluggish trains, would grab a bite on the factory floor, and leave again on the same trains before six every evening."
> Luciano Bianciardi,
> *La vita agra*
> *(A Hard Life)*

> "O what a forest! What colors and what sounds! Such lush greenery and so many animals! In those days there were giraffes in Lombardy, and zebras. There were caymans in the Adda river, and wading birds warbled in the rice fields."
> Guido Ceronetti,
> *Deliri disarmati*
> *(Unarmed Raptures)*

Founded by the Gauls in the 4th century BC, Mediolanum was a city of great importance in the twilight of the Roman Empire, so much so that in AD 286 it was chosen as the capital of the West. It was here in 313 that the Emperor Constantine gave Christians freedom of worship, and here that Saint Augustine of Hippo, the leading philosopher of the new religion, was converted. Not long after, however, with the crisis in Rome, Mediolanum was sacked and fell into decline.

FROM IMPERIAL CAPITAL TO INDEPENDENT COMMUNE. Milan did not prosper again until after the 11th century, when it led the cities in northern Italy in revolt against the Germanic Holy Roman Emperors. Half-destroyed by Frederick Barbarossa in 1162, the city took its revenge in 1176, defeating the imperial army at Legnano ● *36*.

THE VISCONTIS, SFORZAS AND BORROMEOS. At the end of the 13th century the Visconti began their rise to power in what was now a free city, and by the end of 1477 they were firmly in command. The Visconti created the Duchy of Milan, extending its borders to make it the strongest state in 14th-century Italy, and gave it a cathedral and a castle. In 1450, after a brief Republican interlude, power passed into the hands of the Sforza, a family who displayed great far-sightedness in promoting learning and the arts: Leonardo da Vinci ▲ *198*, among others, found work at their court. Foreign forces had now begun to invade Italy, and in 1535 Milan and the surrounding region were annexed by the kingdom of Spain. The nation suffered under Spanish rule, which lasted until 1707, and in the 17th century it was decimated by the plague. It was able to rely, however, on the strength and learning of the Borromeo family, who provided Milan with more than one archbishop ▲ *189*, and the Catholic church with the charismatic figure of Saint Charles Borromeo (see left). Spanish rule did, however, furnish the setting for one of the most important Italian novels: *I Promessi Sposi* (*The Betrothed*) by Milanese writer Alessandro Manzoni.

FROM AUSTRIA TO ITALY. After Spanish dominion Milan was annexed by the Hapsburg emperor. Initially the city benefitted from the enlightened reforms of Maria Theresa, then after the French Revolution it suffered under a less cultivated and more repressive regime. Milan drove out the Austrian garrison during the famous "Cinque Giornate" ("Five Days") of 1848; eleven years later it became part of the kingdom of Sardinia and then in 1861 part of the kingdom of Italy. Almost immediately, the city became the financial hub of the

new nation and, with the industrial booms of the 19th and 20th centuries, Italy's largest center of production. Over the last few decades the city's great industrial enterprises have been largely replaced by tertiary and service industries. Nevertheless, Milan owes its international supremacy in fashion and industrial design today to those years of economic growth and to its long-established artistic traditions ▲ 192.

MASS-MEDIA CAPITAL. In political and administrative terms Milan is the chief city of Lombardy, the wealthiest region in Italy. Culturally the city has always been the capital of the publishing industry and the national media. As early as the Renaissance, when Greek was the educated language, in 1476 Milan published the world's first printed Greek book. This tradition is continued by leading publishing houses such as Rizzoli, Mondadori, Feltrinelli and Garzanti, by the most influential daily newspaper in Italy – the *Corriere della Sera* ▲ 201, which was founded in 1876 – and in the electronic media by the country's highest concentration of private television companies (Mediaset). The main Italian Internet server (Italia Online) is also based in Milan.

URBAN EXPANSION. "Dismantle, demolish, both merry and bold / rings out the ode to whitewash and straight roads": these lines, written in 1866 by Arrigo Boito, clearly express the passion for building that swept Milan in the decade after the unification of Italy. Before this period the center of the city was a crowded area, surrounded by a network of canals that still bore the stamp of the Roman road system – altered in the Middle Ages – and a series of villages (with orchards, gardens and many convents) in the strip of land bounded by the rampart of the 16th-century Spanish walls, which by this time

THE CANALS
As incredible as it may seem today, Milan once sat at the center of a network of man-made canals. Initially excavated to irrigate the fields, as time went by they became vital for communication and an invaluable means of transport across the surrounding plain. Eventually the canals were linked together to form a navigable ring around the walls of the medieval city. These walls were demolished centuries ago, and around 1930 the "ring of water" was covered over with asphalt.

THE FIERA DI MILANO
Dozens of specialist exhibitions of international repute keep this large Milanese exhibition center booked almost all year round. Events connected with these exhibitions often take place in the heart of the city.

was used as a promenade and customs boundary. On the other side of the walls spread the commune of Corpi Santi, which once surrounded the whole of Milan. In 1873 it was annexed by the city, despite the opposition of its inhabitants. Although the commune never expanded very far beyond the city walls (the residents always preferring to rebuild and replace buildings within the same area), in the space of a century Milan was completely transformed and acquired its present appearance.

THE "MORAL CAPITAL". Present-day Milan is the second largest city in the country, a metropolis with 1,300,000 inhabitants, a figure that can be tripled if the densely populated hinterland is included. It is not as large as the great European cities (Greater Rome, for example, is around seven times larger). Milan stands out for its distinctive lifestyle – characterized by hard work, a capacity for initiative, and the pursuit of material comfort – which has often caused it to be described as the "moral capital" of Italy. However, even in the midst of such a frenetic pace of life, it is

11 Palazzo Reale
12 Torre Velasca
13 Università Statale
14 San Nazaro Maggiore
15 Sant'Eustorgio
16 San Lorenzo Maggiore
17 Sant'Ambrogio
18 San Maurizio al Monastero Maggiore
19 Museum of Science and Technology
20 Santa Maria delle Grazie
21 Castello Sforzesco
22 San Simpliciano
23 Pinacoteca di Brera

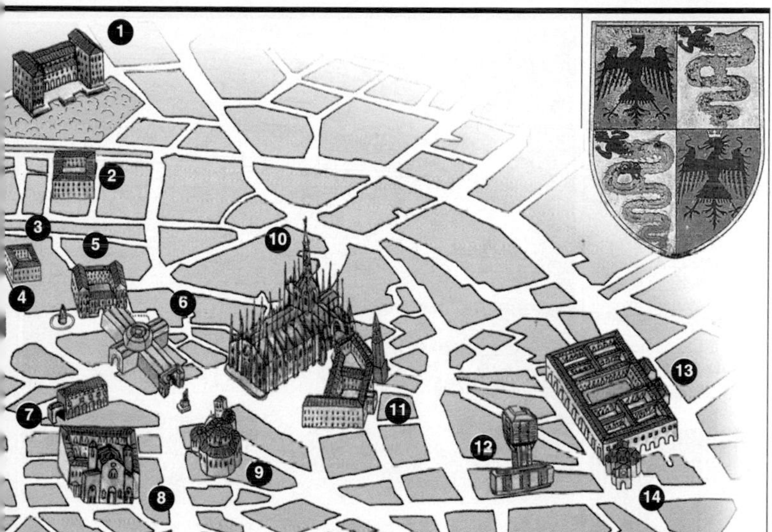

impossible to forget that Milan has played a central role in European history for the last two millennia and that, as a result, it has acquired a rich legacy of monuments and works of art that are more than enough to qualify it as a major cultural city.

The present day. Today terms such as "*cerchia dei navigli*" (canal circle), "*mura spagnole*" (Spanish walls) and "*bastioni*" (ramparts) are still frequently employed in a precise topographical sense: they refer to the concentric roads that circle the city, linked mainly by streets radiating out from the Piazza del Duomo. However, the canals have now been completely covered over; only negligible traces of the ramparts remain; and the development of the modern city makes it difficult to find its most important historical monuments – ancient churches, palaces and houses often being concealed by tower blocks.

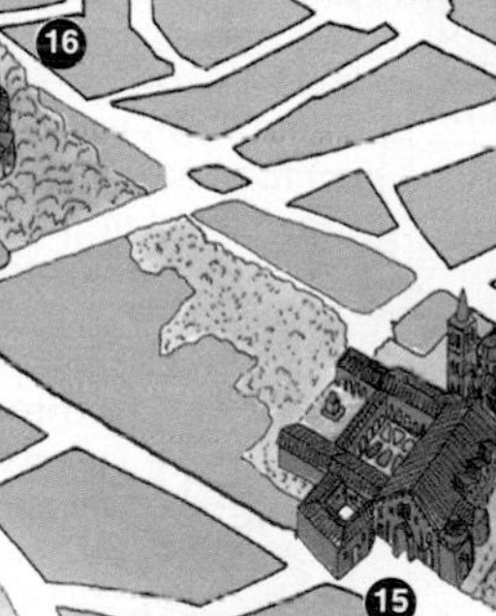

"Panettone"
The four symbols of Milan are the city's coat of arms (a slender red cross on a white field); the Biscione (serpent) of the Viscontis; the Duomo's "Madonnina"; and *panettone*, a Christmas cake shaped rather like a dome. As with all simple but famous objects, its origin remains a mystery, although a variety of legends surround its creation.

THE MADONNINA
Milan's Duomo is dedicated to "Maria nascente", and the Milanese are very fond of the gilded-bronze statue of the Virgin which, since 1774, has stood on top of the cathedral. From the ground the statue really does look like a "little Madonna", even though in reality it is over 13 feet tall. Everyone in Milan (as well as people further afield) knows the dedicatory song by Giovanni D'Anzi, which describes the statue "shining from afar" as it stands high above Milan, protecting and defending the city.

PIAZZA DEL DUOMO

Although enlarged over the last two centuries, which involved flattening an entire district, and embellished with some new buildings and a MONUMENT to Vittorio Emanuele II (the first King of Italy), the Piazza del Duomo remains the true heart of the city, just as it was in the Middle Ages. The defining features of the piazza are now the porticoed buildings erected in the second half of the 19th century, although the ARENGARIO, which houses the tourist office and exhibition rooms, dates from the Fascist period.

DUOMO ★. Milan's Duomo is one of the most famous cathedrals in the world and the largest and most intricate Gothic cathedral in Italy. The magnificence of the rear section (begun in 1386 under Gian Galeazzo Visconti) is matched by the façade – which is Baroque at the base, neoclassical halfway up, and topped by a neo-Gothic upper section completed under Napoleon. Most of the interior dates back to the 16th and 17th centuries, under the Borromei. Inside, the cathedral is 518 feet high and 305 feet across, making it the third largest Catholic church in the world; the gilded statue of the Madonnina, at the top of the main spire, watches over Milan from a height of 358 feet. Passing through the bronze doors, you will find yourself amid a forest of fifty-two columns which over the centuries have been embellished with thousands of works of art (there are over 3,400 statues alone). At the transept crossing is a giant seven-branched candelabrum (13th–14th century); to the right, you will see a dramatic statue of Saint Bartholomew being flayed (1562) and the funerary monument of Gian

Giacomo Medici (1563). In the presbytery the carved wooden choir stalls (1620) and the 16th-century organs, with paintings from the same period, are worthy of note. The ambulatory is bathed in dappled light from huge stained-glass windows dating from the early 15th century; the doorways of the two late 14th-century Gothic sacristies, facing one another, rank among the cathedral's oldest works of art.

MUSEO DEL DUOMO. In one wing of the Palazzo Reale, the Fabbricca del Duomo (the organization that oversaw the centuries-old construction of the church and which is now responsible for its maintenance) displays documents relating to the cathedral's construction. You can take a close look at statues designed to stand at a height of 328 feet and discover designs which helped (or infuriated) the many architects and sculptors who participated in the building of the cathedral.

PALAZZO REALE. Next to the Duomo, on the site of the former Visconti royal palace, stands the elegant neoclassical building erected in 1778 by Giuseppe Piermarini for the Hapsburg rulers. Today, it houses the MUSEO D'ARTE CONTEMPORANEA, displaying the most important artistic movements in 20th-century Italian painting. Major art exhibitions are staged in the SALA DELLE CARIATIDI and on the first floor.

SANTA MARIA PRESSO SAN SATIRO. On Via Mazzini, which leads off from the Piazza del Duomo, next to an ancient belfry, is a chapel that is Renaissance in style but which was already standing in the 9th century. It belongs to a church (whose main entrance is on Via Torino) that contains work by Bramante. It was this great Renaissance architect who was responsible for, among other things, the magnificent trompe-l'oeil presbytery, an inspired solution to the problem presented by lack of space.

PINACOTECA AMBROSIANA. Not far from the Duomo, in Piazza Pio XI (at no. 2), stands the palace built by Cardinal Federico Borromeo (1564–1631) to house a library and an Academy of Fine Arts. This palace was recently restored, and you can now visit its richly stocked LIBRARY (which includes the *Codex Atlanticus* ▲ 198 by Leonardo da Vinci) and its PINACOTECA, which has works by Raphael (the cartoon for his *School of Athens*), Titian (*Epiphany* and *Ecce Homo*) and Caravaggio (*Fruit Basket*), as well as some fine examples of 17th-century Lombard art and works from the Flemish and Dutch schools.

BOCCIONI
The Museo d'Arte Contemporanea at the Palazzo Reale has numerous works by Umberto Boccioni (1882–1916), one of the founders of Futurism and perhaps the most important artist of the Futurist movement. It was in Milan, around 1910, that Boccioni developed the ideas that were to make him famous.

BIBLIOTECA AMBROSIANA
When he became Archbishop of Milan in 1595, Federico Borromeo devoted himself to creating a library that would be a worthy research center for the city. To this end, he sent eight of the most learned scholars to buy manuscripts throughout Italy. He also acquired manuscripts from Europe and the East. When it was opened, in 1609, the library had already amassed some 30,000 volumes, including a 5th-century illustrated *Iliad* and many extremely rare incunabula.

PALAZZO DELLA RAGIONE. Along Via Mercanti, a stone's throw from the Piazza del Duomo, the pillars of a Romanesque portico support the walls of the commune's first city hall, which for centuries served as the main law courts and now houses an exhibition hall. It was built in 1233 by Oldrado da Tresseno, the *podestà* (mayor), who is preserved for eternity on horseback on the façade facing the small square. The upper floor with oval windows was added in the 18th century by Maria Theresa of Austria.

GALLERIA VITTORIO EMANUELE II ★. A magnificent shopping arcade (1867), the work of architect Giuseppe Mengoni, links the Piazza del Duomo to the Piazza della Scala.

PIAZZA DELLA SCALA

In the Middle Ages a church built by Beatrice Regina della Scala, a noblewoman, stood on the site of the present Teatro alla Scala. The opera house and the piazza (1858) took their name from this noblewoman. At the piazza's center is a MONUMENT to Leonardo da Vinci (1872).

TEATRO ALLA SCALA ★. The most famous opera house in Italy, and one of the most important in the history of opera, was commissioned by the Hapsburgs and built in 1778 by Giuseppe Piermarini ● 95. Half-destroyed by the bombings of 1943, it was reopened in 1946 with a memorable concert conducted by Arturo Toscanini. The building is remarkable not so much for its façade as for the magnificent structure and marvelous acoustics of the horseshoe-shaped wooden auditorium, with its four tiers of boxes and two balconies. Provided there are no rehearsals in progress, you can visit the MUSEO TEATRALE ALLA SCALA inside the building itself.

PALAZZO MARINO. Opposite La Scala stands the palace that was built in the mid 16th century for a Genoese banker, Marino. The original parts of the building are the rear façade, the CORTILE and the SALA DELL'ALESSI (the name of the architect); the façade facing the opera house was built in the same style at the end of the 19th century. In 1860 this became Milan's city hall. The Church of San Fidele, which in part dates from the same period, stands on the small square to the rear.

> "MILAN IS TRULY BEAUTIFUL AND SOMETIMES YOU HAVE TO FORCE YOURSELF TO RESIST ITS CHARMS AND NOT BE DISTRACTED FROM YOUR WORK."

GIOVANNI VERGA

POLDI PEZZOLI MUSEUM. Just a short walk from Piazza della Scala, this museum, founded in the 19th century by Gian Giacomo Poldi Pezzoli, is one of several handsome palaces on Via Manzoni (no. 12). It provide the perfect setting for collections of weapons, carpets, textiles, jewelry, gold and silver work, enamel, ceramics, glassware, furniture and clocks dating from the 15th to the 19th centuries. However, the art collection alone would be enough to ensure the museum's reputation. Notable works include *Saint Nicholas of Tolentino* by Piero della Francesca, *Portrait of a Young Woman* by Piero del Pollaiolo, two Botticellis (a *Madonna* and a *Deposition*), many Lombard works from the first half of the 16th century, a *Madonna* by Andrea Mantegna and Venetian works from the 18th century, including the fine *Gray Lagoon* by Francesco Guardi.

Portrait of a Young Woman by Piero del Pollaiolo. Attributed to the Florentine painter (1441–96), this painting is kept in the Poldi Pezzoli Museum.

PARALLEL LIVES
Two of Milan's houses, which have been converted into two of the most outstanding house museums in the world, were built within a few decades of each other during the 19th century by Gian Giacomo Poldi Pezzoli and brothers Fausto and Giuseppe Bagatti Valsecchi respectively – all three of whom had conceived a passion for collecting. Although the former was of noble birth (his mother was a Trivulzio), the two brothers owed their prominence in the city partly to the talents of their father, who was a well-known artist, and partly to their own personal success as lawyers. In other respects their lives followed a similar course, being devoted to a passionate search for masterpieces both in Lombard country residences and from sources in other parts of Europe.

VIA MONTE NAPOLEONE

The name of what is now probably internationally the best-known street in Milan pays tribute to this great emperor, who was in fact made welcome in the city and who chose Milan as the capital of first the Cisalpine Republic (1797) and then the Italian Republic (1805–14). Originally the site of the Monte dei Pegni (pawnbrokers), it was renamed in honor of Napoleon in 1804.

THE "QUADRILATERO DELLA MODA". Almost all the leading designers of Milanese prêt-à-porter, all the celebrated creators of the international styles of the 1980's and 1990's, have their headquarters, or at least one large store, in the "quadrilateral" bounded by Via Monte Napoleone, Via Borgospesso, Via della Spiga and Via Sant'Andrea. The area has also attracted foreign fashion houses, creating a district of key importance to the European fashion industry.

MUSEO BAGATTI VALSECCHI. In the heart of the "Quadrilatero" (at Via del Gesù no. 5 to Via Santo Spiriti no. 10), the Bagatti Valsecchi Museum (1878–87) is interesting for the items of Renaissance art that it contains and for the meticulous restoration of the 19th-century décor. No other house of its type can boast a similar degree of authenticity.

MUSEO BAGATTI VALSECCHI
VIA SANTO SPIRITO 10 MILANO 20121 ITALIA

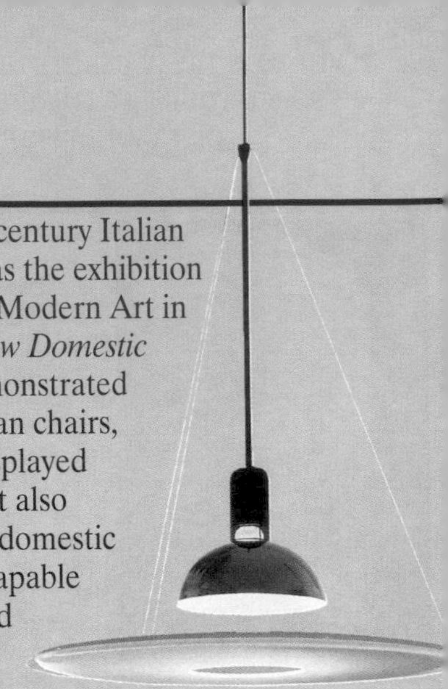

The event that finally put 20th-century Italian industrial design on the map was the exhibition held in 1972 at the Museum of Modern Art in New York entitled *Italy: The New Domestic Landscape*. This exhibition demonstrated not only that the design of Italian chairs, tables, bookcases and lamps displayed extraordinary inventiveness, but also that it promoted the idea of a "domestic landscape" – an environment capable of adapting to social change and of reflecting it in the home, for the benefit of the members of the household. This was an important milestone in the history of popular taste and one that irrevocably influenced Western lifestyles. The greater part of the designers and manufacturers who exhibited in New York were Milanese. Today the Milanese and designers living in Milan still lead the field in the design sector, with the top designers and most prominent Italian companies. Their stores in the city are nearly all clustered around the Piazza San Babila, between the "Quadrilatero della Moda" and the Università Statale.

SHINING DISC
With designs that are mainstream but always innovative (for example the Frisbi lamp, manufactured by Flos), Achille Castiglioni is in some ways the father of Milanese industrial design at the end of the millennium. His ideal has always been "anonymous design", echoing the tradition of the unknown creator who perfected objects such as the hammer or scissors.

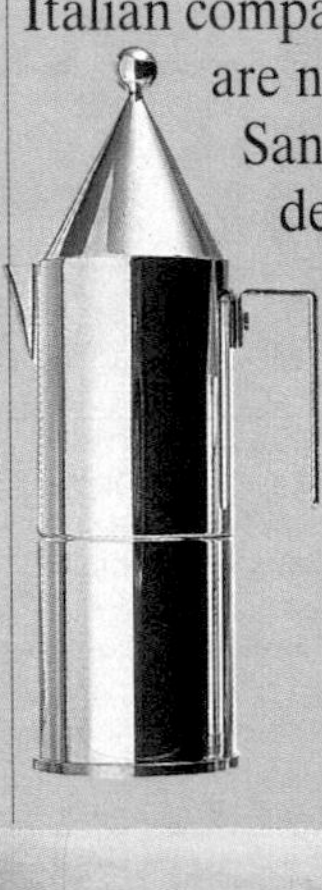

GEOMETRIC COFFEE-POT
Even the most acclaimed large-scale designers, such as Aldo Rossi, have tried their hand at designing household objects. Left: the Caffettiera Conica by Alessi.

AVANT-GARDE OBJECTS IN THE LIVING ROOM
The interest in all kinds of domestic objects began with the avant-garde movement during the first half of the 20th century. It has since encouraged many Milanese town planners and architects to design one-off pieces of furniture. Vico Magistretti, who designed the Sinbad range, manufactured by Cassina, of armchairs and divans with removable covers, is a famous case in point.

FANTASTIC BOOKCASE

The top-class workshop of Enzo Mari has produced a crop of new designers who are as meticulous as their teacher, though occasionally more whimsical. The Vincastro bookcase was designed by Paolo Ulian and made by Driade.

PERSONALIZED COLORS

Leading Milanese designer-architects like Marco Zanuso and Ettore Sottsass Jr have often worked for Olivetti. Sottsass, for example, designed the Elea – the first Olivetti computer – as well as the Praxis 48 and Valentina typewriters. In the last few years this company philosophy resulted in the brightly colored, user-friendly laptops designed by Michele De Lucchi.

SOPHISTICATED PLASTIC

The Kartell range of plastic furniture, like this clothes-stand, is the product of a typically Lombard combination of creative innovation and technical expertise. Originally the company was an industrial manufacturer of laboratory equipment.

FOREIGN INFLUENCES

The Jill lamp shows that Milanese design also thrives on the work of foreign designers, who can give free rein to their creativity in Milan. This lamp was created in Milan by the English designer Perry King and the Andalusian designer Santiago Miranda.

The name Brera comes from the old Germanic word *braida* for "meadow" – from which the adjective *braidense,* meaning "of Brera" (as applied to the Biblioteca Nazionale) – is also derived. Nowadays very little grass is left, but there are still traces of the quarter's venerable history in the cobble-stone streets of Via Fiori Chiari and Via Ciovasso (two well-preserved fragments of the past). It can also be sensed in the atmosphere of the deconsecrated church of San Carpoforo (its stripped interior makes it an excellent venue for temporary exhibitions) and in the curve of Via Madonnina (a short street glittering with elegant shop windows).

BRERA

This area – the main streets are Via Brera, Via Solferino and Via San Marco – now teems with visitors to the countless boutiques and small stores and, by night, with people frequenting the many nightclubs. The Brera Quarter owes its flavor to the fact that between the 19th and 20th centuries it was Milan's equivalent of the Parisian *rive gauche*. Petty crooks, skulking in the old houses and alleyways, rubbed shoulders with the artistic and literary avant-garde, who flocked to the Brera Accademia di Belle Arti – which still thrives in the quarter's main palace.

PALAZZO DI BRERA. From 1572 to 1772 this impressive building inVia Brera (no. 28) served as the Jesuits' "headquarters" in Milan. In the two-tier courtyard (1651), which is the work of Francesco Maria Ricchino, stands a MONUMENT to Napoleon (1811) by Canova (a bronze copy of a larger marble original). Maria Theresa converted the palace into the home of various scientific institutions, with an observatory, a fine library, a botanical garden and, last but not least, the Academy.

PINACOTECA DI BRERA ★. One of the largest art collections in Europe, this originated as a collection of works intended as a study aid for students at the Academy. Its size is largely due to Napoleon, who commandeered paintings and ecclesiastical pictures throughout northern Italy. The major schools of art of central Italy from the 14th to the 16th century are well represented (Ambrogio Lorenzetti, Gentile da Fabriano, Bramante), as are the Venetian school (Bellini, Carpaccio, Lotto) and the Lombard school (Foppa, Bergognone, Luini) of the 15th and 16th centuries. Three masterpieces, which are genuine landmarks in the history of art, date from these centuries: the portrait of *Federico, Duke of Montefeltro* by Piero della Francesca (1472–4), *Dead Christ* by Andrea Mantegna (c. 1480) and *Marriage of the Virgin* (left) by Raphael (1504). The gallery also contains various 18th-century Venetian works (Tiepolo, Piazzetta, Bellotto) and a number of 20th-century Italian works (Modigliani, Medardo Rosso, Boccioni and Sironi).

SAN SIMPLICIANO. A short distance from the center, on Corso Garibaldi, you will come to one of the four churches founded in the 4th century by Bishop Ambrogio (Saint Ambrose) that stood on the roads leading out of the city. The building is Romanesque in appearance, though with some 19th-century additions. The apse contains a large fresco by Bergognone depicting the *Coronation of the Virgin* (c. 1515).

PORTA ROMANA

Around the boundary of the Spanish walls, current place names refer to some twelve gates, each a focal point of a particular quarter. Five of these, including the Porta Romana, still possess their monumental entrance.

UNIVERSITÀ STATALE. The largest public institution erected in Milan under the old regime was the hospital built in 1456 by Duke Francesco Sforza. It has always been called Ca'Granda by the Milanese, and it is indeed huge. Construction was started by Antonio Averulino, who created the right-hand side of the façade on Via Festa del Perdono. It was continued in the 17th century by Francesco Maria Ricchino, who reused 15th-century ornaments in the vast courtyard of the building at no. 7, which is now the headquarters of the university.

SAN NAZARO MAGGIORE. Another of Sant'Ambrogio's four churches, San Nazaro Maggiore is virtually propped up by the university. Rebuilt and restored, it is preceded on the Corso di Porta Romana by the stately TRIVULZIO CHAPEL (1512–50), which has a simple interior containing family tombs.

TORRE VELASCA. This towering 27-story skyscraper (also on Corso di Porta Romana) mushrooms out at the top, so that the upper block overhangs the 18 floors beneath. Because of its distinctive outline, the Torre Velasca stands out boldly from the Milan skyline. The work of L. Belgioioso, E. Peressutti and E.N. Rogers (1956–60), its structural achievements make it one of the most interesting reinforced-concrete buildings.

PORTA ROMANA
Beneath the Torre Velasca and in front of the façade of San Nazaro Maggiore, the long, straight Corso di Porta Romana heads out toward the city boundary. Deep underground, Milan's third subway line now echoes the course of the road – but this is still the same road that 2,000 years ago was laid out in the direction of Rome, the *caput mundi*. At the point where the road crosses the 16th-century city walls stands the arch of the Porta Romana, with its ashlar work still largely intact. It was erected in 1 to commemorate marriage of Ma Margherita of to Philip II of

WATER MUSIC
Along the Naviglio Grande and the Naviglio Pavese, starting from the Darsena, near the city outskirts, there is a host of lively night spots, like the Scimmie (below), that are renowned for their live music. Their model is the Capolinea, a jazz club founded at the end of the 1960's by the drummer Giorgio Vanni and now run by his three daughters.

THE TICINESE QUARTER

The former harbor district of Milan, packed with working-class houses, is located at the outer edge of the network of canals. Until the mid 20th century this was the seediest area in the city, but it is now fast becoming a trendy area, with avant-garde stores, photographic workshops and design studios. The quarter extends as far as the Darsena, where the NAVIGLIO GRANDE, flowing in from the Ticino river, meets the NAVIGLIO PAVESE, which heads toward Pavia.

SAN LORENZO MAGGIORE. For hundreds of years from its foundation in the 4th century, this church – which stands at the entrance to the Ticinese Quarter – must have been the largest in the Western Roman Empire with a circular plan. Sixteen even older COLUMNS, brought here from a temple in imperial Mediolanum, form a portico in front of the building. The church was altered in the Romanesque period (12th century) and assumed its final appearance between the 16th and 17th centuries. However, it still retains its original structure and chapels, which can be reached from inside. The 4th-century mosaics in the CHAPEL OF SANT'AQUILINO, to the right of the entrance, are particularly worthy of note.

SANT'EUSTORGIO. Between the ring of canals, a vast green stretches from the Church of San Lorenzo Maggiore up to this magnificent basilica, named after the Milanese bishop Saint Eustorgio (4th century), which is notable for its 15th-century side chapels. Behind the apse is the superb PORTINARI CHAPEL (1462–6) containing the tomb of Saint Peter the Martyr (1339), built by Giovanni di Balduccio to preserve the remains of a Dominican friar killed by heretics in 1252. On the walls of the chapel, Renaissance frescos (1468) by Vincenzo Foppa recount the story of the saint's life.

SANT'AMBROGIO AND THE MAGENTA QUARTER

To the west of the historical center, our tour takes in two of the city's most important churches, Sant'Ambrogio and Santa Maria delle Grazie, with its refectory painted by Leonardo.

SANT'AMBROGIO ★. This basilica named after the city's patron saint, stands in the piazza of the same name. Renowned for its great age (it was founded in 379), its importance is primarily due to the Romanesque additions, made between 1080 and the mid 13th century, which make it the prototype of Lombardy's Romanesque basilicas ● *87*. As well as a four-sided porticoed atrium, it has an elegant façade with two superimposed loggia, two different campaniles and, inside, a magnificent pulpit and a famous gold altar that is a masterpiece of the goldsmith's art, executed in 835. The seventh chapel off the right-hand aisle provides access to the SACELLO DI SAN VITTORE IN CIEL D'ORO, containing 5th-century mosaics depicting saints. The Museo di Sant'Ambrogio (across the courtyard) has exhibits on the history of the church.

MUSEUM OF SCIENCE AND TECHNOLOGY. At the start of the 1950's the 16th-century Olivetan Convent of San Vittore – not far from Sant'Ambrogio, in Via San Vittore (no. 21) – was converted into the largest museum of science and technology in Italy. It contains hundreds of dioramas and working models,

large engines, railway carriages, airplanes and an entire gallery devoted to the technical inventions of Leonardo da Vinci ▲ *198*.

SANTA MARIA DELLE GRAZIE. Along the nearby Corso Magenta, just outside the ring of canals, you will come to perhaps the most famous church in Milan. From the outside, you will immediately be struck by the difference between the Gothic naves, begun in 1466, and the Renaissance tribune at the rear (probably the work of Bramante), completed later in 1492. Inside, the most fascinating features are the tribune itself, the little cloister (at the rear, to the left) and the old sacristy.

IL CENACOLO (THE REFECTORY OF THE "LAST SUPPER") ★. The Church of Santa Maria delle Grazie is also famous for the former refectory of the adjoining convent, the so-called Cenacolo Vinciano (which has its own separate entrance, to the left of the façade). Here, between 1495 and 1497, Leonardo da Vinci – using the *a secco* in preference to the *a fresco* technique ▲ *198* – painted a mural depicting the *Last Supper*, a work that has been reproduced millions of times.

SAN MAURIZIO AL MONASTERO MAGGIORE. Also in Corso Magenta, the former Monastery of San Maurizio houses the CIVICO MUSEO ARCHEOLOGICO. Its church contains many 16th-century frescos by the Lombard school, including Bernardino Luini's *Life of Saint Catherine*. It is used regularly for classical music concerts.

A VIGOROUS SAINT
The adjective "Ambrosian" has come to be almost synonymous with "Milanese". It is taken from the name of the city's patron saint, Saint Ambrose. Born in Trier (now in Germany), Ambrogio (c. 339–90) was an imperial civil servant who was very popular with the Milanese people – to such an extent that in 374 they appointed him bishop before he had even been baptized. In subsequent years he became involved in the fight against the Arian heresy and paganism. His vigorous defense of the poor and weak, together with his intractable nature, gave rise to legends. It is known that Ambrose compelled the Roman emperor Theodosius to do public penance as punishment for his brutal massacre of the people of Thessalonica – now Salonika, in Greece.

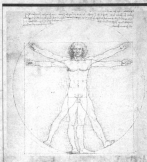

At the age of almost thirty, Leonardo da Vinci (1452–1519) arrived in Milan from his native Tuscany and introduced himself to Duke Ludovico Sforza – "Il Moro", with a letter that he himself had written listing his own abilities. He was warmly received and stayed in the capital of the duchy for almost twenty years. During this time, he produced stage sets for royal entertainments, a large model for the horse of

ULTIMA CENA
The fascination of the *Last Supper* has been augmented by the fact that it has proved extremely difficult to restore and conserve. This is because, when painting it, Leonardo did not use the traditional method of fresco painting, but another technique which bore a greater resemblance to painting on canvas. Although this allowed him to work more slowly and in more detail, it was at the cost of durability. Damp, the settling of the walls and the passage of time have caused lines and pigments to fade, making continuous restoration work essential.

SKETCHES FROM THE CODEX ATLANTICUS
Large spring attached to undercarriage with angled wheels and other springs.

Machine with wings operated manually with the help of screws.

the monument to Francesco Sforza (works which have not survived) and, most importantly, the extraordinary *Ultima Cena* (*Last Supper*) in the refectory of Santa Maria delle Grazie. He also produced a vast number of documents and notes on many different subjects, which were collected together several years later in the *Codex Atlanticus*. Having left the city in 1499 after the Sforza family had fallen from power, Leonardo came back to stay there again between 1506 and 1513. It was during this period that he painted the *Sant'Anna* now in the Louvre in Paris and the *Vergine delle Rocce* in the National Gallery in London.

THE CODEX ATLANTICUS
Throughout his two lengthy stays in Milan, Leonardo was constantly taking notes and drawing sketches, jotting down ideas and inventions, images drawn from life and definitive designs, on thousands of sheets of paper. He left the city an immense technical and artistic heritage. These documents were collected together and bound in a codex which – from the large format of the page – became known as the "Atlantic" codex.

A VENERABLE FACE
A high forehead furrowed with wrinkles, an aquiline nose, a protruding lower lip and a stubborn chin: this was how the elderly Leonardo painted his self-portrait.

MODEL OF "VITE AERFA"
This is regarded as the forerunner of the modern helicopter.

EXHIBITIONS AT LA TRIENNALE
The prestigious series of architectural and design exhibitions held at La Triennale, suspended after the student protest of 1968, were resumed in 1994. Since 1997 La Triennale has also been the home of a permanent exhibition tracing the history of Italian design from 1945 to 1990.

CASTELLO SFORZESCO AND THE SEMPIONE QUARTER

The Castello Sforzesco dominates the view to the northwest of the historical nucleus of Milan. Behind it, the Parco Sempione lies on the site of what was originally the ducal park and subsequently the drill ground.

CASTELLO SFORZESCO ★. Water from the ring of canals was used to feed the castle's moats. The Viscontis began building it in the mid 14th century as a fortress to protect the city against attack and, if need be, to protect the rulers from their own subjects. In fact, as soon as the last member of the Visconti family died, the townspeople destroyed it. In 1466 the Sforzas began rebuilding it, this time creating an elegant Renaissance palace. Under the Spanish, who enlarged it, the Castello Sforzesco was once more used for military purposes; it was then remodeled by Napoleon, and eventually restored during the early 20th century. It is now entirely occupied by libraries, archives, collections of period prints and, most importantly, extensive museums of history and art. Exhibits include fine medieval and Renaissance statues brought here from demolished Milanese churches; countless paintings by the Lombard and Venetian schools (Mantegna, Bellini, Foppa, Bergognone, Lotto, Tintoretto, Magnasco and Canaletto); and large collections of ancient musical instruments and period dress. The castello's crowning glory is undoubtedly the *Rondanini Pietà*, one of Michelangelo's last works.

PARCO SEMPIONE. One of the city's few parks, this is the largest with trees and ponds. It is also the site of the ARENA, a neoclassical stadium dating from the

Napoleonic period, and the TRIENNALE exhibition center
(1933). At the rear of the park stands the ARCO DELLA PACE
(1807–38), a triumphal arch designed by Luigi Canonica that
was built to honor Napoleon.

CIMITERO MONUMENTALE. This vast landscaped cemetery
(1866), northwest of the city center, is the final resting place
of the wealthiest Milanese burghers. Their family tombs,
adorned with statuary by masters such as Medardo Rosso,
Adolfo Wildt, Giacomo Manzù, Fausto Melotti, and Arnaldo
and Giò Pomodoro, reflect changing fashions in Italian art.

PORTA VENEZIA QUARTER

The thoroughfare that heads out from the center toward
Venice (the other major state in northern Italy in the Middle
Ages) and Vienna (the former Hapsburg capital) is still
one of Milan's most elegant streets. Called CORSO VENEZIA,
it is graced with neoclassical buildings and (at no. 47) is the
Art Nouveau façade of the PALAZZO CASTIGLIONI, built in
(1903). The TOLLHOUSES (1828) at the far end of the street
are also neoclassical.

GIARDINI PUBBLICI. Next to Corso Venezia are the public
gardens planted in the 18th century by Giuseppe Piermarini.

The spacious tree-lined
park is also the site of
the imposing building
(1893) that houses
an excellent NATURAL
HISTORY MUSEUM.

VILLA REALE. Next to
the Giardini Pubblici
are the gardens
belonging to the Villa
Belgioioso (1790),
which became the
property of the King
of Italy in 1861 and
then of the city of
Milan. This building
now houses the CIVICA
GALLERIA D'ARTE
MODERNA, which displays paintings and statues from the 19th
and early 20th centuries. The Milanese are particularly proud
of a painting called the *Quarto stato* (*The Fourth Estate*) by
Giuseppe Pellizza da Volpedo (1901).

STAZIONE CENTRALE. After the cathedral, this is probably the
most popular building in Milan. Huge and white, overbearing
and yet familiar, the Stazione Centrale (designed in 1912, but
not completed until 1931) is positively palatial, with its rich
fusion of Art Nouveau and Eclecticism and its abundance of
sculptural detail and mosaics.

THE PIRELLI BUILDING. On the piazza in front of the Stazione
Centrale soars the skyscraper (417 feet high) built for the
famous Milanese manufacturer of rubber and tires, but now
the seat of the regional government. When it went up, in the
1950's, it was one of the tallest reinforced-concrete buildings
ever built. It is remarkable for its ethereal shape (conceived
by Milanese architect Giò Ponti) and for the inspirational way
in which Pier Luigi Nervi met its structural challenges.

**MILANESE
PUBLISHING**
Milan has
an age-old
publishing
tradition,
and there
is a large
number of
leading
publishing
houses ▲ 185
and major
national
newspapers in the
city. Many of
these are based
in the Palazzo
dei Giornali (also
called the Palazzo
dell'Informazione),
built in Piazza
Cavour between
1938 and 1942
to house Mussolini's
newspaper the *Popolo
d'Italia*.

Il Sole 24 ORE

**CORSO
BUENOS AIRES**
The long, busy road
that heads out from
Porta Venezia toward
the northeastern
suburbs is the Corso
Buenos Aires, built
to link Porta Venezia
with the Villa Reale
▲ 207 in Monza.
"Nothing in Milan
looks more like
a river than Corso
Buenos Aires",
wrote Giovanni
Raboni, thinking of
the constant flow
of traffic and people,
drawn here by the
avenue's stylish
boutiques and jewelry
stores, department
stores, patisseries,
fast-food restaurants
and bookstores.

Lombardy is known throughout the world for its long tradition of creativity and productivity. The industrial age was responsible for the first flowering of this tradition, which has its origins in generations of farmers, famous dynasties of craftsmen (such as the medieval Ticinese architects, the 16th-century Milanese armorers, and the stringed-instrument makers of 18th-century Cremona) and in the region's flair for business. Stretching from the Alps to the Po, Lombardy is ideally situated – at the crossroads of central Europe and the Mediterranean. As a result, the region possesses an outstanding cultural and artistic heritage, including castles, villas, abbeys and the remarkable Certosa di Pavia ▲ *208*.

Olona, Ticino and Lake Maggiore

The tributaries of the Po flow down from the Alps, carrying precious water across Lombardy. They are also vital for manufacturing industries and international communications. **CASTIGLIONE OLONA: TUSCAN ART IN LOMBARDY.** Castiglione Olona is a small hillside town that extends along the lush

banks of the Olona river between Lake Maggiore and Lake Como. It owes its charm to Cardinal Branda Castiglioni, who in the 15th century gave the town a facelift, drawing his inspiration from early-Renaissance Tuscan architecture ● *90*. The CHIESA DI VILLA is reminiscent of Brunelleschi's work in shape, while the Gothic COLLEGIATA and the nearby BAPTISTERY both contain wonderful FRESCOS ★ by the Tuscan artist Masolino da Panicale. The Palazzo Branda Castiglioni also has fine decorative frescos, some of which are the work of Masolino.

CASTELSEPRIO AND TORBA: AN ANCIENT PAST. A short distance south of Castiglione Olona stand the ruins of Castelseprio, a late-medieval Longobard (Lombard) fortress, completely razed to the ground by the Viscontis around the end of the 13th century. In the woods, the apse of the millennarian church of SANTA MARIA FORIS PORTAS contains rare frescos from the 7th and 8th centuries showing a Greek-Byzantine influence. Nearby is the equally old and attractive former MONASTERY OF TORBA (originally no doubt a military outpost of astelseprio), with an 11th-century church. **PARCO DEL TICINO: A RIVERSIDE SETTING.** Near Milan's oldest intercontinental airport

**WATER SPORTS
ON THE TICINO**
Recently canoeing
and rafting on the
river have become
popular sporting
activities in the Parco
del Ticino. Anyone
can try their hand at
these activities,
which are enjoyable
in themselves, but
here there is the
additional pleasure
of being able to
view the unspoiled
countryside along the
banks of the "azure
river" from a boat.

(MALPENSA, around 25 miles to the northwest of the city, near
many small industrial towns) a nature reserve of over 220,000
acres protects the moorland, *macchia* (maquis) and woodland
that flank the Ticino river. You can stroll between the river
and the remains of the dense forest that once covered the
entire Po valley ■ *20* or walk alongside the canals, old and
new, that crisscross the countryside.

LAKE MAGGIORE: STRESA AND THE BORROMEAN ISLANDS.

Also known as Lake Verbano, today Lake Maggiore is divided
between Italian Switzerland, Lombardy and Piedmont. The
attractive western shore of the lake between Arona and Stresa
does not belong to the region of Milan – but its entire history
bears the stamp of Lombard influence, from the centuries-old
presence of the Borromeo family to the clusters of Milanese
holiday homes today. Although not the main resort on Lake
Maggiore, STRESA is the lake's crowning glory. As well as the
late-18th-century parish church and the Villa Ducale, Stresa
has lovely gardens and parks renowned for their colorful
shrubs. Other highpoints are the park of the
19th-century Villa Pallavicino (toward
Belgirate) and the botanical gardens of
the Villa Taranto (in VERBANIA, about
10 miles further north), with their rare
species of plants. Between spring and
fall, however, Stresa's main tourist

**STRESA'S SUMMER
MUSIC WEEKS**
For the past forty
years Stresa has won
international acclaim
for its "Settimane
Musicali", a series of
music weeks that are
held in late summer
(during August and
September) either
in Stresa itself or
on the Isola Bella.
These concerts
feature leading
orchestras, soloists
and conductors
from different parts
of the world.

attraction is still a boat trip to the three small BORROMEAN ISLANDS ★. These are so called because in the 16th century they were the property of the great Milanese family of that name, who made the first island the site of a residence, the second a lodge and the third a garden. The Borromeo family's 17th-century palace dominates the ISOLA BELLA, the nearest island to the shore and the most famous of the three. A Baroque masterpiece ● 81, its remarkable Italian garden consists of a series of ten graduated terraces abundantly planted with flowers and rare plants. A little further north, the ISOLA DEI PESCATORI exudes an informal 19th-century atmosphere with its little houses, covered roof terraces, archways and porticos. The largest of the three islands is the ISOLA MADRE. The site of the Borromeo palace is mostly occupied by an extensive botanical garden, populated by peacocks.

ILLUSTRIOUS SONS OF LAKE COMO
Two famous Roman intellectuals were born on the shores of Lake Como. In AD 79 the naturalist, writer and admiral Pliny the Elder (23–79) was in command of the fleet stationed at the Roman naval base of Misenum. He died at Stabiae ▲ 414 while trying to watch the eruption of Vesuvius that buried Pompeii ▲ 412. His nephew and adoptive son – Pliny the Younger (61–112) – was a distinguished orator and man of letters who left behind a fascinating body of correspondence.

LAKE COMO

The Adda river – the largest of the Alpine tributaries of the Po – feeds Lake Como (also known as Lake Lario), the loveliest of Lombardy's great pre-Alpine lakes, which splits into two arms, like a large inverted "Y", extending roughly between La Brianza and La Valtellina. The latter is the name given to the Adda's upper valley, which lies to the northeast of the northern tip of the lake. In this valley you will discover fascinating villages and resorts that evoke time-honored mountain and farming traditions, and also support a thriving modern tourist industry.

> **"O**N THE OTHER SIDE IS MORE RIVER . . . LOSING ITSELF IN A SHINING COIL AMONG THE MOUNTAINS, WHICH FOLLOW IT, UNTIL THEY TOO ARE ALMOST MERGED IN THE HORIZON.**"**
>
> ALESSANDRO MANZONI, *I PROMESSI SPOSI*

COMO: CENTURIES OF ARCHITECTURE. The pretty little town of Como stands at the southwestern tip of the lake, framed by hills. Even more interesting perhaps than the large Gothic Renaissance DUOMO is the Romanesque CHURCH OF SANT'ABBONDIO, an 11th-century masterpiece built by a school of architects known throughout Europe as the "*maestri comacini*". Como's innovative building traditions were continued during the first half of the 20th century by Giuseppe Terragni, perhaps the greatest architect of Italy's Rationalist movement. Between 1932 and 1936 he built the perfect "*parallelepipedo*", behind the cathedral. Originally the Casa del Fascio ● 96, it is now the headquarters of the Customs Service.

FROM COMO TO MENAGGIO. Although it is possible to drive along the winding (though in places spectacular) roads that hug the shores of Lake Como, the best way to enjoy the lake is to take one of the Navigazione Laghi boats – or, if you are in a hurry, a hydrofoil. No matter which you decide on, pay a visit to CERNOBBIO on the western shore, where for over a century the magnificent VILLA D'ESTE, built in the second half of the 16th century by Pellegrino Tibaldi, has housed one of the most exclusive hotels in Europe. With its vast Italian garden adorned with statues, fountains and grottos, it is often used for important international events and conferences. Further along, between Cernobbio and Tremezzo, you will come to Sala Comacina, where you can catch a boat to the ISOLA COMACINA, which has remains of late-medieval settlements. Nearby is the 18th-century VILLA ARCONATI VISCONTI, nicknamed "Villa Balbianello" (usually only accessible by boat). Finally, just outside Tremezzo, the famous VILLA CARLOTTA, which also dates from the 18th century, is now a museum containing paintings of the Lombard school and sculpture by Antonio Canova (1757–1822).

On the northern arm of Lake Como, MENAGGIO has an extremely attractive historical center and is connected by car ferry to the town of VARENNA on the opposite shore (where the Villa Monastero was a Cistercian convent around the end of the 16th century) and to Bellagio at the fork of the lake.

DELICATE AND REFINED
For many centuries Como has been one of the most important centers in the world for the production and processing of silk. This is evident from the stores in the town center, the simple establishments in the suburbs, and the specialist fairs that take place in the area.

LA VALTELLINA
To the northeast of Lake Como, La Valtellina extends as far as the Bernina Glacier and the Parco Nazionale dello Stelvio. The valley's Alpine charm is appreciated by the many people who come to the winter-holiday resorts and skiing championships, for which the area is internationally famous. Beside the attractions of its magnificent mountain scenery, the valley is renowned for its fine terraced vineyards, distinguished culinary traditions, top-quality fruit and the purity of its mineral water. Both historically and architecturally it has much to offer, with the attractive town centers, churches and small-scale palaces of places such as Ponte in Valtellina, Teglio, Tirano and Bormio.

THE IRON CROWN
In the Chapel of Theodolinda in Monza Cathedral (an imposing Gothic basilica, built in the 14th century, that is the work of the Campionese masters) the altar contains the famous Iron Crown, a remarkable piece of early-medieval gold work (possibly 5th century) which is covered with gold,

jewels, enamel and diamonds. According to legend, the crown was made from a nail from the Crucifixion. From medieval times the kings of Italy were all crowned with this relic, up to and including Napoleon.

BELLAGIO ★, THE LADY OF THE LAKE. Geographically at the center of Lake Como, Bellagio is a well-preserved period town with attractive narrow terraced streets climbing between up-market stores. The neoclassical VILLA MELZI has Milanese frescos and stucco work dating from the first half of the 19th century, as well as period furnishings and impressive gardens. But the most important residence, where many European heads of state have stayed, stands just outside the town. This is the 18th-century VILLA SERBELLONI, allegedly built over the ruins of the villa owned by Pliny the Younger ▲ *204*, which now houses the Rockefeller Foundation.

LA BRIANZA, BETWEEN MILAN AND LECCO

A region steeped in history, where the Milanese nobles used to spend their vacations, La Brianza is situated to the north of Milan, between the regional capital and the great pre-Alpine lakes. Dotted with small farms, this area has to a large extent succeeded in conserving its landscape of opulent villas, superb parks and peaceful hills.

THE PARCO DI MONZA: A BLEND OF NEOCLASSICISM AND MODERNITY. One of the largest enclosed parks in Europe, the Parco di Monza is situated just north of MONZA (the capital of La Brianza), which is rich in traces of Lombard influence

"THE SURROUNDING COUNTRYSIDE HAS PLACES WHICH
WILL DELIGHT AND CHARM YOU, SUCH AS MONZA,
MORE A TOWN THAN A VILLAGE.**"**

BONVESIN DE LA RIVA

and major medieval monuments (the cathedral, Arengario, and churches of San Pietro Martire and Santa Maria). Founded in the first half of the 19th century by Napoleon's viceroy, Eugène de Beauharnais, the park was enlarged in 1840 and later equipped with sports facilities such as the hippodrome, polo field and golf course. But the park is primarily famous for the AUTODROMO, or Monza circuit. Opened in 1922, this was one of the first automobile-racing circuits ever built, and it is the only racetrack in the world to have been in constant use for major motor-racing events since its inauguration. The park originally belonged to the VILLA REALE, a huge neoclassical building erected in 1780 by Giuseppe Piermarini, who also built the Teatro alla Scala ● *95*, ▲ *190* and Palazzo Reale ▲ *189* in Milan. This was the royal residence of the Archdukes of Hapsburg-Este, and you can ask to view the chapel, the court puppet theater and the rotunda, which has late-18th-century frescos.

THE VILLAS OF INVERIGO. La Brianza's popularity with the Milanese nobility is illustrated by elegant Inverigo, on the slopes of the valley of the Lambro river. Near the parish church a cobblestone street climbs to the 17th-century VILLA CRIVELLI, which is approached through the dramatic VIALE DEI CIPRESSI, a long straight avenue of cypress trees over a mile long. On another of Inverigo's hills is the ROTONDA, a villa built in the first half of the 19th century by the architect Luigi Cagnola for himself, which is neoclassical in appearance, even though it is an unusual mixture of Greek, Roman, Renaissance and Egyptian elements. The old town of MONTEVECCHIA nearby, now a popular destination for day-trippers from Milan, is no less enchanting.

SAN PIETRO AL MONTE, AN OASIS OF ART AND TRANQUILITY ★. In the upper Brianza – near LECCO, the small town at the southeastern tip of Lake Como ▲ *204* – an hour's climb up the steep mule track from Civate will bring you, as it has done for the past nine hundred years, to San Pietro al Monte in its breathtaking Alpine setting. At the summit of the 1,312-foot rise stand the 11th-century Oratory of San Benedetto and the Church of San Pietro, which may be of Lombard origin. In the church, the ciborium with four granite columns is especially worthy of note.

MANZONI'S LECCO
Alessandro Manzoni (1785–1873) spent most of his childhood and adolescence in the Villa Caleotto which had belonged to his family for two hundred years. The Villa, sold in 1818 to the Scola family, was acquired by the commune around 1960 and now houses the Museo Manzoniano. The ground-floor rooms have been left exactly as they were when Manzoni sold the villa.

MONTEVECCHIA
The oaks and birches of the Valle del Curone (between Inverigo and the Adda) surround the unexpected summit of Montevecchia, the ancient Mons Taegia, which affords some breathtaking panoramic views. Religious processions wind their way up to the 17th-century Church of Beata Vergine del Carmelo and the nearby Via Crucis. However, the hillside paths and the town's attractive 18th-century houses and tempting trattorias are more likely to be the destination of tourists and of outings from Milan.

Prior to the 19th century cemeteries in Italy were not used to the extent that they are today. The dead were generally buried in churches, and the social status of the family concerned was indicated by the opulence of the church. Naturally once the Viscontis ▲ *184* had consolidated their dominion over Lombardy, they were keen to build a church-cum-mausoleum, for the exclusive use of their family, which could be entrusted to a prestigious religious order. In 1396 Gian Galeazzo Visconti commissioned the best architects of the period – the Venetians and the Campionese masters of Ticino – to design and build a *certosa* (charterhouse) adjoining the great park that had been laid out approximately 6 miles from Pavia. The Certosa di Pavia proved to be a lavish and elegant building, which came to be regarded as one of the major landmarks of North Italian art between the Middle Ages and the Renaissance.

THE FAÇADE AND GUEST QUARTERS
The first view of the church is its imposing marble façade, which was erected between the end of the 15th and the middle of the 16th century, the work of Giovanni Antonio Amadeo and then Cristoforo Lombardo, with a portal sculpted by Benedetto Briosco. The upper section of the façade was never completed. To the right of the church, the lodgings intended for distinguished visitors, designed by Francesco Maria Ricchino, were added in 1625.

THE INTERIOR OF THE CHURCH

The majestic interior (which has a Gothic plan reminiscent of that of the Duomo in Milan ▲ *188*) provides a setting for some outstanding works of art, such as the *The Eternal Father* by Perugino (1499) and *Saint Ambrose* by Bergognone (1490), which are in the 2nd and 6th chapels on the left. Also by Bergognone are *Saint Syrus* (in the 6th chapel), the *Crucifixion* (in the 4th), the *Evangelists* (in the 2nd) and the frescos in the recesses behind the 17th-century railings. The inlaid choir stalls (1498) have later frescos (1630), by Daniele Crespi.

THE DUCAL TOMBS

The two arms of the transept contain the Certosa's *raison d'être*: two magnificent tombs, both dating from the end of the 15th century, of two of the dukes of Milan. The tomb on the right is that of Gian Galeazzo himself (though his effigy dates from the mid 16th century). The one on the left was carved by Cristoforo Solari for Ludovico il Moro ▲ *184* and his wife, Beatrice d'Este; he died in France, however, and she was laid to rest in Santa Maria delle Grazie ▲ *197* in Milan.

THE CLOISTERS

From the Little Cloister, adorned with 15th-century terracotta ornament, the Carthusian monks could admire the view of the side and lantern of the church. Beyond the long arcades (spanning 437 yards) of the Great Cloister there are twenty-four secluded cells, ideal for an order devoted to studying and meditation.

209

MORIMONDO

The Abbey of Morimondo (situated between Milan and Vigevano) was almost as important as the Abbey of Chiaravalle for the agricultural development of the area to the south of Milan. It was

founded in 1136 by Cistercian monks from Morimond (north of Dijon), who started building a large church (Santa Maria) in 1182. The stark, atmospheric interior has a single nave and two aisles. Of particular interest are the 14th-century holy-water stoup, a damaged fresco by Bernardino Luini, wooden choir stalls, which date from the first half of the 16th century, and the abbey's chapterhouse. The Chapel of San Bernardo is now an artists' studio.

LOWER LOMBARDY

Lower Lombardy begins where the last hills of La Brianza peter out, far from the Alpine passes, finally giving way to the cultivated plain. Typical of the landscape is an expanse of symmetrical fields, well irrigated or surrounded by rice fields, flanked by the farm complexes called *cascine* ● 83.

CHIARAVALLE AND THE DEVELOPMENT OF THE PLAIN. Built in the open country in 1135, but now on the southeastern fringe of the metropolis, the Abbey of Chiaravalle was named after Saint Bernard of Clairvaux, the Cistercian abbot responsible for introducing the use of canals in Lombardy for irrigation (perhaps the most effective of all medieval agricultural innovations). The church was erected between 1172 and 1221 and – apart from the distinctive color of the Italian brickwork – displays the austerity characteristic of the Cistercian Order.

The building was completed around 1340, including the tower at the transept crossing. The portal, the fresco of the Madonna by Bernardino Luini in the right transept and various other mural paintings date from the 16th century. The nearby Abbey of Morimondo, dating from the 12th century, was also founded by the Cistercians.

Charlemagne's shoe, in the Museo della Calzatura in Vigevano.

RENAISSANCE VIGEVANO.

Vigevano – an attractive small town in La Lomellina, a district of Lower Lombardy that has been widely irrigated since the 14th century – boasts the most beautiful Renaissance square in northern Italy at its heart. According to tradition, the PIAZZA DUCALE ★, elegantly lined on three sides by arcades, was designed in 1494 by Bramante for Ludovico il Moro ▲ 184, Duke of Milan, who commissioned the building of the piazza, together with a flight of steps leading to the entrance tower of his castle. This stairway no longer survives and the piazza now faces the concave Baroque façade, almost like a theatrical backdrop, that was added to the town's cathedral in 1680. The CASTELLO itself has been remodeled over the centuries. Nevertheless, it is still intriguing, with its Renaissance stables and its falconry arcades and the raised covered way that led from the Duke's residence out into the countryside.

MEDIEVAL CREMONA.

If Vigevano has the most beautiful Renaissance square in northern Italy, Cremona has the finest medieval one. Even in the days before the city became part of the Duchy of Milan, under the Visconti, the piazza was dominated by the Torrazzo, a bell tower erected in 1267, rising to a height of 364 feet. The Renaissance LOGGIA DELLA BERTAZZOLA, built during the first half of the 16th century, links the TORRAZZO with Cremona's DUOMO ★, a Romanesque masterpiece dating from the 12th and 13th centuries, which has 16th-century additions and some remarkable medieval reliefs. The interior, which is less severe in appearance, is richly decorated with 16th-century frescos. The octagonal BAPTISTRY is also Romanesque. Opposite the Duomo stand the 13th-century PALAZZO DEL COMUNE, with its 16th-century Arengario, and the LOGGIA DEI MILITI built in 1292. The town's international reputation rests not only on its monuments but also on its long tradition of violin making, which is celebrated in an excellent MUSEUM.

Nuts, honey, sugar and candied peel are the main ingredients of the *torrone* (nougat) that is one of Cremona's delicacies.

STRADIVARIUS
No city in the world has played a more important role in the history of stringed instruments than Cremona. Pioneers whose names are now synonymous with the violin once worked in Cremona: Nicola Amati (1596–1684), Bartolomeo Giuseppe Guarnieri (1698–1744) and Antonio Stradivari (1644–1737), to whom the Museo Stradivariano is devoted. Cremona is the home of the only great school of violin making in Europe. Claudio Monteverdi (1567–1643), who is regarded as the father of opera, was also a native of the city.

"VENETIAN" LOMBARDY

The borders and history of Lombardy were for centuries identical with those of the Duchy of Milan, that powerful political machine created in the Middle Ages by the Viscontis and Sforzas. However, for almost four centuries, from the 15th century to the end of the 18th century, the northeastern part of the region belonged entirely to the Republic of Venice. The pre-Alpine Lake Garda ▲ 238 was also part of the territory owned for three centuries by La Serenissima ▲ 216, although nowadays it is divided between Lombardy and Veneto.

CIVILIZATION IN THE VAL CAMONICA
The Val Camonica, through which the Oglio river flows, is dotted with hundreds of rocks carved with remarkable and puzzling engravings, left by a civilization that dates back

even further than pre-Roman Bergamo and Brescia. The Camuni tribes, who inhabited the Val Camonica between the Neolithic and the paleo-Christian periods, developed a fascinating visual symbolism. One of these engravings, the rose, has become the symbol of the Region of Lombardy.

BERGAMO: MASTERPIECES WITHIN VENETIAN WALLS. On the slopes of the Orobian Alps, between the mouths of the Brembana and Seriana valleys, stands the picturesque city of Bergamo – divided, more clearly than any other in Lombardy, between the old town on the hilltop (1,211 feet high) and the modern town on the plain (more than 300 feet below). The lower town is dominated by industry and commerce, although it is also the site of the influential CARRARA ACADEMY, while the main artistic and historical monuments can be found within the 16th-century Venetian walls of BERGAMO ALTA ★. The most important monuments in the upper town are gathered around the 15th-century PIAZZA VECCHIA – which forms a backdrop for the Palazzo della Ragione (three centuries older) – and around the adjacent PIAZZA DEL DUOMO. The latter is the site of the Romanesque basilica of SANTA MARIA MAGGIORE and of a Lombard Renaissance masterpiece, the COLLEONI CHAPEL, the work of sculptor and architect Giovanni Antonio Amadeo.

ROMAN AND NEOCLASSICAL BRESCIA. The second city of Lombardy, Brescia is now a leading industrial center, which has grown up around the ancient center ● 75. On the slopes of the Cydnean Hills stand the ruins of the CAPITOLINE TEMPLE and Roman theater (both 1st century AD), a castle that has medieval foundations and the MONASTERY OF SAN SALVATORE. Between here and the central PIAZZA DELLA LOGGIA, largely surrounded by Veneto Renaissance buildings, extends the former political and religious heart of the city – with its ROTONDA or Duomo Vecchio, a circular Romanesque building dating from the 11th century, Duomo Nuovo (17th–18th century), BROLETTO ● 78 (13th century) and Torre del Popolo (11th century). The impressive collections of the PINACOTECA TOSIO-MARTINENGO (housed in the palace of the same name) include paintings by Raphael, Lotto, Romanino and Tintoretto. Heading north from Brescia into the Val Camonica, CAPO DI PONTE, together with the Parco Nazionale delle incisioni Rupestri (set up in 1955) at Naquane, make an interesting excursion.

VENICE AND
THE TRIVENETO

VENICE, *216*

1 SIRMIONE 2 VERONA 3 VICENZA 4 TRENTO 5 BOLZANO / BOZEN 6 CORTINA D'AMPEZZO

"In the Lowlands, there is more of sky and plain than people, the days pass without surprise, the silence of the North East is of a special kind, without the little cracklings and interruptions of other European silences. Our tranquility is uninterrupted. Cut off from the world, we exist between sleep and a mysterious happiness."
Sergio Maldini,
La stazione di Varmo
(Varmo Station)

This section of the guide is devoted to the area bounded by the Adriatic Sea, Lake Garda, the Dolomites and the Carso (plateau) of Trieste – an area that has always been culturally, esthetically and linguistically dependent on Venice. This city has been a key player in historical and political events in Italy and Europe, particularly Mediterranean Europe, for almost a thousand years. It boasts one of the most impressive accumulations of artistic and architectural masterpieces in the world, while the varied landscapes of the surrounding regions provide a picturesque setting for some beautiful old cities. The nearest cities to Venice are Chioggia, a working-class version of Venice; Treviso which, threaded with canals, is also reminiscent of Venice's watery vistas; and Padua, which has welcomed almost as many eminent Tuscans as has Venice, among them Giotto, Dante, Petrarch, Donatello and Galileo. The chief attractions in central and western Veneto are Vicenza, "an architect's city" (Andrea Palladio), and Verona with its well-preserved Roman and medieval monuments,

7 Feltre 8 Asolo 9 Padua 10 Strà (Villa Pisani) 11 Chioggia 12 Treviso 13 Venice 14 Vittorio Veneto 15 Udine 16 Palmanova 17 Aquileia 18 Grado 19 Trieste 20 Gorizia 21 Cividale

only 71 miles from Venice and close to the tourist paradise of Lake Garda. Asolo, Vittorio Veneto and Feltre, with their strong Venetian flavor, are the main beauty spots in the Veneto's pre-Alpine region. Our itinerary continues to Trento, city of the bishop-princes; and "Gothic" Bolzano, which never came under the influence of Venice (155 miles away). Continuing through the breathtaking scenery of the "Monti Pallidi", the famous Strada delle Dolomiti leads to the magnificent valley of Cortina d'Ampezzo, providing ample opportunity to enjoy some truly spectacular views. Our journey ends in the northeastern region of Friuli-Venezia Giulia. This tranquil area has several important cities that are rich in art and afford some striking examples of elegant town planning: Udine, the historical capital of the "Patria del Friuli"; Cividale, with its superb Lombard monuments; medieval Aquileia and Grado; the town of Palmanova, with its star-shaped layout; and Trieste, with its somewhat Central European atmosphere, which recalls its past as one of the Hapsburg empire's great maritime trading posts.

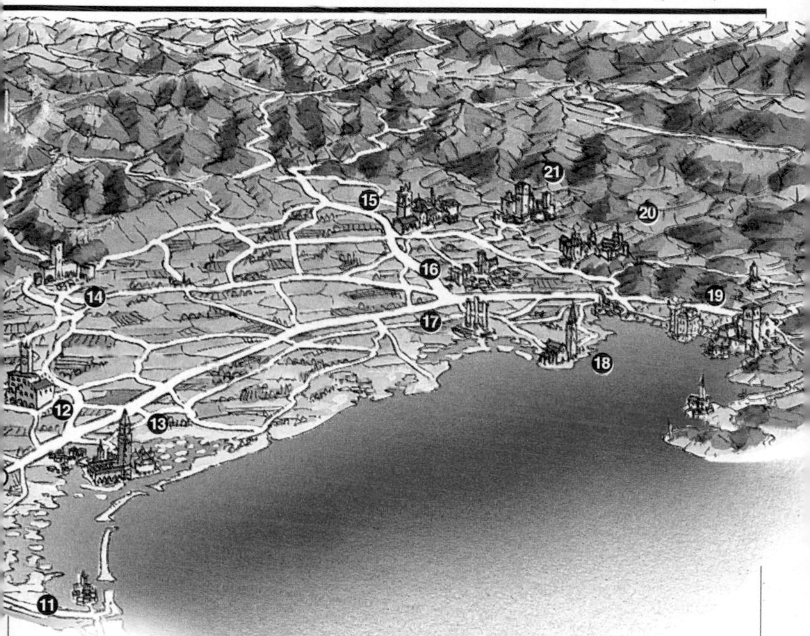

"The pink cloud / And the cold vapors / Are rusted by the evening, / The steamer's hoot interrupts a *largo* of bells. / Through a melancholy window, / Venice drapes her Grand Canal in pink. // The stars have fallen, the rose petals too, / Blown down by the Christmas wind."

Alfonso Gatto, *Natale al caffè Florian (Christmas at Caffè Florian)*

"But that faded Venetian pink, / That harsh violet shading off to the weak / Blue of evening, that sliver / Of light piercing the endless premonition, / It has only to end and winter is here, / The white, the black of its plaster cast / Striking the heart like an eclipse."

Alfonso Gatto, *Paesaggio veneziano (Venetian Landscape)*

▲ VENICE

LA SERENISSIMA AND ITS STATES
"La Serenissima Repubblica"
(the Most Serene Republic) was already in use as Venice's official name in the period between the Middle Ages and the Renaissance when the city was the only large autonomous European State not governed by monarchs or bishops. From the outset, the Republic was divided into two distinct areas of authority: the "Stato da Mar" (the shores and Venetian islands in the Mediterranean) and the "Stato da Tera" (mainland possessions).

NAPOLEON AND VENICE
In 1806 Napoleon introduced a program of architectural and town-planning reforms for the city. On the Punta della Motta, the Convent of Sant'Antonio was demolished to make way for the gardens that are now the site of the Biennale ▲ 228. In San Marco, the 14th-century granaries were replaced by the royal gardens, and the Ala Napoleonica was built in the piazza, on the site of the Church of San Geminiano. The Porta Nuova was opened at the Arsenale, and work began on clearing the port of Malamocco, which was obstructed by sandbanks.

Surrounded by its lagoon ■ *24* (the largest wetland in Italy), just north of the Po delta, Venice is certainly not the only water-bound city on earth. Between the 14th and 16th centuries, however, it was in a league of its own – not only was it the most independent city in Europe, it was also one of the world's leading political and economic centers.
Today Venice is of special interest because its original layout remains intact and many of its buildings date back to its golden age.

ORIGINS. According to tradition, Venice was founded on March 25, 421. This legend is broadly borne out by historical facts: at least, the city's origins can be dated back to the 6th century, when inhabitants of the Roman region of Venetia and Istria moved from the mainland to the islands of the lagoon in order to escape Lombard invasion. By around 770 the lagoon townships had a bishop of their own, and forty years later the political center was moved to the site of what is now the Rialto ▲ *226*.

RULING THE WAVES. By the early Middle Ages the city controlled the trade routes across the Adriatic. As early as the 10th and 11th centuries Venice had begun to conquer the coastline of Dalmatia and rid the seas of pirates. However, it was primarily the Fourth Crusade (begun in 1202, with the specific aim, under pressure from Venice, of taking Constantinople) that made the city a military and economic force to be reckoned with. Bases in Apulia and mainland Greece, the islands of the Ionian Sea, Crete and most of the Peloponnesian islands were all annexed. Genoa ▲ *161* was Venice's great rival during a period that was marked by the construction of magnificent palaces by the merchant families and Marco Polo's first journey to China.

RENAISSANCE VENICE. Although Venice reached its political and commercial zenith in the 14th and 15th centuries (and successfully extended its dominion over inland areas from Udine to Ravenna and from Verona to the Adda river), it was largely in the Renaissance that La Serenissima gained its international reputation. This was also, ironically, the time when the city began to encounter military difficulties: it was defeated at Agnadello in 1509 by the League of Cambrai, and its maritime supremacy was being eroded by the Turks. However,

❝I SPEAK OF THE AUGUST CITY OF VENICE, WHICH IS ALONE IN REPRESENTING THE SEAT OF LIBERTY, PEACE AND JUSTICE TODAY.❞

PETRARCH, *EPISTLES*

the Venetian navy did play a decisive role in the victory over the Ottomans at Lepanto in 1571.

DECLINE AND FALL. Venice was severely affected by a papal interdict during the 17th century, then forced to give up more of the sea to the Turks, even though a good part of the Peloponnese (then known as Morea) had been decisively recovered by Francesco Morosini, who was rewarded with the position of Doge. Then, in the 18th century, the city entered a period of dignified decline. Finally, despite the prestige of figures such as the dramatist Carlo Goldoni and artists such as Canaletto, Bellotto and Francesco Guardi, the last Doge was persuaded by Napoleon to stand down quietly on May 12, 1797.

FROM AUSTRIAN RULE TO ITALIAN UNIFICATION. The city was placed by treaty under Austrian rule, and in 1846 the opening of a railroad bridge meant that Venice lost its total insularity. The anti-Austrian revolt of 1848–9 was followed seventeen years later by a plebiscite that approved Venice's incorporation into the state of Italy. Meanwhile, the first bathing establishment was opened on the Lido. In 1945 the city rose up against the Nazis and Fascists, and on April 28 was liberated by the Allies. In November 1966 it was badly damaged by a high tide.

VENICE TODAY. Venice's main source of income now comes from tourism. La Serenissima is no longer the maritime power it was from the Middle Ages to the 17th century, and the economic recovery enjoyed by Venice after the mid 19th century has ground to a halt. The city is still the venue for cultural events – such as the Biennale ▲ *228*, founded in 1895, and the exhibitions at the Palazzo Grassi ▲ *224* – and it still has its universities. But so far as everyday life is concerned, prices have rocketed and in the center ordinary stores have nearly all been replaced by boutiques, souvenir shops and mask sellers. And yet even this has contributed to Venice's uniqueness.

HIGH WATER AND FOOTBRIDGES
Although it is in effect virtually a living museum, Venice cannot escape the ravages of time. The settling of the lagoon – which until 1797 was meticulously controlled on a day to day basis by the Republic, but which since then has largely been left to run its course – is the basic cause of the city's most notorious hazard, known as *acqua alta* ("high water"). Several times each winter, under the combined effect of tides, wind and low pressure, the lagoon rises for several hours, submerging Piazza San Marco and many other areas.

Footbridges are used to enable people to move around at times of high water.

The modern fancy dress costume of a Moor: the carnival ● *56* still attracts thousands of visitors to Venice.

217

BARGES IN THE "CANAL REGIO"
The Canale di Cannaregio, near to the railroad station, is the second largest canal in the city, after the Grand Canal, and has given its name to the quarter through which it runs. Its name may derive from the luxuriant cane thickets that used to grow there. Until the rail link was built, most of the goods that arrived in Venice from the Veneto mainland (such as vegetables, fruit, meat, and building materials) were transported via the "Canal Regio". Today the canal is still an important means of urban transport.

TAKING THE GRAND CANAL TO SAN MARCO ★

The longest waterway in the city (followed by the Canale di Cannaregio, in the quarter that was the site of the first GHETTO in history) looks like an inverted "S" and is almost 2.5 miles long. It winds its way through scores of noble palaces, from the northwest tip of Venice – where the causeways leading to the mainland are situated (by road from Piazzale Roma and by rail from Stazione Santa Lucia) – to the magnificent St Mark's Basin.

SINUOUS ROWS OF BUILDINGS. The Grand Canal splits Venice into two: the bank of San Marco ("de qua dal Canal") is more patrician, while the other bank ("de là dal Canal") is more working class. There are forty-five tributaries leading off the canal, but it is easier to pick out the bridges over it, which number only three: the PONTE DI RIALTO ▲ 226 (the oldest and most central one), the PONTE DELL'ACCADEMIA (between San Vidal and La Carità) and PONTE DEGLI SCALZI (next to the railroad station).

THE FIRST GHETTO
A quarter crammed with extremely old houses huddles at the back of the east bank of the Canale di Cannaregio. Hard pressed for space, the Jewish community in Venice was forced to inhabit very tall houses. This former ghetto, which was established in 1516, has some fascinating synagogues ("Scole" in Venetian dialect) and collections of applied arts – but it is worth visiting for the claustrophobic atmosphere alone.

A SPECTACULAR INTRODUCTION.

A boat journey along the Grand Canal is always magical – but anyone who comes to Venice for the first time and takes the vaporetto from Stazione Santa Lucia to St Mark's Basin will be enthralled by the fascinating journey along this "triumphal way", where water and architecture combine to create a world of mirror images. Visitors traveling by vaporetto toward La Serenissima's former hub of civic power will be given their first glimpse of Venetian opulence with the 17th-century CHIESA DEGLI SCALZI, designed by Baldassarre Longhena, which has two chapels containing frescos by Tiepolo. This parade of architectural treasures continues with the elegant Renaissance building designed, in 1481, by Mauro Codussi: the PALAZZO VENDRAMIN-CALERGI, Richard Wagner's last home, where he died in 1883, and now the winter abode of the Casino. The vaporetto stops on the two sides of the Grand Canal alternately, but for the moment ignore the particularly arresting array of buildings that will be examined in detail later – including the immense white edifice of Ca' Pesaro ▲ 227, the Gothic traceries of the Ca' d'Oro ▲ 229, the Palazzo Grassi ▲ 224 and the exquisite "jewel box" of the Accademia ▲ 224 – and let your gaze linger over the other noteworthy and highly representative buildings that lead up to two final gems: the 15th-century CA' FOSCARI, on the last bend of the canal, which is a masterpiece of Venetian Gothic architecture, and the PALAZZO CORNER DELLA CA' GRANDA, a lavish but elegant building constructed in 1533 by the great architect and sculptor Jacopo Sansovino, which stands at the mouth of the canal, in St Mark's Basin.

The Renaissance Palazzo Vendramin-Calergi (above) and Ca' Foscari (below), seen from the canal.

BRIDGE OF SIGHS
The Ponte dei Sospiri (Bridge of Sighs) was built at the beginning of the 17th century to link the old prisons in the Palazzo Ducale (Doges' Palace) with new prisons. Legend has it that the bridge owes its name to the laments of the prisoners taken across it. With the passage of time its fortunes have altered. It is now a popular picture-postcard image, and the only sighs that are heard are those accompanying the vows of eternal love sworn by lovers gazing at the view from the bridge.

PIAZZA SAN MARCO

St Mark's Basin – the wide stretch of lagoon beyond the Dogana di Mare ▲ 225, opposite the island of San Giorgio ▲ 230 – is overlooked by Venice's only piazza, the universally famous site of several centuries' worth of remarkable monuments and sights.

PIAZZETTA SAN MARCO. This is the name given to the part of the piazza beside the lagoon. It is graced by two COLUMNS of oriental granite, each topped by a capital supporting the winged lion of Saint Mark, and by a statue of the city's first patron saint, Todaro (Saint Theodore). Standing with your back to the water, on the right you will see the LIBRERIA SANSOVINIANA, designed by Jacopo Sansovino and completed in 1583–8 by Vincenzo Scamozzi. This houses both the

> **"HERE WE HAVE SAN MARCO, THE CAMPANILE, THE PIAZZA, AND THE PALAZZO DUCALE: THIS GEM HAS PROBABLY NO EQUAL IN THE WORLD."**
>
> HIPPOLYTE TAINE

Biblioteca Marciana (the most extensive library in the city, founded with a gift of manuscripts from Cardinal Bessarion) and the ARCHEOLOGY MUSEUM. Set up in the 16th century to display exhibits bequeathed by the Grimani family, the museum has a fine collection of both Greek and Roman sculpture.

THE PALAZZO DUCALE (DOGES' PALACE) ★.

The one-time residence of the Doge and seat of the city's chief magistrates looms over the Piazzetta and St Mark's Basin. Built as a castle in the 9th century, it was radically altered during the reign of Doge Sebastiano Ziani (1172-8), who transformed it into a palace to house the Great and Lesser Councils. Enlarged in Veneto-Byzantine style (in the early 14th century), then in Gothic Renaissance

style, it was rebuilt between 1483 and 1577, after several fires, and restored again during the 17th century. The result is a generally harmonious fusion of styles. The building includes fine 15th-century stonework by Jacobello and Pier Paolo dalle Masegne and also by Giovanni and Bartolomeo Bon. Antonio Rizzo built the courtyard, with its stairway known as the Scala dei Giganti because of the two huge statues added later by Sansovino. The state rooms are on the third floor (Cancelleria, Milizia da Mar, Censura), while the second floor comprises the Doge's private apartments and the vast SALA DEL MAGGIOR CONSIGLIO, with its ceiling painted by Veronese, Bassano and Palma il Giovane, and which contains Tintoretto's *Paradise*, perhaps the largest picture ever painted. The Doges' Palace is now used to mount exhibitions and is also the home of the agency that oversees the city's environment and architecture. The PONTE DEI SOSPIRI (Bridge of Sighs) links the Palace's prisons – which were divided into "Piombi" (those just under the roof, where Giacomo Casanova was imprisoned, before escaping, in 1755–6) and "Pozzi" (those on the ground floor, reserved for serious offenders and political prisoners).

THE "RED PRIEST"
One of the greatest composers of the 18th century, Antonio Vivaldi (1678–1741), taught at the Ospedale della Pietà. The "red priest" – as he was nicknamed, either because of the color of his hair or the livery of the Pietà – was not famous in his own day, although J.S. Bach (1685–1750) studied and transcribed his scores.

HARRY'S BAR
In Calle Vallaresso (opposite the San Marco landing stage) you will find the world-famous Harry's Bar, founded by Giuseppe Cipriani in 1931 and frequented by Ernest Hemingway and other celebrities who loved to visit Venice.

THE LION OF SAINT MARK
The winged lion on top of each of the two columns that tower over the Piazzetta is the official symbol of La Serenissima. Probably oriental in origin, it has an open book between its paws, displaying the words *Pax tibi Marce, Evangelista meus* ("Peace to you, Mark, my evangelist"). In wartime, reflecting this statement, the lion was depicted with the book closed.

ARTISTIC PANORAMAS
The Museo Civico Correr has a copy of the 16th-century wood engraving by Jacopo de'Barbari, which shows a bird's-eye view of Venice. The print combines the fidelity of a topographical map with the accuracy of an aerial photograph and the immediacy of a painting.

PIAZZA SAN MARCO ★. The famous piazza is dominated by the façade of the basilica, which stands between the late 15th-century TORRE DELL'OROLOGIO (Clock Tower), with its two bronze Moors, marking the entrance to the Mercerie ▲ 226, and St Mark's CAMPANILE, an exact replica of the original bell tower that collapsed in 1902. The square is flanked by almost a third of a mile of porticos, made up of the 16th-century arcades of the PROCURATIE along the sides ("Vecchie" on the side of the Mercerie, and "Nuove" toward the Campanile, sheltering the celebrated Caffè Florian), while the ALA NAPOLEONICA ▲ 216 – which dates from the first half of the 19th century – closes it off at the back, in front of another celebrated venue, HARRY'S BAR ▲ 221.

BASILICA DI SAN MARCO ★. Once the private chapel of the Doges, San Marco has been Venice's cathedral since 1807. Its ground plan is in the form of a Greek cross. Features of the basilica include an atrium supported by Byzantine-Egyptian columns, and domes surmounted by Persian-style tridirectional crosses. The interior has a screen with icons in front of the high altar, and extensive highly prized MOSAICS. Begun in the 9th century, San Marco was almost totally rebuilt after the 11th century, given wooden domes in the 13th century, and from then on continually embellished. Major works of art include the 12th-century *Madonna of Nicopeia (*in the left transept) and, behind the altar, the PALA D'ORO, a remarkable masterpiece of Byzantine and Venetian goldwork begun in the 10th century and completed in 1342. Its Gothic frame is inlaid with hundreds of pearls and precious stones. In the small MUSEO SAN MARCO you can see the originals of the four HORSES OF ST MARK'S, cast in gilded bronze, which may be Greek (4th–3rd century BC) or may date from the time of Emperor Constantine (4th century AD).

MUSEO CIVICO CORRER. The entrance to Venice's largest collection of city pictures, period dress, relics, weapons, tapestries, furniture and coins is through the Ala Napoleonica ▲ *216*, the building facing the basilica. The rooms on the second floor, converted in the 1950's by Carlo Scarpa ▲ *244*, display paintings by Carpaccio, Jacopo Bellini and his sons Gentile and Giovanni, Lorenzo Lotto, Antonello da Messina, Cosmè Tura and Alvise Vivarini.

SAN ZACCARIA. Behind St Mark's stands the Church of San Zaccaria, which in former times belonged to the "Convento dei Nobili". Around 1480 an elegant three-arched section was added by Mauro Codussi on top of the two lower parts of the façade, which had been left incomplete. The interior contains paintings by Tintoretto and Tiepolo, frescos by Andrea del Castagno and Francesco da Faenza, and the *Madonna and Child Enthroned*, a splendid altarpiece by Giovanni Bellini. In the nearby CHIESA DELLA PIETÀ the air still seems to resound with the music of Vivaldi ▲ *221*.

THE BRONZE HORSES OF SAINT MARK'S
Brought to Venice from Constantinople in 1204, the four horses were mounted on the upper terrace of the basilica, overlooking the piazza. Damaged by pollution, they were moved to the Museo di San Marco after restoration work, in 1981, and replaced by copies.

THE PALA D'ORO
Now positioned so that it is easier to view it without disturbing the religious services inside St Mark's, this screen is one of the world's most lavish examples of the goldsmith's art.

223

1 PALAZZO CORNER-SPINELLI **2** CÀ FOSCARI **3** PALAZZO GRASSI

LA FENICE
Campo San Fantin is the site of Venice's great opera house, La Fenice, an elegant late-18th-century building where grand premieres of operas by Verdi (*Nabucco, Ernani, Rigoletto, Traviata*) and Wagner (*Lohengrin*) were once staged. After the terrible fire of 1996, which was not the first in the theater's long history, La Fenice is now in the process of rising from its ashes once again.

FROM SAN MARCO TO SANTA MARIA DELLA SALUTE

SANTO STEFANO.
The signs from Piazza San Marco to the Accademia will take you past the walls of LA FENICE into the spacious Campo Santo Stefano, which is closed off at the back by the large church founded by the Augustinians in 1294.

PALAZZO GRASSI
In the 1980's the 18th-century palace built by Giorgio Massari in Campo San Samuele was completely renovated by Gae Aulenti for Fiat and is now used to stage notable artistic and cultural events.

Inside, below the splendid wooden roof shaped like a ship's hull, stands the tomb of Francesco Morosini ▲ *217*, the Republic's last great military commander. A short detour leads to the 15th-century PALAZZO CORNER-SPINELLI.
GALLERIE DELL'ACCADEMIA ★. At the back of the large bridge near Campo San Vidal is Venice's largest art collection – in the former Scuola and Convent of Santa Maria della Carità, which in 1807 welcomed the Napoleonic government's new Accademia di Belle Arti. This museum offers a complete survey of Venetian art through the centuries. Major artists represented include Paolo Veneziano (*Coronation of the Virgin*), Lorenzo Veneziano, Michele Giambono and Antonio Vivarini in the 14th and 15th centuries; Giovanni Bellini (*Sacred Conversation*), Cima da Conegliano, Mantegna (*Saint George*), Giorgione (*The Tempest*) and Lotto (*Portrait of a Young Man*) in the Renaissance; and Veronese (*Christ in the House of Levi*), Tintoretto (*The Miracle of Saint Mark*) and Titian (*Pietà*) at the height of the 16th century. After paintings from the 17th and 18th centuries there are yet more

Renaissance works, including the magnificent series *Miracles of the Relics of the Cross* (by Gentile Bellini, Giovanni Mansueti, Carpaccio and Lazzaro Bastiani) and Carpaccio's own paintings of *The Legend of Saint Ursula*.

GUGGENHEIM COLLECTION
The Palazzo Venier dei Leoni stands between the Accademia and Santa Maria della Salute. In 1949 this fine, though unfinished, 18th-century building became the last home in Venice of the American collector Peggy Guggenheim. After her death in 1979, the house became a museum of contemporary art – the largest in Venice – with works by artists such as Boccioni, Braque, Giacometti, Kandinsky, Klee and Malevich.

THE "ORECCHIONI" OF LA SALUTE
The exterior of the Church of Santa Maria della Salute is rich in elements like the huge spirals that serve as buttresses for the dome. Venetians affectionately call them the "*orecchioni*" ("big ears").

CA' REZZONICO. Overlooking the Grand Canal between the Accademia and Ca' Foscari – and virtually facing the PALAZZO GRASSI (on the other bank), which is the most recent example of Venetian "artistic continuity" – Ca' Rezzonico was started by Baldassarre Longhena for the Bon family around 1650 and eventually completed by Giorgio Massari for the new owners, the Rezzonico family. The palace now houses the MUSEO DEL SETTECENTO VENEZIANO, which makes you feel as if you are intruding into an 18th-century patrician home.

SAN SEBASTIANO. Heading in the direction of the Canale della Giudecca, you will come to a church that is famous for its frescos and pictures – painted by Paolo Veronese in the mid 16th century. His subjects, in accordance with the mission of the Hieronymite monks, revolved around the Virgin Mary and the life of the martyr Saint Sebastian. Veronese is buried in front of the left-hand chapel, in the presbytery.

SANTA MARIA DELLA SALUTE ● *93*. Next to the DOGANA DI MARE (Customs House) – where duties on goods arriving from the Mediterranean had to be paid – is the distinctive profile of the Church of Santa Maria della Salute, or the curlicued "crown for the Virgin", which was how Longhena described it in 1631. This octagonal church, surrounded by statues, side chapels, lateral apses and campaniles, was built in thanksgiving for the people's salvation ("*salute*") from the plague of 1630. In the sacristy there are several pictures by Titian and the *Marriage at Cana* by Tintoretto. Before visiting this opulent church, you should pay a visit to the unobtrusive palace that houses the GUGGENHEIM COLLECTION, a marvelous array of modern art.

225

▲ VENICE

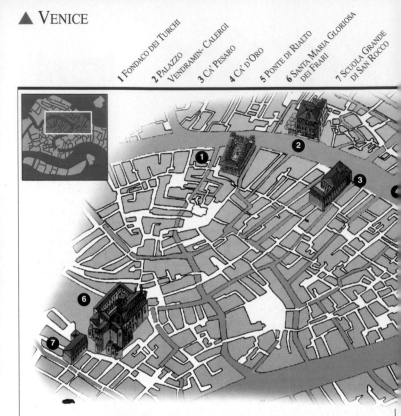

FONDACO DEI TURCHI

Not far from the Ca' Pesaro, on the Grand Canal, stands the warehouse which received Turkish trade delegations in Venice between 1621 and 1838, and now houses the Natural History Museum. In the 13th and 14th centuries, when it was built, it would have been a good example of a Venetian residential warehouse, where the merchant would have lived under the same roof as his stored goods – but its appearance was greatly altered by the restoration work carried out in the 19th century.

FROM SAN MARCO TO THE FRARI

MERCERIE. The Torre dell'Orologio (Clock Tower) ▲ *222* serves as an entrance arch to the Mercerie, which from time immemorial have linked the seat of power (San Marco) with that of the merchants (the Rialto). The streets still bear the names of the type of goods sold by the stores that used to line them. At the entrance, Calle Fiubera leads to the 15th-century Church of Santa Croce degli Armeni, a reminder of Venice's former Oriental community.

THE PONTE DI RIALTO ★. Following the signs and the crowds along the Mercerie, you will come to the oldest bridge on the Grand Canal, which according to tradition was originally built in 1175. A century later a more stable bridge on piles was built (the first had been a pontoon bridge), and this was followed by other wooden versions. The present Rialto Bridge, which dates from 1591, was built by Antonio da Ponte. The bridge has always been regarded as a

great success, not only because it was extremely useful but also because of the various stores that opened their doors on either side of its arch and in the vicinity.

CA' PESARO. Overlooking the Grand Canal, between the Rialto and the railroad station, is the former residence of the powerful Pesaro family, an impressive 17th-century building designed by Longhena. In 1902 it became the home of the MUSEO D'ARTE MODERNA, based on the collections that the city acquired for the first Biennale ▲ *228*. The Ca' Pesaro also houses the MUSEUM OF ORIENTAL ART.

SANTA MARIA GLORIOSA DEI FRARI. One of the most important places of worship in the city, in terms both of social standing and size (almost 328 x 164 feet), this church was built around 1340 for the Franciscan friars (the "frari"). The vaporetto stop for it is San Tomà, which is also the stop for the Goldoni Museum, in Palazzo Centani. Completed in the mid 15th century, the Frari contains some remarkable sepulchral monuments, among them Antonio Rizzo's Renaissance masterpiece for Nicolò Tron (1476), Baldassarre Longhena's macabre Baroque tomb for Giovanni Pesaro (1659), and the neoclassical pyramid designed by Canova for Titian's tomb. Other great works of art include a carved wooden statue of *Saint John the Baptist* by Donatello (c. 1450), two paintings by Titian – the *Assumption* (right) over the main altar and the *Madonna of Ca' Pesaro* over the second altar – and the triptych by Giovanni Bellini above the altar in the sacristy.

CARLO GOLDONI
Served by the same vaporetto stop as the Frari, the Palazzo Centani in San Tomà is the house where the dramatist Carlo Goldoni (1707–93) was born. Since 1953 it has been the home of the Istituto di Studi Teatrali Carlo Goldoni . This museum contains all sorts of mementos associated with the playwright, An inspired reinterpreter of the Commedia dell'Arte, he wrote numerous comedies. His plays include *Arlecchino servitore di due padroni*, *La locandiera* and, in Venetian dialect, *I rusteghi* and *Le baruffe chiozzotte*.

227

THE ARSENALE
Venice extends toward the Lido and the Adriatic with the largest dockyard of all time: the Arsenale (from the Arabian *dar-si-na'a*), which built the war fleet that reigned supreme in the Mediterranean for five hundred years. This industrial complex (113 acres) remains military property – but it can be visited on request, and the vaporetti pass through it.

SCUOLA GRANDE DI SAN ROCCO. After the Black Death (bubonic plague) epidemic of 1477, a "Scuola" was built behind the apse of the Frari. This institution, a cross between a guild and a confraternity, was set up to care for plague victims. The Church of San Rocco and the Scuola's original home are now somewhat overshadowed by the later Scuola Grande, built by Bartolomeo Bon and Scarpagnino at the end of the 16th century. The Scuola itself is internationally renowned for its series of pictures by Tintoretto, painted in 1587, illustrating episodes and characters from the Gospels.

FROM SANTA MARIA FORMOSA TO THE CA' D'ORO

THE BIENNALE
The gardens beyond the Arsenale (on the former Punta della Motta) are the site of the pavilions of the Biennale, one of the leading international

contemporary art exhibitions, opened in 1895 in the presence of King Umberto and Queen Margherita. When the pavilions are in use, they are worth visiting in their lush setting, to see how their various styles of architecture reflected changing national trends over half a century (1907–64). The pavilions designed by Hoffmann (Austria, 1934), Rietveld (Holland, 1954) and Aalto (Finland, 1956) are particularly of note.

Our itinerary takes in some outstanding churches and monuments in the Castello and Cannaregio quarters, leaving behind the easternmost part of the city, the island of St Elena, and the BIENNALE D'ARTE and the ARSENALE – both vital in securing Venice's international reputation over the centuries.
SANTA MARIA FORMOSA. Ruga Giuffa leads from San Zaccaria to Campo Santa Maria Formosa, a picturesque square that takes its name from the church dedicated to the "*formosa*" (beautiful) Virgin who appeared in 639 to Magno, Bishop of Oderzo. This remarkable building was rebuilt in the shape of a Greek cross in the 12th century, then rebuilt by Codussi in the shape of a Latin cross in 1492.
PALAZZO QUERINI-STAMPALIA. The 16th-century palace owned by the Querini family from Stampalia (a Greek island in the family's estate) stands to the right of Santa Maria Formosa. In 1868 Count Giovanni Querini bequeathed the building and its library to the Venetians. The rooms – redesigned by Carlo Scarpa ▲ 244 in 1963, along with interesting gardens – house an outstanding collection of works of art.
SANTI GIOVANNI E PAOLO ★. A short distance from Santa Maria Formosa stands the other great Venetian church which, in common with the Frari, belonged to a preaching order.

After the Dominicans were installed here in 1246, the present building was begun in the first half of the 14th century and completed over the course of nearly a century. Built in Gothic style, with exposed brickwork, San Zanipolo (as it is called by the Venetians) has lovely apses and some remarkable funerary monuments to illustrious Venetian figures, the work of

> **"THE HOUSES OF VENICE ARE BUILDINGS THAT REGRET THAT THEY ARE NOT BOATS."**
>
> PAUL MORAND

Pietro Lombardo, Paolo dalle Masegne and a variety of Tuscan Gothic artists. Other masterpieces here include a polyptych by Giovanni Bellini, a chapel vault with frescos by Piazzetta and *Christ Bearing the Cross* by Alvise Vivarini.

THE COLLEONI MONUMENT
In the square next to the Church of Santi Giovanni e Paolo stands an equestrian monument to the renowned condottiere Bartolomeo Colleoni, a Renaissance work designed by Andrea del Verrocchio in the 1480's. The Tuscan artist did not live long enough to execute it, and the bronze cast was made shortly after his death by Alessandro Leopardi, whose signature can be seen on the horse's harness.

Nearby is the eye-catching white Renaissance façade of the former SCUOLA GRANDE DI SAN MARCO, by Pietro Lombardo and Mauro Codussi, now the entrance to Venice's municipal hospital. Also in this square stands the superb MONUMENT to Colleoni designed by Verrochio.

SANTA MARIA DEI MIRACOLI. The severity of the early-Renaissance Church of Santa Maria dei Miracoli is mitigated by the glowing colors of its marble exterior. Situated near to San Zanipolo and the row of palaces on Rio di Santa Marina, this church was built by Pietro Lombardo in the 1580's to provide a sanctuary for a *Madonna and Child* (1408) venerated by the Venetians.

CA' D'ORO ● 75. The city's most famous Venetian Gothic *palazzetto* overlooks the Grand Canal off the Strada Nuova, toward the station. The name of this well-known palace is derived from the gold ornamental details that Marino Contarini originally used between 1422 and 1440. Bought in 1895 by Baron Giorgio Franchetti, it now houses the GALLERIA FRANCHETTI, which is based around the collection of the Torinese noble who donated it to the state in 1916. Among the most outstanding exhibits are paintings by Vivarini and Mantegna, busts by Tullio Lombardo, medallions by Pisanello, Flemish tapestries, Dutch paintings, Venetian ceramics and two works by Francesco Guardi.

THE CA' D'ORO
Noble Venetian families vied with one another in erecting splendid façades on their palaces along the Grand Canal. Originally owned by the Contarini family, the Ca' d'Oro is the finest example of a private residential building in the florid Venetian Gothic style.

229

THE LAGOON, AN ANCIENT WAY OF LIFE
Pheasants, partridges, stags, foxes and wild boar – the marshes around the Venetian lagoon and the forests that used to mark its boundaries toward the mainland once teemed with game, wildlife and birds. Some of Pietro Longhi's paintings depict the Venetian noblemen's love of hunting, an activity they regarded as healthy sport; the poorer local people, on the other

hand, hunted so they could put food on their family's table.

FRAGILE TREASURE
The Barovier nuptial cup, kept in Murano's Museo dell'Arte Vetraria, is made of enameled blown glass. It depicts the bride and groom and the allegorical fountain of life.

THE ISLANDS

Venice consists of a group of artificial islands, enlarged and connected together by centuries of drainage and land reclamation, scattered along the shores of the LIDO and Pellestrina in the direction of Chioggia ▲ *232*. There are, however, still some real islands in the lagoon.

SAN GIORGIO MAGGIORE. This small island has always been a center of learning: originally (from AD 982) as a Benedictine convent, and now (since 1951) as the home of the GIORGIO CINI FOUNDATION. San Giorgio Maggiore, the church of the former monastery, was designed by Andrea Palladio in 1565–6 and completed, after his death (1580), in the mid 17th century.

LA GIUDECCA. From the island of San Giorgio you can cross to the Giudecca, a string of islands connected together over the centuries by landfills and bridges. In the late 16th century the Republic commissioned the massive CHURCH OF IL REDENTORE, which is the final destination of the colorful procession in one of Venice's most spectacular annual festivals (held on the third Sunday in July). The church is one of Palladio's most important works.

MURANO. Although not far from the center of Venice, the island of Murano was historically "independent" and until 1797 elected its own autonomous Maggior Consiglio. The island owes its fame to the Venetian glassworks, which were moved there from the city because of the danger of fire. The most remarkable buildings are the CATHEDRAL OF SANTI MARIA E DONATO, its floors and walls richly covered in mosaics from the early Middle Ages; and the late-17th-century Palazzo Giustinian, which houses the MUSEO DELL'ARTE VETRARIA, where you can marvel at the creations of master glass blowers.

BURANO. Burano, which lies between Murano and Torcello, is still probably the most traditional island in the lagoon

"[BURANO] AN ISLAND OF LIGHT, OF HARMONIOUS SILENCE, FORGOTTEN BY THE LAND, DEVOTED TO THE WORSHIP OF THE SEA."

MICHEL DESFORGUES

in terms of its architecture and its people. An active trading center (the people of Burano, the "Buranelli", were well known on the mainland as fruit and vegetable merchants), the island is famous for lacemaking, an art developed at the beginning of the 16th century which was popular with the Venetian noblewomen. On this island where time appears to have stood still, the silent streets crowded with brightly colored houses seem a million miles away from the exuberant sights and sounds of La Serenissima.

TORCELLO ★. The Venetian civilization began 1,500 years ago in Torcello when the people of Altinum, the largest city in the region, took refuge from the threat of Barbarian invasion. Among the many reminders of its past splendor are the reused Roman columns and ornaments; the remarkable CATHEDRAL OF SANTA MARIA ASSUNTA, with its priceless Byzantine-Romanesque mosaics; and the CHURCH OF SANTA FOSCA, surrounded by a five-sided portico in the shape of a Greek cross. In the center of the lawn opposite these churches stands the so-called "Chair of Attila", possibly used by the tribunes when passing sentence.

BURANO, THE LACEMAKERS' ISLAND
The island of Burano – whose name recalls the Porta Boreana of Altinum, linking it culturally to nearby Torcello – has perfected the ancient art of lacemaking. As early as the 16th century the invention of the *"punto in aria"* led to the creation of Venetian point, which became the island's specialty. At one time lacemakers, sitting outside their houses, patiently and skillfully producing one of Venice's most highly prized products, would have been a common sight.

THE LIDO
The longest of the sandy islands between the lagoon and the Adriatic, the Lido is now largely a garden city. Once frequented by members of the Viennese court that surrounded Archduke Maximilian of Austria, its expansion dates mainly from the years after World War One. Clustered around the most exclusive part of the island you will find the Casino and numerous luxury hotels, as well as the offices of the Mostra Internazionale del Cinema, which was inaugurated in 1932.

In the first half of the 20th century, during the interwar period, the name Venezia did not just apply to the city in the lagoon, but to the whole of northeast Italy. Today the three regions in this area are known as Veneto, Trentino-Alto Adige and Friuli-Venezia Giulia, but their collective name – Triveneto, or the "Three Venetias" – acknowledges the deep common debt, both artistic and in many areas linguistic, that they owe to the Venetian civilization.

AROUND VENICE

ROSALBA
LA CHIOGGIOTTA
A native of Chioggia, Rosalba Carriera (1675–1757) was renowned for her spirited pastel portraits, which are immediately recognizable among other 18th-century Venetian paintings. Rosalba's own house became the home, some years later, of

As might be expected, La Serenissima's influence is most acutely felt in the resorts that are closest to the region's dominant town: from Chioggia – which even shares Venice's canal-crossed layout – to Padua, where the far-sightedness of the ruling Doges favored not only prosperity and the arts but also education and freedom of thought.

CHIOGGIA, A LAGOON TOWN. In Chioggia, the town that closes off Venice's lagoon to the south ■ *24*, the streets are called "*calli*" and the quays "*fondamenta*", just as they are in Venice. The residential area extends along the Canale della Vena and the parallel Corso del Popolo, where the Duomo (which is almost a thousand years old) was revamped in the 17th century by Baldassarre Longhena. The nearby CHURCH OF SAN MARTINO remains 14th-century Gothic in style, however, and contains a polyptych attributed to Paolo Veneziano. This street is also the site of the old GRANARY (built in 1322) and the Baroque façade of Sant'Andrea, with

Carlo Goldoni, who was inspired by the artist to write his famous comedy *Le baruffe chiozzotte* ▲ 227.

LIVING OFF THE SEA
Chioggia's main resource is fishing, and great care is taken of the boats. Two famous types of boat were the *tartana*, once used for trawling, and the *bragozzo*, a flat-bottomed boat suited to fishing in shallow waters, which replaced it.

its Veneto-Byzantine campanile. At the end of the street you can continue to the right toward SAN DOMENICO, a church dating from the 13th century, although restored several times up to the end of the 18th century. It contains an outstanding painting of *Saint Paul* (1520) by Carpaccio and a 15th-century North European *Crucifixion*. A bridge about half a mile away links the historical center to the island of SOTTOMARINA (the former "Chioggia Minore"), abandoned after the Genoese siege of 1380 but given a new lease of life three centuries later. It is now a modern seaside resort that is popular with tourists.

THE HISTORICAL CENTER OF TREVISO. The Terraglio, an ancient straight road,

> ##### "THE SAILS OF CHIOGGIA, WITH THEIR RED EMBLEMS ON A RED GROUND, ARE LIKE INCAN SHROUD CLOTHS."

PAUL MORAND

over 12 miles long, carries traffic from the congestion of Mestre (part of the mainland in the commune of Venice) to the serene affluence of Treviso. Inside the 16th-century walls the historical nucleus continues to boast some colorful medieval and Renaissance sights. The central PIAZZA DEI SIGNORI is dominated by the massive 13th-century PALAZZO DEI TRECENTO, the former council building, parts of which have been, very obviously, rebuilt as a result of the Allied bombings in World War Two. The nearby Prefettura, a period imitation, is only a century old; but you will see some authentic Roman paving stones near the arcaded CALMAGGIORE, a street lined with elegant stores, which leads from the square through period houses to the DUOMO and its old Romanesque baptistry. Behind the Duomo's incongruous neoclassical façade, the interior is elegantly decorated, with sculptures by Lombardo in the chapel (late 15th century) at the rear of the left nave and frescos from the first half of the 16th century by Pordenone in the corresponding chapel on the right, which has an altarpiece by Titian. The narrow streets between the Palazzo dei Trecento and the nearby LOGGIA DEI CAVALIERI (late 13th century) lead toward the PESCHERIA, an atmospheric fish market on an island in the middle of the Cagnàn Canal, which bisects Treviso's historical center. The eastern districts on the other side of the canal also contain buildings of note, such as the 16th-century Porta San Tomaso or the medieval churches of San Francesco and SANTA CATERINA, the latter deconsecrated but famous for a cycle of 14th-century frescos by Tomaso da Modena, who worked for many years in Treviso. The western district includes another gate, the Porta dei Santi Quaranta; the MUSEO CIVICO LUIGI BAILO, which has a splendid picture gallery; and the huge, brick CHURCH OF SAN NICOLÒ, built for the Dominicans between the 13th and 14th centuries. Its chapterhouse contains some remarkable frescos by Tomaso da Modena. Treviso used to be famous as a "frescoed city", which is evident from the façades of many of the houses in the center, including the 15th-century CA' DA NOAL (now a museum).

PETRARCH AND THE EUGANEAN HILLS
Born in Arezzo in Tuscany in 1304, Petrarch (Francesco Petrarca) was one of the most remarkable innovators in the history of Western literature. This great humanist has given his name to the small town of Arquà Petrarca in the Euganean Hills, near Padua, where he chose to settle, dying there in 1374. The poet's small house and the piazza-cum-churchyard where he is entombed can still be visited, in their attractive medieval setting.

FLORENTINE MASTERS IN PADUA. In the flatland to the west of Venice (less than half an hour away from the provincial capital) stands Padua, a city that has enjoyed a reputation as a major cultural center for centuries. In the 16th century Venice's Stato da Tera ▲ 216 allowed Galileo Galilei to continue teaching at Padua university, one of the first universities in the world (11th century), when the Church was debating whether to condemn him. Over two centuries earlier Francesco Petrarca took refuge in the peaceful Euganean Hills nearby to write. The Brenta Canal is another of the area's main attractions, combining tranquil river views with important monuments like the historical villas ▲ 238. Padua has always prided itself on providing well known artists with a warm welcome, and visitors can now enjoy the fruits of this long collaboration – from frescos by Giotto to sculptures by Donatello. On the way from the railroad station to the center, you will come to a small park on the site of the palazzo owned by the Scrovegni family, demolished in the mid 19th century. The small church belonging to the palace has, however, survived. This is the CAPPELLA DEGLI SCROVEGNI ★, where Giotto began painting one of his most important cycles of pictures in 1303. Other outstanding frescos (although damaged in a World War Two air raid) can be found in the nearby Gothic Romanesque CHIESA DEGLI EREMITANI, built in the 13th century: the remnants in the Ovetari Chapel (to the right of the apse) are by Andrea Mantegna. A short distance away, the former Convent of the Eremitani houses the MUSEO CIVICO, which has some fine collections of archeological artefacts, coins, small bronzes and paintings. The next stop is the university at the heart of Padua. The PALAZZO DEL BO' was the seat of

THE BRENTA CANAL
The highest concentration of La Serenissima's historical patrician villas can be found along the Brenta Canal, the man-made waterway that flows between Padua and Venice. The most popular ones are the 18th-century Villa Pisani in Strà – a particularly spacious and spectacular villa decorated with frescos by Tiepolo – and the Villa Foscari at Malcontenta (between Oriago and Fusina), dating from 1555, which is one of Palladio's most interesting works ▲ 238.

the university in the 16th century; its name is derived from the ox on the sign of a tavern that once stood here. The palazzo has one of the earliest anatomical theaters, dating from 1595. Almost opposite is the CAFFÈ PEDROCCHI, which opened in 1831 and was a breeding ground for the insurrections of 1848,

> **"BUT GIOTTO CAME FROM THE COUNTRY; AND SAW WITH HIS SIMPLE EYES A LOWLIER WORTH."**
>
> JOHN RUSKIN

AN ARCADED CITY
The characteristic stately arcades that line Padua's streets make walking about the town a pleasant experience, come rain or shine. Their historical origins remain unknown, but it is possible that they date back to Roman times, when the city was called Patavium.

although it can no longer be visited. A stone's throw away, the heart of medieval Padua was made up of the Piazza delle Frutta and the Piazza delle Erbe, separated by the massive 13th-century PALAZZO DELLA RAGIONE, once the seat of the city's law courts. The nearby Piazza dei Signori is dominated by the PALAZZO DEL CAPITANIO (16th–17th century) the former home of the Venetian government's representative. Its tower boasts a fine astronomical clock dating from the 15th century. The 16th-century Duomo is next to the older BAPTISTRY, which has a magnificent cycle of frescos painted by Giusto de'Menabuoi at the end of the 14th century. At the southern limits of Padua's historical center stands the BASILICA OF SANT'ANTONIO, called "Il Santo" by the people of Padua. This large Gothic Romanesque church, begun in 1232, is crowned by eight domes. Standing before it on the piazza is Donatello's MONUMENT TO GATTEMELATA, executed in 1453 in honor of Erasmo da Narni, condottiere of the Venetian army. Another masterpiece by Donatello is the high altar inside the basilica, a magnificent assembly of panels, reliefs and sculptures, cast in bronze between 1443 and 1450. Via Luca Belludi leads from Il Santo to the nearby PRATO DELLA VALLE, an attractive, elliptical open space bordered by canals, bridges, trees and statues. This is the site of the colossal 16th-century CHURCH OF SANTA GIUSTINA. The mainland's oldest BOTANICAL GARDEN, founded in 1545, is also nearby.

SAINT ANTHONY OF PADUA
Saint Anthony, a Franciscan monk, born in Lisbon in 1195, is still one of the Catholic church's best-loved and most familiar saints. Anthony (who was acknowledged as a Doctor of the Church in 1946) founded a school of theology in this Euganean city and spent the last months of his life here, before his death in 1231.

THE UPPER VENETIAN PLAIN, BETWEEN THE BRENTA AND THE ADIGE

The Veneto, which is flat in the area of Treviso and Padua, becomes more hilly further upstream along the larger rivers – like the Brenta, which has its source in the Trentino mountains, and the Adige, further to the west. Only the craggy chain of Monte Baldo then stands between the Adige river and Lake Garda, a popular tourist resort with something for everyone, from windsurfing enthusiasts to lovers of literature.
PALLADIAN VICENZA ★. After Padua, the first important port of call for people traveling inland from the Adriatic is the elegant town of Vicenza, whose historical and artistic reputation is based on its many buildings by Palladio. His last work, the TEATRO OLIMPICO, was finished in 1583 (three years after his death) by Vincenzo Scamozzi, who gave it a splendid permanent stage made of wood and stucco. On the same piazza, PALAZZO CHIERICATI was designed by Palladio thirty years earlier; today it houses the MUSEO CIVICO, which exhibits paintings by the Venetian school (including Cima da Conegliano, Tintoretto, Veronese and Tiepolo) and by the North European school (from Memling to Van Dyck). Also by Palladio are the Palazzo Iseppo Da Porto (1552) and Palazzo Barabaran-Porto (1571), in Contrà Porti, and the more mannered PALAZZO VALMARANA-BRAGA (1566) in Corso Fogazzaro. The Palazzo della Ragione, now well known as the BASILICA ★, ● 78, stands at the heart of Vicenza in the Piazza dei Signori. Its Gothic structure was transformed by the false front which the architect began in 1546, and worked on intermittently until his death. Opposite this, Palladio built the LOGGIA DEL CAPITANIATO (1571), an unfinished and controversial work. However, the VILLA ROTONDA ● 90, begun by the great architect in 1567, in the hills just south of Vicenza, is one of his masterpieces.
ROMAN AND MEDIEVAL TRACES IN VERONA. Impressive Roman remains, romantic medieval legends, Gothic vestiges of the ruling Della Scala family and substantial 17th-century palaces make Verona one of the best-loved cultural cities in northern Italy. PIAZZA BRA', once a drill ground on the outskirts of the city, is now the busiest

PALLADIO AND PALLADIANISM
The architectural style of Andrea di Pietro della Gondola (1508–80), known as Palladio, was based on a rigorous reworking of classical themes, creating an aura of harmonious proportions and overall elegance that has served as a model for centuries.

> **"THE PLAIN, IRRIGATED BY PEACEFUL RIVERS, BOUNDED BY MOUNTAINS AND SEA, IS LIKE A ROOMY BED WHERE MOUNTAIN WINDS CONJOIN WITH SEA BREEZES."**

GIOVANNI COMISSO

meeting place in the heart of Verona. The city hall, the 17th-century Palazzo della Gran Guardia (temporary exhibitions) and the Museo Maffeiano (collection of ancient inscriptions) are all here – as is the ARENA ★, one of the largest surviving amphitheaters from imperial times. Behind the Arena, the Via Mazzini, lined with fashionable boutiques, leads to PIAZZA DELLE ERBE ● 77, the site of the Forum during Roman times. The 14th-century Casa dei Mercanti (on the left) and the Case Mazzanti (far right) stand out against the Baroque backdrop of the Palazzo Maffei. Behind the Case Mazzanti, you will come to the PIAZZA DEI SIGNORI, with the Renaissance LOGGIA DEL CONSIGLIO (on the left), built under orders from La Serenissima; and the Palazzo del Comune (on the right), with its soaring Torre dei Lamberti. Also on this side, beyond the 14th-century Palazzo del Capitanio, is the Piazzetta: the site of the ARCHE SCALIGERE, the fascinating tombs of the illustrious Della Scala family, who ruled Verona from 1262 to 1387. A short distance away is the Gothic CHURCH OF SANT'ANASTASIA, begun by the Dominicans in 1290, which contains a remarkable fresco of *Saint George* painted by Pisanello. A ROMAN THEATER (1st century AD) was uncovered about fifty years ago on the opposite bank of the Adige river. Besides the Duomo, which contains an *Assumption* by Titian, the other two most interesting churches are SAN FERMO (near the Roman remains of the Porta dei Leoni), which is on two levels and has a fine wooden ceiling in the form of a ship's hull, and SAN ZENO MAGGIORE ★, which can be reached by following the Adige river upstream past CASTELVECCHIO, with its magnificent bronze-paneled door.

ROMEO AND JULIET Although their story has such a convincing ring of truth, the two main characters of Shakespeare's tragedy never existed.

This throws doubt on the authenticity of the "Casa di Giulietta" in Via Cappello, in Verona, but the powerful appeal of the literary myth seems to have taken precedence over the historical facts. The small building nevertheless remains a good example of Gothic architecture, even though the famous balcony was added in 1935.

VILLAS IN THE VENETO

THE PALLADIAN MODEL
In the 16th century Andrea Palladio developed
several models for villas (such as the Villa Trissino, with
its central manor house, pronaoses on the façades
and servants' wings) that were imitated for centuries.

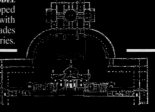

Between the 15th and 18th
centuries, in the regions
governed by La Serenissima the
Venetian nobility built thousands
of country residences. Although they differ greatly in terms of
period, form and size, the villas in the Veneto have certain
characteristics in common: at the time, they functioned both as
a manor house and as the center of an agricultural holding. They
were surrounded by parks or gardens and were sophisticated
enough for society life. Many of them were designed by leading
architects and decorated by artists such as
Veronese and Tiepolo.

THE VENETIAN PALAZZO
Originally the villa was modeled on the
typical Venetian palace in the lagoon.
It had an atrium and large central
reception rooms – illuminated
by mullioned windows with
several lights – and private
quarters at the sides. Later,
under the influence of
Palladio and Scamozzi,
the layout was
adapted for
country life.

VILLA BARBARO
The Villa Barbaro, in
Maser, designed by
Palladio and
containing frescos by
Paolo Veronese, is a
good example of one
of the Veneto's finest
villas. A perfect
fusion of architectural
simplicity and
compositional
elegance in a superb
natural setting, this
villa blends classic
overall design with
decorative detail.
These villas served as
a model for architects
all over the world.

THE IMPORTANCE OF WATER
A large number of
the villas in the
Veneto were built
at the water's edge;
and water was
often regarded as
an important
architectural element,
contributing
greatly to the overall
composition. In some
areas, such as on the
Brenta canal, scores
of villas were built
alongside the water,
their façades being
mirrored in the canal.

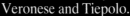

DECORATION

These villas were not simply architectural projects. Teams of painters, sculptors, cabinet makers, carpenters, plasterers and gardeners were employed to decorate and furnish them, joining forces to create a consummate work of art. Several families, such as the Marinali family of sculptors, worked for generations embellishing numerous villas.

"BOSCO DA REME"
East of Vittorio Veneto, in the direction of Friuli, stretches the Bosco del Cansiglio. This magnificent forest is one of the largest in Italy, with nearly 15,000 acres of beech, fir and larch, that can grow at an altitutude of nearly 5,600 feet. The Republic of Venice tended this forest carefully, because it provided valuable raw material for making oars for its fleet.

LAKE GARDA, THE "INLAND SEA" OF THE NORTH. The railroad and highway between Verona and Milan run alongside the largest lake in mainland Italy, Lake Garda or Benacò (the ancient-Roman Lake Benacus), stopping at the fortified citadel of PESCHIERA DEL GARDA, built by the Venetians, and passing close to elegant SIRMIONE, situated at the end of a narrow peninsula. This 13th-century stronghold ● *88* owned by the Della Scala family ▲ *237* includes the remains of a Roman villa, said to have belonged to the poet Catullus in the 1st century BC. Lake Garda is now shared by Lombardy (the western shore, which is richly carpeted with evergreens), Veneto (the eastern shore, notable for its Mediterranean trees and plants, such as lemon trees, planted by man) and Trentino (the northern tip, where the lake resembles a fjord, as if sandwiched between the Monte Baldo chain and the Ledro Alps). GARDONE RIVIERA – the site of "Il Vittoriale", from 1921 the lavish retreat of poet Gabriele D'Annunzio – is in the first of these regions, an area filled with parks and villas. On the Veneto shore you can visit the walled village of LAZISE; then the old town of GARDA, near the panoramic Punta San Vigilio; and MALCESINE, which boasts a castle (built in the 14th and 15th centuries), perched on a overhanging crag high above the lake, and the Renaissance Palazzo dei Capitani del Lago. At the northern tip of the lake, where the shores are steeper and more rocky, is RIVA DEL GARDA, an important tourist resort. Riva has a Central European flavor, as it was one of the Hapsburg's favorite holiday resorts, and also has a sailing center.

Harvest scene from a 15th-century woodcarving.

FROM THE VENETIAN PRE-ALPS TO THE TRENTINO

To the east of the Brenta river and Monte Grappa, the Valdobbiadene separates the hilly terrain of the Venetian pre-Alps and the Asolo Hills from the mountainous strip of land that is the home of the magnificent Cansiglio Forest, the Vittorio Veneto Gorge and the peaks that dominate Feltre.

POETS AND WRITERS IN ASOLO ★. Presented in fief by Venice to the noblewoman Caterina Cornaro in 1489, the delightful small town of Asolo was a famous retreat for intellectuals, including Pietro Bembo and Eleonora Duse. Within its walls you will find an 18th-century DUOMO (containing a *Madonna* by Lotto), on the piazza, and nearby the Loggia del Capitano, which houses the Museo Civico. Above it is the Castello della

Regina, and higher still the ruins of a fortified stronghold.

VITTORIO VENETO, LITTLE VENICE IN THE PRE-ALPS. When, in 1866, Cèneda was united with nearby Serravalle, the new commune took the name of the first king of Italy. The two towns remain divided, by a long street, but both are modeled on Venice. Of note are the 13th-century cathedral, on the PIAZZA DI CÈNEDA, the Loggia del Cenedese (the former city hall) and the huge Seminario Vescovile. The buildings of SERRAVALLE are more spectacular, particularly along the "Calgrande" (Via Martiri della Libertà). The piazza at the end of the Calgrande still looks as it did in the 16th century, with the 15th-century Loggia Serravallese (containing various historical exhibits) and, on the far bank of the Meschio river, the Duomo – notable for the *Madonna and Child* by Titian over the altar.

FELTRE AND THE 16TH CENTURY. Feltre's steep main street, the VIA MEZZATERRA, is lined with centuries-old houses and palaces, some of them with frescos; it climbs to the PIAZZA MAGGIORE, which is on several levels. Here you will find the Palazzo della Ragione (now the city hall), a fountain by Lombardo, the façade of the Church of San Rocco and a clock tower belonging to the impressive castle, which has been rebuilt on several occasions. Paintings by the Veneto school are housed in the nearby museum, while a collection of local wrought-ironwork is displayed in

PROSECCO DI VALDOBBIADENE
The valley between the Piave river and Vittorio Veneto is characterized by rolling slopes covered with vines, from which one of northern Italy's best sweet white wines is made. This is the "strada del vino Prosecco", where winegrowing enterprises are interspersed with small resorts of great artistic interest.

GRAPPA
One of the oldest cultural traditions in the Veneto is that of *grappa*, a distinctive eau-de-vie which, by pure coincidence, has the same name as the mountain that was the arena for some long and bloody battles between the Austrians and Italians in World War One.

GORIZIA
AND THE COLLIO
The small town of
Gorizia, the arena of
fierce fighting in
World War One,
has remained divided
(Gorizia and Nova
Gorica) between Italy
and Yugoslavia
(now Slovenia) since
World War Two.
Gorizia has recently
started to rebuild
its reputation as
the "Austrian Nice",
recalling the days
when it was a famous
resort, under the
Hapsburgs. The
various districts of the
town have been
revitalized, while the
surrounding Collio
region has begun to
be recognized as one
of the peninsula's
most important wine
regions.

the GALLERIA CARLO RIZZARDA. The CATHEDRAL, rebuilt
during the 16th century in Renaissance style, stands outside
the walls.

THE BISHOP-PRINCES OF TRENTO. Virtually a capital of
Christianity during the Council of Trent (1545–63), which

established the canons of the Catholic
Counter-Reformation, Trento still
preserves monuments – the frescoed
houses in the piazza, the 13th-century
DUOMO, the new Museo d'Arte Moderna
in the Renaissance Palazzo delle Albere –
that will delight discerning tourists. For
sheer spectacle, however, the CASTELLO
DEL BUONCONSIGLIO cannot be missed.
The bishop-princes of Trento held court
in this stronghold, built between the 13th
and 16th centuries. A tour of the Castello
will take you from the tall, narrow court of
the Castelvecchio (the original nucleus) to the Magno Palazzo,
commissioned between 1528 and 1536 by Bernardo Clesio,
with its lovely gardens and elegantly decorated salons. But the
castle's finest gem is the 15th-century Gothic cycle *The Frescos
of the Months* in the separate Torre dell'Aquila.

BETWEEN THE PEAKS OF ALTO ADIGE
AND THE BELLUNESE DOLOMITES

MARMOLADA
Now the only true
surviving glacier in
the area, Mount
Marmolada (10,968
feet) towers over
spectacular valleys
and is frequented, in
summer and winter
alike, by hikers and
sightseers. You can
take the cable car up
to Marmolada di
Rocca (10,728 feet).

THE STRADA DELLE DOLOMITI ★. From
BOLZANO (Bozen), the traditionally
German-speaking historical chief town
of the southern Tirol (Südtirol), this
famous road begins to climb upward to
the south of the SCILIAR group ■ *20–21*,
past the Passo di Costalunga (5,725
feet), crossing the Val di Fassa, to reach
the resort of CANAZEI, only 7 miles
away from the slopes of MARMOLADA.
Further on, the Passo Pordoi (7,346
feet) marks the highest point of our
itinerary, just after the alternative road
through the Passo di Sella (7,363 feet),
which will take you to the gorgeous VAL
BADIA with its Ladin minority. After
zigzagging down toward Arabba, the
Passo Pordoi begins to climb again

> **"THIS IS THE ISONZO RIVER / AND HERE I BEST /**
> **APPRECIATED / A QUIET STRAND / OF THE UNIVERSE."**
>
> GIUSEPPE UNGARETTI

toward the Passo di Falzarego (6,906 feet), after which the road, flanked by spectacular views of LAGAZUOI and TOFANE, climbs to CORTINA D'AMPEZZO. The length of this route is 68 miles.
THE AMPEZZO VALLEY. On the eastern stretch of the Strada delle Dolomiti – at a height of 3,973 feet in the province of Belluno, in the Veneto – Cortina d'Ampezzo has been transformed within the span of a few decades from an Alpine village into a world-class tourist resort. The fairy-tale Dolomite landscape will lure you through the Tre Croci Pass (5,951 feet) to the legendary sapphire blue of Lake Misurina, below the spires of the TRE CIME DI LAVAREDO.

FRIULI AND VENEZIA GIULIA

Until the early 20th century the former "Patria del Friuli" came under the jurisdiction of La Serenissima – while in the Venezia Giulia region Gorizia and Trieste (the chief town of the present-day region) were answerable to Vienna, whether they liked it or not.
UDINE, CAPITAL OF A "PATRIA FRIULANA". Although the first Duchy of Friuli had been based in Cividale, by the 13th century Udine had become the capital of Friuli. The town spread in an orderly manner around the hill on which the CASTELLO stands, with its remarkable collections of Venetian and regional art. The liveliest quarters of the town are concentrated between the PIAZZA DELLA LIBERTÀ – with its 15th-century Loggia del Lionello and 16th-century Porticato di San Giovanni – and the former CHURCH OF SAN FRANCESCO. Between them stands the DUOMO, an imposing building (13th–14th century) restored in the 18th century by Manin and embellished with works by Tiepolo. A short distance from it you will come to the PALAZZO ARCIVESCOVILE – containing yet more paintings by Tiepolo, in the new Museo Diocesano. Within easy reach of Udine are the old Lombard town of CIVIDALE DEL FRIULI, the "frontier town" of Gorizia (east of Udine) and the geometrical tour de force of the fortified town of PALMANOVA (to the south).

CIVIDALE DEL FRIULI
The main attractions of this town, which was the capital of Lombard Friuli until 568, are the National Archeology Museum (housed, since 1990, in the Palazzo dei Provveditori Veneti) and the flawless gem of the Tempietto Longobardo, famous chiefly for its 8th-century stuccos depicting female figures. The Duomo, built by the Venetians in the 15th century, also contains some remarkable works, such as the mullioned octagonal chapel of the Baptistery of Callisto and the Altar of Ratchis, both of which date back to the 8th century.

A STAR-SHAPED CITY
Purpose-built by the Venetians in 1593 in order to defend their eastern borders in the event of invasion by the Hapsburgs or the Turks, Palmanova is one of the finest examples of 16th-century town planning. Its perimeter wall in the shape of a nine-pointed star contains a central nine-sided polygon. The streets radiate out from the central piazza. The outer bastions were added in the Napoleonic era.

CARLO SCARPA
A native of Venice, Carlo Scarpa (1906–78) devoted himself to museum design. His most important projects included the remodeling of Ca' Foscari, Museo Correr and Palazzo Querini-Stampalia in Venice; the Museo di Castelvecchio in Verona; and the Museo Revoltella in Trieste.

MIRAMARE
Archduke Maximilian of Austria (brother of Franz Josef and future Emperor of Mexico) chose a scenic promontory just north of Trieste as the site of one of the most graceful residential castles in Central Europe.

ANCIENT BASILICAS IN AQUILEIA AND GRADO. The remains of the vast late-Roman port of Aquilegia, now called AQUILEIA, form one of Italy's most important archeological sites. There are a great many things to see, including the ruins of the Forum, inscribed stone slabs and tablets at the Museo Nazionale, ancient mosaics in the basilica, and the Paleo-Christian Museum. Also on the lagoon is GRADO. Notable monuments there include the 5th-century baptistery and the Church of Santa Maria delle Grazie (4th–6th century).

TRIESTE, A CITY OF COMMERCE AND COSMOPOLITANISM. In addition to the ROMAN THEATER, dating from the 1st and 2nd centuries AD, the Austrian Empire's main seaport preserves many vestiges of its past glory. Facing the sea is the PIAZZA DELL'UNITÀ D'ITALIA, the true heart of the city, surrounded by the Borsa Vecchia (1809), the 18th-century inland landing stage of the CANAL GRANDE (built in the mid 18th century by the Empress Maria Theresa), the neoclassical PALAZZO CARCIOTTI (1803), the Pescheria (1913), which houses the aquarium, and the 19th-century residence of Pasquale Revoltella, transformed by Carlo Scarpa into the handsome MUSEO REVOLTELLA. On the hilltop where the original nucleus of the town once stood, far above the streets where the Assicurazioni Generali and Lloyd Triestino were founded and where James Joyce wrote *Ulysses* and Italo Svevo his *La coscienza di Zeno*, stands the BASILICA DI SAN GIUSTO. Nearby you will see the walls of the CASTELLO and the remains of several other major Roman buildings from the 1st and 2nd centuries. Even older, from the time of Octavian, is the ARCO DI RICCARDO (33 BC). Archduke Maximilian's castle, MIRAMARE (see left), built in 1856, reveals charms of a more recent era.

FROM BOLOGNA TO THE CENTRAL AND EASTERN PO VALLEY

❝I know not nor do I care why, out of so many memories, only the most beautiful come to mind .... All I can remember are the afternoons when the summer heat was at its height in the vast plain, where rows of trees ... bent over as if collapsing under the weight of such violent light. Between one row of trees and another, there were yellow, green or brown fields and canals of stagnant water which, because of the contrast between the brown background and the light falling from above, seemed the color of tawny gold.❞
Dante Arfelli,
*Pomeriggi estivi
(Summer Afternoons)*

Bologna's historical center has one of the highest concentrations of art and culture of all Italian cities, as well as some of the finest restaurants in Italy. Bologna is the capital of the region of Emilia-Romagna, and forms the starting point for this chapter's itineraries which head out to the rich farmland of the Po valley, home to Parma ham and Parmesan cheese. These include the cities of the ancient consular road, the Via Emilia (Emilian Way), as well as Mantua and Ferrara, the centuries-old seats of illustrious ruling families, and Ravenna, once an imperial capital. The city of Modena is well worth a visit for its fine Romanesque cathedral, a symbol of the city's past as an independent commune. The cathedrals of Parma and Piacenza (93 miles from Bologna) boast some stunning examples of medieval art, and conjure up the magnificent years under the rule of the Farnese duchy. Mantua, the former capital of the dukes of Gonzaga, and nearby Sabbioneta, which is a kind of miniature and idealized version of Mantua, part Lombard

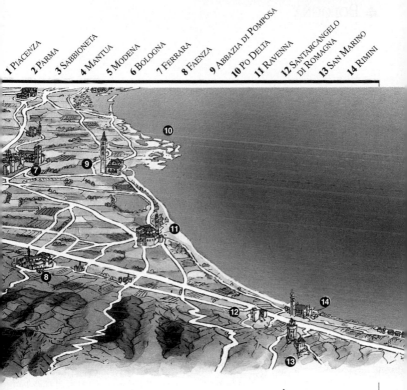

and part Emilian. Ferrara, however, is a wholly Emilian city, and one that bears the stamp of the urban improvement programs that were initiated by the dukes of Este, who successfully added an equally, if not more beautiful, Renaissance city to the original medieval one. Ferrara is ideally placed for two unmissable destinations: the ancient Abbazia di Pomposa, an isolated and austere abbey in the countryside near the sea, and the Po delta, an attractive wetland environment that is shared between Emilia and Veneto. Our itinerary ends in Romagna with a visit to three towns: Ravenna, which in the 5th and 6th centuries was renowned as a city of art without peer; Faenza, which boasts the Museo Internazionale delle Ceramiche, one of the best of its kind; and Rimini (70 miles from Bologna) which, apart from being an attractive, lively seaside resort, preserves a little-known historical center that boasts some important Roman monuments and the Tempio Malatestiano, which is one of the most significant works of Italian Renaissance art.

"The banks of a deserted sand quarry were blocking the street. A tall mechanical structure, its conveyor belts still caked with soil, stood between heath-covered slopes. The trucks had also been abandoned half-full and grass had spontaneously covered two sand dunes. Beyond lay a featureless terrain, the land devastated by these sand or clay quarries which, abandoned (inevitably) to their own devices, revert to heath."
Gianni Celati,
Verso la foce
(Toward the River Mouth)

247

ALONG THE EMILIAN WAY
The city has grown up over the centuries along the ancient Via Emilia (Emilian Way) ▲ *260*, built by consul Marcus Aemilius Lepidus between 191 and 187 BC. Starting from the stronghold of *Ariminum* (modern-day Rimini) at the end of the *Via Flaminia* (Flaminian Way), the Via Emilia linked up with Placentia (Piacenza). Due to this consular highway, now Strada Statale no. 9, many cities that lie approximately along its line have increased in size and importance.

THE PATRON SAINT OF BOLOGNA
As legend has it, Petronius, bishop of this city around 432, was responsible for rebuilding the city and creating the original nucleus of the complex of Saint Stefano. Bologna, whose patron saint he became in the 12th century, celebrates his feast day on October 4.

The largest city between Milan and Florence, the communication center of the peninsula, the heart of a region characterized by pragmatism – that of Emilia-Romagna – and respected for its savoir-faire, Bologna also boasts an historical center packed with medieval buildings, elegant Renaissance architecture and Baroque monuments. Although relatively small, in its provincial way (the Bolognese people remain country-dwellers at heart) the city is known for its financial and administrative efficiency and is renowned for its excellent university, the *Alma Mater Studiorum*, one of the first universities to be founded in the world.

ETRUSCANS AND ROMANS. Originally the cradle of the Villanovan civilization (the most important early Iron Age culture in Italy), Bologna came into its own in the 6th century BC, when, known as *Felsina*, it made a name for itself as one of the main Etruscan towns beyond the Apennines. In 189 BC, Felsina came under Roman rule and was given the Celtic-sounding name of *Bononia*.

SAINT PETRONIUS AND THE MIDDLE AGES. Bologna's future patron saint was elected bishop in the first half of the 5th century, when the region came under the authority of Ravenna ▲ *267*, then the capital of the Western Roman Empire. In the early Middle Ages, Bologna was ruled in turn by Ravenna, the Barbarian kingdoms and then the papacy, but it appears to have been electing its own Consuls by the 11th century. The city acquired power and fame when it became independent and its university was founded. In 1249 Bologna defeated Emperor Frederick II, capturing his son, King Enzo, and, from 1300 to 1500 it had a population of 50,000 inhabitants and was one of the ten principal cities in Europe.

FROM THE BENTIVOGLIO FAMILY TO THE PAPACY. Bologna's last years as an independent commune were troubled by conflicts between rival Guelph and Ghibelline families. In the 14th century, the Pepoli family appeared to emerge victorious but, shortly after, Cardinal Albornoz imposed papal rule. A more stable period ensued when the Bentivoglio family rose to power in the 15th century, but their rule ended in bloody rebellion. This insurrection had been ordered by the papacy who, from then until the 19th century, firmly held the city under sway, relying on the support of other great families such as the Fantuzzi, the Malvezzi and the Poggi: an aristocracy who had acquired their wealth through the silk and hemp trade and the forensic professions (an established Bolognese tradition, associated with the city's time-honored university activities). Although the 17th century was a difficult one, it did witness the birth of an artistic tradition – this was the era of the Carracci family, who painted some magnificent works here – which was to continue into the next century.

FROM NAPOLEON TO THE KINGDOM OF ITALY. On June 19, 1796, Napoleon delivered Bologna from the papacy. This marked the start of boom years for Bologna: various reforms encouraged the growth of textile manufacturing and acted as a catalyst for scientific research, with restructuring of

1 SAN FRANCESCO
2 PALAZZO FAVA-GHISILARDI (MUSEO CIVICO MEDIEVALE)
3 METROPOLITANA DI SAN PIETRO
4 PALAZZO COMUNALE
5 FONTANA DEL NETTUNO
6 MUSEO CIVICO ARCHEOLOGICO
7 SAN PETRONIO

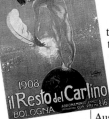

1908
il Resto del Carlino
BOLOGNA
ABBONAMENTO ANNUO CON PREMI L.16

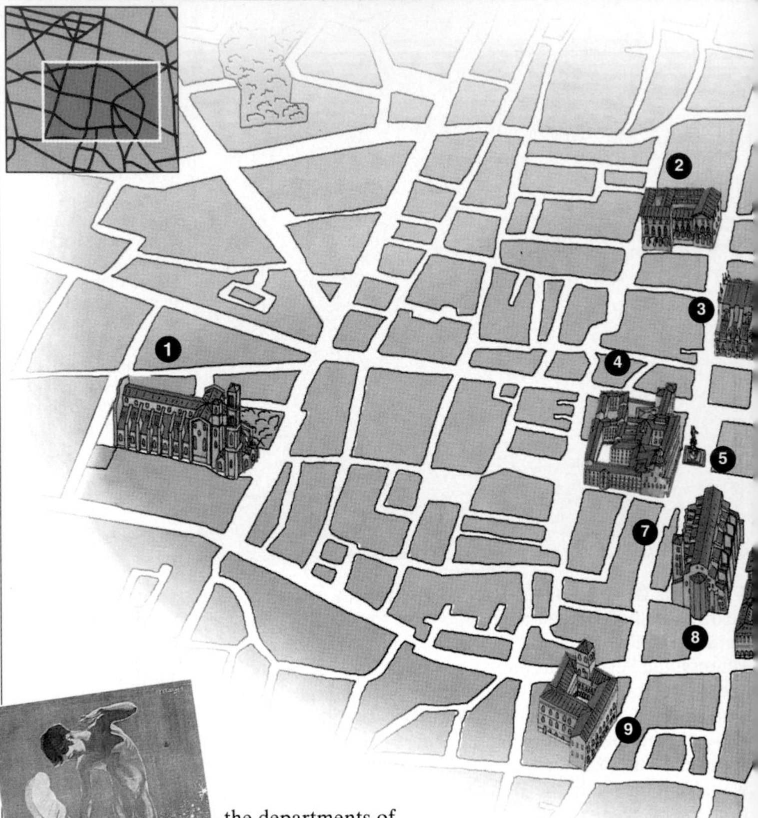

THE "CARLINO"
Bologna's daily newspaper is *Il Resto del Carlino*, founded in 1885. It used to be given by tobacconists in change to customers who came in to buy a cigar and paid with a *carlino* (the cigar cost ¾ of a *carlino*), money of ancient origins still in use in those days.

the departments of the historic university. The Congress of Vienna restored Bologna to papal rule and, as a result, the city experienced its own violent and bloody Risorgimento episode. This culminated in the siege of May 1849, when the Austrians, who had been driven out of the city the previous year, made a triumphant reentry. But the fate of Bologna and Italy was sealed: the time was ripe and, in 1859, a temporary council hoisted the national tricolor.

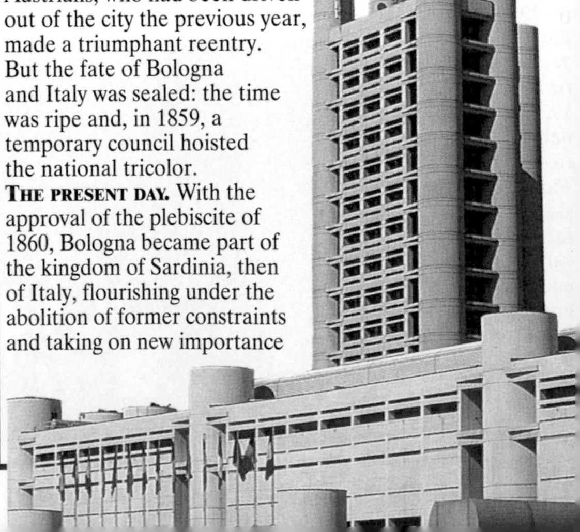

THE PRESENT DAY. With the approval of the plebiscite of 1860, Bologna became part of the kingdom of Sardinia, then of Italy, flourishing under the abolition of former constraints and taking on new importance

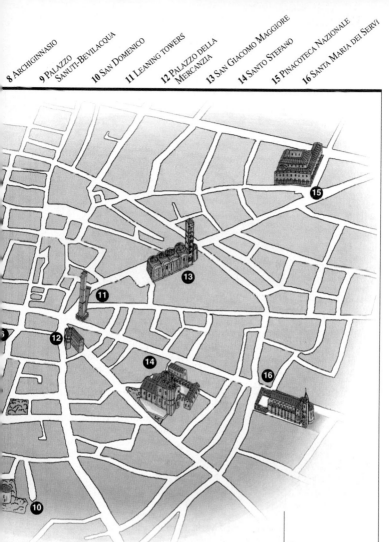

as a communication center (and now a key rail and road junction for private and commercial traffic). Outstanding progress was also made in the fields of education and of science, leading to a wider range of university subjects (medicine, mathematics, physics and chemistry) as well as of literature. Bologna is now one of the country's wealthiest cities, full of thriving businesses and new complexes of buildings – like the Fiera district ▲ *258* – which are at the leading edge of their industries. But throughout its long history, through good times and bad, the city has never forgotten how to greet life with a smile: Bologna is a fine place to live in and to visit.

TWENTY-TWO MILES OF ARCADES
● *77*
Bologna is the most arcaded city in the world. These galleries of stone, in varying architectural styles and sizes, form a continuous pedestrian zone along the streets of the historic city center. The use of arcades is derived from a long tradition of building houses with over-hanging upper floors supported by massive wooden beams.

PIAZZA MAGGIORE ★

The piazza that has always been Bologna's main square was laid out in the center of town by the free commune in the 13th century. Apart from being the seat of Bologna's political power, the square is a meeting place for townspeople, throughout their their daily lives and on holidays.

SAN PETRONIO ★. The square is dominated by the unfinished and undecorated façade – perhaps even more fascinating because of that – of the largest church in the city. Had the project been completed, it would have been even larger than St Peter's in Rome. This Gothic building, originally commissioned by the commune from the Bolognese architect, Antonio di Vincenzo, at the end of the 14th century, is unusual for its immense height. The extraordinary size of the nave posed serious problems: it was not until the mid 17th century that architects could calculate how to complete the roof. Behind the façade, in the center of which is a superb PORTAL carved around 1430 by Jacopo della Quercia, the interior contains a fine *Saint Jerome* by Lorenzo Costa in the sixth chapel on the right, as well as 16th-century inlaid choir stalls in the eighth, a Tribune designed by Vignola in 1548 above the high altar and, turning back along the left aisle, a *Saint Roch* by Parmigianino in the eighth chapel from the entrance and some 15th-century FRESCOS by Giovanni da Modena in the fourth.

PALAZZO COMUNALE. Although the Renaissance façade of the Podesta's palace (opposite San Petronio) was built by the Bentivoglio family, the large

THE BOLOGNESE CALENDAR
Gregory XIII (1572–85) was the pope who reformed the former Julian calendar, replacing it with the Gregorian calendar still in use today. Without this Bolognese Pontiff, there would be no such thing as a leap year.

late 16th-century statue of Pope Gregory XIII decorating the Palazzo Comunale is a reminder that the local seigniory was soon replaced by the authority of the Church of Rome. The part 13th-century and part 15th-century building now houses Bologna's city hall. Passing through a gateway designed by Galeazzo Alessi and under the arcades lining the courtyard, you can climb Bramante's staircase to the COLLEZIONI COMUNALI D'ARTE, which exhibits works of the 13th–16th century largely by Bolognese artists.

FOUNTAIN OF NEPTUNE ★. Between the Palazzo Comunale and the Palazzo Podestà stands the remarkable bronze statue of the god of the sea, cast (like the putti, dolphins and sirens around him) by Giambologna (1563–6). Artistically, this was one of the most important fountains in 16th-century Europe.

GIORGIO MORANDI
The Palazzo Comunale is also the site of the Museo Morandi, a recently opened museum devoted to this famous painter (1890–1964), who was a native of this city. Many of his paintings are of Grizzana, the small Apennine resort where, from 1927, Morandi used to spend his summers.

MUSEO CIVICO ARCHEOLOGICO. The entrance to the city's large archeological collection is just to the left of San Petronio. This museum recreates an accurate picture of Etruscan *Felsina*, Roman *Bononia* and the earlier Villanovan villages. Other sections display artifacts from Ancient Egypt, later Etruscan finds and a collection of antiquities including a remarkable *Athena Lemnia*, a Roman copy in marble of a lost bronze head by Phidias.

ARCHIGINNASIO. In 1562–3, on the site where the left transept of San Petronio should have stood, the papal legate constructed the new Archiginnasio, the seat of the university of Bologna from that time until the first half of the 19th century. The lecture rooms were later replaced by the stores and reading rooms of the MUNICIPAL LIBRARY. You can still see the numerous escutcheons, the inscriptions by the students and the wooden tiers of the ANATOMICAL THEATER where students used to watch the dissection of human corpses.

GALVANI AND THE GALLUZZI
The arcades of the Archiginnasio continue on to Piazza Galvani, which is the site of a monument to the Bolognese scientist, Luigi Galvani (1737–98), one of the first scholars to explore

FROM THE METROPOLITANA TO VIA GALLIERA

Via dell' Independenza is a long straight thoroughfare north of Piazza Maggiore. Laid out in the 19th century to connect the town center to the station, this elegant road is lined with some fascinating stores.

METROPOLITANA DI SAN PIETRO. Bologna's cathedral stands on Via dell'Independenza. This ancient church was rebuilt on several occasions between the 16th and 18th century. Its magnificent interior contains many works of note,

the effects of electrical currents on the nerves. Crossing the piazza and passing under the overhead passageways between old houses, you will come to the Corte dei Galluzzi, a medieval corner of the city, with its 13th-century tower of the same name.

253

THE CITY OF A HUNDRED TOWERS

In the 11th century and for several centuries afterward, Bologna had many more towers than the two (the Due Torri) that remain today. Almost all powerful families built one, regarding it as an essential addition to their house: not for living in, but for military purposes and as a symbol of power.

BONIFACIO VIII

The Bonifacio VIII statue exhibited at the Museo Civico Medievale, executed in 1301 by Matteo Bandini, was perhaps the first to be dedicated to a living person in the city.

including the paintings in the chapels, and the *Annunciation* (1619) by the Bolognese artist, Ludovico Carracci, in the lunette of the presbytery. The two red marble lions, on either side of the main entrance, and the campanile are survivors of the original 13th-century Romanesque structure.

PALAZZO FAVA-GHISILARDI. Virtually opposite each other on Via Manzoni, just off Via dell'Independenza, are the late 15th-century façade of the Madonna di Galliera and the entrance to the MUSEO CIVICO MEDIEVALE, housed within the Palazzo Fava-Ghisilardi, built in 1484. Of particular note is the magnificent collection of sculpture, which includes some 15th-century gems like the tomb slab of Domenico Garganelli, the work of Francesco del Cossa and the superb *Madonna and Child* by Jacopo della Quercia, as well as many important pieces of applied art.

VIA GALLIERA. Via Manzoni leads into Via Galliera, an old Roman road. This quiet street is lined with period palaces, including the spacious Palazzo Aldrovandi (at no. 8, restored in the 18th century) and, almost opposite, the 16th-century Palazzo Dal Monte. Heading further out of the city, you will come to the Palazzo Felicini (at no. 14), its late 15th-century façade embellished with terracotta ornaments.

254

> **"AS YOU COME NEARER TO BOLOGNA, YOU ARE STRUCK BY THE SIGHT OF TWO VERY TALL TOWERS, ONE OF WHICH IS TILTED AT AN ALARMING ANGLE."**
>
> MADAME DE STAËL

FROM THE DUE TORRI TO THE PINACOTECA NAZIONALE

Taking Via Rizzoli from Piazza Maggiore, you will come to the Due Torri. Continue along VIA ZAMBONI (once home to rival families: the Bentivoglio and the Malvezzi) to the university district. The university buildings are clustered around the Palazzo Poggi (no. 33), which was built in 1549. From 1803 this palazzo took over from the Archiginnasio ▲ 253 as the university's headquarters.

THE DUE TORRI ★. These "leaning towers" are a symbol of the city which can be admired in all its panoramic glory from the top of the TORRE DEGLI ASINELLI ● 89, erected at the beginning of the 12th century in what is now Piazza di Porta Ravegnana. This and the nearby TORRE GARISENDA (which tilts even more drunkenly), are the most famous survivors of many other similar structures built in medieval Bologna.

SAN GIACOMO MAGGIORE. A striking building on Via Zamboni is the long, narrow church begun by the Augustinians in the second half of the 13th century. It has a Gothic façade and apse and, facing on to the street, a lovely Renaissance porch, commissioned by the Bentivoglio. The interior contains a *Saint Roch* by Ludovico Carracci in the ninth chapel on the right, the tomb of Anton Galeazzo Bentivoglio (by Jacopo della Quercia, 1435), the BENTIVOGLIO CHAPEL (1486) with superb frescos by Lorenzo Costa and an altarpiece by Francesco Francia. The side portico leads to the ORATORY OF SANTA CECILIA, with frescos by Costa and Francia depicting the lives of the saints. The church backs onto Piazza Verdi, the temple of Bolognese opera and the site of the TEATRO COMUNALE, built in the mid 18th century to a design by Antonio Bibiena.

PINACOTECA NAZIONALE. The former Jesuit college of Sant' Ignazio, now the home of the most important public gallery in the city, is on Via delle Belle Arti, which leads off a lush piazzetta at the end of Via Zamboni. This gallery has a marvelous collection of works by the local schools of painting between the 14th and 18th centuries, as well as Renaissance masterpieces by artists who were not natives of Emilia, including Raphael and Perugino ▲ 320.

THE CARRACCI
The Pinacoteca Nazionale has many paintings by Agostino, Annibale and Ludovico Carracci, members of an artistic family (two brothers and a cousin) who, between the 16th and 17th centuries turned their backs on the excesses of mannerism in favor of a return to more naturalistic and historical subjects.

STRADA MAGGIORE

Lined with elegant porticoed houses and palaces, Strada Maggiore is a section of the Roman Via Emilia that leads in the direction of Rimini from the leaning towers.

PALAZZO BARGELLINI. This is one of the most magnificent examples of the *palazzo senatorio* or senatorial palace. Built at no. 44 on Strada Maggiore in 1638, its doorway is supported by two stone giants and it also has an interesting staircase.

SANTA MARIA DEI SERVI. A wide portico, whose side sections date from the 14th century, leads to the Gothic church of the Serviti, begun in 1346. The understated late Gothic elegance of the interior provides a worthy setting for the opulent marble altar at the rear, which dates from the 16th century and stands in front of an inlaid wooden choir; the third chapel contains a *Maestà* by Cimabue.

PALAZZO HERCOLANI. Continuing down Strada Maggiore after Santa Maria dei Servi you come to the late 18th-century Palazzo Hercolani (no. 45), the most recently built senatorial palace. Now the seat of the university's faculty of political science, it boasts a magnificent stairway lined with statues.

VIA SANTO STEFANO

Like Via Zamboni and Strada Maggiore, atmospheric Via Santo Stefano is another of the old streets radiating from the Due Torri and is lined with churches and palaces.

> **"[BOLOGNA] IS GRACED BY SOME MAGNIFICENT AND LAVISH BUILDINGS . . . FEW CITIES IN EUROPE CAN COMPARE WITH IT IN TERMS OF NUMBER AND SPLENDOR."**
> WILLEM JANSZOON BLAEU, 1640

JERUSALEM BONONIENSIS
The complex of Santo Stefano has been compared to the Holy Sepulcher of Christ and was originally called *Sancta Jerusalem* because its layout reproduced that of the holy sites of Jerusalem.

CARDINAL LAMBERTINI
Palazzo Vizzani-Sanguinetti (near the complex of Santo Stefano) was bought in 1734 by Cardinal Lambertini, a colorful and enlightened ecclesiastical figure who, before he became Pope Benedict XIV, was not above appearing on stage in the guise of Dottore Balanzone (a stock Bolognese character in the Commedia dell'Arte).

PALAZZO DELLA MERCANZIA. The Gothic building at the top of Via Santo Stefano is the Palazzo della Mercanzia, built by the municipal authorities as a chamber of commerce. It was started in 1384, but only the basic structure now survives from the original building.

SANTO STEFANO ★. This attractive religious complex, so-called because it stands on the site of a former abbey named after the first martyr, is made up of three churches, none of which, however, is now dedicated to Saint Stephen. Facing the complex from the piazza, on the right is the CHIESA DEL CROCIFISSO (originally built in the 10th century), in the center (built to a circular plan, probably a paleo-Christian baptistry ● 86) is the so-called SEPOLCRO, and on the left is the Romanesque-style church of SANTI VITALE E AGRICOLA. The cloisters and other buildings are situated behind these three buildings.

TO THE SOUTHWEST

Beyond the Archiginnasio, outside the grid plan of the Roman city, you will come to the piazza which is the site of the church and convent of San Domenico. Further west and just outside the medieval ring of *torresotti* is the building of San Francesco, also from the 13th century.

SAN DOMENICO. Built around 1230, the church was subsequently remodeled in Baroque style. The fascinating ARCA DI SAN DOMENICO – in the chapel dedicated to the saint – contains the body of the founder of the Dominicans, who died in Bologna in 1221. The marble tomb commissioned in 1265 from Nicola Pisano, who worked on it with his pupils, including Arnolfo di Cambio, is crowned by an ornamental lid (1469–73) which earned its sculptor, Niccolò da Bari, the nickname of Niccolò dell'Arca.

THE COLLEGIO DI SPAGNA
Near the Palazzo Sanuti-Bevilacqua stands the college and boarding school which used to house students of the Spanish nobility who came to study in Bologna. It was founded by the Spanish Cardinal Albornoz, who was papal legate from 1353 onward.

Two statuettes on the ornamental lid and the angel holding the candelabrum at the foot of the tomb, on the right, were sculpted by the young Michelangelo. Other noteworthy works include the *Marriage of Saint Catherine* by Filippino Lippi in the chapel to the right of the presbytery and the inlaid choir stalls dating from the mid 16th century.

PALAZZO SANUTI-BEVILACQUA. On Via d'Azeglio, which crosses Via Farini, stands the oldest and best-preserved of Bologna's senatorial palaces, now privately owned. Built in 1474–82, it is Renaissance in style, with a sandstone façade and a courtyard surrounded by a loggia.

PALAZZO ALBERGATI. This palace, which dates back to the first half of the 16th century, stands on Via Saragozza (nos. 26–28) which, near to Via d'Azeglio, wends its way down to the Arco del Meloncello. Its façade and porticos are attributed to Baldassarre Peruzzi.

SAN FRANCESCO. The apse visible on Piazza Malpighi alerts visitors to this church, built in 1236 to a French Gothic design – as can been seen by its flying buttresses and its ring of chapels. The sacristy is 14th century while the Chapel of San Bernardino is late Gothic. The valuable marble reredos was sculpted in 1392.

TOMBS OF THE GLOSSATORI
Piazza Malpighi, from which you can also see the outer wall of San Francesco's apse, is the site of the three fine raised tombs of the famous Glossators, Accursio (Accursius) with his son Francesco, Odofredo and Rolandino de'Romanzi, who were all jurists living in the 8th century. The term *glossatori* is derived from the Latin term *glossa*, which relates to the commentary of ancient Roman law. As *glossae* often differed, Accursius was given the task in 1248 of bringing them together in the *Magna Glossa* to help jurists who were unsure of the correct interpretation.

OUTSIDE THE GATES

Bologna extends into the plain toward the Apennine foothills. On one of these, La Guardia, (some 951 feet above the city) stands the elegant monument of the Madonna di San Luca, with its panoramic views. The lush greenery of the hills also provides a setting for the Monastery of San Michele. Lower down and closer to the city are other key places of interest, such as the exhibition district just north of the railroad station, and the monumental town cemetery, to the northwest, beyond the stadium.

FIERA DISTRICT. Bologna's exhibition and conference venues, built by the town in the 1960's, are concentrated around Piazza Costituzione. The earliest districts (by Leonardo Benevolo, 1967) in the Fiera di Bologna, were already

architecturally important, but the office district added between 1975 and 1984 by the Japanese architect, Kenzo Tange, a master of town-planning, has acquired international renown. Covering two piazzas, the Fiera district provides a contemporary interpretation of two traditional architectural motifs: the portico ● 77 and the tower ● 74.

SAN MICHELE IN BOSCO. Heading out from Porta Castiglione, you will come to the park surrounding the Church of San Michele in Bosco, with its Renaissance façade ascribed to Baldassarre Peruzzi and Biagio Rossetti ▲ 266, and its cloister decorated with frescos by Ludovico Carracci, Guido Reni and other Bolognese artists. A famous orthopedic hospital occupies what was once the adjoining convent.

ARCO DEL MELONCELLO. A remarkable ARCADE, almost 2½ miles long, composed of 666 arches and completed in 1715 after forty years of work, connects Porta Saragozza with the Sanctuary of Madonna di San Luca. Halfway along Via Saragozza, a picturesque arch (1732) designed by Carlo Francesco Dotti spans the street.

MADONNA DI SAN LUCA ★. The ARCADE of San Luca, also the work of Dotti, leads to this intricate sanctuary perched on the hilltop. Built in 1723–57, the form of this elegant, understated building is based upon the ellipse and the pentagon. This church keeps a portrait of the Virgin which is carried to Metropolitana di San Pietro once a year for the Assumption.

CIMITERO ALLA CERTOSA
After a Napoleonic edict prohibited burial in churches, Bologna consecrated the cloisters of the suppressed Carthusian convent as a cemetery. This cemetery contains tombs from different periods, including modern works such as the Monument to the Partisans (by Pietro Bottoni, 1959).

259

RAMPANT HORSE
After Parmesan cheese, probably the most famous Emilian product is Ferrari, founded in 1939, which has dominated the history of motor racing. In general, the whole of the Emilia-Romagna region is passionately interested in cars and has produced many talented mechanics. There are world-class race tracks in Imola (San Marino Grand Prix) and in Misano Adriatico.

FEDERICO THE GREAT
Emilia and Romagna have also produced some top creative movie-makers.

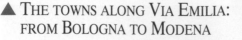

The master, Federico Fellini, came from Rimini, Michelangelo Antonioni and Carlo Rambaldi from Ferrara, Tonino Guerra from Santarcangelo di Romagna and Bernardo Bertolucci from Parma, to name but a few of the most famous.

A long stretch of the Po river marks the administrative border between Lombardy and Emilia-Romagna, with its capital Bologna. However, the river has never formed a hard and fast dividing line: plain and farmland, landscape and climate do not differ greatly north of the Po river, in the area of Lombardy around Mantua ▲ *264,* and south of the river. Although no precise geographical division actually exists, it may well be easier to pinpoint the border between the two regions of binomial Emilia-Romagna, which, from the Renaissance to Italian unification, have led completely separate political lives. While the towns which sprang up at intervals along the Via Emilia were ruled by great families (like the Este in Modena or the Farnese in Parma), Romagna, along with Bologna and Ferrara ▲ *265,* became part of the Stato della Chiesa. This difference in government has left its mark and, even now, it is not unusual to hear people distinguishing between the "ducal" region of Emilia and the former "legations", so-called because these cities were ruled by papal legates. However, common to the whole of the central and eastern Po valley – whether Lombard, Emilian or Romagnan – was the emergence, at the end of the Middle Ages, of many self-sufficient towns, favored by the richly fertile countryside ■ *20–21* and their strategic position with regard to communications and trade.

THE TOWNS ALONG VIA EMILIA

There are no prizes for guessing that the name of Emilia comes from the Via Aemilia, the long road connecting Rimini and Piacenza, built between 191 and 187 BC by the Roman consul Marcus Aemilius Lepidus. Along with the railroad and the highway, the consular road is still one of the main links between northern Italy and the rest of the country.
MODENA, AN INDEPENDENT COMMUNE. The largest town in Emilia and the historical rival of Bologna, Modena, ancient

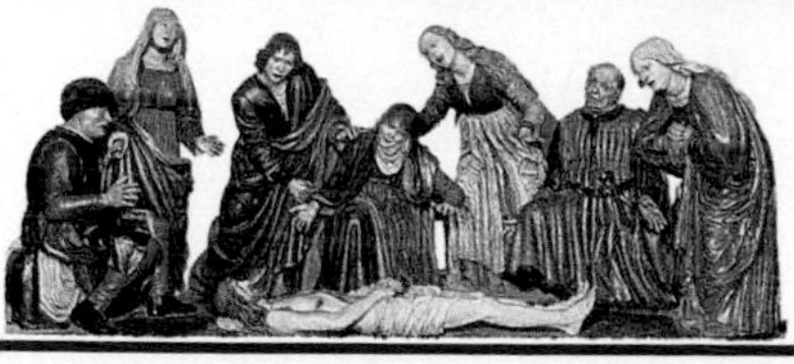

The *Descent from the Cross* (1476), a polychrome terracotta group by Guido Mazzoni in the church of San Giovanni Battista in Modena: the masterpiece of an artist whose work can also be seen in the town's cathedral.

Mutina, was the capital of the Este Duchy between 1598 and 1859, except in the Napoleonic period. Long famous for Lambrusco wine, balsamic vinegar and *zampone* (stuffed pig's trotter), it is now no less famous as the birthplace of Enzo Ferrari and Luciano Pavarotti. Another of the town's main attractions is the Military Academy, housed since 1862 in what was the 17th-century Palazzo Ducale degli Este. The town's skyline is dominated by the Ghirlandina, a bell tower which rises 282 feet beside the apse of the CATHEDRAL, the latter a superb example of Romanesque architecture begun in 1099 by Lanfranco and completed in the 14th century by the Campionese masters. The statues and reliefs (particularly *Scenes from the Book of Genesis* on the façade) carved in the early stages of construction by Wiligelmo, are remarkable for their depth of expression. Historically, the church is a symbol of the Po valley's civic independence (the Este, in fact, did not come to power in Modena until 1288), but the interior contains some later works of art, like the *Saint Sebastien* by Dosso Dossi (1522) along the left aisle and the *Madonna della Pappa*, a polychrome terracotta statue (1480) by Guido Mazzoni. The art collections are almost all housed in the Palazzo dei Musei on Piazzale San'Agostino. The most important of these museums is the GALLERIA ESTENSE, which contains art from the early Emilian and Veneto periods (Tommaso da Modena, Cosmè Tura, Dosso Dossi, Tintoretto, Veronese, Scarsellino, the Carracci family and Guido Reni) and a bust of Francis I carved in 1651 by Gianlorenzo Bernini. Another important institution is the Biblioteca Estense on the first floor of the Palazzo dei Musei, which has illuminated manuscripts from the 14th to 16th century.

LUCIANO PAVAROTTI
The Modenese singer, Luciano Pavarotti, is the finest exponent today of Italian bel canto in the tradition of Benjamino Gigli, Caruso and Di Stefano. Pavarotti's only difference is that he has combined his huge talent with a gift for promoting opera and projecting a love of spectacle, which has won him a worldwide audience.

THE BIBLE OF BORSO D'ESTE
The Biblioteca Estense in Modena also contains the *Bible of Borso d'Este*, which takes its name from the first Duke of that family. The Bible was illuminated for him (1455–62) by Taddeo Crivelli.

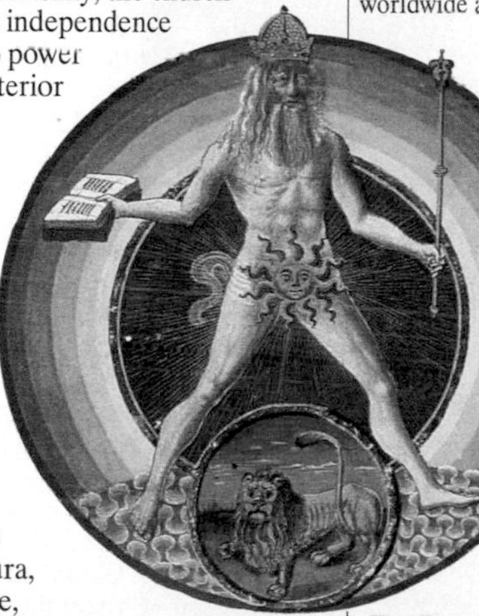

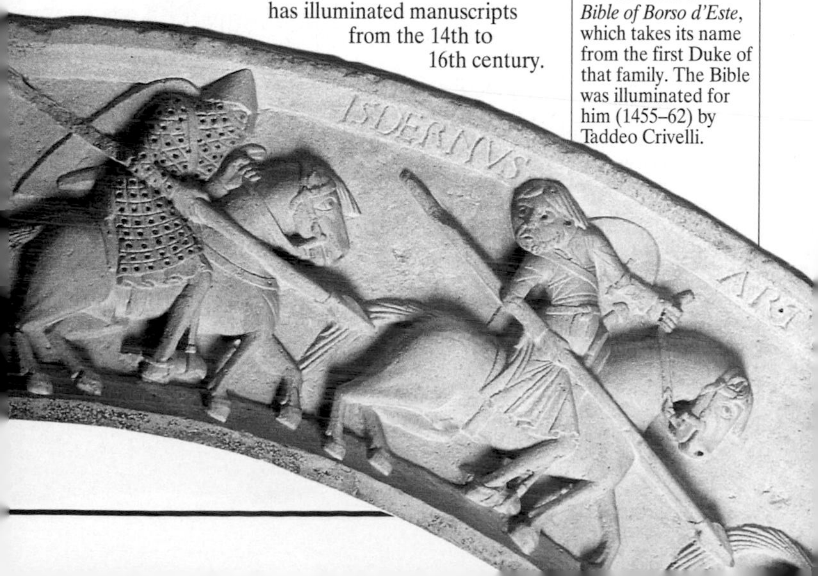

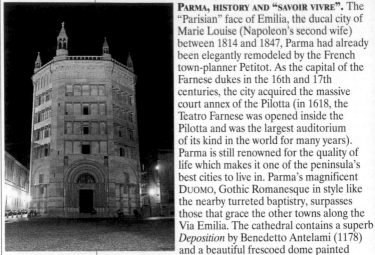

PARMA, HISTORY AND "SAVOIR VIVRE". The "Parisian" face of Emilia, the ducal city of Marie Louise (Napoleon's second wife) between 1814 and 1847, Parma had already been elegantly remodeled by the French town-planner Petitot. As the capital of the Farnese dukes in the 16th and 17th centuries, the city acquired the massive court annex of the Pilotta (in 1618, the Teatro Farnese was opened inside the Pilotta and was the largest auditorium of its kind in the world for many years). Parma is still renowned for the quality of life which makes it one of the peninsula's best cities to live in. Parma's magnificent DUOMO, Gothic Romanesque in style like the nearby turreted baptistry, surpasses those that grace the other towns along the Via Emilia. The cathedral contains a superb *Deposition* by Benedetto Antelami (1178) and a beautiful frescoed dome painted around 1530 by Correggio, which is remarkable for its rich colors and pioneering use of perspective. On the lower part of the exterior of the remarkable BAPTISTRY (in the niches), you can admire magnificent statues by Antelami which are generally regarded as masterpieces of Italian Romanesque sculpture and, inside, the 13th-century frescos in the dome and the other sculptures by Antelami, including the *Mesi* (months), the *Stagioni* (seasons) and the *Segni zodiacoli* (signs of the zodiac). Behind the Duomo, more frescos by Correggio can be found in the Church of SAN GIOVANNI EVANGELISTA (near the old Benedictine Pharmacy – "spezieria"), which dates from the Renaissance, as does the Church of the MADONNA DELLA STECCATA, the Farnese mausoleum, which can be seen clearly from the central thoroughfare of Strada Garibaldi (the site of the Teatro Regio, the neoclassical "temple" of opera). In between the Steccata and the Torrente Parma, stands the PALAZZO DELLA PILOTTA, looming impressively over the city. The museums which it now houses include the remarkable National Archeology Museum with finds unearthed at the 1760 excavations of Roman *Velleia* (between Parma

VERDI AND TOSCANINI Giuseppe Verdi, one of the most important Italian composers, was born at Roncole di Busseto, some 19 miles from Parma.

The house where he was born can be visited, as can Toscanini's house in Parma itself (on Via Tanzi) ▲ *190*, which contains writings, mementos and paintings of the famous conductor. The Regio di Parma is one of the most important opera houses in the country.

> **"FROM PIACENZA TO RIMINI [YOU ARE GREETED BY] THE HUMAN SPECTACLE OF WORKING-CLASS LIFE WHICH STILL COMBINES STRONG PASSION WITH A WARM AND JOYOUS COURTESY."**
>
> RICCARDO BACCHELLI

and Piacenza, some 19 miles west of the Via Emilia); and the GALLERIA NAZIONALE (with works by Correggio, Parmigianino, Van Dyck, Canaletto, Tiepolo and Piazzetta).

The Camera di San Paolo, on nearby Via Melloni, has other famous frescos by Correggio.

PIACENZA, THE FIRST FARNESE CAPITAL. Piacenza, ancient *Placentia*, the first capital of the Farnese Duchy of Parma and Piacenza (the court was moved in 1556), is certainly the least Emilian of all the cities in Emilia and only separated from Lombardy by the Po river. On the other side of the barricade of large installations along the Po river that hide the historical nucleus, stands the incomplete but attractive massive brick structure of the Palazzo Farnese and, in the heart of the city, Piazza Cavalli, the focus of all the city's main roads. This square is the site of the Palazzo del Comune, nicknamed IL GOTICO, and the EQUESTRIAN MONUMENTS to Duke Alessandro (left) and Ranuccio (his son, on the right), dating from 1620–5 which commemorate its Farnese rulers. Of interest are the DUOMO, a Romanesque building from the 12th–13th century, the Romanesque basilicas of San Savino and Sant'Antonino, the GALLERIA DI ARTE MODERNA RICCI-ODDI (with a collection largely of Italian paintings from the Romantic era to the 20th century) and – further away but still within the city walls – the Renaissance MADONNA DI CAMPAGNA, with its collection of paintings by Pordenone. Along the Via Emilia in the direction of Parma, the Galleria Alberoni boasts an extremely beautiful *Ecce Homo* by Antonello da Messina.

BETWEEN EMILIA AND LOMBARDY

Another of the powerful ruling families in northern Italy was the Gonzaga, who ruled Mantua and Piedmontese Monferrato. From the 14th to the 18th century, the Gonzaga succeeded in blocking the expansionism of Visconti-ruled Milan and in withstanding the might of the great European powers, made Mantua the learned capital of a stable, independent and highly respected Lombard duchy.

THE FARNESE
Pope Paul III created the new duchy of Parma and Piacenza in 1545 for his son, Pier Luigi Farnese, from territory which at the time came under papal authority. A few years later, due to the marriage of his successor, Ottavio, to the daughter of Emperor Charles V, the family became part of the ruling aristocracy of the Western Roman Empire. The fortunes of the Farnese of Parma reached their apogee between the 16th and 17th centuries.

LA CAMERA DEGLI SPOSI
The north tower of the Castello di San Giorgio, part of Mantua's Palazzo Ducale, contains the "Camera degli Sposi". This is the room in which Andrea Mantegna's frescos (1465–74) depict scenes from the life of Ludovico Gonzaga and his family.

MANTUA'S HISTORICAL SQUARES. Some 9 miles before it converges with the Po river, the Mincio river forms the vast lake system which encloses Mantua and provides its natural setting. Between the three lakes, the extensive historical center boasts a fascinating mix of neoclassical, Renaissance and medieval architecture. Time appears to have stood still in the huge Piazza Sordello, lined by the massive bulk of the PALAZZO DUCALE ★ on one side and enclosed on the other by the DUOMO. The palazzo complex is more like a city within a city than a single building, comprising palaces, churches and inner squares enclosed between gardens and porticos. Important works (apart from Mantegna's frescos in the Camera degli Sposi) include a series by Pisanello and tapestries designed by Raphael. The Duomo was founded in the Middle Ages and preserves a Romanesque campanile, but has a 16th-century interior by Giulio Romano and an 18th-century façade. A short distance away is the second largest historical square in Mantua, the PIAZZA DELLE ERBE, which is the site of the medieval Rotonda di San Lorenzo (11th century), the 15th-century clock tower, the Palazzo della Ragione (13th century, but restored) and the Palazzo del Podestà, remodeled in the 15th century. The nearby arcades of Via Broletto stand adjacent to the city's most important church, SANT'ANDREA, a remarkable building started in 1472, and only completed in the mid 18th century. The splendid interior contains the chapel where Mantegna is buried. Among Mantua's many other historical buildings are the remarkable PALAZZO TE ★, the suburban villa of Federico II Gonzaga, built between 1525 and 1535 by Giulio Romano and regarded as his masterpiece. Many of the rooms in the four sections of the building

> **"A** DELICATE VEIL OF MIST SHROUDS [MANTUA'S] SKYLINE COMPLETELY, RENDERING ALL COLORS DULL AND FADED.**"**
>
> NINO GIANNANTONI

surrounding the courtyard contain grotesque figures and frescos dealing with mythological and profane subjects.

SABBIONETA: THE "LITTLE ATHENS" OF THE 16TH CENTURY ★. In the second half of the 16th century, Vespasiano Gonzaga, a brilliant man-at-arms from a younger branch of the great family, built a small "ideal city" not far from the Po river, whose rational layout reflected its founder's humanistic philosophy. Sabbioneta's reputation as a "Little Athens" rests particularly on the beautiful TEATRO OLIMPICO, a masterpiece by Vincenzo Scamozzi of 1588 and the PALAZZO DUCALE that towers over the piazza and whose interior boasts inlaid ceilings, trompe-l'oeil frescos and equestrian statues. The chapel by Antonio Bibiena in the parish church, the octagonal church of the Incoronata and the series of rooms with grotesque figures and frescos in the Palazzo del Giardino are also extremely beautiful.

THE FERRARA REGION

This region gives evidence of an ancient civilization, as can be seen by the Roman centuriation ● *80* of the countryside, the ancient Abbazia di Pomposa ▲ *267*, the medieval and Renaissance architecture of Ferrara and the region's close links with *La Serenissima*, north of the Po delta.

FERRARA, A MONUMENT TO THE MIDDLE AGES AND THE RENAISSANCE. Popularly regarded as the most beautiful city in Emilia-Romagna, Ferrara is indebted to its former rulers, the Este family, for many of the town's treasures, for its long tradition of civic tolerance (it welcomed Ariosto, among others), and for its remarkable urban layout. The long straight thoroughfare formed by Viale Cavour and Corso della Giovecca cuts through the center of the city. In the medieval districts to the south are the huge CATHEDRAL of Romanesque origin (1135), and many picturesque streets such as VIA DELLE VOLTE; but the highest concentration of monuments can be found in the quadrant of the city behind the cathedral. This is the site of the 13th-century Church of San Francesco, renovated in 1494 by Rossetti; the nearby 15th-century Casa Romei; the PALAZZO SCHIFANOIA, also remodeled by Rossetti, whose interior has frescos

TAZIO NUVOLARI (1892–1953)
The nickname of this famous racing driver was the "flying Mantuan". His trophies and mementos are on display in the small museum dedicated to him next to the Piazza delle Erbe in Mantua.

FERRARAN TREASURES
Cosmè Tura, Carpaccio, Gentile da Fabriano and Mantegna are some of the artists whose works form part of an ever-expanding collection, started in 1836 and kept in the Palazzo dei Diamanti in Ferrara.

LUDOVICO ARIOSTO
The poet who wrote *Orlando Furioso* lived in Ferrara from 1525 to 1533, in a house whose address is now 67 Via Ariosto. Here he worked for Alfonso d'Este, studied, wrote poetry and prepared stage works. His peaceful life and his affection for his home can be seen by the famous Latin epigraph over the door, which in English declares: "Small but suited to me, not indebted to anyone, not poor and yet built with my own money."

showing mythological and court scenes by Francesco del Cossa and Ercole de'Roberti; the Palazzo di Ludovico il Moro, also by Rossetti, which is now the seat of the excellent MUSEO ARCHEOLOGICO NAZIONALE (National Archeological Museum) that contains Etruscan finds from Spina; and last but not least, the Palazzina di Marfisa on Corso della Giovecca, which was the home of Princess Marfisa d'Este in the late 1500's. On the other side of the massive, turreted CASTELLO ESTENSE, built between the 14th and 15th centuries, is the more regular, spacious and stately northern part of Ferrara. This is, in fact, the result of an urban improvement program (the so-called HERCULEAN ADDITION, commissioned by Duke Ercole I in 1492 and carried out by Biagio Rossetti), which doubled medieval Ferrara, making Corso della Giovecca into a kind of axis of rotation. The pivotal point

of this "half-city" is the corner of Corso Porta Mare and Corso Ercole d'Este, the site of the PALAZZO DEI DIAMANTI. This palace, one of the most interesting buildings of the Italian Renaissance, with its 8,500 diamond-shaped ashlar stones, houses the Pinacoteca Nazionale (National Art Gallery).

THE TRANQUIL SILENCE OF THE PO DELTA. Traveling down the waterways remains the best possible way to explore the wetlands of the Po delta, a vast almost triangular area of 215 square miles. Formed by the longest river in Italy, it has been advancing into the Adriatic Sea for over 2,000 years. Boat trips into the Riserva Naturale Bocche di Po, along the outer edge of the delta, are enjoyable and highly recommended.

Fishing in the wetlands and (inset) a little egret. This bird is a common sight on the Po delta.

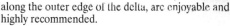

ROMAGNA

RAVENNA, A CITY RICH IN MOSAICS. The small city of Ravenna which, almost 16 centuries ago, was chosen as the capital of the Western Roman Empire, is one of the oldest in the Romagna region and still retains some ancient buildings. The instability caused by the Barbarian invasions and the formation of precarious Barbarian-Roman kingdoms did not stop the daughter of Emperor Theodosius, Galla Placidia, and later the Barbarian-Roman kings, Odoacer and Theodoric, embellishing it with beautiful buildings, often decorated by mosaics ▲ 268. In 553, the Byzantine emperor, Justinian, reconquered Italy and Ravenna acquired more fine buildings and mosaics. The city center, which still reflects the layout of the medieval road network, boasts the 17th-century Palazzo Comunale, the Duomo (5th century, but remodeled in Baroque style in the 18th century, with the Archiepiscopal Museum) and, next to the cathedral, the octagonal, early medieval NEONIAN BAPTISTRY, with its mosaics ▲ 268. Further out, but a must for any visitor to the city, are the Basilica di SAN VITALE and the nearby TOMB OF GALLA PLACIDIA, 5th- and 6th-century buildings whose interiors are richly decorated with fabulous mosaics. The former Benedictine monastery of San Vitale houses the National Museum, with

POMPOSA'S CHARM
Heading toward the coast from Ferrara, you will join the Roman road that connects Ravenna with the Venetian Lagoon. Here, the architecture of Ravenna is echoed by the lofty Lombard campanile of the Abbazia di Pomposa, founded in the 8th century as a Benedictine monastery and suppressed in the

17th century due to a malaria epidemic. This delightful complex has a fine atrium adorned with terracotta ornaments and 14th-century frescos by Vitale da Bologna.

267

THE MOSAICS OF RAVENNA

Forming a very valuable artistic heritage, due to their thematic richness and compositional quality, these mosaics were used in the 5th and 6th centuries to decorate walls, vaults, the domes of basilicas and baptistries. The mosaics also form part of the historical record of Ravenna, which was ruled respectively by the Romans, the Barbarians and the Byzantines for over seven centuries.

"IL CORTEO DELLE VERGINI" (c. 560)
On the left wall of the central nave of Sant'Apollinare Nuovo, built in the 5th century by Theodoric and dedicated to the Catholic religion in the 6th century, the long procession of virgins, similar to that of the 26 martyrs on the right wall, reveals the transition from the Hellenistic-Roman style with scenes of characters and landscapes to the more abstract tendencies of Byzantine art, which favored stylized figures against a gold background.

"CRISTO REDENTORE"
(first half of the 6th century)
Sitting on a blue globe, the Redeemer, surrounded by archangels, offers the crown of martyrdom to San Vitale and receives a model of the church from the Bishop. The mosaics of the Basilica di San Vitale, characterized by naturalistic elements, are perhaps the final manifestation of Roman culture.

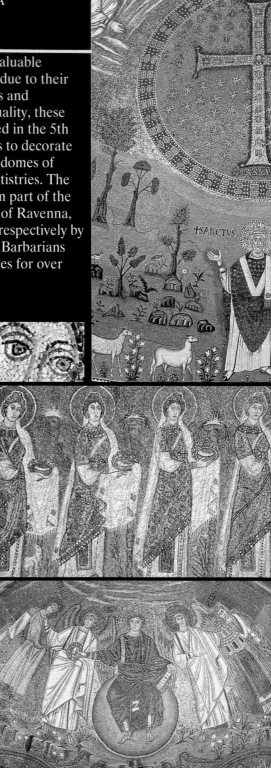

"Colombe che si abbeverano" (Drinking Doves) (425–450. Tomb of Galla Placidia). Like the stags drinking from the fountain of life, the doves symbolize the soul drinking from the true faith and the water of eternal life.

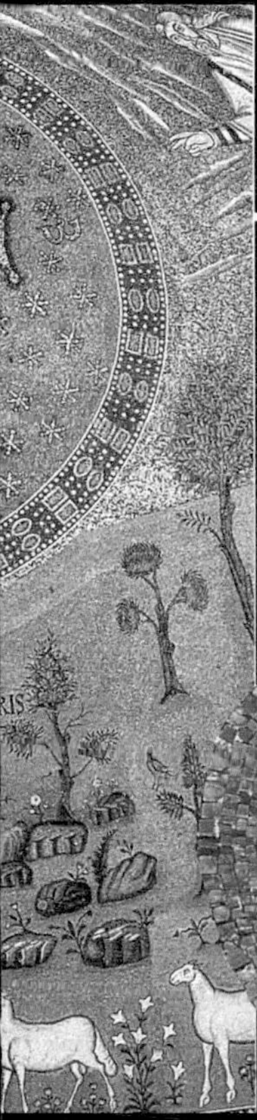

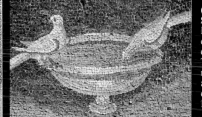

"Il Buon Pastore" (The Good Shepherd)
Lunette over the entrance to the tomb of Galla Placidia. These mosaics, a marvel of rich color and attention to detail, are a legacy of Roman figurative art.

ransfiguration"
h century)
e bowl-shaped vault of the
se of Sant'Apollinare in
asse. In this allegorical
ion, Christ is represented
a large Latin cross within a
r-studded blue circle.
low the cross, at the center
a meadow scattered with
ks, flowers, grass, plants
l trees, an allegory of
radise, is Sant'Apollinare,
ssed as a Bishop and
ying in the midst of 12
ite lambs which represent
faithful.

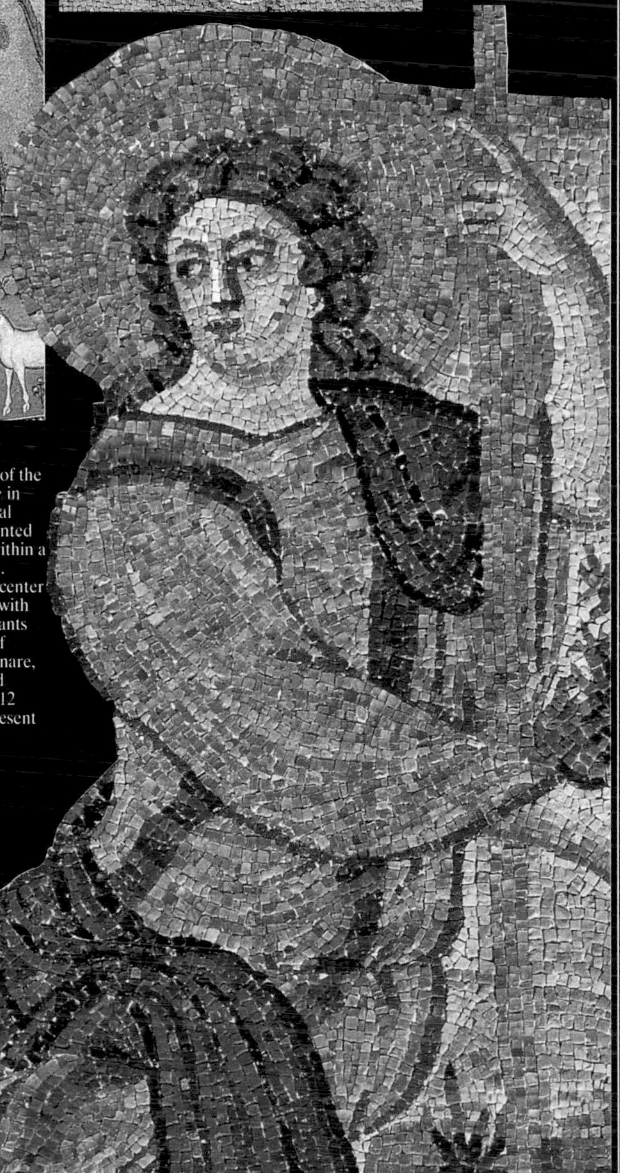

The ivory throne of Maximian, from the 6th century, in the Archiepiscopal Museum in Ravenna.

SAN MARINO AND SANTARCANGELO
Some 12 miles from Rimini, San Marino is a small, foreign, independent Republic, founded ten centuries ago, perched high on the slopes of Monte Titano. Santarcangelo di Romagna, however, which clings to the slopes of the nearby Monte Giove, is an historical town famous for its medieval center, its 15th-century Rocca dei Malatesta, the ancient game of Il Tamburello and the International Theater Festival held there every July.

its Roman and paleo-Christian artefacts. Another of Ravenna's famous churches is SANT'APOLLINARE NUOVO, built by Theodoric between the 5th and 6th centuries, and graced with the original mosaics. SANT'APOLLINARE IN CLASSE, outside the city, is dedicated to the same saint and dates from a similar period. This church stands near the site of the former port of Classis, built by Augustus. The MAUSOLEO DI TEODORICO is on the northern outskirts of the city. It was built using huge slabs of stone from Istria and is almost a symbol of the Barbarian-Roman kings.

FAENZA, THE POTTERY CENTER. To find out why the word *faience* is universally synonymous with decorated pottery, visit Faenza's MUSEO INTERNAZIONALE DELLE CERAMICHE, which pays tribute to the great local manufacturing tradition, showcasing a remarkable range of majolica, porcelain, glazed terracotta and pottery from all periods and countries in almost forty rooms. Aside from the ceramic industry, Faenza is well worth a visit in its own rights. Of particular interest is the central Piazza del Popolo, with its 15th-century CATHEDRAL designed by Giuliano da Maiano and the many historic streets around it.

RIMINI, CITY OF ART AND HOLIDAY RESORT. Rimini, a popular holiday resort with beaches lapped by the Adriatic Sea, is also within easy reach of the delightful inland hills which are the site of San Marino and Santarcangelo di Romagna. For all its tourist trappings, the city still preserves traces of Roman *Ariminum* (like the remains of the AMPHITHEATER, or the elegant ARCH OF AUGUSTUS which marked the junction of the Via Emilia with the Via Flaminia ▲ *248*) as well as vestiges of the time it was ruled by the Malatesta. The TEMPIO MALATESTIANO ★ erected in honor of the ruler's mistress, Isotta, is the most important monument from this period. This temple was designed (1477–60) by Leon Battista Alberti as an external shell to be dropped down over an earlier Gothic Romanesque Franciscan church. The building also has an attractive interior, with sculptures by Agostino di Duccio and a damaged fresco by Piero della Francesca.

THE ADRIATIC RIVIERA
This has been a prime tourist destination for decades. From the north to south of Rimini, all beach resorts, however small, offer a range of facilities which may vary considerably in price, but are always extremely efficient and competitive.

FLORENCE AND THE REGIONS OF TUSCANY

The distinctive blend of history, culture, art and landscape which has assured the universal fame of Tuscany and its capital has been thousands of years in the making. The itineraries suggested in this chapter will explore all aspects of this age-old civilization, starting with unique Florence and its most beautiful neighbor, Fiesole, then heading toward the sea, stopping at Prato, with its castle built by Frederick II; Pistoia, whose Church of Sant'Andrea contains a pulpit by Giovanni Pisano that would be enough to justify a visit alone; Lucca, an exquisite gem encircled by 15th–16th-century ramparts; and Pisa (59 miles from Florence), a city of art which has a great deal more to offer than just its noted Piazza del

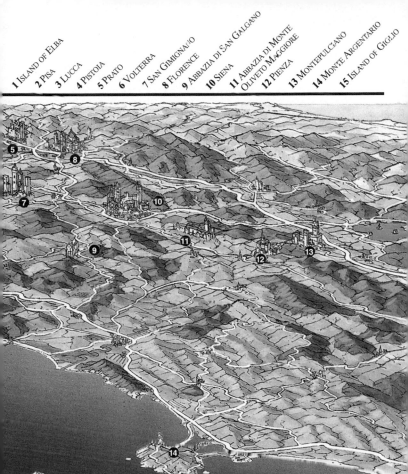

Duomo. In the
Tyrrhenian Sea, that the dashing city of Pisa
dominated until the Battle of Meloria (1284),
when it was defeated by Genoa, are the island
resorts of the Tuscan Archipelago while, in the
heart of the region, we will visit three fine
communes: the austere Volterra, the turreted
San Gimignano and Siena, described by Taine
as a "medieval Pompeii". The historical abbey
of Monte Oliveto Maggiore and the dramatic
ruins of San Galgano are followed by two pearls
of southeastern Tuscany: Pienza, the
sophisticated creation of Renaissance
Humanism, and Montepulciano, the furthest
city from Florence (88 miles away), an enclave
of Florentine style in the Siena province.

> "The air sparkled
> above the chalky
> banks, the dry grasses
> trembled and
> shimmered; the cars
> on the road, hidden
> from my sight, sent
> up long plumes of
> dust which barely
> rose above the diners.
> This dust looked
> yellow; but, gradually
> dispersing, it began to
> sparkle just as it was
> about to disappear
> completely."
>
> Federigo Tozzi,
> *Bestie (Beasts)*

273

In the 9th century BC, Villanovans settled on the site where the Arno river meets the Mugnone, but it was not until the Romans settled there that this area began to look like a real city. The navigability of the Arno and the colony's close proximity to the Via Cassia favored the growth of *Florentia* which, by the 3rd century, numbered over 10,000 inhabitants. Byzantines and Lombards in turn ruled this small city, whose intellectual and economic dignity was restored by the Carolingian dynasty. In 1173, the city's growth required construction of a new circle of walls.

"ALTA FIOR SEMPRE GRANATA" (NOBLE FLOWER FOREVER STRONG). In the 13th century, despite bitter conflict between Guelph and Ghibelline factions and strife between the wealthy merchant classes and poorer lower classes, the city's supremacy was assured by its success in trade and banking, which in turn led to a surge of building activity and a general opening up to culture: Florence was described as a *"pomegranate tree"*, overflowing with fruit, by the poet Guittone d'Arezzo (1235–94). Over the brief space of a century, the city became a hotbed of new ideas and artistic development, in which Cimabue, Arnolfo di Cambio and the poets of the new style worked side by side, fired by a passion for innovation. The reins of government were held even more firmly by the merchants and the artisans, who had formed guilds called Arti.

"SFIORATA FIORE" (FADED FLOWER). Dreams of expansion were dashed in the 14th century: the plague of 1348, immortalized by Boccaccio in the *Decameron*, was the most serious in a succession of disastrous events

MONEY AND BUILDING SITES
In 1252, the city began to mint its own gold coin, the florin, and the Florentine moneylenders dominated the European money market: between 1296 and 1299, this wealth was used to build the Palazzo della Signoria and the Duomo which, being financed by the City and not the Church, became a proud symbol of the city's new identity.

> **"I SAW DANTE, PETRARCH, MACHIAVELLI, PAZZI, POLITAN, MICHELANGELO AND THOUSANDS OF OTHERS GAZING OUT FROM THE WINDOWS OF THE GLOOMY PALACES WHICH LINE THE STREETS AND BLOCK OUT THEIR LIGHT."**
>
> ALPHONSE DE LAMARTINE

(the fire of 1306, the famine of 1315–17, the flood of 1333) which decimated the population and seriously damaged the economy. However, this was also the century in which Dante and Giotto developed a new language, revolutionizing poetry and painting, and in which, soon after, Boccaccio wrote his deeply realistic and insightful "human comedy". In the last twenty-five years of the century, however, the winds of change began to blow: there was renewed interest in *studia humanitatis* or "studies of humanity", when Florence became the cradle of civic Humanism after the failure of the rising of the *Ciompi*, the wool-carders (1378), and embraced Republican freedom. The future looked bright, with economic recovery and territorial expansion paving the way for the enlightened 15th century and the Renaissance with Brunelleschi, Donatello and Masaccio.

THE MEDICI ERA. Infighting within the oligarchy of bankers and merchants contributed to the rise to power (1434) of Cosimo de' Medici (Cosimo the Elder) who handed his family three centuries of power over the city, although this dominion was not always peaceful or glorious. Under his son, Lorenzo, nicknamed Il Magnifico (1449–92), Platonic Humanism and the Renaissance flourished in a variety of different forms: the new ruler's charismatic personality and reputation for learning acted as a catalyst for the most prolific intellectual and artistic movement ever witnessed in Italy. Private commissions began to play a more influential role and this was symbolized in architecture by the palazzo ▲ *286*. The censorious sermons of Fra Girolamo Savonarola in the last years of the 15th century paved the way for the restoration of the Republic. During this brief Republican interlude, Florence welcomed the return of Leonardo and Michelangelo, the inspired theories of Machiavelli, the arrival of the young Raphael and, after 1520, the Mannerism of Pontormo and Rosso Fiorentino. Cosimo I came to power in 1537 under the Spanish aegis and in 1569 became the first Grand Duke of Tuscany. He left the stamp of his own brand of absolutism on the

THE PRIORS
The priors, or "masters" of the Florentine Arti in 1293 held the political, legal and diplomatic reins of the city. Their term of office lasted only two months and they were not permitted to give private audiences.

THE "BONFIRE OF THE VANITIES"
To encourage the Florentines to cleanse themselves, Savonarola built a pyre in the Piazza della Signoria where jewels, books, precious objects and works of art that were considered too "pagan" were put to the flame. His terrible prophecies and attacks on corruption, after inflaming the people, eventually led to his own execution: on May 23, 1498, the friar was burned to death in the very same square.

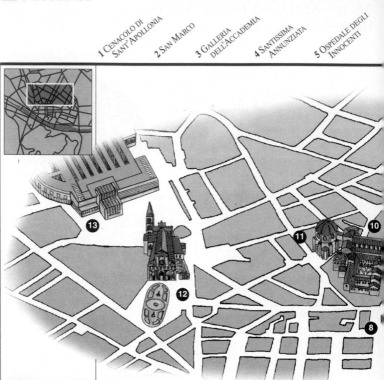

PIETRO LEOPOLDO
Grand Duke Pietro Leopoldo, the future Emperor Leopold II, was an enlightened sovereign and, during his reign (1765–90), Florence became one of Italy's new cultural beacons: in deference to the theories of laissez-faire, he abolished constraints on the export of grain outside the Grand Duchy as well as those relating to the transfer of real estate. He also restructured the fiscal system, initiated a reform of criminal legislation, abolishing torture and the death penalty, and encouraged studies in economy and agriculture at the Accademia dei Georgofili.

city (which had a population of 60,000) when he commissioned Vasari to build the Uffizi and convert the Palazzo Vecchio into a ducal palace. His reign coincided with the final years of the city's supremacy; by the 17th century, the finest art was being produced outside Florence and only the frontiers of science were being pushed back by the discoveries of a physicist from Tuscany, Galileo Galilei ▲ *298*.

ENLIGHTENED GOVERNMENT. After the fall of the Medici dynasty, in 1737 the power passed into the hands of the Grand Dukes of Lorraine who, influenced by the progressive ideas of the *philosophes* and the "Age of Enlightenment", launched a far-reaching economic, administrative and civic reform program. After the Vienna Congress, the climate of tolerance inherited from the Enlightenment made Florence an ideal meeting place for moderate liberals, whose discussions led to the birth of the *Antologia*, the most important Italian review of the Risorgimento. Leopold II, the last Grand Duke, also initiated an artistic revival.

CAPITAL OF ITALY. Proclaimed capital of Italy in 1865 (which it remained until 1870), Florence's new role called for an urgent facelift. The city initiated an extensive building program to make use of the surrounding land and hills: the 14th-century walls were replaced by ring roads, the *lungarni* (roads following the banks of the Arno river) were laid out and the Piazzale Michelangiolo and the Viale dei Colli were built ▲ *293*. The program for clearing the center continued after 1871, when the Mercato Vecchio, the Ghetto and various buildings once owned by the nobility were demolished; with the dawning of the new century, the role of tourism became more decisive; no longer an elitist pastime, as had been the case with the 18th-century Grand Tour, tourism was identifying Florence as one of the most important places to visit in Italy. Within this social and environmental context, the city developed for many years in an uncontrolled and fairly disorganized fashion. This was to continue even after the disastrous flooding of the Arno river in 1966 ▲ *292* which seriously damaged the city's artistic heritage along with the churches and museums in which it was kept.

THE PRESENT DAY. Over six million tourists visit Florence every year and this has caused the service sector to expand, with all the attendant problems of heavy traffic and overcrowded streets. Nevertheless, this Tuscan capital, whose emblem is the fleur-de-lys, is still a remarkably lively cultural and social center and the seat of various Italian and foreign universities and cultural institutes.

THE MUSEO DI FIRENZE COM'ERA
Housed in the former Oblate convent at Via dell'Oriuolo 24, the museum of Florence As It Was illustrates the changing face of the city over the centuries. Among the various documents and accounts are the twelve remarkable *Vedute delle Ville Medicee* (1599) by the Flemish painter, Giusto Utens, which depict the architecture and gardens of the Grand Duke's villas around Florence ● *80*.

FILIPPO BRUNELLESCHI
The most innovative young Florentine artist in the first half of the 15th century was Brunelleschi, who used classical principles to create new and exciting forms, full of harmony and beauty; he was not only responsible for bringing Renaissance ideals to bear on architecture but also for rediscovering perspective and providing artists with the mathematical means to achieve it ▲ *289*, a discovery that was destined to dominate art for centuries to come.

PIAZZA DEL DUOMO

The two squares, Piazza del Duomo and Piazza di San Giovanni, which surround the Duomo and the baptistry, did not acquire their present aspect until the 19th century.

BAPTISTRY OF SAN GIOVANNI ★. Reconsecrated in 1059, this may well be the oldest religious building in the city. The clear-cut lines of its octagonal shape are emphasized by the green and white striped geometric design of the exterior marble facing. This Florentine Romanesque building shows an obvious classical influence in its windows with their triangular and curvilinear pediments and in its interior. It is richly decorated with 13th-century mosaics in the apse and has bronze doors adorned with biblical figures by Andrea Pisano and Lorenzo Ghiberti ▲ *295*.

DUOMO (SANTA MARIA DEL FIORE). Not only was the cupola of the Duomo an inspired architectural achievement, it was also a symbol of Florence's great ambitions. The indefatigable Arnolfo (who designed the Duomo and began work on it in 1296) and Francesco Talenti (who continued it in 1357) had bequeathed the Florentines a magnificent church but one that lacked a cupola. The solution to this challenging problem became Brunelleschi's life work. Drawing on his enthusiastic research into Roman architecture, he resolved the difficulties

it posed with two extremely daring innovations: the abolition of the centering (the traditional armature or huge wooden skeletal framework) and the construction of a self-supporting double vault with a usable space between the two shells; all this without, however, undermining Arnolfo's original inspiration, which was based on a skillful marriage of Gothic elements (ogival arches, tall two-light windows) with extended, harmonious and brightly lit spaces that, like the cupola, were evocative of classical buildings.

GIOTTO'S CAMPANILE ★. Giotto was responsible for the design and the first floor; Andrea Pisano continued the work up to the second cornice, and Francesco Talenti completed it, replacing the pyramidal apex of the original design with a horizontal crowning ● *86*. Giotto's design was totally original compared to traditional models: the tall building is defined by

> **"SUCH A LOFTY CONSTRUCTION [THE DOME], HIGHER THAN THE SKY ITSELF, SO HUGE THAT IT CASTS ITS PROTECTIVE SHADOW OVER ALL THE PEOPLE OF TUSCANY."** LEON BATTISTA ALBERTI

corner buttresses and lightened by two rows of two-light windows and one large three-mullioned window at the top.
MUSEO DELL'OPERA DEL DUOMO. This museum presents an assortment of Florentine sculpture from the late 13th century to the 15th century, with original works that once adorned the Duomo, the baptistry and the campanile: statues from the old façade of the cathedral (Arnolfo di Cambio, Donatello, Nanni di Banco); Michelangelo's uncompleted *Pietà*; the two *cantorie* (marble choir balconies) by Luca della Robbia and Donatello; panels (Andrea Pisano, Luca della Robbia) and statues (Andrea Pisano, Donatello, Nanni di Bartolo) from the campanile and the anguished wooden *Mary Magdalen* by Donatello (who also sculpted the statue of *Habakkuk*).

A MEDICI ENCLAVE

Between the 15th and 16th centuries, the area north of the Duomo was transformed into a Medici enclave with their family palace (owned by the Riccardi family after 1659), the complex of San Lorenzo, the monastery of San Marco and other minor buildings.
PALAZZO MEDICI-RICCARDI. After Cosimo rejected Brunelleschi's overly bold designs, he gave the commission (1444–62) to Michelozzo, who created the prototype of the aristocratic palace in Renaissance Tuscany ▲ *286*. Traditional medieval motifs were given a new lease of life by the geometric design of the building, its rhythmic rows of windows, the repetition of the horizontal lines and the use of different facings (rusticated stone, smooth stone, plain brick) to emphasize the progression of the three floors.
SAN LORENZO. The simple gray stone façade gives no indication of the magnificent interior of this basilica (1420–70), a symbol of the vast power of the Medici who could lay claim to an entire church rather than the

▲ *286*

THE OPERA DEL DUOMO
This was an executive organization, consisting of four representatives from the commune and two from the Arte della Lana (the wool merchants' guild that financed the project), responsible both for the construction of the Duomo and its maintenance, an activity in which it is still involved to this day.

"ZUCCONE"
The Prophet Habakkuk, carved by Donatello for the campanile of the Duomo, is now kept in the Museo dell'Opera: the artist created a figure so realistic that, as the story goes, he kicked it, exclaiming "Say something, you idiot!"; perhaps this is why Florentines still call it "Lo Zuccone" (*The Dunce*).

279

conventional family chapel. Its ground plan was designed by Brunelleschi in accordance with strict laws of proportion and perspective. The same relentlessly logical approach is apparent in the plan of the Old Sacristy (1421–6), a simple cube-shaped room topped by a vaulted dome: the purity of the geometric forms is offset by the dark moldings and stucco ornaments by Donatello, which were not to Brunelleschi's liking, however, as they disrupted the architectural harmony.

MEDICI CHAPELS ★. Michelangelo had taken the rejection of his design for the façade of San Lorenzo as a personal affront. As a result, almost as if to compensate the artist for four years of hard work, the commissioners, Leo X and Giulio de' Medici, asked him in 1520 to build the new Sacristy, a funerary chapel for the family of Lorenzo Il Magnifico. Its structural plan and the use of gray stone is in clear homage to Brunelleschi, but here pure geometry is replaced by a more versatile, monumental style of architecture, suitable both for glorifying the Medici dynasty and for the individual tombs of the young dukes, Lorenzo and Giuliano (respectively the grandson and third son of Il Magnifico). These statues, with their qualities of virtue and solitude, resemble classical heroes facing their inevitable fate. The opulent octagonal mausoleum known as the Chapel of the Princes was built later (1640) by Matteo Nigetti under San Lorenzo's impressive dome. Entirely faced with porphyry, rare granite and semi-precious stones provided by the Opificio delle Pietre Dure, this was the most lavish example of Florentine Baroque and the last monument to the glory of the Grand Dukes.

> "THE GREATEST ARTIST HAS NO SINGLE CONCEPT
> WHICH A ROUGH MARBLE BLOCK DOES NOT CONTAIN
> ALREADY IN ITS CORE: THAT CAN ONLY BE ATTAINED
> BY A HAND THAT SERVES THE INTELLECT."
>
> MICHELANGELO, SONNET 83

AROUND PIAZZA DELLA REPUBBLICA

This piazza was the nucleus of the Roman city, whose orthogonal plan can still be glimpsed in the surrounding road system which "survived" Giuseppe Poggi's urban improvement program in the late 19th century.

VIA DEI CALZAIUOLI. This busy street connecting the two most important monuments in Florence is one such product of that 19th-century improvement program: its name is all that remains of its medieval past.

PIAZZA DELLA REPUBBLICA. This vast empty square bears eloquent witness to the creative poverty of the 1881 program, which demolished the old Mercato Vecchio (built over the Roman Forum) to make it bigger and more "decorous".

ORSANMICHELE. An almost unique example in Florence of the influence of the ornamental style of European late Gothic, this building replaced the former Loggia of the Grain Market (Arnolfo di Cambio, 1290). Its upper level, with high vaults and windows, was used as a storehouse; the lower level, after the arcades with their elegant three-mullioned windows with interwoven arches were bricked up, became a church dedicated to the Virgin. The niches on the exterior contain 15th-century statues of the patron saints of the Arti.

PALAZZO DAVANZATI. The period rooms of this elegant 14th-century palace and the Museo della Casa Fiorentina (housed here since 1956), recreate the atmosphere of daily life in a medieval nobleman's palace.

PIAZZA DELLA SIGNORIA ★

As in Siena ▲ *304* and Bologna ▲ *252*, the true center of political and civic life in Florence was originally, in the 13th century, a completely "secular" piazza, in which buildings of municipal power stood independently from the bishop's palace and the cathedral.

PALAZZO VECCHIO ★, ● *79.* In 1540, Cosimo I began living in the palace which had been the seat of the Republican government, thereby emphasizing that the city's power was concentrated in his hands; in 1565, when Cosimo I moved into the Palazzo Pitti, it became known as the "old" palace. Designed by Arnolfo di Cambio as a fortress, the interior celebrates the absolute power of the

OPIFICIO DELLE PIETRE DURE
Founded in 1588 by Ferdinando I de' Medici, the workshops of the Opificio were generally dedicated to the restoration of inlaid work using semi-precious stones. Over the centuries, it has widened its area of competence and is now one of the most prestigious art restoration institutes in the world, with a famous school and a well-equipped scientific laboratory.

PALAZZO DAVANZATI
This is a typical Florentine medieval palace: the arcaded first floor was occupied by stores and workshops and opened out onto the street; the reception rooms and the owner's private apartments were on the second floor; the rooms of the other family members were on the third floor; the servants' quarters were on the fourth floor; and the kitchen was at the top.

GIORGIO VASARI
Not a first-class artist
although extremely
prolific, a talented
architect, a man of
culture and a great
entrepreneur, Vasari
monopolized artistic
activity in the city.
With the first edition
of his *Vite* (1550)
(*Lives of the
Painters,
Sculptors and
Architects*) he
gave Cosimo the
most effective
manifesto of
Florentine
supremacy in the
history of Italian
art: an ideological
template which,
widened to
include
literature
and
language,
continued
to have a
considerable
impact until
after Italian
unification.

Medicis, particularly that of
Cosimo I, who relied on
Vasari's remarkable
inventiveness to do full justice
to his ambitions. With great
sensitivity, Vasari left the heavy
façade unaltered and instead
completely remodeled the
building's interior, coordinating
the work of a large team of artists:
they decorated the Quartiere degli
Elementi (1555–8), then the Quartiere di Leone X (1555–62)
and di Eleonora (1558–65) and, last but not least, the opulent
Salone dei Cinquecento (1563–72), the
elegant, private closets of the Tesoretto of
Cosimo I and the Studiolo of Francesco I
(1570–5). The winds of change had,
however, already begun to blow. In 1534, the
year in which Michelangelo left Florence for
good, the statue of *Hercules and Cacus* by
Baccio Bandelli had been erected in front of the
Palazzo Vecchio: its triumphant and violent
show of muscular strength, placed in front
of the copy of Michelangelo's *David*
(the original is in the Galleria
dell'Accademia), clearly symbolized the
changing climate of Florentine culture.

LOGGIA DELLA SIGNORIA. This is also
known as the Loggia dell'Orcagna or dei
Lanzi, because in the 16th century the
Lanzichenecchi (German bodyguards)
employed by Cosimo I had their quarters
here. Its three lofty pointed arches (1376–82)
reveal a taste for bright,
sunlit, open spaces that
prefigures Brunelleschi's
first classical essays.
Built to house public
ceremonies, it
then became
a sculpture
studio and
finally an
open-air museum. It is now
the home of Giambologna's
Rape of the Sabines
(Benvenuto Cellini's *Perseus*
was moved to the Uffizi in
December 1996).

> **T**HERE IS NO PLACE [IN FLORENCE] THAT IS NOT IMBUED WITH THE NOBLE, MAGNIFICENT SPIRIT OF THE MEDICI.
>
> FRANZ GRILLPARZER

"ALBERTO DELLA RAGIONE" COLLECTION OF CONTEMPORARY ART. Dazzled by so much Renaissance art, this collection (temporarily located at no. 5 on the Piazza) marks a welcome return to the 20th century, offering a chance to admire the work of the most important Italian artists of this century.

THE UFFIZI

THE PIAZZALE AND THE PALAZZO. In 1560, next to the Palazzo Vecchio, Vasari started work on a building for Cosimo I which was to bring together all the administrative offices under one roof. Two parallel buildings, with elegant Doric porticos, connect the Piazza della Signoria with the Arno river, enclosing a long, narrow space, like an open-air drawing room. This is closed off at the back by a light and airy three-mullioned window in the style of the architect San Serlio, and crowned by a loggia commanding splendid views on both sides. Francesco I (1580) used the third floor as a private museum. His art collection was greatly augmented by later members of the family.

THE GALLERY ★. The art collection originally consisted of ancient statues and historical finds, but was extended by the insatiable curiosity of the Medicis, who also collected items of natural history, weapons and objects of scientific and technical interest. At the end of the 18th century, the Dukes of Lorraine began reorganizing this incredible amount of material, which ranges from antiquity to the 18th century (and up to the 20th century if you take a walk through the CORRIDOIO VASARIANO). A drastic restructuring of the exhibition rooms is planned which will also make good the damage caused by the bomb explosion of May 27, 1993.

THE CORRIDOIO VASARIANO
The final stage (1565) of Vasari's plan was to create a spectacular passageway connecting the Piazza della Signoria and the Palazzo Pitti. This functional corridor allowed the Grand Duke to keep an eye on things while ensuring his personal safety. Coming from his residence, he could take advantage of a secret window to watch audiences at the Palazzo Vecchio unseen and, in case of rebellion, he could quickly reach the Boboli Gardens, which led to the safety of the Palazzina del Belvedere.

1 PALAZZO RUCELLAI
2 SANTA TRINITA
3 PALAZZO STROZZI
4 ORSANMICHELE
5 MUSEO NAZIONALE DEL BARGELLO

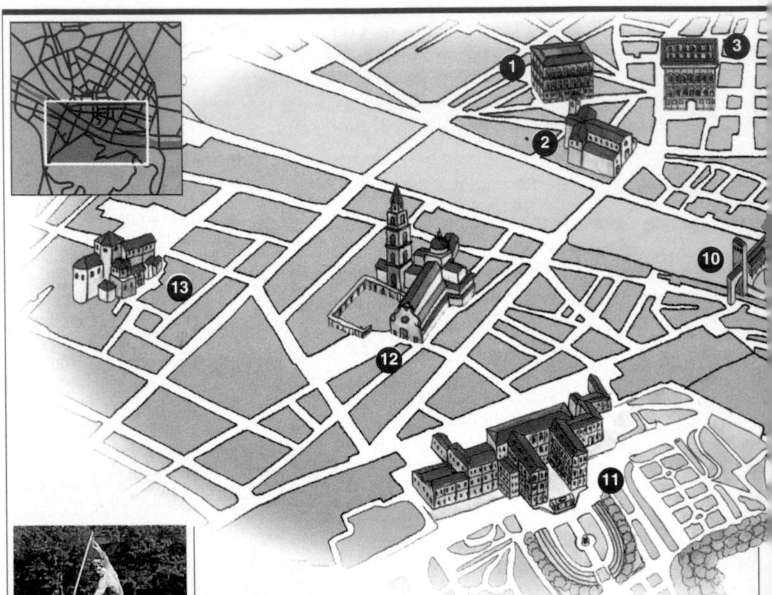

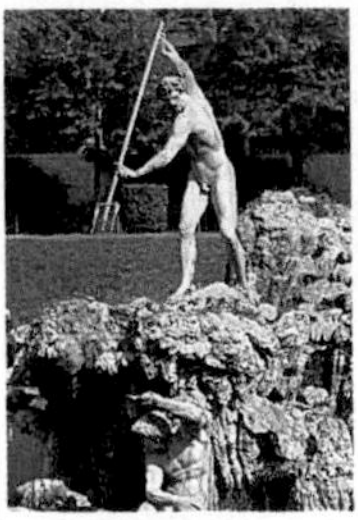

THE BOBOLI GARDENS
Fountains and water features, groves, avenues of cypress trees, grottos and terraces, an amphitheater, a little island and countless classical statues, both grotesque and bucolic. The gardens originally served as a "botanical laboratory" for the Grand Duke's court: potatoes, mulberry bushes, dwarf pear trees and other exotic fruit trees from all over the world were grown here for the first time.

THE OLTRARNO: PITTI

Until the early Middle Ages, when the Ponte Vecchio was the only bridge in the city, the left bank of the Arno river was clustered with markets and workshops. The former working-class nature of the Oltrarno, so colorfully described by Palazzeschi and Pratolini, has left its mark on the appearance of this quarter, forming a sharp contrast with the austerity of the Palazzo Pitti, the religious centers of Santo Spirito and Santa Maria Del Carmine and the façades of the palaces.

PONTE VECCHIO ★. A bridge would certainly have stood here at the narrowest part of the river since antiquity. The present one, built in 1345, is one of the symbols of the city and was fortunately not destroyed during the German retreat in 1944. It is crowded with goldsmiths' shops (which in the 16th century would have been butchers and greengrocers) and is overlooked upriver by the Corridoio Vasariano.

PALAZZO PITTI ▲ *286*. The largest palace in Florence, begun in 1458 for the banker Luca Pitti, was the residence of the Medici and the House of Lorraine for three centuries and then of the House of Savoy when Florence was the capital of Italy (1865–70), a few years after it was completed. The stark, somewhat oppressive courtyard, that was built between 1558 and 1570 by

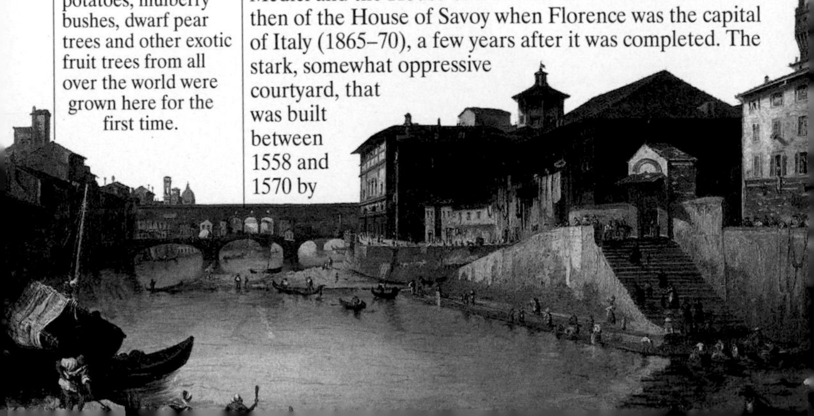

Bartolomeo Ammannati for Cosimo I and his wife, Eleonor of Toledo, should be seen in context with the magnificent Boboli Gardens, for which the palace complex provides an uncluttered backdrop.

THE PITTI PALACE MUSEUMS. The Palazzo is also a prestigious museum complex, housing the Galleria Palatina, a splendid example of a prince's picture gallery, with masterpieces of Italian and European painting from the 15th to the 17th centuries; the Appartamenti Reali, which for centuries accommodated princes and kings; the Galleria d'Arte Moderna, the Museo degli Argenti and the Museo delle Porcellane, with pieces from important Italian and European factories (Naples, Doccia, Tournai, Meissen); and the Museo delle Carrozze with its collection of carriages.

CROSSING BACK OVER THE ARNO

Variety is the keynote in the part of the city between the Palazzo Pitti and San Frediano: the stately architecture of Via Maggio is little more than a stone's throw away from the lovely medieval buildings on Borgo San Jacopo, while not far from the elegant palaces lining Lungarno Guicciardini you will be plunged into the noisy, working-class atmosphere of the district around Borgo San Frediano, which is also the site of two Renaissance gems: Santo Spirito and Santa Maria del Carmine.

SANTO SPIRITO. In this church, Brunelleschi progressed from the linear purity of the plan of San Lorenzo to a more elaborate use of space: the curved profile of the side chapels guides the eye constantly back to the central axis of the nave while the use of the design in the presbytery transforms it into a centrally planned building of classical influence.

SANTA MARIA DEL CARMINE. This 13th-century building, completed in the 15th century, was entirely rebuilt in 1775 after a fire. Its fame is largely due to the frescos in the BRANCACCI CHAPEL ★ where Masaccio's collaboration with Masolino da Panicale enabled him to formulate a revolutionary new style of painting.

MASACCIO AND MASOLINO
The recent restoration (1990) of the paintings in the Brancacci Chapel have clearly identified the distinctive styles of these two artists. They reveal Masaccio's

authentic colors, which are unexpectedly similar to those used by Fra Beato Angelico ▲ *290*, and Masolino da Panicale's consummate use of form. Masolino's delicate settings and courteous gestures, which echo the grace of the international Gothic style, are in striking contrast to the noticeable force and realism of Masaccio's work.

The Florentine architects of the 15th century developed the blueprint for an elegant urban residence – the palazzo – which then spread throughout Italy, becoming one of the country's most typical and enduring features. Palaces were essentially based on the plan of the Roman *domus* (a square courtyard surrounded by four main buildings), but the Florentine palace was built higher, which gave it a cubic shape, and had a set of windows overlooking the street. This placed a great deal of emphasis on the façade, which was characteristically constructed according to classical architectural orders.

PALAZZO PITTI

Built around 1458, probably to a design by Filippo Brunelleschi, the Palazzo Pitti was an example of the early style of Florentine palace, a three-storied, cube-shaped building with a rusticated façade. The sides were later extended, altering its original proportions.

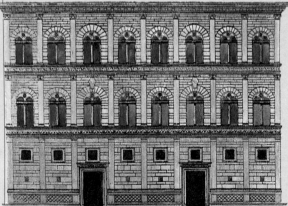

PALAZZO RUCELLAI

Designed by Leon Battista Alberti and built around 1460 by Bernardo Rossellino, this was the first fully realized attempt to construct the façade using classical architectural orders to indicate upward progression. The palace retained traditional elements such as two-light windows under arched lintels and a rusticated façade.

THE CORNICE

This crowning element was one of the key features of the palace's new type of façade.

THE WINDOWS

The arched two-light windows, enclosed within a heavy arched lintel, were gradually replaced by more elegant openings, such as Michelangelo's design for the Palazzo Medici-Riccardi.

PALAZZO MEDICI

Cosimo de' Medici commissioned the new Palazzo from Michelozzo, who designed a three-story building with a colonnaded ground floor surrounding an inner courtyard and an architraved loggia on the upper floor; the façade of each of the three floors has a different facing: rusticated (beveled) ashlar for the first floor, smooth ashlar for the second and plain stone for the third. In the 17th century, its new owners, the Riccardis, enlarged the building, altering the elegant proportions which had made it a model for subsequent Renaissance palaces.

PALAZZO STROZZI

Begun in 1489 by Benedetto da Maiano and completed by Simone del Pollaiuolo, nicknamed Il Cronaca, this is a magnificent building with a completely rusticated façade with evenly spaced arched windows. The rustication becomes less marked with each successive floor, although this variation is more subtle than that of the Palazzo Medici. The stringcourses and heavy "Roman-style" cornice, modeled on classical moldings, make the building look even more imposing.

**PALAZZO GUADAGNI-RICCARDI
then STROZZI DI MANTO**
Built in the 17th century, this th
story palace has rusticated windows
architraves or tympanums and rust
entrances on both f

Some examples from the Mineralogical Museum near St Mark's.

GIOVANNI RUCELLAI
This wealthy merchant had found a reliable architect in Alberti who designed his Florentine palace, as well as the façade of Santa Maria Novella and the small temple of Santo Sepolcro for the Rucellai Chapel in San Pancrazio. This church (deconsecrated in 1808), of which Giovanni Rucellai was the protector, is now the home

of the Museo Marino Marini, with a varied selection of works by the Pistoian artist (1901–80).

SANTA TRÌNITA. Beyond the reconstructed arches of Ammanati's original SANTA TRÌNITA BRIDGE (1567–9) stands the basilica of Santa Trìnita. Its severe Mannerist façade (Buontalenti 1593–4) conceals one of the oldest Gothic interiors in the city (14th century). In the frescos (1483–6) of the SASSETTI CHAPEL, Ghirlandaio married the Florentine tradition with the stylized Flemish elements that had become fashionable after the arrival in Florence of the *Portinari Triptych* by Hugo van der Goes (now in the Uffizi).

VIA DE' TORNABUONI. It is virtually mandatory for any international fashion designer to have a retail outlet on this street.

PALAZZO STROZZI ★. This famous Renaissance palace ▲ 287, inspired by Michelozzo's Palazzo Medici but far taller, was designed by Benedetto da Maiano in 1489. The cornice and elegant inner courtyard surrounded by two orders of loggia are the work of Simone di Pollaiuolo, nicknamed Il Cronaca (the chronicle).

PALAZZO RUCELLAI. This Renaissance palace ▲ 286, built by Rossellino to a design by Alberti, is a powerful affirmation of geometric purity and classicism.

PIAZZA SANTA MARIA NOVELLA

It was here, in the 13th century, at the opposite end of the city from the Franciscan complex of Santa Croce, that the Dominicans chose to found the Church of Santa Maria Novella. An order of great erudition, religious intolerance and political conservatism, the Dominicans left their mark on the city with this richly decorated building, begun in 1278. With a Florentine juxtaposition of different architectural styles, Alberti's innovative treatment of the church contrasts with the functional continuity between the interior and exterior of the railroad station. There is always something going on in this vibrant area of the city and the nearby Teatro Comunale di Firenze and the Fortezza da Basso offer a lively program of cultural and theatrical events.

SANTA MARIA NOVELLA. Commissioned by Giovanni Rucellai to complete the 14th-century façade of the church, Leon Battista Alberti came up with an inspired solution to the problem of linking the new pediment to the preexisting lower part and concealing the Gothic buttresses of the arches: he "invented" the two large scrolls on the sides, creating a model which was to be widely imitated and successfully integrated the Romanesque heritage (dichromatic decoration) with the architectural tradition of Ancient Rome. The interior contains many priceless works including the frescos by Ghirlandaio in the TORNABUONI CHAPEL, those by Nando di Cione in the Strozzi Chapel, an early *Crucifix* by Giotto, one by Brunelleschi, and the outstanding *Trinity* (1424–7) by Masaccio, a secular meditation on the relationship between mankind and God, here depicted on an almost equal footing.

THE RAILROAD STATION. Designed by Giovanni Michelucci with a team of pupils (1933–5), the station of Santa Maria Novella is one of the most successful products of Italian functionalism. It was rare, indeed, in the 1930's, for a large public building to blend in with the preexisting urban layout; more often than not, it would simply be inserted brashly into an area cleared by demolition work; in this case, however, the architect successfully managed to strike a balance between the building and its urban setting.

PIAZZA SAN MARCO

The walls of the monastery of San Marco still resound with Savonarola's castigating sermons and exhortations to asceticism. The Medicis did not escape his barbs and Cosimo

Il Vecchio spent a good part of his huge revenue from money lending on completely remodeling the Dominican complex in order to square his account with God. The commission was given to Michelozzo, who supplemented the stark monastic architecture with the

PERSPECTIVE
The Greeks were not aware of the mathematical laws according to which an object will seem to become smaller and smaller as you move away from it; no classical artist had succeeded in depicting a row of trees disappearing into the distance. Brunelleschi ▲ 278 provided other artists with these laws; the *Trinity*, painted by his friend, Masaccio, for Santa Maria Novella, is one of the first examples of this new technique.

289

BEATO ANGELICO
This was the sobriquet of Fra Giovanni da Fiesole, whose real name was Guido di Pietro (1400–55). It has nothing to do with a real ecclesiastical beatification, but

refers specifically to his style of painting, which clearly showed the influence of Masaccio's innovations and already revealed the new trends in Florentine art as codified in Leon Battista Alberti's treatise *De pictura* (1435).

light, airy elegance of an unusually long library, intended for use as a school.

MUSEO DI SAN MARCO ★. The artist commissioned to paint the convent was Giovanni da Fiesole, known as Beato Angelico, a man more capable than any other of translating the strict doctrines of the Dominican order into color and form. As early as the *Linaiuoli Altarpiece* (1433–4), he had adopted Masaccio's ethics although rejecting his realism and had attained a new depth of serenity in his treatment of religious imagery. His work showed further development in the *Enthroned Madonna and Six Saints* (1437–40), the first example of a "sacred conversation" executed in intimate, thoughtful tones that were accentuated even further in the frescos lining the walls of the monastery's cells, the true pinnacle of his achievements. Here the paintings are truly meditative in theme, like the famous *Annunciation* of 1442.

CENACOLO DI SANT'APOLLONIA. The refectory of the convent of Sant'Apollonia contains Andrea del Castagno's painting of the *Last Supper*, which became the model for all subsequent Renaissance interpretations of the theme until Leonardo ▲ 198. The architectural setting of the picture was designed as a continuation of the real space in the refectory and the eyes and gestures of the disciples all focus on the dramatic central group in which Judas, the only figure on this side of the table, stands out in the foreground, his dark face looming over that of the Master (due to Castagno's use of perspective): a daring solution.

GALLERIA DELL'ACCADEMIA. Although it also houses some important Florentine paintings from between the 14th and the 17th centuries, the gallery is widely regarded as the "Museo di Michelangelo", and possesses many of his original casts. His *David* (1502–4) is closely associated with Medici ideology and with the prevailing passion for antiquity: the iconography is that of Hercules, the Florentine rulers' favorite hero, but when the statue was placed in front of the Palazzo Vecchio, it also

290

> **"A NOBLEMAN'S HOME SHOULD BE ELEGANTLY DECORATED [AND] SHOULD BE MORE PLEASING THAN OSTENTATIOUS."**
> LEON BATTISTA ALBERTI, *DE RE AEDIFICATORIA*

became a symbol of the new republic's strength and liberty, a cause Michelangelo supported. Other masterpieces, in various stages of completion, are the four gigantic *Prigioni* (c. 1530), intended for Pope Julius II's tomb, and the *Saint Matthew* (1506).

PIAZZA DELLA SANTISSIMA ANNUNZIATA

OSPEDALE DEGLI INNOCENTI. The only part of the original design for the piazza built by Brunelleschi was this building, the Hospital of the Innocents which was begun in 1419. It is not only a masterpiece of civic architecture, but also a monument to Florence's social conscience, since the city employed one of its top engineers in the service of its most underprivileged citizens; children and babies. Brunelleschi's customary meticulous attention to geometric proportion produced a functional and attractive building (and a superb COLONNADE).

SANTISSIMA ANNUNZIATA. The largely Baroque interior of this basilica contains some of the most important frescos of the 16th century. The ones in the CHIOSTRINO DEI VOTI, in particular, clearly reveal the unsettling and innovative response of Pontormo and Rosso Fiorentino to the erudite and flawless classicism of Andrea del Sarto, described by Vasari as the "faultless" painter. This new language had a marked impact on Andrea del Sarto himself, as can be seen by the naturalism and spontaneity of his *Madonna del Sacco*, painted in 1525 for the CHIOSTRO DEI MORTI.

MUSEO ARCHEOLOGICO. This museum, which grew out of the Medicis' interest in antiquity, was supplemented by the Lorraine collection and also includes various Egyptian pieces collected by Leopoldo II (this is the second largest collection in Italy after the Egyptian Museum in Turin ▲ *145*). The most outstanding collection is that of Etruscan art and the museum is a must for students of this ancient civilization.

THE MAGGIO MUSICALE IN FLORENCE
The most famous and longest-running opera and orchestral festival in Italy (the first session took place in 1933) is held between April and June; its main venue is the Teatro Comunale at Corso Italia 10, a neoclassical building (1862) not far from the railroad station.

PAST TREASURES
The Etruscan finds at the Museo Archeologico in Florence create a telling and

down-to-earth picture of a race too often described as "mysterious". The *François Vase* from Chiusi (570 BC), the *Mater Matuta* from Chianciano (470 BC), the famous *Chimera* from Arezzo (4th century BC), the *Sarcophagus of the Amazons* (4th century BC), the Roman-influenced *Arringatore* (*Orator*) of the late 2nd century BC and countless other finds chart the history of a nation that once governed a large territory in central Italy ▲ *326* which extended north toward Spina and Chioggia.

THE FLOOD OF 1966
On November 4, the Arno flooded, sweeping away everything in its path. The disaster hit Florence particularly hard, causing incalculable financial and artistic damage. Santa Croce was the worst hit: flood waters rose to a height of 16 feet and completely ruined the *Crucifix* by Cimabue.

GIOTTO IN SANTA CROCE
Giotto's expansive and confident treatment of space show that his work had developed even further since his time in Padua ▲ *234*. His warm, subtly varied colors create a mood of intense serenity, the last flowering of a successful period.

THE SANTA CROCE DISTRICT

For centuries, this has been the most populous district of Florence, packed with merchants and manufacturers and the seat of the magistracy (first the Bargello, then Palazzo Castellani and finally San Firenze).

PIAZZA SAN FIRENZE. Behind the Palazzo Vecchio, near the heart of the medieval city, is Piazza San Firenze, the home of some of Florence's most important buildings.

BADIA FIORENTINA. Founded in 978 (which makes it the oldest monastery in the city), this building was remodeled by Arnolfo da Cambio (1285) and then again in the 17th century. The Baroque interior, in the form of a Greek cross, contains various works of art, including the remarkable *Virgin Appearing to Saint Bernard* (1485) by Filippino Lippi. The church is also known for another famous vision: it was here that Dante saw Beatrice for the first time.

PALAZZO AND MUSEO NAZIONALE DEL BARGELLO ★. The Bargello (a synonym of the more prosaic "sbirro" or policeman) was the Capitano di Giustizia or Chief of Police, who lived here from 1574. Built in several stages between 1255 and 1345, restored in the 19th century, it is now a MUSEUM ▲ *294* housing one of the world's finest collections of applied arts and medieval art.

SANTA CROCE ★. The fame of this church as the last resting place of many illustrious men, such as Michelangelo, Alfieri, Galileo and Foscolo, sometimes overshadows the number of remarkable works of art it also contains. One prominent figure buried here is Leonardo Bruni, the humanist and chancellor of the Florentine Republic, whose

"THE CHURCH OF SANTA CROCE ... CONTAINS THE TOMBS OF MACHIAVELLI, MICHAEL ANGELO, GALILEO GALILEI AND ALFIERI ... I DID NOT ADMIRE ANY OF THESE TOMBS – BEYOND THEIR CONTENTS."

LORD BYRON

monument, built by Bernardo Rossellino in 1444–5, was to become the model for countless Renaissance tombs. There are two of Donatello's works here, both displaying the artist's anti-classical tendencies: the tranquil *Annunciation* (1435) and the hyper-realistic *Crucifixion* (1425) which was criticized by his friend, Brunelleschi, who accused him of "putting a peasant on the cross". There is also one of Giotto's last series of paintings: the frescos in the BARDI and PERUZZI CHAPELS (1320–6).

THE PAZZI CHAPEL AND THE MUSEO DELL'OPERA DI SANTA CROCE. Before the conspiracy of 1478, the Pazzis financed a funerary chapel which enabled Brunelleschi to revert to his beloved centrally planned ground plan ● *91*. The museum's collections were seriously damaged in the flood of 1966: Cimabue's *Crucifix* was the most poignant loss.

THE HILLS

Overlooking the left bank of the Arno river, traversed by the winding Viale dei Colli, these hills afford some stunning panoramic views.
PIAZZALE MICHELANGIOLO. This square was built by Giuseppe Poggi (1875), the architect who spearheaded the urban improvement program during the brief time that Florence was the capital of the kingdom of Italy. This is not one of his most successful projects, in view of the overblown rhetoric of its architecture and its disastrous monument to Michelangelo. From here, you can climb up to San Salvatore al Monte, with its simple yet fascinating façade.
SAN MINIATO AL MONTE. Like the Baptistry of San Giovanni, this church (1018–1207) displays some of the most distinctive features of Florentine Romanesque with its allusions to ancient Roman architecture and the clear-cut linear design of the bicolored inlaid work; the potential monotony of the repetitive geometrical motifs is avoided by the introduction of a vivid mosaic of *Cristo Benedicente*.
FORTE DEL BELVEDERE. Designed by Bernardo Buontalenti and Giovanni de' Medici, the fortress was built between 1590 and 1595 by order of Grand Duke Ferdinand I and surrounds the Palazzina del Belvedere (1560–70) which is occasionally open to the public for exhibitions.

CALCIO STORICO
One of the most popular Florentine traditional festivals takes place in Piazza Santa Croce: this is "historical soccer", an older (dating back to the end of the 15th century) and more violent version of today's sport. From mid-June, teams from the four districts of the old city center battle it out in semi-finals and a final.

SAN SALVATORE AL MONTE
The steps from Piazzale Michelangiolo lead up to one of the most beautiful churches in the city: San Salvatore al Monte (1499–1504), the work of Il Cronaca. This was a favorite of Michelangelo, who called it "la bella villanella" (his pretty country lass); the interior displays the innovative use of two superimposed orders of pilaster strips.

The façade of San Miniato al Monte.

In 1865, just after Florence had become the capital of the kingdom of Italy, the city opened a new museum dedicated to applied arts and medieval art. This was housed in the city's oldest purpose-built civic building: the 13th-century Palazzo del Capitano di Giustizia. This impressive palace had, since the 16th century, been the seat of the Bargello ▲ 292, and consequently of the law courts and the prisons. Bequests and donations have made this one of the most famous museums in the world.

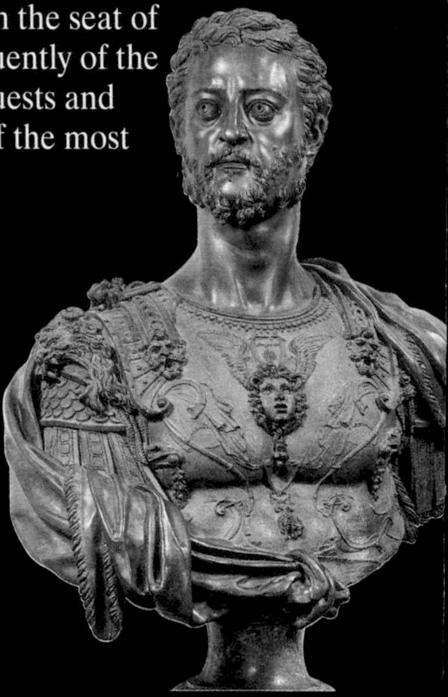

BUST OF COSIMO I
This splendid bronze (1545-7), the work of Benvenuto Cellini at the height of his technical powers, combines classical formality with telling psychological detail.

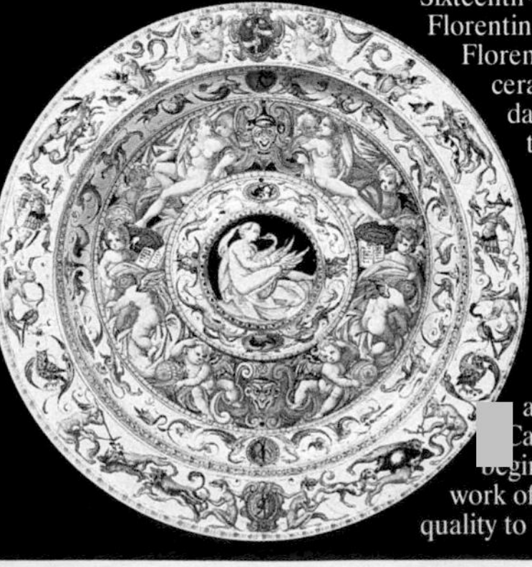

"LEDA AND THE SWAN"
Sixteenth-century Florentine majolica. Florence's long ceramic tradition dates back to the 15th century; only in the later 16th century did various neighboring towns (particularly Montelupo and Cafaggiolo) begin to produce work of a superior quality to the capital's.

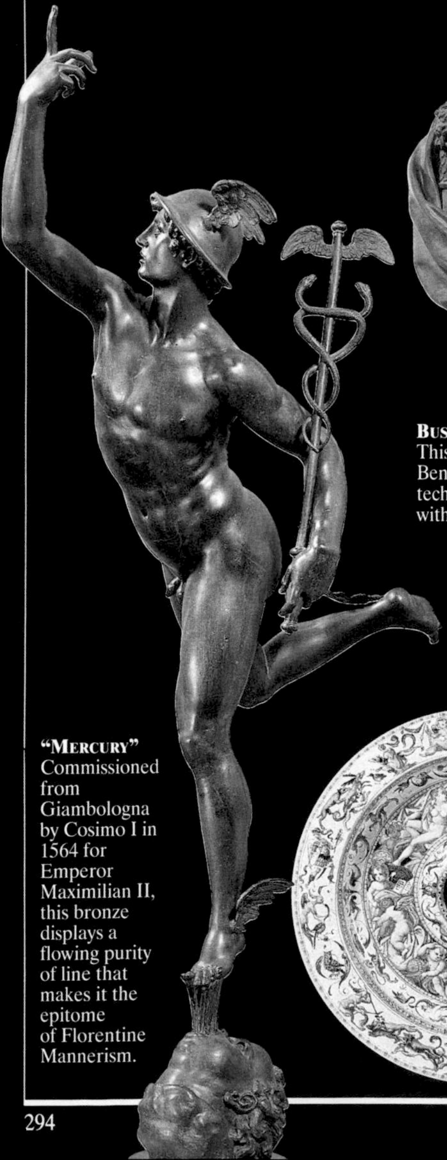

"MERCURY"
Commissioned from Giambologna by Cosimo I in 1564 for Emperor Maximilian II, this bronze displays a flowing purity of line that makes it the epitome of Florentine Mannerism.

"BACCHUS"

Michelangelo was little more than twenty when he sculpted this swaying *Bacchus* (1496–7), whose eyes, in the words of Ascanio Condivi (the artist's pupil and biographer), "are in the overwhelming grip of his love of wine".

THE COMPETITION OF 1401

The finalists of this competition, for the commission of the north door of the baptistry, were Filippo Brunelleschi, who produced the panel below, and Lorenzo Ghiberti, the winner with his entry above. These two panels, depicting the *Sacrifice of Isaac*, are among the earliest examples of Renaissance sculpture.

"SAINT GEORGE SLAYING THE DRAGON"

On the bas-relief at the base of his magnificent *Saint George* (1416), Donatello provided the first example of a *stiacciato* relief; the scene, with the holy crusader at the center, is flanked by a colonnade depicted in geometric perspective.

THE MUSEO BANDINI AT FIESOLE
This museum houses a collection amassed by the 18th-century scholar, Canon Angelo Maria Bandini. There are pieces of majolica, furniture, terracottas by the Della Robbia family and paintings from between the 13th and the 15th centuries, including a small *Crucifixion* by Lorenzo Monaco.

Prehistoric fishermen and miners from Elba, Etruscans and Romans, pilgrims from the Via Francigena, grape and olive farmers from every period, enthralled foreign travelers doing the Grand Tour: Tuscany is a multifaceted, independent-minded region, set in a diverse landscape ranging from the Sienese *Le Crete* ("crests") region to the shores of the Tyrrhenian Sea, from the wild Apennines to the hills of Chianti, Valdarno and the Maremma.

AROUND FLORENCE

FIESOLE ★, A PERFECT FLORENTINE HILL TOWN. The countryside around Florence is characterized by a remarkable symbiosis of mankind and nature. In Fiesole, this close union

AN UNUSUAL SALOME
The frescos in the choir of the Duomo at Prato (1452–64) have all the hallmarks of Filippo Lippi's best work: well-spaced, solemn composition, skilled use of perspective, sophisticated colors and delicate figures rendered by flowing, harmonious lines, like his modest Salome dancing for Herod's guests.

is of ancient origin, dating back to the harmonious relationship initiated by the Etruscan rulers between the urban aristocracy and the agricultural society. The Romans wisely maintained this system of organization. From the 15th century to the present day, Fiesole's beautiful setting and abundant local archeological and artistic monuments have attracted many admirers. The town's archeological area (north of Fiesole, at the start of Via Duprè) is particularly notable, as is its museum. No less valuable is its heritage of Renaissance art. Even though, despite their names, Mino da Fiesole and Fra Giovanni da Fiesole (Beato Angelico) were not born here, they gave the town some priceless works: the former in the Duomo (the tomb of Leonardo Salutati, c. 1464), the latter in the church of San Domenico (*Crucifix, Madonna and Child*, c. 1425), several miles south of Fiesole.

FREDERICK'S NORTHERN CASTLE IN PRATO. Two inspired and famous dance scenes in the

cathedral – Donatello's dancing children on the Pulpit of the Sacred Girdle and Filippo Lippi's elegant fresco of Salome in the *Stories of Saint Stephen and John the Baptist* in the apse – would be enough to assure the artistic importance of this town. Prato has many fine examples of Romanesque, Gothic and Renaissance art, but this is to be expected in Tuscany. What is

> **"THE GOD WHO CREATED THE HILLS OF FLORENCE WAS AN ARTIST:
> A GOLDSMITH, A SCULPTOR, A SKILLED WORKER IN BRONZE;
> AND A PAINTER TOO. IN SHORT, HE MUST HAVE BEEN A FLORENTINE."**
>
> ANATOLE FRANCE

exceptional is the CASTELLO DELL'IMPERATORE (1237–48), built by Frederick II, who unexpectedly succeeded in creating a little corner of Apulia or Sicily here. Giuliano da Maiano and Giuliano da Sangallo designed the sharp, clear lines of SANTA MARIA DELLE CARCERI, an early Renaissance gem. The town's rich artistic heritage includes some prestigious names such as Paolo Uccello, Michelozzo, Agnolo Gaddi, Andrea della Robbia, Luca Signorelli and Giovanni Pisano. Finally, the Museo d'Arte Contemporanea Luigi Pecci is a must for connoisseurs of 20th-century art; the Museo del Tessuto's collection of textile art and technology is just as fascinating.

"PISTORIA"
According to one theory, the name Pistoia is derived from the Latin term *pistoria* meaning "bakers", which might have indicated the presence of an army supply station.

AN UNFORGETTABLE CAMPANILE
The campanile of the Duomo in Pistoia is one of the most beautiful bell towers in Italy, with three floors of loggias and marble statues in Pisan style (12th–13th centuries). The coats of arms confirm its dual function as a bell tower and the seat of the town's magistracy.

THE CITIES OF ART IN THE NORTHWEST

GIOVANNI PISANO'S PULPIT IN SANT'ANDREA AT PISTOIA. In the 15th century, Pistoia was known as the "city of the pulpits" because it had no less than three medieval pulpits of the highest artistic quality. The oldest, in the church of San Bartolomeo in Pantano, was begun by Guido da Como in 1240, while San Giovanni Fuorcivitas, a masterpiece of Pistoian Romanesque (12th–14th centuries), contains the one by Fra Guglielmo da Pisa (1270). The most famous pulpit, however, and justifiably so, is the one sculpted by Giovanni Pisano (1298–1301) for the Romanesque church of Sant'Andrea. Its hexagonal plan is modeled on the one executed forty years earlier by his father, Nicola, in Pisa, but here the slender columns and pointed arches display a marked Gothic influence, which is underlined by the dramatic and emotional impact of the scenes.

297

▲ From the ramparts of Lucca to Romanesque Pisa

LUCCA, THE OUTLINE OF A "CITY-STATE". The regular plan of the city's historical center betrays its Roman origins as does the name of San Michele in Foro. But nowhere is this presence more obvious than in the highly unusual Piazza del Mercato, built at the beginning of the 19th century when buildings that had stood on the remains of a Roman amphitheater were demolished and replaced by others that traced the elliptical outline of the monument. The city's flourishing silk trade and banking activities created an economic boom in the 12th and 13th centuries that can be seen in civic buildings (for example, the attractive Via Guinigi) and numerous Romanesque churches (the Duomo, San Michele in Foro and San Frediano are the most famous). In 1369, after violent conflicts with Pisa, civil strife and a succession of different rulers, Lucca regained its independence and, except for thirty years under Paolo Guinigi, remained an oligarchic republic until 1799. During these four centuries of political autonomy, the city was wealthy, peaceful and tolerant: the cultural open-mindedness of the ruling class promoted the spread of Lutheran ideas and the publication of books which, in the dark years of the Counter-Reformation, had only been printed in Venice. Various elegant palaces were built between the 15th and 16th centuries (like the Palazzo Cenami, Palazzo Mansi or those lining the busy Fillungo). After Italian unification, projects to demolish the CINTA MURARIA were put forward, but ignored: built between the 16th and 18th centuries, Lucca's ramparts form its most important monument ● *74, 75*.

THE PIAZZA DEL DUOMO IN PISA ★, A "MUSEUM OF THE ROMANESQUE". Pisa reached the height of its glory around the 11th century, but this golden age did not last long: its defeat in 1284 by Genoa ▲ *164* marked the end of its supremacy in the Tyrrhenian Sea and the beginning of a decline which culminated in its subjugation by Florence (1405). But in 1063, when the Pisan fleet had

THE RAMPARTS OF LUCCA
The ramparts form a circuit around the city for a distance of nearly 2½ miles which can be walked or cycled. Any military purpose they had was lost when Maria Luisa of Bourbon (1819–64) converted them into a public promenade.

YOUNG GALILEO
During his years as a student at the University of Pisa, Galileo began his research into the theory of motion. According to a famous anecdote, he discovered the phenomenon of the pendulum's isochronism by watching a swinging lamp in the Duomo at Pisa and he experimented with his theories about gravity by dropping heavy objects from the top of the Leaning Tower.

> **"STRANGELY ENOUGH, THE BUILDINGS [IN THE PIAZZA DEL DUOMO] REPRESENT THE COMPLETE CYCLE OF HUMAN LIFE: IN THIS SQUARE ARE THE BAPTISTRY, THE CATHEDRAL, THE LEANING TOWER, THE HOSPITAL AND THE GRAVEYARD."** H. FRIEDLANDER

returned victorious from the expedition against the Muslims at Palermo, the city gave its navy a triumphal welcome and ordered the construction of a cathedral dedicated to the Virgin who had given the enterprise her protection. The location they chose was on the outskirts of town, safe from the Arno's flood waters. They began to build the largest architectural complex in Romanesque Europe, the "Square of Miracles". *Non habet exemplum niveo de marmore templum* (this white marble temple has no equal): with these proud words engraved on Buscheto's tomb (to the left of the entrance), the Pisans extolled the inspired designer of the Duomo, which became even more ornate in the 12th century when Rainaldo added the façade. The work is a harmonious fusion of many traditions: the columns and capitals are classical in inspiration, the basilican plan displays a paleo-Christian influence, the loggias of the façade are Lombard in style, the black and white striped design, the elliptical dome and the ogival arches draw their inspiration from Oriental art, while the diamond-shaped blind arches are inspired by Armenian art. At the heart of this Romanesque gem, there are already intimations of a new culture: Giovanni Pisano's pulpit (1301–11), whose structure seems incapable of containing the exuberance of the sculpted reliefs, marks the artist's conversion to the Gothic style. Begun in 1153 by Diotisalvi, the baptistry blends in well with the cathedral next to it. It is encircled by a ring of blind arches and has four doors which are decorated with an exceptional variety of ornamental motifs. The façade of the Duomo also inspired the colonnaded tiers of the original structure of the campanile (the "leaning Tower of Pisa", built between 1173 and the late 14th century), world-famous for its age-old inclination which stopped its architects building it to the planned height of 230 feet. Although a later addition (1277–1464), the marble arcade of the Camposanto (Cemetery) with its pure, clean lines and characteristic blind arches, is in keeping with the other buildings on the piazza.

TWO CONTRASTING GENERATIONS
The intricate carved figures on Nicola Pisano's pulpit (1260) in the baptistry at Pisa, which appear to be classical in inspiration, mark the sculptor's departure from the Romanesque tradition and his creation of a new and innovative figurative language which was to be fully developed by his son, Giovanni (in the photo above), half a century later in the Duomo. The Gothic style provided Giovanni with an expressive medium that enabled him to create intense figures capable of communicating a keen sense of drama.

SINOPIAS
The Camposanto at Pisa has the largest collection of medieval mural paintings. Seriously damaged in the air raids of 1944, the frescos were removed from the walls to be restored: this led to the discovery of the sinopias, or preparatory drawings for the frescos, which are now kept at the Museo delle Sinopie.

Chianti: this one word refers not only to a famous wine but also to the district that produces it, an excellent olive oil, a special type of cuisine, and a beautiful yet still unspoiled wooded landscape. In the Middle Ages the district was divided between Florence and Siena – the Guelphs and the Ghibellines – leading to some bloody battles, including the infamous Battle of Montaperti in 1260, which claimed the lives of around 10,000 Florentines. The political climate having quieted in the Renaissance, Chianti was able to dedicate itself to farming: the work of generations of farmers created a close-set mosaic of family-run share-cropping farms, which have now almost all been replaced by large vineyards owned by specialist firms.

BARON BETTINO RICASOLI
Known as the "iron baron", not only because of his intransigent character, but also because he would often prop his ancestors' armor against the walls of his castle, Ricasoli was also interested in agronomy. It was he who, in 1837, selected the blend of grapes which produced "Chianti Classico", a heady, flavorful yet robust wine: 70 percent San Giovese, 15 percent Malvasia and Trebbiano, 15 percent Canaiolo, leaving out Malvasia in the good vintages.

A FAMOUS OIL AND A TASTY CUISINE
Chianti also produces the oil made largely from the "Moraiolo", "Leccino" and "Frantoio" olives, which is best in the first few months after pressing ("new oil"), when it has a powerful "fruity" smell and is used to season Tuscan dishes with a very strong flavor like soups made of bread and black cabbage and beans *al fiasco* ("in a flask").

Typical dishes from the Chianti district: *pappardelle* (broad noodles) "over" rabbit or "over" wood pigeon, *crostini* (fried bread) with game or spleen, *cibreo* (fricassee of giblets and cockscomb), pork sausage and pig's liver or thrush on the spit, Pecorino cheese with fresh broad beans.

THE HISTORY OF A WINE

Chianti is a world famous wine: the traditional flask remained in use until fairly recently, becoming almost a symbol of Italian wine. The name "Chianti Classico" refers not only to wines from the areas that produce the "Classico" label, with its emblem of the black rooster on a gold background, and those in the "Putto" consortium, founded in 1927, but to others, including the Chianti dei Colli Senesi, Aretini, Fiorentini, delle Colline Pisane: all of which use a similar blend of grapes, but differ in flavor due to the different terrain.

THE ISLANDS OF TUSCANY

IN SEARCH OF NATURE
Guided boat tours will enable you to discover beautiful creeks inaccessible by land, ancient cliffs high above the sea, islets, ravines and caves, ruined towers buried in thick vegetation, crystal-clear water and unusual birds: a true delight for nature lovers.

THE ISLAND OF ELBA: FROM MINING TO TOURISM. The coastline of the largest island in Tuscany is fairly rugged, a picturesque succession of inaccessible cliffs and beautiful coves with sandy beaches. Inland, the terrain is largely mountainous, dotted with secluded villages and ruins of fortresses. The Etruscans once exploited Elba's iron mines, the Romans built villas in the island's loveliest spots, Pisa, Genoa, Lucca and Florence were attracted by its mining resources and strategic position and it suffered raids by the Turks and dominion by the Spanish and English. From 1814 to 1815, Napoleon was imprisoned here after his abdication at Fontainebleau, and the Corsican exile's presence can still be felt in Portoferraio, the island's chief town. Another illustrious figure who had already left his mark on the town was Cosimo I de' Medici. He remodeled and fortified it in 1548. In response to this Medici bastion, the Spanish erected (1603) the huge star-shaped stronghold of Porto Azzurro, dominating one of the most beautiful bays.

PROTECTING THE MARINE HABITAT. Besides Elba, the Tuscan Archipelago comprises a handful of small islands scattered along the coast between Leghorn, Grosseto and Corsica. Their names (Gorgona, Capraia, Pianosa, Giglio, Montecristo and Giannutri) are suggestive of isolated landscapes and ancient myths, but particularly of an unspoiled natural heritage which, in 1989, was made part of a specially protected reserve, the Parco Nazionale dell'Arcipelago Toscano. The largest and most widely developed island (after Elba) is Giglio (opposite Monte Argentario), whose biggest village is Giglio Castello, enclosed within turreted Pisan walls; the rockiest and most untamed island is Montecristo, where the count of the same name, created by Alexandre Dumas *père*, acquired the fabulous treasure which enabled him to pursue his relentless vendetta.

CAPRAIA
Part of the Parco dell'Arcipelago Toscano, but closer to Corsica than Elba, the island of Capraia is completely unspoiled, due in part to its long history (1873–1986) as a penal colony and the fact that it has only half a mile of street. A boat trip around the island will take half a day and affords panoramic views of gray and pink rocks, cliffs high above the sea, and the small white houses of Capraia and its little port; all set against the backdrop of the Tyrrhenian Sea.

> **"WE HAVE PASSED THROUGH PLACES THRONGING WITH FISHERMEN, SIMPLE, HOSPITABLE, CHEERFUL PEOPLE NO DIFFERENT FROM THOSE WHO WOULD HAVE INHABITED THE PORTS DESCRIBED IN THE ODYSSEY."** JEAN GIONO

THE CITIES OF ART IN INLAND TUSCANY

ETRUSCAN CIVILIZATION AND CIVIC INDEPENDENCE IN VOLTERRA. Anyone approaching Volterra from the northwest will be greeted by a fantastic lunar landscape, the Balze, a vast stretch of badlands caused by huge landslides of clayey soil that have swallowed up buildings. This was a thriving Etruscan stronghold, which owed its wealth to its profitable trade in metals and the production of wood, grain and particularly alabaster, as can be seen by the remarkable collections at the Museo Etrusco Guarnacci, which include the important *Urna degli Sposi* as well as pottery, bronzes and goldwork. The town's second golden age was during its years as a free commune when the Palazzo dei Priori, the Duomo and the *case-torri* (towers built for living in) were constructed. In 1361, the city came under the rule of the Medici, who built one of the most formidable Renaissance fortresses in Italy, which has long been used as a prison. Today, besides farming and tourism, Volterra's economy depends on the thriving craft industry.

SAN GIMIGNANO ★, A WELL-PRESERVED MEDIEVAL TOWN. In 1282, a law was passed in San Gimignano prohibiting the demolition of houses unless replaced by buildings that were

MUSEO ETRUSCO MARIO GUARNACCI This is one of the principal Etruscan collections in Italy and its huge range of artefacts bears witness to the golden age of Volterra which, between the 5th and 4th centuries BC, was at the head of one of the twelve noble houses of the Etruscan nation, numbering 25,000 inhabitants and exporting iron and alabaster artefacts throughout the Mediterranean basin. The so-called *Evening Shadow*, a statuette that dates from the 3rd century BC, is of surprisingly modern appearance.

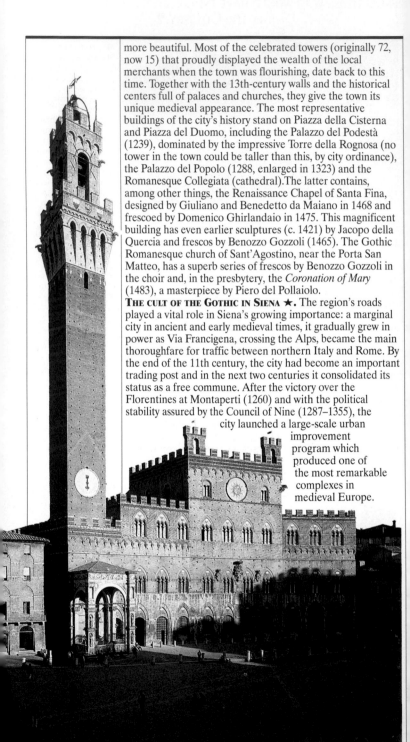

more beautiful. Most of the celebrated towers (originally 72, now 15) that proudly displayed the wealth of the local merchants when the town was flourishing, date back to this time. Together with the 13th-century walls and the historical centers full of palaces and churches, they give the town its unique medieval appearance. The most representative buildings of the city's history stand on Piazza della Cisterna and Piazza del Duomo, including the Palazzo del Podestà (1239), dominated by the impressive Torre della Rognosa (no tower in the town could be taller than this, by city ordinance), the Palazzo del Popolo (1288, enlarged in 1323) and the Romanesque Collegiata (cathedral).The latter contains, among other things, the Renaissance Chapel of Santa Fina, designed by Giuliano and Benedetto da Maiano in 1468 and frescoed by Domenico Ghirlandaio in 1475. This magnificent building has even earlier sculptures (c. 1421) by Jacopo della Quercia and frescos by Benozzo Gozzoli (1465). The Gothic Romanesque church of Sant'Agostino, near the Porta San Matteo, has a superb series of frescos by Benozzo Gozzoli in the choir and, in the presbytery, the *Coronation of Mary* (1483), a masterpiece by Piero del Pollaiolo.

THE CULT OF THE GOTHIC IN SIENA ★. The region's roads played a vital role in Siena's growing importance: a marginal city in ancient and early medieval times, it gradually grew in power as Via Francigena, crossing the Alps, became the main thoroughfare for traffic between northern Italy and Rome. By the end of the 11th century, the city had become an important trading post and in the next two centuries it consolidated its status as a free commune. After the victory over the Florentines at Montaperti (1260) and with the political stability assured by the Council of Nine (1287–1355), the city launched a large-scale urban improvement program which produced one of the most remarkable complexes in medieval Europe.

"Siena, the only surviving example of a medieval city."

RANUCCIO BIANCHI-BANDINELLI

The Palazzo Pubblico, begun at the end of the 13th century, was later completed by the slender Torre del Mangia which, according to governmental decree, had to be taller (289 feet) than the campanile of the cathedral (built at the highest point in the city, near the former seat of the bishops), thereby emphasizing the equal importance of state and church.

The gracefulness of the structure, the delicacy of the colors and the harmonious interplay of the lines are typical features of Sienese art. However, the relationship between the building and the vast square Campo ● *77*, that stretches before it is absolutely unique. This square slopes gently down from the Fonte Gaia (1419, Jacopo della Quercia) toward the Palazzo Pubblico which appears to embrace it with its curving wings. The Virgin Mary has always been worshipped devoutly in the city, which styled itself the *civitas Virginis*, and there was not a Sienese painter who did not dedicate a work to her: the *Maestà* by Duccio di Buoninsegna (from 1308–11, intended for the Duomo and now in the Museo dell'Opera Metropolitana), the one by Simone Martini (1315, in the Palazzo Pubblico) and the many Madonnas by Pietro and Ambrogio Lorenzetti are merely the most famous of a huge collection of devotional works. The Palazzo Pubblico is the epitome of civic pride: in the same room as the *Maestà* is the fresco, painted in 1328 and attributed to Simone Martini, of *Guidoriccio da Fogliano*, who rides like a ghostly knight through a barren, almost lunar, landscape. The Sala della Pace contains Ambrogio Lorenzetti's fresco, the *Effects of Good and Bad Government*, in some ways a political manifesto of the Council of Nine who commissioned the series. In the late 13th century, work was once again started on the Duomo, founded in the 12th century, and Giovanni Pisano was commissioned to build the façade. His ambitious design (1284–99) resulted in a harmonious fusion of architecture and sculpture, inspired by the model of French Gothic churches, although Pisano's interpretation of this model was completely original and his figures did not play any kind of structural role. Only the lower part of the façade was built to his design.

THE TWO "MAESTÀ"
In 1315, four years after Duccio's *Maestà* was completed, Simone Martini tackled the same subject (above) in his fresco in the Palazzo Pubblico, but in a completely different spirit. With his images of aristocratic elegance, Martini turned his back on static mysticism to portray with great lyricism the chivalric ideals that were still popular despite the decline of the feudal system.

The lofty interior of the Duomo in Siena.

rider: this contest, which is extremely dangerous for the horses and jockeys, who ride bareback, consists of three laps of the huge Piazza del Campo. This takes little more than a minute, but the celebrations can last for several days. The Palio is held on July 2 and August 16.

The Palio magically recreates the atmosphere of the medieval city, not only with the colors of the traditional costumes worn by the jockeys but also by rekindling the partisan spirit and bitter rivalries between the old quarters or *contrade*. Only ten of the seventeen *contrade* take part, each entering a horse and

THE CARROCCIO
The Carroccio (chariot), drawn by four oxen and escorted by the seven riders from the *contrade* who have not been lucky enough to take part in the race, follows the parade of the *contrade* into the Piazza. The Carroccio bears the hoisted standard and "palio", the "rag", which will be awarded to the winning *contrada*.

"VA' E TORNA VINCITORE"
(GO FORTH AND WIN)
Before the race, in the local church of each *contrada*, a priest blesses the horse and jockey with holy water.

A FRANTIC RACE
The three laps of the Piazza are completed at an incredible speed in little more than a minute. Particularly dangerous are the right angles at the downhill San Martino bend and the uphill Casato bend.

RIDERLESS HORSES
Occasionally the jockey falls off or is unhorsed. The riderless horse continues to race and can win the Palio.

GUEST OF HONOR
The victory celebrations are concluded with a great banquet: tables are set in the main street of the *contrada* and thousands of people sit down to eat. At the place of honor is the horse, which is given its favorite fodder.

INTARSIA WORK
The use of wood inlays as a decorative technique spread in the 15th century from Florence throughout Italy. Development of this technique, which used strips of various woods cut into intricate shapes and fixed to a preliminary design, was closely linked to the illusionist effects of perspective in art. The Venetian practice of staining wood to obtain a greater variety of vivid colors was adopted by Fra Giovanni da Verona in the choir of the abbey of Monte Oliveto Maggiore, resulting in work of extraordinary finesse.

THE CISTERCIANS
While the temporal power of the Church was conveyed by magnificent, lavishly decorated buildings, certain Benedictine monks from the abbey at Cîteaux (*Cistercium*) in Burgundy opposed the wealthy Cluniacs, advocating strict asceticism and poverty. These austere principles, preached by Bernardo di Chiaravalle from 1112, were reflected in the simplicity of the Cistercian monasteries.

MONASTIC TUSCANY

THE "LIFE OF SAINT BENEDICT" AT MONTE OLIVETO MAGGIORE.
High and isolated, on the edge of the arid Sienese landscape of Le Crete, stands the abbey which was the home of the first Olivetan Benedictine monks. This building is essentially late Gothic in structure, with Renaissance motifs and remarkable Baroque additions.

The heart of the monastery is the Great Cloister, with two orders of arcades, which contains stories from the *Life of Saint Benedict*, one of the largest Renaissance cycles of frescos. Eight of these stories were painted between 1497 and 1498 by Luca Signorelli, whose grave style and complex iconography can be admired in the later celebrated frescos in the Duomo at Orvieto ▲ *329*, his masterpiece; twenty-six other episodes were painted by Sodoma from 1505. At the same time, Fra Giovanni da Verona, one of the most highly respected intarsia specialists of the period, created some of his most valuable works for the abbey, particularly the inlaid choir stalls of the church.

SAN GALGANO ★, THE MOST FASCINATING RUIN IN TUSCANY. With its lofty, roofless nave, its incomplete façade and its columns weakened by thousands of cracks, the Cistercian abbey of San Galgano, standing alone in the Sienese countryside, is as evocative as a Greek temple and even more awesome as it thrusts its way toward heaven.

Around 1180, a nobleman, Galgano Guidotti, withdrew to Monte Siepi to lead a life of penitence, building a small circular Romanesque church there, with a simple campanile. After his canonization (1185), a Cistercian community settled at the foot of the mountain. This led to the foundation of the monastery (1224–88) of San Galgano, which soon became very large and powerful. Its slow decline began in the 16th century and culminated with the collapse of the campanile and vaulting in the 18th century; in 1789, the building was deconsecrated and finally abandoned. Like other Cistercian abbeys in central Italy (for example, Fossanova and Casamari ▲ *384*), San Galgano bears a close resemblance to the French models, with its emphasis on verticality and spatial clarity.

> **"THE FRENCH HAD NO KNOWLEDGE OF THIS COUNTRY,**
> **IN WHICH THE ART OF SO MANY CENTURIES CONSPIRED**
> **WITH THE SHEER BEAUTY OF THE NATURAL ENVIRONMENT TO**
> **CREATE A PARADISE ON EARTH."**

JULES MICHELET

THE CITIES OF ART IN THE EAST

PIENZA ★, THE "IDEAL CITY" OF THE RENAISSANCE. When Aeneas Silvius Piccolomini, the future Pope Pius II, was born in this town in 1405, it was called Corsignano and it looked like many other fortified medieval villages in the Valdorcia. During a visit of 1459, the well-read, humanist pope decided to revamp his place of birth in accordance with Leon Battista Alberti's theories about town-planning and architecture and appointed Bernardo Rossellino to carry out the work. Piazza Pio II was built in line with strict criteria governing the use of perspective and dramatic effect: the Duomo stands at the back, the Casa dei Canonici, the home of the Museo di Arte Sacra, and the old, completely remodeled Palazzo dei Priori are on the left and the immense Palazzo

Piccolomini is on the right. This latter is virtually a replica of Alberti's Palazzo Rucellai ▲ 286, 288 in Florence, with its innovative inner courtyard and airy loggia overlooking the valley. The façade of the cathedral reworks elements of the Tempio Malatestiano ▲ 270 in Rimini, Alberti's masterpiece, while the interior, divided into a nave and two aisles with tall clustered columns, draws its inspiration from the German late Gothic *Hallenkirchen* (hall churches) by specific order of the pope, who had admired such buildings on his travels in Germany. Pius II also built a public hospital and housing for the poor. This architectural and urban complex, still much admired today, took just over three years to build before it came to an abrupt halt with the death of the pope (1464), followed unexpectedly by the demise of Rossellino. However, Pienza still remains the most compelling example of that great humanist and Renaissance dream of an "ideal city" ● 90.

MONTEPULCIANO, A FLORENTINE ENCLAVE IN SIENA. Politian's home town has one of the richest collections of 15th- and 16th-century monuments

GOTHIC SOLITUDE
In San Galgano, the winds from the upper Valdimerse caress the ogives and pointed arches of the roofless nave of the former abbey. It stands in peaceful countryside, as befits a place of worship founded by the austere Cistercians.

PIENZA: A BUILDING PROGRAM
For his ideal city, Pius II instructed his cardinals and court to construct or remodel various buildings.

in Italy: some of the best architects worked on their construction, giving the town an unmistakably "Florentine" flavor and creating one of the most beautiful and harmonious Renaissance complexes. The main street, the Corso, is made up of Via di Gracciano, Via di Voltaia and Via di Opio and is lined with many patrician palaces, like the Palazzo Tarugi, the Palazzo Avignonesi (Via di Gracciano) attributed to Vignola, and the Palazzo Cervini (Via di Voltaia) ascribed to Antonio da Sangallo the Younger. Via di Gracciano is graced by the magnificent façade of the 15th-century church of Sant'Agostino, in which Michelozzo harmoniously married Gothic motifs with a Renaissance design. The same architect designed the Palazzo Comunale, which resembles the Palazzo della Signoria ● 79 in Florence: this building towers over the Piazza Grande, Montepulciano's center, bordered by Renaissance buildings like the elegant Palazzo Contucci (by Antonio da Sangallo the Elder and Baldassarre Peruzzi), the austere Palazzo Nobili-Tarugi with its first-floor arcading, and the majestic Duomo (1592–1630) which contains works by Taddeo di Bartolo, Michelozzo and Sano di Pietro. The Museo Civico (Via Ricci) preserves Tuscan paintings from the 13th to 18th centuries, illuminated choir books and terracottas from the Florentine school by the Della Robbia family. Another important building is the Church of San Biagio, reached by taking Via San Biagio after leaving Montepulciano through the Porta della Grassa to the east. This domed church, in the form of a Greek cross, was built between 1518 and 1545.

AN ISOLATED GEM
Outside the walls of Montepulciano, set apart on the hillside, stands what is perhaps the town's most beautiful monument: the Church of San Biagio (1518–45), a masterpiece by Antonio da Sangallo the Elder. Even from a long way off, the church does not look any smaller but continues to tower over the other buildings in the town. The building is in the form of a Greek cross topped by a magnificent dome and is completely made of travertine which has, over the years, turned to colors ranging from gold to pink.

PERUGIA,
THE HILLS OF UMBRIA
AND THE MARCHES

PERUGIA, *314*

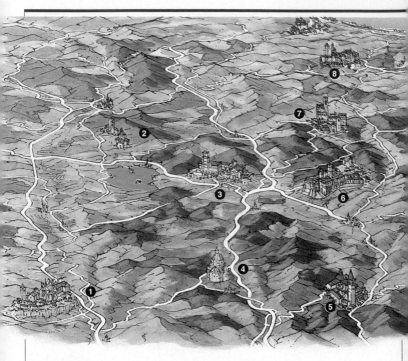

Perugia, the smallest of the twelve cities selected as interesting centers from which to explore the surrounding countryside, is a favorite destination for those interested in culture, both for its historical and artistic heritage and for the quality of its buildings. Around the city are the fascinating hills of Umbria and the Marches. Leaving the Umbrian capital, we pass briefly into Tuscany to Cortona, then head back into Umbria to Orvieto and Todi. These three centers, all within a 50-mile radius of Perugia, have a distant Etruscan past, but they also display the uniquely Italian knack for remodeling a city's face that was especially evident in the medieval and Renaissance period. Passing from the Tiber to the Umbrian valley, we visit Spoleto, where centuries of history, art and culture are intertwined, as well as Assisi, much closer to Perugia, which combines with its history and art a religious ambience due to its association with Saint Francis. Finally there is Gubbio, the last and

1 ORVIETO 2 CORTONA 3 PERUGIA 4 TODI 5 SPOLETO 6 ASSISI 7 GUBBIO 8 URBINO 9 ANCONA 10 LORETO 11 ASCOLI PICENO

most beautiful stop in Umbria, similar in many ways to the places that come before it, yet marked even more strongly by a medieval stamp. At Urbino, barely 40 miles from Gubbio but on the other side of the Appenines, the Marches welcome each visitor with "palace-city" of Federico da Montefeltro, the epitome of Renaissance perfection. At Ancona there's the spectacular sight of the majestic Basilica of San Ciriaco, towering high above the city and the Adriatic Sea. On nearby Mount Conero, dark wooded pathways offer dizzyingly framed views over the Adriatic. The close ties between art and religious devotion are visible once again at Loreto, where the famous sanctuary of the Holy House recalls the rustic simplicity of the "little home come by air from Nazareth". Finally, at Ascoli Piceno, in the far south of the Marches region, the scenic journey that commenced in Perugia comes to a fitting end in the Piazza del Popolo, a square that is surrounded by beautifully proportioned medieval and Renaissance buildings.

"He went to the back of the carriage and peered at a railway map of Italy. He looked for Urbino and compared it with Pesaro, to see if it was in smaller print. When he looked out of the window once more, the train was running along the seaside, through the canefields below Mount Ardizio. He kept looking at the sea all the way to Ancona, and when he saw it disappear among the ugly gantries of a dock, he went to look for a spot in another compartment.**"**

Paolo Volponi,
La strada per Roma
(*The Road to Rome*)

313

SALVS NRA IN MANV TVA ES

THE WELL OF THE ETRUSCANS
At the center of Piazza Piccinino, a few steps from the Cathedral of San Lorenzo, is the Sorbello Well. An unmarked entrance in the adjacent Piazza Danti provides access into the bore of the well, which is lined with travertine blocks right down to the little bridge spanning

the water, about 100 feet down. The well, dating from the same period as the city's first walls, is one of the few public works dating from the Etruscan period that have survived.

The ring of walls made of blocks of travertine, the well in the town center and the many graveyards in the various neighborhoods, are reminders that Perugia was inhabited by the Etruscans ▲ *326* until the 6th century BC. Even before that, this high ground facing onto the valley of the upper Tiber was the site of prehistoric Umbrian settlements.

THE DECLINE OF THE ETRUSCANS. The city grew up around the river, which in ancient times was the natural dividing line between the spheres of influence of the Umbrians (to the east) and the Etruscans (to the west). Situated on the trade route between the Tyrrhenian and the Adriatic Seas, Perugia acquired a dominant position in the Etruscan federation from the 4th century BC and soon came up against Roman expansionism. Then followed an increasingly intense economic and military squeeze – studded with defeats, fragile alliances and reversals of fortune – until the tragic year 40 BC when, having sided with Antony against Octavian, Perugia was sacked and burned to the ground. A few years later the acropolis was rebuilt by Octavian and named Augusta Perusia. This was written over the entrance gates to the city and can still be seen today.

FROM CLERICAL TO SIGNORIAL RULE. Following centuries of barbarian invasions (the Goths destroyed it in 547) and Byzantine sway, the city returned to exercising economic and military control – this time under protection of the papacy – over the area between the Apennines and the Valdichiana. The age of the *comuni* (free towns) ● *36* – from the 12th to the 14th centuries – saw the birth of new districts, encircled inside the new and larger ring of walls, with majestic churches and imposing civic buildings. This period of political autonomy and economic growth drew to a close at the end of the 14th century. Following this, throughout the course of the 15th century, the leading families fought among themselves in

> **"It is a rough, fierce, mountain of a city with its tall houses of dark stone, an eagle's nest which broods from afar over the immense horizon where Assisi, Foligno and Spoleto sleep."** Paul Bourget

ENRAPTURED BY THE PANORAMA
From beside the Palazzo del Capitano del Popolo you gain access to the terrace of the covered market. It is worth spending some time contemplating the magnificent view of Perugia from the terrace. To the right, you can see the southern end of the town, with the bell towers of San Domenico and San Pietro; in the middle, Assisi blazing white on the foothills of Mount Subasio; and on the left, all by itself, the little church of San Bevignate.

a bloody struggle for control of the city, which at one time or another brought to power soldiers of fortune like Braccio Fortebraccio ▲ *319* (1416–24) and influential houses like the Oddi and the Baglioni.

THE RISORGIMENTO, AN ANTICLERICAL RISING. The year 1540 was decisive for the civil and political freedoms of Perugia. To quell a popular revolt against a tax on salt planned by Pope Paul III, his nephew, Pier Luigi Farnese, put the city to the sword and the torch. On the still-smoking ruins of the residences of the Baglioni family was erected the imposing Rocca Paolina, which from then on became the symbol of Rome's power over Perugia. For more than three centuries, apart from the Napoleonic period (1798–1814) and the brief interlude of the Roman republic (1848–9), the scepter of authority remained firmly in the hands of the popes, who governed its subject provinces through proxies often unseen by the people. In 1859 a popular uprising installed a provisional government, which a few days

THE ROCCA PAOLINA
This fortress was designed by Antonio da Sangallo the Younger on behalf of Pope Paul III, in 1540, for the area where the medieval quarter of the Baglioni family ▲ *317* had stood. By erecting a powerful fortress, the pope aimed to reinforce his rule over rebellious Perugia. Ringed with massive ramparts and battlements, Rocca Paolina stretched to the city wall and had a fortified corridor that guaranteed communications with the outside. Following the suppression of the Papal States, the Rocca Paolina was demolished, in just a few days, in 1860.

315

SWEET TRADITION
You have to be nostalgic, romantic and gluttonous, all at once, to truly appreciate the "Baci"

made by Perugina, the first confectionery factory founded in Perugia, in 1907. "Baci" literally means "kisses", and each of these traditional chocolates has a small piece of paper inscribed with a different saying, conveying good wishes. In 1997 a museum was opened at Perugina's premises at San Sisto, to celebrate the firm's ninety years of business.

later was drowned in blood by a garrison of Swiss Guards sent by Pope Pius IX. But the Risorgimento had already borne its fruit: the following year the *bersaglieri* (sharpshooters) of Victor Emanuel II took possession of the city, greeted by a rejoicing throng; a plebiscite ratified its annexation to the Kingdom of Sardinia and then to Italy.

THE FACE OF THE PRESENT. Even Umbria, often called the "*cuore verde*" (green heart) of Italy, has experienced the economic and social upheavals of the 20th century. Agriculture, which until 1930 employed almost two-thirds of the population, declined steadily in the following decades, while industry – notably in the foodstuffs, textiles and construction sectors – grew, as did the tertiary sector. Perugia changed profoundly, though not in the same traumatic way as Terni and

THE GRIFFIN
The symbol of the city is a griffin with a crown on its head. This device probably dates from Etruscan times.

4

5

6

7

9

8

10

11

12

"In the red light
the still and surging /
Mountains chase
each other, / Giving
off smoke in sweet
swells / With vapors
of violet and gold
inside."

Giosue Carducci

ART SHOWS
Going up the
escalators from the
Piazza Partigiani
to the upper city,
you enter the
Bagliona ▲ *325*,
the foundations
of the Rocca Paolina
and the rest of the
medieval quarter.
The area now
hosts international
art shows.

some other cities in central
Italy. Toward the end of the
19th century the region's capital
began to expand outside its walls, filling the
surrounding plain – and, in more recent
decades, the foothills – with new residential
and industrial districts. In the 20th century
the historic center has undergone important
restoration work, although it still retains its
medieval feel, with its stone houses tumbling
over each other, winding streets, looming bell
towers and noble palaces. Indeed, for the
sensitive traveler Perugia and the many other
centers of Umbria and the Marches still
maintain the feeling and appearance of the
past, elsewhere lost forever, and of the
landscape in which little trees in the distance
"lent to the countryside a down which
thickened beneath the hills" (Paolo Volponi).

FONTIVEGGE:
STYLISTIC INNOVATION
The seat of the
Umbrian regional
government, with the
Piazza Nuova and
the other buildings
designed by Aldo
Rossi close to the
railroad station,
provide the nucleus of
an administrative
center at the foot of
Perugia's hills. It
exhibits the
metaphysical
geometry of a
De Chirico painting
but with echoes
of traditional colors,
materials and
architectural styles.

PIAZZA IV NOVEMBRE

Every historic city has its heart, a focus for civic activities or perhaps a sacred place where the people come together in worship. The heart of Perugia has always been in Piazza IV Novembre, from the time of the Etruscans and Romans, who built their Forum here. Throughout the Middle Ages and the Renaissance, generation after generation of citizens pooled resources to build the cathedral. The piazza is still the main meeting place for the local people today, as well as the venue each summer for the international "Umbria Jazz" festival.

FONTANA MAGGIORE ★. Built in 1275–8 to carry water to the city from the new Mount Pacciano aqueduct, the fountain is a cultural treasure and the symbol of medieval Perugia. The task of designing it was undertaken by Nicola and Giovanni Pisano, who conceived of the fountain as elegantly rising in tiers, consisting of a pair of twenty-four-sided pools, made of white and red stone, topped by a bronze basin; from this rose three nymphs or virtues, drawn from theology, which are now housed in the National Gallery of Umbria. Yet the fountain

"UMBRIA JAZZ"
Each year since 1973, during the first half of July jazz has left the clubs to invade the squares and streets of Perugia. Thousands of fans gather for live concerts both in the central square and in venues such as San Francesco al Prato in the northwest and the Frontone Gardens in the southeast. Jazz "greats" who have performed at these concerts include Dizzy Gillespie, Charlie Mingus, Miles Davis, Gerry Mulligan, Sarah Vaughan, Sam Rivers, Keith Jarrett and – in an effort to bring together jazz and rock – Phil Collins and Sting.

> **"T**HEY WANDERED TO AND FRO, ACCORDINGLY, AND LOST
> THEMSELVES AMONG THE STRANGE PRECIPITATE PASSAGES WHICH,
> IN PERUGIA, ARE CALLED STREETS.**"**
>
> NATHANIEL HAWTHORNE

was also designed to represent the life and history of Perugia: around the lower pool are fifty small figures performing agricultural tasks, as well as scenes drawn from political and moral history, and not least of all the symbols of the city (the griffin), the Guelf party (the lion) and the empire (the eagle). Completing the collection are the seven Liberal Arts and Philosophy. The upper pool is decorated with characters, both real and imaginary, who have made Perugia great: from the mythical Trojan founder Eulistes to Saint Herculanus, the bishop who defended the city against the Goths. At present (1997) the fountain is being restored, but you can admire it through the Plexiglas dome protecting it.

SAN LORENZO. Work on the construction of the cathedral, built on top of an earlier Romanesque church, lasted from 1345 to 1587. The building runs along the southern side of the piazza, while the unembellished façade with its Baroque doorway faces onto the neighboring Piazza Danti. In fact, the southern side, with its stairways constantly crowded with tourists, holds the most interest: a delicate floor paved with white and red marble from Mount Subasio is overshadowed by the great wall in rusticated stone pierced by large Gothic windows. The 15th-century wooden chancel in the apse is San Lorenzo's greatest masterpiece: it includes an interesting *Deposition from the Cross* by Federico Barocci (1567–9) and the venerated *Madonna of the Graces*, attributed to Giannicola di Paolo. The cathedral's MUSEO CAPITOLARE holds the magnificent *Panel of Saint Onofrius* by Luca Signorelli (1484), as well as paintings such as Bartolomeo Caporali's *Pietà* (1486), the *Tryptych* of Meo di Guido da Siena, illuminated manuscripts, and other precious artworks. Close to Piazza Danti is one of Perugia's oldest sites, an ETRUSCAN WELL (the Sorbello Well ▲ *314*), dating from the same period as the walls (6th century BC).

LOGGIA OF BRACCIO FORTEBRACCIO. The Loggia of Braccio Fortebraccio forms a continuation of the left side of the cathedral. Dating from 1423, this elegant balcony was originally intended by the lord of Perugia as an adornment for the adjoining palace, now long since vanished. Under the four arches of the balcony is a cast of the "Stone of Justice", with which the city commemorated the decision in 1234 to write off public debt.

PALAZZO DEI PRIORI ★. Opposite the side of San Lorenzo stands the magnificent and imposing Palazzo dei Priori (1293–1444) – the seat of Perugia's magistracy in the age of the *comuni* ● *36* – which is now the seat of the city council. The battlements and Gothic three-mullioned windows along its façade and flank give the piazza its characteristically medieval feel. A picturesque staircase fans out from the doorway, above which are set two consoles bearing the griffin

BRACCIO DA MONTONE, KNOWN AS "FORTEBRACCIO" OR "STRONG ARMS".
This soldier of fortune (1368–1424) was hounded out of Perugia with his family when he was scarcely in his twenties. He returned as undisputed lord after the battle on the Tiber in 1416. Both the balcony on Piazza IV Novembre and the ancestral coat of arms in the Palazzo dei Priori commemorate him.

THE HOLY RING
Kept under lock and key in a priceless tabernacle of gilded copper in San Lorenzo's Chapel of the Holy Ring is which, according to legend, belonged to the Virgin Mary. An object of popular devotion, it was pilfered from the Church of San Francesco di Chiusi by a friar and given to the city of Perugia in 1473. Perugino's painting *The Wedding of the Virgin* (1499) – now in France – was commissioned to decorate the chapel.

PERUGINO
Described by Vasari as a painter of great grace and delicacy, Pietro Vannucci (c. 1448–1523), better known as Perugino, was active in Perugia, Florence and Rome. His paintings, almost always religious in theme, were the archetype of Umbrian landscape art – with their softly sloping hillsides, bejeweled with trees, brilliantly caught by the keen eye of the miniaturist.

A SUCCESSFUL "FAKE"
In Perugia some modern additions to the historic fabric of the city harmonize so well with their ancient surroundings that

of Perugia and the Guelf lion, two of the best examples of casting in Italian sculpture anywhere. The doorway leads to the second-floor Hall of Notaries whose lively 14th-century frescos recount biblical scenes and moral fables. On the Corso Vannucci side, the building's main doorway leads into the Hall of the College of Merchants ▲ *321*, engraved in 1326 with allegorical scenes.

NATIONAL GALLERY OF UMBRIA. The fourth floor of the Palazzo dei Priori houses the most outstanding collection of the region's art, documenting its development from the 13th century through to the 18th century. A wooden crucifix from 1236 is the oldest work in the gallery, which also features the paintings of the Maestro di San Francesco, Meo di Guido da Siena, Duccio di Buoninsegna, the Giotto-like Puccio Capanna, Benedetto Bonfigli, Gentile da Fabriano and Fra Angelico. The climax of the collection is Piero della Francesca's remarkable *Polyptych of Saint Anthony*, together with works by

Perugino (including *The Madonna of Consolation*, *Adoration of the Shepherds* and *View of Mount Rapido*) and by one of Perugino's pupils, Pinturicchio (*Polyptych of Saint Mary of the Ditches*). These last two painters are also credited with the eight tableaux illustrating the *Miracles of Saint Bernard*, a high point in 15th-century Umbrian art. So far as sculpture is concerned, the gallery has on display some priceless reliefs from a fountain sculpted by Arnolfo di Cambio (1281).

MAESTÀ DELLE VOLTE. This picturesque street leads from Piazza IV Novembre – past the Loggia di Braccio Fortebraccio – and snakes its way down among arches, vaults and overhanging medieval houses.

only an expert would look twice. One notable addition is the fountain in the medieval Via Maestà delle Volte – which looks convincingly medieval but was in fact built in 1927.

CORSO VANNUCCI AND PIAZZA MATTEOTTI

The Corso Vannucci is the favorite haunt of Perugians for their *passeggiata* (the traditional evening stroll) – past former aristocratic residences, dating from the 16th and 17th centuries, for the most part now occupied by banks, insurance brokers and other businesses.

HALL OF THE COLLEGE OF MERCHANTS.

The records of the Merchants' Guild date from as early as 1218, but it was during the course of the 14th century that the society began to take a strongly active part in the city's life, electing its own representatives to the magistracy under the rule of the priors. In 1390 the city granted this influential professional organization a hall on the first floor of the Palazzo dei Priori (situated to the right of the main entrance), which in the first half of the 15th century was redecorated with inlaid paneling.

COLLEGE OF THE EXCHANGE.

Further along the Corso Vannucci, at the far end of the Palazzo dei Priori, is the seat of the medieval Moneychangers' Guild. Its representatives were expected to ensure that moneychanging was both legitimate and clearly regulated and to adjudicate in any financial disputes. The proceedings took place in the AUDIENCE HALL, itself one of the city's greatest works of art, with wooden furnishings and frescos (1498–1500) by Perugino. On the ceilings and floors can be seen likenesses of mythological characters and illustrious figures from the past, interspersed with depictions not only of the cardinal virtues, but also prophets, prophetesses, the Nativity, and God the Father bestowing His blessings. Near the Audience Hall, the CHAPEL OF SAINT JOHN boasts frescos (1513–28) by Giannicola di Paolo.

PIAZZA MATTEOTTI.

A few steps from Corso Vannucci, heading east, is the square formerly called Piazza del Sopramuro. It rises above the Etruscan walls toward the new part of the city on the hillside.

PALAZZO DEL CAPITANO DEL POPOLO.

This building, on the eastern side of the square, blends Gothic with Renaissance elements (1472–81) and has a fine doorway, double windows and a balcony. It is now used for public lectures.

A JEWEL IN WOOD
The rectangular hall of the College of Merchants, in late-Gothic style with a double cross-patterned vault, is completely covered on all sides by a precious wood inlay, consisting of square and quatrefoil panels. Also in wood is a small pulpit with exquisite columns, as well as a bench and statues of the Virtues.

SAN PROSPERO
A walk along Via della Cupa and out beyond the walls leads to the Church of San Prospero. Often overlooked by tourists in a hurry, it offers a pleasant surprise for those taking the time to visit (ask for the key from the Salesian priests next door). Inside is a ciborium (7th–8th century) of Lombard make; and frescos from 1225, the oldest in the city yet barely studied to this day.

PLASTERWORKS
As well as paintings by Umbrian artists from the last two hundred years, the Accademia di Belli Arti (next to the little Church of San Bernardino) has around three hundred items of plasterwork. These include slabs worked by Michelangelo, and an original plaster version of the *Three Graces* donated by the sculptor, Antonio Canova (1757–1822), who was one of the greatest exponents of neoclassicism.

VIA DEI PRIORI

Starting from the Palazzo dei Priori, this street leads down between stately houses toward Lake Trasimene. Branching off it are typically medieval alleyways, among them Via Ritorta and Via della Cupa, which in turn are crisscrossed by inviting passageways that lead to lesser-known monuments. A walk along Via dei Priori unveils a succession of the most dazzling jewels of Renaissance and Baroque architecture.

SAN FILIPPO NERI. With its grandiose façade (1665), this is the most interesting Baroque building in the city; the interior also has a marvelous unity of style, though frescoed by various 17th-century artists. Displayed above the great altar is *The Conception of Mary*, a tableau by Pietro da Cortona (1662).

TOWER OF THE SCIRI. Continuing down the street, you come to the only tower house surviving from the 12th and 13th centuries. Some 150 feet high, it proclaimed to the countryside all around the wealth of the family that built it.

MADONNA DELLA LUCE. In the picturesque square of the same name, this church is a lesser but nonetheless interesting example of Renaissance architecture. The travertine façade, with a rose window embellished with festoons, is from 1512–18. Inside, the frescos on the dome (1532), painted by Giovan Battista Caporali, and the *Madonna with Baby and Saints* by Tiberio d'Assisi (on the altar) are remarkable works that are highly prized.

SAN BERNARDINO ★. Nearby, in Piazza San Francesco, stands the most beautiful Renaissance church in Perugia. The enchanting pink-and-blue façade (1457–61) by Agostino di Ducchio celebrates the popular Franciscan preacher who was frequently seen in this Umbrian city. The interior, where a

4th-century Roman sarcophagus serves as the high altar, is as simple and unimposing as the exterior is fussy.

THE NORTHERN QUARTERS

Toward the north, outside the gate stretch the poorer districts of Sant'Angelo, Sant'Antonio and Fonte Nuovo, built at the beginning of the 13th century to house people drawn to the city from the countryside. In medieval times the northern quarters lying along the Corso Garibaldi were actually part of the city proper, enclosed within the outer city walls. Yet these districts retain a lively and popular atmosphere, and a vitality that is sometimes lacking in cities where the historic center has virtually become a museum. Beyond the walls, toward the east, lies an unexpected jewel: the CHURCH OF SANTA MARIA DI MONTELUCE.

THE ETRUSCAN ARCH. Dating from the 3rd century BC, the Etruscan arch here is the main gate of the Etruscan and Roman cemetery. Its importance is evident from the two robust buttresses spanned by the arch, decorated with friezes, escutcheons and small Ionic columns. In the 2nd century BC the motif of Colonia Vibia underlined Perugia's effective submission to Rome. The inscription Augusta Perusia ▲ *314* emphasized its later integration into Augustus' empire. On the same square as the Etruscan arch stands the UNIVERSITÀ ITALIANA PER STRANIERI (Italian University for Foreigners).

SANT'ANGELO. At the end of the Corso Garibaldi, beyond the MONASTERY OF THE BLESSED COLOMBA and before the medieval gate, is this unusual circular paleo-Christian church dating from the 5th century. The interior is equally surprising, with its round ambulatory; and the exposed roof has a central rotunda supported by sixteen Roman Corinthian columns.

SAN SEVERO. In Piazza Raffaello, to the northeast of the historic center, this little oratory has one of the city's most startling surprises: the only fresco (1505–8) executed in Perugia by Raphael. The lower part (six saints) was done by the aging Perugino, after his great pupil's death

SAN DOMENICO

SAN PIETRO

THE "MIRACULOUS BANNER"
Crippled by a plague epidemic in 1494, the city begged the help of the Dominican abbess Colomba. On her suggestion, Giannicola di Paolo painted a banner which was carried in procession by the people of Perugia for three days running. In spite of this, the plague was not moved to pity.

BLESSED COLOMBA
Saint Francis and Saint Dominic met each other in 1220 at the Monastery of the Blessed Colomba, in what is now the Corso Garibaldi. Fact or legend? Dante seems to have believed that such a meeting did take place, as he mentions it in Canto XI of his *Paradiso*: "One in his zeal was truly seraphim-like; / the other, so wise while on this earth, / was a dazzling vision of cherubic light".

THE SOUTHERN QUARTERS

A stone's throw from the center, on a spur sloping down from the hillside, Corso Cavour runs southeast, through the XX Giugno district. This "corridor" of houses, churches and grand buildings, between Porta Marzia and Porta di San Costanzo, makes up the city's southern suburbs, which are rich in art and dotted with reminders of history. In contrast, heading southwest, toward the railroad station, you reach the modern district of FONTIVEGGE ▲ *317*. This venture is Perugia's response to the challenge of the new millennium, and after careful planning the area will be redesigned in a daring attempt to integrate the modern city with the historic center that overlooks it.

PORTA MARZIA. A short distance from the central Piazza Italia, this gate dating from the 2nd century BC has suffered from the urban planning changes of an earlier age. In this case the architect Antonio da Sangallo the Younger, while building the fortress of Rocca Paolina ▲ *315* for Pope Paul III in 1540, summarily cut the gate out of the city's Etruscan walls in order to put it together again, piece by piece, about 4 yards further outside the ramparts of the new papal fortress. The old walls were swallowed up by this new project; they were razed to the ground and, along with them, the houses and towers of the Baglioni family.

VIA BAGLIONA. At the opening of the Porta Marzia, you enter the ancient subterranean Via Bagliona. This winds along the perimeter of the Rocca Paolina and takes in a number of sights.

SAN DOMENICO. The great rugged façade of this Dominican church, dating from the 14th and 15th centuries, dominates the first stretch of Corso Cavour. Inside, the Gothic windows in the apse are second in size only to those of the Duomo in Milan ▲ *188*. The Renaissance chancel (1470–98) and the funeral monument (1324–5) of Benedict XI, an elegant tomb in the Italian Gothic style, are also prized.

NATIONAL ARCHEOLOGICAL MUSEUM OF UMBRIA. Situated next to the former Convent of San Domenico, the museum has displays of prehistoric, Umbrian, Etruscan and Roman finds from the region and from the neighboring Marches and Tuscany. Of particular interest are the objects recovered from the various graveyards – which have made it possible, through studying the funeral rites of the Umbrian and Etruscan populations, to reconstruct the development of the two civilizations over the centuries. The museum's crown jewel is the COLUMN OF PERUGIA (3rd–2nd century BC), one of the longest and most revealing Etruscan inscriptions to come to light. For a fuller appreciation of Perugia's Etruscan past, the BURIAL VAULT OF THE VOLUMNI, a little way out of the city toward Assisi, is well worth a visit.

SAN PIETRO. After the PORTA SAN PIETRO, a fine but incomplete example of Renaissance elegance, you come to the Benedictine abbey of the same name. Tradition has it that the church and the monastery were both consecrated in 968. All that remains from this time are the foundations of the original basilica. The body of the building, the imposing hexagonal bell tower and the monastery cloisters were built in the 15th to 17th centuries. The interior of the church has a surprising number of canvases and frescos, among which are paintings by Sassoferrato, Guercino, Guido Reni and the cycle of great paintings (1592–4) by Aliense – a student of Veronese – and four small canvases (1496) by Perugino that were found in the sacristy. In the apse is a marvelous wooden chancel (1525–6). At the rear of the chancel a small doorway leads to a loggia with a magnificent panorama of Assisi, Spello, Montefalco, Bettona and, in the distance, the Apennines.

A HOUSE FOR THE AFTERLIFE
An Etruscan tomb (dating from the 2nd century BC) in the form of a Roman house: this is what makes

the burial vault of the Volumni (near the San Giovanni Bridge) so fascinating. Discovered in 1840, the "house" – with an atrium, staircase and rooms – contains priceless funerary urns in travertine and marble.

▲ THE ETRUSCANS

An aura of enduring mystery shrouds the Etruscans, whose origin is unknown. They may have been indigenous, or perhaps settlers from Asia Minor. Present in Italy from the 8th century BC, the Etruscans were a highly cultured people and Italy's first major civilization. They based themselves in an area between the Arno and Tiber rivers, along the shores of the Tyrrhenian Sea and the plains of the Po. Their culture, which flourished around the 6th century BC, when they organized a system of fortified city-states, made an enduring impression on large swathes of the Italian countryside. Conquered by the Romans in the 3rd century BC, the Etruscans left a profound artistic legacy, capable, even today, of surprising archeologists and researchers of the classical Italian past.

ETRUSCAN TOMBS
Burial chambers began to appear from the 8th century BC, dug out of the ground or built of great blocks of stone. The Tomb of the Bulls, in the Monterozzi cemetery at Tarquinia, is one of the oldest, dating from the 6th century BC. It has two funerary "cells" and a main chamber, with pictorial decorations drawn from Greek mythology.

SARCOPHAGUS OF THE AMAZONS
This decorated coffin, which was found at Tarquinia, dates from the 4th century BC. On the sides is an Amazon scene, while on the pediment Atheon is in the process of being torn apart by dogs. The sarcophagus provides proof of the profound influence of Greek mythology on the upper classes of the Etruscan world.

326

A DANCE FOR THE DECEASED
Dance scene on a small burial urn. Bas-reliefs of this kind, relating to the cult of the dead, were common in Chiusi during the second half of the 6th century BC.

SARCOPHAGUS OF THE HUSBAND AND WIFE
The couple depicted on this sarcophagus from Cerveteri (6th century BC) are half-reclining on a couch. The wife appears to be pouring perfume into her husband's hand. Their gestures and the harmony of the composition convey the strong bonds of affection that united them.

DISPLAY OF RANK
Plate, in silver and gold, with scenes and figures with an Egyptian feel. Found in the royal Tomb of Bernadini di Palestrina, it testifies to the influence of near Eastern styles on Etruscan art of the 7th century BC.

THE FICORONI "CISTA"
Found at Palestrina and signed "Novius Plautius" (a Greek artist active in Etruria from the end of the 4th century BC to the beginning of the 3rd), this bronze *cista* (casket) is decorated with episodes from the legend of the Argonauts. Carousing figures of Dionysus and two satyrs form the elegant handle on top of the lid.

TEMPLE FRAGMENTS
grand pediment adorned
the temple at ancient
lamone. Fragments of
ive work from it (2nd
BC) depict episodes
e war of "The Seven
against Thebes".

▲ FROM PERUGIA TO VALDICHIANA AND THE TIBER VALLEY

BETWEEN THE ARNO AND PAGLIA RIVERS
In effect a southward continuation of the Casentino valley, the Valdichiana rolls on for 60 miles, taking in the valleys of the Arno and Paglia. Grapes and other fruits are grown here, but this fertile land is known above all for raising a breed of cow known as the *chianina*. White and well built, it is highly prized for the quality of its beef.

A MEMORABLE CHANDELIER
In the Museo dell' Accademia Etrusca, in Cortona, a bronze Etruscan chandelier (5th–4th century BC), weighing 128 lbs and measuring 2 feet in diameter, is a truly outstanding exhibit. In the center is a carving of a gorgon, and the sixteen candleholders have the form of satyrs and sirens.

❝It has a restful appearance, free of dramatic colors. Most people look at it solely from the point of view of artistic and natural beauty. Foreigners have a very simple, pleasant idea of it: a dense crown of little cities and wonderful textures, blending the beautiful countryside and tales of Saint Francis with inhabitants who are elegant and refined by nature.❞ This is how author Guido Piovene, traveling around Italy in the middle of the 1950's, recalled the fascinating essence of this triangle of territory, centering on Perugia and wedged between Tuscany, the Marches and Lazio.

FROM THE VALDICHIANA TO THE TIBER VALLEY

CORTONA'S ETRUSCAN MEMORIES. It was with the publication in 1724–36 of *On royal Etruria*, by the Scottish scholar Thomas Dempster, that Cortona became known as the "queen of Etruria". A fulsome title, to be sure, but not unwarranted, since Cortona was one of the foremost cities of the Etruscan confederation, along with Perugia, Arezzo, Volterra, Orvieto, Chiusi and Tarquinia. Cortona was at the height of its splendor in the last centuries before Christ, and a reminder of its power in ancient times can be seen as you come into the town. You are immediately hemmed inside the gigantic town walls (which in part follow the line of the original ones) at the foot of Mount San Egidio, towering over the Valdichiana and the road linking Arezzo with Perugia. Once ho[me] to the first Etruscan Academy of Italy (1727), Cortona hosts the MUSEO DELL'ACCADEMIA (in Palazzo Pretori[o] in the Piazza della Repubblica), wh[ere] archeological finds of considerable interest are housed. The town is a[lso] rich in masterpieces dating from

> **"T**HE FACADE [OF ORVIETO CATHEDRAL] WITH ITS DAZZLING MOSAICS BRINGS TO MIND THE RISING SUN. WHATEVER RESTORATION MAY HAVE TAKEN PLACE IN THE 17TH AND 18TH CENTURIES HAS NOT HAD THE SLIGHTEST IMPACT.**"**
> STANLEY T. WILLIAMS, *ITALY IN A FIAT TOPOLINO*

14th and 15th centuries, such as the painted crucifix by Pietro Lorenzetti and the *Annunciation* by Fra Angelico in the MUSEO DIOCESANO, in Piazza Duomo. Below, about 2 miles from the old town, stands the CHURCH OF THE MADONNA DEL CALCINAIO (1485–1513), a Renaissance jewel created by Francesco di Giorgio Martini in the last decade of his life.

ORVIETO'S SUBLIME ARCHITECTURE ★. Following the trail of Etruscan sites, you come to Orvieto, gently seated on the plateau of a volcanic rock face and dominating the Paglia plain. Another ancient Etruscan city, Orvieto was destroyed by the Romans in 265 BC and its population deported to Volsinii (modern-day Bolsena). Reborn in the Middle Ages under the name Urbs Vetus, the city appears today as a citadel of bedrock and basalt rising up from massive walls on the hillside's spur. With its crisscross of narrow streets that snake like trenches to let in shafts of light between the house fronts, Orvieto retains a medieval feel. It has the town-center culture typical of the 13th century, of which the PALAZZO DEL POPOLO (in the Piazza del Popolo) and the CATHEDRAL are the

THE WELL OF SAN PATRIZIO
For Orvieto's well, the architect Antonio da Sangallo the Younger designed an ingenious double-helical stairway by which people and their mules could reach the water, 203 feet down, without getting in each other's way while descending or coming back up. Without knowing it, today's tourist who throws a coin in the well is performing the same gesture as penitents two centuries ago, who gave an offering to the friars in the hope of getting to heaven.

supreme architectural expressions. The cathedral attracted generations of visitors on the Grand Tour, who lingered to describe the mosaics, the bas-reliefs and the Orcagna rose window blazing in the façade at sunset. A Gothic masterpiece, the building was begun in 1290 and continued by Lorenzo Maitani in the 14th century. On its façade both sculpture and painting are used to illustrate the triumphs and tragedies of the Old and New Testaments. Inside, one of the chapels is decorated with an awesome *Last Judgement* (left) by Luca Signorelli.

THE MIRACULOUS COMMUNION CLOTH
Legend has it that in 1263 a doubting and libertine priest celebrating mass in Bolsena saw blood drip from the host on to the communion cloth while he was serving the Eucharist. The rumor reached Pope Urban IV, who was in Orvieto at that time. The communion cloth was displayed to the public and on August 11, 1264 the Pope inaugurated the feast of Corpus Domini. Today the communion cloth is kept in a reliquary inside the high altar of Orvieto Cathedral.

JACOPONE DA TODI
"O Pope Boniface, you have played a great joke on the world / What with all that laughing, take care not to split in two." The famous insult hurled by Jacopone da Todi (c. 1235–1303) sheds light on only one aspect of this remarkable religious poet. Unforgettable, too, are his songs of

praise, which exalt divine love and the "sorrowful mysteries" of the Passion.

This clifftop town is like a city of tunnels carved out of the soft volcanic rock: a close network of stone has opened up over a long period of time. Here you will find Etruscan wells, medieval pits under the houses, full of crockery from the period, and deep cellars dug on every level. In underground Orvieto the most famous monument is the WELL OF SAN PATRIZIO ▲ *329*, which Pope Clement VII had built between 1528 and 1537 so that the city would never be without water in the event of siege.
UMBRIA'S MIDDLE AGES, IN TODI. If you had to choose a square that summed up in its buildings the spirit of the Middle Ages in Umbria the prime candidate would be the Piazza del Popolo in Todi. Enclosed by public buildings and the cathedral, the square is situated in the middle of the town, which is laid out in a triangular pattern, on a pleasant little hill, within walls dating from three distinct periods (Etruscan, Roman and medieval). The PALAZZO DEL POPOLO (1214–28) and the adjoining PALAZZO DEL CAPITANO (1290) make up a single medieval structure. The flight of stairs, shared by the two buildings, leads to the Sala del Capitano del Popolo (Hall of the Captain of the People), the throbbing pulse of public life in the age of the *comuni* ● *36*, while the arcade below was the venue for the market and the place where the people's often lively disputes were thrashed out. In front of this complex of public buildings rises the solemn flight of stairs leading up to the CATHEDRAL (12th–14th centuries), on whose façade the three rose windows and the three imposing doorways rise further still in a triangular pattern. On the south side of the Piazza del Popolo, and of profound architectural significance, is the PALAZZO DEI PRIORI (first half of the 14th century, with

> **"TWO STAIRCASES, AMONG THE NOBLEST IN CENTRAL ITALY – ONE A TESTIMONY TO RELIGIOUS POWER, THE OTHER SECULAR – CONFRONT ONE ANOTHER ON THE PIAZZA [DEL POPOLO, IN TODI], POLES APART, MUTUALLY EXCLUSIVE TO THIS DAY."**   ENZO SICILIANO

Renaissance modifications), which housed the magistracy during the period of papal rule. To appreciate the complex power relations, both secular and religious, that underpinned the life of a medieval town, one need only visit the nearby CHURCH OF SAN FORTUNATO (in Piazza Umberto I), built by Franciscan Friars Minor from 1292 onward. Buried in the crypt is Jacopo da Todi, a combative defender of the Franciscan Order in its struggle with the papal Curia in Rome – for which he was excommunicated and imprisoned – and one of the earliest and most interesting composers of vernacular poetry. Outside the walls is SANTA MARIA DELLA CONSOLAZIONE (1508–1617), in the form of a Greek cross, whose surprising harmony conveys a feeling of the utmost elegance.

FROM THE UMBRIAN VALLEY TO THE PLATEAU OF GUBBIO

EARLY CHRISTIAN SPOLETO AND THE FESTIVAL OF TWO WORLDS. Already important in the Roman era, and later the capital of a Lombard duchy, Spoleto has the most noteworthy early-Christian churches in the region. Of these, the CHURCH

OF SAN PIETRO (probably 5th century, but with medieval additions) has a finely sculpted late-Romanesque stone façade. The central doorway is also special, being embellished with floral motifs and elegant bas-reliefs depicting biblical scenes. At the foot of the Luciano Hill nestles the BASILICA OF SAN SALVATORE, built in the 4th and 5th centuries, which still has its original apse; of particular interest is the façade, in which you can discern some of the earliest Oriental influences on Italian art. In addition to these two buildings, there are important early-Christian and Romanesque churches, evocative Roman ruins and the dizzying Ponte delle Torri – but even these cannot eclipse the fascinating frescos (1467–9) of Filippo Lippi in the apse of the cathedral, itself a magnificent structure. Spoleto, however, does not live on devotion alone: a whole world of culture has been welcomed here since 1958, when composer Gian Carlo Menotti inaugurated the Festival of Two Worlds, one of the most prestigious international get-togethers of music, dance, theater and figurative art.

THE FESTIVAL'S NAME
"I was coming from the United States, a famous composer, well-connected, with a real possibility of getting together the funds to set up a very prestigious artistic event. But why should it take place in the United States ? I was, after all, an Italian composer, not an Italian-American one. It was only right, therefore, to emphasize this side of me and, at the same time, make my Italian compatriots familiar with the art of that other great country."
  Gian Carlo Menotti

PONTE DELLE TORRI
This bridge was erected in Spoleto during the 13th and 14th centuries on the remains of a Roman aqueduct. Some 250 feet high and 250 yards long, it has ten oval arches. Along the bridge runs a small road protected by a low wall and by the rampart of the ancient aqueduct.

TODAY'S FRANCISCANS

There are altogether approximately 35,000 Franciscan friars, divided into three orders: the Minors, the Conventuals and the Capucins. The first (about 20,000 members) keep alive the order's historical continuity, and devote themselves to helping the poor and needy. The second (around 3,000 friars) split off from the Minors in 1517 and live in the cities. The Basilica of Saint Francis in Assisi and that of Saint Anthony ▲ 235 in Padua are entrusted to their care. The third order (about 12,000), which was recognized in 1528, maintains the discipline and poverty of the original friars.

ASSISI, ART AND SPIRITUALITY. The starting point for a tour around the legend of the Pauper of Assisi, the BASILICA OF SAN FRANCESCO ★ is composed of two churches, sheltered from the valley by the great building of the Holy Convent. The Lower Church – begun in 1228, the year of the canonization of Francis – has Romanesque features and low, crossed and barrelled vaults. The saint's remains are kept in the sarcophagus below the altar. On the shoulders of the Lower Church rises the Upper Church, the interior of which is lofty and filled with light – as if calling the visitor to the Franciscan gaiety of the *Canticle of the Creatures*. In the two churches are cycles of frescos, which juxtapose eye-witness scenes from the saint's life, drawing a deliberate parallel between episodes from Christ's life and Francis'. Particularly worth seeing – in the Upper Church – are the twenty-eight scenes from the celebrated cycle that Giotto began in 1296. As you view them in order, the life of Francesco di Pietro di Bernadone passes before your eyes: from his birth in 1181 (or 1182) until his death, as a pauper (his order is characterized by poverty), in Porziuncola (1226). Tragically, the church was struck in October 1997 by a series of earthquakes which rocked Umbria and the Marches, sustaining serious structural damage. Much of the roof collapsed, killing two friars and a pair of government heritage experts who were surveying the harm done to the artworks by the first

> **"PRAISE TO YOU, MY LORD, AND ALL YOUR CREATION, ESPECIALLY BROTHER SUN, THE LIGHT OF DAY BY WHICH YOU SHOW US OUR WAY."**
>
> SAINT FRANCIS OF ASSISI

tremors. It would appear that Giotto's famous cycle of frescos, while suffering some cracking, was relatively spared and can be restored, although the artist's *Saint Jerome* was not so fortunate. In addition, Cimabue's frescoed vault of Saint Matthew from *The Four Evangelists* collapsed completely. The precise extent of the damage will not be known until detailed surveys are complete. In all likelihood, however, the church will be closed for restoration for some time to come. The forested place where the saint lived was later completely encased inside the grandiose BASILICA OF SANTA MARIA DEGLI ANGELI, a little outside the city. Francis was baptized in the CATHEDRAL (in Piazza San Rufino), begun in 1134, as was Saint Clare. The BASILICA OF SANTA CHIARA (1257–65), houses the body of the saint who founded the Franciscan Order of Poor Clares. Reports suggest that the basilica also sustained earthquake damage, although the exact nature of this awaits the findings of the survey team. Leaving the city by the Capucin gate, after 2½ miles clambering up Mount Subasio, you will at last arrive at the EREMO DELLE CARCERI, the forest hermitage to which Saint Francis and his friends and followers used to retire, in order to meditate and pray in the solitude of the caves.

GUBBIO, A CITY BUILT ON A SLOPE. The medieval areas of this town – which was first an ancient Umbrian center and then a Roman city – remain largely intact, though they look somewhat austere thanks to the local gray limestone. From the Piazza dei Quaranta Martiri you can see the whole of the town, built on a slant on the foothills of Mount Ingino. At the foot of the slope stands the LOGGIA DEI TIRATORI, overlooked by the 13th-century CHURCH OF SAN GIOVANNI BATTISTA, its façade adorned with a wide Gothic doorway and flanked by a beautiful bell tower. Raising your eyes up over the crags, you will spot the Palazzo dei Consoli and the Palazzo Pretorio, which face onto Piazza della Signoria, the center of the town's public life. The PALAZZO DEI CONSOLI (1332–49) is one of Italy's most beautiful public buildings. A fan staircase leads to the doorway, with its frescoed lunette and an inscription on the architrave attributing the work to Angelo da Orvieto. Inside, the

▲ From the hills of Gubbio to Urbino and the Adriatic

Fe Dux
This abbreviation stands for *Federicus Dux* (Duke Federico). Along with the eagle from the family coat of arms, it is carved, almost obsessively, all over the interior of the splendid Palazzo Ducale in Urbino: on balustrades, skirting boards, architraves and ceilings. Here and there you see a slightly different monogram: FC. This provides a valuable historical clue, since it affords evidence that certain decorations were carried out before 1474, the date when Count Federico da Montefeltro (*il conte*, hence the C) was transformed into Duke Federico or *il duca* (in Latin, *dux*) by papal grant.

magnificent Great Hall, the seat of the people's assembly, has a barrel-vaulted ceiling and many Roman and late-medieval relics along the walls. The other rooms house the town's MUSEO CIVICO (where the famous Tablets of Gubbio are kept ▲ *333*) and the rich PINACOTECA COMUNALE (municipal art gallery).

Unfinished to this day, the PALAZZO PRETORIO (1349) opposite is now the seat of the town council. Raising your eyes up further, you can make out the battlements of the PALAZZO DUCALE. Built on the orders of Federico da Montefeltro from 1476 onward, this gorgeous building put the seal on the Montefeltro family's rule over Gubbio, which had begun in 1384. In front of the Palazzo Ducale stands the sober bulk of the DUOMO, rebuilt in the Gothic style at the beginning of the 14th century. A network of steps and stairways, sometimes with a central handrail, lead the visitor uphill from one level of this picturesque town to the next.

BETWEEN URBINO AND THE ADRIATIC

THE PALACE-CITY OF THE MONTEFELTRO FAMILY AT URBINO. Whether Duke Federico wanted to assure his family a great destiny in the form of an unforgettable monument, or whether he simply wanted to create an eyrie from which to look out over the undulating countryside of his ducal lands, what is certain is that during his reign (1444–82) he turned the little hill town of Urbino into a model city. The heart of this masterpiece of a city is the PALAZZO DUCALE ★, ● *78* (begun in 1465), the work first of the Dalmatian architect Luciano Laurana and then of Francesco di Giorgio Martini, with the collaboration of the most important artists of the time. In front of the palazzo's façade rises the TORRIONE DELLA DATA, an ingenious construction in which Francesco di Giorgio Martini built a huge helical gallery of stairs to enable pedestrians (and, in those days, horses) to come up from the level of Piazza del Mercatale to the level of the town center.

COURTLY CODE
It was during his years in Urbino, in the service of Guidobaldo da Montefeltro (1504–8) and Francesco Maria Della Rovere (1508–16), that Baldesar Castiglione gathered material for *The Courtier*, a bible of Renaissance taste, behavior and style.

> **"GUBBIO IS SUPERB. IT LOOKS AS IF IT WERE PLACED THERE BY THE HANDS OF A FRIENDLY GIANT."**
>
> GUIDO CERONETTI

Urbino is also the home of the NATIONAL GALLERY OF THE MARCHES, where masterpieces such as the *Flagellation* and *Madonna of Senigallia* by Piero della Francesca, the famous *Ideal City* attributed to Luciano Laurana and Raphael's *Portrait of a Lady* (sometimes called *"The Silent Woman"*) are kept.

ROMANESQUE AND 18TH-CENTURY ART IN ANCONA.

Goethe wrote that from Piazza Sangallo you can see "the most beautiful sunset in the world". It's not all that hard to believe him if you think about Ancona's position which, facing onto the sea but sheltered in a cosy elbow bend (in Greek, *ankos* – hence the name of the city), stretches like an amphitheater around the northern foothills of Mount Conero. Engaged in a constant struggle with the neighboring cities of the Marches, besieged by Frederick Barbarossa and again by the Venetians, Ancona ended up being absorbed (1532) into the Papal States. All the same, it is in fact to one of the popes, Clement XII, and to his penchant for patronage, that the city's 18th-century artistic flowering is owed, as typified in the works of Vanvitelli: the LAZZARETTO or MONOLITH OF VANVITELLI, begun in 1733, a majestic pentagonal structure; the ARCO CLEMENTINO (1738), which adorns the port area; and the picturesque façade (1743) of the CHURCH OF JESUS. But surpassing everything in Ancona, thanks not least to its panoramic situation, is the CATHEDRAL OF SAN CIRIACO, one of the most important Romanesque buildings in central Italy. Built between the 11th and 13th centuries, it recalls the influence of Byzantine architecture, but combines this with Gothic elements; over a floor on the plan of a Greek cross swells a harmonious twelve-sided dome dating from the 13th century. Not far away, in the rooms of the elegant Ferretti residence, home of the NATIONAL ARCHEOLOGICAL MUSEUM OF THE MARCHES, you can retrace the history of the region from paleolithic times to the Roman age, wandering among magnificent black-and-red-figure vases from Attica (6th–4th centuries BC), bronzes from the Etruscan period and items in gold from Gallic tombs.

"PIERO THE GREAT"
Born in Sansepolcro in 1420, Piero della Francesca began to paint in Florence with Domenico Veneziano some time before 1440. Around the middle of the 15th century, the artist was first in Ferrara and Rimini and then in Arezzo. The contact with the court of Urbino that followed brought him fortune and fame. Finally, after returning to Sansepolcro, he died there in 1492.

THE LIONS OF SAN CIRIACO
Before entering the Ancona Cathedral on the patron saint's feast day, there was a tradition of children daring each other to put their hands inside the gaping jaws of the two enormous lions that form the base of the columns of the great doorway. Resplendent in their red granite from Verona, they are poised to devour a bird and a snake.

The Quintana

Every first Sunday in August history takes a leap backward, as banners, standards, pikes and halberds, horses and horsemen advance over the sun-baked beaches of Ascoli Piceno. This is the tournament of the Quintana, a test of skill in which the champions face each other in a contest of tilting at a revolving target.

CAVE THEATER

On the coast above Sirolo, where marble and stone have long been quarried, is the Theater of the Caves, a transportable structure that can seat as many as 1,800 people. Dreamed up by the actress Valeria Moriconi, a native of Sirolo, in memory of the director Franco Enriquez, it hosts a summer festival with productions by some of Italy's most famous theater companies.

Woods and sea of Mount Conero. In the Middle Ages the steep white cliffs and limestone rocks that lend a touch of magic to this somewhat wild and wooded environment attracted hermits and monks; more recently they have protected the coast from thoughtless development and despoliation. A haven for wildlife and a rare natural oasis, stretching from Portonovo to Sirolo and Numana, this part of the Adriatic boasts a wide range of evocative spots – from the White Pebble Beach, in front of which the triangular Sail Reef breaks the waves, to the tiny Pillars of the Two Sisters (only accessible by sea).

The southeastern Marches

The Holy House of Loreto. Inside the basilica (15th–16th century), covered by the octagonal dome built by Giuliano da Sangallo, is the reliquary of the Holy House ★ – the room in which, according to Christian tradition, the Archangel Gabriel brought news of the forthcoming birth of Jesus to the Virgin Mary. The legend goes that, miraculously escaping the Muslim invasion of Palestine, the Virgin's house was carried aloft by angels first to Fiume, in Dalmatia, and then in 1294, to the Hill of Loreto, where it became a site of pilgrimage. Only three walls are left of the house; covered in very old frescos, they are enclosed within an amazing marble covering.

The architectural center of Ascoli Piceno. The symbol of the town of Ascoli Piceno is the Piazza del Popolo. Low Renaissance buildings encircle the serene space of the square. These buildings, dating from the start of the 16th century, are enhanced with porticos and battlements. The 13th-century tower of the Palazzo dei Capitani del Popolo looms formidably over them all. Here too is the Gothic Church of San Francesco; begun in 1258 and finished in the 15th and 16th centuries, it is embellished with the elegant Loggia of the Merchants dating from 1513. Finally, stroll along the Corso Mazzini, once a Roman decuman.

ROME
AND THE REGIONS OF
LAZIO AND ABRUZZO

ROME, *340*

"Only in Rome could a church be so . . . absent-minded, to take under its wing a scruffy and obviously pagan arch; or to rent out a temple whose god has retired to the countryside, because of the climate.**"**
  Giorgio Manganelli, *Lunario dell'orfano sannita (The Samnite Orphan's Almanac)*

"I see pale herons, their singed wings/ Black among black olive-trees . . ./From the shadows, the smoking tale pursues me,/ Caresses pour down from the jagged rocks./Ulysses spent many hours here/ Trying to pluck the rose from Circe's bosom,/Here they frolicked through the garden caves,/There Medusa quivered, purple, evil.**"**
   Libero de Libero, *Monte Circeo (The Mount of Circe)*

The cultural and natural beauty of the regions of Lazio and Abruzzo, (both of which can be visited from the capital), may seem of secondary importance to a visitor, as Rome's own magnificence – historical and artistic, religious and civic – towers so far over everything else. But the destinations in Lazio and Abruzzo covered in this section provide the tourist with an interesting and varied itinerary. The first trip, along the Tiberian Way and the Aniene valley, takes you past Tivoli to the imperial Villa of Hadrian, an evocative archeological site, and to Subiaco, a place of intense spirituality. The second tour, by way of contrast, heads southeast from the capital to Ciociara and Agro Pontino, and certainly merits the visitor's attention for several reasons: first, there are the remains left at Alatri and Ferentino by pre-Roman Italian civilization; next, the striking architecture of the Cistercians at Casamari and Fossanova, both about 60 miles from Rome; then, the mix of woods, lakes and sea in the Circeo National

Park. The third trip, to the northeast of the *Urbs,* leads into the so-called Roman Tuscia: to Tarquinia, where the National Museum is a must for those who want to understand Etruscan culture; to the Church of San Pietro and Santa Maria Maggiore in Tuscania, whose importance goes beyond the purely regional; and to Viterbo, a city with impressive buildings and streets that follow a plan first laid down in medieval times. The final journey, in lovely Abruzzo, leads to the region's most artistically interesting city, L'Aquila (70 miles from Rome); its church, San Clemente in Casauria, is renowned and nearby is one of Italy's famous nature reserves, the National Park of Abruzzo.

"The sirocco began before Christmas, stirring up the leaves which lay abandoned on the footpaths of Via Lagrange and Via Kircher. It brought the hot, sweaty air of the African deserts, and red dust, carried by the Mediterranean breezes rained down ... It was a chaotic but decipherable city, and even if the odd person gave an impression of a chilly unfriendliness ..., underneath it all, the warmth of the city folk made itself felt."

Sergio Maldini,
La casa a Nord-Est
(The House to the North-East)

Two centuries ago, Johann Gottfried Herder, a forerunner of the Romantic movement, wrote: "The images of ancient and late ancient Rome swirl together in my mind with those of the Rome of today, creating an unbelievable and sometimes fatal confusion; not only that, but frustrating as it is to ponder all the time the origins of everything around me, I am afraid that my head will end up being overwhelmed, so that I run the risk of leaving Rome knowing less than I did when I got here." Rome, *caput mundi*, "eternal city", "the world's navel", has had 27 centuries to build itself and its legend. To visit Rome is to completely immerse yourself in history, and the city will constantly fascinate all who visit it.

THE LEGEND OF THE FOUNDING OF ROME
After a coupling with the god Mars, the vestal virgin Rea Silvia – a descendant of Aeneas, the Trojan hero who was himself the son of Venus and Anchises – gave birth to the twins Romulus and Remus. Thrown into the Tiber by an uncle, the twins were saved and suckled by a she-wolf. They founded Rome on April 21, 753 BC. After killing his brother, Romulus gave shelter to undesirables. He kidnapped the Sabine women as wives for the Romans, and peopled the city. Six kings ruled after him.

RISE AND FALL OF A GREAT EMPIRE. Eight centuries before becoming the controlling force in the Mediterranean, Rome was a modest group of villages within the Palatinate. It was not until 200 years later that it took the form of a city, due mainly to the Etruscan kings. After the founding of the republic in 509 BC, and the struggles between the patricians and the plebeians ▲ *351*, the city gradually subdued the peninsula and, beginning in the 3rd century BC, undertook the conquest of the Mediterranean, which ended with the annexation of Cleopatra's Egypt by Octavian in 31 BC. Contact with Greek civilization transformed Roman art, architecture and culture so profoundly that, to quote the poet Horace, "Conquered Greece conquered its savage victor." Octavian Augustus, first of the emperors (27 BC–AD 14), had the task of adapting Rome to its role as the capital of a vast State. His long-lasting achievements in urban planning were listed in his will, where he boasted of having transformed a city of wood and bricks into one of marble. His successors could do nothing but add the finishing touches and, under the emperors Trajan, Hadrian and the Antonines, Rome could

Pope Gregory XI returns to Rome in 1377 after exile in Avignon, France.

boast many wonderful and imposing buildings. But from the end of the 2nd century AD the supremacy of the *Urbs* began to be undermined. This was a result of economic crisis, social tensions and barbarian raids on the frontiers of an empire that was becoming more and more difficult to govern, as well as the spread of Christianity and other eastern religions. The great ring of city walls built by the emperor Aurelian (AD 270–5) is a clear sign of the empire's growing military weakness. There was a revival of building activity under Diocletian (AD 284–305), but he nevertheless abandoned Rome as the imperial capital. Constantine reinstituted the divine right of emperors, supported by the Christian movement, which, growing in strength and popularity, was by now virtually the official religion throughout the empire. He made Constantinople a "new Rome," moving the center of power eastward for good. But first the Visigoths (410), then the Vandals (455) sacked Rome's grand buildings and monuments and

in 476, Hodoacres overthrew Romulus Augustus, the last Roman emperor in the East. The ancient city was destroyed, but from its ruins rose a new city every bit as splendid – Christian Rome.

THE MIDDLE AGES. Between the 5th and 10th centuries, the face of Rome changed: the population declined dramatically, pagan temples were converted into churches, the urban fabric decayed and cultural life disappeared. It was not until the 9th century that an alliance between the papacy and the Carolingians developed that brought with it the hope of a political and spiritual rebirth. But all too soon it was interrupted by a long struggle between the various noble families and by divisions between the emperor and the city authorities. However Pope Innocent III (1198–1216) managed to restore the Church's moral standing, which contributed to the city's cultural and artistic renaissance. Rome, in the 13th and 14th centuries, attracted artists of great renown and a fundamental change in the city's architecture took place in the 15th century, when the Church decided to make the ancient capital of the empire the dazzling symbol of its supremacy.

SACKINGS OF ROME
The sudden pillagings of Rome are recorded with dismay by historians and witnesses. In 390 BC, the Gauls, under Brennus, put the city to the sword and the torch; centuries later it was the turn of Alaric's Visigoths (AD 410), Genseric's Vandals (455) and the Saracens (846). But the worst destuction was carried out in 1527 by the army of Charles V, which ravaged Rome for weeks, leaving over 4,000 victims. This event was interpreted by the Lutherans as the wages of the New Babylon's sin, and struck terror into the hearts of the whole Christian world.

THE "TRISTILOQUIUM"
Or, the "vulgar common tongue", was Dante's harsh opinion of the Roman vernacular which in his day was a dialect similar to Neapolitan. Two centuries later, as a result of the influence of Florentine language and culture, the everyday language was the Tuscany dialect, which was more distinguishable than those of south-central areas.

Julius II, pope from 1503 to 1513, in an engraved portrait by Raphael.

SIXTUS V
Pope Sixtus V (1585–90) engaged the services of the architect Domenico Fontana and by so doing realized a far-sighted urban vision which made Rome the foremost modern city in Europe. In order to build, however, he also had to knock down, and thus Sixtus V became one of ancient Rome's most enthusiastic destroyers ▲ 353.

PASSION FOR THE OLD
Love for the past reached its peak in the 18th century, when an enthusiasm for collecting antiques spread abroad and Johann Joachim Winckelmann laid the foundations of the history of ancient art.

THE "RESTAURATIO URBIS" DURING THE RENAISSANCE AND BAROQUE PERIODS. The *restauratio imperii* (restoration of the empire), took the tangible form of the magnificent structures of the *restauratio urbis* (restoration of the city). Papal patronage encouraged grand roads, sanitation works, buildings and urban planning and, although Rome was sacked by imperial troops in 1527, its Renaissance continued. Many glories of the past were rediscovered such as Michelangelo's Capitol ● 77, while the population and number of foreign visitors grew. The Counter-Reformation and the support of the Spanish monarchy consolidated the power of the popes, who throughout the 17th century were the main investors in the city's cultural and architectural development. The Caracci family together with other artists such as Bernini, Borromini and Pietro da Cortona, helped to transform Rome as the center of the elaborate Baroque style. This period also saw the burning of Giordano Bruno at the stake and the excommunication of Galileo Galilei ▲ 298. The works of Pannini, Piranesi and Vanvitelli illustrate the spirit of the aristocracy and the papal court, the antique esthetic and the panoramic architectural vision of early 18th-century Rome. The ideals of the French Revolution and later the short Napoleonic rule, however, exposed the political weakness of the papacy and its inability to meet the demands of a secular State.

NEW WAYS FIND NO PLACE IN ROME. Liberal ideas and economic stagnation created a gulf between the government

> **"HE WHO HAS SEEN ROME HAS SEEN EVERYTHING."**
>
> JOHANN WOLFGANG GOETHE

and the people: cultural life languished, sanitary conditions were appalling, administration was hopeless ("... a slovenly, dissipate, patternless city," wrote Leopardi ▲ *375* in 1823; "... new ways find no place in Rome," the Russian writer Gogol observed in 1838). Despite this, Rome was becoming more and more crowded with visitors and sought consolation for its troubles in the restoration of its great architectural heritage. After defeating Mazzini and Garibaldi's Roman republic, the French prevented the annexation of Rome by unified Italy. However, this eventually came about in September 1870, following the fall of Napoleon III. Soon afterward, the city was declared the capital of Italy.

ROME TODAY. Geographical factors and Rome's ancient ruins strongly dictated the course of post-unification urban development. Today, as in centuries past, what is striking about the city is the contrast between the dense, irregular pattern of the medieval residential quarters and the grandeur of the surviving ancient monuments. The latter have

SATIRICAL SONNETS
Giuseppe Gioachino Belli (1791–1863) and Trilussa (1871–1950) are two of the greatest exponents of Roman dialect poetry. Belli's sarcastic and piquant verses reflect knowingly the life of everyday Roman people, often oppressed by the obstructive and out-of-date papal government. Trilussa commented wittily on the Giolitti, Fascist and post-War eras, and with melancholy on the decadence and corruption of Rome.

THE POLITICAL CULT OF ROMAN-NESS
The myth of Rome, which since the Middle Ages had served as a prop for political ambitions, was taken to the point of hysteria by the Fascist regime. The combined force of rationalist architecture and the momentum given to classical studies constituted the "pickaxe of the regime." To give the capital a makeover and to exalt the role played by archeology, the whole district between Piazza Venezia and the Colosseum was razed to the ground, while the "Empire Way" replaced part of the Forum. Unfortunately, the Fascist approach to archeology often did Rome's antiquities a lot more harm than good.

THE BERBER RACE

Piazza Venezia was the finish-line for the race of the Berber horses at carnival time. The course of the race was festooned with flags from Piazza del Popolo along Via del Corso. The carnival was inaugurated by Pope Paul II in 1465.

A PRESTIGIOUS INSTITUTE

Palazzo di Venezia is the headquarters of the National Institute for Archeology and History of Art. It houses 300,000 books and 15,000 papers, drawings and manuscripts: a legacy of incalculable value. For years it has been awaiting recataloging and rehousing somewhere more spacious.

stood in the way of the development that the city's role as a modern metropolis necessitates. The various regulatory schemes for the capital, and the demolitions that many of these have entailed, betray an uncertainty between the city's heritage and its present. What is modern day Rome? It is a capital city, with over two and a half million people, burdened with traffic problems, and caught between a past that refuses to disappear (despite the jackhammers) and the needs of a metropolis heading for the third millennium. Such needs are made even more compelling by the festivities of the upcoming Millennium jubilee. Rome is a city of glaring contrasts: it is Italy's biggest city, but also the only European capital to have kept its old defensive walls (the Aurelian Walls); it is the city of the Farnese palace and of the Garbatella, of parks and of unchecked urbanization, of decay and yet of examples of "miraculous" conservation.

PIAZZA VENEZIA

This square – today choked with traffic – was where vast numbers of people gathered for Fascist rallies. Here, in the "forum of Italy," in the shadow of the cumbersome "typewriter" (one of the less irreverent names for the Victor Emmanuel monument), Mussolini harangued the crowd from the balcony of the Palazzo di Venezia. The area was first laid out during the Renaissance, but its present appearance is largely the result of heavy-handed renovations in the 19th century and during the Fascist period.

PALAZZO DI VENEZIA. In the courtyard and the interior decoration of this building, the Renaissance ideals of Leon Battista Alberti ● *91*, still visible above the doorway, were accepted in Rome for the first time. The Palazzo di Venezia was built in 1455 as the residence of the Venetian cardinal, Pietro Barbo, who later became pope under the name of Paul II. He later enlarged it with the new façade taken from the basilica of San Marco and the *viridarium* (today's PALAZZETTO VENEZIA), and inside added the Hall of the Map of the World. Expropriated in 1916 by the Italian government, the palazzo was designated for the most part as a MUSEUM, which exhibits collections of paintings, porcelains, sculptures and works in glass and silver. At the corner of the square, near the Palazzetto Venezia, there is a bust of a woman popularly known as Madama Lucrezia.

VICTOR EMMANUEL MONUMENT ● *94*. This imposing monument (1885–1911), designed by Giuseppe Sacconi, was dedicated to Victor Emmanuel II, the first king of unified Italy. It inflicted great damage on the ancient remains of the Capitol and destroyed many medieval buildings. The monument embodies the principles of classical Roman architecture, in which you can identify the foundations of a national style of art as yet undefined. The monument was once regarded as being very symbolic – it was inaugurated in 1921 on the 50th anniversary of Unification. But it is now considered to be an obsolete "altar" consecrated to the Fatherland.

SAN MARCO. The stones used to build the elegant façade of the basilica were taken from the Colosseum and the Teatro di Marcello. Dating from the early Christian period, the basilica was completely renovated by Pope Paul II. The precious coffered ceilings date back to the time of Pope Barbus, while the mosaics in the apse (9th century) and the Romanesque bell tower represent the building's medieval phases.

MADAMA LUCREZIA
This is the only statue of a woman in the group known as the "talking statues" ▲ *365*. They are so called because under cover of darkness, people used to stick on them satirical sayings and quips critical of the papal government. The gigantic bust may represent the goddess Isis or perhaps Lucrezia, Alfonso of Aragon's most beautiful lover.

A SYMBOLIC PLACE
To make room for the monument to Victor Emmanuel II, the ruins of the Capitoline Arx were seriously damaged and the greater part of medieval Rome was knocked down. On the right, just after the Museum of the Risorgimento and to the left of the tomb of Publicius Bibulus, are some of its remaining traces. This marks the perimeter of the old Servian and the start of the Flaminian Way.

THE CAPITOL

At a height of 150 feet above sea-level, surrounded by inaccessible cliffs, and with its strategic position (overlooking the Tiber island and the river crossing), the Capitol was certainly the best-suited of the Roman hills to become the citadel. Its two peaks (*Capitolium* and *Arx*) can still be identified. The dip which separated them (*Asylum*) corresponds to today's Piazza del Campidoglio, to the left and right of which two flights of stairs lead to the Church of Santa Maria in Aracoeli (*Arx*) and to the gardens on Via del Tempio di Giove (*Capitolium*). The name of this street recalls the hill's principal building and the most important shrine in the State religion of ancient Rome. This was the temple dedicated to Jupiter, Juno and Minerva, and the remains can be viewed in the Museo Nuovo Capitolino (on the right of the square). Its extraordinary dimensions (175 feet x 205 feet) indicate the power of the "Great Rome" of the Tarquins, the Etruscan kings who built it in the 6th century BC. Another prestigious monument was the *Tabularium*, whose imposing façade still dominates the Forum. Erected in 78 BC to house the public archives of the State, it epitomizes Roman architecture, both in the judicious use of the pavilioned vault ● 85 and in the invention of the squared, half-columned arch, which has been used in architecture ever since.

PETRARCH ON THE CAPITOL
On April 8, 1341, Francesco Petrarca was solemnly declared a poet on the Capitol. This distinction also conferred on him the immunities, titles and prerogatives of the professors of the faculty of arts.

THE IMAGE OF POWER
The colossal head of the emperor Constantine, in the courtyard of the Palazzo dei Conservatori, originally adorned the apse of the Basilica of Massentius. Only the uncovered parts of the figure (the head, arms and legs) were marble; the rest was gilded bronze.

> **"THE CAPITOL! IMMORTAL NAME, SUMMING UP ALL THE GLORIES OF THE *RES PUBLICA*."**
> *ITALY IN WORDS AND PICTURES*, 1838

PIAZZA DEL CAMPIDOGLIO ★.

After work on Charles V's triumphal parade (1536) was completed, Pope Paul III entrusted to Michelangelo the construction of a monumental square that would transform the ancient remains into a modern setting. The artist's spectacular solution to the problem ● 77, 91 was a trapezoidal terrace from which one can gaze out over the past (the Roman Forum) and the present (the modern city). Like the wings of a theater, it flanks the horseback statue of Marcus Aurelius, with the Palazzo Senatorio, the Palazzo dei Conservatori and the Palazzo Nuovo at its foot. Also part of Michelangelo's scheme are the ramp, which leads up to the piazza, and the balustrade, both of which are made all the more dramatic by raised statues. While modifying the original design, the subsequent additions by Giacomo della Porta and those by Girolamo and Carlo Rainaldi are not out of keeping.

MUSEI CAPITOLINI. In 1471 Pope Sixtus V inaugurated the world's first public museum, which contained every *objet d'art* gathered on the Capitol. Housed in two buildings to the side of the square, it includes famous relics such as the *Lupa capitolina*, dating from the

THE RESTORATION OF MARCUS AURELIUS

Although one of only a handful of ancient bronzes which escaped destruction or melting down (because it was mistakenly thought to depict the first Christian emperor, Constantine), the statue of Marcus Aurelius has not been spared from pollution and corrosion. Demanding rescue-work was called for and was carried out by the prestigious Central Institute for Restoration. Today the statue, which has recovered the luster of its ancient gilding, can be admired in a room at the Musei Capitolini.

THE EMPEROR AUGUSTUS
Represented here as a high priest, Augustus has his head covered by a strip of his toga, like one performing the sacrificial rite. Throughout his life Augustus bore the title of pontifex maximus, head of the Roman religion, with which he legitimized his power. With the coming of Christianity, the high priest's title passed to the popes.

THE TEMPLE OF MARS ULTOR
A stately flight of stairs led up to this temple. Eight enormous Corinthian columns formed the façade, and eight more held up the sides: only three remain.

5th century BC, the *Galata morente* (a Roman copy of a Hellenistic work from Pergamon), the statue of Marcus Aurelius on horseback, which until a few years ago adorned the square (where a copy ▲ *347* has stood since 1997), as well as portraits of emperors and figures from the ancient past. The PINACOTECA CAPITOLINA houses works of Italian and European painting from the Middle Ages to the 18th century.
SANTA MARIA IN ARACOELI. This was built by the Franciscans in the 13th century on the spot where, according to legend, the Emperor Augustus had a vision of the Madonna and Child, and subsequently erected an altar. The 14th-century staircase is a homage to the Virgin for having put an end to the Black Death. Among the many notable works there are those bearing the signatures of Donatello, Pietro Cavallini and Benozzo Gozzoli; Pinturicchio's cycle of the *Stories of Saint Bernard* also stands out.

VIA DEI FORI IMPERIALI

By the 1st century BC, Rome was the capital of an empire that stretched from Spain to Asia Minor. There were up to a million inhabitants, and the republican Forum was no longer up to the task of carrying out its administrative functions. The first ruler to do something about this was Julius Caesar. He decided to enlarge the zone of public buildings, initiating a program of construction that would last for almost 150 years, breathing life into that grand complex that was the imperial Forums. The *forum Iulii* was, like all those that came after it, a wide colonnaded square closed in by a temple that Caesar had consecrated in honor of Venus Genitrix, founder of the *gens Iulia*. The Forum of his successor and adopted son Augustus, on the other hand, was dominated by the temple of Mars Ultor, or Mars the Avenger, because he had helped

> **"THIS EPIC IN STONE [TRAJAN'S COLUMN] STILL STANDS BEFORE US TODAY, ONE OF THE MOST COMPREHENSIVE AND MOST PERFECT VISUAL NARRATIVES EVER KNOWN."**
>
> ITALO CALVINO

Octavian at Philippi (42 BC) to wipe out Brutus and Cassius, the murderers of Caesar – who after his death had been made a god. The emperors Vespasian and Nerva also created their own triumphal areas on the same site and, last of all, Trajan constructed the grandest of all the Forums.

FORUM AND MARKETS OF TRAJAN. When the Byzantine emperor Constantius II visited Rome, he was spellbound by the Forum of Trajan: the triumphal arch, the gigantic basilica, the libraries and the markets backing onto the Quirinal gave him the sense of being in "the world's sanctuary." The statue of the emperor on horseback struck him so deeply that he resolved to construct one equal to it in Constantinople. The entire building program (107–13) was made possible by a genius of an architect, Apollodorus of Damascus, and the stupendous booty plundered from the Dacians, who were routed by Trajan.

TRAJAN'S COLUMN ★, ● 85. The inscription on the base of the column reveals that it served to indicate the original height of the hill, which had been levelled to make way for the new and immense building-complex. Its main function, however, was to hold, according to ancient tradition, the emperor's ashes.

Up the trunk of the column winds a long, spiral relief (originally multi-colored) bearing a minutely-detailed depiction of the Dacian campaigns, perhaps inspired by the emperor's war diary. The formal elegance, the typically Roman running storyline and the expressive tension of the frieze, which captures tragic and brutal moments in several of its scenes, make this monument one of the great masterpieces of sculpture.

AN EMPORIUM ON SEVERAL LEVELS
In the Trajan Markets, people sold a wide array of foodstuffs; also found here were the imperial stores, which handed out food to the poor.

COLOSSEUM ★. Almost 165 feet high and 205 yards in diameter at its widest point, the Colosseum is made of more than 130,000 cubic yards of travertine and 300 tons of iron bracing, with a capacity for 50,000 spectators. The "magic circle," as Byron described it, is the largest amphitheater in the world. It was begun by the Emperor Vespasian in AD 72 on the site of the manmade pool of the Domus Aurea, as if to restore to the people the part of the city that had been occupied by Nero's scandalously vast residence. The name, which dates from the Middle Ages, comes from a colossal statue of Nero depicted as the sun god, which used to stand there and which, at 115 feet high, was the biggest bronze statue ever made. In the building itself, gladiatorial contests and wild animal kills took place until the time of Teodoricus (523). Before heading eastward, no visit to the Piazza del Colosseo would be complete without a look at the magnificent stone-carving on the ARCH OF CONSTANTINE (in the opposite corner).

SAN CLEMENTE. About 440 yards from the Colosseum, on the road toward San Giovanni in Laterano, stands the basilica dedicated to Pope Clement (88–97), founded in the 4th century AD on Roman foundations. It was burnt down by the Normans in 1084, but Pascal II (1099–1118) built another church on the site, in which Rome's marble-workers created a sumptuous interior. The basilica's present appearance dates from the 18th century. The splendid mosaic in the apse

❝The pillared arcade [of Domus Aurea] ran for a whole mile. An enormous pool, more like a sea than a pool, was surrounded by buildings made to resemble cities, and by a landscape consisting of ploughed fields, vineyards, pastures and woodlands . . . Parts of the house were overlaid with gold and studded with precious stones and nacre. . . . When . . . Nero dedicated it, [he] condescended to remark: 'Good, now I can at last begin to live like a human being.**❞**

Suetonius

ARCH OF CONSTANTINE
This commemorates the emperor's triumphal procession after the victory over Massentius in 312. It is made up of about a hundred reworked sculptures from monuments dating from the periods of Trajan, Hadrian and Antoninus. Only a few of the decorative parts and the six reliefs over the lower supporting arches are from the time of Constantine. Because of its composite nature, the arch is, in effect, a storehouse of official Roman sculpture.

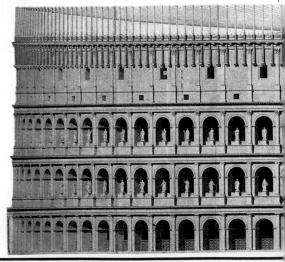

The apse of the Basilica of San Clemente, dazzling with gold and vivid colors, houses one of the finest works from the Roman school of the 12th century, a mosaic with the image of the Crucifix surrounded by twelve doves, which are allegorical representations of the twelve apostles.

(*The Triumph of the Cross* ★) has all the natural freshness of the frieze on the Ara Pacis. Between 1428 and 1431, Masolino da Panicale frescoed the Chapel of Santa Caterina, possibly with the help of Masaccio.

ROMAN FORUM

In the first period of Rome's history, the valley between the Palatine and the Capitol was flooded swamp. Only around 600 BC, thanks to land reclamation and the construction of the Great Sewer by the Etruscan king Tarquinius Priscus, did it form part of the inhabited town. Throughout the republican period, it was the political and religious center of the city, while in imperial times it became a place for audiences.

THE BASILICA EMILIA AND THE BASILICA GIULIA. Sole survivor of the republican basilicas, the BASILICA EMILIA, restored several times in the imperial period, was founded in 179 BC. Even more grand was the Basilica of Caesar (the BASILICA GIULIA, on the opposite side).

COMIZIO AND CURIA. The northern corner of the Forum was occupied by the COMIZIO, the oldest seat of the city's political life. The popular assembly met in the central square; the CURIA hosted the Senate; and the magistrates spoke from the *Rostra*, the platform decorated with the rams from the prows of captured ships.

ARCH OF SEPTIMIUS SEVERUS. This imposing arch with three supporting arches was built in 203, on the 10th anniversary of the coming to the throne of the African emperor. The four grand panels above the lower uprights depict scenes from the battle against the Parthians, according to the technique (by then employed countless times) of the running storyline.

THE TEMPLE OF CONCORD. In 367 BC, Furius Camillus had this sanctuary erected to mark a crucial event in Rome's history: the end of the struggle between the patricians and the plebeians ▲ *340*, which brought about laws that balanced the rights of both.

THE VESTALS
Separated from their families at a very early age, the vestals had to stay in the priesthood for thirty years, preserving their virginity. A vestal who lost her virginity was buried alive and her lover was flogged to death.

TEMPLE OF VESTA AND THE HOUSE OF THE VESTALS. Situated in front of the *Regia,* this was the ancient sanctuary of religious rites associated with the ruler. The Temple of Vesta with its ever-burning flame acted as the king's "hearth", and represented the "hearth" of the State. Originally entrusted to the ruler's daughters, custodianship of the fire later fell to a group of priestesses from noble families, the vestals, who lived in the large adjoining building which, according to tradition, was inaugurated by the second king of Rome, Numa Pompilius.
BASILICA OF MASSENTIUS. The barreled vaults, which made such an impression on artists of the Renaissance, can only hint at the great richness of the basilica begun by Massentius and finished by Constantine (308–12), as they have long since been looted of their multi-colored marble, stucco and statues.

THE ARCH OF TITUS
This rises up near the Basilica of Massentius and commemorates the Romans' victory (AD 70) at Jerusalem, which began the Jewish diaspora. The two magnificent panels inside the supporting arches depict Titus' triumphal parade and are some of the finest examples of Roman narrative relief.

IL PALATINO

The Palatino hill, to the south of the Forum, is the site of some legendary events in Rome's history: here Evander and Pallas' Greeks settled, and here Hercules and then Aeneas found them. At the foot of the hills was the Lupercal, the grotto where Romulus and Remus were suckled by the she-wolf; here also was Romulus' house, near where Augustus built his. When excavations in 1948 brought to light three Bronze Age huts, there was an outpouring of emotion: archeology had proved the myth right. During the republic, the little hill became the residential quarter of the Roman ruling class (the CASA DEI GRIFI and the AULA ISIACA are magnificent testaments to this). In the imperial period, it played host to one emperor's residence after the other: after the palace of Augustus, who was born here, came those of Tiberius, Nero (the Domus

"GIVE EAR TO ME, MOST BEAUTIFUL QUEEN OF A WORLD WHICH BELONGS TO YOU ALONE . . . THANKS TO YOUR TEMPLES WE ARE CLOSER TO HEAVEN."

RUTILIUS NAMATIANUS

FAÇADE COTÉ DV GRAND CIRQVE

Aurea ▲ *350* stretched all the way to here), the Flavi and Septimius Severus. The name *Palatium* (Palatino) came in this way to refer to the imperial residence and the word passed into many European languages. In 1535, Vignola built a villa with stupendous gardens (the ORTI FARNESIANI) for Alessandro Farnese and later the dukes of Parma excavated (and looted) the palace of Domitian.

HOUSE OF LIVIA AND HOUSE OF AUGUSTUS. In 36 BC, Octavian, not yet "Augustus", decided to live in the house of Hortensius, which he later expanded by buying up neighboring houses. One of these, the so-called House of Livia, was possibly reserved for the emperor's wife. Both houses show traces of magnificent murals in the Pompeiian style, but on the whole their rooms are not sumptuous, matching the description given to us by Suetonius. To honor the god Apollo, who had helped him crush his enemies, Octavian dedicated a temple (36–28 BC) to him, which was linked to his house and decorated with statues and fine tiles of multi-colored terracotta.

PALACE OF DOMITIAN. From the end of the 1st century, this occupied the whole of the central part of the hill and remained the imperial residence *par excellence* until midway through the 5th century. It was divided into three distinct parts: the Domus Flavia, or the audience wing; the Domus Augustana; the private wing characterized by a very detailed floor-plan; and the STADIUM, a circular garden used as a private racetrack for horses. There were also the Baths of Severus and the DOMUS SEVERIANA.

"[Augustus'] new palace was not larger nor more elegant than the first; . . . the living rooms were free of marble . . . he slept in the same bedroom all year round for over forty years . . . The couches and tables . . . were scarcely fit for a private citizen."

Suetonius

THE DOMUS SEVERIANA
A bare shell is all that remains of the palace of Septimius Severus. On the side facing the Appian Way was the Septidozium, demolished by Pope Sixtus V ▲ *342*, a façade with several tiers of columns, intended by Septimius Severus to impress his fellow Africans.

THE VATICAN

A tiny state in its own right, the Vatican is also one of the most visited sites, both as a sacred place for Christians and because it has an outstanding collection of Italian art. The immense wealth of paintings is housed within an endless procession of architectural wonders. The home of the pope is a unique and appropriate citadel of faith.

JULIUS II ON HIS LITTER
In this detail from the *Hunt of Heliodorus* (1514), in the so-called Room of Heliodorus, the pope is pictured at the scene carried aloft by two bearers. Raphael, asked by Julius II to decorate his apartments at the end of 1508, portrayed himself as the figure in the long black outfit to the side of the litter.

PETER'S KEYS
"I will give you the keys to the kingdom of Heaven . . ." (Matthew, 16:19). On the papal coat-of-arms are combined the tiara (the triple crown of the pope, signifying ruler of rulers, king of the world and Vicar of Christ) and the keys to the kingdom of Heaven.

1. ST PETER'S SQUARE
2. ST PETER'S BASILICA
3. SISTINE CHAPEL
4. BELVEDERE COURTYARD
5. COURTYARD OF PINES
6. ENTRANCE TO THE VATICAN MUSEUM
7. PINACOTECA VATICANA
8. HOUSE OF PIUS IV
9. VATICAN APOSTOLIC LIBRARY
10. PALACE OF THE GOVERNORSHIP
11. VATICAN RADIO
12. RAILROAD STATION
13. HALL OF PAPAL AUDIENCES
14. PASSAGE
15. VIA DELLA CONCILIAZIONE
16. CASTEL SANT'ANGELO
17. PALACE OF JUSTICE
18. PIAZZA CAVOUR

Called on by Julius II to complete the decoration of the chapel first commissioned by Pope Sixtus V, Michelangelo commenced work in May 1508 and finished it in October 1512. Out of this came what Vasari called "a shining light on all our art": a work of immense proportions (8,600 sq ft) which comprises sculptural, pictorial and architectural elements. In the central area are painted nine biblical stories symbolizing the ascent of the soul toward God, framed by a marble structure "inhabited" by copies of *Naked Figures* with worked medallions; in the lower part, the architectural design continues in a series of seven *Prophets* and five *Prophetesses*, all seated.

THE "LAST JUDGEMENT"
Twenty-four years after the frescos on the vault, Michelangelo was recalled to Rome by Clement VII. But it was Paul III who entrusted to him the task of painting the *Last Judgement*, in 1534. The disappearance from the fresco (1536–41) of all trace of Renaissance optimism is a sign of how much the climate had changed after the sack of Rome (1527) and the politico-religious crisis. The cyclone in which the figures in the *Judgement* are caught has at its eye Christ the Judge in an angry pose: no longer do the chosen ones, from whom Christ averts his gaze, radiate peace. The Renaissance was by then over.

The vault of the Church of Sant' Ignazio: with the fresco's amazing use of perspective, the Jesuit Andrea Pozzo created the illusion of a dome.

VIA DEL CORSO

The long street which joins Piazza Venezia to Piazza del Popolo corresponds to a continuation of the Flaminian Way, the former Via Lata. Its present name has its origins in the carnival races which took place here until the end of the 19th century ▲ *344*. It did not take long for this vehicular axis to assume great importance in the life of the city and the Roman aristocracy built or transferred their luxurious residences here.

GALLERIA DORIA PAMPHILI. The building of the same name (on the left-hand side of the Corso) contains a wonderful collection of more than 400 paintings from Italy and abroad. It was opened in 1651 by Innocent X Pamphili and there are portraits of him inside painted by Velázquez and sculpted by Bernini. The palace is still owned by the Doria Pamphili, and exceptional paintings by Bronzino, Titian, Caracci and Claude are beautifully displayed in its magnificent rooms and halls.

SANT'IGNAZIO. The Rococo produced some of the most refined urban designs in Rome: the PIAZZETTA DI SANT' IGNAZIO (1727–8), on the right-hand side of the Corso, is one of the most original. The adjoining Church of Sant' Ignazio was begun in 1626 and dedicated by Gregory XV to the founder of the Society of Jesus. Its façade and interior imitate those of the Church of Jesus ▲ *363*. In the decoration of the vault, the Jesuit Andrea Pozzo expressed the Baroque dream of conquering infinite space with the techniques of optical illusion.

PIAZZA COLONNA. Facing onto the piazza is the Palazzo Chigi – seat of the President of the Council – with a late-16th-century façade. The galleria Colonna (1922) was built on the area formerly occupied by the Palazzo Boncompagni Piombino, destroyed in 1873 when the Corso was widened. It embodies once more the 19th-century planning formula already used to dramatic effect in Milan and Naples ▲ *190, 397*. In the center stands the COLUMN OF MARCUS AURELIUS (180–93) ● *85*. Its narrative frieze recounts the emperor's wars against the Sarmats and the Germans. The statue of the emperor, lost in the Middle Ages, was replaced, at the pope's request, by one of Saint Paul.

PALAZZO DELLA RINASCENTE
This was built on the Corso facing the Palazzo Chigi in 1885–7, along the lines of Parisian commercial buildings of the period. Escalators were installed here for the first time in Rome.

PALAZZO DI MONTECITORIO
Standing in the square of the same name, this has been the seat of the Chamber of Deputies since 1871. It was commissioned in 1653 by Innocent X for the Vatican Tribunals. The elegant, curving façade was designed by Bernini.

MAUSOLEUM OF AUGUSTUS AND ARA PACIS AUGUSTAE. After defeating Antony and Cleopatra at Azio in 31 BC and conquering Egypt, Octavian Augustus began work on a grand burial monument for himself and his family. His MAUSOLEUM suffered centuries of looting. The mausoleum is near the ARA PACIS, originally closer to the Via Lata (the Corso) and not situated, as it is today, alongside the Tiber. Its decoration celebrates the peace finally reached, thanks to Augustus, after decades of civil war.

THE ARA PACIS (ALTAR OF PEACE)

Peace is depicted as a blooming woman in a luxuriant country setting, alongside the goddess Rome; the mythical scenes recall the origins of the capital ▲ 340 and of Augustus; the long procession of figures from the Julian clan alludes to the importance of dynastic continuity for the stability of the empire. Since the 1930's, the Ara has been kept in a glassed pavilion.

Caffè Greco

A.D. 1760
Roma, via Condotti 86

VIA CONDOTTI

A walk along here is a must for anyone who wants to keep up to date with the latest fashion. Among the flashy shop-windows of world-famous designers and jewelers, you will also come across the Caffè Greco, which has welcomed artists, musicians and people of letters since the 18th century.

PIAZZA DI SPAGNA ★

Perhaps the most picturesque of the additions of the Roman late-Baroque, the piazza (accessible from the Corso by the elegant VIA CONDOTTI) owes its name to the Palazzo di Spagna, site of the first permanent embassy to be established in Rome. In the 17th century, it became the center of artistic and tourist life in the city. In the first century BC, the grand Villa of Lucullus (the general famous for his banquets) stood on the site, with a series of terraces linked by grand staircases. The triumphal STAIRCASE by Francesco de Sanctis (1726) known as the 'Spanish Steps', which leads up to Bernini's BARCACCIA (old boat) FOUNTAIN, thus had an ancient predecessor.

PALAZZO DI PROPAGANDA FIDE. Built in 1586 and the headquarters of the congregation of the same name since 1626, this benefited from modifications by Bernini and, later, by Borromini. Borromini's work can be seen in the CHURCH OF THE MAGI, and in the superb tiburium of the neighboring Church of SANT'ANDREA DELLE FRATTE.

CORSO VITTORIO EMANUELE II

Stretching from the bridge of the same name to the Piazza del Gesù, and cutting through part of what is known as the "Renaissance quarter," Corso Vittorio Emanuele II was constructed at the end of the 19th century to provide access to the Vatican City. It divides the area that in Roman times was called the Field of Mars, where electoral and military activities originally took place and which was later to become the site of grand public buildings.

1 ARA PACIS AUGUSTAE
2 MAUSOLEUM OF AUGUSTO
3 PALAZZO CHIGI AND COLUMN OF MARCUS AURELIUS
4 TREVI FOUNTAIN
5 SANT'IGNAZIO
6 PALAZZO (GALLERIA) DORIA PAMPHILI
7 CHURCH OF JESUS
8 PANTHEON
9 PIAZZA NAVONA
10 PALAZZO MASSIMO ALLE COLONNE
11 PALAZZO DELLA CANCELLERIA
12 PALAZZO FARNESE

CHURCH OF JESUS. In the design of this building (1568–71), Vignola gave form to the devotional style of the Counter-Reformation. His work reflects the influence of Leon Battista Alberti, the architectural forms of ancient Rome and the Renaissance idea of the central place of the dome (modified by Giacomo della Porta) as the symbol of the soul's ascent to God. A century later, the Jesuits decided to also have the interior decorated. Andrea Pozzo designed the sumptuous CHAPEL OF SAINT IGNATIUS, who is buried here, and, in 1679, Baciccia painted the *Triumph of the Name of Jesus* which can be found in the vault.

SACRED AREA OF LARGO DI TORRE ARGENTINA. The four buildings in the area provide a valuable summary of the temple architecture of the republican period, from the beginning of the 3rd to the end of the 2nd century BC. The dedication of three of the buildings to water divinities (Feronia, Giuturna, Lari Permarini) and the identification of the complex with the two *Porticus Minuciae* have led some (F. Coarelli) to suspect that this was the site of the government departments in charge of aqueducts and the distribution of grain.

PALAZZO MASSIMO ALLE COLONNE. The curving line of the façade recalls the curve of the Odeon of Domitian, whose only visible element is the large bulbous column in Piazza de' Massini. Baldassare Peruzzi rebuilt it (1532–6), taking great liberties with classical tradition.

ROME'S SECOND DOME

Sant'Andrea della Valle (1591–1665), close to the Palazzo Massimo alle Colonne, is symbolic of developments in Roman artistic style during the transition phase from Mannerism to the Baroque. Maderno gave it a master's touch: the grand, towering dome is second in size only to that of St Peter's.

CIRCVS

PALAZZO DELLA CANCELLERIA. The identity of the building's architect is still not known, but Bramante's imprint is evident, especially in the lines of the COURTYARD. The façade, in travertine, is noteworthy for the elegant balcony in the corner toward CAMPO DE' FIORI; inside are frescos by Vasari and Perin del Vaga.

PALAZZO FARNESE. The Palazzo Farnese project (in the square of the same name), entrusted to Antonio da Sangallo the Younger by Cardinal Alessandro Farnese, reached its final, grand stage of accomplishment in the year that the man who commissioned it became Pope Paul III (1534). Antonio's maturity is seen in the originality with which he recast the palace's Florentine model ▲ 286, boldly defining the space with curved ashlars and accentuating the relief of the doorway which leads on to the theater-like layout of the ATRIUM (divided into three magnificent naves) and the courtyard. Michelangelo heightened the sculptured quality of the superb façade by adding the CORNICE.

THE "RENAISSANCE QUARTER"

PIAZZA NAVONA ★. Commissioned by Innocent X, this occupies the site of the stadium of Domitian, whose foundations and dimensions can still be made out. It was Gian Lorenzo Bernini who had the idea of placing the three fountains, one of which is the FONTANA DEI FIUMI (1648–51), along its central axis. In 1653, Borromini succeeded Girolamo Rainaldi in the construction of the Church of SANT'AGNESE IN AGONE, creating the effect of motion in the concave façade and adding high, lone towers.

CAMPO DE' FIORI
Home since the 19th century to a bustling market, this is one of the city's liveliest and most popular places, and constitutes a unique example of urban continuity. Close to the square stands the grandiose theater of Pompey, whose curved shape is echoed by the ring of houses around the Piazza di Grotta Pinta.

SAN LUIGI DEI FRANCESI. The church owes its fame to the chapel ★, decorated (1599–1602) by Caravaggio. The three works (*Saint Matthew and the Angel*, *The Martyrdom of Saint Matthew* and *St Matthew's Calling*) attest to a totally new way of conceptualizing painting and the message of the Gospels: the holy story is rendered in the idiom of the everyday, while light takes on a dramatic and essential significance.

SANT' IVO ALLA SAPIENZA. This is one of many strokes of genius by Francesco Borromini, who built the church around 1650 for the former university of Rome (which until 1935 was housed in the Palazzo della Sapienza). The interior has an unusual star-shaped floor-plan. The exterior is even more extraordinary: the snail-shaped capstone surmounted by a metallic, aerial-like structure thrusts skyward.

SANTA MARIA SOPRA MINERVA. The church (very close to the Pantheon) is renowned more for the artistic treasures it houses – from the statue of the risen Christ (1519–20, Michelangelo), to the frescos of the Carafa Chapel (1488–93, Filippino Lippi) and the burial monuments of Clement VII and Leo X (1536–41, Antonio da Sangallo the Younger) – than for the building itself, which has been restored several times, not always happily. On the square, supported by a marble elephant designed by Bernini, stands an Egyptian obelisk from the 6th century BC.

PANTHEON ★, ● 85. Built in 27 BC, the Pantheon was altered in the 2nd century BC, and its appearance has changed over subsequent centuries. The colonnaded façade originally stood higher so that the dome (at more than 130 feet in diameter, the widest ever vaulted with stonework) was practically invisible from the approach. Once inside the church, this added an element of surprise to the effect of the first view of the dome, stunning in the simplicity of its proportions: it is a perfect sphere, held in a cylinder of equal height and radius. In 1878 it was declared a tomb for Italy's kings, and Vittorio Emanuele I and Umberto I are buried here.

PASQUINO
Backing on to the rear of Palazzo Braschi (near Piazza Navona), this is the most famous of the "talking statues" and stood near the house of an artisan by the name of Pasquino, famous for his denunciations of the vices of the powerful. After his death, anonymous authors got into the habit of sticking antipapal witticisms to the statue (where the Italian word "pasquinata" comes from).

BREAD, BREAD, BREAD!
A bitter *pasquinata* near the Fontana dei Fiumi contrasts this display of splendor with the real-life position of everyday Roman people: "In place of spire and fountainhead; it's bread we want, bread, bread, bread."

The buildings near the Trident, designed by Valadier, house two famous and crowded cafés, the Rosati (on the corner of Via di Ripetta, opened by Leo X) and the Canova (on the corner of Via del Babuino, begun by Clement VII). From their terraces, you can enjoy the panoramic layout of the square at its very best.

THE PINCIO
From the Piazza del Popolo, you can reach the Pincio ● 95, which until the beginning of the 20th century was the classic public entertainment spot for the people of Rome, where concerts were given by the city band. The beautiful promenade was built by Valadier with a clever use of balconies and colonnades, which lead to the scenic terrace in the middle of the lawn. The freedom with which the architect used the language of neoclassicism is neatly expressed in the Casina Valadier, a little building executed with casual classical references and housing a café-restaurant since its opening in 1817.

PIAZZA DEL POPOLO

For a long time this square has been a theater for popular performances, games and fairs. Into here, through the PORTA DEL POPOLO, flows the Flaminian Way and from here, on the south side, at the beginning of the 16th century, the TRIDENT was opened up, formed by Via di Ripetta, Via del Babuino and, in the middle, Via del Corso framed by two identical 17th-century churches. It was Sixtus V who had the obelisk of Ramesses II (circa 1200 BC), a "spoil of war" that Augustus had put in the Circus Maximus, placed instead by the fountain in the center of the square. At the beginning of the 19th century, Giuseppe Valadier gave the square its definitive appearance, in a neoclassical key.

SANTA MARIA DEL POPOLO ★. This church is medieval in origin but was rebuilt in the 15th century. Bramante redid the chancel (1500–9), which houses two notable burial monuments (1505–7) by Andrea Sansovino, overlooked by superb stained-glass windows (1509), fire-dyed by Guillaume de Marcillat. Pinturicchio frescoed the vault (1508–10); the Chigi Chapel (1513–14) and the mosaics of the dome (1516) were executed according to drawings by Raphael; Bernini was involved in the decor in various ways; and Carlo Fontana designed the Cybo Chapel (1682–7). Particularly noteworthy are works by Caravaggio, who painted in the chapel to the left of the presbytery the *Crucifixion of Saint Peter* and the *Conversion of Saint Paul* (1601–12).

THE PARK OF THE VILLA BORGHESE ★

This is the largest and most central of the city's public parks, with a perimeter of nearly 4 miles. The entire area is set to become a MUSEUM PARK with tended lawns and reorganized museums.

> **"THE PINCIO GARDEN OVERLOOKS THE COURSE OF THE TIBER AND THE SURROUNDING FIELDS FROM A HEIGHT OF ALMOST 100 FEET: THE VIEW IS SUPERB."**
>
> STENDHAL

ETRUSCAN MUSEUM OF VILLA GIULIA. The museum has been housed since 1889 in the suburban villa (1551–55) of Julius III, which is a showcase of mannerist architecture by Ammannati and Vasari (in the nymph's gallery) and Vignola (on the façade). The collections include exhibits from Etruscan and Faliscan

culture, as well as Greek material. Outstanding among these are the gold tables of Pyrgi (Etruscan and Carthaginian inscriptions), the multi-colored terracotta statues from the Temple of Portonaccio at Veio, the SARCOPHAGUS OF THE HUSBAND AND WIFE (530 BC) from Cerveteri ▲ *327*, the FICORONI URN (4th century BC) ▲ *327*, the works in gold from the Collezione Castellani and the rich burial furnishings of *Praeneste* (Palestrina). The new Venus Room was opened in June 1997.

NATIONAL GALLERY OF MODERN ART. The Palazzo delle Belle Arti houses the largest collection of modern and contemporary art in Italy. Every school of painting, sculpture and the graphic arts of the 19th and 20th centuries is represented in its newly refurbished rooms.

BORGHESE MUSEUM AND GALLERY. The collections display ancient works of sculpture alongside masterpieces from the Renaissance and Baroque, and many works up to the end of the 19th century. The cool sensuality of Canova (*Paolina Borghese*, which has become the symbol of the museum) and the carnality of Correggio (*Danae*), the masterly sculptural technique of Bernini (*David Loosing His Slingshot, Apollo and Daphne, Rape of Proserpine*), Titian's colors (*Sacred Love and Profane Love*), Caravaggio's shades (*John with Basket of Fruit, Madonna of the Grooms, David with Goliath's Head*) and the intensity of Antonella da Messina (*Portrait of Man*) would merit a visit on their own. Also represented are Botticelli, Raphael, Pinturicchio, Bronzino, Lotto, Carracci, Guercino, Rubens and Bellini. After thirteen years of restoration and refurbishment work, the Gallery reopened in June 1997.

VIA VENETO
The famous winding street, whose full name is Via Vittorio Veneto, was the symbol in the 1950's and 1960's of the "dolce vita". It is built on top of the foundations of the Villa Ludovisi, which was demolished after 1870, causing outrage throughout Europe.

PIAZZA DI SIENA
An annual date in fashionable Rome's calendar is the famous horserace which takes its name from the piazza where it takes place. This piazza, was first opened in the Park of the Villa Borghese by Mario and Antonio Asprucci at the end of the 18th century and is designed along the lines of an ancient Roman amphitheater.

367

PIAZZA BARBERINI

The square, named after
the family in 1625, is
embellished by two fountains which
are among Bernini's most resounding
works: the FOUNTAIN OF TRITON (1642–3), in the
middle, and the FOUNTAIN OF THE BEES (1644), at the
junction of VIA VENETO ▲ *367*.

PALAZZO BARBERINI. The Barberini had chosen the
architect Carlo Maderno for their residence in Rome.
After his death, they called upon Gian Lorenzo Bernini
to carry the façade through to completion. Helping first
Maderno and then Bernini was Francesco Borromini, while
Pietro da Cortona painted the roof of the main salon with the
fresco of the *Triumph of Divine Providence* (1633–9). Since
1949 the building has housed the NATIONAL GALLERY OF
ANCIENT ART, which contains the works of painters from the
13th to the 18th centuries from both Italy (Raphael, for
example, with *The Little Baker Girl*) and abroad.

IL QUIRINALE

The hill's first inhabitants were probably Titus Tatius' Sabines,
who later mingled with the Latin city, and the etymology
of the name seems to link it with the Sabine god *Quirinus*.
In earlier times shrines stood here but from the end of the
republican period the hill became residential.
THE QUIRINAL SQUARE AND PALACE. The square's former
name, Monte Cavallo (Horse Hill), comes from the statues of
the Dioscuri mounted on their steeds, originally
on the baths of Constantine, which stood on the
grand FOUNTAIN that adorns the square. The
QUIRINAL PALACE, the residence of the king of
Italy after 1871, has been the official house of
the President of the Republic since 1947. It was
originally the popes' summer residence at the
beginning of the 16th century. Its interior was
completed in 1740, providing work in the
process for renowned architects such as
Fontana, Bernini and Maderno.

SANT' ANDREA AL QUIRINALE. Standing a few feet apart, the churches of Sant'Andrea al Quirinale ● 92 and San Carlo alle Quattro Fontane exemplify the different personalities of the two most appealing architects (and most stubborn rivals) of the Roman Baroque: Bernini and Borromini.

TREVI FOUNTAIN ● 92
The theatrical esthetic of Bernini's legacy is echoed in this famous fountain (1732–62). The work of Nicola Salvi, it stands between the Corso and the Quirinal. Each day coin after coin is thrown into the fountain by the huge numbers of tourists hoping to come back to the "eternal city", courtesy of this gesture. For many, the Trevi fountain is synonymous with Rome itself, having been made world famous as the setting for Anita Ekberg's nocturnal dip in Federico Fellini's movie, *La Dolce Vita*.

369

In Sant'Andrea, the pinnacle of the religious architecture of the Baroque age, Bernini employed an elliptical floor plan, his preferred technique for achieving the bulging

DOME OF SAN CARLO ALLE QUATTRO FONTANE
The lacunae, in the shape of crosses, octagons and hexagons, create an ensemble of sweeping movement but at the same time absolute geometrical purity, recalling a beehive.

effect he was after. Your gaze never strays to the side-chapels of the ellipse but is drawn unfailingly toward the central sanctuary, which contains the spectacular vision of the saint being carried up to heaven.

SAN CARLO ALLE QUATTRO FONTANE ★. Borromini started work on the Monastery of St Charles Borromeo in 1638. The space available to him was minimal (hence the building's nickname of San Carlino). The church's elliptical apse is towered over by the complex geometry of the oval dome, creating an effect of exaggerated height. The exterior has one of his trademark bell towers and the façade was the great architect's last creation.

TOWARD SANTA MARIA MAGGIORE

"BIRTH OF APHRODITE"
Of all the works in the National Museum of Rome, the most outstanding are those from the collection of the Ludovisi family, sold to the State at the beginning of the 20th century. The front of the *Ludovisi Throne*,

with its depiction of the birth of Aphrodite, thought by some to be an obvious fake, may date from the middle of the 5th century BC.

BATHS OF DIOCLETIAN. The city's biggest baths (they could accommodate more than 3,000 people) were built in less than eight years, between 298 and 306. A gigantic enclosure with semicircular exedra contained the bathing complex, set out according to the classic plan: central bathing area, *caldarium*, *tepidarium*, *natatio* along the lesser axis, *gymnasia* either side of the greater axis. The best-preserved are the rooms converted into the Basilica of Santa Maria degli Angeli, those modified to house the National Museum of Rome and the two circular wings (one became the Church of San Bernardo alle Terme).

NATIONAL MUSEUM OF ROME. Founded in 1889, this is one of the largest collections of ancient art in the world. At present, the historical home of the museum is in the process of being reorganized. The main nucleus of the collection has been transferred to a new site, the building of the former Collegio Massimiliano Massimo in Piazza dei Cinquecento, and another part of it can be seen at Palazzo Altemps.

SANTA MARIA DEGLI ANGELI ★. In 1561, Pius IV agreed to turn several rooms of the baths into a church consecrated to the angels and Christian martyrs. The building works, entrusted to Michelangelo and finished by Vanvitelli (1750), preserve inside the appearance of the ancient complex, from which the eight enormous granite-monolith columns and the three great cross-vaults of the roof have been kept.

TERMINI RAILWAY STATION ● 96. The name comes from the spring which fed the baths, called "botte di termini". The 19th-century building was completely rebuilt in 1937, but its inauguration did not take place until 1950. Its long, low structure is punctuated by windows, and clad in travertine, with a canopy of reinforced concrete known as the "dinosaur". In front of the station, the SERVIAN WALLS represent the final barrier to the city for those who arrive by train.

SANTA MARIA MAGGIORE. Do not be fooled by the Baroque façade by Ferdinando Fuga (1741–3), because, inside, the basilica houses priceless evidence of its early-Christian

THE SERVIAN WALLS
In Piazza dei Cinquecento, you soon run into the grandest remaining relic of the republican walls. The first to set about building them was Servius Tullius (6th century BC), although the wall there today was built two centuries later.

ROME UNDER UMBERTO
Between Termini and Santa Maria Maggiore lies one of the first "Piemontese" districts built after Rome became the capital, which served as a model for the new construction sites in the center.

THE "TRAGEDY OF THE TOMB"
This is how Michelangelo described the mausoleum of Julius II, built in 1545 in San Pietro in Vincoli to a somewhat scaled-down design after forty years of arguing with the pope. In the proud anger of *Moses* (1514–16), in the middle of the tomb, the artist developed the impassioned tension seen on the faces of the prophets in the Sistine Chapel and, perhaps, expressed his own anger over the design that never was.

origins. The mosaics in the central nave and those of the grand triumphal arch go back to the time of Sixtus III (432–440). The mosaics in the apse, where Jacopo Torriti, a devoted pupil of Cavallini, depicted the *Coronation of Mary*, date from 1295. The 14th-century bell tower is the highest in Rome (nearly 250 feet). Following Via Cavour, you come to the Church of SAN PIETRO IN VINCOLI, which houses Michelangelo's celebrated *Moses*, placed in the middle of the mausoleum of Pope Julius II.

PIAZZA DI SAN GIOVANNI IN LATERANO

Sixtus V reorganized this district – first given to the bishops of Rome by the wife of Constantine – and its palace, which had been abandoned by the popes (by then firmly settled in the Vatican) for two centuries. He entrusted the supervision of the works (1586–9) to Domenico Fontana. Up to the end of the 19th century, the buildings stood in isolation, surrounded by fields, leading to the rise of the traditional feast of Saint John: the "festival of the snails". The LATERAN PALACE was finished in great haste, in keeping with the frenetic pace of all Sixtus' building programs. It cost very little, thanks to the use of marble and stone taken from those most convenient of quarries – the ancient ruins – and to excellent organization. Nevertheless, it is one of Fontana's greatest works, and one of the

❝I BURN TO TELL YOU THAT THIS NEW ROME . . . SO ADORNED WITH PALACES, CHURCHES AND OTHER BUILDINGS, WAS BUILT WITH MORTAR MADE FROM ANCIENT MARBLE.❞

RAPHAEL, *LETTER TO LEO X*

finest of the period in Rome. Since 1967 it has been the seat of the Vicarage of Rome (the doorway was damaged by a bomb in 1993), and home to the Vatican Museum of History since 1987.

BAPTISTERY. The original appearance of the building, founded by Constantine and modified by Sixtus III (5th century), was revealed by radical 17th-century restoration. Inside, several mosaics (5th–7th centuries) and elements of the Chapel of St John the Baptist belong to the oldest phases in its construction.

SAN GIOVANNI IN LATERANO ★. This is known as the "mother of all churches" because it is the cathedral of the bishop of Rome. Constantine's original basilica, dazzling with gold mosaics, enjoyed a degree of prestige greater than that of the two apostolic basilicas and was considered the true psychological center of Christianity. Destruction in the 17th and 18th centuries occasioned long-running restorations and rebuilding. Its long history is revealed by the rich decor inside, while the cloister created (1215–32) by Vassalletto is a masterpiece of art in the Cosmati style ▲ *379*.

CASTEL SANT'ANGELO ★

Nerva was the last emperor to be buried in the mausoleum of Augustus ▲ *362*. Hadrian wanted a new tomb ● *89* for himself and his family and had it built in the *horti* of Domitia in the Vatican, where all the Antonine and Severine emperors up to Caracalla were buried. Its incorporation into the Aurelian Walls (275) brought a new role as a fortress, capable of withstanding the Visigoths' assaults in 410. Various popes strengthened its military capacity and lavishly refurbished its interior chambers. The upper terrace is towered over by the colossal bronze statue of the archangel Michael who, according to legend, appeared to Gregory the Great to announce the end of the plague (590).

NATIONAL MUSEUM OF CASTEL SANT'ANGELO. This contains collections of art and antique weapons. Worthy of note are the lavish papal apartments decorated with plasters, grotesques, friezes, tapestries, frescos and ceramics.

PONTE SANT'ANGELO. The old Elius bridge built (133–4) by Hadrian became an obligatory route for the throngs of pilgrims heading for St Peter's, leading to the collapse of the parapets during the Jubilee of 1450. The statues of the angels were designed by Bernini (1669).

THE "FESTIVAL OF THE SNAILS"
On the night of June 24 (the birth of John the Baptist), the main attraction was the hundreds of snails eaten in the taverns and in huts specially built for the purpose in the fields near the Basilica of San Giovanni in Laterano. Today the tradition lives on only in 19th-century paintings.

FROM EGYPT TO ROME
The obelisk of San Giovanni in Laterano was first erected by the pharaohs Tutmoses III and IV (15th century BC) in front of the temple of Amun in Thebes and was transported to Rome by Constance II in 357. Re-erected in the Circus Maximus and toppled by an earthquake, it was rediscovered in 1587 and set in the center of the square by Domenico Fontana. It is the oldest and, at 154 feet, the tallest obelisk in Rome.

"St Peter's left me truly dumbfounded by its vastness and its indescribable splendor. And yet I had the impression more of an imperial palace than of a temple of the living God. There's something pagan in all this pomp."
Friedrich Schlegel

St Peter's Square ★

The colonnade which opens its imposing arms to welcome pilgrims (and tourists), granting them access to the Vatican, is the product of a somewhat lively collaboration between Bernini and Alexander VII (1655–67). Once again the artist opted for the "ovate shape", defined by four rows of columns which appear as one to a visitor standing at either of the focal points of the ellipse, in the center of which rises the obelisk.

St Peter's ★, ● 90. Between AD 64 and 67, Peter was martyred in the circus of Caligula (where the obelisk in the Vatican originates). Around 320, Constantine built an enormous basilica on the site of the apostle's much-venerated tomb. By the time of the popes' return from Avignon (1377), the thousand-year-old church was falling apart. In 1506, Julius II launched a new building program under the direction of Bramante. Raphael, Baldassarre Peruzzi and Antonio da Sangallo the Younger supervized the work one after the other, but the turning-point came in 1546 when Michelangelo increased the sweep and height of the future dome, supported by the upward thrust of gigantic pillars. The Latin floor plan and the forward prolongation of the building demanded by Paul V again triggered arguments, since this modification would have lessened the impact of the volume of the dome. Yet, faced with a papal order, Carlo Maderno had no choice but to obey and, with the completion of the façade, the church was opened in 1626 by Urban VIII.

TREASURES OF SCULPTURE
It is impossible to enumerate all the masterpieces in St Peter's Basilica: from Michelangelo's *Pietà* to Bernini's canopy, over the throne of St Peter, once again by Bernini, to the burial monuments of the popes, built throughout the centuries by the most illustrious of artists.

VATICAN MUSEUMS ★. Rather than trying to take in the complete history of art from ancient Egypt to the 20th century, visitors can select instead a themed itinerary focused on a single period, following a color-coded route. Highlights include the SISTINE CHAPEL and the RAPHAEL ROOMS ▲ *354–60*.

TRASTEVERE

The popular character of this neighborhood dates back to the Roman age when it was jam-packed with merchants, generally foreigners and Jews, who were attracted here by the goings-on of the river port (businesses which continue to this day in the Porta Portese market). Indeed, perhaps this population's

essential foreignness to Rome lies at the root of Trastevere's character. In order to guarantee a better link with the Vatican, Bramante built Via Lungara for Julius II, but it was not until Rome was made the capital that the tranquil harmony was shaken by the opening of Viale Trastevere and the Tiber embankment.

THE GIANICOLO ★. From Etruscan times onward, the hill served as a gate against invaders, witnessing the assaults of the Saracens and the strenuous defense of the re-established republic in 1849. The little hill nevertheless kept the appearance of calm, with its profile of pines and cypresses, and at sunset it fairly blazed, so much so that the Romans called it the "golden mountain", *Mons Aureus* or *Montorio*; it was a favorite spot for loners and thinkers, such as Tasso or Chateaubriand, and noble families (the Lante, the Corsini, the Pamphilj) clothed its foothills in gardens.

SAN PIETRO IN MONTORIO. The rulers responsible for the discovery of America, Ferdinand and Isabella of Spain, were also responsible for the rebuilding of this church (1481–1500), most likely founded in the 9th century. They also commissioned a "memorial", that is, a LITTLE TEMPLE on the spot where tradition had it Saint Peter was crucified. The tiny building in the middle of the cloister, by Bramante, had an enormous influence on the architecture of the new century, through its emphatic affirmation of the central floor plan.

LEOPARDI IN TRASTEVERE

On the occasion of his visit to the tomb of Torquato Tasso, the poet Leopardi had the opportunity to get to know the area, the sole pleasure to befall him in Rome: "It echoes with the creaking of looms, the song of women and of artisan's at work. . . Even the expression and manners of the people whom one meets in the streets have something, . . . it seems simpler and more human, and expresses the character and habits of people . . . who are living by work, and not by intrigue, imposture and deceit, like the greater part of this population."

THE PROMENADE ON THE GIANICOLO ★

Created at the end of the 19th century to commemorate the Roman republic (1849), on either side are busts of Garibaldi's followers and monuments to the Cairoli brothers, to Garibaldi himself and to his wife Anita. The most panoramic spot is on the terrace.

The Farnesina, today the council headquarters of the Accademia dei Lincei.

THE FARNESINA. The villa that Baldassarre Peruzzi built (1506–10) for the humanist patron of the arts Agostino Chigi had to be a "villa of delights", dedicated to pleasures both worldly and contemplative, to parties, to gatherings of intellectuals and to the owner's rich collection of art. The balcony and the two *avant-corps* expressed the harmony between architecture and nature, although today this is less clear since the magnificent gardens sloping down toward the river were obliterated by the Tiber embankment. Part of the building's attraction is in the painted decorations. Secular images from ancient mythology are interwoven with astrological motifs. Sebastiano del Piombo, Sodoma and Raphael all worked on these.

PSYCHE AND GALATEA Brilliantly interpreting the architecture-nature relationship created by Baldassarre Peruzzi, Raphael transformed the roof of the Farnesina's balcony into a pergola: among the festoons of flowers and fruit, against the sky, is painted the myth of Psyche, executed by the master's apprentices. From his own hand, however, comes the luminous and sensual *Galatea*, the nymph who led Polyphemus to fall for her.

SANTA MARIA IN TRASTEVERE According to legend, when Jesus was born, a spring of oil bubbled up here all day from the earth. A church was built on the spot in 222 and was called Santa Maria in Fons Olei.

SANTA MARIA IN TRASTEVERE ★. Only the papal basilicas are historically more significant than this one, which stands in the heart of Trastevere and was once, before Santa Maria Maggiore, a center of worship of the Madonna. Its present appearance is due to Innocent II (1138–48) who gave it the bell tower, the transept and the MOSAICS in the apse, executed some time after 1143; in 1291, the cycle featuring Pietro Cavallini's *Stories of the Virgin* was added above the windows.

FROM TRASTEVERE TO THE AVENTINE AND THE BATHS OF CARCALA

TIBER ISLAND ★. Closely linked to Rome's origins and early fortune, the Tiber island gave rise to various legends. The most famous relates to its ship-like shape, which is said to come from the boat of Aesculapius, god of medicine, from whom the Romans sought advice about putting a stop to a plague. Its reputation as a place of welcome for the sick led to it being converted into a leper colony during the plague of 1656.

THEATER OF MARCELLUS. Dedicated by Augustus (11 BC) to his nephew and designated successor Marcellus,

THE GHETTO
On the shoulders of the Theater of Marcellus, in the neighborhood of Sant'Angelo, was where the Jews of Rome were shut in from 1555 to 1848. In its dense concentration of buildings, the "islands" of the Mattei and of the Cenci Bolognetti stand out, as well as the arcade of Octavian (146 BC) and the new synagogue (1899–1904). In the latter, a permanent display commemorates the Nazi persecutions and the deportation to extermination camps suffered by the Jews.

MOUTH OF TRUTH
In the colonnade of Santa Maria in Cosmedin is an ancient manhole, with the face of a river god, made, according to legend, by the sage Virgil. Even today people believe that if a liar puts his hand in, he will never pull it out.

the theater was turned into a quarry in the Middle Ages for construction and fortification materials. In the 16th century, it became the property of the Savelli and Orsini whose family palace (1523–7), which sits on top of the Roman colonnades, is the work of Peruzzi.

SANTA SABINA. Past Piazza Bocca della Verità, onto which faces the Church of SANTA MARIA IN COSMEDIN, you reach the silent and highly elegant Aventine. The Basilica of Santa Sabina was built here in the 5th century, expanded in the 9th and again in the 13th, when it was dedicated to Saint Domenic who, so the story goes, had planted the first orange tree in Rome. Its real gem is the original wooden DOOR, decorated with scenes from the Old and New Testaments.

TERME DI CARACALLA. The grandest imperial baths, although well preserved, must have been even more magnificent when they were first built (AD 217), with all the sculptures, marble, plasters and mosaics adorning them. Their function as a bath could not have justified the complex layout of the structure, which provided Romans with opportunities for both entertainment and rest.

A CAPITAL IN MINIATURE
The Museum of Roman Civilization (in the EUR, Piazza Agnelli) has on display, besides dozens of casts, reconstructions and maps, a gigantic model of ancient Rome which evokes the look of the monuments and the city's layout in the 4th century.

THE TREASURES OF ST PAUL'S ★
The fire of 1823 (thirty years after the basilica was faithfully rebuilt) spared the ciborium by Arnolfo di Cambio, the Pascal candelabrum by the Vassalletto family and the 4th-century mosaic in the apse. Also by the Vassallettos is the elegant, enchanting 12th-13th-century cloister, with columns of different patterns.

THE EUR DISTRICT

The "metaphysical" layout of the EUR, the district designed by the Fascist regime to celebrate its 20th anniversary and brought to a halt in 1943, reveals some interesting examples of 20th-century Italian rationalist architecture.

PALAZZO DELLA CIVILTÀ DEL LAVORO. The impressive gleam of the "Square Colosseum", with its six rows of colonnades (1943), is the undisputed symbol of the district; it was designed by the architects Giovanni Guerrini, Ernesto Bruno La Padula and Mario Romano. Four groups of Dioscuri adorn the staircase, one of the regime's self-aggrandizing tributes to the classical age.

PALAZZO DELLE SCIENZE. Two prestigious institutions are housed here: the MUSEO NAZIONALE LUIGI PIGORINI and the MUSEUM OF THE LATE MIDDLE AGES. The first exhibits one of the foremost ethnographic collections in Europe, as well as displays dealing with the protohistory and prehistory of Italy; the second allows you to understand better the history and art of the 4th to 10th centuries.

PALAZZO DELLO SPORT ● *96.* Pier Luigi Nervi and Marcello Piacentini built (1958–60) one of the capital's most interesting engineering feats, a circular structure topped by a dome 330 feet in diameter.

THE GATES AND OUTSIDE THE GATES

PORTA SAN PAOLO, SAN PAOLO FUORI LE MURA AND OSTIA ANTICA ★. St Paul's Gate, fortified by two heavy round towers and walls in a pincer formation, is the best preserved of the Aurelian Walls, along with St Sebastian's Gate. The ancient Via Ostiense started here, heading straight to Rome's port, and along it stood the BASILICA OF ST PAUL OUTSIDE THE WALLS, the biggest after St Peter's. The EXCAVATIONS AT OLD OSTIA ● *75* provide a historical walk unparalleled in

Italy: the city, which was the commercial heart of Rome in the first centuries of the empire, is a precious archive of facts on every aspect of Roman life, especially for the period following the destruction of Pompei (AD 79) 412.

PORTA SAN SEBASTIANO AND THE VIA APPIA ANTICA ★.
St Sebastian's Gate, in the Aurelian ring of walls, is a great

arch flanked by two stout, crenelated towers. From here you can follow the evocative walk which runs along the line of the walls, or venture onto the Old Appian Way, built in 312 BC. This was once lined with burial monuments and the houses of the influential, in a natural setting of cypresses, pines and olive trees. Miles of underground CATACOMBS spread out beneath here. From the Middle Ages, the path through them was lost and it was only in the 19th century that they were restored. Since March 1997, the whole area has become a pedestrian walkway.

PORTA MAGGIORE AND SAN LORENZO FUORI LE MURA. The Porta Maggiore was constructed out of the arches holding up two aqueducts from the reign of Claudius (AD 38–52). The 13th-century appearance of the Basilica of St Lawrence Outside the Walls is the result of reconstruction after bombing in 1943. The interior clearly reveals two different phases: the front part dates back to the 13th century, the back part to the 6th. The paving, the ambos, the Pascal candelabrum, the ciborium and the splendid episcopal throne (1254) are the product of the Cosmati school's extraordinary creativity with colors.

PORTA PIA, SANT' AGNESE FUORI LE MURA AND MAUSOLEO DI SANTA CONSTANZA. The Porta Pia was commissioned by Pius IV Medici and designed (1561–4) by Michelangelo. It is the only gate with its main façade facing toward the city, forming the backdrop to the Holy Road. Inside is the Museum of the History of the Bersaglieri. On Via Nomentana, the BASILICA was dedicated in the time of Constantine to Agnes, the youngest of martyrs, although it was significantly altered in the 16th century. The mosaic in the apse (7th century) represents one of the finest examples of Byzantine art in the capital. From the garden you enter the MAUSOLEUM designed for Constantine's daughters, and turned into a church in 1254, which contains ancient mosaics.

THE CATACOMBS
The theory that these were a refuge for persecuted Christians or secret places of worship is groundless. The catacombs were in fact burial-grounds until the 6th century and were then turned into places of devotion. Those on the Old Appian Way (the catacombs of Domitilla, San Callisto and San Sebastiano) are among the biggest in

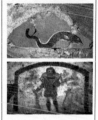

Rome and still have some beautiful paintings. A visit to these caverns is also a pleasant way to cool down during hot days in Rome.

THE MARBLE-CRAFTSMEN OF ROME
These were most active between the 12th and 13th centuries, sometimes working individually but more often organized together in family groups (the Cosmatis or the Vassallettos), who handed their skills down from generation to generation. Their specialty was ecclesiatical interiors (for example, partitions, pavements, ambos, thrones, tombs, ciboriums and candelabra). The interior of St Lawrence Outside the Walls represents an important example.

"TIME AND WORK"
After spending several years as a hermit at Subiaco, in around 525 Benedict of Norcia (480–547) founded the monastery of Montecassino, welcoming men of every class and culture. The *Rule*, drafted for them, was based on communal prayer and manual labor, as "idleness is the enemy of the soul." Saint Benedict was buried at Montecassino.

A journey from the capital toward the Tyrrhenian Sea or the Adriatic takes you past ancient reminders of imperial power, and religion; westward, the trip covers the territories of the Etruscan peoples, while eastward, the route takes a geographical and chronological leap into the preserved natural landscape of the Abruzzo.

ALONG THE ANIENE VALLEY

History has seen the development of some highly attractive towns in the valley of this important tributary of the Tiber. These settlements flourished in the Middle Ages, some even earlier, because of the abundance of water (it is enough to recall the Tivoli waterfalls, painted by so many who have seen them). These towns suffer nevertheless by comparison with the beauty of the architectural legacy of two quite contrasting figures: Hadrian, emperor and intellectual, and Saint Benedict, mystic and "rule-maker" of monasticism.
HADRIAN'S VILLA, SHINING MEMORY ★. The fascinating and many-sided personality of the Emperor Hadrian, combined with his well-known dilettante's passion for architecture, is reflected in the varied and whimsical articulation of the layout of the villa's buildings ▲ *382*, near Tivoli. Their arrangement has actually been compared to King Louis XIV's magnificent palace of Versailles in France. Here, too, nature was allied to culture, but in much more explicit ways.

BENEDICTINE SPIRITUALITY AT SUBIACO ★. The name Subiaco (from Sublaqueum, "below the lake") is derived from the three artificial lakes that were created by the Emperor Nero for his villa, which was actually washed away in 1305 following a

"THE TRAVELER'S PILGRIMAGE TO THE ETERNAL CITY WOULD BE INCOMPLETE WITHOUT A SHORT TRIP TO TIVOLI."

ITALY IN WORDS AND PICTURES, 1838

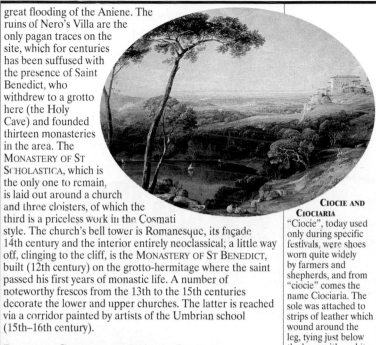

great flooding of the Aniene. The ruins of Nero's Villa are the only pagan traces on the site, which for centuries has been suffused with the presence of Saint Benedict, who withdrew to a grotto here (the Holy Cave) and founded thirteen monasteries in the area. The MONASTERY OF ST SCHOLASTICA, which is the only one to remain, is laid out around a church and three cloisters, of which the third is a priceless work in the Cosmati style. The church's bell tower is Romanesque, its façade 14th century and the interior entirely neoclassical; a little way off, clinging to the cliff, is the MONASTERY OF ST BENEDICT, built (12th century) on the grotto-hermitage where the saint passed his first years of monastic life. A number of noteworthy frescos from the 13th to the 15th centuries decorate the lower and upper churches. The latter is reached via a corridor painted by artists of the Umbrian school (15th–16th century).

BETWEEN CIOCIARIA AND AGRO PONTINO

Many people call Ciociaria the "soul of Lazio". Typical of this region and Agro Pontino are the unforgettable hill-top strongholds and the slender linearity of the religious architecture. It is a region which seems to live also in legend, as in the mythical dominions of Circe that are protected by the Parco Nazionale del Circeo spreads along the Tyrrhenian coast.

THE ACROPOLISES OF ALATRI AND FERENTINO.
These two ancient centers of the Ernici people originally profited considerably from their commanding strategic position and later grew rich in public buildings and shrines. Both towns contain ruins that are of pre-Roman origin, while at the same time the old urban fabric of the medieval city has, for the most part, been preserved. Yet by far the most fascinating monuments are the majestic acropolises of the two cities. These are broad terraces that have been built on the top of the hill, cutting into and flattening the rock, and arranging it into embankments and really imposing superstructures.

CIOCIE AND CIOCIARIA
"Ciocie", today used only during specific festivals, were shoes worn quite widely by farmers and shepherds, and from "ciocie" comes the name Ciociaria. The sole was attached to strips of leather which wound around the leg, tying just below the knee with a white piece of cloth.

A PERFECT WALL
The ring of walls around the acropolis at Alatri is completely intact and at several points reaches 56 feet in height. The gigantic blocks (up to 14 feet long and more than 7 feet high) fit perfectly together.

Built between 118 and 134, the villa was Hadrian's trip down memory lane, as he reconstructed places that made the greatest impression on him during visits to the empire's provinces: the Pecile recalled the *Stoá Poikíle* in Athens, the Valle di Tempe evoked the countryside of Thessaly; and with the Canopus, the sad emperor tried to keep alive the memory of Egypt: in 130, the waters of the Nile had engulfed Hadrian's favorite Antinous.

A VAST COMPLEX
Emperor Hadrian (above, in a portrait kept in the Musei Capitolini) designed his residence himself. It appears to have covered around 740 acres, thereby making it the largest villa built in ancient times. It is arranged into pavilions, which are positioned in the surrounding natural environment with a keen sense of drama.

THE MOSAIC OF THE DOVES
A copy of a 2nd-century BC original, it is a priceless example of a highly skilled technique: ry small tiles of irregular shape which render the gaps in between invisible. This mosaic was scovered in the area around the Accademia and today is in the Musei Capitolini ▲ 347.

CENTAUR
Exquisite creations of Aristeas and Papias (2nd century), the two centaurs (in the photo, the older of the two) in gray marble made up part of the villa's decorative furnishings and are found today in the Musei Capitolini ▲ 347.

383

THE SORCERESS CIRCE
The island where the palace of this Homeric figure stood was long identified with the Circeo promontory, which was then cut off from dry land. Today the impenetrable grotto of Circe, accessible only by sea, is the sole reminder of the enchanted surroundings which attracted Ulysses and his companions.

THE "LESTRA" OF THE PONTINE REGION
Before the draining of the Pontine marshes (1926–35), a vast area was inhabited in the winter season by woodsmen, coal-miners, hunters, fishermen and cattle farmers: they lived in a clearing, the "lestra", in clusters of huts made of wood, straw and brush in an oval shape, with a coned or domed roof.

THE CISTERCIANS AT FOSSANOVA ★ AND CASAMARI. The Cistercian abbeys of Lazio are distinctive for their close ties with the monuments of Burgundy, where the order was born before spreading all over Europe. The name "FOSSANOVA" comes from the land improvement undertaken by the monks in 1135 with the building of a 'new canal' or 'fossa nova'. The façade of the church (1208), which is brought to life by a rose-window and a doorway decorated in the Cosmati style, suggests the most light-filled of interiors, yet it is one of absolute sobriety, which is in keeping with the strict and rather severe principles of the community. In the abbey, the Romano-Gothic cloister, onto which face the chapterhouse and the refectory, is worthy of note. The accentuated verticality of the church at CASAMARI (1217), with three naves separated by towering pillars supporting sharp arches, is even closer to French Gothic lines, as is the imposing chapterhouse facing onto the cloister.

THE WOODS, LAKES AND SEA OF THE PARCO NAZIONALE DEL CIRCEO ★. South of Rome, stretching from the foot of the Lepini mountains to Terracina, were the Pontine marshes, an inhospitable place, but one where nature remained unspoiled. Today the marshes barely exist, wiped out by the reclamation of the 1930's. To safeguard the forest and marshes that remain, the Parco Nazionale del Circeo was created in 1934. The preservation area covers the coastal lakes, the forest and the Circeo promontory. As a result of this diversity of environments, the appearance of plant life also

varies, with a kaleidoscopic array of wetlands and
Mediterranean scrublands, of sand dunes and imposing
woods. Equally varied is the animal population, with
fascinating fish and migratory birds. There are also the
imprints of human presence, from the neanderthal grottos
of "Circeo man" to the settlements and reminders of the
Romans. Outstanding among these are Domitian's Villa and
the swimming pools of Lucullus. The Park Museum houses
an exhaustive display documenting everything associated with
the history and environment of this exceptional area.

THE ROMAN TUSCIA

Of the territory that the Etruscans controlled at the peak of
their splendor, the Roman Tuscia (corresponding to northwest Lazio) represents only a very small part. Nevertheless,
after more than two millennia, the Etruscans still maintain a
powerful cultural presence. In the 8th century, after the grant
of Sutri, this region became the main base of the Church's
temporal power with Viterbo as its capital. This often led
the most powerful families of the Roman aristocracy to
fight here against each other. Fortifications proliferated
in the Middle Ages while, from the 16th to the 17th
centuries, architects produced Villa
Lante at Bagnaia, Palazzo Orsini at
Bomarzo, and also Palazzo Farnese
at Caprarola.

PALACES OF TARQUINIA
There are many
beautiful palaces in
the city, but the most
beautiful of all is the
Palazzo Comunale
(11th century, then
modified in the
Baroque period).
The Palazzo dei
Priori encompasses
four medieval towers.
Similarly, the 16th-
century Palazzo
Sachetti incorporates
a low tower dating
from some time
earlier.

THE MONSTERS OF BOMARZO
In 1552, Vicino Orsini
withdrew to live at
Bomarzo where, to
decorate the park's
terraces, he had
enormous stone
figures of exotic and
imaginary animals
sculpted, perhaps
creatures of the devil,
or creations of a
refined sensibility.

THE MUSEO NAZIONALE TARQUINIESE: THE ETRUSCANS IN A 15TH-CENTURY PALACE.
The
necropolis at Monterozzi ▲ 326 has given us a
pictorial legacy of unparalleled value and an
eyewitness account of the daily life, the burial and
religious customs, and the cultural evolution of the
Etruscan people. The museum offers an opportunity to
become familiar with the history, and not just romance,
of this civilization. Not to be missed is the beautiful
Gothic-Renaissance palace (1436–9) by the Vitelleschi,
which gave Corneto (at that time the name of the town)
its age of magnificence. The courtyard is lined with
sarcophagi and burial stones; on the first floor are bronzes,
golds, ceramics and the vivid WINGED HORSES; on the second
floor, there are several frescos removed from the walls of the

TARQUINIA HORSES
The terracotta horses
come from the Altar
of the Queen.

A ROMANESQUE JEWEL
At Tuscania, on the hill of volcanic rock outside the walls, and standing alone and evocative amid the medieval towers, is the Basilica of San Pietro, one of the most beautiful creations of the Romanesque with its Cosmati doorway and stupendous rose-window. It sits at the far end of a lonely, grassy square.

CONCLAVE AT VITERBO
One of the longest and liveliest conclaves was that which led to the election of Pope Gregory X (1271–72). After many months of meetings the cardinals were shut in the Bishop's palace, but differences of opinion continued. The city captain decided to remove the roof of the hall and to ration the provisions: as a result, tormented by the dog-days of August and by hunger, the argumentative prelates wasted no time in coming to an agreement, and in subsequent conclaves the cutting off of supplies became law.

tombs and, not to be outdone, a wide view over the country and the sea, to which Tarquinia's fortune has been tied.

THE OLD CHURCHES OUTSIDE THE GATES OF TUSCANIA.
Tuscania has been active on the same site for 2,600 years. Not even the severe earthquake of 1971, which rendered the town almost uninhabitable, succeeded in cutting short this record longevity. Tuscania's two jewels are to be found outside the modern town, on the isolated hill of San Pietro. The starting date of construction is uncertain, but is probably around the 8th century. The foundations of the great building projects of SAN PIETRO and SANTA MARIA MAGGIORE coincided with the economic revival and renewed political role of Tuscania, which in 787 had become part of the pope's domain. Standing on ancient and often-reworked ruins, the churches were mainly rebuilt in the 12th century, assuming their present-day Romanesque form.

VITERBO: STORIES OF THE MIDDLE AGES, POPES AND CONCLAVES. The Etruscan and Roman history of the city has barely left an impression compared to the flowering which followed when, after being fought over for a long time between the papacy and the empire, the town began to play frequent host to popes and conclaves in the 12th century. The presence of the papal court coincided with the period of

the greatest growth in construction which, between the Romanesque and Gothic, has left important reminders. The airy and panoramic balcony of the Gothic PALACE OF THE POPES is one of the city's most well-known images, but the medieval colors and atmosphere are more vivid in the 13th-century district of San Pellegrino, where the towers, dark houses, overhead walkways and barred arch windows are almost completely preserved.

> **"I**T IS AS IF [THE ETRUSCANS] DREW THEIR VITALITY FROM DEPTHS WHICH NOW, WITH OUR STEADY STREAMS OF BASE WATER, ARE DENIED US.**"**
>
> D.H. LAWRENCE, *ETRUSCAN PLACES*

THE MOUNTAINS AND VALLEYS OF ABRUZZO

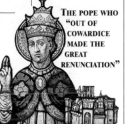

THE POPE WHO "OUT OF COWARDICE MADE THE GREAT RENUNCIATION"

Spartiacque, with the Gran Sasso, between the Adriatic and the Tyrrhenian – the land of Ovid, D'Annunzio, Croce, Silone and Flaiano – long ago lost its reputation as a place across which whole peoples migrate, but it is still a crossroads between north and south. It is a region "on a high", with a countryside shaped by hills, studded with artistic gems set in an environment that, especially in the Parco Nazionale d'Abruzzo, man has decided to preserve.

L'Aquila's Basilica of Santa Maria di Collemaggio was built at the wish of the hermit friar Pietro da Morrone, who in the same basilica was crowned pope under the name of Celestine V (1294), exciting high hopes of renewal and a return to morality. Just six months later, perhaps feeling himself incapable of ruling over such a great political power, he instead made "the great renunciation" (Dante) and returned to the ascetic life.

L'AQUILA, FOUNDED IN THE 13TH CENTURY. According to tradition, L'Aquila was formed in the 13th century by the coming together of 99 smaller towns, each of which had a castle, a square, a church and a fountain. Strategically sited on the Naples-Florence axis, it benefited from a wide degree of autonomy and from wealth, thanks to its flourishing wool industry and its trade in saffron. The FOUNTAIN OF THE 99 SPOUTS (1272) proudly recalls the castles which gave rise to the city. Here the Romanesque has its greatest masterpiece in Abruzzo: SANTA MARIA DI COLLEMAGGIO ★. High up and standing alone, it dates back to 1287 and has a superb façade with white and red geometric patterns, as well as a rich central doorway. The rough bulk of the CASTLE (1530–1635), on the stout foundation of the Gran Sasso, recalls the period of Spanish control. It houses the National Museum of Abruzzo, rich in works of art and with a

THE FESTIVAL OF THE PARDON
This festival takes place in L'Aquila each year on August 28, to mark the plenary indulgence given by Celestine V to all who visit the basilica.

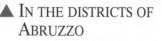
paleontology section (preserved here is a fossilized elephant found in the town).

SAN CLEMENTE A CASAURIA ★, THE MOST BEAUTIFUL CHURCH IN ABRUZZO. The lie of the region's land allows you to distinguish, in the valleys between the rivers running to the coast, the principal sites of local cultural development in the Middle Ages. Most noteworthy of all is a school of sculptors elaborating a language all their own, neatly expressed in a series of pulpits in churches scattered throughout the Pescara river valley. The abbey of San Clemente at Casauria (12th century), entered through an elegant colonnade and beautiful doorway with bronze knockers, contains one of the most characteristic example, with extremely rich floral friezes and lively rosettes bearing a classisistic touch. In the crypt are the remains of the original foundations (9th century), built on a Roman *vicus*.

FLORA AND FAUNA OF THE PARCO NAZIONALE D'ABRUZZO. At the far southern end of the Appenines is one of the most fascinating inland regions in the peninsula: the Abruzzo National Park, established in 1923. The wide expanses of forest, pasture, valleys and clearings, splashed with abundant springs, support a precious floral and animal heritage. Great stands of trees cover two thirds of the total area, a mixture of oak, maple, flowering ash and ash, while the higher regions are home to thickets of pine. The flora is the park's richest asset, with a full 150 indigenous varieties: here flowers the rarest and most beautiful of the wild orchids, the "slipper of Venus". The fauna owes its presence to the ice ages, which scattered Nordic-type animals, which have found safety and protection here, as far as the Appenines. The original object of the park was safeguarding Abruzzo's Marsican bear and chamois, but now the Appenine wolf is a protected species as well. The most outstanding of the Park's birds is the golden eagle, and foremost among its reptiles is the tiny, rare Orsini viper. Such a rich array of fauna, with 300 species of bird, 40 mammals and 30 reptiles and amphibians, is probably without comparison in the other parks of Europe.

THE MARSICAN BEAR
A solitary and tireless walker and climber, brown in color and imposing in build, the bear has a gentle character and feeds on tubers, fruit and small animals, rarely posing a danger to flocks or shepherds. A typical adult can stand over 3 feet 6 inches at the withers and reach 5 feet 11 inches from muzzle to tail.

FROM NAPLES TO COASTAL AND INLAND CAMPANIA

NAPLES, *392*

▲ From Naples to Coastal and Inland Campania

A visit to Naples offers an intoxicating combination of cultural heritage – the city has exceptional monuments and art collections – and vibrant daily life – a consequence of the city's individualistic history as the former capital of Italy's Mezzogiorno. Popular with tourists since the days of the Grand Tour, Naples is also an ideal starting point for visiting the islands in its gulf and its enchanting hinterland. The excursions in this section radiate from Naples: first to the mythical Campi Flegrei, where the agricultural countryside is scattered with architectural reminders of classical times; next, to the idyllic islands of Procida, Ischia and Capri; then to Herculaneum and Pompeii, buried in a catastrophic fall of volcanic ash and lava nineteen centuries ago but which today reveal amazing details of their ancient culture, preserved in time; and finally to Sorrento, high on the southernmost peninsula of the Gulf of Naples, looking over to the city itself in the north. Refined Positano, old Amalfi and silent, dignified Ravello punctuate the melting beauty of the Amalfi Coast. To the south-east lies the

Gulf of Salerno and
the lively city itself, which provides
a link to the far south of Campania. Along
this wilder coast is found Paestum (57 miles
from Naples), whose dazzling temples recall the
civilization of Magna Graecia, evidence of which
appears everywhere along this coast. Beyond,
the wooded cliffs of unspoilt Cilento stand out
proudly against the sea. To the north of Naples
the productive farmlands of *Campania felix*,
called "happy" in Roman times because of the
extraordinary richness of its soil. Prominent in
this wealthy region are Santa Maria Capua
Vetere, Capua and Caserta. This region once
also belonged to one of the most important pre-
Roman civilizations in Italy, the Sannites, whose
history can be explored in the museums at
Benevento and Isernia (68 miles from Naples).

"There are cities
which rise out of
water, others out
of thin air. Naples
stands on a mound
of volcanic rock
riddled with caverns,
underground caves
and lost channels.
The earthquake
brewing underneath it
finds pockets of air in
which to boom, sing
and ring. . . . Every
so often, the great
stone beams sink into
the ground and the
subsoil rises up."
Erri De Luca,
In alto a sinistra
(Top Left)

MAGNA GRAECIA
For those who come down from the North, Naples is the gateway to Magna Graecia, the start of that long

strip of the Tyrrhenian and Ionian coast which, between the 8th and the 6th centuries BC, became "Greater Greece" for the Hellenic colonies on the peninsula.

THE GORGON
This head of a Gorgon, a female monster from Greek mythology, comes from Santa Maria Capua Vetere.

Even though it sits in the middle of a magnificent gulf, Naples represents more for tourists than just its spectacular and internationally famous position: its attraction is also – and above all – the accumulation, indeed the tangle, of presences left by its extraordinary history as a metropolitan melting-pot fronting onto the belly of the Mediterranean.

A WORLD UNTO ITSELF. The uniqueness of Naples' present-day culture has always provoked discussion and has given rise to a well-defined "napoletanità" (the state of being Neapolitan). The prevailing culture is in fact the result of the influence of a succession of different periods and styles of government throughout its history. Each different rule brought new yardsticks by which to judge and evaluate both duty and pleasure. Aspiring political powers, Italian and foreign, have come and gone, leaving behind vague relics, architectural lines and street routes. These, unlike richer legacies, give a sense of impermanence. Naples gave an appearance of indeterminacy and idleness to the invader, although notable exceptions like the 17th-century Masaniello revolt, and the anti-Nazi Forty Days in 1943 exist. The people of Naples seem to have internalized, in ways not observed anywhere else in Europe, and perhaps the world, an instinct for survival and a capacity for overcoming restrictions imposed from above.

PARTENOPE AND "NEAPOLIS". The origins of what has today become a city of nearly three million inhabitants, almost unbroken from Pozzuoli to Castellammare di Stabia, lie in Greek colonies which came from Euboea toward the middle of the 8th century BC. The first colony on the sea was Cumae ▲ *411*, which in the 7th century founded Partenope and in the 5th *Neapolis* (the "new city"). Neither then nor in the Roman period was Naples important in

its own right. The whole of Campania, under the dominion of Rome, constituted no more than a rich granary for the empire, even if various members of the aristocracy of the City chose to build magnificent villas in the region, not only at Herculaneum and Pompeii but also in more "protected" places, hedonistic havens of *buen retiro*, for example Capri ▲ *411*.

FROM THE ROMAN AGE TO THE 16TH CENTURY. After the fall of Rome, the coasts of the region remained tied to the Byzantine empire: Gaeta, Naples, Sorrento and Amalfi enjoyed a time of great prosperity that saw the construction of buildings that still recall an era of culture and commerce, even if it was in the shadow of the barbarian invasions (the Goths of Alaric

and the Vandals of Genseric). In the feudal period, the French descended on Campania and, constantly under the threat of the Saracens' marauding bands of pirates, the population of Campania and the citizens of Naples witnessed the arrival of Norman knights in the 11th century. They conquered all of the South. In Campania, Robert le Guiscard made himself Lord of Salerno, as did Roger II over Amalfi, Capua and Naples (1139). The Norman-Swabian dynasty was highly civilized – under

Frederick II ▲ *447*, it gave Naples the first university in the South – but in the mid 13th century it was ousted from power. Straightaway the new rulers, the Angevins, victorious at Benevento (1266) and Tagliacozzo (1268), signaled the decisive turnaround in the city's history, moving their capital here from Palermo. A period of splendor dawned, which did not come to a close until 1442, when the Aragonese from Spain succeeded the Angevins.

SPANIARDS AND BOURBONS. In 1503, power over Naples was assumed by newly unified Spain: the whole of the South would be ruled by Spain until 1707. Naples was filled with churches and convents, while never losing its ability to rebel – as Masaniello (right)

CITY OF "CONCENTRATION"
Naples was not always as densely populated as it is today. The foundations for its current congestion were laid in the 16th century under Spanish rule, when fear that the province's nobility would escape central control convinced the empire to gather its feudal vassals into the capital. The workforce ended up following them.

MASANIELLO
Around the fishmonger Tomaso Aniello (1620–47) crystalized the discontent of a population overburdened with taxes not spent by the authorities and rightly considered by the taxpayers to be unjust and excessive: a new levy on fresh fruit brought them to the point of rebellion. The fate of Aniello, the ringleader, was tragic (he was decapitated, after ten days of fighting and bargaining, on July 16, 1647, in the Church of Carmine), but the episode was one of the exceptions to the Neapolitans' instinct for "idleness" (almost an instinct for survival) when faced with oppressors.

393

▲ Naples

1 The Floridiana 2 Villa Pignatelli 3 Castel Sant'Elmo 4 Charterhouse of San Martino 5 Church of Monteoliveto (Sant'Anna dei Lombardi) 6 San Giacomo degli Spagnoli

SCIUSCIÀ
The figure of the shoe-shine boy (his Neapolitanized name is a corruption of the English shoeshine), symbolic of Neapolitans forced to do any job they could to survive, recalls the memory of the Allied occupation at the end of World War Two and of the 1946 De Sica film *Sciuscià*, a masterpiece of cinema neorealism.

showed in 1647. Barely ten years had passed since Masaniello's upheaval before the entire city was laid low by a terrible outbreak of the plague. The "cause of the distress", according to many, was the Spanish overlords themselves who, by means of such inhuman tactics, attempted to eradicate any remaining dreams of revolution. One thing for sure is that the calamity (more likely caused by poor sanitary conditions and overpopulation) killed 350,000 Neapolitans, or seven out of every ten inhabitants. At the turn of the 18th century, the State of Naples passed to the Hapsburg empire, only to be handed over in 1734 to the Bourbon dynasty.

1799–1860. Naples responded to the French Revolution and its cry for freedom by giving birth in 1799 to the Neapolitan republic, which was immediately put down with English backing and, for the rest of the period, was supported only by enlightened nobles, not by the common people, who in fact violently opposed it. Once Napoleon's epic and the reign of Joachim Murat had come to an end, the Bourbons got their State back, adopting for it the old name of the Kingdom of the Two Sicilies. In 1860, the victorious campaign of Garibaldi's "Thousand" ● *44*, along with the ensuing plebiscite, meant the state was annexed to Italy.

"NEW NAPLES"
Outstanding among developments undertaken for the city's renewal is the reuse of the site previously occupied by the Bagnoli steelworks, where the City of Science now stands. The Naples Ninety-Nine Foundation, born in 1984, is reviving the city's historic heritage, playing a vital civic role.

THE FACE OF TODAY. The city approaches the bicentenary of 1799 with a great awareness of how much the defeat of the Neapolitan republic went on to weigh down its history and that of the country. With about 1,100,000 inhabitants, Naples is today the third biggest city in Italy after Rome and Milan. The major center of the South, it combines the scatter-gun ebullience and headstrong, passionate insistence of its people with an ambivalent rapport between undirected urban development and the cultural legacy of a secular, pluralist European capital.

The long, green, gently rising expanse from the Harbor Terminal all the way to the seat of the city council, together with the towers of Castel Nuovo on one side, bring together much of the city's history and can be thought of as the true center of Naples. Leaving the Harbor Terminal, you quickly come to the enormous PIAZZA DEL PLEBISCITO, grandly laid out by Joachim Murat.

PALAZZO DI SAN GIACOMO. Piazza del Municipio, where the offices of airlines, shipping companies and various travel agencies recall the time when tourists mostly arrived by sea, is bounded on the uphill side by this grand building, built between 1819 and 1825 to house the Bourbon ministers and today the town hall. San Giacomo is the church on its right.

SAN GIACOMO DEGLI SPAGNOLI. Erected in 1540, originally as a chapel for the military hospital serving the Spanish Quarters ▲ *398*, this church is rich in works of art from the 16th century and in reminders of Iberian rule. Behind the altar is the beautiful tomb of the viceroy Pedro de Toledo, who during his long tenure (1532–53) rejuvenated the city's justice system and town-planning.

CASTEL NUOVO ★. This is the largest civic structure from the Angevin and Aragonese periods, commissioned in 1279 by Charles of Anjou as his royal residence (Castel dell'Ovo ▲ *409* and Castel Capuano were no longer suitable for Naples' role as capital) and completed in 1284. Its present appearance is the result of its final reconstruction in 1443 by the Aragonese ruler Alfonso the Magnanimous, for whom the grand TRIUMPHAL ARCH

THE BARONS' HALL
From the courtyard, you go up to a large room with a ceiling covered in stars, which appears to conjure up just as many associations with central-plan Roman architecture ● *90* as with Spanish Gothic. The hall (today the seat of the city council) takes its name from the feudal vassals arrested here in 1486 for conspiring against the sovereign.

JOACHIM MURAT
Brother-in-law to Napoleon, whose sister he married, he was ruler of Naples and its State from 1808–15. During his period in power, Joachim Murat rationalized the education system and set in train a wide-reaching program of reform.

OF ALFONSO was built in 1468. The arch, confirming the transition from Gothic to Renaissance in southern Italy, is the castle's most interesting artistic feature, but other important works (F. Laurana, D. Gagini) are to be found in the CITY MUSEUM. Several of these come from the PALATINE CHAPEL, the only remaining part of the Angevin castle (the frescos that Giotto painted have been missing for centuries).

ROYAL PALACE. In front of the Doric semicircle commissioned by Murat for Piazza del Plebiscito is enthroned the main façade of the royal palace of Naples, a vast, mostly 16th-century complex, rearranged afterward bit-by-bit until the 19th century. Today it houses offices of public authorities and cultural institutes, among them the Vittorio Emanuele III National Library. You can go up from the courtyard to the MUSEO DELL'APPARTAMENTO STORICO, which despite wartime damage and restoration – including windows, tiles and frescoed walls – recaptures the building's royal atmosphere. Among the individual works, the most outstanding are canvases by Luca Giordano and the altar from the 1690's.

SAN FRANCESCO DI PAOLA. The colonnade in front of the Royal Palace must have struck Ferdinand I as too obvious a sign of the Napoleonic period, so much so that he had a monumental neoclassical basilica, completed in 1846, inserted in its center. The church, modeled on the Pantheon in Rome ▲ 365, was presented as a votive offering by the sovereign in thanks for his restoration to the throne of Naples.

TEATRO SAN CARLO ★. Built in a short space of time in 1737, the city's opera theater was one of the first innovations introduced by Charles of Bourbon. It was inaugurated on the sovereign's name day: hence its name. One of the most important premieres that San Carlo has hosted was that of Gaetano Donizetti's *Lucia di Lammermoor*, in 1835.

GALLERIA UMBERTO I ● 95 Twenty years younger and smaller than the one in Milan, this is named after Vittorio Emanuele II ▲ 190 . However, both are similar in their style and use of iron and glass.

Votive offering to Giuseppe
Moscati (1880–1927),
biochemist and doctor
canonized in 1987, in the
Church of Gesù Nuovo.

THE SPANISH QUARTERS
The opening up of
Via Toledo in the
16th century enabled
the development of
new districts to the
west which, until
the middle of the
17th century, were
used mostly to house
the Spanish troops
garrisoned in Naples.
Today this is an
extremely lively
neighborhood where,
according to the
collective
imagination, you see
"napoletanità" ▲ 402
at its best: cordiality,
the art of getting by,
clothes strung out to
dry, the characteristic
"bassi" (poorer
districts) and
community life
on the streets.

PIAZZA DANTE
Between San Michele
and the 17th-century
Port'Alba opens
Piazza Dante, the
former Mercatello
dramatically arranged
in a semicircle by
Luigi Vanvitelli in
1765. Under the
name of Forum
Carolinum, it was
meant to frame a
monument to Charles
of Bourbon which was
never finished. In the
middle of the piazza
is the statue of Dante
Alighieri, the work of
the Neapolitan artist
Tito Angelini, erected
in 1872.

VIA TOLEDO

Running from Piazza del Plebiscito, this is
one of the most important streets in Naples,
commissioned by the viceroy Pedro de Toledo.
The street is packed with stately buildings and
elegant shops (GALLERIA UMBERTO I ▲ 397
opens out here, and links Via Toledo with Via
Verdi), then takes on a more low-brow feel.
LA CONCEZIONE A MONTECALVARIO. Toward the
hill of Vomero, Via Montecalvario brings you
to two churches which give their names to the
surrounding streets and district. The oldest dates
from the 16th century but the more recent, la Concezione,
designed by Vaccaro, is more noteworthy.
PALAZZO CARAFA DI MADDALONI. This faces onto one side of
Via Toledo (the entrance is in Via Maddaloni) and is one of
the grandest and most elegant residences from the Neapolitan
Baroque, commissioned in 1582 by the d'Avalos family and
passing to a ducal branch of the Carafas. Next door, on the
corner of Via Sant'Anna dei Lombardi, is the 18th-century
PALAZZO DORIA D'ANGRI, designed by Luigi Vanvitelli.
LO SPIRITO SANTO. On the opposite side of Via Toledo from
Palazzo Carafa and Palazzo Doria stands this important
church, founded in the 16th century and rebuilt in 1774 by
Mario Gioffredo. It retains several works of art from inside
the original building.
SAN MICHELE A PORT' ALBA. A little past the end of
the street, and one of the jewels of early 18th
century in Naples, this is the work of Vaccaro
and is a renovation of a church that actually
dates from nearly two centuries earlier,
paintings from which have been preserved.

SPACCANAPOLI

The old lower decuman of the Roman city
appears to cut the urban layout in two:
hence the name of the axis along which Via
Benedetto Croce and Via San Biagio dei
Librai run ("Spaccanapoli" means "splits
Naples"). This long route links two of the most

important churches in the city, Monteoliveto and l'Annunziata, the latter in the Forcella neighborhood, and opens out onto squares in front of one holy building after another.

CHIESA DI MONTEOLIVETO ★. Also called Sant' Anna dei Lombardi, this represents a sort of museum of the sculpture of Renaissance Naples. Particularly noteworthy are three chapels in the Tuscan style: the Piccolomini (with the tomb of Mary of Aragon, the work of Antonio Rossellino and Benedetto da Maiano), the Terranova (with an *Annunciation* by Benedetto da Maiano) and the Capella Tolosa (in the style of Brunelleschi, with Della Robbia medallions). Also outstanding are the *Lament*, an ensemble in terracotta by Guido Mazzoni, in the oratory to the right of the altar, and the wooden marquetry by Fra Giovanni da Verona kept in the old sacristy, whose walls boast frescos by Giorgio Vasari.

PALAZZO GRAVINA. On Via Monteoliveto, and famous for its Tusco-Roman design, is this residence built in the early 16th century for the Gravina branch of the Orsini family. Today it houses the university's faculty of architecture.

GESÙ NUOVO. The unusual ashlars on the façade of this church, the second to be commissioned in the city by the Jesuits (the first, Gesù Vecchio, on Via B.Croce, is next to the university), were taken from the 15th-century Palazzo dei Sanseverino di Salerno which the church replaced at the end of the 16th century. The greatest Neapolitan artists of the age decorated the interior. The *Hunt of Heliodorus* by Francesco Solimena is on the inside façade.

SANTA CHIARA ★. On one side of the Piazza del Gesù Nuovo is this church-mausoleum of the house of Anjou, a grand Gothic building begun in 1310, and at one time the center of an entire monastic neighborhood of Poor

The axis of Spaccanapoli divides the city in two.

THE SPIRE OF THE IMMACOLATA
On Piazza del Gesù Nuovo, the obelisk erected by the Jesuits in the mid 18th century to celebrate their order, one of the most important spots for preaching, looks like a petrified "party popper".

CLOISTER OF THE POOR CLARES
The greater part of the area occupied by the Convent of St Clare is taken up by the fabulous cloister which stretches out behind the church. The facelift carried out on it in the 18th century by Domenico Antonio Vaccaro was based on a liberal use of majolica along rural themes, in yellow, green and blue tones similar to the lemons and grapevines tended here (or else the sky); out of these elements, Vaccaro produced a rustic, secular effect almost unique among cloistered places.

399

THE TERRIBLE 1600'S
Besides the plague of 1656 ▲ *394*, which cut down 70 percent of the population (not to mention the anti-Spanish revolt of Masaniello ▲ *393* a decade before), the 17th century also brought to Naples the dramatic return of Vesuvius' eruptions in 1631 and the run of destruction caused by the earthquakes of 1688. The spire of San Domenico Maggiore was built as a thanksgiving offering for the end of the pestilence of 1656.

Clares (and, to a lesser degree, Franciscans) which covered the whole of the enormous block behind. Engulfed in flames during the bombing raids of 1943, the church lost its magnificent mid-18th-century interiors. Similarly, only scorched fragments could be reassembled from the giant TOMB OF ROBERT OF ANJOU, the magnificent creation of the Tuscan school which forms the far end of the single nave. Nonetheless, many important works are left (among them other royal tombs), as well as the solemn space of the CHANCEL OF THE POOR CLARES (a sort of separate church, closet-like and hidden behind the public one), the magnificent CLOISTER ▲ *399* and the collections in the new MUSEO DELL'OPERA DI SANTA CHIARA, which contains Roman baths.

SAN DOMENICO MAGGIORE. Piazza San Domenico is near the university neighborhoods. Turning its shoulders toward the square is this large 13th–14th-century church, commissioned by Charles II of Anjou. Its monastery played a role in the life of the university and, among others, hosted Thomas Aquinas and Giordano Bruno. The most notable BURIAL MONUMENTS are those of the Carafa family, as well as the 16th-century Pandone tomb.

CAPPELLA SANSEVERO. Near San Domenico (in Via De Sanctis) is this genteel 16th-century chapel, reconstructed in the mid 18th century on the orders of prince Raimondo di Sangro. To his powerful personal skills as scientist and man of

GIAMBATTISTA VICO
Number 31 Via San Biagio dei Librai is the house in which Giambattista Vico (1668–1744), the philosopher who opposed Descartes' *cogito*, was born. Vico valued the knowledge of facts (which are truth) over logical deduction and enunciated a theory of reality imposed on the phases (occurrences and recurrences) of historical evolution.

THE STREET OF CRIBS
Via San Gregorio
Armeno, the center
of Naples' craftsmen,
offers the amazing
sight of its figurine-
makers' workshops.
Gathered together
here are molders and
decorators of little
sculptures depicting
famous personalities
and of the figures
which bring to life
Naples' traditional
Nativity cribs.

letters, not to mention mason, we owe both the designs for the iconography of the Sangro tombs, as well as the very fame of the building, which grew in a somewhat shady manner on account of the macabre anatomical machines in the crypt. The *Christ Wrapped in the Shroud*, sculpted by Giuseppe Sanmartino in 1753, is famous.

PALAZZO CARAFA DI MADDALONI. Running through to no. 121 VIA SAN BIAGIO DEI LIBRAI ★ , this is one of the most important civic buildings dating from 15th-century Naples, built on the wishes of the humanist Diomede Carafa.

MONTE DI PIETÀ. The austere palace of Monte di Pietà, finished in the early 17th century, faces onto Via San Biagio dei Librai, at the top of Via San Gregorio Armeno. The CHAPEL at the end of the courtyard has sculptures that date from the same time as the interior façade, frescos and stuccos.

SANTI SEVERINO E SOSSIO. Most blocks south of Monte di Pietà were taken up by a Benedictine monastery of the late Middle Ages (from 1835 it has housed the State Archives), of which only this church, rebuilt in the 16th century, remains.

SAN GREGORIO ARMENO. This large, rich monastic complex was founded in the 8th century by monks fleeing from Byzantium. The most notable features of the church's present-day decoration, which dates from the 16th century, are the wooden ceiling from 1580, the frescos by Luca Giordano over the entrance and the great altar from the mid 17th century. The monastery has a splendid 18th-century CLOISTER.

PALAZZO COMO. This Renaissance residence of the Como (in Naples, Cuomo) family, bankers from Florence, is on Via del Duomo. At the end of the 19th century, the building was moved to conform to the new lie of the street.

CHURCH OF THE SANTISSIMA ANNUNZIATA. This church, rebuilt in the 18th century after a fire, stands in the neighborhood of FORCELLO. In 1318, ʰe Holy House for ᵇabandoned infants ᵃs established this site.

PIAZZA DEL MERCATO
On the southern edge
of the neighborhood
of Forcella, an exedra
and the church of
Santa Croce al
Mercato, both from
the 18th century,
provide the backdrop
for the marketplace,
one of the richest
places in the city
when it comes to
historical events.
Public executions
took place here
(including that of
Conrad of Swabia, in
1268, which signaled
the end of the
Norman-Swabian
dynasty in the South),
and the revolt of
Masaniello was
begun here as well.

An ancient sign, the horns, to ward off the evil eye.

No other Italian city, not even Rome, has a culture as distinctive as that of Naples. There are those who go further and claim that the Neapolitan culture is in fact quite separate from that of the rest of the peninsula. Down through the centuries – in spite of the obstacles that everyday life has always placed in front of the populace, or perhaps because of these and the stimuli generated by them – "napoletanità" has been expressed in ways that have sometimes been transformed into international hallmarks. To understand the phenomenon, just a few of the foods and cultural features that Naples has been responsible for are shown on these pages.

SPAGHETTI
The invention of spaghetti has been claimed even by the Chinese.

In the absence of a firm place of origin (and without getting into an argument over the merits of the products), you have to concede that it was in Naples, at the court of Ferdinand II, that Gennaro Spadacini invented the four-pronged fork specifically for spaghetti.

PIZZA
The idea of flattening out dough, putting tomato and salt on top, adding oil and baking it in the oven might not seem all that appetizing, but it ended up conquering the planet. As everybody knows, there are almost always other ingredients, sometimes in extra-ordinary variety, but the basic pizza is the classic *Margherita*. To make this you should use chopped San Marzano tomatoes and buffalo's-milk mozzarella.

RELIGIOUSNESS

The most ancient of features – perhaps just as much as the superstitions basic to the Neapolitan cabal, linked to dreams and lucky numbers – pervade the city's popular religious beliefs. The phenomenon of the liquification of the blood of Saint Gennaro, which takes place twice a year in the cathedral (if it does not, it is a bad omen), might well be an extraordinary case of a recurring miracle (and one which excites a large following).

THEATER

According to Benedetto Croce, the Pulcinella routine (in English, *Punch*, in French, *Polichinelle*) was created in 17th-century Naples by a certain Puccio d'Aniello. In this century alone, the broad-based expressiveness and energy of the medium are the roots of plays by Edoardo Scarpetta and Raffaele Viviani, the populist comic appeal of Totò (Antonio de Curtis), the ironic humanity of Eduardo de Filippo and, today, the musical theater of Roberto de Simone.

MUSIC

The tarantella, opera stars such as Enrico Caruso, the evergreen success of classics like *Te voglio bene assaje*, *'O sole mio* or *Torna a Surriento* are the fruits of a musical tradition going back perhaps a thousand years. Napoletanità has also produced instruments, especially percussion, like the *putipù*, the *scetavaiasse* and the *triccheballacche*.

'o Sole Mio!

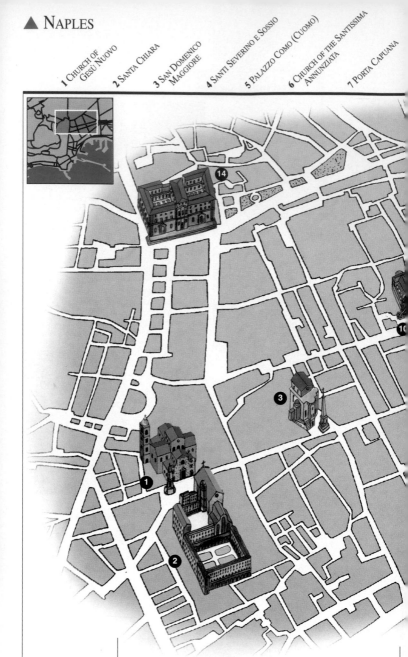

1 CHURCH OF GESÙ NUOVO
2 SANTA CHIARA
3 SAN DOMENICO MAGGIORE
4 SANTI SEVERINO E SOSSIO
5 PALAZZO COMO (CUOMO)
6 CHURCH OF THE SANTISSIMA ANNUNZIATA
7 PORTA CAPUANA

CONSERVATORY OF MUSIC
Attached to San Pietro a Maiella is its former monastery, where an important conservatory of music has operated since 1826. The institute brings together the traditions of composers such as Scarlatti, Paisiello, Spontini and Pergolesi.

FROM VIA DEI TRIBUNALI TO PORTA CAPUANA

The city's central axis, Via dei Tribunali, is so named because it is bounded to the east by Castel Capuano, which from the 16th century housed the main law courts.

SAN PIETRO A MAIELLA. This 13th-century church, with its characteristic three-pronged and steepled bell tower, stands close to Piazza Dante at the narrow end of the street. It was dedicated to the hermit of Maiella, Pietro Angeleri, who in 1294 became pope under the name of Celestine V ▲ 387, before making the "great renunciation" and returning to a life of meditation. Inside, 17th-century canvases by Mattia Preti,

8 Castel Capuano
9 San Lorenzo Maggiore
10 San Paolo Maggiore
11 Cathedral
12 Santa Maria Donnaregina
13 San Giovanni a Carbonara
14 National Archeological Museum

illustrating
the *Stories of
Saint Celestine*, have
been incorporated into
the ceiling. The
Conservatory of Music is housed
in the adjoining Celestine monastery.

PONTANO CHAPEL. This private place of
devotion for the 15th-century humanist Giovanni
Pontano stands on the corner of Via del Sole and was
probably built according to the design of the architect
Franceso di Giorgio Martini in his old age.

SAN PAOLO MAGGIORE. Standing on the raised site of the
ancient temple of the Dioscuri (from which only a pair of
columns is still visible), this church was founded between the
8th and 11th centuries. It was later annexed to the Theatine
Monastery, established here in 1538 by Saint Gaetano Thiene.

SAN LORENZO MAGGIORE. This church, the first in the city by
the Franciscans and rebuilt some time after 1270 on the
wishes of Charles of Anjou, overlooks a square which possibly
witnessed the founding of *Neapolis*. The striking apse frames
an ANCONA with 16th-century statues of Saint Lawrence, Saint
Anthony and Saint Francis. Also oustanding is the TOMB OF
CATHERINE OF AUSTRIA, a 14th-century creation by Tino di
Camaino near the altar.

**BOCCACCIO
AND FIAMMETTA**
It was in San Lorenzo
Maggiore that the
writer Giovanni
Boccaccio (1313–75),
staying at the
monastery while
working in the city as
a clerk in a subsidiary
of Florence's Bardi
bank, met the
daughter of Robert
of Anjou, Maria of
Aquin. This noble
lady fascinated him,
and he immortalized
her under the poetic
name of Fiammetta.

405

CHAPEL OF THE TREASURY OF SAN GENNARO
Forming part of the cathedral is this sumptuously rich Baroque structure, with decorations and works of art in gold which constitute the Treasury of the patron saint of Naples. The *reliquary bust* and the *reliquary of the blood* are displayed on the occasion of the regular festivals of Saint Gennaro and the liquifying of his blood.

CATHEDRAL ★. Running across the eastern stretch of Via dei Tribunali, the cathedral has a neo-Gothic façade from the 19th century, although the doorways are 14th century. Inside, where for pillars there are 110 paired columns recycled from ancient times, the most interesting features are the Gothic frescos in the MINUTOLO CHAPEL (at the back of the right transept), and the hollowed effigy carved between the 15th and 16th centuries (possibly to a design by Donato Bramante) to hold the relics of Saint Gennaro. The sumptuous 17th-century makeover of the early Christian Basilica of SANTA RESTITUTA (with access via the left nave) and the associated BAPTISTRY, from the late Middle Ages, with its mosaics, are also worth seeing.

CASTEL CAPUANO. This ancient fortress became, first of all, a Norman palace and then, in 1540, was expropriated by the viceroy Pedro de Toledo to house the city's tribunals. Inside, the CAPPELLA DELLA SOMMARIA contains grotesques, stuccos and frescos from the mid 16th century.

PORTA CAPUANA. Beyond the castle, typical of Aragonese Naples, is a truly beautiful marble arch (to a design by Giuliano da Maiano, 1484) between two towers which form part of the city walls.

FROM CARBONARA TO THE NATIONAL ARCHEOLOGICAL MUSEUM

ANCIENT ART IN NAPLES
At least a few supreme examples of especial beauty should be singled out from the huge collections in the National Archeological Museum: the statue of the so-called Farnese Hercules (discovered in Rome in the baths of Caracalla), the Farnese bowl (a 2nd-century BC cameo from Alexandria), the marbles of Armodius and Aristogitone (Roman copies of 5th-century BC Greek statues), the Psyche brought to light in the amphitheater of Santa Maria Capua Vetere and the mosaics from the House of the Faun in Pompeii.

The axis of Via Santi Apostoli and Via Anticaglia, with its extensive ruins from a Roman theater, corresponds to the upper decuman of ancient *Neapolis*.

SAN GIOVANNI A CARBONARA. At the furthest reach of the Carbonara (a medieval garbage-dump and jousting-ground), stands the 15th-century Augustinian Church of San Giovanni, which was the mausoleum of the last Angevin rulers. The CARACCIOLO DI VICO CHAPEL, to the left of the presbytery, is a fine early-16th-century structure.

SANTA MARIA DONNAREGINA. The front of this 17th-century convent church, which surrounds an earlier one from the beginning of the 14th century, looks down onto Via Santi Apostoli. The burial monument of the

monastery's founder, Maria of Hungary, a 14th-century masterpiece by Tino di Camaino, will be placed in the Diocesan Museum, along with the frescos from the nuns' chancel.

NATIONAL ARCHEOLOGICAL MUSEUM ★. Housing some of the antiquities from the Farnese collection ▲ *408* and finds from excavations at Herculaneum and Pompeii ▲ *412*, this large building is one of the finest museums in the world.

CORSO UMBERTO I (THE RETTIFILO)

Corso Umberto I is joined to Piazza Municipio by Via Sanfelice and by the street which takes its name from the viceroy Medina. The most interesting sights in this area are the 14th-century frescos in SANTA MARIA INCORONATA, the church of SANTA MARIA LA NOVA, with its painted ceiling from the end of the 16th century, and the 15th-century PALAZZO PENNA. Running east, the Rettifilo passes the church of SANT'AGOSTINO ALL ZECCA, with 18th-century canvases in the apse, and SANTA MARIA DEL CARMINE, whose bell tower from 1631 (246 feet, the highest in Naples) is festively "set alight" with fireworks every July 16.

TOWARD CAPODIMONTE

The route links the National Archeological Museum with the palace of Capodimonte, culminating in a magnificent park which overlooks the city.

SANTA MARIA DELLA SANITÀ. The church of the Sanità, known also as "San Vincenzo" because of the statue of Saint Vincenzo Ferreri venerated here, stands halfway up the slope, on top of the early-Christian catacombs of San Gaudioso. Archeologically complex inside, with twelve small domes, its high altar is positioned above the chapel at the entrance to the underground galleries, which you can visit.

REORGANIZATION OF THE CITY
Following an outbreak of cholera in 1884, some of the "bassi" (poorer districts) between the old city and the harbor were cleared away. As a result a straight new thoroughfare was carved out, enabling people to cross town in a hurry: this is Corso Umberto I, known as "the Rettifilo".

CATACOMBS OF SAN GENNARO
These are the most extensive catacombs in the South. Saint Gennaro was laid here at the beginning of the 5th century. The frescos, painted throughout the caves' entire period of use (2nd–9th century), are of great importance.

ROYAL PALACE OF CAPODIMONTE. Near an old hill-town, which in those days stood all by itself in the woods, Charles of Bourbon commenced the construction of a new and grand building where he could display the collections of the Farnese family (and from where, about 80 years later, the antiquities were moved to the present-day National Archeological Museum). The surrounding 300 acres of forest still make up the CAPODIMONTE PARK, with its radial pattern of pathways. A different fate befell the MUSEUM AND GALLERIES OF CAPODIMONTE ★. Some of its exhibition rooms have been reopened with new displays, including paintings by Masaccio, Giambellino, Mantegna, Raphael, Titian, Correggio, Caravaggio, Luca Giordano and Matti Preti.

VOMERO

As the cable-car climbs to the higher stations, the cityscape changes unexpectedly: not so much in the style of the buildings as in the clearly higher standard of living. "Well-to-do Naples" tends to live here rather than in the historic center and, in a certain sense, the two cities appear to ignore each other.

CASTEL SANT' ELMO. This star-shaped stronghold has stood on the hilltop since the 16th century, preceded on the same spot by a 14th-century Angevin fort. Designed to protect the city from outside attack, it was more often used against it (for example, during the Masaniello uprising ▲ *393*).

CHARTERHOUSE OF SAN MARTINO. Just beneath the castle, this immense Cistercian complex, which took shape on Vomero between the 14th and 17th centuries, is of exceptional interest both for its history and its view. Beside the magnificent space of the GREAT CLOISTER (with busts of Cistercian saints and the little graveyard's balustrade) and in addition to smaller open areas and passages, you can visit the fascinating historical collections of the NATIONAL MUSEUM OF SAN MARTINO (mostly maps, costume and Nativity cribs).

THE WATERFRONT AND THE RIVIERA DI CHIAIA

The SANTA LUCIA DISTRICT, named for its church, was famous for its hotels and for its natural beauty, at least until the strip of sea facing it silted up in the 19th century. As a result, the present-day waterfront of VIA PARTENOPE ★ is much further away from the waterline than it once was. Opposite this, CASTEL DELL'OVO, the oldest fortified site in the city, sits on a tiny island which by Roman times hosted a nobleman's

residence. Just to the west, the RIVIERA DI CHIAIA borders the wide, green expanse of the Villa Comunale. Just past the Riviera di Chiaia, more greenery surrounds the neoclassical VILLA PIGNATELLI, built in 1826 by the Actons and now state property, housing period furniture and a collection of carriages.

MERGELLINA AND POSILLIPO

The old suburban center of MERGELLINA ★ is now known primarily as a tourist port and as a neighborhood with an important railroad station. A little uphill, in the small Parco Virgiliano, is a site thought to be that of Virgil's tomb. From Mergellina, heading inland from the promontory of POSILLIPO, Via Mergellina affords a view of the unfinished 17th-century Palazzo Donn'Anna. On the promontory's point is the little square of MARECHIARO, while beyond the Nisida breakwater lies BAGNOLI ▲ 395.

THE FLORIDIANA
This suburban villa, the most outstanding historic building on Vomero, was given by Ferdinand I to the duchess of Floridia, his morganatic wife. Restructured in the early 19th century and today state property, it houses collections of applied arts.

LA GINESTRA
The remains of Giacomo Leopardi, who died in Naples in 1837 and who named one of his most famous *Canti* after the *ginestra* (broom) flower he saw at the foot of Vesuvius, were transferred to the Parco Virgiliano in 1939.

THE SIBYL OF CUMAE
Although there were many other sources of prophesy around the sacred places of the ancient Mediterranean, the Sibyls were noted for their ability to counter the most

obscure questions – with even more obscure answers. The fame of the Sibyl of Cumae even featured in the Jewish and Christian traditions.

THE CIRCUMVESUVIANA
An integral part in the metropolitan public transport network is played by the old line which winds around Vesuvius. It is useful for getting to the major archeological sites.

Out of all the South over which it once held sway, all that Naples has left to administer is Campania, a region which is not particularly large even if it is very populous. Its hinterland is pleasantly hilly and in some cases ruggedly mountainous, but of greatest attraction to visitors are the regions along the Tyrrhenian Sea, 224 miles of mostly stunning coastline from the mouth of the Garigliano to the Gulf of Policastro.

THE GULF OF NAPLES

Around Naples, attractive landscapes alternate with concrete wastelands. Fortunately the image of the earthly garden still predominates, and the islands and coast around Sorrento are not spoiled by these jarring contrasts. Meanwhile, you only have to take the Circumvesuviana down to its stops at Herculaneum and Pompeii to go back to the 1st century AD, when an eruption of Vesuvius engulfed the Roman cities at the volcano's foot and stopped time dead.

THE HISTORIC CENTERS OF THE CAMPI FLEGREI ★.
The name of this hinterland to the west of Naples, inland from the coastline on the Gulf of Pozzuoli, comes from the Greek word *flegraios* ("burning"), because of its characteristic volcanic phenomena. It is an area abundant in mythical reminders from classical antiquity – from the helmet of Misenus, named for Aeneas' herald, to the cave of the Sibyl at Cumae – where in Roman times the villas of the imperial aristocracy clustered. POZZUOLI flourished in the period of the Flavian emperors, when it served as a landing port for the grain trade from Egypt to Rome. Of exceptional interest in the upper part of the

> **"ALL THE ISLANDS . . . , DOWN THERE IN THE SEA OF NAPLES, ARE BEAUTIFUL."**
> ELSA MORANTE

GROTTA AZZURRA CAPRI

town are the Flavian Amphitheater (still with its underground functional areas), the great Carditus pool (a reservoir) and the baths of Neptune, arranged on terraces facing the sea. Below, the Serapeus (temple of Serapidis, in reality a commercial *macellum*, or slaughterhouse) appears half-sunken on account of the shifting ground. Grand ruins from an imperial palace, with buildings for bathing, make the archeological park at BAIA similarly extraordinary. The palace lies below an Aragonese castle now refitted to house the new Archeological Museum of the Campi Flegrei. CUMAE, founded around the middle of the 7th century BC, had as its original center the acropolis, where ruins from the Greek, Sannite and Roman eras are layered one on top

of the other. Before heading up here, you will come across the entrance to the den of the Sybil, a series of underground chambers explored in the early 19th century by the archeologist Amedeo Maiuri.

THE ISLANDS IN THE GULF.
Fertile and picturesque PROCIDA ★, formed by an outcrop from the rims of four craters, and the more mountainous ISCHIA, which has a reputation as a place for spa therapies, are both products of the volcanic activity of the Flegrei. Going further south along the Sorrento peninsula, a lone limestone block, peaking at a height of 1,932 feet at Mount Solaro, forms the island of CAPRI ★, so magnificent that Tiberius transferred his imperial court here in the 1st century AD. The town of Marina Piccola stands at the bottom of the twisting path of Via Krupp, which drops steeply from the 14th-century charterhouse of San Giacomo. From here you have a view of the famous sheer rockfaces of the PILLARS, the symbol of Capri. It is only a short stroll to the vast excavations at Villa Iovis, the former residence of Tiberius.

THE BLUE GROTTO
Near the northwest corner of the island of Capri, you can visit by boat (the opening to the Tyrrhenian is only a few feet high) a magical marine grotto known since ancient times and rediscovered in the early 19th century. As it sinks very, very slowly, the light that penetrates has been reduced to a glimmer. When this light filters through the water, it produces a fairytale color.

POMPEII

Buried in AD 79 by an eruption of Vesuvius, Pompeii was brought to light again in the 18th century, revealing before the eyes of an enlightened Europe the structure and life of a Roman city. The excavations continued from then on, with methods ever more scientific, into the 19th and 20th centuries. Thanks to the preservative effect of the volcanic ash, the city was "frozen" as it was at the moment of the catastrophe. As such, its ruins represent not only a fascinating visit but also a unique tool for gaining an "inside" understanding of ancient Roman civilization. Its discovery helped to spread the new neoclassical esthetic.

POMPEII AND VESUVIUS
Vesuvius had been dormant for centuries. In AD 62, an earthquake struck the city, a prelude to the eruption which buried the area in ash and volcanic rock.

ROMAN DECORATION
A very lively hunting scene, indicative of the high level of technical and artistic skill which Roman decoration of the 1st century AD attained.

412

THE MYSTERIES OF DIONYSUS
The meaning of many of the scenes in the Villa of Mysteries is still unclear, but they are related to the myth of Dionysus: a cult shrouded in mystery, even in ancient times.

THE VILLA OF MYSTERIES
This villa, opening onto a broad terrace toward the sea, is interesting for its layout and the cycle of paintings that decorate the walls of the triclinium, which to date is the most extensive to survive from antiquity. Depicted here is a representation of Orpheo-Dionysiac rites (where the name of the villa comes from), possibly painted from a live ensemble model. These pictures are fundamental to the study of Roman pictorial art.

THE ROMAN HOUSE
The excavations have recovered a large number of dwellings, complete with their decorations and furnishings. These are an incomparable means by which to study the way of life of the ancient Romans. Particularly important are the domus, that is, the most sophisticated and involved structures, like the House of the Faun, the largest of the residences of the nobility in Pompeii.

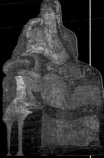

WIFE AND MOTHER
The paintings, mosaics and furnishings in Pompeii are a veritable mine of information on the clothes, jewelry and intimate relationships of the ancient Romans.

Every view of the gulf of Naples is inevitably dominated by the volcanic cone of Vesuvius, now no longer topped with the plume of smoke with which it used to appear until March 1944, the date of its most recent eruption. That "fateful day" in August AD 79 suffocated Pompeii with toxic fumes, covering it with ash and volcanic rock, and overwhelmed Herculaneum with a stream of mud and detritus. Today, even though grapevines blanket the volcano's foothills, a similar emergency could still occur, forcing hundreds of thousands of people to flee.

THE TIME CAPSULE OF HERCULANEUM AND POMPEII ★. The great eruption of AD 79 smothered the coastline around Vesuvius, leading to the preservation, under the layer of volcanic material, of four population centers with an advanced degree of civilization (Oplonti, Stabiae, Herculaneum and Pompeii). After their accidental rediscovery (at Herculaneum in 1709) and after the first, burrowing excavation campaigns had paid off with recoveries that enriched royal collections or were recycled in new building works, the means of bringing things to the light of day was perfected. From 1927 onward the archeological zones assumed the appearance they have today. Particularly impressive is HERCULANEUM, where houses, shops and streets look as they did nineteen centuries ago, still in their original state of construction. The roads are parallel to the coast (decuman), crossing in directions which correspond to the points of the compass. The houses, subdivided further into apartments, are built up vertically. The many wall-paintings, the mosaics in the baths and the surviving wooden beams are what strike you most of all here. The excavations at the city of POMPEII ▲ *412* are more extensive and require a more demanding visit, preserving as they do even the most minute details of daily life in Sannite and Roman society, which are impossible to find elsewhere. Like Herculaneum, Pompeii was discovered by accident at the end of the 16th century during the construction of a canal. The earliest explorations were begun in 1748. Out of all the buildings, the most outstanding (inside the walls and beyond the Porta Marina) are the entire Forum complex, the district around the Theater, with the gladiators' barracks and the Temple of Isis standing behind it, the long Via dell'Abbondanza with the baths and the Great Gymnasium (next door to the

amphitheater) and, further north, the scattering of private dwellings (the Houses of the Faun, the Vettii, the Golden Cupids and the Surgeon). Further away, toward the sea, is the most famous villa of all, the Villa of Mysteries.

THE NATURAL ENVIRONMENT OF MONTE FAÌTO. From the Circumvesuviana station at Castellammare di Stabia to the foot of the Sorrento peninsula runs an aerial cable-car which in summer goes down to one of the finest panoramas on the Gulf of Naples from the lookout (3,444 feet) of Faìto, in the Lattari mountains. The area, rich in broadleaved trees, conifers and pastures higher up, is ideal for walks.

THE EVOCATIVENESS OF SORRENTO. On the peninsula which forms the southernmost limit of the Gulf of Naples, perched on a veritable bastion of volcanic rock, ancient *Surrentum* (whose name is tied in with the cult of the sirens) is today mostly a tourist town. Besides the cathedral, rebuilt in the 15th century but with a modern façade, and the little structure of the Sedile Dominova (a rare example of a genre formerly widespread throughout the region and related to the Sedili Nobiliari, officials who administered the city from the Angevin period onward), the town's most interesting building is the 18th-century villa where the MUSEO CORREALE DI TERRANOVA is set up. Rearranged after its closure following the earthquake of 1980, it has maintained the patrician character of the collection. It houses archeological finds, paintings, 19th-century Sorrentine furniture, porcelains, Venetian glassware, crystalware and clocks. From Sorrento come pieces of marble from the 10th–11th century, with abstract motifs and motifs of animals of Sassanid origin.

THE AMALFI COAST

Running along the southern side of the Sorrentino peninsula, cut through the rock, is the state Highway 163, which corresponds to the carriage-way opened in 1840 and which is one of the most panoramic, winding roads in the world, with spectacular sheer drops and wonderful views over to Capri or the closer cliffs of li Galli.

ELITE TOURISM IN POSITANO. The coast's inhabitants live closely together on the sea-cliffs of the valleys between one mountain and the next. Positano, one of the most exclusive of these spots, clings to a slope plunging down to the sea, amid narrow, often-staired streets.

AMALFI'S MEMORIES. Rich in history, from the 10th–12th century Amalfi was the first of a string of maritime republics ● *38*. Dominating

TORQUATO TASSO
From the cathedral to the sea, Sorrento's main thoroughfare is dedicated to Torquato Tasso. He was a great, tormented poet who was born here in 1544. In his later years, Tasso rewrote in a tone of gloomy moralism his masterpiece, *Jerusalem Set Free*, renaming it *Jerusalem Conquered*.

FLAVIO AND THE COMPASS
The invention of the compass – the revolutionary idea of putting a magnetic pointer, floating on a few drops of fluid, inside a purpose-built container – is traditionally attributed to the legendary navigator from Amalfi, Flavio Gioia.

TERRACING
Especially wonderful in the valley leading up to Ravello, but spread here and there all the way along the coast, are the steep terraced slopes carved out of the mountainsides through centuries of work. Grapes, citruses and fruit grow on them.

THE SALERNO SCHOOL
Salerno's importance in the late Middle Ages is evidenced by the Medical School which operated here from the 9th century on, possibly the first "university" ever opened.

the square is the entrance staircase of the CATHEDRAL. This is an 18th-century building but its façade was redone at the end of the 19th century. However, its Chapel of the Crucifix is still identifiable with the 10th-century cathedral. Next door, the 13th-century CLOISTER OF PARADISE was the burial place for prominent citizens. The church is built from rock pocked with air-holes. RUGA NOVA MERCATORUM, which runs parallel to the main street, Via Capuano, is almost completely covered with similar rock. The period urban fabric is woven out of colorful Mediterranean houses backing one onto the other, amid stairs, alleyways and courts.

THE ELEGANCE OF RAVELLO ★. Further uphill, another very interesting town is Ravello, which at the turn of the millennium was an autonomous diocese and in the 13th century an important center of trade with the East. Its stately atmosphere, which over the centuries fascinated Boccaccio as much as Wagner, is still to be seen, starting from the end of the peaceful square in front of the CATHEDRAL, founded in 1087, with a magnificent gate with little casts dated 1179, a pair of fantastic ambos (the one on the left being of Byzantine origin) and the treasures of the museum in the crypt. Next door to the church, broad views over the Gulf of Salerno open up from the gardens of VILLA RUFOLO, and the villa itself (even if reduced to a *pastiche* of styles) still bears traces of the elegant group of residences which it must have been between the 13th and 14th centuries. The narrow streets lead inland to the medieval decoration of SAN GIOVANNI DEL TORO, while from the opposite side you reach VILLA CIMBRONE,

"EVERYONE WHO SAW PAESTUM, MARVELED AT THE THREE SUPERB RUINS."

GUY DE MAUPASSANT

a "whimsical copy" by English eccentrics; there are grand gardens as well as views of quite remarkable beauty.

SALERNO, ACTIVE REGIONAL CENTER. The thriving economy and harbor of Salerno, second city of Campania, contrasts neatly with the cosseted climate of the coast. All the same, there are still some streets to be found which are strong in character in the city's ancient center, such as VIA DEI MERCANTI, and noteworthy historic buildings like the CATHEDRAL, which was begun in 1080 by Robert le Guiscard. The cathedral has an arcaded atrium and an Arab-Norman bell tower, while inside the two wall pulpits, the sanctuary screen in mosaic and the towering 13th-century Pascal candelabrum survived the Baroque refit. Also of interest are the city's museums – in the cathedral (with paintings, reliquaries and codices) and the provincial museum of archeology – while the nearby VIETRI SUL MARE takes you back to the peace of the Gulf of Salerno.

FROM THE SELE PLAIN TO THE GULF OF POLICASTRO

The coastal regions of Campania south of Salerno have fewer people and are much wilder than around the Gulf of Naples. On the plain of the Sele river, where the remains of Paestum contain some of the most dazzling temples in all of Magna Graecia, are coves, beaches, crags and promontories typical of the Cilento coast, today a national park ▲ *418*.

MAGNA GRAECIA AT PAESTUM ★. A ring of ancient walls, fascinating in themselves, still protects what from the 6th century BC was the Greek colonial city of Poseidonia – in honor of the god of the sea – and from 273 BC the Latin Pacstum. To the north of the archeological area

VIETRI'S CERAMICS
Near Salerno, Vietri sul Mare comprises a maze of streets onto which the windows of a great many decorative ceramic and clothing stores open, the product of a long-running local tradition of craftsmanship.

A " VER" AT THEMUSEUM
In the exquisite National Museum of Paestum are displayed 5th-century BC wall-paintings from the "tomb of the Diver". They provide an example of extremely rare frescos preserved in their ancient Greek setting.

THE CILENTO PARK Stretching from the Tyrrhenian coast to the feet of the Appennines at Luca is the vast protected zone of the Parco Nazionale del Cilento and Vallo di Diano. It also takes in the peaks of the Alburni (with the grottos of Castelcivita and Pertosa, whose course follows that of an underground river) and the 6,224 feet summit of Mount Cervati, Campania's "rooftop", with its two expanses of lavender.

stands the TEMPLE OF CERES (effectively, of Athena, dating from the end of the 6th century BC), but the true milestones in the architectural history of Magna Graecia – one next door to the other in the southern sector – are what is known as the

BASILICA (probably from the second half of the 6th century BC) and the TEMPLE OF NEPTUNE ● *85* (dedicated in reality to Hera or to Zeus, from the middle of the 5th century BC), well preserved and perfect examples of the Doric style. A building near the archeological area houses the interesting NATIONAL MUSEUM of Paestum.

CILENTO'S HISTORY AND NATURE. Wooded cliffs stretch along the part of southern Campania which juts out into the Tyrrhenian. Only occasionally is the countryside interrupted by ancient presences such as the archeological ruins of VELIA (the former Elea, founded in 540 BC), or historic ones such as the Byzantine town of AGROPOLI, or more recent ones like the tourist settlements of MARINA DI CAMEROTA. Mythical memories surround CAPO PALINURO, which takes its name from Aeneas' unfortunate helmsman.

MARINA DI CAMEROTA Among the first holiday spots to raise the Cilento coast from anonymity was Marina di Camerota, with its vacation villages, its grottos and now – as part of innovative measures linked to the Parco del Cilento – the new ecomuseum.

"CAMPANIA FELIX"

North of Naples, the Volturno crosses a fertile strip of hinterland which, because of the bounty of its crops over thousands of years (the harvest here contributed substantially to keeping Rome fed), has born the name since classical times of *Campania felix*. The area is also known as the Terra di Lavoro – referring not to man's deeds (in Italian, "lavoro" means "work") but to the ancient *Terra Leboriae*, or land inhabited by the Leborini people.

THE TWO CAPUAS. If today *Campania felix*'s principal town is Caserta, in the past this role fell to Capua or, more precisely, at first to the Capua which is today called SANTA MARIA CAPUA VETERE. An Etruscan and later Sannite center, the Anfiteatro Campano is the second largest structure of its type after the Colosseum, alongside other important Roman

CHANGE OF COMMAND With the battle of Volturno, a conclusive defeat for the Bourbon troops which took place on October 2, 1860, Giuseppe Garibaldi completed the expedition of the "Thousand" ● *44* in the Kingdom of the Two Sicilies. Southern Italy was symbolically handed over to Vittorio Emanuele II of Savoy 24 days later, during a meeting of the two at Teano.

ruins. Oldest of all, however, is the cathedral, begun in the 5th century (the columns in the nave remain), even if it does have a 17th-century apse and a neoclassical façade. It was Lombard people in the 9th century who founded present-day Capua, a few miles away on a bend of the Volturno, and they were also responsible at that time for the first work on its associated cathedral. This cathedral, however, rebuilt several times and then destroyed by bombs during World War Two, has mainly modern features. More interesting are the Renaissance town walls and the Museo Campano, with important archeological and medieval collections and works of art from successive centuries. A third place not to be missed in the area is what is today the Benedictine Basilica of SANT' ANGELO IN FORMIS, which stands next door to the little village of the same name 2½ miles from Capua. Its Romanesque frescos (which depict episodes from the Old and New Testaments, prophets and prophetesses, and a Last Judgement) constitute the most important cycle of its type in the whole of the South of the peninsula.

CASERTA, ROYAL CITY. A little over 20 miles north of Naples, medieval Caserta – interesting to this day and very well preserved, with a cathedral from the 12th century – took the name of Casertavecchia when construction work on Charles of Bourbon's new palace commenced in 1752. Under Luigi Vanvitelli, the most dramatic ROYAL PALACE ★ in all Italy was completed in 1774 (a year after the architect's death). Around 250 yards wide, it is built around four identical courtyards defined by buildings five floors high, making up a total of 1,200 rooms. The lower vestibule and the grand

"MATRES MATUTAE"
The Museo Campano in Capua has a collection of around 200 statuettes in gray tufo, dating from the 5th to the 1st century BC, depicting mothers with babies in their arms. They were votive offerings given in thanks to Matuta, the Italian goddess of fertility.

The cathedral bell tower at Casertavecchia.

SAN LEUCIO
In 1789, Ferdinand IV of Bourbon founded at Caserta the silk factory of San Leucio, whose charter provided for a strictly equal share among each resident. Today, several private businesses, which you can visit, still have looms dating from the 19th century.

POLITICAL AND MILITARY VICTORIES
Lucius Cornelius Silla (138–78 BC), from a patrician family, fought in the political field with Caius Marius, a supporter of the popular faction in the Senate. After seizing Rome by force, causing his opponent to flee, he confirmed himself as a great general in the wars against Mithridates of Pontus (85 BC) and the Sannites, allies of Marius' popular party (82 BC).

staircase of honor work to great effect, as does the Palatine Chapel – clearly (as is the rest of the complex) inspired by the French example of Versailles – and the royal apartments, with decoration on the cusp between Rococo and neoclassical. Also beautiful is the small court theater on the left-hand side of the second courtyard, against the backdrop of the amazing prospect Vanvitelli provided over the PARK leading up to the palace. The lawn takes as its central axis a sequence of pools, fountains and waterfalls that are about 2 miles long.

THE SANNITES

By the 5th century BC, the Sannite people, organized into federations and at that time settled in an area between southern Abruzzo, Molise and Beneventano, had already set their sights on *Campania felix* ▲ *418*. The Sannites spread out as far as Capua, finding common cause there with Rome in defending the latter against the Gauls' invasion attempt (in the middle of the 4th century BC), but then coming into

conflict with the growing power of the Romans. The Sannites and Romans fought for almost forty years, from 343 to 290 BC. The former were defeated but remained independent. Hostilities erupted once more in 90 BC and it took Silla's military skills to defeat the Sannites eight years later. They were still granted Roman citizenship.

THE MUSEUM COLLECTIONS OF ISERNIA AND BENEVENTO. One of the leading towns during the Sannite period, ISERNIA (the former *Aesernia*), in Molise, stands on a spur overlooking a tributary of the Volturno. The Town Museum, in the ex-

Benedictine Monastery of Santa Maria Assunta (the church was destroyed in World War Two), displays archeological finds from the Paleolithic, Sannite and Roman ages. Another important collection of Italian antiquities is the one in the Museo del Sannio at BENEVENTO, the major town in the inland district of Campania, once an important Roman city (from which time the theater and the Arch of Trajan, among other things, remain), later the capital of a thriving Lombard duchy (during which time the central-plan Church of Santa Sophia was founded), and then until 1860 almost always a papal enclave inside the Kingdom of the Two Sicilies.

BARI AND THE LANDS OF APULIA AND BASILICATA

BARI, *424*

"[His] journey went on for some 24 hours after reaching the middle of Taranto's 'turning bridge'. A note suggesting an amorous encounter had drawn the young count to visit Alberobello, the famous city of the Trulli. ... It was a brief visit; a turn around the quarter of the Trulli noting the cleanliness of the streets and roofs, the whiteness of the *calcina* and the poor condition of the houses."

Paolo Volponi,
Il sipario ducale
(The Duke's Curtain)

After Naples, the most important city in southern Italy is Bari – a city of two halves. Its subtle charm comes from the old city, which is as tiny in dimensions as it is great in art and history. Alongside is the new city, which is characterized by the lucid urban planning of the early 1800's. Of the stimulating itineraries that branch off from here, the first one is a trip of great interest that heads toward the northwest: to the Romanesque Apulian cathedrals, built between the 12th and 13th centuries in the Roman and Swabian ages. The route runs from the nearby Baronto to the faraway Troia (92 miles), passing through Ruvo, Trani and Barletta. As a variation, from Ruvo there is a brief diversion through Castel del Monte, the fascinating castle constructed by Frederick II that has dominated the landscape of the Murge for 750 years. The next itinerary leads us to the Gargano region, a promontory of great natural significance protected by the

National Park opened in 1991. Monte Sant'Angelo is the most interesting site historically, and on the nearby Tremites the quality of light on sea and sky is wonderful. The grottos of Castellana, the Trulli of Alberobello and the Baroque buildings of Martina Franca begin the trip to southeast Apulia.

"When the day is mild and the weather clement/The great falcons of Puglia, Lubecca and Malta/ File by . . .Tufts of brooms colour the vast plain, the newly harvested earth is flat/ With the great seabirds calmly wheeling overhead . . .// This is a world of feathers, of gloved hands/ Of bells, of beaks, of tongues, of heads of beasts,/ Dogs bark at the sound of the horn// And squires, knights and imperial masters/ Sit astride good-natured horses/ All gazing into the far distance,//

In addition there is Basilicata, which lists among its attractions the dramatically picturesque landscape of Sassi di Matera and the vivid panorama of the Magna Graecia of Metaponto. The fascinating art and culture of the Magna Graecia is reflected in the archeological museum of Taranto. In the Salento region there is Lecce which has been called the "Florence of the Baroque age" because of its rich and beautiful architecture; the medieval center of Gallipoli; and Otranto (121 miles from Bari), where the cathedral has a floor mosaic that is well worth seeing.

Among the multitude of birds, see the falcon: /Launched all of a sudden,/ Holding itself high above the mountain/ Then boldly attacking.// The motionless victim's eye closes./ Between this and the sparrow's strongly beating wing/ Is skill, single-mindedness and an intense cruelty.// And the Voice of the falconer, calling out on the slope . . ."
Nelo Risi,
I fabbricanti del "bello"
(The Makers of the Beautiful)

▲ THE FANTASTIC MEDIEVAL AGE

Proud hippopotamuses support the columns of
the principal great door of San Nicola, instead of
the lions which decorate the southern door.

Eagles eye you from the pulpit, griffins keep watch
over the great doors, lions threaten to rip the
brains out of men, and snakes suffocate their prey:
the Apulian cathedrals house Romanesque
sculptors' most fantastical and terrible creatures.
Typical of the medieval period which had a
fascination for the monstrous and the bizzarre, the
great beasts sculpted in stone reveal the cathedrals
of Romanesque Apulia to be the meeting place of a
wide variety of different styles and traditions. These
range from ancient art to the imaginative work of
the peoples of northern Europe, to the formal
rigidness of the Byzantine style, to Arabic decorativeness.

THE EAGLE
Symbol of San
Giovanni (and of
imperial power),
the eagle is often
an element of
the support in
the missal, as in
the refined
pulpit of the
Cathedral of
Bitonto (1229),
work of the
magister
Nicolaus, who
was proud to
sign the piece.

THE LION
The entwined limbs over the right column of
the principal portal of the Cathedral of Trani
(above) reveal one of the many variations
on the theme of the carnivorous
lion. The same
imagery

THE ELEPHANT
Two of these animals
(1080–9), sculpted by
Romualdo, support
the episcopal
cathedral of Canosa.

An eagle in the form of a support of the canopy in the Church of Santa Maria Maggiore at Monte Sant'Angelo.

is on the back of the Cathedral of Elia (and in the Cathedral of San Nicola, at Bari). The obvious distress of the figures supporting the chair above contrast with the formal, composed nature of the seat.

Tomatoes and chilies bring out
the flavors of Apulian cooking.

THE MAZE IN STREETS OF THE OLD CITY

Many old Bari
houses preserve the
atmosphere of the
medieval quarter. In
the little streets it is
easy to come across

On the tiny triangular-shaped island, locked in between the
modern Corso De Tullio, the Emperor Augustus coastal road
and the Corso Vittorio Emanuele II, beats the heart of the
old city of Bari. The complexity of streets invites you to follow
your inclinations and explore at random the intriguing
alleyways and
little piazzas.

SAN MARCO.
You can arrive
quickly at
San Marco
from San
Nicola by
taking the
Strada delle
Crociate. It was
erected in the
12th century by
the Venetians.
SAN GREGORIO.
Near San
Nicola, is
San Gregorio
built in a
romantic
Apulian style,
with unusual
windows.
In the elegant

arches that have
legendary origins,
such as the arch
called Meraviglia, in
the shape of a
bridge, that is said
to have been built in
one night to allow
two lovers to meet.
Often the alleyways
converge into a
closed courtyard
that allows the
houses to enjoy the
air and the light.
Alleys may even
suddenly open up
onto piazzas with
irregular shapes.
From the courtyards
rise the external
staircases by which
you reach the
residential quarters,
while the rooms at
ground level that
give onto the narrow
streets are used as
living rooms, stores
or for deliveries.

three-naved interior, two lines of columns show off fantastical
and diverse decorations.
SAN GIOVANNI CRISOSTOMO. A tiny 14th-
century church to the west of San Nicola,
today restored and used as a chapel for
Greek services. Outside are the remains
of a Gothic arch while inside there is a
marble sculpture (11th century)
depicting a griffin and a lion with wings.
VIA VENEZIA. Suspended between
the Adriatic and the old city, it runs
along behind San Nicola following
the ancient bastions which were
licked by the sea until 1930.
PIAZZA MERCANTILE.
You can get there from
Via Fragigena. The
widest square of the old
city, fairs were once held
there. The SEDILE DEI
NOBILI, constructed in
1543 and rebuilt in the
1600's, was the
meeting place of the
local council. The
porch area was
used as a theater
in the 1800's.

PIAZZA DEL FERRARESE. Today the site of a local market, it opens onto the wide area in front of an old gate to the city. It takes its name from a merchant of Ferrara who lived in Bari in the 1600's; to the right the apse of the Romanesque CHIESA DELLA VALLISA is recognizable, with its medieval foundation which has been restored.

THE MODERN CITY TO THE SOUTHEAST

Nestled between the old city, the railroad and the sea, the modern city's layout is rigorously geometric, interspersed by piazzas with gardens and treelined streets.

THE IMPERATORE AUGUSTO COASTAL ROAD ★. Constructed in the 1930's, it follows the outside line of the old walls along the eastern side of the city, from Piazzale Colombo to the beginning of the Nuovo Molo Foraneo and the square of the Eroi del Mare (Heroes of the Sea), coasting along the Porto Vecchio. The stroll offers panoramas between the bell towers and the cupolas high above the old city and the wide arm of the sea that frames it on the outside. At the end of the wall of Sant'Antonio Abate rises the little fort with a great view.

CORSO VITTORIO EMANUELE II. A busy passageway, it is an important thoroughfare that separates the old city from the walled quarter. On the first house on the left a stone plaque records that this is the site where the first stone of the new city was placed in 1813; as it widens it becomes the Piazza of Liberty, with the great PALAZZO DELLA PREFETTURA and the Teatro Piccinni.

TEATRO PICCINNI. A neoclassical building dedicated to the Bari

COLUMN OF JUSTICE
Right of the Sedile dei Nobili (the Nobles' Place) rises a column with a stone lion next to it. This is where bankrupts and thieves were brought and tied up.

THE PROCESSION OF THE MYSTERIES
From the Chiesa della Vallissa the Good Friday procession makes its way through the city to the mournful sound of a funeral march. Two days later the atmosphere is more joyful as Easter songs accompany the exchange of sweets called *scarcedde*.

THE FLAME OF SAINT ANTHONY
In the small fort of Anthony a chapel recalls the saint who, according to legend, handed out an oily perfumed cream that could heal animals and sooth the burns caused by ergotism, a disease which is also called Saint Anthony's fire .

In eclectic style, Palazzo Mincuzzi houses a haberdashery of the same name which opened in 1927.

musician, Niccolò Piccinni (1728–1800), it opened in the mid-1800's after 14 years of work. Initially used only for recitals, the theater later staged operas and operettas.

VIA SPARANO DA BARI. An elegant pedestrianized walkway declared a traffic-free passageway for city dwellers. It is the heart of the commercial center with expensive shops, running at a right angle to the Corso Vittorio Emanuele II for half a mile. Before reaching the vast Piazza Aldo Moro where the street ends, Via Sparano crosses the treelined Piazza Umberto I, where the Ateneo building (1868–89, Giovanni Castelli) houses the important MUSEO ARCHEOLOGICO (Archeological Museum) which holds an extensive collection of material from the ancient Apulian city.

CORSO CAVOUR. A wide treelined avenue, parallel to Via Sparano, where the TEATRO PETRUZZELLI (1898–1903) is situated. It is one of the greatest Italian lyrical theaters, the interior of which was completely destroyed by a fire in 1991.

LUNGOMARE NAZARIO SAURO. Along this coastal walkway you will find the Rotonda, a terrace that offers a wide view of the promontory of the old city. There is a series of buildings including is the Province building erected in 1930–2, in a neo-Renaissance style by Luigi Baffia, with an elegant portico and bell tower.

PINACOTECA PROVINCIALE. Set up in 1928 in the San Domenico building, it was transferred in 1936 to the newly built Province building. There you will find oil paintings, pastels, and engravings by artists of the 1800's and of the early 1900's (Fattori, Morandi), icons, frescos and sculptural fragments from the 11th and 12th centuries; canvases of the Venetian school of the 1500's (Tintoretto, Veronese) and works of the Neapolitan and Apulian painters, and ceramics and nativities from the 1600's and 1700's.

MUSEO ARCHEOLOGICO
The Archeological Museum set up in 1875 and endowed with private donations. It has over 30,000 pieces, ranging from the prehistoric age to the Apulian civilization as well as Greek imports (Corinthian and Attican vases) from the 7th and the 8th centuries BC. The museum reveals the history of the Daunian province in Foggia), of essapia (Salento) d of Peucezia ovince of Bari).

> **"IN THE WINDING STREETS OF THE OLD CITY YOU WILL FIND ALL THE COLOR OF THE SOUTH, A PICTURESQUE CONFUSION AT ONE REMOVE FROM THE BUSTLE OF MODERN LIFE."**
>
> GUIDO PIOVENE

THE MODERN CITY TO THE WEST

This area expanded from the beginning of the 1900's when the city, crossing the railroad, started to develop rapidly in a semicircular wave from the coast to inland areas. Industry, in particular expanded toward the west, in the direction of Bari-Santo Spirito and Bari-Bitonto. Corso Vittorio Veneto runs along the wide basin of the Porto Nuovo (New Port), from the old city to the point at San Cataldo, defining the limits of the modern city from the coastal side.

LUNGOMARE STARITA. Continuing along Corso Vittorio Veneto, after having rounded the point at San Cataldo and the lighthouse, the Lungomare takes us to the Piazza Vittorio Emanuele III, which stands just in front of the area set aside for fairs. Planned and erected in the 1930's, the buildings are set out in chessboard style with wide avenues, generous green spaces and a magnificent entrance. Further on, the Fiera del Levante houses numerous shops.

FIERA DEL LEVANTE. The fair takes place every year in September. Begun in 1930, it follows the model of international and national exhibitions, and is one of the most important commercial and international shows. It is specially designed to strengthen exchanges between Europe and the East, in which Bari forms an essential link with her traditional ties stretching back a thousand years.

MONUMENTAL CEMETERY. Situated at the end of the long Via Francesco Crispi, it was created in 1842 by Francesco Saponieri in an 1800's style which is rarely seen in southern Italy.

LATERZA EDITORS
For the publishers of the 20th century, Bari means Laterza, a publishing firm founded at Putignano in 1885 which transferred to the capital four years later. The long association with Benedetto Croce, the works of whom it published in 74 volumes, and the prestigious collaborations with De Ruggiero, Einaudi, Garin and Luigi Russo, as well as wide cultural interests have contributed its reputation.

SAN NICOLA STADIUM
Planned by Renzo Piano for the soccer World Cup in 1990, it has a light and articulated structure. It is among the most interesting achievements of the Genovese architect.

A FAMILY OF COLLECTORS
Giovanni Jatta (1767–1844), was a cultivated lawyer and influential magistrate, who together with his brother Giulio, created a "collection of beautiful and chosen things". They amassed a collection of vases appreciated for its richness and the variety of forms and decoration. His archeologist son, Giovanni Jatta Jnr (1832–95), increased his father's collections and arranged the immense family vase collection in the family palace at Ruvo di Puglia. Today, the National Jatta Museum displays more than 2,000 Corinthian, Attican, Peucezian, Apulian, and Daunian ceramics from the period between the 8th and 3rd centuries BC.

CATHEDRAL OF TRANI
This is one of the most significant examples of Romanesque Apulian architecture. Dedicated to Saint Nicola Pellegrino, it stands in an imposing position, isolated in front of the sea.

The Luccan writer Giustino Fortunato defined the Mezzogiorno as the "promised land" for its grandeur, which emanates as much from the solitary ruins of Greek civilization as from the beauty of a land bathed in light. From Bari to Capitanata there are pale fields of wheat, whereas the Murge is dotted with grottos and gorges. There are many varied landscapes in this region that are well worth visiting. These include the inhabited valleys of Itria, that are punctuated with Trulli, the Sassi di Matera as far as coasts swept by the Ionian Sea, and Salento sandwiched between two seas.

"FLOWERS OF STONE" IN THE LAND OF BARI AND CAPITANATA

The imposing medieval cathedrals of Apulia are proof of the exchanges between West and East, as well as between the north and south of Europe. Norman, Byzantine and even Saracen motifs are woven into the rose windows, while archways and columns feature emblematic and fantastical animals.

BITONTO. Among Romanesque cathedrals, the one which stands above the medieval center of Bitonto is reminiscent of the Church of San Nicola at Bari ▲ *429, 430*; the interior has a pulpit that is signed by Nicolaus *sacerdos et magister*, dated 1229, and a stone carving that depicts characters of the house of Swabia, possibly including Frederick II.

RUVO DI PUGLIA. About 10 miles to the west, Ruvo boasts a cathedral begun in the 12th century and completed in the 13th century in Gothic and Romanesque styles. Other notable reminders of Ruvo's past are in the MUSEO NAZIONALE JATTA (the Jatta National Museum).

CASTEL DEL MONTE ★. Erected in splendid isolation between 1229–49 following the wishes and, perhaps, the plan of Frederick II, the most celebrated of Frederican castles is situated 13 miles to the west of Ruvo and reflects the fascinating personality of the Emperor. The number 8, symbol of the union between God and man, features in the structure of the entire building:

The priceless inlaid rose window of the Cathedral of Troia.

on the octagonal plan (which is repeated in the interior courtyard) punctuated by eight octagonal towers, a portal opens to the east that links classical elements on an arch with lions supported on male figures.

TRANI ★. You arrive in Trani after heading 20 miles toward the coast; the scene is unforgettable: the sea breaks at the feet of the resplendent Romanesque cathedral, built (12th–14th century) in the light and hot-colored local brick. A stairway with a double ramp leads to the door sculpted by Barisano da Trani (12th century) with thirty-two small decorative pieces.

BARLETTA. Eight miles from Trani, the Romanesque-Gothic duomo (12th–14th century) of Barletta deserves a visit. It has a Renaissance portal and bell tower windows that have one or two openings. In the city center, by the church of Santo Sepolcro, which is of French inspiration, is the famous bronze Colossus of the 4th century.

TROIA. In Capitanata, 14 miles to the southwest of Foggia, is the Cathedral of Troy made of rose stone (11th–12th century). Above the portal with sculpted bronze shutters by Oderisio da Benevento in 1119, is the large airy rose window with eleven arms linked by small marble arches. The interior is characterized by thirteen columns that symbolize Christ and the twelve apostles.

FROM THE GARGANO TO THE TREMITE

MONTE SANT' ANGELO. The promontory of the Gargano region jutting into the Adriatic, is an immense bowl of lime that plunges heavily into the sea with a high and rocky coastline. Monte Sant' Angelo is inland, 80 miles from Bari, at the edges of the Foresta Umbra (Umbra forest), at an altitude of almost 2,400 feet. The

THE LAST EMPEROR
Dante calls Frederick II the "last Emperor of the Romans", and in the *Commedia* evokes this several times: through the voice of Farinata who, with his sovereign, mixes with the heretics; with the suicide of the gatekeeper Pier delle Vigne, who held "both the keys" to the heart; in the meeting with Manfredi, natural son of the Emperor, beaten and killed by Carlo d'Angio; in the Moon, where the soul of Mother Costanza, last heiress of the Norman kings, shines.

HUNTING WITH THE FALCON
We owe a debt to Frederick II for one of the most precious and vivid works on falconry, *De arte venandi cum avibus*, of which twelve miniature manuscript copies remain.

CASTEL DEL MONTE
The castle rises up on the island hill of the Murge in the northwest and is one of the most famous Frederican castles. It was used as a hunting, and holiday retreat or defense castle and the architecture has a relaxed feel to it.

SANTUARIO DI SAN MICHELE (Sanctuary of
St Michael the Archangel) rises up in the grotto
where miraculous apparitions are said to have
appeared in the 5th century. It became a sort of
"national sanctuary" of the Longobards and was
visited by pilgrims, popes, saints, and sovereigns
over the centuries. Note the bronze doors, that
were cast in Constantinople in 1076, and the
marble statue of the archangel, attributed to
Andrea Sansovino (16th century). The nearby
TOMBA DI ROTARI (Tomb of Rotari) is in reality
a baptistry that by virtue of its name evokes the
memory of the Longobardan power.

THE ARCHIPELAGO OF THE TREMITE. White
fragments of lime turning green in the azure sea:
here lies Diomedes, the king of Etolia sung
about by Homer and killed by Daunus, son of
Licaone. But the Tremite Islands (San Nicola,
San Domino and Caprara, with the rocks of
Cretaccio and of Vecchia, at little more than
12 miles from the Gargano coast) are above
all synonymous with vacations, in a scene where
the sea, an unspoiled environment and history
unite. The islands can be reached by boat
and hydrofoil principally from Rodi Garganico
and Termoli.

THE BARI AND TARANTO MURGE

GROTTOS OF CASTELLANA ★. In a landscape
marked by depressions and limestone caves to
the southeast of Bari and not far from the
Adriatic, is the township of Castellana-Grotte. Its grottos
open around one mile from the village and constitute the
most famous Italian cave complex. The caves stretch for
almost two miles at a depth of about 200 feet and with a
temperature of about 59°F. The spectacular sight of the
grottos, as well as the fascinating shapes of the stalactites
and stalagmites, is a result of the faded tonality of crystalline
colors that change in the light from ocher to bright white,
and rusty red to green.

THE TRULLI OF ALBEROBELLO AND THE VALLEY OF ITRIA.
Alberobello ★ is 35 miles from Bari, and set
between tranquil olive groves, vineyards,
almond trees and old farmhouses. In the
countryside, where the stone walls without
mortar mark out the fields, the trulli
(round stone
buildings) stand
out in their
picturesque
simplicity ▲ 83.
The conical shape
of the roofs which
are constructed
of stone without
lime becomes
more promine[nt]
from Putigna[no]

THE TRULLI
The principle behind
the Apulian trullo is
that of a false cupola:
the covering is
achieved with
concentric circles of
stone, one on top of
the other, protruding
inward, closed at the
top by a stone topped
by a decorative
pinnacle; there are
about a thousand
Apulian trulli built
in the late 1500's,
although some
may be of
more
ancient
origin.

> **"WHEN WE STUDIED DANTE AT SCHOOL AND TRIED TO IMAGINE WHAT HIS HELL WAS LIKE, IT WAS THESE INVERTED CONES, THESE FUNNEL-SHAPED ROCKS THAT CAME TO MIND."**
>
> CARLO LEVI

toward Martina Franca, along the limestone valley of Itria.

MARTINA FRANCA ★. The Prince of Taranto, Filippo d'Angio, founded Martina between 1294 and 1310, and began cultivating the terrain; the peasants farmed the land and for three centuries, it prospered. Duke Petracone V Caracciolo was a patron, and the area was dramatically transformed, giving the city the Baroque appearance that distinguishes it today. Noble families, such as the Blasi, Motolese, Grassi, Gioia, Marinosci and Barnaba erected buildings with façades featuring little porches and balconies, that faced onto the streets of the historical center, dominated by the PALAZZO DUCALE. The palazzo, with its iron balcony, is on two floors and is one of the jewels of the old city, containing frescos from the 1700's. Alongside the aristocrats' houses is the collegial Church of SAN MARTINO and, next to it, the PALAZZO DELLA CORTE (the building of the Court) with the Watch Tower (1734). Nearby is the Church of SAN DOMENICO (1746) with its large rococo façade and various paintings, among which is the *Madonna del Rosario* by Domenico Carella (1723–1813); and the CHIESA DEL CARMINE (1730) with an octagonal cupola, an altar in colorful marble and a *Madonna* (1760) by Pietro De Mauro of 1760.

MATERANO AND THE GULF OF TARANTO

THE ROCKS OF MATERA ★. At Basilicata, in the center of a high lime plain dotted with deep depressions is Matera. Here the eye roams over a desolate and grandiose desert-like landscape that is also famous for the SASSI. These are groups of ancient habitations carved out of the vibrant ocher-colored rock of two enormous crater-like holes, Barisano (toward Bari) and Caveoso, toward the Gulf of Taranto. Considered a national shame, and abandoned in the 1950's and 60's, they have, more recently, been the object of study and have been made habitable. Historians have examined the many ruined churches which coexist with the late Romanesque cathedral and the Baroque Chiesa del Purgatorio. In this region, traditional buildings seem outclassed by the "dream-like" qualities of the Sassi, described as long ago as 1569 by Leandro Alberti: "Deep valleys where the families, with the sun gone down, show the lantern in front of their houses, from where it seems to those above the hill, that they see under their feet the sky full of beautiful stars." Among the ruined churches in the immediate surroundings, often dating from ancient Greek and Latin communities, Santa Maria della Colomba and Santa Maria della Valle, both with Roman façades are worth seeing.

THE OLIVE
One of the most valuable crops in southern Apulia is the olive. Trees that may be centuries old characterize the landscape. The need to export the oil in the 19th century saw the advent of the crushing machine and the manufacture of bottles and wooden containers.

THE RUPESTRIAN CIVILIZATION
In Apulia and Basilicata you will find grottos where people once lived, little churches and villages carved out of the soft rock. They served the farming community as refuges in isolated places when they fled the Longobard and Islamic invasions.

439

TARANTO AND ITS GOLD. Founded in 706 BC by the Spartans, Taras, as it was first known, was one of the most powerful Greek cities by the sea. Although the resistance of the Messapians blocked a link-up with Salerno, Taranto was a great political and cultural center, which flourished as a result of its businesses: in the 5th century BC it was considered the richest city of Magna Grecia (Greater Greece). It took the might of Rome to break its power in 272 and 209 BC, when Massimo conquered it. It was razed to the ground but later reconstructed by the Byzantines in 967. The city, however, has preserved hardly any of its ancient buildings. The MUSEO ARCHEOLOGICO NAZIONALE ★ (the National Archeological Museum), which has its premises in the ex-monastery of the Alcantarini fathers, houses finds from the necropoli: toiletry objects, vases, gymnastic equipment and large amphorae which were presented to winners at the Panatanaic games and have been found in the tombs of athletes. Particularly famous is the jewellery, the "gold of Taranto", some of which was part of funeral vestments, and dates from the 4th to the 1st century BC.

ANCIENT MEMORIES OF METAPONTO. Diogene Laerzio records that "Pythagoras died in the temple of the Muses at Metaponto, where he had sought refuge, after starving himself for forty days". Tradition has it that the city was founded in 773 but archeologists favor the end of the 8th or the beginning of the 7th century BC. Of Achean origin, Metaponto rises up in the fertile region between the Bradano and Basento rivers: it welcomed Pythagoras fleeing from Crotone, became part of Taranto, was aligned by Pyrrhus and Hannibal against Rome, and was devastated by the bands of Spartacus. After so much history, all that remains today are the columns of the temple of Hera, better known as the Palatine Tables (6th century BC), ten on the east side, five on the west side. This temple, along with the nearby one of Apollo Licio (both of Dorian origin) and other temples and little chapels in the area, formed an extensive sanctuary.

necklaces, diadems, rings, and precious bracelets; these are just some of the many gold pieces of Taranto, discovered in the necropoli and arranged in a room of the Museo Archeologico Nazionale. These valuable pieces are only a fraction of the great quantities of silver and gold, statues and paintings that, according to Livy, fell to Quinto Fabio Massimo when he conquered the city in 209 BC.

TAVOLE PALATINE
At Metaponto, the remains of the Dorian temple from the end of the 6th century BC are called *Tavole Palatine* (Palatine Tables) or the *Scuola di Pitagora* (School of Pythagoras) in memory of the mathematician who founded his school of philosophy at Crotone, further south in Italy, around 530 BC.

SALENTO

LECCE, FESTIVAL OF BAROQUE. The best time of day in Lecce is sunset, when the sinking sun lights up the color and emphasizes the grandeur of the buildings. "In no other city have I seen doors, windows, porches, pedestals, balustrades all in stone" wrote the amazed George Berkeley in 1716. Gregorovius, more prosaically but no less surprised, defined it in the 9th century as "the cleanest locality in the kingdom of Naples". Known throughout the world as the "Florence of the Baroque", Lecce is situated on a limestone table at the center of a rich agricultural area, particularly known for its production of oil, wheat and wine. In the heart of the Salento region, of which it is also the capital, Lecce has had a remarkable development from the end of the 15th century to the 1700's. The period which left the most lasting impression on the city was the 17th century. Many buildings in the historic center date from this period and their "Leccian Baroque style" gives the city a unique architectural flavor. The Leccian stone is a limestone with compact grain, "the color of honey, that one can work with the chisel" (Cesare Brandi). There are magnificently decorated façades, little columns, capricious ornamental tops of columns, curves with net-shaped or curled motifs, flowers, large masks, statues and other strange patterns. "At Lecce one needs to stop longer," wrote the poet Alfonso Gatto, "to really know who it is, like a person." The DUOMO was built around 1100 and restored by Giuseppe Zimbalo (1659–70), who also built the 223-foot high bell tower. To the right is the PALAZZO VESCOVILE (Episcopal Palace, 1632), and in front you will find the sumptuous PALAZZO DEL SEMINARIO (1709). Further on, past the Roman ampitheater and Piazza Sant 'Oronzo (where a

COOKING
Leccian cooking has dishes which use local produce such as olive oil, vegetables, eggplant, "lampascicini" (coarse onions) and sun-dried tomatoes.

**THE MOSAIC IN THE
CATHEDRAL OF OTRANTO**
The mosaic covers the central floor, the side aisles and the presbytery. It was created in 1166 by local artists from a design by a monk called Pantaleone.

The façade of the Basilica of Santa Croce: the decorations on the highest part make it the most famous example of Leccian Baroque.

OCCUPATIONS AND BATTLES
The castle and the walls that surround the town are a reminder of Gallipoli's history, which is one of occupation and battle with many different protagonists: the Vandals in the 5th century, the Turks in 1481, the Venetians in 1484. The castle, built by the Angevins on Byzantine foundations, was rebuilt in the 16th century, and it is this building that you can see today.

column stands, raised at the point where a branch of the Via Appia probably terminated) is the center of the old city, with the Seggio Palace (1592), formerly the town hall, in pride of place. The highest expression of the Leccian Baroque style is found in the Basilica of SANTA CROCE ★ (1548–1646): this imposing building presents an ornate façade with two rows of Corinthian columns and a balcony, held up by fantastic figures, that stretches across its full width; the interior consists of three naves with a wooden ceiling, and is magnificently decorated.

WHITE WALLS OF ORANTO. This is the easternmost town in Italy, 28 miles from Lecce. The old city is almost entirely enclosed by defensive walls; at the highest point is the mighty Aragonese CASTELLO (15th century). The city's most important building is the CATHEDRAL (15th century), with a crypt that is held up by 68 columns. Of particular interest is the floor mosaic, with a crowd of characters (among them King Arthur) and animals. Another notable building is the little Basilica of SAN PIETRO (10th–11th century), which has a Greek cross and Byzantine frescos inside.

GALLIPOLI, THE "BEAUTIFUL CITY". It was called "KALLE POLIS" (beautiful city) by the Greeks and is a port on the Ionian Sea. The old city at its center has today, as it did in 1767, about 8,000 inhabitants, while the new city, which stands behind it and was built in the 19th century, has 12,000. Inhabited from the earliest times, its importance grew during the imperial age. Destroyed by Totila, it was a Byzantine city for five centuries. I was conquered by the Normans in 1071, and the castle was then rebuilt by the Angevins. It has maintained a medieval and Mediterranean feel. Among the buildings the Cathedral of SANT' AGATA stands out, with its 17th-century façade and a three-naved interior with a Latin cross; it is richly decorated with frescos and Baroque paintings by Salentine artists. The 18th-century Church of SAN FRANCESCO D'ASSISI, with a view of the triumphal arch, is opposite the castle on the main street that divides the city. The narrow streets that lead off it invite you to lose yourself in the ancient heart of this delightful city, which lives up to its name.

PALERMO, SICILY AND SOUTHERN CALABRIA

The image of Palermo, immersed in the extensive green plantations of citrus trees which was made famous by landscape painters and engravers, now belongs to the past. Yet the attractions of its beautiful position embraced by the sea, its gentle climate and its unique monuments are still very real, and have made the city one of the most popular tourist destinations. Sicily and its numerous attractions are selectively described in the itineraries on the following pages. We begin in the west of the island: the Cathedral of Monreale, artistic pinnacle of Sicily's Norman period; the Zingaro Nature Reserve tenaciously resisting man's encroachment on the coastline; the dazzling, isolated Greek temple of Segesta; fascinating Erice, perched above the Mediterranean; and ancient Selinunte reduced by sackings and earthquakes to a theatrical silence. We set off again on the tour of Sicily toward the east: with Cefalù, where Norman and Byzantine cultures meet in the cathedral; the sunny Aeolian islands; and Messina (146 miles from Palermo) with its important regional museum. Then a digression (with the boat-ferry from Messina) to Southern Calabria where we look at the National Museum of Reggio, among the most important archeological collections of the Mezzogiorno, and the Cattolica di Stilo (93 miles from Reggio), a rare and delightful example of a miniature Byzantine church. The itinerary continues: back in Sicily, in the busy urban landscape of Catania against which the immense Mount Etna leans; in the picturesque and charming Taormina; in the Ionic lands of Syracuse, an incomparable open-air museum of art and in Noto with its ingenious Baroque planning; in the Ragusan countryside, with the fantastic churches of Modica (42 miles from Syracuse) and in Ragusa itself. We explore the powerful and mysterious fortifications of Gela and Piazza Armerina, where the late Romanization left some of the most precious mosaics. The itinerary ends at Agrigento, whose splendid reminders of Greek civilization in Sicily compete with those of Syracuse.

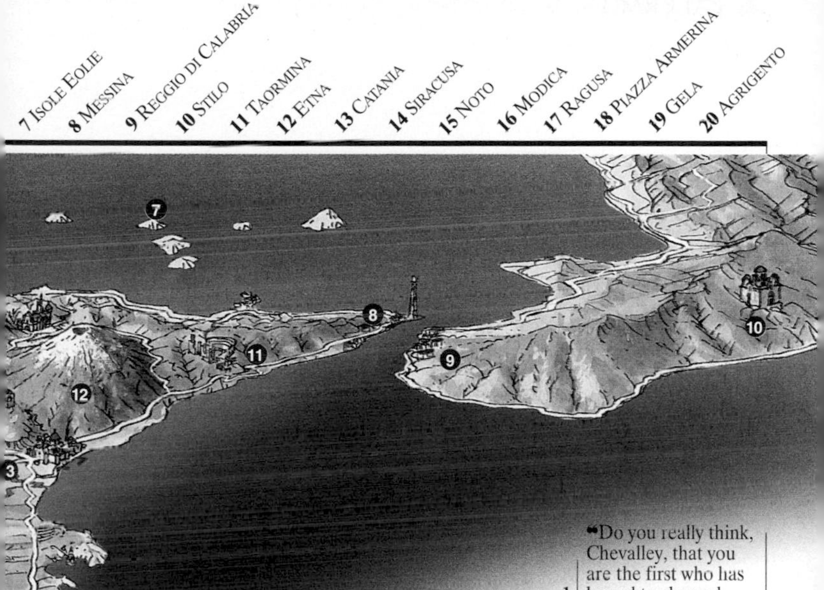

"Do you really think, Chevalley, that you are the first who has hoped to channel Sicily into the flow of universal history? I wonder how many Moslem imams, how many of King Robert's knights, Swabian scribes, Angevin barons and jurists of the most Catholic King have conceived the same fine folly; and how many Spanish viceroys too, how many of Charles III's reforming functionaries! And who knows now what happened to them all! Sicily wanted to sleep in spite of their invocations; for why should she listen to them if she is rich, wise, civilized and honest, if she's admired and envied by all, if in a word, she's perfect?"

Giuseppe Tomasi
di Lampedusa,
The Leopard

"It was instinct that drew us toward the occupation our father and his father had had, that carried us toward our destiny, the sea, il Stretto, the swordfish, ... it carried us on, with our spears and our long cloaks."

Vincenzo Consolo,
Neró metallicó
(Metallic Black)

ARAB PALERMO
The fortified quarter of Kalsa (al-Halisah, in Arabic "the chosen") represents the first expansion beyond the walls of the Punic and Roman city. In 937 it became the headquarters of the emirate, with its troops, government offices, prisons and military building yards.

ROGER OF HAUTEVILLE
Capable of predicting the future and gifted with extreme tolerance in political and social spheres, King Roger created what is considered by historians as the first modern reign of a still barbaric Europe. Upon the death of his eldest brother Robert Guiscard, Roger assumed command of the Norman forces (1087–91) to defeat the last Saracen resistance in Sicily, and received the title of "Great Count" from Pope Urban II.

Giuseppe Garibaldi, at the head of the Thousand, enters Palermo on May 27, 1860.

The city's ancient name, Panormus, literally means "all-port." Founded by the Phoenicians in the 8th century BC, but never won by the Greeks, it was conquered by the Romans in 254 BC. The settlement was made up of two fortified centers: the Paleapolis (the original nucleus) and the Neapolis (developed in the 4th and 5th centuries). The Romans occupied a rocky peninsula that was bounded north and south by two rivers, which have disappeared today, that flowed into the sea at a deep and well-protected natural harbor.

FROM THE ARABS TO THE NORMANS.
The Arabs conquered the city in 831, calling it Balarmu. The Arab period saw the extraordinary development of agriculture and trade in Palermo, making the city one of the major trade centers in the entire Mediterranean. The internal rivalries of the Arabs however, hastened the arrival of the Normans in Sicily and, in 1072, Roger of Hauteville and Robert Guiscard took control over Palermo. The 500 mosques in the city were replaced by an assortment of places of worship that represented the various faiths that were followed by the different populations (Greek, Catholic, Arab and Jewish).

SWABIANS, ANGEVINS AND ARAGONESE. When the Norman reign in Sicily concluded in 1194, the future emperor of the Holy Roman Empire, Frederick II of Swabia (who reigned for fifty years) made Palermo a hub of exchange between the Byzantine East, Muslim Africa and the Catholic Empire. Upon the death of Frederick, however, the pope supported Charles of Anjou, to prevent any attempt to restore an emperor. Under Angevin rule, Palermo went into decline.

Continually subjected to abuses by the French, the Sicilians rebelled in 1282 with the Vespers revolt, but the nobility solicited and supported the intervention of the Aragonese with a guarantee of former privileges.

TOWARD ITALY. It was in Bourbon Palermo, in 1812, that the first constitution was proclaimed on Italian soil. The revolutionary movements of 1820 and 1848 started in Palermo, and

> **"THIS RICH AND ELEGANT CITY, SPLENDID AND GRACEFUL... IT RISES FROM ITS SQUARES AND THE COUNTRYSIDE THAT SURROUNDS IT, SUPERB, AS IF FROM A GARDEN."**
>
> IBN GIUBAIR, 12TH CENTURY

FREDERICK II OF SWABIA
Thirteenth-century historians defined the age they lived in as a "stupor mundi". With his free and illuminated spirit, Frederick sought to harmonize three civilizations: the Latin-Germanic, the Siculo Norman and the Arab cultures. At his court in Palermo he surrounded himself with wise men of the time and "the Sicilian poetic school" was the source from which, via Tuscany, we ended up with the first national language: Italian.

in 1860 Garibaldi found in the thousands of *picciotti* (rebel Sicilians) the key for defeating a superior army.

On December 1, 1860 Sicily finally became Italian.

THE MAFIA. The region has often been associated with the Mafia. Palermo is considered the city of crime *par excellence* and is a base for the struggle between the Mafia and the state. From an historical point of view, organized crime in Sicily started in the 15th century, when the "honored societies" existing in Spain headed for Italy. The development of the Mafia passed through three periods: the rural Mafia (1860–1946 involved the control of an economy still linked to rural ownership), the urban Mafia (1946–77, concerned with building speculation and public works), and finally the international Mafia (from 1977 onward, with the trafficking of drugs). Following the murders of judges Falcone and Borsellino in 1992, with the breakdown of the protective and complicit links of the political world and the use of collaborating penitents, the fight against the Mafia has finally taken an encouragingly positive turn.

PALERMO TODAY. With almost 700,000 inhabitants, present-day Palermo demonstrates the contrasts and typical contradictions of a big southern city: alive and active, but with great sociocultural differences and huge areas of backwardness and underdevelopment. The brightness of the new residential quarters and the Viale della Libertà only accentuate the degradation of certain areas. In the last few years the council has proposed (with good results) a plan for the regeneration and conservation of the historic center, which was approved in 1989.

THE VESPERS
It is said that the revolt began with the following episode: the Angevins had forbidden the

Sicilians to carry arms. On March 30, 1282, while the bells were ringing for Vespers, a French soldier, Drouet, on the pretence of conducting a meticulous search, interfered with an attractive local girl. This sparked a reaction from her husband and passersby. The consequence was that the Angevins were hunted from the city. The kingdom then passed to Peter of Aragon, who eventually gave the capital to Naples.

447

AN UNUSUAL PLACE FOR A DEBATE
The popular insurrection of August 1647 against the misrule of the Spanish viceroy was headed by Giuseppe Alessi, a goldsmith who had taken part in the revolt in Naples led by Masaniello ▲ 393. Elected Captain General, Giuseppe Alessi assembled the people twice, in the Church of San Giuseppe dei Teatini, to discuss the requests imposed on the viceroy: equal rights in the Senate for nobles and the lower classes and the lifting of heavy government taxes. Giuseppe Alessi's luck lasted eight days: like Masaniello he was massacred by his enemies.

QUATTRO CANTI

Piazza Vigliena, better known as the "Quattro Canti" (Four Corners) was created in 1600 when Via Maqueda was built at right angles to what is now Corso Vittorio Emanuele. The four corners of the piazza are richly adorned with fountains, windows, statues, and decorative niches in the walls, forming an elaborate architectural backdrop to one of the pulsing centers of the city.

FONTANA PRETORIA
The fountain of Francesco Camilliani (1554–55) was originally intended for the Florentine city of Don Pedro di Toledo. It was then acquired by the Senate of Palermo and installed in 1575 on the Piazza Pretoria. Circular in shape, raised on small steps and surrounded by a balustrade, the fountain is also called the "fountain of shame" because of its nude figures.

SAN GIUSEPPE DEI TEATINI. Standing in the southwestern corner is this imposing church erected around 1612. It is characterized by a fine sloping cupola and a simple Baroque façade that looks out on to Corso Vittorio Emanuele.

PIAZZA PRETORIA. This "garden of stone" is located a few feet from the Quattro Canti. Its centerpiece is the grand FOUNTAIN of the same name. The imposing PALAZZO SENATORIO (Senate Building), commonly called "the Eagles", headquarters of local government since the 14th century, fronts the southern edge of the square. On the eastern side you will find the 16th-century Church of SAN CATERINA, with its extraordinary interior decorations along the walls and the columns with figures and allegorical compositions.

PIAZZA BELLINI OR THE PIANO DI SAN CATALDO. You reach this small square (site of the Council in medieval times) via the little street of Santa Caterina. It features the Teatro Carolina (now a restaurant) and the Church of SAN CATALDO, constructed around 1160 by the Admiral Majone di Bari.

THE MARTORANA ★. Also facing onto Piazza Bellini is the Church of Santa Maria dell'Ammiraglio, known as La Martorana because it was given in 1435 to the nearby convent founded by Goffredo and Eloisa Martorana. Built in 1143 by George of Antioch, great admiral of King Roger, its Norman bell tower is in striking contrast to the Baroque façade.

MARTORANA FRUIT
Tradition has it that the cloistered monks of the Monastery of Martorana invented

these candies, made of almond paste and sugar, shaped and colored like pieces of fruit.

The Church of San Cataldo is characterized by three small Arab-style cupolas.

Sicilian cuisine is a triumph of strong aromas and flavors: dishes vary from village to village, but imagination is always an ingredient.

FEELING HUNGRY?
In the streets it is easy to find the vendors of *stigghiole* (lamb intestines cooked over coals).

IL PALAZZO DEL GATTOPARDO
In the Ganci-Valguarnera palace, director Luchino Visconti shot the famous ball sequence for the movie *The Leopard*, 1963, based on the novel by Tomasi di Lampedusa.

VIA MAQUEDA

The so-called "New Street", dedicated to Bernardino di Cardines, Duke of Maqueda, was opened in 1600.
SAN NICOLÒ DA TOLENTINO. A little further toward the south of the Piazza Pretoria you will notice the imposing façade of the church. This was erected in 1609 with the nearby Agostinian convent.
CIVIL ARCHITECTURE. Among numerous noble residences along the street, the PALAZZO COMITINI (today the Province's seat of government), the enormous PALAZZO SANTA CROCE and the majestic PALAZZO FILANGERI DI CUTO are of particular interest. The ground level of the ancient buildings is made up of numerous clothing and fabric shops.
THE MARKETS. This area of Palermo attracts many small traders, selling everything from objects in aluminum, zinc, brass, iron and wood in Via Calderai, to exotic fruits and vegetables in the Ballaro market which runs down Via del Bosco or Via Ponticello.

CORSO VITTORIO EMANUELE WEST

The modern street follows the "Cassaro" (from the Arab al-qasr, or castle), the oldest thoroughfare of the city, which leads from the castle to the port of Cala. This is an imposing street of Renaissance and Baroque churches, convents and palaces. In recent years the corso has been taken over by a lively and colorful mix of stores selling secondhand clothes and antique dealers, antiquarian bookshops and craft shops selling dolls ● 58, terracotta, silver, nativity scenes and straw bags. In the western part of the street stands the CHIESA DEL SANTISSIMO SALVATORE, the Baroque work of Paolo Amato built at the behest of the Basilian monks. Opposite is the imposing COLLEGIO MASSIMO DEI GESUITI, erected in 1586–8 as

> **"THE CONQUERING MUSLIMS ARRIVED IN PALERMO IN THE 9TH CENTURY AND, UNDER THEIR INFLUENCE, THE REGION PROGRESSED FURTHER TOWARD CIVILIZATION AND PROSPERITY THAN ANY OTHER PART OF ITALY."** MICHELE AMARI

an institute of higher learning near to the cathedral. After educational reform, it became the premises of the university and in 1778 it was adapted as a library. Today it houses the Regional Sicilian Library and contains illuminated codices, books, manuscripts and collections of correspondence that date back to the 11th century, and which attract scholars from around the world.

PIAZZA DELLA CATTEDRALE

Formerly a cemetery, a trysting-place for knights and a venue for grand religious celebrations, the square today is dominated by the cathedral and the grandiose 18th-century PALAZZO ARCIVESCOVILE (Archbishop's Palace). Its annex, the Diocesan Museum, preserves 17th- and 18th-century works of art from churches that were destroyed during World War Two. Around the Piazza Peranni you can find secondhand clothes, books, prints and many other curiosities in the flea market.

THE CATHEDRAL ★. There have been countless modifications to the complex and elaborate construction founded by the Archbishop of

Palermo, Walter of the Mill, in 1184. The magnificent PORTICO with it three arches at the southern entrance is a veritable masterpiece of Catalan inspiration. Inside the cathedral are the tombs of Frederick II, Roger II and various other members of the Sicilian royalty which have been preserved, while the presbytry is ornamented by the complex wooden CHOIR which is beautifully carved in a Gothic-Catalan style. On the side of the sacristy the rich TREASURE of the cathedral is on show, while the crypt contains twenty-three sarcophagi.

THE JESUITS AT PALERMO
The Collegio Massimo (Great College) is the emblem of the cultural domination that the order enjoyed from the 1600's until 1767, when the Bourbons expelled the Jesuits and confiscated their goods. In 1603 it was linked directly to the Casa Professa, the father-house of the order, and since 1775 it has housed the Biblioteca Comunale (City Library).

PROCESSIONS AND POPULAR FEASTS
In the 16th and 17th centuries the tradition of celebratory processions became established,

to mark events such as the arrival of the Emperor Charles V in 1535, or religious occasions such as the Feast of Santa Rosalia ▲ *457* or Lent. Sometimes the processions were organized by religious orders or craftsmen.

THE "PUPPET OPERA"
Orlando, Angelica, Rinaldo and King Carlo are just a few of the characters of the "Puppet Opera", the theater of wooden marionettes. Dressed in armor and extravagant costumes, the figures are maneuvered by strings and iron poles by the *pupari* (puppeteers). The shows have lost some of their popularity but examples of the art can be seen in the International Museum of Marionettes in the precincts of Santa Maria della Catena.

PIAZZA DELLA VITTORIA

This open space in front of the Palazzo dei Normanni was formerly used as a military parade ground as a livestock market, as a venue for popular festivals in honor of the patron saint or sovereign, and also for executions. The present name commemorates the victorious revolt of the Palermitan people in 1820 against the local Bourbon garrison. In the adjoining Piazza Giovanni Decollato stands the PALAZZO SCLAFANI (1330) which has a splendid doorway surmounted by the coats of arms of the Sclafani family, the city, Sicily and the Aragonese. The palazzo was passed over to the Spanish viceroys and it was used as a hospital from 1435. The atrium was decorated with frescos, including the famous *Trionfo della Morte* (Triumph of Death) which was removed after World War Two and can be found today in the Regional Gallery of Sicily ▲ *454*. On the piazza stands the monumental PORTA NUOVA, which was built to celebrate the arrival at Palermo of Charles V from his victorious campaigns in Tunisia.

PALAZZO DEI NORMANNI ★. This palace occupies the western side of Piazza della Vittoria. Once the seat of emirs, kings and viceroys, today it houses the Sicilian Assembly.
PALATINE CHAPEL ★. King Roger had the chapel constructed between 1130 and 1132 within the palace. It is a true jewel of Norman art that blends marvelously with the complex decorative Islamic motifs of the splendid ceilings, the vast gold-based mosaics of Byzantine origin and an extraordinary geometrically designed pavement.

Refined mosaics of the 12th century with animal and plant motifs decorate the room of King Roger in the Palazzo dei Normanni.

SAN GIOVANNI OF THE HERMITS. In the nearby Via dei Benedettini, is one of the most visited places of the city. It is an extraordinary example of a Christian adaptation of elements typical of the Arab *Quba*. After lengthy work to eliminate recent additions, the convent complex of the ancient church, the colonnaded cloister and several of the adjoining buildings of the convent are once again open to the public.

THE SOUTHEASTERN QUARTERS

SANT'ANTONIO ABATE. This building stands on the wide Via Roma, almost on the corner of Corso Vittorio Emanuele. On the side is the bell tower built by Chiaramonte (its bells call for the Senate council to assemble.

"VUCCIRIA" MARKET. This lively, popular market takes place in the little square and in the small streets at the back of the Church of Sant'Antonio. Crossing the Corso Vittorio Emanuele you will find the Church of SAN FRANCESCO D'ASSISI with its beautiful 14th-century doorway, standing in the square of the same name.

ORATORY OF SAN LORENZO. The building stands on the adjacent and narrow Via San Francesco and is an example of the bright and enjoyable decorative talent of the great sculptor Giacomo Serpotta ▲ 455.

SANTA MARIA DELLA CATENA (ST MARY OF THE CHAIN). This church, in Gothic-Hispanic style, is on the nearby Piazzetta delle Dogane and takes its name from the chain that closed the ancient port; its elegant loggia has been used as a model for several other Palermitan churches.

PALAZZO AJUTAMICRISTO. A network of streets and alleyways leads into Via Garibaldi and the 16th-century residence of the Pisan merchant.

LA "VUCCIRIA"
Pari'na Vucciria: this is how the Palermitans indicate in dialect a place where confusion, noise and chaos reign. Make a trip to the market of the *Vucciria* and you will encounter a jumble of stalls laden with every kind of food, a maze of narrow alleyways and a throng of people.

PALAZZO CHIARAMONTE (STERI). In Piazza Marina, this palace is typical of the architecture of Palermo in the 14th century. It belonged to the powerful family that in 1392 led the Sicilian barons against King Martin of Aragon.

GALLERIA REGIONALE DELLA SICILIA. At the side of the Steri, the Regional Gallery is housed in the PALAZZO ABATELLIS. It has a collection of works of medieval Sicilian and 16th–17th-century artists. It is worth noting the important *Annunziata* by Antonello da Messina.

VILLA GIULIA. The tour of Piazza Marina ends at Villa Giulia, a vast and extremely popular Italian garden. Established in 1778, it was the first public green space of the city.

ORTO BOTANICO. Adjacent to Villa Giulia, the botanical garden was opened in 1785, two centuries after its inception. It is still a scientific, educational institution of exceptional importance. The buildings of the gymnasium, with the herbarium, the library, the classroom, and the nearby premises of the *tepidarium* and the *calidarium* are also worthy of note.

THE END OF THE CHIARAMONTE
Andrea, son of Manfredi III Chiaramonte, count of Modica and great palace official, led the barons who opposed the conquest of Sicily on behalf of Martin I of Aragon. On May 17, 1392, forced to surrender after a long occupation of the city, he was beheaded in front of his house – the Fortezza dello Steri. All his goods and his land were divided between the victors.

THE CENTRAL EAST QUARTERS

SAN DOMENICO. This church, built in 1724, faces onto a piazza of the same name. It is one of the most sumptuous Baroque monuments of the city, and it is regarded as Palermo's "pantheon" because from the 14th century the city's most famous men were buried there (among them Emerico and Michele Amari, Giovanni Meli, Pietro Novelli, Francesco Crispi and Roger VII who assembled the Sicilian Parliament here).

ORATORIO DEL SANTISSIMO ROSARIO DI SAN DOMENICO ★. At no. 2, Via dei Barberini, the oratory was used by the company of the Santissimo Rosario which welcomed the rich artisans and businessmen of the city, such as the painter Pietro Novelli and the sculptor Giacomo Serpotta. The

❝A CITY AT ONCE BEAUTIFUL AND VAST, PALERMO HAS SUCH A
REPUTATION FOR THE MARVELS OF ITS ARCHITECTURE, THAT
PEOPLE TRAVEL FROM FAR AND WIDE TO SEE IT.**❞**

AL-IDRĪSĪ

splendor of the oratory owes much to Serpotta's work. At the altar you will see the *Madonna del Rosario con San Domenico e le patrone di Palermo* by Van Dyck, commissioned in 1624.

ORATORIO DEL SANTISSIMO ROSARIO DI SANTA CITA. This is another masterpiece of the Palermitan sculptor Serpotta who worked there between 1687 and 1718 creating an extraordinary fantasy of stuccos with allegorical statues and a swathe of *putti* on the entrance wall, the paintings of the fifteen *Misteri del Rosario* and that of the battle of Lepanto ▲ *217*. The oratory is situated in Via Valverde on the left side of the Church of SANTA CITA or SANTA ZITA, dedicated however to San Mamiliano. This church, in Via Squarcialupo, houses notable sculptures by Antonello Gagini and the finely decorated Chapel of Maria Santissima del Rosario.

SAN GIORGIO DEI GENOVESI. Situated in the eponymous piazza, it is a rare example of unspoiled 16th-century architecture. It was built around 1576 by the community of Genoese merchants in Palermo. A large part of the floor is covered with tombstones dating from the 16th and 17th centuries. The church is now deconsecrated and periodically houses temporary exhibitions.

MUSEO REGIONALE ARCHEOLOGICO. The Regional Archeological Museum is located in Via Roma, in the convent house of the Filippini order. It was founded at the beginning of the 19th century as the University Museum and was transferred in 1866 to its current quarters. It is one of the most important in Italy for its size and the quality of the collections, which are exhibited over three floors. It is particularly well known for its sculptures from Selinunte ▲ *462*. Less well known, but just as interesting is the Etruscan collection from Chiusi. The exceptional Greek vases, decorative for the most part, are painted with black figures. Among the many classic sculptures of note are *l'Ariete,* a bronze bull dating from the 3rd century BC from ancient Syracuse; and the second *Ariete* was destroyed by the cannons during the revolts of 1848. Other rooms in the museum house interesting prehistoric collections, mosaics and Roman frescos.

GIACOMO SERPOTTA
The great Palermitan sculptor and stucco artist, the son of a humble marble sculptor, was born in 1656 in the poor quarter of Kalsa da Gaspare. His decorative carvings were so fine they give his works unmistakable character, weaving wonderful fantasies and emphasizing the brightness of the marble. His masterpieces are in

the oratories of the Santissimo Rosario di San Domenico and of Santa Cita. Serpotta signed his works with a *sirpuzza* (lizard, in Sicilian).

A room of the Museo Regionale Archeologico is dedicated to the sculptures which decorate the temples of Selinunte.

The carriage drawn by four horses and the high relief sculptures that crown the Teatro Politeama.

THE FLORIO DYNASTY
In the 19th century this family symbolized Sicilian capitalism. Bold and innovative entrepreneurs, the opposite of the bourgeoisie and the Palermitan nobility of the time, the Florios reinvested their

MODERN PALERMO

From Piazza Verdi to the Viale della Liberta is the city entertainment center with theaters, historical hotels, luxurious shops, meeting places, villas and gardens.

TEATRO MASSIMO. The great theater was built in 1897 by Giovan Battista Basile and finished by his son Ernesto. Situated between the old city and the new southern development, it is one of the greatest theaters of Europe. It was closed for lengthy restoration works and reopened in 1997.

TEATRO POLITEAMA. This neoclassical building stands in Piazza Ruggiero Settimo and was built between 1867 and 1874. The CIVICA GALLERIA D'ARTE MODERNA EMPEDOCLE RESTIVO occupies the top-floor rooms and displays works by 19th- and 20th-century southern artists.

LIBERTY AT PALERMO. Along the Viale della Liberta and in the neighboring districts there are numerous villas and palaces in Liberty-style such as the Palazzo Dato di Vincenzo Alagna or the numerous

profits in further initiatives. They dealt in spices, medicinal drugs, exports of Marsala wine. Their other interests included tuna, foundries, ships, sulphur, hotels, newspapers and impressive buildings like the Liberty-style villa in Viale Regina Margherita. They also promoted the Targa Florio, the famous automobile race. In the early 20th century they lost the entire fortune in less than ten years.

works of Giovan Battista and Ernesto Basile: Villa Bordonaro (Via della Croci 7), Villa Favarolo (Piazza Virgilio), Villino Ida-Basile (Via Siracusa 15) and the extraordinary VILLA FLORIO (Viale Regina Margherita 38), which is considered to be the absolute masterpiece of Ernesto Basile.

THE OUTLYING DISTRICTS

There are many different buildings of architectural interest, originally constructed in the rural outskirts Palermo but which now form part of the modern city.

THE PLEASURES OF VIALE DELLA LIBERTÀ
In Piazza Croce on summer evenings, the
Palermitans like to stop and sit down for
a taste of prickly pear, carefully
peeled on the spot by one of the local
Palermitan street vendors.

SANTUARIO DI SANTA ROSALIA ★. The sanctuary, built in
1625, stands on Mount Pellegrino at an altitude of 1407
feet. The adjoining rock contains the grotto (82 feet
deep) where the saint prayed, and the water which drips
from it is said to have miraculous properties.

FIERA DEL MEDITERRANEO. Via Monte Pellegrino leads along
the foot of the mountain to a showground that is the venue
for the annual festival in May and June.

PARCO DELLA FAVORITA ★. The park extends to the foot of
Mount Pellegrino and was intended as a hunting reserve and
place for agricultural experimentation by Ferdinand III, the
Bourbon king who took refuge in Palermo in 1799 after
having been exiled from Naples by the Napoleonic troops.
This park is the "green lung" of the city, and is frequently
visited by the local Palermitans, especially
at weekends, and is also a venue for open-
air concerts.

PALAZZINA CINESE. This was a favorite
palace of Ferdinand III and Queen Maria
Carolina during their enforced stay in
Sicily. The Chinese Palace is found in the
northwestern zone of the Parco della
Favorita. It is a very colorful and bizarre
construction, the product of a taste for
chinoiserie at the end of the 19th century.
In the buildings adjoining the palace the
MUSEO ETNOGRAFICO GIUSEPPE PITRÈ
houses a very rich collection of objects
documenting the life, ways and customs of
the people of Sicily.

LA ZISA ★. In the piazza of the same
name (from Al-aziz, in Arabic "glorious")
this palace in the form of a parallelepiped,
with splendid architectural lines, was
erected by the Norman kings William I
and William II (using Muslim artistry). It
is situated at the center of a great park

containing a small lake and was primarily used as a
summer residence.

LA CUBA. A little further from La Zisa, mostly within the
Tuköry barracks of Corso Calatafimi, stands another splendid
example of William II's architecture. Built in 1180, the
pavilion was used as a retreat and has a compact rectangular
shape, surrounded on four sides by a pool and the shady
green of a park.

**ROSALIA,
LA "SANTUZZA"**
At Palermo, the feast
of the city's patron
saint Rosalia occurs
in mid-July. It
commemorates the
discovery in 1624 of
her remains, which
were carried in
procession, putting
an end to the plague.
Born in the 12th
century of a noble
family, the young girl
had refused marriage
to a Norman and all
honors, to live and
pray in a grotto on
Mount Pellegrino.

GIUSEPPE PITRÈ
Born at Palermo in
1841 and a graduate
in medicine, he
studied the Sicilians
and wrote numerous
books about them
including the
*Biblioteca delle
Tradizioni Popolari
Siciliane* in twenty-
five volumes). He
organized the
Ethnographic
Museum and, until
his death (in 1916),
occupied a chair of
psychology at the
University of
Palermo.

Founded in 1174, the monastic complex of Monreale was the citadel of Norman power in Sicily. Next to the church rose the royal palace: a complex, the historians say, of "multa dignum admiratione", worthy of great admiration, such that no king could boast of another similar. Every single culture of the composite Norman kingdom left a trace there: the cathedral's façade and layout are Norman, the 64,000 square feet of mosaics are of the Byzantine school, the altar decorations are of Arab-Norman origins, the columns classical and in the cloister, Lombard, French and Islamic designs intermingle.

THE FLOOR
The whole church is full of beautiful mosaics which are at their finest in the high section of the walls. The original floor is still in place and is also in mosaic style. It was worked on through successive periods and completed in the 1500's. The wooden ceiling, on the other hand, was rebuilt after the fire of 1811.

COMPOSITE ARCHITECTURE
In the architecture of the cathedral, Lombard, French, Islamic and Byzantine traditions blend, a testimony to the fusion of civilizations in Sicily at the time. It is built in the style of a basilica, with three naves supported on columns that mostly come from ancient buildings; the interior mosaic decoration is typically Byzantine; the exterior reveals, particularly in the decoration, the Arab influences.

ALTAR AND NAVE
The upper part of the walls of the cathedral are decorated with mosaics by Greek and Byzantine craftsmen. Behind the altar is the Virgin Mary, flanked by saints, apostles and angels. The wooden ceiling is elaborately decorated, and there are mosaics set into the marble floor. Columns support ogival arches along the nave.

THE MOSAICS

The great half-figure of Christ Pantocrator, in the Byzantine tradition, covers the vault of the central apse and appears to look at you no matter where you stand. The rest of the upper walls around the altar and along the nave are covered with mosaic pictures from the Bible on a gold ground: over 64,000 square feet of mosaic.

THE CLOISTER

The beautiful cloister of the Benedictine monastery next to the cathedral also dates from the Norman period. It is a great square surrounded by a continuous portico with arches supported by 228 twin columns. The columns are in a wide range of different designs and are topped by capitals with intriguing carvings. A graceful fountain in the form of a stylized palm sits in the center.

"SAINT PAUL IS LOWERED FROM THE WALLS OF DAMASCUS"

A detail from one of the mosaics on the walls.

DETAIL OF A PANEL

THE MAIN DOORS

The great doors of the duomo are masterpieces of sculpture from the period. The ogival-shaped central pair, within a carved arch with mosaic insets, are faced with beautiful bronzework divided into forty two little panels worked by Bonanno Pisano in 1186. The door on the left has twenty eight bronze panels decorated with figures of saints sculpted and signed by Barisano da Trani between 1186 and 1190.

"William II offers the Duomo of Monreale to the Virgin", bas-relief of a column of the cloister.

POWER GAMES
To diminish the power of the Archbishop of Palermo, Offamilio, William II had the Abbey of Monreale constructed, vesting it with even greater powers when it was made an archbishopric, thereby removing considerable territory from Palermitan control.

Sicily still has an air of mystery, even as the island approaches the year 2000. The evocative stones of antiquity continue to attract travelers on the Grand Tour, giving them much food for thought and providing insights through unique panoramas and thousand-year-old traditions. In Calabria, too, the precious treasures of the Archeological Museum of Reggio, the Byzantine architecture of Cattolica de Stilo and the many evocative remains of former times invite the traveler to reflect upon the debt we owe to the past.

WESTERN SICILY

The Sicilian countryside to the west of Palermo contains many jewels of art and architecture from successive periods (Segesta, Monreale, Erice) in a natural, unspoiled setting, typified by the Zingaro Nature Reserve. To the southwest, Selinunte still stands as a silent witness to an ancient trading power and the earth-shattering forces that continue to devastate the region.

THE NORMANS AT MONREALE ★. In 1174, 5 miles to the southwest of Palermo, the Norman king William II wanted to erect one of the most sumptuous creations of medieval Italy: the Duomo of Monreale ▲ *458*. The façade, squeezed between two towers, frames the extraordinary PORTA REGIA, crowned by woven arches and decorated with carvings and mosaic surfaces. The walls of the interior, with three naves divided by eighteen imposing columns in granite from the Roman era, are covered with magnificent MOSAICS from the 12th and 13th centuries. These complex designs on a gold background represent the cycle of the Old and the New Testaments, while in the dome over the central altar the figure of the blessing Christ rises up like a giant. There you can admire the sarcophagi

Built in the 3rd century, at 1,312 feet the theater of Segesta faces toward north to allow the spectators to enjoy spellbinding view of the hills and the distant sea.

of kings William I and William II. From the chapel of the Crucifix you can move on to the Treasury: of particular interest is the Baroque urn of Sacra Spina (in which remains are preserved), a valuable small drawer made of wood from the Norman period and a precious vase in silver from the 12th century. The abbey developed around the CHIOSTRO (cloister) of the convent of the Benedictines: a true miracle of architecture and color. The arches of the square colonnade are pointed, with double ferrules, held up by 228 columns that are encrusted and carved. The superior part of the column is decorated with images from history that are seen together with sacred objects, vegetable figures, animals and fantastic and symbolic motifs that create a cultural anthology which is incomparable.

THE LONE DORIAN TEMPLE OF SEGESTA ★. About 15 miles to the south of Scopello, you come upon a bare hill that leans on Mount Barbaro; it is a strategic position for the domination of a vast territory. It was built in the 5th century BC by the Elimes, a people who possibly came from Anatolia, using the lines of the great Greek temples of the rival Selinunte and "Akragus", to give solemnity and power to a place of an indigenous cult. The temple is formed by a base with steps upon which rises an internal courtyard of thirty six tall columns ● *84* with two large features, with smooth spaces in between without a single decoration. Nearby the temple is the THEATER dating from two centuries later.

NATURAL RESERVE OF THE ZINGARO
This beautiful reserve extends for about 37 miles to the west of Palermo – to the north of Scopello, in the gulf of Castellamare – and safeguards one of the last complete stretches of coast on Sicily. A path of 4 miles crosses it, allowing you to reach the white beaches of the magnificent harbors which still exist. The dwarf palm is the true symbol of the reserve, but the area also contains examples of a wide variety of Mediterranean vegetation, and includes oak. The reserve is also the nesting site of the rarest Bonelli eagle and of the peregrine falcon.

"To have seen Italy without having seen Sicily is not to have seen Italy at all, for Sicily is the key to everything."
Johann Wolfgang Goethe

461

ANCIENT TEMPLE
In the past, Erice was famous for its temple dedicated to Astarte by the Phoenicians, to Aphrodite by the Greeks, and finally to Venus Ericina by the Romans. The latter imposed an annual tax on seventeen Sicilian cities for the maintenance of the sanctuary; in addition, all the consuls and generals had to make offerings to the goddess. The temple was located where the Norman castle stands today: it was Frederick of Aragon who decided to build the original church far from the ancient site of the pagan cult.

ERICE, THE SILENCE AND THE MEDIEVAL AGE. The city, founded by the Elymians on the top of the isolated Mount San Giuliano, is situated about 31 miles from Segesta, toward the west. It is the only Sicilian town where the medieval urban fabric has remained intact. Typical features are the geometrical plan of its many alleyways and narrow streets; the 260 Moorish-style courtyards; the remains of the city walls, some of which are inscribed with Phoenician letters; the many towers, fortified gateways, and palaces; and the Norman CASTLE. A surreal atmosphere envelops the city, just as mist can often shroud it from the sun, even in full summer. The CHIESA MATRICE is a masterpiece of medieval art that blends the Gothic style of the portal and ornate rose window with the that of the bell tower which was once used as a lookout.

SELINUNTE. Further south and 55 miles from Erice, colonists from Megara Hyblaea founded Selinunte in 628 BC on two low hills overlooking the sea. Its ruins are preserved today within an archeological park. It was sacked in 40 BC by the Carthaginians, allies of the rival Elymians of Segesta. It was finally destroyed in the Byzantine age by a disastrous earthquake. Excavations, which began in 1823, have revealed a number of monuments covering a wide area. On the acropolis, the remains of Doric TEMPLES are of interest, as is the main road (*plateia*) dividing the settlement from north to south.

MATTANZA AT FAVIGNANA
Tuna fishing takes place ■ *30* in the waters around the Egadi islands, 10 miles from Trapani. Straining boats and nets, the tuna are forced to the center of what becomes a "room of death" where they are easily hooked.

The figure of Christ Pantocrator in the Cathedral of Cefalu makes a blessing with the three fingers of the right hand to represent the mystery of the Trinity.

On the plain to the east, only three grandiose temples remain; the latter, dedicated to Zeus, is one of the most colossal constructions of the Greek world. Another important site at Selinunte is the CAVE DI CUSA, where you can easily picture the toil of the slaves who dragged stone from these quarries to the temple contruction sites.

TYRRHENIAN SICILY AND SOUTHERN CALABRIA

The sea dominates the landscape in this region. The coastline has been inhabited by man from ancient times, from the prehistoric settlements of the Aeolians to the lively town of Messina. The latter represents the artistic achievements of subsequent centuries and was reconstructed after the earthquake of 1908. Taking a detour just across the Strait (il Stretto), Reggio di Calabria welcomes the visitor to the Italian peninsula.

BYZANTINE TRACES IN CEFALÙ. Legend has it that King Roger, having escaped from a shipwreck near Cefalù (41 miles east of Palermo), wanted to thank the Madonna by building a cathedral. Roger's original plan in 1131 was to build a Norman "pantheon", but his successors William I and William II had different ideas. So the cathedral, with its two imposing square towers, was to take much longer to complete, although the extraordinary mosaics that can be seen over the apse were finished by 1148. In Byzantine style on a gold background, the figure of Christ Pantocrator sits enthroned, one of the most sublime representations of Christ in the whole of Christian art. In the Museo Mandralisca which is 220 yards from the cathedral, is Cefalù's other exceptional work of art: the *Ritratto di ignoto* (Portait of an unknown man) by Antonello da Messina (c. 1430–79).

MOZIA,
A PHOENICIAN CITY
Almost opposite Favignana, on the island of San Pantaleo, the Phoenicians founded Mozia in the 8th century BC. It became one of the most prosperous colonies in the Mediterranean, but was destroyed in 397 BC by Dionysius II of Syracuse. The survivors founded the present day Marsala.

NATURE ON THE AEOLIAN ISLANDS
The six small islands of the Aeolian archipelago abound with natural color and unusual forms: the

helichrysum and the caper grow freely and lobsters swim in the sea. Lipari is the most populated and its coastal roads can be followed by car, but the most charming places can only be reached on foot, between the points of Crepazza and Levante to the south.

SCILLA AND CHARYBDIS
Today the Strait of Messina can be crossed quickly and safely but its currents generated the myth of the monsters of Scilla and Charybdis. Also the official Napoleonic Courier, in the vain hope of organizing a fleet to invade the island held by the English, was disheartened and noted from Calabria that as incredible as it seemed, the currents made it difficult to cross a stretch of sea that was no wider than the distance between the Tuileries and Faubourg Saint-Germain.

MARINE VIEWS OF THE AEOLIAN ISLANDS. "We arrived at the Aeolian island, the floating island : an entire wall of bronze, indestructible, stark, the rock rose up and surrounded it" is how Ulysses described to the Phesians his arrival at the island of Aeolus, god of the winds. This place is perhaps identifiable as one of the seven volcanic summits overlooking a sapphire-colored sea about 16 miles to the northwest of Milazzo. This archipelago has long been recognized as an exceptional natural environment. In addition to the active volcanos which color the craters an intense yellow with sulphur crystals, there is the splendor of the fragrant Mediterranean vegetation that grows between the black lava rocks and the deep marine waters, among the most colorful of the Mediterranean. Accessible from Milazzo, Messina, Palermo or Naples, the seven Aeolian islands are Alicudi (the westernmost island), Filicudi, Salina, Lipari (the largest, with the Aeolian Archeological Museum and Archeological Park with evidence of the local culture going back to 4000 BC), Vulcano, Panarea (the smallest) and Stromboli (the easternmost island). At Salina, the area around the highest peak of the archipelago (Mount Fossa delle Felci, 3,156 feet) is unspoiled and has been declared a protected reserve.

> **"THROUGH THEIR RESERVE, THE SICILIANS EMPHASIZE THE CONTRAST BETWEEN THEIR CLOSED MINDS AND THE LUMINOUS OPENNESS OF THEIR NATURAL SURROUNDINGS."**
>
> LUIGI PIRANDELLO

MESSINA AND THE PAINTERS OF THE LIGHT. The REGIONAL MUSEUM of Messina houses Antonellos' great work of 1473, the *Polittico di San Gregorio*, commissioned by Frabia Cirino, abbess of the convent of Santa Maria alle Monache (San Gregorio). There are also works by Michelangelo Merisi, known as Caravaggio, including the *Risurrezione di Lazzaro* (Resurrection of Lazarus) and *L'Adorazione dei pastori* (The Adoration of the Shepherds), painted in 1609 respectively for the Chapel of the Lazzarines in the Chiesa dei Crociferi and for the Church of the Cappucines. Painters far apart in time and circumstances – the first left Sicily for Venice and Flanders, while the second left the Lombardian plain for the south – they shared in their art a common element: light. In Antonello, it is cold and sharp, nevertheless it anticipated Caravaggio since "it exalts the plastic value of form, instrument of synthesis in the hands of the powerful builder" (A.Venturi).

SOUTHERN CALABRIA. The ferry takes you to this land of pure color. For a long time, southern Calabria remained more isolated from the rest of Italy than Sicily itself, which is divided from it by the Strait of Messina. For the Greeks, however, it was part of Magna Graecia (Greater Greece) and many treasures from this period are preserved in the MUSEO ARCHEOLOGICO NAZIONALE DI REGGIO DI CALABRIA (National Archeological Museum of Reggio di Calabria). Among the exhibits are the statues of two warriors known as the "Bronzi di Riace", Greek masterpieces of the 5th century BC. Greek style gives way to Byzantine architecture in the CATTOLICA DI STILO, to the northeast of Reggio, a tiny cube with a Greek cross, with three altars on the eastern side and five cupolas, a design which was frequently reproduced in the Byzantine world during the 11th and 12th centuries.

UNDER THE VOLCANO: CATANIA AND ETNA

The capital of the Etna region and the communities on the slopes of the "muntagna" coexist uneasily with Mongibello: a relationship combining gratitude for the fertility of the soil with a deep respect for the forces of nature.

THE APPEARANCE OF CATANIA. The 18th-century reconstruction, following the earthquake of 1693, focused on the intersection of two roads, the present day streets of

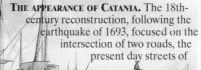

THE HEROES FROM THE SEA
Discovered by chance in 1972, only 330 yards from the Calabrian coast of Riace and at a depth of only 26 feet, are two great bronze warriors dating from the 5th century BC. They belong to the Fidian school and may even be the work of Fidia himself. Possibly intended as a votive offering of Milziade at the temple of Delphi to celebrate the victory of Marathon, they were later removed by the Romans and lost in a shipwreck on the voyage to Rome. Now restored, the sculptures are today on display at the National Archeological Museum of Reggio di Calabria.

ETNA AND CATANIA
There are about 135 recorded eruptions; one of the earliest was in 12 BC, when the molten lava reached Catania, but this was nothing compared with the eruption of 1669 when parts of the city and the port were completely destroyed by 3 days of earthquake and 122 days of volcanic activity. The countryside around Catania was devastated and the city was

Sangiuliano and Etnea (forming an area like the Quattro Canti in Palermo ▲ *448*). East of Via Etnea the city expanded unobstructed in the 19th century. New districts sprang up as urbanization continued and the State acquired ecclesiastical properties and redeveloped open spaces and old buildings. Despite work to strengthen the port, the development of the railroad actually separated the city from the sea. Ancient walls were demolished to make way for two wide roads – Marina and Plebiscito – and the post-war period has seen an intense building program. Catanians did not, however, lose ther vivacity and their spirit of initiative, and the city has successfully acquired a new look.

PIAZZA DEL DUOMO. *Voyage pittoresque*, a magnificent book illustrated by the 18th-century French artist Houel, contains a splendid picture of Catania's main piazza, showing preparations for a procession, with the elephant of the fountain standing out magnificently against the sky. At this point where the main streets of the town converge, the central view is dominated by the FONTANA DELL'ELEFANTE ★ (the elephant fountain). Created by Giovan Battista Vaccarini in 1736, it has become a symbol of the city, and it inspired a similar work by Bernini, the Minerva in Rome ▲ *365*. The artist made use of various archeological finds, including an elephant in volcanic stone from the Roman period, an Egyptian granite obelisk, and a column from the Roman circus. Notice the Baroque Council building, the early 18th-century former seminary of the Chierici, and the cupola of the Convent of Sant'Agata as you approach the DUOMO. Described as *Ecclesia Munita* because of its robust walls, the duomo was founded by Count Roger and was dedicated to Saint Agatha (the patron saint of Catania). It was constructed between 1078 and 1093 on the site of a Roman spa. After being damaged in the 1693 earthquake, it was sympathetically rebuilt using original materials. Its numerous attractive features include the façade by Caccarini, completed in 1761 in the style of Borromini; the 16th-century portal; Antonio Bataglia's cupola constructed at a slightly later date; the mid-19th-century bell tower; and the striking interior with three colonnaded naves, a Norman apse, the Treasury, and the Chapel of Saint Agatha with early 16th-century works that are behind a wrought-iron gate.

swamped by destitute refugees.

"U LIOTRU"
The black elephant of the fountain was supposed to ward off the dangers of Etna, according to the Arab geographer Al-Idrisi, writing in the mid 12th century.

> **"No-one can look at this city without admiring it, so often has it risen from volcanic fires, reborn like a phoenix from the ashes, more beautiful than before."**
>
> *Italy In Words And Pictures*, 1838

VIA VITTORIO EMANUELE II. The other axis of the urban reconstruction planned by Giuseppe Lanza, Duke of Camastra, was called the "street of the Corso" before the Unification. It runs in a straight line from east to west past the Piazza del Duomo, and is one of the most elegant streets of Catania. There are many civil and ecclesiastical examples of the Catanian Baroque: the Gravina-Cruyllas Palace (birthplace of Vincenzo Bellini), dating from the early 18th century; the churches of San Placido (1769), of Sant'Agata alle Sciare (reconstructed in 1720) and of the Trinity, with the concave façade flanked by Francesco Battaglia's bell towers; the building of the convent of Sant'Agostino and the adjacent church, as well as the neoclassical Cutelli college. At the highest point on Via Landolina, a brief walk takes you to the Biscari palace which was built in the mid-18th century and used as a museum housing a collection that has since been transferred to the Museo Comunale (City museum).

CHIESA SANT'AGATA. Vaccarini's masterpiece of harmony and elegance was built between 1735 and 1767 in the form of a Greek cross with a majestic curved façade. The cupola is on top of an octagonal tower. The interior is of striking contrast between the white stucco, the yellow marble altars and the elegant designs on the floor paving in white marble against a gray background.

TEATRO BELLINI (TEATRO MASSIMO). The theater was opened on May 31, 1890 with a gala performance of the opera *Norma* and was dedicated to its Catanian composer Vincenzo Bellini. The theater was the work of Carlo Sada, who adapted an unfinished building, in an eclectic style.

MUSEO BELLINIANO. Based in the Gravina Palace, which is reached by way of Piazza San Francesco, the museum was opened in 1930 and houses various items relating to the life of the early 19th-century composer Vincenzo Bellini.

ladies". Born in 1801, Bellini ended his brief life in 1835 at Puteaux, in the Paris suburb; his remains were transfered for burial to the city of his birth in 1876.

GIOVAN BATTISTA VACCARINI
This Palermitan architect (1702–1768), who studied at Rome at the school of Carlo Fontana, reached Catania in 1730. His work embraced the liveliest aspects of Roman Baroque and the style of Borromini. He was one of the major architects involved in the reconstruction of the city following the earthquake of 1693.

▲ THE LITTLE SICILIAN CART

In many Italian regions the farm carts were the pride and joy of their owners, who decorated them with paintings and carvings. Only in Sicily, however, have they reached the status of masterpieces in wood, painting and wrought iron. The typical Sicilian *carretto* has two wheels and is drawn by a single animal. The load box is made of panels painted with lively historical scenes or episodes from stories of the Paladin Knights of France, also a source of inspiration for the puppet theater ▲ 58. The connecting parts are usually carved.

The decoration of the Sicilian *carretto* combines diverse elements of folk art with one of the richest and most vital imaginative traditions in Europe.

Antique carts and period pieces of decoration are avidly sought by collectors, but artisans today are still producing work which is worthy of the tradition.

The connecting panel at the back, called the "key", consists of a bas-relief made of wood.

In the most elaborate examples, no part of the *carretto* is left undecorated. The designs are often planned around the structural function of the part.

The expertise of the artisan is given free rein in the wrought-iron decorations.

"I MALAVOGLIA"
Aci Trezza is one of the seven localities to the north of Catania that have Aci as a prefix. Here Giovanni Verga set his novel *I Malavoglia,* the story of a family of fishermen whose world ends with the death of the patriarchal civilization and the ancient wisdom that is no longer needed. Luchino Visconti was inspired by the novel and, in 1948, at Aci Trezza, he made the film *The Earth Trembles*.

REALISM
Catania is known as the cradle of Italian realism; here Verga and Luigi Capuana lived, and Federico De Roberto stayed here. These writers knew how to marry Sicilian culture with Italian and European traditions, creating a new and powerful literature.

THE ROMAN THEATER. The semicircular Roman theater, the seating of which is raised by strong walls, held seven thousand spectators. It is on the southern side of the slope of the ancient acropolis; the gradations of limestone were divided into nine sectors by access corridors made of lava stone.The structure has only been partially explored as it is buried under more recent constructions. Adjacent is the smaller odeon, also in semicircular form, which is constructed entirely in lava rock, with seating for 1,300.

VIA GARIBALDI. Originally called Strada San Filippo, then Ferdinanda, the street was finally named after the hero of the Thousand ● *44*. It is lined with elegant palaces and crowded shops, noble residences and cultural buildings, mostly in an 18th-century style, sometimes with 19th-century decorations. As it runs from Piazza del Duomo to the Garibaldi door it cuts through the square-shaped Piazza Mazzini, surrounded by airy porticos with balustrades, supported by thirty two columns of marble from a Roman basilica.

GIOVANNI VERGA'S HOUSE. This late 1700's building with an entrance on Via Sant'Anna (a street between Via Vittorio Emanuele and Via Garibaldi), is where the writer lived, and then died there in 1922. The second floor, used as a museum, preserves furniture and artefacts belonging to Verga, such as the two thousand volumes of the library of foreign and Italian authors often with a dedication, while a good part of his correspondence is collected in the university library.

CASTELLO URSINO. Built by Frederick II between 1239 and 1250 on a promontory once surrounded by the sea, to reinforce the defence system of the eastern part of the island. It has walls over 6 feet thick and angular towers 100 feet high. The entrance is an acute arch surmounted by the Swabian eagle catching a hare in its claws.

Head of "kouros" of the 5th century BC, from the collection of the princes of Biscari.

The castle has seen a lot of changes: the Aragonese modified the original castle, making it a more comfortable place to live. In the 16th century it was enclosed by walls and the bastion of San Giorgio was added to the south; next, it was fortified on the city side; it was partly covered by lava in the eruption of 1669 and damaged by the earthquakes of 1693 and 1818. The building was restored somewhat inadequately in 1934, in an attempt to restore it to its former grandeur. In the grounds of the castle the MUSEO COMUNALE was opened in 1934, bringing together works from various state collections (including those in the Biscari Palace) and ecclesiastical ones. In addition to numerous Greco-Roman archeological finds and works from the medieval, Renaissance and Baroque periods, there are collections of weapons, coins, gold artefacts and antique furniture.

VIA DEI CROCIFERI. This street has some of the most beautiful 18th-century architecture, much of an impressive testimony to the economic and social power of Catholicism. Along its brief length there are five churches and four convents and the statues on these buildings are made more visible by the slope of the path. Past the Convento dei Crociferi (Convent of the Crossbearers) and the Church of San Camillo, the street ends at the entrance to the 18th century Villa Cerami. From there you can comfortably reach, on the piazza of the same name, the CHIESA SANT'AGATA AL CARCERE, erected upon the Roman prison in which the patron of Catania was incarcerated. The building has a beautiful 13th-century portal taken from the old duomo which collapsed in the earthquake of 1693. The arch of the Church of SAN BENEDETTO at the beginning of the street unites the two buildings of the Badia Grande and the Badia Piccola: tradition has it that it was erected in one night in 1704 to make the joining of the two parts of

THE PATRON SAINT OF CATANIA
In the rich Catanian literature on saints, the figure of Sant'Agata stands out. According to tradition the beautiful child, having refused the Roman proconsul Quinziano, was put in prison and was martyred in 251. The cell where she died is incorporated into the Church of Sant'Agata al Carcere. The remains of the saint, locked inside a box, are preserved in the

cathedral and are carried every year in a procession through the old city. The feast lasts three days from February 3, with alternate sacred and secular celebrations.

THE EARTHQUAKE AND THE RECONSTRUCTION
Already half destroyed by the eruption of 1669 ▲ 466, in 1693 Catania was struck by an earthquake which razed the whole urban area to the ground. Only a few private houses and several churches remained. The city was rebuilt with wide streets and wide piazzas, spaced out to permit escape in the event of further earthquakes.

THE CIVIC LIBRARY
To the right of the façade of San Nicolo, after a little tree-filled piazza and a small arch, you enter Via della Biblioteca where, up stairs of lava stone, you find the Civic Library. This Baroque building has the famous Vaccarini room, a wide rectangle illuminated by oval windows. The library has 170,000 rare books, codices and manuscripts.

ON THE SLOPES OF ETNA
For thousands of years man has lived with the fire of the volcano, and entire generations have worked the land and cultivated the lower slopes. These lower slopes were thickly wooded until the 1800's, but now only 37,000 acres of woodland remain, mostly oak, ancient chestnut and conifers. Etna is a desert of ashes, lava and yellow sulfur pinnacles. At Sant'Alfio is the legendary "chestnut tree of a hundred horses" which is reputedly more than a thousand years old: in the 14th century, Giovanna of Anjou and her hundred knights are said to have sheltered under its branches.

the monastery a *fait accompli* for the city authorities. To the left rises an early 18th-century church of the same name, with a high staircase closed in by an iron grate and a great wooden door depicting scenes from the life of the saint. The Baroque Church of SAN GIULIANO, in front of the ex-college of the Jesuits, is attributed to Vaccarini. Its cupola is surrounded by a balcony and has a convex façade. Within the octagonal interior is the major altar, resplendent with precious marble, golden bronze and a 14th-century painted cross. The Church of SAN NICOLO and the convent of the same name are approached by Via dei Crociferi which runs into Via dei Gesuiti and should be followed to Piazza Dante, where the imposing unfinished façade of the grandiose building emerges. Work was begun in 1687 but was interrupted by the earthquake of 1693, then continued by the architects Francesco Battaglia and later Stefano Ittar; the latter is responsible for the cupola. The sober and austere interior houses 7 of the 11 richly engraved and colored church candles that are carried in procession during the festival of Sant' Agata ▲ *471*. On the left of the church is the Benedictine Monastery of San Nicolo l'Arena. Built in the middle of the 15th century, damaged by the eruption of 1669, restored and then almost completely destroyed by the earthquake of 1693, it was rebuilt by the great architects of the Catanian reconstruction. Nearby the church is the Civic Library, a center of culture.
VIA ETNEA. This street, sloping slightly and with the bulk of Mount Etna in the background, bisects the city in a north-south direction. It crosses a varied succession of piazzas and intersections and is so full of life that, as Antonio Aniante wrote, "even the central crater of the volcano seems dead by comparison". It was once paved with squares of volcanic rock, as if to symbolize the destructive force of nature.

Red Valerian (far left) is often found growing on the slopes of Etna, as is wild Iris.

The patient and determined reconstruction work of the inhabitants of the plain has helped it to become the main stage of daily life in Catania, animated at all hours by its shops, meeting places and the many ice-crea 1 parlors. Of particular interest are the examples of 18th-century architecture, such as the classical façade of the Chiesa dei Cappuccini which can be found in Piazza Stesicoro. This contrasts with the remains of the Roman amphitheater at the edge of the ancient city which dates from the 2nd century. Now covered with shells of volcanic rock, it was capable in ancient times of housing 16,000 spectators.

PIAZZA DELL'UNIVERSITA represents the cultural center of the city. The Palazzo Sangiuliano was reworked by Vaccarini who contributed the great door and the great staircase in the courtyard. The building of the university was modified in the early 19th century according to a plan by Battaglia. The library is one of the finest in Sicily with over 210,000 volumes, among which are precious codices and manuscripts of the works of Horace and Savonarola.

LA COLLEGIATA (REGIA CAPELLA), erected in the early 1700's by Antonio Amato according to plans by Angelo Italia, is a jewel of the Catanian late Baroque. It is noted for its decorative finesse and the balanced proportions of the façade, the work of Stefano Ittar (1758); frescoed surfaces decorate the interior, with its Latin cross and three naves. The gardens of the Villa Bellini, opened at the end of the 1800's by Giuseppe Sciuti at the center of a prosperous residential zone, are a triumph of botany and fantasy, cultivated with gentle flowering slopes, with 100-year-old trees, date palms and a swan pool behind the bust of Bellini. The two small artificial hills, with a pavilion and cloister in the Moorish style, are dominated by the wide view of Etna.

FROM CATANIA AROUND ETNA ★. Leaving Catania it is possible to complete a circumnavigation of the Etna region in an anticlockwise fashion from the coast as far as the plain.
In the green, fertile countryside the village houses stand in dense rows against the slopes of the great volcano, which are protected today by the Regional Park of Etna.

TAORMINA ★. In 1880 its hotels had twenty beds in total, but in 1896 Kaiser William II, won over by its charm, spoke of it in glowing terms, paving the way for its development as an exclusive tourist destination. The ancient "Tauromenion" sacred to Apollo stands on a far spur of Mount Tauro, jutting

THE REGIONAL PARK OF ETNA
Etna, the highest active volcano in Europe, is 10,902 feet high and stands within the 198,000 acres of the Regional Park of Etna, which was created in 1981.
The active section of the central crater includes the Great Gorge and the New Mouth. There are also two secondary craters, one on the northeast side, one on the southeast.

THE ALCÀNTARA GORGE
The river has carved a 60-foot deep channel through an old lava flow. The impressive effect confirms how in Sicily "the idyllic is always mixed with the wild" (Ugo Ferroni).

THE GRECO-ROMAN THEATER
It is the biggest in Sicily after that of Syracuse. Having extended the original construction, the Romans held hunts, gladiatorial shows, and possibly shows of nautical combat. From the top of the spectator area the view extends from the snows of Etna to Aspromonte in Calabria.

out into the Ionian sea. The elegant network of ancient streets converges on the Greco-Roman theater, which is magnificently situated in one of the most celebrated landscapes of Sicily. During the summer season the theater comes alive with many performances and there is a continuous show of entertainment from various actors, comedians and artists, with the public and the city itself acting as a backdrop.

RANDAZZO. Founded by the Byzantines at the divide of the Alcantara (with its amazing gorge cut by the flow of water) and Simeto rivers. This city has an urban profile which is reminiscent, like all the villages found within the Etna region, of the Norman and Baroque periods. Although it was modified in the 16th and 19th centuries, the 13th-century Basilica di Santa Maria, built in volcanic rock, still has a grandiose 15th-century door on the right side. The Museum of Natural Sciences houses one of the most important ornithological collections to be found in the whole of Italy.

ADRANO. Founded by Dionysius of Syracuse, this town carries the name of the pre-Hellenic god to whom a famous sanctuary on the slopes of Etna was dedicated. The castle, which is a bare, four-sided fortress, dates back to the Norman period; Adelasia, niece of King Roger, sponsored the construction of Santa Lucia (1158) and various other churches in the city. The collections of the local archeological museum encompass prehistoric times through to the medieval age.

PATERNO. Although coming to prominence during the Norman period, the town of Paterno had previously been noticed and recorded by the Arab geographer Al-Muquaddasi. Having occupied it, the Hauteville family built the imposing castle whose massive structure is attractively relieved by a loggia and four 14th-century windows.

IONIAN AND RAGUSAN SICILY

Land of Greek legends and home of Baroque art and architecture, the Ionian coast was the heartland of Magna Graecia and Syracuse was its capital; later, the area was a center for the Baroque.

SYRACUSE, THREE MILLENNIA OF HISTORY AND ART. The island of Ortigia, once inhabited by the Greeks, is joined to the mainland by two bridges. Here the nymph Aretusa was reached by Alfeo; here the ten remaining columns of the

temple of Athena competed for the glory of Christ; they are included in the perimeter of the DUOMO; here Frederick II built the Castello Maniace. Here Caravaggio stopped and painted the *Seppellimento di Santa Lucia* (Burial of Santa Lucia) which is preserved, like the *Annunciazione* of Antonello da Messina, in the Regional Gallery. An east coast city with a thousand smells and colors, Syracuse (38 miles from Catania) was the most splendid and proud Greek city of Sicily, so powerful as to emerge victorious from the war against Athens. According to Greek historians its walls extended for 180 "stages" – almost 22½ miles, as a Greek "stage" measures 641 feet, but archeologists maintain that the walls were just 17½ miles long, culminating in the fortress of CASTELLO EURALIO (5th–4th century BC), an intricate labyrinth of galleries. Only the power of Rome with Carthage conquered Syracuse. Today, all that remains of the city sacred to Artemis and to Apollo Karneios is the extensive PARCO ARCHEOLOGICO DELLA NEAPOLI on the mainland. Here is a huge Roman amphitheater; the altar of Ierone II; the Greek theater where Aeschylus' plays were premiered; and the mines of Latomie, which provided five million tons of rock for buildings. To understand the civilizations that have ruled this historical land, visit the MUSEO REGIONALE PAOLO ORSI (Paolo Orsi Regional Museum) in the park of Villa Landolina.

THE DUOMO OF SYRACUSE

Damaged by the earthquakes of 1542 and 1693, the duomo stands on the highest point of the island of Ortigia, on a site where the Siculi had a sacred building even before the Greeks built a temple in the 5th century BC. The cathedral was built over the Greek temple, using parts of it in its own structure. Inside are rich marble decorations, wrought iron, spiral columns and a grandiose Baroque altar supported by columns from the Greeks' temple of Athena.

GALLERIA REGIONALE DI SIRACUSA

Housed in the Parisio and Bellomo palaces, the Regional Gallery of Syracuse preserves statues, paintings, and sacred vestments from the churches of the townships. Here it is possible to see the 14th-century painted beam from the ceiling of the duomo. There are major paintings by Antonello da Messina and Caravaggio in the art gallery on the second floor.

**THE BAROQUE
SPLENDOR AT
NOTO ★.** "Noto
is a honeycomb of
gold stone"
writes Vincent
Cronin, and
indeed the
Sicilian Baroque
seems to be worked in
honey. A few miles inland
and 20 miles from Syracuse, Noto was the headquarters of
Vallo until 1817. The present town was built following the
destruction of an earlier town by the earthquake of 1693.
A commission headed by Giuseppe Lanza di Camastra saw
to the planning and reconstruction. Engineers, soldiers,
civil architects and religious people of many different
nationalities took part. The result, creating the centers
of Avola and Ferla, was the most interesting and innovative
urban experiment during the 17th and 18th centuries.
There are two piazzas, that of the Mercato (Market) and
the Duomo (with the church dedicated to San Corrado);
they form part of a rational structure based on the square,
a scheme in chessboard style with a grid of streets on which
flourish superb Baroque buildings. The architectural details
and harmonious decorations reflect the highly personalized
styles of the local guilds of workers. The original plans of
the architects who designed the new Noto are held in the
local library, housed in the Nicolaci-Villadorata building.
Here too is a reminder that on March 13, 1996 the cupola
and the ceiling of the central nave of the DUOMO of San
Corrado fell down, drawing public attention to the need
to restore the whole of Noto.

THE CHURCHES OF SAN GIORGIO AT RAGUSA AND AT MODICA.
After the earthquake of 1693 that devasted eastern Sicily,
Ragusa and Ibla were forced to live together, united by an
ancient staircase until 1926, when the two cities joined
together in the name of RAGUSA. Today the city boasts a
cathedral built in the early 1700's and, in the old part of Ibla,
a beautiful duomo dedicated to San Giorgio, built between
1738 and 1775. Set against its 140-foot high cupola is the
neoclassical Circulo di Conversazione on the square. The

**THE CAPITAL OF
THE BAROQUE**
The earthquake of
1693 was catastrophic
for the region, but
even more so for
Noto and Vallo,
where the Baroque
flourished.
Nevertheless, the
Baroque of Noto
which remains has an
element of bizarre
fantasy drawn from
an earlier period. Sir
Anthony Blunt, in
fact, wrote that many
of its ornamentations
"would be perfect on
the façade of a late
Gothic church".

**THE IBLEAN
FARMHOUSE**
Around Ragusa
and Modica it is easy
to recognize these
buildings ● *83* built
in various styles
around an uncovered
courtyard where
grain was winnowed.
In addition to the
farm buildings
and workers'
accommodation,
there was the owner's
house, lived in only
during the harvest.

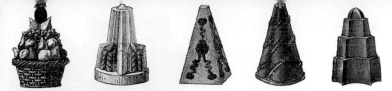

cupola of the duomo is overwhelmingly Baroque. The original Church of MODICA (25 miles from Noto and 10 from Ragusa), is also dedicated to San Giorgio, the fighting saint. Modica was until 1816, the capital of the area of the same name. It was rebuilt after the earthquake of 1693 in sumptuous Baroque around which swirl the serpentine forms of rococo. The church has a bold façade with a tower, high up on the hill of the Eagle.

Metallic molds from a 19th-century engraving for sweets and ice cream. This is a traditional Sicilian treat.

THE IBLEAN HONEY
Hailed as very sweet by the Greek and Latin poets, the honey produced in the Ragusan area was plentiful and was still produced by wild swarms in the 1800's. Until World War Two a liqueur was distilled from it that is not found today. The honey still exists, no longer produced by wandering groups of bees but in properly constructed beehives.

FROM THE GULF OF GELA TO AGRIGENTO

The following summary of the area takes in Greek and Roman history in Sicily and concludes in ancient Trinacria, which is of both historical and artistic interest.

THE WALLS AND THE ACROPOLIS OF GELA. Here in 456 BC Aeschylus died, killed, according to a popular legend, by a turtle dropped by an eagle that was flying high in the sky. Gela, 35 miles west of Ragusa, was founded in 689 BC by Rhodian-Cretian colonies. Today, beaten by the waves of the Sea of Sicily, it sits alongside the petrochemical complex of the ANIC. By leaving the center and traveling just 2½ miles to the west to Cape Soprano, you can get in touch with the ancient past: almost 300 yards of MURA CICLOPICHE (cyclopic walls), 43 feet high and perfectly preserved in the sand over the centuries, evoke the past. They date back to around 338 BC when, with the works of Timoleonte, the city achieved its greatest development. Much of its history was uncovered by a series of archeological excavations in 1948–54. Greek Gela can be found preserved in the rooms of the REGIONAL ARCHEOLOGICAL MUSEUM, in the east of the city.

▲ TOWARD AGRIGENTO

Conversation between men wearing the "coppola", the traditional Sicilian beret at Piazza Armerina.

WHO LIVED AT THE VILLA DEL CASALE? The vastness of the building, its opulence and the elaborate mosaics have favored the hypothesis of a senatorial or imperial presence. The building dates back to the years of the tetrarchs and of Constantine, but the names of Massiminiano and his son Massenzio have also been proposed. This attribution is reinforced by an illustration which depicts Eutropia, wife of Massiminiano, escorted by two servants, together with her children Fausta and Massenzio.

LA VILLA ROMANA DEL CASALE. A few miles west of PIAZZA ARMERINA and around 30 miles from Gela is the Villa Romana. On one point the archeologists agree: the grandiose, colorful and vivid floor mosaics of this immense patriarchal villa of the 3rd and 4th centuries are the result of patience and the skill of groups of African artisans. The exotic animals, the hunters, the great heavily laden boats speak of vast spaces reunited under the empire of the Caesars; the actors, the dancers in revealing costume, the circus races tell of a refined society suspended in the light of a long sunset. The great springs with conduits for running water, the colonnades of the courtyards and of the dining room – the porticos and the rooms testify to a civilization that a short time later would disappear following the barbaric invasions. The villa was to be submerged under river sediment that preserved it until excavations were carried out from 1929 to 1960.

AGRIGENTO, AN ARCHEOLOGICAL SITE OF WORLD IMPORTANCE. At 47 miles from Gela (or 80 miles from Palermo) appear the concrete buildings of present day Agrigento. With approximately 740 acres of development it only occupies the area that was the acropolis of "Akragus", one of the most important Greek cities, spread in the valley underneath for over 4,500 acres. The VALLE DEI TEMPLI ★ (valley of the temples) offers amazing traces of the past: the temple of Hercules (from the ruins rise up eight columns that were re-erected in 1924), the majestic temple of Concordia (one of the best preserved in the entire Greek world), the temple of Juno Lacinia (only partially destroyed by an earthquake in the Medieval period), the vast Hellenistic-Roman quarter (in the houses with courtyards or atriums there are well preserved mosaics and elegant wall decorations), the *bouleuterion* and the temple of the Dioscuri.

THE TEMPLE OF CONCORDIA The temple is well preserved because it became a church around the 6th century. The building became in fact a basilica, with three naves. Mass was celebrated here until 1748 when the church was deconsecrated and it was returned to its original form.

Cagliari
and Sardinia

▲ CAGLIARI AND SARDINIA

1 COSTA DEL SUD   2 NORA   3 CAGLIARI   4 SU NURAXI (BARUMINI)   5 GIARA DI GESTURI   6 THARROS

Cagliari, the capital city and port, stands at the center of Sardinia's largest bay, which lies at the southern end of the island.

"The women followed one another along the narrow street, stiff in their festive costumes, their hands folded on their embroidered aprons, or with children in their arms . . . the sun made the gold of their belts sparkle and illuminated their beautiful Grecian profiles, but the doctor's eyes were on Zana alone, as if she were gifted with magical powers, and the malicious old women thought: 'The daughter of Tomas Acchittu has given him the magic potion to drink!' . . .**"**
Grazia Deledda,
La volpe
(The Wolf)

Ancient fortifications, impressive monuments and delightful open spaces enhance the city's appeal as the starting point for a holiday on this beautiful and historically fascinating island. Sardinia is internationally renowned for its charm and hospitable atmosphere. It also has a richness of landscape and heritage that extend far beyond the beauty of its resorts and its coastline's succession of picturesque inlets and beaches. The rugged interior, dotted with unspoilt lakes, adds one dimension to enjoy. Another can be found in the ancient sites, such as Nora, where there are extensive archeological excavations of the Phoenecian and Roman site. Exploring the island begins with Nora and continues along the Costa del Sud, where inlets are interspersed with deserted beaches. The second itinerary leads northward from Cagliari to the hills of Marmilla and the Sinis peninsula, stopping first at the prehistoric site Su Naraxi, continuing through the unspoilt landscape of the Giara dei Gesturi, then going on to Tharros, which competes with Nora in archeological importance. The third itinerary explores the isolated northwest coast, a spectacular setting for medieval Bosa (143 miles from Cagliari) and Alghero, whose 14th-century Catalan origins can still be perceived. The fourth itinerary includes megalithic remains from the Nuraghic period, and a succession of splendid Romanesque-Pisan churches between Sassari and Ozieri. Finally, the fifth itinerary explores the Gallura region in northeast Sardinia, passing through wild granite mountains to the exclusive Costa Smeralda, where the dazzlingly beautiful Maddalena archipelago stretches through the cobalt blue sea towards Corsica in the north.

"He too became quiet: it seemed . . . that he heard only the murmur of the wind on the shores, like the far off beating of the sea. Antioco felt the flutter of wings above his head. He turned to look and saw on the rocks the old hunter, the tame eagle, with its beautiful stong beak like a little horn and the black fan of his wings opening wide and beating slowly."
Grazia Deledda,
La madre
(The Mother)

"The Nuraghs bear testimony not only to a prosperous and historically useful civilization, but also to a spiritual idea that left signs of a monumental and enduring nature. No other example of island architecture, either from antiquity or even from recent times, reveals the sense of power, majesty and religious faith that emanates from the Nuraghic buildings."
Giovanni Lilliu,
Le vie d'Italia
(The Lives of Italy)

481

**THE "CITY OF
THE DEAD"**
In the necropolis of
Tuvixeddu you can
visit numerous
excavated
Carthaginian tombs,
10 feet deep. Among
the most beautiful,
going back to the 6th
and 7th centuries BC,
are those of Ureo and
of the Warrior, in
which the Punic god
Sid is depicted. The
funeral vestments
found in the tombs
are now located in

the National
Archeological
Museum of Cagliari.

**ELEONORA
OF ARBOREA**
Of the four ancient
subdivisions of
Sardinia, Arborea,
with its capital of
Oristano, was ruled
from 1383 to 1404 by
Eleonora. For the
Sardinians she

became the symbol
of liberty and of wise
administration: her
Carta de Logu was an
ensemble of judicial
norms that remained
in force for about
four centuries.

The area that corresponds to
the modern city was
inhabited from Neolithic times by
people who lived in the grottos of
Sant'Elia, on Mount Urpino and Mount Claro. It also
attracted the Phoenicians, Carthaginians, Romans, the
maritime republics ● *38* and finally the Spanish and
Piemontese. Around the 8th century BC, the Phoenicians used
it as an anchorage but it was not until the 6th century BC that
the Carthaginians developed the first nucleus of the city.

A CITY OF SEA AND STONE. At that time it was known as *Karalis*
(or *Caralis*), a name which has been linked by some to the
Phoenician god *Quaral*, and by others to the Mediterranean
word *cara*, meaning rock or rock worker. It was precisely in
the rocks of the limestone ridges between the port and the
interior that the Carthaginians excavated the characteristic
underground tombs of the Tuvixeddu necropolis, and where
the Romans, succeeded by the Carthaginians in 238 BC,
carved out the vast amphitheater.

FROM BYZANTIUM TO PISA. At the close of the Roman era,
the Vandals, Goths, Byzantines and Arabs fought over
Cagliari with varying degrees of success. Liberated
from ties with far off Byzantium, the Sardinian city
became one of the principal centers of judicial
power in the period from 1000 to 1200. Cagliari
was the only autonomously governed city in
Sardinia, the island being divided into four
territories: Cagliari, Torres, Gallura to the north
and Arborea in the center. The city went further
into decline when, for reasons of safety, the judge
of Cagliari chose as the premises for his
government the peripheral city of Santa Igia, in the
lagoon of San Gilla. This autonomy was destined to
clash with the interests of Genoa and above all Pisa (at
the time powerful maritime republics), and around 1217 saw
the fortification of the city, works which are still visible today
in the walls and in the towers of the Castello quarter. The
Pisan stronghold resisted until 1326, the first year of a long
feudal Aragon domination, under which Cagliari became one
of the crucial ports for the aggressive Mediterranean politics
of the Spanish monarchy, culminating in 1535 with the
expedition of Charles V against Tunis ▲ *488*.

> **"A** SUPERB, VAST GULF STRETCHES OUT IN FRONT OF CAGLIARI,
> ITS MOUTH TURNED TO THE SOUTHEAST WIND."
>
> *ITALY IN WORDS AND PICTURES,* 1838

THE "PERFECT FUSION". In 1720, after a brief period of Austrian occupation, the history of Cagliari and the island entered its "Italian" period with the arrival of the Savoys. The island population had been excluded from public life during the period of Spanish rule; after several significant anti-Savoy moves on the wave of the French Revolution, the people regained the right to participate in political life under Carlo Felice and Carlo Alberto, who in 1847 conceded the "perfect fusion" of the island with Piedmont. Sardinia was no longer burdened by vice-regal powers and customs restrictions, and the civil and penal codes of the Savoy states were extended to the island. When Sardinia ceased to be a Piedmont colony around 1860, the fortified barrier around the quarters of Stampace, Marina and Villanova was knocked down, allowing the development of the bourgeois city beyond its historical confines and the opening of the grand avenues, some tree-lined, such as the Viale Trieste, Via Roma and Via Sonnino.

ITALIAN CAGLIARI. The passage of Cagliari from fortified piazza to a city of the kingdom and then of the republic marks the inclusion of Sardinia in the historical events of the new nation. A period of industrial development followed, that was based on oil refining and mineral resources. One of the major ports of Italy for freight movement, Cagliari, with its 176,000 inhabitants, remains essentially tied to commercial activities and to the service industry.

THE PRESENT DAY APPEARANCE. The tragic bombings of 1943 and the considerable damage wrought by the building boom in the post-war period were not enough to destroy Cagliari's charm. From the air, one of Cagliari's most striking features is the surrounding lagoon, but sadly this is ever decreasing as residential building spreads further outward. Decorated in 1947 with the gold medal as a reward for military valor, Cagliari has been the capital of the autonomous region of Sardinia since 1949.

THE SAVOYS AND SARDINIA
In 1836 at Turin, Carlo Alberto was thanked for having pulled the island from a state of abandon and negligence: "Already one of the fastest points of embarkation it takes just hours to cross the sea, so that the desired novels are more certain to arrive on time. Because of the nearness, good communications and comfortable rooms, there is no doubt that they will pull in crowds from far and wide. There will be erudite researchers, and those who want the innocent amusement of festive hunts . . ."

VIA ROMA AND THE PORT
The Pisan and Spanish bastions overlooking the harbor were demolished in the 1800's to make way for a porticoed coast road, an appropriate stage for the *passegiata* of Cagliari families. At the front of Via Roma the port opens out, a source of life to the city since Phoenician times, and divides into the basins of Levante and Ponente (east and west). Today thirty million tons of merchandise and about half a million passengers pass through it every year.

483

"KASTRUM KARALIS"

The story of Castello has its beginnings in 1217, when the hill was surrendered to the Pisans. The center of the city is characterized by a dense network of streets and noble buildings beside modest dwellings and craftsmen's shops.

CASTELLO

For the Sardinians, Cagliari is "su Casteddu", the Castle. Ancient fortress and historical seat of political and religious power, for centuries it has expressed the aristocratic and administrative spirit of the capital. Today, Castello is the city's treasure house of monuments and provides a superb view not only of the Villanova, Stampace and Marina districts, but also of the port and the marsh of Molentargius.

SANTA MARIA ★. As you ascend the steps that lead to Piazza Carlo – the ancient "plazuela" of the Spanish – with the Piazza Palazzo above, the cathedral comes into view. It is without doubt the most important monument

of Cagliari for the richness of its interior, divided into three naves. Among the many works the PULPITO (pulpit) stands out, placed against the contrafaçade with the sides of the main great door, work of Guglielmo da Pisa. Built for the cathedral of the Tuscan city in 1159–62, it was donated to Cagliari in 1312. To adapt it to its new premises, the pulpit was dismantled in the 1600's into two parts, while the four splendid lions supporting it were placed together at the feet of the raised PRESBITERIO (presbytery). Under the presbytery the 17th-century SANTUARIO (sanctuary) contains three chapels designed to house the

"What symbol the Pisans wanted this forest creature to embody is not clear. What is clear is that, in Medieval times, the elephant carried great prestige and the *Bestiari*, in part repeating Pliny, reported marvelous things about it. Clemente Alessandrino was convinced that it waved its trunk to greet the sun in the morning and the moon in the evening."
    Francesco Alziator

TERRACES LOOKING OUT ON THE CITY
The most obvious Savoy addition to the fortress of Castello is the fort of St Remy which takes its name from the first Savoy viceroy. It was built between 1899 and 1902 as a panoramic promenade. A neoclassical viewpoint takes you through a triumphal arch to the stairway up to the terrace of Santa Caterina. Higher still, another terrace dedicated to Umberto I provides an impressive panorama of the city below. On Sundays a fleamarket is held here.

martyrs' relics previously kept in the Church of San Saturno. The major chapel is decorated with 584 Baroque rosettes.
THE TOWERS. Of the four towers erected by the Pisans to fortify Castello, only the towers of San Pancrazio and that of the Elephant remain, dating from the early 1300's. The latter takes its name from the marble elephant on a ledge, about 30 feet high, overlooking the Via dell'Universita.

485

Bracelet in gold with winged scarab from Tharros, 7th–6th century BC.

LA PURISSIMA. This 16th-century church stands in Via Lamarmora, the ancient "Ruga Mercatorum" of Castello. Along with a convent (closed in the 19th century) it was built by the Cagliari noblewoman Gerolama Rams. Clearly visible on the Gothic portal is the coat of arms of the church.

LA CITTADELLA DEI MUSEI

The open spaces on Mount Castello, which were used from 1825 for Carlo Felice's Arsenal, are today occupied by the Citadella dei Musei, which integrates Punic and Roman remains with the modern museum structures planned by Pietro Gazzola and Libero Cecchini. The Citadella houses, besides several university premises, the National Archeological Museum, the National Painting Gallery, the Siamese Cardu Museum and the collections of anatomical waxworks of Clemente Susini. Emerging from the Cittadella and passing the public gardens to the north, you reach the GALLERIA COMUNALE D'ARTE MODERNA (The District Gallery of Modern Art).

NATIONAL ARCHEOLOGICAL MUSEUM. This museum is the most important in Sardinia and houses evidence of the island's successive cultures from the Neolithic age (6000 BC) to the late Medieval period (8th century). The collection of major interest is, however, that of the Nuraghic civilization (1600–500 BC), where you can admire the bronze statues,

weapons, casts, tools and ceramics. The remains of the Phoenician-Punic occupations are displayed, such as the inscriptions of Nora ▲ 492, which together with the funereal vestments of the necropolis of Sulci (Sant'Antioco) and the jewels of Tharros ▲ 494 give a good idea of the level of skill and the trading activity prevalent on the island from the 11th to the 2nd centuries BC.

ANCIENT BRONZE FIGURINES Created between the 11th and 6th centuries BC and preserved in the National Archeological Museum of Cagliari, they constitute a fascinating artistic testimony to Sardinian prehistory. The figurines, made by the lost wax method, represent tribal chiefs, warriors, mothers and devoted shepherds offering animals or crops, or even supernatural beings with four eyes and four arms.

GALLERIA COMUNALE D'ARTE MODERNA The gallery's premises are in the small neoclassical building that served as a munitions depot and which was readapted at the end of the 1920's. It is located at the end of the public gardens and houses sculptures and paintings of artists of the Italian neo-Avant garde and works of 20th-century Sardinian authors. It is used for temporary exhibitions. The building also houses the civic library and the historic archives of the Council.

> "A CITY WITHOUT TREES, WITHOUT COVER, RISING RATHER BARE AND PROUD, REMOTE AS IF BACK IN HISTORY, LIKE A TOWN IN A MONKISH, ILLUMINATED MISSAL."
>
> D.H. LAWRENCE

PINACOTECA NAZIONALE. The National Art Gallery holds collections of Sardinian works of art, of predominantly Spanish inspiration, dating from the 1400's to the 1700's, with an additional annex of pictures and sculptures of the 19th and 20th centuries. The beautiful collection of 15th-century tables ▲ *496* deserves special attention.

PIAZZA YENNE, MARINA AND STAMPACE

In the district of Stampace, Piazza Yenne, dedicated to the Savoy Viceroy, runs down as far as the coastal road and the small square of Carlo Felice. It is the true center of the city. The neighboring quarters of Marina, the ancient Roman commercial "castrum", and Stampace, whose inhabitants are called "cuccuru cottu" (hard heads), because of their argumentative nature, still preserve the atmosphere of the bygone Cagliari.

SANT' EFISIO is dedicated to the Christian martyr, sent to Sardinia by Diocletian to fight the Barbaracini. He was killed in Nora in 303 for having refused to renounce the Christian faith. In 1652, to save the city from the plague, the saint's protection was invoked. Every year a great procession in traditional costume uniting religion and folklore leaves from the church ▲ *492*, in an rite of thanksgiving.

LARGO CARLO FELICE. Running between the statue of the King of Savoy and the arcades of Via Roma is the small square of Carlo Felice, a product of 19th-century town planning. At no. 10, in Palazzo Accardo, you will find the CRIPTA DI SANT'AGOSTINO (Crypt of Saint Augustine, 4th–5th centuries). Legend has it that in 496 the relics of the saint were brought here from his birthplace of Ippona. In the 8th century the remains were sent to the Church of San Pietro in Ciel d'Oro in Pavia.

SANT'AGOSTINO. The beautiful church – one of the few late Renaissance examples remaining in Sardinia – was planned in 1577 by Giorgio Palearo, called Frattino. It has a sober façade and an interior with a Greek cross, where the golden altar and a medieval statue of the saint will be relocated after restoration work. The excavations have revealed Roman remains which seem to link the whole area to a thermal bath complex.

THE DISTRICTS
Castello, Marina, Stampace and Villanova are the four historical districts that once defined the four souls of the city; they have now merged to form modern Cagliari.

CARLO FELICE
The statue in Roman style of the viceroy of Sardinia (eventually the Savoy king) is strangely pointing away from the road which he had constucted in 1822–9 and which joins Cagliari to Porto Torres. The nearby milestone column indicates the exact beginning of Strada Carlo Felice.

THE VIPER'S GROTTO
Eternally preserved here is the love of Attilia Pomptilla who begged the gods to exchange her own life for that of her husband Cassio Filippo. The two vipers sculpted on the front of the tomb (1st century) are a symbol of fidelity and amorous pleasures.

LAKE OF MOLENTARGIUS
Under threat today from the pressure of urban expansion from Cagliari and Quartu, the lake of Molentargius (1,200 acres) was already used by the Phoenicians for the collection of salt. Today it is a refuge for many varieties of bird life, particularly the elegant pink flamingo.

SAN MICHELE. At the lower end of Via Azuni, in the heart of the Stampace district, stands what is perhaps the most beautiful Baroque church on the island (12th century), constructed by the Jesuits. The porticoed area in limestone opens onto a wide atrium, where the PERGAMO (pulpit) (formerly in San Francesco di Stampace) is preserved. Charles V would have listened to mass here before the expedition to Tunis, which set off from Cagliari in 1535 ▲ *452*.
ROMAN MONUMENTS. The most important monument of the long Roman domination on the island is the AMPHITHEATER (2nd century), in Viale Fra Ignazioda Laconi. The steps and the auditorium are preserved in good condition. Restoration has facilitated its use as a venue for shows once more. A little further on, across the botanic gardens, you can visit the remains of the VILLA DI TIGELIO, named for a Sardinian friend and musician of Caesar and Cleopatra, who lived in the 1st century BC. The building consists of three "domus" in the four-columned atrium which still contains fragments of decoration of the period. In the precincts is the necropolis of Tuvexiddu ▲ *482*, but this is more of a curiosity than an item of artistic interest. Finally to the east, toward the Punic necropolis, is the GROTTA DELLA VIPERA (the Viper's grotto).

VILLANOVA AND BEYOND

The historic quarter of Villanova, with the modern building expansion toward the STAGNO DI MOLENTARGIUS (the lake of Molentargius) and the land in between, left by the destruction of the Spanish walls, has a rural character unlike the other quarters of Cagliari. It is not clear why the inhabitants of Villanova gained the epitaph of "inforca Cristus", "Christian's fork", perhaps because the fusion of ethnic groups of this new district spread the belief that in former times it was a Jewish ghetto.

> **"A** NAKED JEWEL OF AMBER WHICH SUDDENLY OPENS UP PINK, IN THE DEPTH OF THE WIDE BRANCH OF THE SEA WHICH HEADS INLAND."
>
> D.H. LAWRENCE

SAN DOMENICO. The beauty of the church, built in 1254 and remodeled in Gothic-Aragonese form in the 15th century, is apparent in the ancient parts of the building, which were incorporated into the new building after the war. In the Gothic church which acts as the crypt is the notable CAPPELLA DEL ROSARIO (1580, fifth from the left) containing the standard that the Sardinian torch-bearing soldiers raised in the battle of Lepanto of 1571. From the adjacent convent you can reach the beautiful chiostro (cloister) square, which was saved from wartime bombing. It was originally constucted in Renaissance style in the 16th century.

SAN SATURNO ★. Not far from Villanova , in Piazza San Cosimo, stands the Paleochristian Basilica of San Saturno (also dedicated to Cosma and Damiano) built between the 5th and 6th centuries on the site of the martyrdom of the Cagliaritan saint. Originally with a Greek cross, it was transformed into a basilica by the Vittorini monks of Marseilles, and was charged by the pope in 1089 with introducing the Latin rite in the place of the African-Eastern one, which had dominated the first centuries of Christianity in Sardinia. The church is currently under restoration and excavation works.

OUR LADY OF BONARIA ★. From Viale Armando Diaz, a picturesque stairway leads from the sea to the hill of the sanctuary and the Basilica of Bonaria. The SANTUARIO was built between 1324 and 1326 by the Aragonese. On the main altar stands the wooden statue of the Madonna, Catalan work of the mid-1400's, which is said to have fallen into the sea during a storm in 1370, from a boat traveling from Spain to Italy. A small column marks the point where the statue is said to have been found. It is now popularly revered as the protector of navigators. The monumental BASILICA at its side dates from 1704, built from the plans of Felice De Vincenti and Giuseppe Viana.

HOLY WEEK AT VILLANOVA
The main religious brotherhoods organize the rites of Holy Week, based on the ceremonial of their Spanish ancestry: The processions of the Mysteries and of the dead Christ, which leave from Piazza San Giacomo, are urged on by the fervent encouragement of the people.

Legend has it that God, having finished creating the world, found Himself with a handful of left-over stones which He threw into the sea. In this way Sardinia and the minor islands were created. One of the finest rocky archipelagos is that of Maddalena, off the northeastern point of Sardinia, which has seven main islands and a number of minor ones. The islands are predominantly made of granite, with sharp and rough rocks, sometimes worked into strange shapes by the wind and rain. Together with the islands of the French-controled archipelago of Lavezzi, they constitute the Parco Internazionale delle Bocche di Bonifacio.

RED MULLET "MULLUS SURMELETUS"
This species, related to the mud catfish, is widespread along the Atlantic and Mediterranean coasts. It has pale red scales and fins that can be yellow, golden yellow or bright red. It is 12–15 inches long.

COMMON OCTOPUS "OCTOPUS VULGARIS"
It has a short, round body, with eight tentacles charged with poison, and a tube for jet propulsion. It often hides between the rocks and, if disturbed, changes color, turning gray to dark brown.

STONE FISH "SCORPAENA SCROFA"
It has a big head, thorny cheeks and is a reddish color marbled with brown. It reaches 10 inches in length. The first rays of the dorsal fins are linked to poison glands and can give a painful stab if trodden on.

MORAY EEL "MURAENA HELENA"
A species typical of the rocky coastal zones, it lives in holes and narrow recesses. Often only its head protrudes. It has a large mouth with sharp teeth. It can reach up to 5 feet in length and is rather aggressive.

CONGER EEL "CONGER CONGER"
It is similar to the Moray eel and reaches
6½ feet in length. Endowed with a strong set
of teeth, it crushes the shells of
molluscs on which it feeds. It is
usually found in shallow waters
along rocky and sandy
coasts.

SOLE "DIPLODUS SARGUS"
It reaches 16 inches in length and weighs
up to 4½ pounds. It has sharp, cutting
teeth which point forward. It is a beautiful
silver color with black stripes.

COMMON DOLPHIN "DELPHINUS DELPHIS"
This is the most common dolphin in the Mediterranean. The best time
to see it is in the spring, when there are fewer tourists around. It
reaches 7 feet in length and has dark flippers and a distinctive
yellowish patch on the side. It is a gregarious species and lives in
family groups of up to thirty.

**SARDINE
"SARDINELLA
PILCHARDUS"**
A typical reef fish,
it can grow up to
1 foot in length,
and is greeny-blue
with beautiful purple
overtones. It is
found throughout
the Mediterranean.

MONK SEAL "MONACHUS MONACHUS"
The only seal present in the Mediterranean, it is in grave danger of
extinction. Even though it is seen from time to time around the coasts
of Sardinia, you can no longer speak of a population, but of single
wandering individuals. It is generally a little less than 10 feet long and
weighs up to 750 pounds.

**MANTIS SHRIMP
"SQUILLA MANTIS"**
Also called a
canocchia, it can reach
a size of 10 inches.
The species is
declining as a result
of polluted waters.

Paeonia mascula, a splendid
pink peony, native
to Sardinia.

If Sicily is the "island-crossroad", a melting pot of cultures, Sardinia is the "island-emporium" invaded by many (from the Phoenicians to the Savoys) who sought to strip it of its assets. With its 1,100 miles of coast, the island was unable to defend itself from invaders. Its people could only take refuge inland.

FROM THE GULF OF CAGLIARI TO SULCIS

NORA, THE MOST ANCIENT. Nora was perhaps the first Phoenician center in Sardinia and, indeed, the first city on the island. It is here that the oldest Phoenician inscriptions, dating back to the 9th century BC, have been found. But very few traces of the peoples of Tyre and Sidon remain. The Nora that can be seen today is the

SANT' EFISIO
Every year, on May 1, the procession of Sant' Efisio leaves from the Church of Sant' Efisio in Cagliari ▲ 487 and ends some 20 miles later, near the little Roman Church of Sant' Efisio in Nora, where it remains for three days.
The participants, in traditional costume, who gather from all corners of the island, file past on foot or in carts.

Roman one, which was built over the Phoenician site, destroying it and other structures, including the Punic TEMPIO DI TANIT or the "TOPHET" behind the little Church of Sant' Efisio, and the Phoenician acropolis. In their place, the Romans erected TERME (baths), temples, the FORO (forum), and the splendid TEATRO (theater).
THE CHARM OF THE SOUTH COAST. For those who approach from Cagliari it is a surprise, after miles of beaches, marshes and reeds, to find cliffs which offer stunning views. Along the route from Capo Spartivento to Capo Teulada, the Costa del Sud provides a contrasting perspective to the Costa Smeralda, in the northeast of the island.

BETWEEN MARMILLA AND SINIS

THE MOST IMPORTANT NURAGHIC COMPLEX: SU NURAXI ★.
At Barumini, in Marmilla, close to the Giara di Gesturi plateau, excavations have revealed a fortified village (*nuraghe*) built around a central tower and defended by walls

The first *tophet* was found in the ruins of Carthage in 1820, then others were discovered in Sicily and Sardinia. It was once thought that the Phoenicians and Carthaginians used the *tophet* to sacrifice their first born to the gods, burying the child's ashes in an urn together with sacrificed animals. The suggestion today is that stillborn babies and children who died in the first few years of life were cremated here in a rite designed to stave off future battles.

and angular towers. Of the almost seven thousand Nuraghs spread around Sardinia, that of Barumini is one of the best preserved. The central complex still has two of the three original levels and rises to a height of 45 feet amid the surrounding buildings. The discovery of weapons made of stone and bronze, of cisterns, pestles and mortars, pottery and knives of volcanic glass has enabled the reconstruction of the historic development of the village. Erected around 1500 BC, the great Nuragh was the residence of the king-pastor, surrounded by a series of lower dwellings where his subjects lived. Between the 9th and 8th centuries BC the waves of invaders who were interested in Sardinia made it necessary to fortify the building with four angular towers. After it was partially destroyed in the 7th century BC, the bastion was surrounded with walls and another five towers were built, making it unconquerable for many centuries. It was inhabited until the Roman age, when it started to be filled in with earth.

GIARA DI GESTURI ★: SCENERY AND ATMOSPHERE. This scenic basalt plateau, 5 miles north of Barumini, rises to a height of around 1,600 feet, and Nuraghs have been found on it. What makes the site particularly interesting is its wildlife. Free from buildings, the *giara* is like a great table (7½ miles long and 2½ miles wide) covered by dense Mediterranean vegetation, with occasional woods of oak trees and swamps of water called *paulis*. Here with a bit of luck, you will run into herds of wild Sardinian ponies.

PONIES OF GESTURI
At the right season it is possible to see ponies with almond-shaped eyes and thick manes, grazing in small herds. The French poet, Paul Valéry, encountered the ponies on a trip to Sardinia in 1837 and recalled an unlikely anecdote: "I was told that at times they were put to bed in their owner's bed, instead of going to the stable."

UNDERGROUND TOMB OF SAN SALVATORE
Through a trapdoor in the little Church of San Salvatore of

Sinis, not far from Tharros, you can reach the underground sanctuary dedicated to the pagan cult of water. Rebuilt in the Constantine period, the underground tomb contains decorations from ancient times to the Spanish domination.

SAN PIETRO, THE ANCIENT CATHEDRAL
Just 1 mile from Bosa, up the river Temo, is the Romanesque-Gothic Church of San Pietro, built between the 11th and 13th centuries. The façade is worth noting, divided by acutely shaped arches and softened by three rose windows. In the apse are walls with pagan inscriptions from the nearby Roman and medieval necropoli.

THARROS, PHOENICIAN CITY. Founded by the Phoenicians in about the 8th century BC, then developed as a Punic city and finally (from 238 BC) as a Roman town, it was a port of call on the routes from the East to Marseilles and the Spanish peninsula. Saracen incursions led to Tharros being gradually abandoned in favor of the nearby city of Oristano. The ruins are predominantly from Roman Tharros, with the TERME (2nd-century baths), the CASTELLUM AQUAE (the reservoir for the city's aqueduct) and the CARDO MAXIMUS, which has well-preserved sewer pipeworks. The popular image of Tharros, seen on many of the postcards, is of the two Roman columns built on Turkish foundations by the sea. They were erected in the course of a partial reconstruction of a temple dating from 50 BC. Next to the columns are the remains of the TEMPIO DELLE SEMICOLONNE DORICHE, constructed in the Punic period (4th–3rd century BC). To the north, on the hill of Su Murru Mannu, are traces of a Nuraghic village and Phoenician *tophet*. Still further north is SAN SALVATORE DI SINIS, with its ancient underground tomb.

THE WEST COAST

MEDIEVAL BOSA. Myth has it that the city was founded by Calmedia, daughter of the divinity Sardus Pater. Documented history, however, begins with a Phoenician inscription found nearby which dates back to the 9th century. Present-day Bosa, by the river Temo, was rebuilt around the 12th century after it was destroyed by the Arabs. CASTELLO DI SERRAVALLE stands above it, erected in 1112 by the Malaspina marquis. The walls and towers remain, while in the military piazza is the little 14th-century Church of Nostra

"TOURISTS OF A ROMANTIC DISPOSITION WERE PASSIONATE ABOUT ALGHERO, DRAWN THERE BY THE GROTTOS [OF] CAPO CACCIA ... NEPTUNE'S GROTTO IS THE MOST FAMOUS AND THE MOST SECRET."

GUIDO PIOVENE

Signora di Regnos Altos, with its collection of Italo-Provençal frescos (1350–70). Admiring the city from the stairs of the castle, you can see the extended levels of the roofs belonging to the late medieval buildings of SA COSTA, clinging to the slopes of the hill of Serravalle.

ALGHERO ★, THE BEAUTIFUL CATALAN ENCLAVE. Alghero is an attractive WALLED TOWN surrounded by ramparts and towers built by the Spanish during their long rule, which started in 1354 and finished almost four centuries later when power passed to the Savoys. The Spaniards left their mark on civic and ecclesiastical architecture and on local customs. A language derived from Catalan, in fact, is the one still most commonly used by the Algherese, and in much of its phrasing is closer to Barcelona than to Rome. The historic center which attracts tourists is where the two main 16th-century buildings are located – the CATTEDRALE (Piazza del Duomo) and the church-convent of SAN FRANCESCO (Via Carlo Alberto). The second, in particular, is considered with good reason to be the finest building in the city, combining Gothic-Catalan and late Renaissance architectural touches.

THE CHURCH OF SAN FRANCESCO AT ALGHERO
Of particular interest, in addition to the elaborate decorations of the interior and the hexagonal bell tower, is the cloister made out of sandstone, with fantastic tops to the columns. In this charming setting, concerts and other cultural events are held throughout the summer.

MEILOGU AND LOGUDORO

THE MEGALITHIC REMAINS IN THE VALLEY OF THE NURAGHS. In the triangle defined by Thiesi, Bonorva and Mores we have one of the most interesting concentrations of megalithic structures in Sardinia, of which the neolithic necropolis of SANT'ANDREA PRIU (3000–1800 BC) and the Nuraghic complex of SANTU ANTINE are the finest examples. Built probably in the 9th century BC, Santu Antine is the tallest building from antiquity which has been discovered on Sardinia. Originally 69 feet high, it still stands at 57 feet, despite weathering. The central tower is surrounded by well-preserved fortifications.

THE MYRTLE
Evergreen shrub of the Mediterranean. A sweet liqueur is created by marinating the fruit in alcohol.

ROMANESQUE-PISAN CHURCHES ★. In the space of some 12 miles on the drive from Sassari to Ozieri, you will see the largest concentration of Romanesque architecture on the island. Built in the 12th and 13th centuries as the Camaldolese, Vallombrosans, and Cistercians advanced inland, these churches reinvent the Romanesque Pisan style, incorporating the ideas of local artists in their colors and decorations. In the Basilica of the SANTISSIMA TRINITA DI SACCARGIA, at the top of a column in the portico, is a bas-relief of two cows hiding. This relates not only to the origin of the place (*s'acca àrgia* means "mottled cow"), but also to the miracle of a cow that used to get down on its knees on the site of the church to offer its milk to the brothers of a nearby monastery. In the Basilica of Nostra Signora or SANTA MARIA DEL REGNO DI ARDARA, the façade in dark volcanic rock is most striking. Finally, the splendid Basilica of SANT'ANTIOCO DI BISARCIO is worth a visit, to see the façade decorated with pieces of black and red glassy volcanic rock and an archway with a little rose window, supported on a column which rests on a curled up lion.

THE ART OF "RETABLO"
Of Spanish derivation, these shiny handmade objects in marble, stucco, metal and wood, decorated with paintings and reliefs, are fixed behind the altar. The latin term *retro tabula* means literally "behind the table". In Santa Maria del Regno, at Ardara, are fine examples.

THE HOUSE OF GARIBALDI
Giuseppe Garibaldi withdrew to Caprera in 1856, where he died on June 2, 1882. The "White House", which he built himself, is now part of the museum that holds a collection of his belongings, including books, an armchair (a gift from Queen Margherita), weapons, his legendary red shirt ● *44* and a "poncho" from his South American adventure.

LA GALLURA

This part of Sardinia is best known for its sea and windy weather, but between the mountainous ranges and high plains, the rocks and granite, the Gallura region conceals the traces of a civilization which has its root deep in prehistory.

COSTA SMERALDA ★, TOURISM IN THE SANCTUARY OF NATURE.
Following the coastal road from Olbia to Palau, you pass through the well-known tourist resorts of PORTO ROTONDO, CALA DI VOLPE, PORTO CERVO, and BAIA SARDINIA. Here sailing boats float on a sea of turquoise clarity and the villas lie camouflaged amid Mediterranean vegetation, in surroundings that combine to create one of the most exclusive resort complexes of the Mediterranean.

MARINE LANDSCAPES OF THE MADDALENA ARCHIPELAGO.
Close to Corsiza, the Maddalena archipelago is composed of the seven main islands (not counting rocks and islets) of Maddalena, Caprera, Santo Stefano, Spargi, Budelli, Razzoli, and Santa Maria, which can be reached by ferry from Palau. The islands' splendid underwater landscapes and wildlife have ensured that the archipelago is included as one of the outstanding features of the region's National Park.

PRACTICAL INFORMATION

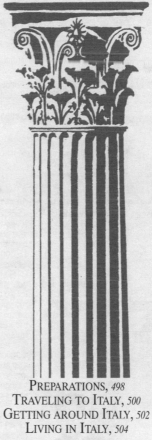

◆ PREPARATIONS

Lying in the center of the Mediterranean, bordered by the Alps in the north and traversed by the Apennines, the Italian peninsula, the "Bel Paese", offers visitors an extraordinary variety of different landscapes and types of architecture. Italy's historic and artistic heritage, its rich background of folk tradition, not forgetting its superb food and excellent wine, make a trip to Italy an unforgettable experience.

ENTRY REGULATIONS

On October 26, 1997, Italy joined France, Spain, Germany, Portugal and the Netherlands in adhering to the regulations of the Schengen Convention for free circulation in Europe.

For citizens of EU countries an identity card or valid passport is all that is required for entry into Italy. All other visitors will need a valid passport and a visa, which is limited to a three-month stay.

PETS

Following EU regulations, dogs and cats are allowed into Italy without restriction, provided they have a veterinary certificate attesting to their good health and a record of necessary vaccinations.

USEFUL INFORMATION

ITALIAN CONSULATES IN THE UK
◆ 38 Eaton Place
London SW1
Tel. 0171-235 9371

◆ 32 Melville Street
Edinburgh E3
Tel. 0131-226 3631

IN THE US
◆ 690 Park Avenue,
New York, NY 10021
Tel. (212) 737 9100

◆ ITALIAN EMBASSY
1601 Fuller Street
NW, Washington DC
20009
Tel. (202) 328 5500

ITALIAN TOURIST OFFICES
IN THE UK
◆ 1 Princes St,
London W1
Tel. 0171-408 1254

◆ ITALIAN INSTITUTE
39 Belgrave Square
London SW1
Tel. 0171-235 1461

IN THE US
◆ 630 Fifth Avenue,
Suite 1565
New York, NY 10111
Tel. (212) 245 4822

◆ 401 North
Michigan Avenue
Chicago, IL 60611
Tel. (312) 644 0990

◆ 12400 Wilshire
Blvd, Suite 550
Los Angeles
CA 90025
Tel. (310) 820 0098

CUSTOMS
For EU citizens, all customs and fiscal regulations for the import and export of goods have been suspended since July 1, 1993. Certain products such as artworks,

antiques, weapons and ammunition will need to be accompanied by the necessary documentation and export authorization.

YOUNG PEOPLE
Foreign students can join the *Centro*

Turistico Studentesco e Giovanile (CTS) and obtain an ISIC membership for 15,000 lire, which allows access to CTS services: youth hostel membership for 20,000 lire; an Agis card which permits a discount for movies, shows, museums, exhibitions and hotels; plus discounts on flights and some rail journeys. Young foreigners under 26 years old who are not students can obtain a CTS Member Card for 43,000 lire, which gives similar concessions to the ISIC card. The CTS can also be joined by groups such as schools, communities and other associations. The card is valid for one calendar year, and so always expires on December 31. CTS offices in Italy:
◆ TURIN
Via Montebello, 2/H
Tel. 011-812 45 34, 812 51 49 or 812 55 65
◆ GENOA
Via S. Vincenzo, 119

Tel. 010-56 43 66
◆ MILAN
Via Sant'Antonio, 2
Tel. 02-58 30 41 21
◆ VENICE
Dorsoduro
Ca' Foscari 3252
Tel. 041-52 056 60, or 520 56 55
◆ BOLOGNA
Largo Respighi, 2/F
Tel. 051-26 18 02 or 23 75 01
◆ FLORENCE
Via dei Ginori, 25/R
Tel. 055-28 5 70, 28 97 21 or 28 97 36
◆ PERUGIA
Verdumbria
Via del Roscetto, 21
Tel. 075-572 70 50 or 572 2 84
◆ ROME
Via Genova, 16
Tel. 06-46791
◆ NAPLES
Via Mezzo
Cannone, 25
Tel. 081-552 79 60 or 552 79 75
◆ BARI
Movida
Via Vito Fornari, 7
Tel. 080-521 32 44
◆ PALERMO
Teen Ager
Via Nicolò Garzilli, 28/G
Tel. 091-33 22 09 or 32 57 52
◆ CAGLIARI
Gio Tour,
Via Balbo, 4
Tel. 070-48 82 60

CLIMATE

Despite the traditional image of Italy as a sunny country, the temperature varies considerably between the summer and winter months. So much so that winter in northern Italy is comparable to the cold climates of northern Europe. Even so, Italy benefits from its enviable climatic conditions of hot, dry summers and mostly mild winters. Italy roughly divides into three different types of climate: continental in the North; temperate in the inland areas; and Mediterranean along the coast. For those who dislike extreme temperatures, the best time to visit Italy is between May and June, or once the extreme heat of summer is over (September and October). These are also the months when the natural beauty of the Italian landscape is at its most magnificent. Visiting cities at these times of year is ideal as it makes it possible to avoid the cold and rainy days of winter, and also the stiflingly hot, tourist-packed days of summer. To truly appreciate the cities of Italy and the rich variety of Italian architecture, take the time to wander through the streets of the older parts of the cities and pay a passing visit to any of the many extraordinary Italian churches and cathedrals.

AVERAGE TEMPERATURES (MIN/MAX) IN °F

	Spring	Summer	Fall	Winter
Turin	46/63	66/80	50/61	27/37
Genoa	54/63	70/82	59/70	41/50
Milan	46/64	66/80	50/64	28/39
Venice	50/46	68/86	52/64	34/43
Bologna	46/64	68/86	52/64	28/41
Florence	46/68	64/90	50/68	34/46
Perugia	45/61	64/84	50/64	36/45
Rome	48/66	66/88	54/72	37/52
Naples	52/66	68/84	55/72	43/54
Bari	52/63	66/86	55/72	41/52
Palermo	52/68	70/88	59/77	45/59
Cagliari	52/66	66/86	54/73	43/57

CLOTHES

For a trip to Italy, make sure you pack the appropriate range of clothing. In spring and fall it is advisable to take medium-weight clothes, a light jumper and a light-weight raincoat. The Italian summer usually means extremely hot, sunny weather, so take sleeveless tops and shorts, but be careful to meet the dress requirements for visits to religious buildings (often covered knees and shoulders are a requirement). A hat is advisable if you are going to be

walking around in the sun, as is a good sunblock cream. In winter, bring warm clothes and a thick jumper, with a jacket, waterproof if possible.

TIME

From around the start of spring the whole of Italy adopts "legal time", which moves the clocks forward an hour from Greenwich Mean Time, which is then restored in early fall. This practice first began during the two world wars in order to try and save electricity. It has been definitively adopted in Italy since 1966.

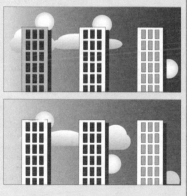

ITALY ON THE INTERNET

You can get useful information about visiting Italy, especially about artistic sites, by surfing the internet. The *Instituto Poligrafo e Zecca di Stato* has put out a website with lots of up-to-date information which is, however, supplied only in Italian:
http://www.ipzs.it/enit/enitel.html
With this address you can access two new sites:
Museums in Italy: http://www.ipzs.it/enit/ita.html
Cultural events: http://www.ipzs.it/enit/all.html
e-mail: infoipzs@ipzs.it
Other useful addresses: Arcanet – Italian museums,
in Italian and in English:
http://www.arcanet.it/cultura/musei-it.htm
Culture and science – a virtual trip to Italy:
http://www.repubblica.it/cultura-scienze/musei/gui/gui.html
Museums and institutions in Italy:
http://www.giramondo.com/fra/framusei.htm

The number of European cities connected by direct flights is constantly increasing. Partnerships between airlines of different European states mean that any corner of this continent is now easily accessible. Alitalia, for example, has agreements with airlines such as Air France, British Airways and Finnair, who have collaborated to guarantee a first-rate service. From the US there are direct flights from most major cities to Rome and Milan, with connecting flights through to other cities.

BY AIR

FROM THE UK
Air fares from the UK tend to be cheaper in winter than in summer. The best deals can usually be obtained by traveling midweek (Monday to Thursday) and staying over a Saturday night. Fares are much higher over Easter or Christmas holiday periods and in August.
◆ ALITALIA
Tel. 0171-602 7111

◆ BRITISH AIRWAYS
Tel. 0345 222 111
◆ MERIDIANA
Tel. 0171-839 2222
◆ Or contact the AIR TRAVEL GROUP
Tel. 0181-745 7575
FROM THE US
There are regular and charter flights to Rome, Milan and Venice from the US with connecting flights to other destinations.
◆ ALITALIA
Tel. (800) 223 5730
◆ AMERICAN AIRLINES
Tel. (800) 433 7300
◆ CONTINENTAL AIRLINES
Tel. (800) 231 0856
◆ DELTA AIRLINES
Tel. (800) 241 4141
◆ US AIRWAYS
Tel. (800) 428 4322

BY COACH

Eurolines is the main European coach company and it runs services to Italy from numerous European cities. For many destinations, departures are two or three times a week or sometimes even daily, depending on the time of year. During the summer months are more frequent services are available. Eurolines offers a network of services between almost a hundred different cities throughout Europe (including some internal services within Italy itself). Coach journeys allow the traveler to appreciate the beauty of the Italian landscape and to take the opportunity to visit sites of cultural and natural interest along the way. The coach journeys to Rome and Venice, for example, stop at around eight of Italy's most beautiful cities. To get to some of the the less important cities in Italy, you will need to take a coach to Rome and then change to a local bus or train to arrive at your destination. For information and reservations contact:
◆ EUROLINES
Tel. 0171-730 8235
(London)

INTERNAL FLIGHT CONNECTIONS

The table below shows the average time taken on flights between the twelve major Italian cities which head the chapters of this guide. Other major regional towns can also be reached by flights from these airports.

no connection ✳
flight duration ▨
change in Rome ★

	Turin	Genoa	Milan	Venice	Bologna	Florence	Perugia	Rome	Naples	Bari	Palermo	Cagliari
Turin												
Genoa	✳											
Milan	✳	✳										
Venice	✳	✳	45min									
Bologna	✳	✳	45min	✳								
Florence	✳	✳	55min	✳	✳							
Perugia	✳	✳	✳	✳	45min	✳						
Rome	1hr 5min	1hr	1hr 5min	1hr 5min	55min	1hr	✳					
Naples	1hr 20min	1hr 40min	1hr 15min	1hr 10min	1hr 30min	1hr 15min	✳	50min				
Bari	2hr 50min ★	3hr 5min ★	1hr 25min	3hr ★	3hr 5min ★	2hr 55min ★	✳	1hr	3hr ★			
Palermo	2hr 45min ★	2hr 50min ★	1hr 35min	1hr 40min	1hr 20min	2hr 55min ★	✳	1hr 5min	50min	1hr 15min		
Cagliari	1hr 20min	2hr 45min ★	1hr 20min	2hr 50min ★	2hr 45min ★	3hr 25min ★	✳	1hr	1hr		50min	

BY RAIL

From the UK trains depart daily from London's Victoria station for Italy's major cities, such as Rome, Bologna, Venice and Florence. Alternatively, take the Eurostar train to Paris, departing from London's Waterloo station. This service operates hourly throughout the day. After arriving at Paris Gare du Nord, transfer to Gare de Lyon for trains to Italy. A luxury option is to travel to Italian on the Orient Express from London (see below).

INFORMATION AND RESERVATIONS
International Rail Enquiries:
Tel. (0990) 848 848 – Eurostar
Tel. (0345) 30 30 30

BY SEA

There are relatively few ferry crossings to Italy from the surrounding countries, apart from those that operate in the Adriatic, where connections can be made from Greece to Ancona, Bari and Brindisi. There are also ferries to Genoa from the southern coast of France and from Spain to Italy via Sardina and Corsica.

IN ITALY
INFORMATION
◆ Milano Viaggi Wasteels
Via Angelo Belloni, 1 Milan
Tel. 02-66 10 10 90
Fax 02-66 10 11 00

BY CAR

The principal roads entering Italy from Europe have to go via Alpine passes (mainly tunnels), which join the main freeways, signposted as E in Europe and A in Italy. Names of roads and passes that link Italy with its neighboring countries include:
◆ E80 A8/A10 Genoa.
◆ Colle del Frejus E70 A32 for Turin.
◆ Colle di Tenda E74.
◆ Traforo del Monte Bianco E25 A5 for Aosta.
◆ Gran S. Bernardo Pass E27 for Aosta.
◆ Sempione Pass (Switzerland) E62.

◆ A8/26 for Milan.
◆ Bernina Pass (Switzerland) 29 38 for Tirano. S.
◆ Bernadino Pass (Switzerland) E35 N13 A9 for Milan.
◆ Spluga Pass E40 for Lake Como.
◆ Resia Pass SS40 for Bolzano.
◆ Brennero Pass E45 A22 for Bolzano.
◆ Tarvisio Pass E55 A23 for Udine.
The mountain passes are generally open all year round. However, to cross most passes in the Alps, especially in the winter months, it is obligatory to carry snow tires or snow chains.

THE ORIENT EXPRESS

The Venice–Simplon Orient Express runs from March to November along the routes London–Paris–Venice, Venice–Florence–Rome and Venice–Prague–Paris–London. The journey, stopping at major European cities, crosses splendid Alpine countryside, vineyards, forests and rolling hills. The uniqueness and beauty of the Orient Express train is in itself fascinating. The three splendid restaurant coaches are rare antiques, and the carriages are decorated with original 1920's fittings. The refined cuisine by select French chefs and the attentive service add to the exclusivity of this voyage across Europe.
INFORMATION
◆ Milano Travel United, Viale Montenero, 6 Tel. 02-55 18 00 03
◆ Venezia Royal Tour, San Marco 4590 Tel. 041-522 17 46
It is advisable to confirm reservations 48 hours before departure.

RAIL PASSES

If you plan to travel around Italy or around Europe, the Italian-run tour operator CIT will give information and advice on fares and rail passes that can be purchased before leaving home
UK
Tel. 0181-686 0677
US
Tel. (212) 697 2100
Train timetables are available from most railway stations throughout Italy for around 4,500 lire.

ITALIAN RAILWAYS

The Italian state railroads (FS or *Ferrovie dello Stato*), guarantee connections between the major European cities and Italy. Long distance intercity trains offer the traveler various menus, catering for traditional European tastes as well as for special dietary needs, such as those of vegetarians or of Muslims. They also provide a good selection of newspapers and a mini-bar for the whole journey.
INFORMATION
FS
Tel. 1478-88088 (toll-free)

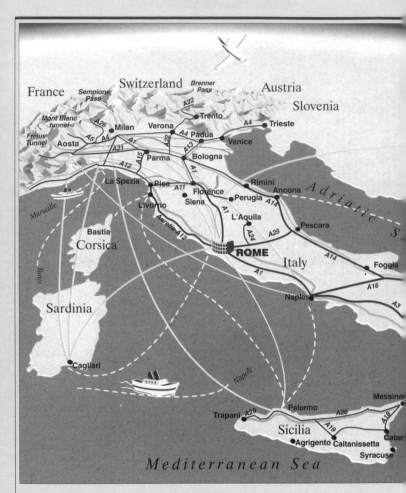

BY AIR

Alitalia is the national company, servicing the entire peninsula.
RESERVATIONS
Tel. 06-65641 (Rome)
Tel. 02-26851 (Milan)
INFORMATION
Tel. 06-65643 (Rome)
Tel. 02-26853 (Milan)
Meridiana airlines connect Sardinia (Cagliari, Olbia, Alghero) with the main Italian cities.
RESERVATIONS AND INFORMATION
Tel. 06-47 80 41 (Rome)
Tel. 02-86 47 71 (Milan)
Air One Airlines links some of the major Italian cities (Rome,

Milan, Turin, Bari, Naples), and also offers some flights to London. There are around 14 flights a day between Rome Fiumicino and Milan Linate airports. Prices vary according to the day of the week. A one-way ticket from Rome to Milan costs between 140,000 lire and 190,000 lire.
RESERVATIONS AND INFORMATION
Tel. 06-47 87 66
The Televideo RAI (◆ 508) service (teletext on the national channel) will give flight information (teletext page 432).

BY RAIL

Trains are classified in Italy according to their speed: the high-speed Pendolino ETR 450 is the fastest option; the Intercity links large cities; the Expresso stops at major towns; the Diretto stops at more places than the Intercity, and the Locale stops at every tiny station along a route and tends to be very slow!

Eurocity trains link Italian cities with major European centers. Long-distance trains have either a restaurant or self-service carriage, mini-bar service, public telephone, sleeping cars and sleeping berths (4 to 6 beds). Tickets are valid for two months from date of issue.
NOTE: all tickets must be stamped with the time of departure (both outward and return tickets), at the machines provided in the stations.

Freeways

Railway lines

Ferry routes

Flight routes

BY CAR

Italy is served by an extensive freeway system. These are almost all toll-paying freeways: the payment at the toll gates can be made in cash, or else by a pre-paid card valid for the entire network (available from Viacard or Telepass). Other types of payment, such as Fastpay, are linked to Bancomat network services. Road signs conform to international regulations.

STREET SIGNS
Main roads are marked with white writing on a blue

background, while freeways are signposted with white writing on a green background. Drivers and front-seat passengers must wear their safety belts. The national speed limits are: 30mph in built-up zones, 55mph on country roads, 70mph on main roads and 110mph on freeways. The Automobile Club

Italiano (ACI) provides a rescue service for car breakdowns. This service is free for cars with foreign number-plates. In the event of a breakdown the number to call is 116.

CAR RENTAL
The major car rental companies (Hertz, Avis, Maggiore, Europcar), all have outlets in most airports and large hotels. You will need a credit card and must be over 21 years of age in order to rent a car. Your driving license (preferably an international one), must be valid for at least one year.

PUBLIC TRANSPORT

Italian cities are well served by comprehensive public transport systems, often including buses, trains, trams and subways. Venice's canals are serviced by a network of *vaporetti* (water-taxis). Public transport is run by various local authorities in Italy,

but ticket prices remain more or less the same throughout the peninsula. Special-price day tickets for tourists are available. Tickets for public transport can be purchased at newsagents, tobacconists, at automatic ticket machines and in

some bars. Some cities are also served by a subway system.

BY BOAT

The principal Italian islands are connected to the mainland by regular ferry services, which carry both cars and passengers. The timetables vary according to the season.
INFORMATION
◆ TIRRENIA
Rione Scrignano, 2
Naples
Tel. 081-720 11 11
A service between the smaller islands (Aeolia, Ustica, Egadi, Pantelleria, Linosa and Lampedusa), is provided by:
◆ SAREMAR,
Via Principe di

Belmonte, 1/c
Palermo
Tel. 091-58 26 88
Ferry service between Naples and Capri or Ischia:
◆ ALILAURO
Via Caracciolo, 11
Naples
Tel. 081-761 42 50
Ferry between Elba to Piombino:
◆ NAVARMA
Piazzale Premuda
Piombino
Tel. 0565-27 60 77
Boats on Lakes Maggiore, Garda and Como:
◆ NAVIGAZIONE LAGHI
Via Ariosto, 2
Milan
Tel. 02-48 12 08

BY BUS

Eurolines is the bus company which links the major Italian cities with the main centers in Belgium, France, the UK, the Netherlands, Poland, Spain and Hungary.
RESERVATIONS AND INFORMATION
◆ Florence
Via Mercadante, 2/B
Tel. 055-357110
Other Italian companies:

◆ AUTOSTRADALE VIAGGI
Piazza Castello, 1
Milan
Tel. 02-72 00 13 04
Covers Lombardy and central Italy.
◆ AUTOLINEE LAZZI
Via Mercadante, 2
Florence
Tel. 055-36 30 41
Covers Tuscany and central Italy.
◆ SITA
Viale dei Cadorna, 105
Florence
Tel. 055-47821
Covers the entire peninsula, except Sicily and Sardinia.

Greece

Brindisi

Lecce

Taranto

ggio di Calabria

Although not a particularly large country, Italy offers its visitors unlimited possibilities – artistic masterpieces, stunning architecture, beautiful cities and a delightful, varied countryside. Each region has its own character, a unique culture and a particular dialect. Italy prides itself on being a welcoming country, traditionally used to receiving visitors and provided with good facilities for travelers. Wherever you decide to go, you can be confident of enjoying warm hospitality, excellent food and good local wine.

ACCOMMODATION

HOTELS

Hotels are graded by stars, from one star (*) to the luxury five-star category (*****L). Small one- or two-star family-run hotels (*pensioni*), basic and friendly, often offer surprisingly good value for money.

In every establishment, from the most modest to the grandest hotels, hoteliers are obliged by law to display a list of prices for each room. Beware, however, that these can vary considerably according to season, or if there are important events or shows held in town at any given time. In the main art cities, high season runs from Easter to October; on the coast the busiest time is in July and August; in the mountains the busiest times are the skiing season (Christmas to Easter), and August; throughout Italy, Christmas and Easter vacations are considered high season. While it is normally advisable to reserve in advance, during high season it becomes absolutely

essential. Tourist offices can help by providing lists of hotels, plus and can

be asked to make advance reservations on your behalf.

FARMHOUSES (*AGRITURISMO*)

INFORMATION
Agriturist,
Corso Vittorio
Emanuele II, 101,
Rome
Tel. 06-685 23 42
You can buy a guide to farmhouse accommodation, published by Agriturist and entitled *Guida dell'Ospitalità Rurale*, which contains all the necessary information for those wishing to stay in a farmhouse in Italy.

YOUTH HOSTELS (*OSTELLI DELLA GIOVENTÙ*)

Youth hostels offer good value budget accommodation. There are over fifty youth hostels throughout Italy. To stay in any one of them you must be a member of the AIG (Associazione Alberghi per la Gioventù). There are no age limits, but if the hostel is almost full, then under-25s are given priority.

INFORMATION
AIG
Via Cavour, 44
Rome
Tel. 06-487 11 52.

CAMPING AND TOURIST VILLAGES

Italy has around 2200 camping sites and tourist villages, usually open from Easter to September. Camping means tourists can stay in environments of special natural beauty or interest, often in places where it would be impossible to build a hotel, large or small. A guide entitled *Campeggi e villaggi turistici in Italia* (Camping and Tourist Villages in Italy), published by Touring Club Italiano, contains a list of sites plus other necessary information. You can camp anywhere on public ground, provided that you have the local government's permission; to camp on private ground, you must obtain the owner's permission.

INFORMATION
Almost all local tourist offices will supply camping information;
◆ ENIT
Federcampeggi
Via Vittorio
Emanuele, 11
50041 Calenzano
(Florence)

RESTAURANTS

Unlike hotels, restaurants have no system of classification. There is a vast choice of eating places on offer: from the family-run *trattoria* or *osteria*, to restaurants which serve refined and exclusive cuisine. Eating out is still reasonably good value for money. Prices are usually displayed outside restaurants, and it is best to consult them first as expensive restaurants can look very unassuming from outside. It is advisable to reserve ahead in well-known restaurants. The check will show a price for *pane* (bread), at around 2000 lire, and *coperto* (cover charge), at around 4000 lire. Tipping is common practice throughout Italy, as service is not included in the check. Add approximately 10% to the total price paid.

Il Gambrinus, one of the most famous cafés in Naples.

BARS AND OTHER PLACES TO EAT

In Italy, breakfast at the bar is a real tradition. From small bars, generally not very comfortable but often with great character, to the luxurious bars in city centers, all these offer an ample choice of drinks, sandwiches and hot and cold snacks. Prices for coffees and drinks are fairly consistent, but can vary enormously for food and table service. Many bars also sell tobacco, cigarettes and stamps. Most bars are open from 7am to 8pm, some stay open even later. For an after-dinner drink one can choose between the classic *birreria* (brasserie/bar), which may stage live shows (music, cabarets, floor shows), and bars inspired by foreign traditions (such as pubs, disco pubs, American-style bars and taco bars). These all close around 2am to 3am. Nightclubs or *discoteche* are in a category of their own. They frequently play different styles of music according to the night of the week, and are generally open from 10pm until between 4am and 6am.

"LO SCONTRINO"

By law a receipt (*lo scontrino fiscale*) must be issued with every purchase in Italy. Both seller *and* buyer are liable to be fined if a receipt or *scontrino* cannot be produced on demand.

GLOSSARY

◆ OSTERIA
Traditionally an inn or tavern; these modest restaurants offer a good choice of wines but usually have a very limited food menu.

◆ RISTORANTE
Restaurant serving hot, complete meals at table.

◆ ROSTICCERIA
Serves hot and cold food to eat in or take away.

◆ TAVOLA CALDA
Serves hot or cold fast food, to be eaten at the bar.

◆ TAVOLA FREDDA
The same as above, serving cold dishes only.

◆ TRATTORIA
Modest, family-run eateries serving hot meals at table. Usually extremely good value for money.

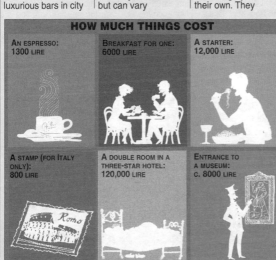

HOW MUCH THINGS COST

AN ESPRESSO: 1300 LIRE	BREAKFAST FOR ONE: 6000 LIRE	A STARTER: 12,000 LIRE
A STAMP (FOR ITALY ONLY): 800 LIRE	A DOUBLE ROOM IN A THREE-STAR HOTEL: 120,000 LIRE	ENTRANCE TO A MUSEUM: c. 8000 LIRE

MONEY

In Italy the currency is the lira (plural lire, symbolized by £ or lit.). Bank notes are in denominations of 1000, 2000, 5000, 10,000, 50,000, 100,000 and 500,000 lire, and coins are 50, 100, 200, 500 and 1000 lire. Bank opening hours are from 8.30am to 1pm or 1.30pm, and from 2.45pm to 3.45pm or 4.30pm.

CHANGING MONEY
Bureau-de-change booths can be found outside most major banks, in larger railway stations, in airports and in places much frequented by tourists. Beware of people offering to change your money in the street, or at railway stations: this is an illegal practise.

CASH CARDS AND CREDIT CARDS

Major credit cards such as American Express, Diner's Club, Visa and Mastercard are accepted throughout almost all Italy, with the exception of a few small restaurants and stores, especially in smaller towns. Another valid and easy way of paying for foreign tourists is with international cash cards (*bancomat*), issued by the visitor's own bank in their country of origin. There are automatic tellers outside most major banks. If you see the Eurocheque symbol (EC) on automatic tellers, you can key in your PIN number to obtain Italian money.

TELEPHONES

There are around 100,000 public telephones in Italy, which operate using 200 lire tokens (*gettone*), telephone cards, credit cards or account cards. Emergency numbers may be dialed toll-free from all public telephones.
Telephone charges are as follows: local calls are charged at 200 lire plus 200 lire for each successive unit. National calls are charged at 400 lire plus 200 lire for each successive unit.

TELEPHONE CARDS
Cards (5,000, 10,000 or 15,000 lire) are available from Telecom Italia agencies, public telephone centers, tobacconists', automatic dispensers, post offices and newspaper sellers.

TELEPHONE CREDIT CARDS
These cards allow you to call internationally through an operator (dial 170). The card costs 2000 lire + tax for two months' usage. Contact Italy Direct customer services:
Tel. 167-156 156.
Pre-paid international telephone cards can be used for international calls to and from Italy. Dial 1740 from Italy and the appropriate code from all other countries to for access to an automatic guide in English and Italian.

The card is sold in sealed envelopes and costs 12,500, 25,000, 50,000 or 100,000 lire, plus UDT (*tariffa Unità di Traffico*) and tax. Cards are on sale in major airports and railway stations, post offices, on board international Alitalia flights, in travel agencies, ACI (*Automobile Club Italiana*) offices, at border crossings and at major banks.
INFORMATION
Tel. 167-293822

(toll free)
Lines are open 24 hours with a recorded message in English.

TELEPHONING FROM A PTA
Posti Telefonici Pubblici (PTP) – public telephone centers – have soundproofed booths from which you can make local, national and international calls. You pay after making your call. There are PTPs in most major cities throughout Italy.

COST OF A TELEPHONE CALL

ITALY	DAYTIME RATE	EVENING AND WEEKEND RATE
FRANCE	950 LIRE PER MIN.	700 LIRE PER MIN.
GERMANY	950 LIRE PER MIN.	700 LIRE PER MIN.
UK	770 LIRE PER MIN.	680 LIRE PER MIN.
US	1310 LIRE PER MIN.	1120 LIRE PER MIN.
JAPAN	2890 LIRE PER MIN.	2370 LIRE PER MIN.

MAIL

TELEPHONING FROM ITALY

UK

To telephone the UK from Italy dial 00 44 followed by the regional code (dropping the initial zero), then the number you require.

US

To telephone the US from Italy dial 00 1 followed by the regional code (dropping the initial zero), then the number you require.

Post offices throughout the country are open from 8.30am to 1.30pm.

POSTAL CHARGES

◆ The basic price for a stamp (*francobollo*) for inland letters or postcards is 800 lire; for fast delivery, add another 3600 lire; recorded delivery 4000 lire; ordinary postal orders 0000 lire; giro fee 1200 lire.

◆ The basic price for a stamp for a letter or postcards sent abroad is 900 lire. For fast delivery add another 3,600 lire; recorded delivery 4000 lire; ordinary postal orders 4000 11,000 lire; giro fee 1200 lire. Mail boxes are red (inland) or blue (international) and are located near post offices.

SHOPPING

STORES

Italy has a huge variety of stores. Thanks to the great tradition of Italian fashion, the windows of the larger stores are often masterpieces of creativity and good taste. But it's not just clothing stores which make a good impression along city streets: from high-tech design to antiques, from typical crafts to simple, everyday products such as food and paper, Italian stores offer you every kind of merchandise, to satisfy even the most demanding

customer. Normal opening hours are from Mondays through to Saturdays from 9am to 1pm and 3.30pm to 7.30pm. In the center and south of Italy: winter from 9am to 1pm, and 3.30pm to 7.30pm; summer from 9am to 1pm and 4pm to 8pm. Sunday is

traditionally a day of rest, and many stores have half-day closing one day during the week. In recent years, particularly in the north, there has been a growing trend for some stores to remain open all day, from 7am to 7pm, in an "*orario continuato*", and sometimes even on Sundays (especially in supermarkets and megastores).

SALES

Shopping in Italy can be an amazing experience, and there is no better time to buy than during the sales. When the seasons change, especially at the end of winter and at the end of summer, store owners hold so-called "end of season sales" (*saldi*), with reductions of up to 50% off the original prices.

MARKETS

Wandering around the lively markets held in towns can be fascinating. A vital part of the local scene, they often sell a huge range of products, from antiques to curiosities, from clothes to books. Information on market days and sites can be obtained from local tourist offices.

HEALTH

Citizens of the European Union can obtain an E111 form their local post office or health authority, which is in line with the U.S.S.L. (*Unità Socio Sanitaria Locale*), and so entitles them to free Italian health care. In all the major hospitals in the larger cities there is 24-hour emergency assistance, also open to those who are not entitled to free health care.

PHARMACIES

In city centers throughout Italy there is a pharmacy on almost every street corner. As a general rule pharmacies have the following opening hours (with some minor variations): during the day from 8.30am–12.30pm and 3–7pm; night opening hours are from 9pm–9am. If the pharmacy is closed, a list of other

pharmacies open in the neighborhood with their telephone numbers is posted on the entrance door. In the main rail stations there are 24-hour pharmacy services.

◆ For emergency pharmaceutical assistance dial 118.

EMERGENCY SERVICES

◆ Public emergencies: 113 (only resort to this number in cases of real danger, serious injuries or when the

other emergency numbers are unavailable).

◆ *Carabinieri* (military police): 112

◆ Fire service: 115
◆ Forest rangers: 1515
◆ Road accidents (ACI): 116

MEDIA

TELEVISION

The national television network is called RAI: it broadcasts three stations, RAIUNO, RAIDUE and RAITRE (with some regional broadcasts). They show various programs, with slots dedicated to documentaries, films, comedy shows, family and children's shows. The major independent TV companies are Canale5, Italia 1, Rete4, belonging to the Mediaset group, and the two networks belonging to the Cecchi Gori group, TMC and TMC2. The differences between the public and privately owned stations, both in terms of reception and quality of programs, have now become imperceptible. Satellite television, receiving major international stations such as BBC, CNN and Eurosport, is available in many large hotels.

NATIONAL PAPERS

Despite Italy's long journalistic tradition and the enormous number of daily papers available (almost one for each major town), they do not sell in large quantities. The main daily newspapers are the *Corriere della Sera* in Milan, and *La Repubblica*, whose head office is in Rome. These each sell around 800,000 copies per day.

INTERNATIONAL NEWSPAPERS

Major international newspapers are sold in railway stations and in most towns' main piazzas.

RADIO

Italian national radio broadcasts news in Italian and three foreign languages (French, English and German), giving information on cultural events, traffic updates, weather forecasts and international news. Information on opening times, which can vary according to the season, can be found in the daily papers, which also give television and radio program listings.

MUSEUMS

Italy is a country rich in art treasures. There are also many interesting exhibitions, mostly held in the larger cities. However, small towns often host prestigious displays of national and international interest as well. Opening hours of Italian cultural institutions (museums, churches, and art galleries), vary considerably from region to region and depending on the time of year. Generally, they are open throughout the day, or are only closed for lunch, which in the south, especially in summer, is later and extends for half an hour more than in the north. Many museums are closed one day during the week, so it is best to check beforehand.

The following table shows some of the major cultural events held in Italy during the summer.

CULTURAL EVENTS

INTERNATIONAL EXHIBITION OF CINEMATOGRAPHIC ART	movies	Venice	early September
MYSTFEST	detective and horror movies	Cattolica	early July
FLORENTINE MAY MUSIC FESTIVAL	classical music	Florence	May–July
ROSSINI OPERA FESTIVAL	opera	Pesaro	August
UMBRIA JAZZ	jazz	Perugia	July
TWO WORLDS FESTIVAL	theater, music and dance	Spoleto	June–July
MILANOLTRE	theater and music	Milan	October–Nov.
TAORMINA FESTIVAL	theater, dance and movies	Taormina	June–July
GREEK THEATER FESTIVAL	classical theater	Syracuse Segesta	May–August
PALERMO DI SCENA	music, theater and dance	Palermo	June–July
TEATRO DELL'OPERA SUMMER OPERA SEASON	opera	Rome	July–August

USEFUL ADDRESSES

DIALING CODE 011

KEY

★ **SPECIAL INTEREST**

🄲 **CENTRAL LOCATION**

⊡⋯ **ISOLATED**

⌂ **QUIET**

🔆 **VIEW**

🅿 **PARKING**

🚙 **SUPERVIZED PARKING**

🏊 **SWIMMING POOL**

🧍 **REDUCTIONS FOR CHILDREN**

🐾 **NO PETS**

♫ **MUSIC**

🎸 **LIVE BANDS**

💳 **CREDIT CARDS ACCEPTED**

📺 **TELEVISION**

PRACTICAL INFORMATION

POSTAL CODE
10100

DIALING CODE
011

TOURIST INFORMATION
◆ APT and IAT
Via Roma, 226
Tel. 53 51 81,
or 53 59 01
Fax 530 00 70
◆ APT
Stazione Porta Nuova
Tel. 53 13 27

◆ Vetrina per Torino
Piazza S. Carlo, 161
Tel. 442 47 40
or 1670-15475
(toll-free)
◆ INFORMACITTÀ
Via Palazzo di Città,
24/B
Tel. 422 28 88,
422 21 21
or 422 22 44

MAIN POST OFFICE
Agenzia P.I. Torino
Via Maria Vittoria, 24
Tel. 88 96 61
Open 8.30am–1.30pm

EMBASSIES AND CONSULATES
UK
International House
Via Saluzzo, 60
Tel. 650 92 02

EMERGENCIES

AMBULANCE SERVICE
Tel. 118

MEDICAL SERVICES
Free emergency
service
Tel. 5747
Italian Red Cross
Tel. 244 54 11
Anti-poison center
Tel. 663 76 37

POLICE
Central headquarters
Tel. 55881
Highway patrol
Tel. 56401

FIRE SERVICE
Tel. 115

TRANSPORT

AIR
TORINO CASELLE
AIRPORT
9 miles north of
the city.
Information and
enquiries:
Tel. 567 63 61
Open 6am–
midnight
◆ ALITALIA
Via Lagrange,
35
Tel. 57691
Fax 576 94 00

RAIL
STAZIONE DI
PORTA NUOVA
Corso V. Emanuele II,
53
Information
Tel. 665 11 11

CAR
ACI-AUTOMOBILE
CLUB D'ITALIA
Via Giolitti, 15
Tel. 57791
Fax 577 92 86
Assistance for members
Tel. 577 92 51
or 577 92 53
Car rental:
Via S. Francesco
da Paola, 20/A
Tel. 562 5 14
Fax 561 30 03

CAR RENTAL
AVIS
– Corso Turati, 15/G
Tel. 50 11 07, 50 08 52
or 50 55 68
– Aeroporto Caselle
Tel. 470 15 28
Fax 567 80 20
MAGGIORE-BUDGET
Reservations:
Tel. 1478-67067

PUBLIC TRANSPORT
A.T.M. AZIENDA TRANVIE
MUNICIPALI
Corso Turati, 19/6
Tel. 57641
or 167-01 91 52 (toll-free)
Tourist information:
Tel. 576 42 22

TAXIS
RADIOTAXI
Tel. 5730 or 3399
PRONTO TAXI
Tel. 5737

HOTELS

ALEXANDRA★★★
Lungodora Napoli, 14
Tel. 85 83 27
Fax 248 38 05
*Very near the historic
center, this hotel has
well-equipped, large
quiet rooms. Closed
August.
Air conditioning.*
🄲 🚙 💳 📺

AMADEUS E TEATRO★★★
Via Principe Amedeo,
41A
Tel. 817 49 51
Fax 817 49 53
*Well situated (near
Mole Antonelliana),
a good hotel for
business travelers,
offering comfort and
modern facilities.*

*Air conditioning,
conference room.*
🅿 💳 📺

GIADA★★
Via Barbera, 6
Tel. and fax 348 93 83
Closed throughout
Aug.
*Easily accessible from
the main road, this
hotel is comfortable
and friendly. Air
conditioning.*
🅿 💳 📺

GRAND HOTEL SITEA★★★★
Via Carlo Alberto, 35
Tel. 517 01 71
Fax 54 80 90
*Situated in the city
center, this elegantly
furnished hotel
boasts one of the
best restaurants in
the city, the "Carignano".
Air conditioning, garden,
conference room,
disabled access.*
🄲 💳 📺

JOLLY HOTEL AMBASCIATORI★★★★
Corso V. Emanuele II,
104
Tel. 5752
Fax 54 49 78
*Large, well-positioned
hotel. Bedrooms are
spacious and very
comfortable. Air
conditioning,
conference room,
disabled access.*
🄲 💳 📺

JOLLY HOTEL PRINCIPI DI PIEMONTE★★★★
Via Gobetti, 15
Tel. 562 96 93
Fax 53 54 38
*Elegant hotel with
luxurious bedrooms
and attractive public
rooms. Good
restaurant,
"Gentilhom".
Air conditioning,
conference room.*
🄲 🚙 💳 📺

LIBERTY★★★
Via Pietro Micca, 15
Tel. 562 88 01
Fax 562 81 63
*An Art Nouveau palazzo
right in the historic
center, very
welcoming.Family-run
restaurant. Air
conditioning.*
🄲 🄿 ▭ ▢

STATUTO★★
Via Principi d'Acaja, 17
Tel. 434 46 38
Fax 434 43 80
*Despite its slightly
austere appearance,
this hotel offers very
comfortable rooms.
Disabled access.*
♿

YOUTH HOSTEL

**OSTELLO DELLA
GIOVENTU**
Via Alby, 1
Tel. 660 29 39

RESTAURANTS

AL BUE ROSSO
Corso Casale, 10
Tel. 819 13 93
Closed Mon., Sat.
lunchtimes and
throughout Aug.
*Warm and intimate
restaurant. Authentic
Italian flavors and
stylish presentation.*
▭

BALBO
Via Andrea Doria, 11
Tel. 812 55 66
Fax 812 75 24
Closed Mon. and
for a period July–Aug.
*Traditional regional
cookery in a 19th-
century palazzo.
Beautiful furnishings
and good service.*

DEL CAMBIO
Piazza Carignano, 2
Tel. 54 6 90
Fax 53 52 82
Closed Sun. and Aug.
*Founded in 1757, Del
Cambio is distinguished
by its elegance and
impeccable service.
Classic Italian and
Piedmontese cuisine.*
▭

GATTO NERO
Corso F. Turati, 14
Tel. 59 04 14
Fax 59 04 77
Closed Sun. and
throughout Aug.
Good classic cuisine is

*guaranteed here. The
Vannelli family have run
this restaurant for over
60 years.*
▭

GHIBELLIN FUGGIASCO
Via Tunisi, 50/B
Tel. 319 61 15
Closed Sun. evenings
and Mon., part of Aug.
and throughout Jan.
*House specialties are
fish and mushroom
dishes. Elegant setting.*
▭

VECCHIA LANTERNA
Corso Re Umberto, 21
Tel. 53 70 47
Fax 53 03 91
Closed Sat. lunchtime
and Sun.
*An elegant early-20th-
century setting, good
service and excellent
gourmet cuisine by
Armando Zanetti.
Carefully considered
wine list.*
▭

CULTURE

CIVIC BUILDINGS
◆ CASTELLO DEL
VALENTINO
Viale Mattioli
Tel. 669 93 72
Closed Mon.
Open 7am–9pm
◆ PALAZZO REALE
Piazzetta Reale
Tel. 436 15 57
or 436 4 55
Closed Mon.
Open 7am–9pm,
guided tours only.
◆ TEATRO REGIO
Piazza Castello, 215
Tel. 88151
or 167-807064 (toll-free)

RELIGIOUS BUILDINGS
◆ BASILICA DI SUPERGA
Strada della Basilica
di Superga, 73
Tel. 898 00 83
Open 8.30am–noon,
3–6pm
◆ DUOMO (CATHEDRAL)
Piazza San Giovanni

Tel. 436 15 40
Open Mon.–Sat.
7am–noon, 3–7pm

MUSEUMS
◆ GALLERIA CIVICA
D'ARTE MODERNA
E CONTEMPORANEA
(MUNICIPAL GALLERY OF
MODERN ART)
Via Magenta, 31
Tel. 562 99 11
Open 9am–7pm;
usually paid entrance,
except for the first Fri.
of each month when
entry is free.
◆ GALLERIA SABAUDA
Via Accademia delle
Scienze, 6
Tel. 54 74 40
Closed Mon.
Open 9am–2pm
On Sun. the upper
floor may only be
visited by guided tour
at 9.30am, 10.30am,
11.30am and 12.30pm
◆ MUSEO ARMERIA
REALE (ROYAL ARMORY)
Piazza Castello, 191
Tel. 54 38 89
Closed Mon.
Open Tue. and Thur.
2.30–7.30pm; Wed.,
Fri., Sat., Sun. and
public holidays
9am–2pm; guided tours
for groups on Sun. at
9.45am, 10am,
10.45am, 11.30am,
12.45pm and 1pm
◆ MUSEO DI ANTICHITÀ
(MUSEUM OF ANTIQUITY)
Corso Regina
Margherita, 105
Tel. 436 30 82
or 521 22 51
Closed Mon.
Open Tue.–Sat. 9am–
7pm; Sun. and public
holidays 2–7pm; guided
tours on Sun. morning
◆ MUSEO NAZIONALE
DELL'AUTOMOBILE CARLO
BISCARETTI DI RUFFIA
(AUTOMOBILE MUSEUM)
Corso Unità d'Italia, 40
Tel. 67 76 68

Closed Mon
Open 10am–6.30pm
◆ MUSEO EGIZIO
(EGYPTIAN MUSEUM)
Via Accademia
delle Scienze, 6
Tel. 561 26 77
or 561 7 76
Closed Mon.
Open Tue.–Sat.
9am–7pm; Sun. and
public holidays
9am–2pm
◆ MUSEO NAZIONALE DEL
RISORGIMENTO ITALIANO
(CONTEMPORARY ART
MUSEUM)
Via Accademia
delle Scienze, 5
Tel. 562 37 19,
or 562 11 47
Closed Mon.
Open Tue.–Sun.
9am–7pm
◆ MUSEO STORICO
NAZIONALE DI
ARTIGLIERIA (MUSEUM
OF ARTILLERY)
Mastio della Cittadella
Corso Galileo Ferraris
Tel. 561 28 37
Open for temporary
exhibitions and by
previous arrangement
for groups.
◆ RIVOLI-MUSEO
D'ARTE CONTEMPORANEA
CASTELLO DI RIVOLI
Piazza del Castello
Tel. 958 15 47
or 958 72 56
Closed Mon.
Open Tue.–Fri.
10am–5pm; Sat. and
Sun. 10am–7pm; first
and third Thur. of each
month 10am–10pm

OTHER MONUMENTS
◆ MOLE ANTONELLIANA
Via Montebello, 20
Tel. 817 04 96
◆ STUPINIGI
APT
Corso Ferrucci,
122/128
Torino
Tel. 335 24 40

★ **DO NOT MISS** ★
SALONE DEL LIBRO
The *Salone del Libro* is a publishing institution.
Apart from promoting books (over 1000 publishing
houses are represented), it offers a varied calendar
of seminars, talks, presentations and meetings with
authors. Each year a specific theme runs through
the various events. The *Salone* also covers comic
books, home videos and entertainment.
Takes place during the second half of May.
INFORMATION
Via Susa, 32
Tel. 433 70 54
Fax 433 10 56

DIALING CODE 010

PRACTICAL INFORMATION

POSTAL CODE
16100

DIALING CODE
010

TOURIST INFORMATION
◆ APT
Via Roma, 11/4
Tel. 54 15 41, 58 13 71
or 58 14 07
◆ IAT
Stazione FFSS Principe
Piazza Acquaverde
Tel. 26 26 33
◆ SERVIZIO REGIONALE
DI PROMOZIONE
TURISTICA
Via Fieschi, 15
Tel. 54851

MAIN POST OFFICE
Agenzia P.I. Genova
Succursale, 1
Via Sal. S. Giovanni di
Pré, 7/A/R
Tel. 246 35 92
Open 8.30am–1.30pm

EMERGENCIES

AMBULANCE SERVICE
Tel. 570 59 51

MEDICAL SERVICE
Tel. 35 40 22

POLICE
Central headquarters
Tel. 53661
Highway patrol
Tel. 37011

FIRE SERVICE
Tel. 115

TRANSPORT

AIR
CRISTOFORO COLOMBO
AIRPORT:
4 miles from the city
Tel. 60151
◆ ALITALIA
Via XII Ottobre, 12
Tel. 54931
Fax 549 32 51

RAIL
STAZIONE PORTA
PRINCIPE
Piazza Acquaverde
STAZIONE DI BRIGNOLE
Piazza Verdi
Information:
Tel. 28 40 81

CAR
ACI-AUTOMOBILE CLUB
D'ITALIA
Via le Brigate
Partigiane, 1
Tel. 56 70 01
Enquiries:
Tel. 56 16 65
Car rental:
Tel. 56 70 01
24-hour emergency
breakdown:
Tel. 116
Via Casaregis, 53
Tel. 362 15 27

CAR RENTAL
◆ AVIS
– Uffici di Genova
Via Pionieri and Aviatori
d'Italia
Tel. 651 51 01
or 651 60 44
Fax 651 50 88
– Aeroporto Cristoforo
Colombo
Tel. 650 72 80

PUBLIC TRANSPORT
A.M.T. AZIENDA
MUNICIPALIZZATA
TRASPORTI
Via L. Montaldo, 2
Tel. 59971

TAXIS
RADIOTAXI
Tel. 5966

HOTELS

AGNELLO D'ORO***
Via delle Monachette, 6
Tel. 246 20 84
Fax 246 23 27
This attractive, family-run hotel has a delightful terrace with a good view. Attractive lobby and comfortable bedrooms.
🅿 ▱ ❑

ALEXANDER***
Via Bersaglieri d'Italia, 19/R
Tel. 26 13 71
Fax 26 52 57
A classic city building with a lovely view over the port. Air conditioning.
🚗 ▱ ❑

BRISTOL PALACE****
Via XX Settembre, 35
Tel. 59 5 41
Fax 56 17 56
Late-19th-century aristocratic residence with sumptuous public rooms. Air conditioning, conference room, disabled access.
🄲 🚗 ▱ ❑

BRITANNIA****
Via Balbi, 38
Tel. 26991
Fax 246 29 42
Smart hotel in the historic center, very near Principe station. Top-floor rooms enjoy spectacular views. Impeccable service. Air conditioning. Conference room, gym, solarium, sauna.
🄲 🚗 ▱ ❑

CITY****
Via S. Sebastiano, 6
Tel. 55451
Fax 58 63 01
In the heart of the old city; combines comfort and modernity. Air conditioning, conference room.
🄲 🚗 ▱ ❑

MEDITERRANÉE***
Via Lungomare, 69
Pegli
Tel. 697 38 50
Fax 696 98 50
An attractive period home transformed into a hotel. Quiet bedrooms. Air conditioning, disabled access.
🚪 🚗 ▱ ❑

METROPOLI***
Piazza delle Fontane
Marose
Tel. 28 41 41
Fax 28 18 16
In a central location, offering good service and well-equipped rooms. Conference room.
🚗 ❄ ▱ ❑

SAVOIA MAJESTIC****
Via Arsenale di Terra, 5
Tel. 26 16 41
Fax 26 18 83
This sophisticated modern hotel is situated near the Porto Vecchio basin and Principe station. Large comfortable bedrooms, many with views. Air conditioning, conference room, disabled access.
🚗 ▱ ❑

YOUTH HOSTEL

A.I.G. GENOVA
Via Costanzi, 120
Tel. 242 24 57

CAMPING

**CAMPING VILLA
MASNATA S.N.C.**
Via Creto, 119
Tel. 80 33 11

**CARAVAN PARK
LA VESIMA**
Strada Statale (highway)
Aurelia
exit at 547 km
Voltri
Tel. 619 96 72
Fax 619 96 86

VILLA DORIA
Via al Campeggio Villa
Doria 15N
Pegli
Tel. and fax 696 96 00

RESTAURANTS

**ANTICA OSTERIA
DEL BAI**
Via Quarto, 12
Quarto dei Mille
Tel. 38 74 78
Fax 39 26 84
Closed Mon., part of Aug. and part of Jan. Gianni and Renata Malagoni serve wonderful traditional Genoese fish dishes in this attractive restaurant with views over the sea. Air conditioning.
▱

BRUXABOSCHI
Via F. Mignone, 8
S. Desiderio
Tel. 345 03 02
Closed Sun. evening and Mon.; through Aug. Just outside the city limits, where you can get a first taste of the bracing mountain air;

natural, wholesome food; in particular try the delicious mushrooms.

CICCHETTI 1860
Via Gianelli, 41/R
Quinto al Mare
Tel. 310 03 91
Closed Tue., Wed. and part of Aug.
Classic Genoese inn ("osteria"), serving traditional Genoese food.

DA MARIA
Via Testadoro, 14/R
Tel. 58 10 80
Closed Mon. evenings, Sat. and part of Aug.
A small and pleasant eatery on two floors. Maria (the namesake), creates traditional dishes from ancient recipes, including such specialties as "trenette al pesto" and "burrida di seppie".

GRAN GOTTO
Viale Brigata Bisagno, 69/R
Tel. and fax 56 43 44
Closed Sat. lunchtime, Sun. and part of Aug.
Traditional regional cooking served by the Bertola family. Specialties include seafood antipasti, and kidneys.
▭

IL PAMPINO
Via Ruspoli, 31/R
Tel. 58 84 02
Closed lunchtimes; Sun. and 3 weeks in Aug.
This wine bar offers around 400 different wines. Enjoy delicious food in simple surroundings.

LA BITTA NELLA PERGOLA
Corso F. Turati, 14
Tel. 590414
Fax 590477
Closed Sun. evenings, Mon. and part of Aug.
Carefully presented, traditional Ligurian

dishes and a well-stocked cellar. Elegant setting. Air conditioning.
▭

RINA
Mura delle Grazie, 3
Tel. 20 79 90
Closed Mon.; Aug.
Since 1945 the Traverso family has been serving tasty traditional dishes in this friendly trattoria, favored by artists.

SAINT CYR
Piazza Marsala, 4
Tel. 88 68 97
Closed Sat. lunchtime and Sun., Christmas and part of Aug.
Classic Ligurian cuisine is served in three small wood-paneled rooms by a long-established management. Attentive and friendly service. Air conditioning.
▭

ZEFFIRINO
Via XX Settembre, 20
Tel. 59 19 90
Closed Wed.
Internationally, one of the city's best-known restaurants where you can sample excellent traditional Italian cuisine. Modern decor. Air conditioning.
▭

CULTURE

CIVIC BUILDINGS
◆ ACCADEMIA LINGUISTICA DI BELLE ARTI
Piazza De Ferrari, 5
Tel. 58 19 57
Closed Sun.
Open 9am–1pm
◆ ACQUARIO
Porto Vecchio district, Ponte Spinola
Tel. 248 12 05
◆ TEATRO CARLO FELICE

Piazza De Ferrari
Reservations:
Tel. 58 93 29
or 59 16 97

MUSEUMS
◆ GALLERIA DI PALAZZO BIANCO
Via Garibaldi, 11
Tel. 29 18 03
Closed Mon.
Open Tue.–Sat. 9am–7pm; Sun. 9am–noon
◆ GALLERIA DI PALAZZO REALE
Via Balbi, 10
Tel. 20 60 51
Open 9am–1.30pm
◆ GALLERIA DI PALAZZO ROSSO
Via Garibaldi, 18
Tel. 28 26 41
Closed Mon.
Open Tue.–Sat. 9am–7pm; Sun. 9am–noon
◆ GALLERIA DI PALAZZO SPINOLA
Piazza Pellicceria, 1
Tel. 29 46 61
Open Tue.–Sat. 9am–5pm; Sun. and Mon. 9am–1pm
◆ MUSEO AMERICANISTICO FEDERICO LUNARDI
Salita Santa Maria della Sanità, 43

Tel. 81 47 37
Closed Mon.
Open 9.30am–noon, 3–5.30pm; Sun. 3–5.30pm
◆ MUSEO CHIOSSONE
Piazzale Mazzini, 1
Tel. 54 22 85
Closed Mon., Tue., first and fourth Sun. of each month. Open 9am–1pm
Free entry on Sun.
◆ MUSEO DEL TESORO DI S. LORENZO
Cathedral
Piazza San Lorenzo
Tel. 20 86 27
Closed Sun. and Mon.
Open 9.30–11.45am, 3–5.45pm

For all monuments and cultural institutions not listed here contact:

SERVIZIO REGIONALE DI PROMOZIONE TURISTICA
Via Fieschi, 15
Tel. 54851

★ DO NOT MISS ★
INTERNATIONAL BOAT SHOW

A prestigious commercial boat show with yachts, touring boats, leisure-craft, off-shore and speed boats, prototypes. Apart from being of historic interest, the show will appeal to all boat lovers, who can admire the latest models manufactured by the major Italian and international ship-builders.
Takes place in mid-October
INFORMATION
UCINA
Piazzale Kennedy
Tel. 37 51 10 01

513

DIALING CODE 02

PRACTICAL INFORMATION

POSTAL CODE
20100

DIALING CODE
02

TOURIST INFORMATION
◆ ENIT
c/o Aeroporto Linate
Tel. 73 30 91
Open Mon.–Sat.
8am–8pm
◆ UFFICIO INFORMAZIONI DEL COMUNE DI MILANO
Galleria V. Emanuele
Tel. 87 83 63
or 62 08 31 01
Open Mon.–Sat.
8am–8pm
◆ APT
Via Marconi, 1
Tel. 80 96 62
Open 8am–8pm;
Sun. 9am–12.30pm,
1.30–5pm
Stazione Centrale
Piazza Duca D'Aosta
Tel. 669 05 32
Open 8am–8pm;
Sun. 9am–12.30pm,
1.30–5pm

EMBASSIES AND CONSULATES
US
Via Principe Amedeo 2/10
Tel. 29 03 51
UK
Via San Paolo 7
Tel. 72 30 01

MAIN POST OFFICE
Piazza Cordusio, 4
Tel. 246 35 92
Open 8.30am–1.30pm

EMERGENCIES

AMBULANCE SERVICE
Tel. 118

MEDICAL SERVICES
Tel. 34567

ANTI-POISON CENTER
Tel. 66 10 10 29

POLICE
Central headquarters
Tel. 62261
Highway patrol
Tel. 32 67 81

FIRE SERVICE
Tel. 115

TRANSPORT

AIR
AIRPORTS:
AEROPORTO DI LINATE
4 miles east of the city
Information:
Tel. 756 11 72
AEROPORTO INTERCONTINENTALE MALPENSA
28 miles northwest of the city
Via Malpensa, 1
Information:
Tel. 40 09 99 35
◆ ALITALIA
Via XIV Maggio, 6
Tel. 24991
Fax 24 99 28 90

RAIL
FERROVIE DELLO STATO
STAZIONE CENTRALE
Piazza Duca d'Aosta FS
Information:
Tel. 1478-88088
FERROVIE NORD MILANO
Piazzale Cadorna, 14/16
Information:
Tel. 48 06 67 71

CAR
ACI-AUTOMOBILE CLUB D'ITALIA
Corso Venezia, 43
Tel. 77451
Emergency breakdown service
Tel. 116

CAR RENTAL
◆ AVIS
– Via Gasparotto, 4
Tel. 67 07 08 84,
or 67 07 09 92
– Piazza Diaz, 6
Tel. 86 34 94,
or 89 01 06 45
– Aeroporto di Linate
Tel. 717 22 14,
71 72 14 or 71 51 23
– Aeroporto di Malpensa
Tel. 40 09 93 75,
or 40 09 93 45
◆ EUROPCAR
Reservations and information:
Tel. 70 39 97 00
◆ MAGGIORE-BUDGET
Reservations:
Tel. 229 15 30

PUBLIC TRANSPORT
A.T.M.
Information office
Duomo (subway station)
Tel. 89 01 07 97
or 87 54 95
Stazione FS Centrale
Tel. 669 70 32 or

669 70 81

TAXIS
COOPERATIVA ESPERIA
Tel. 8383
RADIOTAXI
Tel. 6767
RADIO TAXIDATA
Tel. 5353
TAXI MALPENSA

Tel. 40 09 90 29

HOTELS

ARIOSTO***
Via Ariosto, 22
Tel. 481 78 44
Fax 498 05 16
A good hotel very near the Fiera. Attractive courtyard. Air conditioning.
⬜

DEI CAVALIERI****
Piazza Missori, 1
Tel. 8857
Fax 72 02 16 83
Elegant, comfortable hotel in the center of town. Air conditioning, disabled access.
🅲 🚗 ⬜

GALA***
Viale Zara 89
Tel. 68 80 08 91
Fax 68 80 04 63
An early-19th-century villa with period fittings, set in a quiet garden. Air conditioning.
🅿 ⬜

★GRAND HOTEL ET DE MILAN*****
Via Manzoni, 29
Tel. 72 31 41
Fax 86 46 08 61
The Grand Hotel's prime location next to La Scala has earned it the patronage of many celebrities, divas and royals. The excellent "Don Carlos" restaurant is ideal for an intimate meal, while the "Caruso", open at midday, is the perfect place for a working lunch. Air conditioning, conference room.
🅲 🚗 ⬜

HERMITAGE****
Via Messina, 10
Tel. 33 10 77 00
Fax 33 10 73 99
Comfortable, stylish hotel with a pleasant veranda overlooking the garden. The "Il Sambuco" restaurant specializes in seafood. Air conditioning, conference room.
🚗 ✗ ⬜

JOLLY TOURING****
Via Tarchetti, 2
Tel. 6335
Fax 659 22 09
Built in the 1920's, this comfortable hotel has now been completely renovated. Air conditioning, disabled access.
🚗 ⬜

KING***
Corso Magenta, 19
Tel. 87 45 45
Fax 34 6 49
A modern and comfortable hotel with good amenities. Air conditioning.
⬜

PRINCIPE DI SAVOIA*****
Piazza d. Repubblica, 17
Tel. 62301
Fax 659 58 38
A historic Milanese hotel, very near the Central Station. An imposing neoclassical façade hides a stylish and elegant interior. Air conditioning, gym, solarium, sauna.
🚗 🏊 ⬜

RESTAURANTS

AIMO E NADIA
Via Montecuccoli, 6
Tel. 41 68 86
Fax 48 30 20 05
Closed Sat. lunchtime, Sun. and Aug.
This quiet restaurant in the suburbs serves a balance of traditional and innovative cuisine. Wonderful food and an inspiring wine list.
⬜

ANTICA TRATTORIA MONLUÈ
Via Monluè, 75
Tel. 761 02 46
Closed Sat. lunchtime; Sun.; Aug.
Perhaps the oldest Milanese trattoria in an

old "borgo" (village) at the gates of Milan.
🖂

BICE
Via Borgospesso, 12
Tel. 76 00 25 72
Closed Mon.; Tue. lunchtime, and Aug.
Famous restaurant established in the 1920's. Specializes in Tuscan cuisine. Good regional wine list.
🖂

BISTROT DI GUALTIERO MARCHESI
Via S. Raffaele, 2
Tel. 87 71 20
Fax 87 70 35
Closed Sun. and Mon. lunchtime and part of Aug.
Enjoy an inspiring view over the spires of the

Duomo while sampling creative Lombard cuisine. Great desserts.
🔆 🖂

BOEUCC
Piazza Belgioioso, 2
Tel. 76 02 02 24
Fax 79 61 73
Closed Sat.; Sun. lunchtime, and Aug.
Built in the old stables of the 18th-century Palazzo Belgioioso. Classic Lombard cuisine and an excellent wine list. Tables on the veranda in summer.
🖂

CALAJUNCO
Via Stoppani, 5
Tel. 204 60 03
Closed Sat. lunchtime; Sun. and part of Aug.
Traditional cooking from the Aeolian islands. The restaurant is decorated in the typical colors of the islands.
🖂

CINQUE TERRE
Via Appiani, 9
Tel. 657 51 77
Fax 65 30 34
Closed Sat. lunchtime; Sun.; part of Aug.
Traditional Ligurian cuisine. Good choice of Italian wines.
🖂

★ DO NOT MISS ★
TRIENNALE
The *Triennale* houses a permanent collection of architecture entitled *Collezione permanente del museo del design Italiano 1945–90* (permanent collection of the Italian Design Museum 1945–90). It dedicates its space to exhibitions of various types and themes, from architecture to costume, from movies to photography. It also houses permanent assets, of which the design collection is part, together with the archives of the network of town planning.
INFORMATION:
Ente Autonomo La Triennale di Milano
Viale Alemagna, 6 Milano
Tel. 72 43 42 40 or, 72 43 42 41
Fax 72 43 42 39

GIANNINO
Via Sciesa, 8
Tel. 55 19 55 82
Fax 55 19 57 90
Closed Sun. and Aug.
A fusion of regional cuisines in one of the city's oldest restaurants.
🖂

JOIA
Via Panfilo Castaldi, 18
Tel. 29 52 21 24
Closed Sat. lunchtime, Sun. and Aug.
Chef Pietro Leemann has created an imaginative menu of delicate vegetable and seafood dishes.
🖂

IL MONTALCINO
Via Valenza, 17
Tel. 89 40 37 83
Closed Sun. and part of Aug.
Exquisite Tuscan cuisine in a family-run restaurant. Specialties include game, venison and red meats. Regional wine list.
🖂

SAVINI
Galleria V. Emanuele II
Tel. 72 00 34 33
Fax 86 46 10 60
Closed Sat. lunchtime; Sun. and Aug.
Established in 1867, this is one of Milan's most famous restaurants. Sumptuous interior, rich cuisine and wonderful desserts.
🖂

CULTURE

CIVIC BUILDINGS
◆ CASTELLO SFORZESCO
Piazza Castello
Tel. 62 08 35 52
◆ PINACOTECA E BIBLIOTECA AMBROSIANA

Piazza Pio XI, 2
Tel. 86 45 14 36
◆ PINACOTECA DI BRERA
Via Brera, 28
Tel. 86 46 35 01
Closed Mon.
Open 9am–5.30pm;
Sun. and public holidays
9am–noon

RELIGIOUS BUILDINGS
◆ BASILICA DI S. AMBROGIO
Piazza S. Ambrogio, 25
Tel. 805 73 10
Open 9.30am–noon, 2.30–6pm
◆ BASILICA DI S. EUSTORGIO
Piazza S. Eustorgio, 1
Tel. 58 10 15 83
Open 8am–noon, 3–7pm
Portinari chapel may be visited on request.
◆ BASILICA DI S. LORENZO
Corso di Porta Ticinese
Tel. 832 29 40
◆ DUOMO
Piazza del Duomo
Tel. 86 46 34 56
Paleo-Christian finds
Closed Mon.
Open 10am–noon, 3–7pm
Ascent to the roof.
Open from 9am–5pm;
Oct.–Feb. 9am–4.30pm

MUSEUMS
◆ CENACOLO VINCIANO (DA VINCI'S "LAST SUPPER").
Piazza S. Maria delle Grazie, 2
Tel. 498 75 88
Closed Mon.
Open 8am–1.45pm
◆ CIVICA GALLERIA D'ARTE MODERNA (MUNICIPAL GALLERY OF MODERN ART)
Via Palestro, 16
Tel. 76 00 28 19
Closed Mon.
Open 9.30am–5.30pm

◆ CIVICO MUSEO ARCHEOLOGICO (ARCHEOLOGICAL MUSEUM)
Corso Magenta, 15
Tel. 86 45 06 65
Closed Mon.
◆ CIVICO MUSEO D'ARTE CONTEMPORANEA (MUNICIPAL MUSEUM OF CONTEMPORARY ART)
Palazzo Reale
Piazza del Duomo
Tel. 62 08 35 04
Closed Mon.
Open 9.30am–5.30pm
◆ CIVICO MUSEO DI STORIA NATURALE (NATURAL HISTORY MUSEUM)
Corso Venezia, 55
Tel. 62 08 54 05
Closed Mon.
Open 9.30am–5.30pm;
Sat. and public holidays
9.30am–6.30pm
◆ MUSEO BAGATTI VALSECCHI
Via S. Spirito, 10
Tel. 76 00 61 32
Closed Mon.
Open 1–5pm
◆ MUSEO DEL DUOMO
Palazzo Reale
Piazza del Duomo
Tel. 86 03 58
Closed Mon.
Open 9.30am–12.30pm, 3–6pm
◆ MUSEO NAZIONALE DELLA SCIENZA E DELLA TECNICA (NATIONAL MUSEUM OF SCIENCE AND TECHNOLOGY)
Via S. Vittore, 21
Tel. 48 01 00 40
Closed Mon. except on public holidays
Open 9.30am–4.50pm
◆ MUSEO POLDI PEZZOLI
Via Manzoni, 12
Tel. 79 48 89
Closed Mon.; public holidays; Sun. afternoons April–Sep.
Open 9.30am–12.30pm, 2.30–6pm
◆ MUSEO TEATRALE ALLA SCALA
Piazza della Scala
Tel. 805 34 18
Closed Sun.; Nov.–April.
Open 9am–noon, 2–6pm

For monuments and cultural institutions not listed here, contact:
APT
Via Marconi, 1
Tel. 72 52 43 00
Fax 72 52 43 50
Open 8am–8pm

515

DIALING CODE 041

PRACTICAL INFORMATION

POSTAL CODE
30100

DIALING CODE
041

TOURIST INFORMATION
◆ APT
S. Marco, 71/c
Tel. 522 63 56
Fax 529 87 30
Stazione F.S.
Tel. 71 90 78
Gran Viale S. Maria
Elisabetta, 6/A
Tel. 526 52 71
Fax 529 87 20

MAIN POST OFFICE
Via Cannaregio, 1
Tel. 71 65 94

EMERGENCIES

AMBULANCE SERVICE
Tel. 523 00 00

MEDICAL SERVICES
Tel. 534 44 11

POLICE
Central headquarters
Tel. 271 55 11
Highway patrol
Tel. 534 34 34

FIRE SERVICE
Tel. 115

TRANSPORT

AIR
AEROPORTO
INTERNAZIONALE
MARCO POLO-TESSERA
8 miles north of the city
Information:
Tel. 260 92 60
◆ ALITALIA
Via Sansovino, 7
Mestre
Tel. 258 11 11

RAIL
STAZIONE SANTA LUCIA
Fondamenta S. Lucia
Information:
Tel. 71 55 55

CAR
ACI-AUTOMOBILE
CLUB D'ITALIA
Via Ca' Marcello, 67/A
Mestre
Enquiries:
Tel. 531 03 48
Car rental:
Tel. 531 03 48
Emergency breakdown
services:
Tel. 116

CAR RENTAL
◆ AVIS
– Piazzale Roma, 496/H
Tel. 522 58 25,
or 523 73 77
– Aeroporto Marco Polo
Tel. 541 50 30
◆ EURODOLLAR
– Piazzale Roma, 468/B
Tel. 528 95 51
Fax 520 83 96
– Aeroporto Marco Polo
Tel. and fax 5411570
or 167-018668 (toll-free)
◆ EUROPCAR
– S. Croce, 496/H
Tel. 523 73 57,
or 523 86 16
◆ HERTZ
– S. Croce, 496/E
Tel. 528 35 24,
or 528 40 91
– Aeroporto Marco Polo
Tel. 541 60 75
◆ MAGGIORE-BUDGET
– Stazione F.S.-Mestre
Tel. 93 53 00
– Aeroporto Marco Polo
Tel. 541 50 40

PUBLIC TRANSPORT
A.C.T.V. AZIENDA DEL
CONSORZIO TRASPORTI
VENEZIANO
Corte dell'Albero
Casella Postale 688
Fax 520 71 35
Information office
Tel. 528 78 86
Open 7.30am–8pm,
also public holidays

TAXIS
TAXI A VENEZIA TAXI
CONSORZIO
public motorboat service
S. Polo, 2583
Tel. 72 31 12
TAXI COOPERATIVA
SAN MARCO
Via Dorsoduro, 167
Tel. 522 23 03
TAXI COOPERATIVA
SERENISSIMA
in front of Danieli hotel
Tel. 522 85 38
RADIOTAXI
Via Piave, 208
Mestre
Tel. 93 62 22
Fax 93 61 37
Taxi station:
Mestre Ferrovia
Tel. 92 94 99

HOTELS

ABBAZIA★★★
(CANNAREGIO)
Calle Priuli, 68
Tel. 71 73 33
Fax 71 79 49
*The name is from the
old abbey ("abbazia")
upon which it was built,
the convent of the
Scalzi Carmelites. A
fascinating place to
visit. Garden, air
conditioning.*
🅲 ✂ ⬜ 🅳

AGLI ALBORETTI★★
(ACCADEMIA)
Rio terrà A. Foscarini,
884
Tel. 523 00 58
Fax 521 01 58
*This lovely hotel with a
pleasant courtyard
garden offers simple,
friendly hospitality.*
🚗 ⬜

AMADEUS★★★★
(CANNAREGIO)
Lista di Spagna, 227
Tel. 71 53 00
Fax 524 08 41
*A luxury hotel just a few
steps from the main*

stations. It boasts
two of the city's
best restaurants,
"Papageno" and
"La Veranda". Garden.
Air conditioning,
conference room.*
🚗 ⬜ 🅳

ATENEO★★★
(SAN MARCO)
Calle Minelli, 1876
Tel. 520 07 77
Fax 522 85 50
*A modern hotel which
has the use of a private
landing-stage and is
very near La Fenice.
Recently restored.
Air conditioning.*
🅲 ⬜ 🅳

BISANZIO★★★
(CASTELLO)
Calle della Pietà, 3651
Tel. 520 31 00
Fax 52 04 41 14
*A small, quiet hotel
in the historic center.
Attractive bedrooms.
Private landing-stage
for gondolas and
motorboats. Air
conditioning.*
🅲 ⬜ 🅳

CASANOVA★★★
(SAN MARCO)
Frezzeria, 1284
Tel. 520 68 55
Fax 520 64 13
*A few steps from
St Mark's Square;
welcoming and
comfortable. Air
conditioning.*
🅲 🚗 ⬜ 🅳

CAVALLETTO & DOGE ORSEOLO★★★★
(SAN MARCO)
Calle del Cavalletto,
1107
Tel. 520 09 95
Fax 523 81 84
*Equipped with a
gondola and motorboat
landing-stage, this
complex has been built
over the remains of a
14th-century inn.
Air conditioning,
conference room.*
🅲 ⚔ 🚗 ⬜ 🅳

CIPRIANI★★★★
(GIUDECCA)
Fondamenta
S. Giovanni, 10
Tel. 520 77 44
Fax 520 39 30
*Luxury complex with
private tennis court,
Olympic seawater
swimming pool, private
moorings. Sumptuous*

rooms. Air conditioning, sauna, conference room, disabled access.
C ⅍ 🚗 ⌕ ▭ ☐

★DANIELI★★★★★
(CASTELLO)
Riva degli Schiavoni, 4196
Tel. 522 64 80
Fax 520 02 08
A luxurious hotel in the splendid 14th-century Palazzo Dandolo. Peaceful and elegant, with sumptuous decor. Impeccable service. Air conditioning, conference room.
C ⅍ 🚗 ▭ ☐

DES BAINS CIGA HOTEL-ITT SHERATON★★★★
(LIDO)
Lungomare Marconi, 17
Tel. 526 59 21
Fax 526 01 13
Internationally renowned hotel immortalized in Thomas Mann's "Death in Venice". All the rooms have balconies or terraces with sea views. Garden, air conditioning, conference room, beach, tennis, sauna.
⅍ P ⚒ ⌕ ▭ ☐

LA FENICE & DES ARTISTES★★★
(SAN MARCO)
Campiello della Fenice, 1936
Tel. 523 23 33
Fax 520 37 21
Typical Venetian furnishings in a peaceful setting. Favored by opera singers. Garden, air conditioning.
C ▭ ☐

GABRIELLI SANDWIRTH★★★★
(CASTELLO)
Riva degli Schiavoni, 4110
Tel. 523 15 80
Fax 520 94 55

★ **DO NOT MISS** ★
LA MOSTRA
(INTERNATIONAL CINEMATOGRAPHIC ART EXHIBITION)
This exhibition is for both commercially released movies and those not on general release. It is the most prestigious cinematographic festival in Italy, and (together with those in Berlin and Cannes), one of the most important in Europe.
Winners are awarded the Leone d'Oro.
Takes place in early September.
INFORMATION
Ufficio attività d'istituto, Ca' Giustinian/San Marco
Tel. 521 88 63

Housed in 13th-century Palazzo Gabrielli, this elegant hotel is furnished in 18th-century Venetian style. Lovely internal courtyard. Air conditioning.
C ⅍ 🚗 ▭ ☐

GIORGIONE★★★
(CANNAREGIO)
Campo SS. Apostoli, 4587
Tel. 522 58 10
Fax 523 90 92
In a peaceful position, this beautifully renovated palazzo has retained its garden and internal courtyard. Air conditioning, disabled access.
▭ ⚒ ☐

★GRITTI PALACE ITT SHERATON★★★★★
(SAN MARCO)
Campo S. Maria del Giglio, 2467
Tel. 79 46 11
Fax 520 09 42
The original fittings have been preserved in this splendid 15th-century doge's residence on the Canal Grande. A real gem. Air conditioning, conference room.
C ⅍ ⚒ ▭ ☐

★LIDO DI VENEZIA EXCELSIOR★★★★★
(LIDO)
Lungomare Marconi, 41
Tel. 526 02 01
Fax 526 72 76
An early 20th-century Lido hotel, exclusive and sophisticated and favored by celebrities. Garden, air conditioning, conference room, beach, tonnis, golf, solarium, disabled access.
⅍ 🚗 P ⌕ ▭ ☐

LONDRA PALACE★★★★
(CASTELLO)
Riva degli Schiavoni, 4171
Tel. 520 05 33
Fax 522 50 32
A few steps from St Mark's, this is known as "a hundred windows over the lagoon". Stylish bedrooms and wood-paneled bathrooms. The restaurant, "Do Leoni" is well worth a visit for its regional dishes and beautiful views. Air conditioning.
C ⅍ 🚗 ⌕ ▭ ☐

LUNA HOTEL BAGLIONI★★★★
(SAN MARCO)
Calle larga dell'Ascension, 1243
Tel. 528 98 40
Fax 528 1 60
In one of the most elegant palazzos in Venice with frescos in the bedrooms and paintings by well-known artists, this hotel is the

oldest in the city. It was already known in the Middle Ages as a stop for Knights Templar. An excellent restaurant, the "Canova", offers Venetian specialties. Air conditioning, conference room, disabled access.
C 🚗 ⚒ ▭ ☐

METROPOLE★★★★
(CASTELLO)
Riva degli Schiavoni, 4149
Tel. 520 50 44
Fax 522 36 79
A patrician residence which was transformed into a small hotel in the early 19th century. Comfortable and charming, it has period fittings and an

interesting collection of antiques. Air conditioning, conference room.
C ⅍ 🚗 ▭ ☐

MONACO & GRAND CANAL★★★★
(SAN MARCO)
Calle Vallaresso, 1325
Tel. 520 02 11
Fax 520 05 01
A splendid position (where the Grand Canal meets St Mark's basin), and a warm welcome characterize this lovely hotel. Stunning views. Garden, air conditioning, conference room.
C ⅍ ⚒ ▭ ☐

PAUSANIA★★★
(DORSODURO)
Fondamenta Gherardini, 2824
Tel. 522 20 83
Fax 522 29 89
A charming old patrician house, tastefully renovated, with a truly beautiful veranda. Garden, air conditioning.
C ▭ ☐

DIALING CODE 041

YOUTH HOSTEL

OSTELLO A.I.G. VENEZIA
Giudecca, 86
Tel. 523 82 11

CAMPING AND TOURIST VILLAGES

CAMPING AL BOSCHETTO
Via delle Batterie
(Ca' Vio)
Tel. 96 61 45
Fax 530 11 91

CAMPING CA' PASQUALI
Via Poerio, 33
Treporti
Tel. 96 64 81
Fax 530 07 97

CAMPING CA' SAVIO
Via di Ca' Savio,
Località Ca' Savio
Treporti
Tel. 96 60 17

CAMPING CAVALLINO
Via delle Batterie, 164
Tel. 96 61 33
Fax 530 08 27

CAMPING ITALY
Via Fausta-Cavallino,
272
Tel. 96 80 90
or 537 00 76
Fax 537 03 55

CAMPING MARINA DI VENEZIA
Via Montello Punta
Sabbioni, 6
Tel. 530 09 55
Fax 96 60 36

CAMPING RESIDENCE VILLAGGIO TURISTICO ALBERGHIERO
Via F. Baracca-
Cavallino, 47
Tel. 96 80 27
Fax 537 01 64

CAMPING SAN NICOLO-LIDO
Riviera S. Nicolò, 65
Lido di Venezia
Tel. 526 74 15

★ DO NOT MISS ★
THE ISLANDS OF THE LAGOON

In the islands of Venice, art and the landscape combine to perfection. The larger islands (Murano, Burano and the more distant and silent Torcello), as well as the smaller ones (such as San Lazzaro degli Armeni, so loved by Byron) offer splendid art treasures and sublime views, which have been a source of inspiration to generations of sightseers. To all this, Murano and Burano add their ancient traditions of craftsmanship: they have both been home to specialized glass workshops since the 13th century; and Burano has been famed for lace-making since the 1500's.
A tour of the three islands takes a whole day.

INFORMATION
APT
S. Marco 71/c
Tel. 522 63 56

CAMPING VILLAGE DEI FIORI
Via Batterie, 38
Treporti
Tel. 96 64 48
Fax 96 67 24

CAMPING VILLAGE GARDEN PARADISO
Via F. Baracca-
Cavallino, 55
Tel. 96 80 75
Fax 537 03 82

CAMPING VILLAGE JOKER
Via Fausta-Cavallino,
318
Tel. 537 07 66
Fax 96 82 16

CAMPING VILLAGE MEDITERRANEO
Via delle Batterie, 38
Ca' Vio
Treporti
Tel. 96 67 21
Fax 96 69 44

CAMPING VILLAGE VELA BLU
Via Radaelli-Cavallino, 10
Tel. 96 80 68

RESTAURANTS

A LA VECIA CAVANA
(CANNAREGIO)
Rio Terrà Santi

Apostoli, 46214
Tel. 528 71 06
Closed Thur. and
throughout Aug.
*Once a gondola
shelter, this is
now one
of the
smartest
places to
eat in
Cannaregio.
A taste of
ancient Venice
both in the décor
and the menu.*

ANTICA CARBONERA
(SAN MARCO)
Calle Bembo, 4648
Tel. 522 54 79
Closed Sun. and Thur.
in high season;
Feb. 1–15 and July
*Late 19th-century
setting with furnishings
from the yacht
belonging to Duke
Rudolph of Habsburg,
and precious paintings
by well-known artists.
Traditional fare.*

ANTICA TRATTORIA ALLA MADDALENA
(BURANO)
Mazzorbo, 7/A
Tel. 73 01 51
Closed Thur. and
Dec. 20–Jan. 20
*On the small island of
Mazzorbo (reached
via bridge
from
Burano), this
trattoria has
been here
for over*

---

forty years. Simple,
fresh food. Specialties
include soups, fish and
rice, duck and game.

ANTICO MARTINI
(SAN MARCO)
Campo S. Fantin, 1983
Tel. 522 41 21
Fax 528 98 57
Closed Tue., and Wed.
lunchtime.
*Founded in 1720.
The Baldi family have
served first-class local
cuisine here since 1920.
Good wine list.*

BACARETO
(SAN MARCO)
San Samuele, 3447
Tel. 528 93 36
Closed Sat. evenings,
Sun. and Aug.
*Founded at the end
of the 19th century,
this is one of the last
traditional Venetian
"osterie" (inns)
where the ritual
of "ombra"
♦ 519, is
still practised.
The limited
menu
(cuttlefish, liver,
salt cod), offers
exclusively
traditional dishes.*

BENTIGODI DA ANDREA
(CANNAREGIO)
Calesele, 1423–24
Tel. 71 62 69
Closed Sun.
*A recently opened
osteria serving
traditional dishes; the
bar-top is crammed with
"cicheti" (nibbles) ♦ 519,
vegetables and main
course are chosen at
the buffet, while starters
(soups and risottos) are
served at the table.*

CAMPIELLO
(SAN MARCO)
Calle dei Fuseri, 4346
Tel. 520 63 96
Fax 520 63 96
Closed Mon. and part
of Aug.
*Interesting seafood
cuisine, drawing on
traditional dishes. Much
frequented by artists.*

★CORTE SCONTA
(CASTELLO)
Calle del Pestrin, 3886

Tel. 522 70 24
Fax 522 75 13
Closed Sun. and Mon.,
for a period Jan.–Feb.
and for a period
Jul.–Aug.
*Excellent traditional
fish cuisine in a simple,
lively restaurant.
Impressive antipasti.*
▱

Covo
(CASTELLO)
Campiello della
Poccaria, 3968
Tel. 522 38 12
Closed Wed. and Thur.
*Fish specialties are
cooked by the owner
with the simplicity of
authentic Italian cuisine.
Excellent selection of
wines. Memorable
desserts.*
▱

> ★ **DO NOT MISS** ★
> THE "OMBRA" RITUAL
>
> The ritual of *ombra*, a glass of red or white
> wine (it should be light, not full-bodied), drunk
> as an aperitif, is the typical calling-card of
> traditional Venetians, who love socializing and
> conversation. If you know any Venetians, get
> together with them for an *ombra* and *cicheti*,
> the snacks which accompany the aperitif:
> sardines (*sarde*), Venetian fried fish ("*saor*"),
> baby squids (*calamaretti*), baby cuttlefish
> (*seppioline*), mussels (*cozze*), and in winter
> boiled artichokes (*carciofi*).

HARRY'S BAR
(SAN MARCO)
Calle Vallaresso, 1323
Tel. 528 57 77
Fax 520 88 22
Closed Mon.
*The famous Harry's
bar offers unique
cocktails and great food.
A good atmosphere,
if inclined to be touristy
in summer.*
▱

★OSTERIA DA FIORE
(SAN POLO)
Calle del Scaleter, 2202
Tel. 72 13 08
Fax 72 13 43
Closed Sun. and Mon.
*A charming and very
popular restaurant
serving high-quality
cuisine. Wonderful
risotto. Select wine list.
Advance reservation
essential.*
▱

OSTERIA DEL PAMPO
(SANT'ELENA)
Calle Chinotto, 24
Tel. 520 84 19
Closed Fri.

*In the Castello (castle)
area, this is one of the
most popular and
authentic trattorias in
the city. Delicious fish
risottos, salt cod and
cuttlefish dishes.*

TESTIERE
(CASTELLO)
Calle del Mondo Novo,
5801
Tel. 522 72 20
Closed Sun.
*Between the Rialto and
Santa Maria Formosa,
this former wine tap-
room is decorated
with old bedheads
and transformed
into a tiny trattoria.
Specialties: traditional
dishes, all fish-based.
Reservations are
essential.*
▱

CULTURE

CIVIC BUILDINGS
◆ ARSENALE
Piazza Castello
Tel. 62 08 35 52
◆ BIBLIOTECA MARCIANA
(NATIONAL LIBRARY)
Piazzetta San Marco, 7
Tel. 520 87 88
Closed Sun.
Open 9am–7pm; Sun.
9am–1.30pm
◆ PALAZZO DUCALE
Piazzetta San Marco
Tel. 522 49 51
Open 9am–4pm
◆ PINACOTECA
QUERINI STAMPALIA
(PICTURE GALLERY)
Campiello Querini-
Stampalia 4778
Tel. 520 34 33,
or 522 52 35
Closed Mon.
Open 10am–12.30pm

◆ SCUOLA GRANDE
DI SAN ROCCO
Campo di
San Rocco 3054
Tel. 523 48 64
Open 10am–1pm; Sat.
and Sun. 10am–4pm

RELIGIOUS BUILDINGS
◆ BASILICA DI
SAN MARCO
Piazza San Marco
Tel. 522 56 07
Open 9.45am–5pm
(summer); Sun. 2–5pm;
10am–4pm (winter);
Sun. 2–4pm
◆ IL REDENTORE
Tel. 523 14 15
Open 8am–noon,
4–6.30pm
◆ SANTA MARIA ASSUNTA
(TORCELLO)
Tel. 73 00 84
Open 10am–12.30pm,
2–5pm
◆ SANTA MARIA
DELLA SALUTE
Tel. 522 55 58
Open 9.30am–noon,
3–5pm
◆ SANTA MARIA
GLORIOSA
DEI FRARI
Tel. 522 26 37
Open 9.30am–noon,
2.30–5.30 (winter);
9am–noon, 2.30–6pm
(summer).
◆ SANTI GIOVANNI
E PAOLO
Tel. 523 75 10
Open 7.30am–12.30pm,
3.30–6pm
◆ SANTA MARIA E
DONATO (MURANO)
Tel. 73 90 56
Open 8am–noon,
4–7pm

MUSEUMS
◆ CA' D'ORO-
GALLERIA FRANCHETTI
Calle Ca' d'Oro 3933
Tel. 523 87 90
Open 9am–2pm; Sun.
and public holidays
9am–1pm
◆ PEGGY GUGGENHEIM
COLLECTION
Calle San Cristoforo,
701
Tel. 520 62 88
Closed Tue.
Open 11am–6pm;
Sat. 6–9pm
◆ MUSEO D'ARTE
MODERNA
Santa Croce 2078
Tel. 72 11 27

(INTERNATIONAL GALLERY
OF MODERN ART)
Closed Mon.
Open 10am–4pm
(winter); 10am–5pm
(summer).
◆ GALLERIE
DELL'ACCADEMIA
Campo della
Carità 1050
Tel. 522 22 47
Open 9am–2pm; Sun.
and public holidays
9am–1pm
◆ MUSEO
ARCHEOLOGICO
(ARCHEOLOGICAL
MUSEUM)
Piazzetta San Marco, 17
Tel. 522 59 78
Open 9am–2pm; Sun.
and public holidays
9am–1pm
◆ MUSEO CIVICO
CORRER
Piazza San Marco, 52
Tel. 522 56 25
Closed Tue.
Open 10am–4pm
◆ MUSEO D'ARTE
ORIENTALE (MUSEUM OF
ORIENTAL ART)
Santa Croce 2076
Tel. 524 11 73
Closed Mon.
Open 9am–1.30pm
◆ MUSEO DELL'ARTE
VETRARIA (GLASS

MUSEUM, MURANO)
Fondamenta Marco
Giustiniani
Tel. 73 95 86
Closed Wed.
Open 9am–4pm
◆ PALA D'ORO AND
THE TREASURES OF
SAN MARCO
Basilica di San Marco
Tel. 522 56 97
Open 10am–4pm;
Sun. and public
holidays
1.45–4pm

DIALING CODE 051

PRACTICAL INFORMATION

POSTAL CODE
40100

DIALING CODE
051

TOURIST INFORMATION
◆ APT
Piazza Maggiore, 6
Tel. 23 96 60
Stazione FS
Piazza Medaglie
d'Oro, 4
Tel. 24 65 41
Aeroporto G. Marconi
Tel. 647 20 36

MAIN POST OFFICE
Agenzia P.I. Bologna
Succursale 1
Viale Pietramellara, 18
Tel. 24 34 25
Open 8.30am–1.30pm

EMERGENCIES

AMBULANCE SERVICE
Ambulances Cinque
Tel. 50 50 50
Bologna soccorso
Tel. 33 33 33
Italian Red Cross
Tel. 23 45 67

MEDICAL SERVICES
Blood transfusion center
Ospedale Maggiore
Tel. 647 81 11
C.O.S. emergency
medical help
Tel. 22 44 66
Toxicology unit
Ospedale Maggiore
Tel. 33 33 33
Ospedale Santa
Orsola
Tel. 636 44 29
Ospedale Maggiore-
Sezione d'Azeglio
Tel. 33 10 00

POLICE
Emergency
intervention
Tel. 23 33 33
Highway patrol
Tel. 649 20 20

FIRE SERVICE
Tel. 115

TRANSPORT

AIR
AEROPORTO G. MARCONI
4 miles northwest of
town
Borgo Panigale
Via Triumvirato, 84
Tel. 38 39 44,
or 31 15 78
Fax 56 33 63
◆ ALITALIA
Via Riva Reno, 65
Tel. 630 01 11

RAIL
STAZIONE FS
Piazza Medaglie D'Oro, 4
Tel. 246490

CAR
ACI (AUTOMOBILE CLUB
D'ITALIA)
Via Marzabotto, 2
Tel. 38 99 08,
or 38 14 78
Fax 38 26 82
Car rental:
Via Calori, 10/D
Tel. 55 10 48
or 55 61 55
Emergency breakdown
service:
Tel. 116

CAR RENTAL
◆ AVIS
Via Marco Polo, 91/A
Tel. 634 16 32
Fax 634 64 20
◆ EURODOLLAR
Viale Masini, 4/3
Tel. 25 55 46,
or 25 41 26
Fax 25 52 26
Aeroporto G. Marconi
Tel. 647 20 27
Fax 647 20 52
◆ EUROPCAR ITALIA
Via Boldrini, 3/A/B
Tel. 247230
◆ HERTZ ITALIANA
Via Amendola, 17
Tel. 25 37 43
or 25 48 52
Aeroporto G. Marconi
Tel. 647 20 06
Fax 647 20 14
◆ MAGGIORE-BUDGET
Via Fratelli Cairoli, 4
Tel. 25 25 25

PUBLIC TRANSPORT
A.T.C. AZIENDA
TRASPORTI CONSORZIALI
Via Saliceto, 3
Information:
Tel. 24 70 05
or 24 83 74
Open 7am–7pm

TAXIS
CO.TA.BO.
Tel. 37 27 27
RADIOTAXI
Tel. 53 41 41

HOTELS

AL CAPPELLO ROSSO★★★★
Via de' Fusari, 9
Tel. 26 18 91
Fax 22 71 79
This building has been a hotel since the 14th-century, and now offers comfortable modern fittings. Ask for an en-suite in the attic, on the fourth floor.
Air conditioning, conference room, disabled access.

ASTORIA★★★
Via Fratelli Rosselli, 14
Tel. 52 14 10
Fax 52 47 39
In a good location, this hotel has a friendly bar, and a delightful garden.
Air conditioning.

CITY HOTEL★★★
Via Magenta, 10
Tel. 37 26 76
Fax 37 20 32
Well situated for tourists and business travelers, this is a comfortable hotel with good facilities. Garden, air conditioning, conference room.

CORONA D'ORO★★★★
Via G. Oberdan, 12
Tel. 23 64 56
Fax 26 26 79
Recently renovated, the building is a synthesis of different architectural styles and eras, from the 14th to early 20th centuries, with an Art Nouveau staircase and hall. Air conditioning, conference room.

DEI COMMERCIANTI★★★
Via de' Pignattari, 11
Tel. 233052
Fax 224733
This 13th-century palazzo is antique in style, yet its rooms are comfortable with modern fittings. Air conditioning, disabled access.

HOLIDAY INN BOLOGNA TOWER★★★★
Viale Lenin, 43
Tel. 601 09 09
Fax 601 07 00

Well equipped for business guests, this hotel is pleasant and comfortable and has a good restaurant, "La Caveja". Air conditioning, conference room, sauna, disabled access.

INTERNAZIONALE★★★★
Via dell'Indipendenza, 60
Tel. 24 55 44
Fax 24 95 44
This classic example of a Bologna palazzo is now renovated as a modern hotel. Air conditioning, conference room, disabled access.

SAN DONATO★★★★
Via Zamboni, 16
Tel. 23 53 95
Fax 633 23 66
Highly recommended for business travelers, this handsome 17th-century palazzo is equipped with every comfort. Air conditioning.

OROLOGIO★★★
Via IV Novembre, 10
Tel. 23 12 53
Fax 26 05 52
An ancient palazzo right in the historic center of Bologna; some rooms have a view of the Piazza Maggiore. Air conditioning.

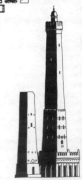

TOURING***
Via de' Mattuiani, 1/2
Tel. 58 43 05
Fax 33 47 63
This hotel has a large terrace with a magnificent view. Recently renovated. Air conditioning, solarium.
☀ 🚗 ▭ □

YOUTH HOSTELS

A.I.G. DUE TORRI-SAN SISTO 2
Via Viadagola, 5
Tel. and fax 50 18 10

OSTELLO DELLA GIOVENTÙ SAN SISTO
Via Viadagola, 14
Tel. and fax 51 92 02

CAMPING AND TOURIST VILLAGES

CAMPING PICCOLO PARADISO
Leona di Sasso Marconi
Tel. 84 26 80

CITTÀ DI BOLOGNA
Via Romita, 12/4A
Tel. 32 50 16
Fax 32 53 18
Open all year

RESTAURANTS

ANTICA TRATTORIA DEL CACCIATORE
Via Caduti di Casteldebole, 5
Tel. 56 42 03
Fax 56 71 28
Closed Mon. and Sat. evenings and part of Aug.
An out-of-town eatery, with a friendly rustic atmosphere and a garden and veranda ideal for lunches in the countryside. Typical Emilian cuisine. Air conditioning.
🍴⋯ ▭

CANTINA BENTIVOGLIO
Via Mascarella, 4/B
Tel. 26 54 16
Closed Mon.
An "enoteca" (wine cellar) offering a choice of more than 200 different wines. Starters of fresh pasta and various Italian specialties, from cheese to salami to desserts. Good jazz bands.
🍴 ▭

CARLO
Via Marchesana, 6
Tel. 23 32 27
Closed Tue. and Sun. evening, part of Jan. and part of Aug.

Situated under the portico of an 18th-century palazzo, this wonderful setting is ideal for tasting the delicious cuisine on offer, both regional and classic. Air conditioning.
▭

CARRACCI
Via Manzoni, 2
Tel. 22 20 49
Closed Sun. and throughout Aug.
Authentic Emilian cuisine is the mainstay of this attractive, elegant restaurant. Air conditioning.
▭

★DIANA
Via dell' Indipendenza, 24
Tel. 23 13 02
Closed Mon., part of Jan. and part of Aug.
One of Bologna's best-known restaurants, Diana is distinguished by its typically 1930's style. Excellent food. Very pleasant garden which is open in summer. Air conditioning.
▭

FRANCO ROSSI
Via Goito, 3
Tel. 23 88 18
Closed Sun. (always open during the Fiera).
Classic Bolognese cuisine in one of the most acclaimed restaurants in the city. Air conditioning.
▭

GRASSILLI
Via dal Luzzo, 3
Tel. and fax 22 29 61
Closed Wed., public holidays in the evenings and mid-July–mid-Aug.
This long-established restaurant was once frequented by stars of the theater, as the pictures on the walls attest. Great food. Air conditioning.
▭

★PAPPAGALLO
Piazza Mercanzia, 3
Tel. and fax 23 28 07
Closed Sun.
A long-established restaurant housed in a 14th-century palazzo; elegant and exclusive. Local cuisine. Garden, air conditioning.
▭

RODRIGO
Via della Zecca, 2/H
Tel. and fax 22 04 45
Closed Sun. and part of Aug.
The wood decor gives this restaurant a warm, comfortable atmosphere. Classic Bolognese cuisine. Air conditioning.
▭

ROSTERIA LUCIANO
Via Sauro, 19
Tel. 23 12 49
Fax 26 09 48
Closed Wed. and mid-July–mid-Aug.
This elegant restaurant is traditional both in its furnishings and its wine selection. Excellent regional dishes. Air conditioning.
▭

CULTURE

CIVIC BUILDINGS
◆ ARCHIGINNASIO
Piazza Galvani, 1
Tel. 23 64 88
Closed Sun.
Open Mon.–Fri. 9am–7pm; Sat. 9am–2pm
Library
Open 9am–6.45pm; Sat. 9am–1pm
◆ TEATRO COMUNALE
Largo Respighi, 1
Tel. 52 90 11

RELIGIOUS BUILDINGS
◆ SAN PETRONIO
Piazza Galvani, 5
Tel. 22 54 42, or 23 42 64
◆ SAN STEFANO
Via San Stefano, 24
Tel. 22 32 56
Open 9am–2pm; Sun. and public holidays 9am–1pm

MUSEUMS
◆ COLLEZIONI COMUNALI D'ARTE
Piazza Maggiore, 6
Tel. 20 35 26
Closed Mon.
Open 10am–6pm
◆ MUSEO CIVICO ARCHEOLOGICO (ARCHEOLOGICAL MUSEUM)
Via Archiginnasio, 2
Tel. 23 38 49
Closed Mon.
Open 9am–2pm; Sat. and Sun. 9am–1pm, 3.30–7pm
◆ MUSEO CIVICO MEDIEVALE (MEDIEVAL MUSEUM)
Via Manzoni, 4
Tel. 22 89 12
Closed Tue.
Open 9am–2pm; Sat. and public holidays 9am–1pm, 3.30–7pm
◆ MUSEO MORANDI
Palazzo comunale
Piazza Maggiore, 6
Tel. 20 36 46
Closed Mon.
Open 10am–6pm
◆ PINACOTECA NAZIONALE (PICTURE GALLERY)
Via delle Belle Arti, 56
Tel. 24 32 22
Closed Mon.
Open Tue.–Sat. 9am–2pm; Sun. 9am–1pm

For all monuments and cultural institutions not listed here contact:
APT
Piazza Maggiore, 6
Tel. 23 96 60

★ DO NOT MISS ★
FIERA CAMPIONARIA INTERNAZIONALE
A market exhibition of crafts and other wares, where you can find everything from antique furniture to homemade cheese, or simply wander among the stands to look and learn.
INFORMATION
Bolognafiere
Piazza Costituzione, 6
Tel. 28 21 11
Fax 28 23 32
Takes place during the first half of June.

DIALING CODE 055

PRACTICAL INFORMATION

POSTAL CODE
50100

DIALING CODE
055

TOURIST INFORMATION
◆ APT
Via Manzoni, 16
Tel. 23320
Fax 234 62 86
Stazione FS Santa
Maria Novella
Tel. 21 22 45
◆ APT PROVINCIA
COMUNE
Via Cavour, 1R
Tel. 29 08 32
◆ UFFICI INFORMAZIONI
DEL COMUNE
Chiasso Baroncelli,
17/19R
Tel. 230 21 24

EMBASSIES AND CONSULATES
US
Lungarno Amerigo
Vespucci 38
Tel. 239 82 76
UK
Lungarno Corsini 2
Tel. 28 41 33

MAIN POST OFFICE
Agenzia P.I. Firenze
Succursale 1
Via Galliano, 27–31
Tel. 35 77 58-35 78 83
Open 8.30am–1.30pm

EMERGENCIES

AMBULANCE SERVICE
Misericordia
Tel. 21 22 22
Fratellanza militare
Tel. 21 55 55
Fratelllanza popolare
Tel. 31 13 11
Misericordia SPM
Campo di Marte
Tel. 66 65 55
Humanitas
Tel. 33 11 11
or 71 11 11

MEDICAL SERVICES
Please check which
district you are in:
◆ Historic center
Tel. 28 77 88
◆ San Jacopino-
Puccini-Cascine
Tel. 27 58 27 14
◆ Le Cure-Faentina-
Trespiano-Campo di

Marte-Bolognese
Tel. 57 13 33
◆ Bella Riva-
Coverciano-Rovezzano-
Settignano-Oberdan-
Varlungo
Tel. 67 92 93
◆ S. Frediano-S.
Spirito
Tel. 215616
◆ Galluzzo
Tel. 232 00 82
◆ Gavinana-Sorgane
Tel. 653 03 33
◆ Isolotto-Soffiano-
Argingrosso-S. Bartolo
a Cintoia-Ponte a
Greve
Tel. 71 39 63
◆ Rifredi-Careggi-
Romito-Vittoria-Le
Panche-Tre Pietre-
Castello
Tel. 436 15 41
◆ Ponte di Mezzo-
Firenze Nova
Tel. 41 97 79
◆ Novoli-Peretola-Rozzi-
Osmannoro
Tel. 31 52 25

POLICE
Central headquarters
Tel. 49771
Highway patrol
Tel. 57 77 77

FIRE SERVICE
Tel. 115

TRANSPORT

AIR
AIRPORT: AEROPORTO
AMERIGO VESPUCCI
2 miles northwest of
the city
Via del Termine, 11
Information:
Tel. 37 34 98
◆ ALITALIA
Lungarno Acciaiuoli,
10/12R
Tel. 27888

RAILWAY STATION
STAZIONE FS
Santa Maria Novella
Tel. 28 87 85

CAR
ACI-AUTOMOBILE CLUB
D'ITALIA

Via Amendola, 36
Information:
Tel. 248 62 02
Fax 234 32 57
Breakdown services:
Via Panciatichi, 26/3
Tel. 422 25 33
Breakdown services:
Tel. 116

CAR RENTAL
◆ AVIS
Via di Villamagna, 34R
Tel. 68 42 02
Aeroporto Peretola
Tel. 31 55 88
◆ EURODOLLAR
Via il Prato, 80/R
Tel. 238 24 80
or 238 24 81
Fax 238 24 79
Aeroporto Peretola
Tel. 238 24 80
or 167-01 86 68
(toll-free)
◆ EUROPCAR
Borgo Ognissanti, 53
Tel. 236 00 72
or 236 00 73
◆ HERTZ
Via Maso Finiguerra,
33/R
Tel. 239 82 05
Aeroporto Peretola
Via del Termine, 1
Tel. 30 73 70
◆ MAGGIORE-BUDGET
Via Maso Finiguerra,
31/R
Tel. 29 45 78
or 21 02 38
Aeroporto Peretola
Tel. 31 12 56

PUBLIC TRANSPORT
A.T.A.F. CONSORZIO
INTERCOMUNALE AREA
FIORENTINA
Via dei Mille, 115
Tel. 56501
Fax 565 02 09

TAXIS
TAXI AUTORADIO
Tel. 4242
TAXI RADIO CO.TA.FI.
Tel. 4390
TAXI RADIO SO.CO.TA.
Tel. 4242

HOTELS

ALEXANDER**
Viale Guidoni, 101
Tel. 437 89 51
Fax 41 68 18

*A modern hotel in the
commercial center of
the city, well suited to
business guests.
Air conditioning,
conference room,
disabled access.*
🇨 🚗 ▭ 📺

ALBANI**
Via Fiume, 12
Tel. 26030
Fax 21 10 45
*Early 20th-century
palazzo with a stunning
interior and attractive
furnishings. Air
conditioning,
conference room,
disabled access.*
🇨 🚗 ▭ 📺

AMBASCIATORI**
Via Alamanni, 3
Tel. 28 74 21
Fax 21 23 60
*This well-placed hotel
is notable for its warm
hospitality and the
quality of service. It
houses a permanent
exhibition of modern
paintings and sculpture.
Air conditioning.*
🇨 🚗 ▭ 📺

ANDREA**
Piazza dell'
Indipendenza, 19
Tel. 48 38 90
Fax 46 14 89
*In a tree-lined piazza
in the city center, this
hotel offers comfortable
and quiet rooms, from
which guests can enjoy
a view of the Duomo.
Air conditioning.*
🇨 🇵 ☒ ✄ ▭ 📺

ANGLO-AMERICAN**
Via Garibaldi, 9
Tel. 28 21 14
Fax 26 85 13
*In an 18th-century
palazzo, renovated
but with an original
period interior and
furnishings. Lavish
comfort and dedicated
service. Good
restaurant, "Il
Granduca". Garden,
air conditioning,
conference room.*
🇨 🚗 ▭ 📺

ASTORIA PALAZZO GADDI****
Via del Giglio, 9
Tel. 239 80 95
Fax 21 46 32
Luca Giordano painted the frescos which adorn the inside of this old palazzo, now an attractive hotel. Air conditioning, conference room, disabled access.
C 🚗 ▭ ☐

BERNINI PALACE****
Piazza San Firenze, 29
Tel. 28 86 21
Fax 26 82 72
Situated in the center of town, this is a charming hotel. Light meals are available in its snack bar. Air conditioning, conference room, disabled access.
C 🚗 P ▭ ☐

BRUNELLESCHI****
Piazza San Elisabetta, 3
Tel. 56 20 68
Fax 21 96 53
This hotel successfully blends the old and the new. Attractive public rooms and bedrooms. Air conditioning, conference room.
C ▭ ☐

CALZAIUOLI***
Via Calzaiuoli, 6
Tel. 21 24 56
Fax 26 83 10
A typical Florentine palazzo, between Piazza del Duomo and Piazza della Signoria. Air conditioning, disabled access.
C � ▭ ☐

CASCI**
Via Cavour, 13
Tel. 21 16 86
Fax 239 64 61
This 15th-century building, in which the famous musician Gioacchino Rossini once lived is today an intimate little hotel.
C 🚗 ▭ ☐

CROCE DI MALTA****
Via della Scala, 7
Tel. 21 83 51
Fax 28 71 21
An ancient convent which today houses a tasteful modern hotel. Garden, air conditioning, conference room, disabled access.
C 🚗 ⊃ ✱ ▭ ☐

DAVID***
Viale Michelangiolo, 1
Tel. 681 16 95
Fax 68 06 02
This beautifully renovated 19th-century villa offers traditional warm hospitality. Garden, air conditioning.
C P ✱ ▭ ☐

EXCELSIOR*****
Piazza Ognissanti, 3
Tel. 26 42 01
Fax 21 02 78
This Renaissance-style building houses a plush hotel. Grand lobby and large bedrooms. Right in the historic center, it has a very good restaurant, "Il Cestello". Air conditioning, conference room, disabled access.
C ↘ 🚗 P ▭ ☐

GRAND HOTEL*****
Piazza Ognissanti, 1
Tel. 28 87 81
Fax 21 74 00
Florentine Renaissance style is the setting for an exclusive well-equipped hotel. Air conditioning, conference room, disabled access.
C 🚗 P ✱ ▭ ☐

GRAND HOTEL VILLA CORA*****
Viale Machiavelli, 18
Tel. 229 84 51
Fax 22 90 86
A lovely neoclassical-style 19th-century villa with a plush interior on a grand scale. Air conditioning, conference room, disabled access.
C 🚗 ⊃ P ✱ ▭ ☐

GRAND HOTEL VILLA MEDICI*****
Via il Prato, 42
Tel. 238 13 31
Fax 238 13 36
In an 18th-century patrician villa, this hotel has a peaceful atmosphere and a good restaurant, "Lorenzo de' Medici". Garden, air conditioning, conference room.
C 🚗 ⊃ ▭ ☐

HELVETIA E BRISTOL*****
Via dei Pescioni, 2
Tel. 28 78 14
Fax 28 83 53
Opposite Palazzo Strozzi in a late 19th-century villa, this luxury hotel has been equipped to meet modern requirements. Air conditioning.
C ✱ ▭ ☐

HERMITAGE***
Vicolo Marzio, 1 corner of Piazza del Pesce
Tel. 28 72 16
Fax 21 22 08
This unique hotel has a suspended garden with a view of the Ponte Vecchio, and offers comfortable rooms, unusually situated on the lower floors. Air conditioning.
C ↘ 🚗 ☐

LOGGIATO DEI SERVITI***
Piazza SS. Annunziata, 3
Tel. 28 95 92
Fax 28 95 95
Rooms are individually furnished with period pieces in this small 16th-century palazzo. Air conditioning.
C 🚗 ☐

LUNGARNO****
Borgo San Jacopo, 14
Tel. 26 42 11
Fax 26 84 37
This hotel incorporates the medieval Torre dei Marsili and houses a collection of paintings and antique furniture. An enchanting view of the Arno can be enjoyed from the top rooms. Garden, air conditioning, conference room.
C ↘ 🚗 ▭ ☐

LIANA**
Via Alfieri, 18
Tel. 24 53 03
Fax 234 45 96
When Florence was the capital of Italy (albeit briefly), this palazzo was the English ambassador's residence. Now it is a popular family-run hotel. Garden, disabled access.
C P ▭ ☐

MONTEBELLO SPLENDID****
Via Montebello, 60
Tel. 239 80 51
Fax 21 10 67
In a tranquil position (hidden away in the greenery of an Italian-style garden), this attractive, soberly elegant hotel is housed in a 19th-century building. Air conditioning, conference room.
⌂ ↘ 🚗 ▭ ☐

REGENCY*****
Piazza d'Azeglio, 3
Tel. 24 52 47
Fax 234 67 35
In a 19th-century villa, this luxurious hotel has a few select rooms and a superb restaurant, "Relais le Jardin", with some of the best Tuscan cuisine in the city. Garden, air conditioning.
C 🚗 ▭ ☐

RIVOLI****
Via della Scala, 33
Tel. 28 28 53
Fax 29 40 41
A few steps from Santa Maria Novella station, this hotel, a converted

DIALING CODE 055

15th-century Franciscan convent, combines stylish modern interiors with period style. Garden, air conditioning, conference room.

🆑 🚗 ♨ ✂ ☎ ▭

YOUTH HOSTEL

EUROPA VILLA CAMERATA IYHF
Viale Righi, 2/4
Tel. 60 14 51
Open all year
Reservation in advance is essential for visits between April and October.

CAMPING AND TOURIST VILLAGES

PARCO COMUNALE
Viale Michelangiolo, 80
Tel. 681 19 77
Open seasonally

VILLA CAMERATA
Viale Righi, 2/4
Tel. 60 14 51
Fax 61 03 00
Open all year

RESTAURANTS

ALLE MURATE
Via Ghibellina, 52/R
Tel. 24 06 18
Closed Mon. and throughout Aug.
One of the best wine cellars in town, offering innovative Tuscan cuisine, with an emphasis on dishes from Lucca. Air conditioning.
☎

BUCA LAPI
Via del Trebbio, 1/R
Tel. 21 37 68
Closed Sun., Mon. lunchtime, Aug. and for a period Nov.–Dec.
A traditional Florentine restaurant in the vaults of Palazzo Antinori. Delicious Tuscan food, and local wines.
☎

CANTINETTA ANTINORI
Piazza Antinori, 3
Tel. 29 22 34
Fax 235 98 77
Closed Sat., Sun. and throughout Aug.
A historic palazzo, a warm welcome, and elegant presentation. Local specialties and classic wines. Air conditioning.
☎

★CIBREO
Via dei Macci, 118
Tel. 234 11 00
Closed Sun., Mon. and throughout Aug.
Authentic Tuscan cooking based on "cucina povera" and soups. The homemade bread and desserts are highly recommended. Garden, air conditioning.
☎

DA SERGIO
Piazza S. Lorenzo, 8/R
Tel. 28 19 41
Closed Sun. and public holidays, and Aug.
Although only open for lunch, this trattoria deserves a mention for the freshness of the ingredients used. Serves a selecti choice of traditional Tuscan dishes, in generous portions.

DON CHISCIOTTE
Via Ridolfi, 4/R
Tel. 47 54 30
Fax 48 53 05
Closed Sun.; Mon. lunchtime, and throughout Aug.
Innovative Tuscan cuisine. The hero of La Mancha (Don Quixote) and his famous traveling companion are the protagonists of the decoration in this eatery. Air conditioning.
☎

ENOTECA PINCHIORRI
Via Ghibellina, 87
Tel. 24 27 77

★ DO NOT MISS ★
ALL'ANTICO RISTORO DI CAMBI
The specialties of Tuscan cuisine, from *pappa al pomodoro* and *crema di verdure* (both soups), to *crostini* and red wines. Rustic, friendly, warm, great cooking, good house wine.
Via San Onofrio, 1/R
Tel. 21 71 34

Fax 24 49 83
Closed Sun.; Mon. and Wed. lunchtimes and Aug.

With one of the most original cellars of world wines, this restaurant offers a great sampling menu even at lunchtime. Garden, air conditioning.
☎

FUORI PORTA
Via Monte alle Croci, 10/R
Tel. 234 24 83
Closed Sun. and throughout Aug.
Open until 3am, this "enoteca" (wine cellar) is a haunt of young Florentines who enjoy good wine. A fabulous wine list (over 600 different labels) is accompanied by a limited but delicious choice of local dishes. Homemade liqueurs. Garden.
☎

LOGGIA
Piazzale Michelangelo, 1
Tel. 234 28 32
Fax 234 52 88
Closed Wed.
This splendid loggia, with its elegant dining-rooms and view over the entire city, is the ideal setting for excellent Tuscan cuisine. Extensive selection of wines. Garden, air conditioning.
☎

MARIONE
Via della Spada, 27/R
Tel. 21 47 56
Closed Sun. and part of Aug.
A Tuscan trattoria which has been doing steady business since the 1960's. Simplicity and authenticity characterize the dishes.
☎

LE MOSSACCE
Via del Proconsolo, 55/R
Tel. 29 43 61
Closed Sat. and Sun. and throughout Aug.
This is an excellent trattoria for a quick lunch, with a good selection of traditional Florentine dishes.
☎

OLIVIERO
Via delle Terme, 51/R
Tel. 288 76 43
Fax 230 24 07
Closed Sun. and throughout Aug.
In this restaurant, classic regional cuisine is combined with more avant-garde gastronomy, from tasty fish dishes to "cucina povera". Air conditioning.
☎

SABATINI
Via de'Panzani, 9/A
Tel. 21 15 59
Fax 21 02 93
Closed Mon.
Excellent Florentine cuisine served in attractive surroundings. Popular with locals and tourists. Air conditioning.
☎

TRE SOLDI
Via Gabriele D'Annunzio, 4/R-A
Tel. 67 93 66
Closed Fri. evenings, Sat. and throughout Aug.
In the Campo di Marte area, attractive surroundings and solidly traditional Tuscan cuisine.
☎

CULTURE

CIVIC BUILDINGS
◆ PALAZZO RUCELLAI
Via Vigna Nuova, 16

Tel. 21 91 10
◆ PALAZZO STROZZI
Piazza degli Strozzi
Tel. 21 59 90
◆ PALAZZO VECCHIO
Piazza della Signoria
Tel. 276 83 25
Closed Sat.
Open 9am–7pm; Sun.
and public holidays
8am–1pm

RELIGIOUS BUILDINGS
◆ BASILICA DI
S. CROCE
Piazza di S. Croce
Tel. 24 46 19
Open 8.30am–12.30pm,
3–6pm; public holidays
3–6pm
◆ BASILICA DI
S. LORENZO
Piazza S. Lorenzo
Tel. 21 66 34
Open 8am–noon,
3.30–5.30pm; public
holidays 3.30–5.30pm
◆ BASILICA DI S. MARIA
DEL FIORE (DUOMO)
Piazza del Duomo
Tel. 29 45 14
Open 10am–5pm;
public holidays
7am–noon, 2.30–6pm
Crypt of S. Riparata,
Open 10am–5pm;
closed public holidays.
Cupola del Brunelleschi,
Open 10am–5pm;
closed public holidays.
◆ BATTISTERO DI
S. GIOVANNI (BAPTISTRY
OF S. GIOVANNI)
Piazza di S. Giovanni
Tel. 230 28 85
Open 1–6pm; public
holidays 9am–1pm
Baptistery.
◆ CENACOLO
DI S. APOLLONIA
Via XXVII
Aprile, 1
Tel. 238 86 07
Closed Mon.
Open 9am–2pm
*Da Vinci's "The
Last Supper".*
◆ CHIESA DI
S. MINIATO AL
MONTE
Via Monte Croci, 34
Tel. 234 24 22
Open 8am–noon,
2–7pm (summer);
8am–noon,
2.30–6pm (winter);
public holidays
2.30–5.30pm

◆ S. MARIA DEL CARMINE
Piazza del Carmine
Tel. 21 23 31
Open 9.30am–5.30pm
◆ S. MARIA NOVELLA
Piazza S. Maria Novella
Tel. 21 01 13
Open 7–11.30am,
3.30–6pm
◆ S. TRINITA
Piazza S. Trinita
Tel. 21 69 12
Open 8.30–11am,
4–6pm; public holidays
4–6pm

MUSEUMS
◆ GALLERIA D'ARTE
MODERNA DI PALAZZO
PITTI (MODERN ART
GALLERY)
Piazza de' Pitti, 1
Tel. 28 70 96
Closed Mon.
Open 9am–2pm
◆ GALLERIA
DEGLI UFFIZI
Piazza degli Uffizi, 6
Tel. 238 86 51
Closed Mon.
Open 9am–7pm; public
holidays 9am–2pm
◆ GALLERIA
DELL'ACCADEMIA
Via Ricasoli, 60
Tel. 238 86 12
Closed Mon.
Open 9am–2pm
◆ GALLERIA
DELL'OSPEDALE DEGLI
INNOCENTI
Pza SS. Annunziata, 12
Tel. 24 91 71
Closed Wed.

Open 8.30am–1.30pm;
Sun. 8am–12.30pm
◆ MUSEO
ARCHEOLOGICO
(ARCHEOLOGICAL
MUSEUM)
Via della Colonna, 38
Tel. 248 04 74
Closed Mon.
Open 9am–2pm;
public holidays
9am–1pm
◆ MUSEO DELL'OPERA DI
S. MARIA DEL FIORE
Piazza del Duomo, 9
Tel. 239 87 96
Closed public holidays.
Open 9am–6pm
◆ MUSEO DELL'OPERA
DI S. CROCE, CHIOSTRI
E CAPPELLA PAZZI
Piazza di S. Croce, 16
Tel. 24 46 19
Closed Wed.
Open 10am–12.30pm,
2.30–6.30pm (summer);
10am–12.30pm,
3–5pm (winter).
◆ MUSEO DELLA CASA
FIORENTINA ANTICA
Palazzo Davanzati
Via Porta Rossa, 13
Tel. 238 86 10
Closed Mon.
Open 9am–2pm
◆ MUSEO DI FIRENZE
COM'ERA
Via dell'Oriuolo, 24
Tel. 239 84 83
Closed Thur.
Open weekdays
9am–2pm;
public holidays
8am–1pm

◆ MUSEO DI S. MARCO
Piazza S. Marco, 1
Tel. 238 86 08
Closed Mon.
Open 9am–2pm
◆ MUSEO NAZIONALE
DEL BARGELLO
Via del Proconsolo
Tel. 238 86 06
Closed Mon.
Open 9am–2pm
◆ RACCOLTA D'ARTE
CONTEMPORANEA
ALBERTO DELLA
RAGIONE
Piazza della
Signoria, 5
Tel. 28 30 78
Closed Tue.
Open 9am–2pm,
public holidays
8am–1pm

OTHER MONUMENTS
◆ GIARDINO DI BOBOLI
Piazza de' Pitti
Tel. 21 34 40
Closed first and last
Mon. of each month.
Open from 9am;
closing times vary
according to the
season.

For all monuments
and cultural
institutions not listed
here, contact:
APT
Via Manzoni, 16
Tel. 23320
Fax 234 62 86

★ **DO NOT MISS** ★
MAGGIO MUSICALE FIORENTINO
Classical music and opera performed by
internationally famous singers, conductors and
directors. Emerging young talent is often
showcased here. A high-quality event. A different
musical theme is chosen each year.
Runs from May to the beginning of July.
INFORMATION
Ente Autonomo Teatro Comunale
Via Solferino, 15
Florence
Tel. 2779 and 2771
Fax 239 69 54
Reservations and ticket office:
Corso Italia, 12
Florence
Tel. 21 11 58
Fax 277 94 10
Open 1–7pm from Tuesday to Saturday

DIALING CODE 075

PRACTICAL INFORMATION

POSTAL CODE
06100

DIALING CODE
075

TOURIST INFORMATION
◆ APT
Via Mazzini, 21
Tel. 572 53 41
Fax 573 68 28
◆ INFORMATION OFFICE
Piazza IV Novembre, 3
Tel. 573 64 58

MAIN POST OFFICE
Agenzia P.I. Perugia
Via Innamorati
Tel. 42391

EMERGENCIES

AMBULANCE SERVICE
Tel. 572 11 11

MEDICAL SERVICES
Emergency home
service
Tel. 34024
Policlinico S. Maria
della Misericordia-
Ospedale Silvestrini
Tel. 5781

POLICE
Central headquarters
Tel. 56891

FIRE SERVICE
Tel. 115

TRANSPORT

AIR
AIRPORT:
AEROPORTO
REGIONALE UMBRO,
S. EGIDIO
9 miles west of the town
Information:
Tel. 692 94 47
◆ ALITALIA
Via Fani, 14
Tel. 573 12 26

RAIL
STAZIONE FS
Piazza Vittorio Veneto
Tel. 500 74 67
Stazione Ferrovia
Centrale Umbra
Via Sant'Anna
Tel. 572 91 21

CAR
ACI-AUTOMOBILE CLUB
D'ITALIA
Via M. Angeloni, 12
Tel. 500 73 94
Car rental:
ACI Service
Via Angeloni, 19
Tel. 500 01 22

24-hour breakdown
services:
Tel. 116

CAR RENTAL
◆ AVIS
Via Settevalli, 42
Tel. 500 03 95
Aeroporto S. Egidio
Tel. 692 97 96
or 692 93 46
◆ HERTZ
Stazione FS
Piazza Vittorio
Veneto, 4
Tel. and fax
500 24 39

◆ MAGGIORE-BUDGET
Aeroporto S. Egidio
Tel. 692 92 76

PUBLIC TRANSPORT
A.T.A.M. AZIENDA
TRASPORTI
AUTOFILOVIARI
MUNICIPALIZZATA
Località Pian Massiano
Tel. 505 24 41
Fax 505 42 48

TAXIS
RADIO TAXI
Tel. 500 48 88

HOTELS

BRUFANI***
Piazza Italia, 12
Tel. 573 25 41
Fax 572 02 10
*Glorious 19th-century
hotel. Rooms enjoy
splendid panoramic
views. Lovely central
courtyard and
comfortable rooms.
Elegant restaurant,
"Collins".
Air conditioning,
conference room,
disabled access.*
🇨 ⛄ 🚗 🅿 ⬜ 🖵

GIO ARTE E VINI**
Via R. d'Andreotto, 19
Tel. and fax 573 11 00
*A modern construction
recently annexed to a
shopping mall. The
hotel also has a good
traditional restaurant
serving regional-style
food and a well-
selected wine list.
Air conditioning,
conference room,
garden, disabled access.*
🅿 ⬜ 🖵

GRIFONE*
Via Pellico, 1
Tel. 583 76 16
Fax 583 76 19
*Close to the historic
center, this modern
hotel is convenient for
those with their own
means of transport.
The restaurant, with
its large French-Gothic
fireplace, is delightful.
Air conditioning,*

*conference room,
disabled access.*
🇨 🚗 🅿 ⬜ 🖵

ILGO*
Via A. Di Duccio, 1/A
Tel. 573 66 41
Fax 572 07 20
*Located out of the
city center, but linked
with the
town by the
hotel's free
shuttles. Air
conditioning,
conference
room,
solarium.*
☀ 🚗 🅿
⬜ 🖵

IDEAL
Via Tuderte,
1/G
Tel. and fax
30869
*Surrounded by a
huge garden, this is
a welcoming, family-
run hotel.*
🚗 🅿 ⬜ 🖵

**LOCANDA
DELLA POSTA****
Corso Vannucci, 97
Tel. 572 89 25
Fax 572 24 13
*Situated within an old
patrician palazzo, this
long-established hotel
dates back to the
1700's. Traditional
service and modern
comfort. Air
conditioning.*
🚗 ⬜ 🖵

**PERUGIA PLAZA
HOTEL****
Via Palermo, 88
Tel. 34643

Fax 30863
*This elegant hotel lies
in the shelter of the
Hill of Prepo, in an
oasis of green and calm.
The "Fortebraccio"
restaurant
is good, offering
specialties typical of
traditional regional
cuisine. Air conditioning,
conference room,
solarium,sauna,
disabled access.*
🇨 🏠 🚗 🅿 ⬛
⬜ 🖵

**SANGALLO PALACE
HOTEL****
Via Masi, 9
Tel. 573 02 02
Fax 573 00 68
*In a good location (near
the Rocca Paolina), this
hotel is notable for its
architecture and the
decorative interior, in
the style of the high
Perugian Renaissance.
Air conditioning,
conference room,
disabled access.*
🇨 🚗 🅿 ⬛ ⬜ 🖵

SIGNA
Via del Grillo, 9;
corner of
Corso Cavour
Tel. 572 41 80
Fax
572 23 93
*A small
hotel in
the center,
frequently used
by students in
transit; it also
has some
self-catering
apartments.
Garden, disabled
access.*
🚗 🅿 ⬜ 🖵

YOUTH HOSTEL

**OSTELLO DELLA
GIOVENTÙ**
Via Bontempi, 13
Tel. 572 28 80

CAMPING

**CAMPING
IL ROCOLO**
Via Trinità, 1/A
Tel. 517 06 75

RESTAURANTS

ALADINO DEL SOLE
Via delle Prome, 11
Tel. 572 09 38
*Open evenings only,
closed Mon. and Aug.
Typical offerings from*

this restaurant include Sardinian recipes, such as "linguine con pere e pecorino" (linguini with pears and cheese), and "cinghiale alla vernaccia" (wild boar). Also has a good wine list. Air conditioning.

🗔

BOCCA MIA
Via Rocchi, 36
Tel. 572 38 73
Closed Sun. and throughout Aug.
Right in the city center, this is mainly patronized by young people. Tasty fish dishes and a vast choice of great desserts. Air conditioning.

🗔

CESARINO
Via della Gabbia, 13
Tel. 573 62 77
Closed Wed. and throughout Feb.
A trattoria which has always been a popular with those who love typical Perugian cuisine. Great desserts and 120 different types of whisky.

🗔

GARIBALDI
Via Caporali, 12
Tel. 572 77 88
Closed Mon.
An "osteria" (inn), serving dishes using largely forgotten Umbrian recipes. Once a simple wine bar serving snacks, it has extended its menu to include salamis, preserves in oil, roasts and desserts.

IL GUFO
Via della Viola, 18
Tel. 573 41 26

Closed Sun. and Mon., and for a period Aug.–Sep.
A good atmosphere which harks back to that of the old "osterie": – marble tables, walnut benches, a visible kitchen. Interesting food, with traditional recipes served alongside imaginative inventions.

OSTERIA DEL BARTOLO
Via Bartolo, 30
Tel. 573 15 61
Closed Fri. and for a period from Aug.–Sep.
Care and good taste in both decor and cuisine make for a pleasing ambience. Interesting menu with Umbrian specialties. Air conditioning.

🗔

PAIOLO
Via Augusta, 11
Tel. 572 56 11
Closed Wed. and part of Aug.
Located in a 16th-century palazzo, furnished in a rustic style, this restaurant is also a pizzeria.

🗔

CULTURE

CIVIC BUILDINGS
◆ COLLEGIO DEL CAMBIO (COLLEGE OF THE EXCHANGE)
Palazzo dei Priori
Corso Vannucci, 25
Tel. 61379
Closed Mon.
Open 9am–1pm, 2.30–5.30pm (Mar.–Oct.), Sat. until 6.30pm; 8am–2pm (Nov.–Feb.), public holidays 9am–1pm
◆ COLLEGIO DELLA MERCANZIA
Palazzo dei Priori
Corso Vannucci, 15
Tel. 573 03 66
Closed Mon.
Open 9am–1pm, 2.30–5.30pm (Mar.–Oct.), Sat. until 6.30pm;

8am–2pm (Nov.–Feb.); public holidays 9am–1pm
◆ PALAZZO DEI PRIORI
Corso Vannucci
see Collegio della Mercanzia and Galleria Nazionale dell'Umbria for opening hours.

RELIGIOUS BUILDINGS
◆ ORATORY OF SAN SEVERO
Via Raffaello
Tel. 573 38 64
Closed Mon.
Open 10.30am–1.30pm, 2.30–6.30pm (Apr.–Sep.); 10am–1.30pm, 2.30–4.30pm (Oct.–Mar.), Sat. until 5.30pm, Sun. 10.30am–1.30pm

MUSEUMS
◆ GALLERIA NAZIONALE DELL'UMBRIA
Palazzo dei Priori
Corso Vanucci
Tel. 574 12 47
Closed first Mon. of each month.
Open 9am–7pm, public holidays 9am–1pm

◆ MUSEO ARCHEOLOGICO NAZIONALE DELL'UMBRIA
Piazza G. Bruno, 10
Tel. 572 71 41
Closed Sun. afternoons and Mon. Open 9am–1pm, 2.30–7pm
◆ ACCADEMIA DI BELLE ARTI
Piazza S. Francesco al Prato
Tel. 572 65 62
Closed Sun.
Open 10am–1pm, 3–5.30pm Sat. and Sun. (July and Aug.); 2.30–5.30pm (Sep.); during the rest of the year from 10am–1pm

OTHER MONUMENTS
◆ POZZO ETRUSCO (ETRUSCAN WELL)
Piazza Danti, 18
Closed Mon.
Open 10.30am–1.30pm, 2.30–6.30pm (Apr.–Sep.), 10am–1.30pm, 2.30–4.30pm (Oct.–Mar.); Sat. until 5.30pm; Sun. from 10.30am–1.30pm

For all monuments and cultural institutions not listed here contact.
APT
Via Mazzini, 21
Tel. 572 53 41
Fax 573 68 28

★ **DO NOT MISS** ★
UMBRIA JAZZ FESTIVAL
This festival constitutes the most important annual event for music lovers. At *Umbria Jazz* you can listen to a range of musical genres, such as soul, rock, hip hop and Latin, even if the star of the show is indisputably jazz.
INFORMATION
Associazione Umbria Jazz
Via S. Andrea, 2
Tel. 573 24 32
Fax 572 26 56
Open Mon.–Fri.10am–1pm, 3.30–5.30pm
Ticket office and reservations: Ceccherini
Via Boncambi, 21
Tel. 572 33 66
Open 9.30am–1pm, 4–7.30pm
Takes place during the first half of July.

DIALING CODE 06

PRACTICAL INFORMATION

POSTAL CODE
00100

DIALING CODE
06

TOURIST INFORMATION
◆ ENTE PROVINCIALE PER IL TURISMO
– Information office:
Via Parigi, 5
Tel. 48 89 92 55
or 48 89 92 53
Closed Sun.
– Stazione Termini
Tel. 487 12 70
or 482 40 78
– Aeroporto di Fiumicino Leonardo da Vinci
Tel. 65 95 44 71
or 65 95 60 74

MAIN POST OFFICE
Agenzia P.I. Roma succursale 1
Via Sicilia, 191/197
Tel. 474 56 49
or 474 57 90

EMBASSIES AND CONSULATES

AUSTRALIA
Via Alessandria, 215
Tel. 832 721

CANADA
Via Zara, 30
Tel. 440 30 28

IRELAND
Largo Nazareno, 3
Tel. 678 25 41

NEW ZEALAND
Via Zara, 28
Tel. 440 29 28

SOUTH AFRICA
Via Tanaro, 14/16
Tel. 855 44 85,
844 32 41, or 844 08 48

UK
Via XX Settembre, 80a
(Porta Pia)
Tel. 482 54 41

US
Via Veneto, 119a
Tel. 46 74 1

EMERGENCIES

AMBULANCE SERVICE
Tel. 5510

MEDICAL SERVICES
Tel. 118
URGENT BLOOD TRANSFUSIONS
Policlinico Umberto I
Tel. 49 97 08 60,

49 97 8 61
or 85 79 55 36
S. Giovanni
Tel. 77 05 55 63
ANTI-POISON CENTERS
Policlinico A. Gemelli
Tel. 305 43 43
Policlinico Umberto I
Tel. 49 06 63

POLICE
Central headquarters
Tel. 4686

FIRE SERVICE
Tel. 115

TRANSPORT

AIR
AIRPORT: AEROPORTO INTERCONTINENTALE LEONARDO DA VINCI DI FIUMICINO
16 miles southwest of the city
Information:
Tel. 65951
◆ ALITALIA
Via Bissolati, 20
Tel. 65621
Information:
Tel. 65643
Reservations
Tel. 65621
Stazione Termini
Piazza dei Cinquecento
Tel. 65 62 82 44
or 65 62 82 46

RAIL
STAZIONE TERMINI
Piazza dei Cinquecento
Tel. 1478/88 08 81

CAR
ACI-AUTOMOBILE CLUB D'ITALIA
Via Cristofoto Colombo, 261
Tel. 51 49 71
Breakdown services:
Via Solferino, 32
Tel. 44595
Breakdown services:
Tel. 116

CAR RENTAL
◆ AVIS
Via Sardegna, 38A
Tel. 72 82 47 28
Information:
Tel. 41998
Aeroporto Leonardo Da Vinci di Fiumicino
Tel. 65 01 15 31,
65 95 41 46
or 65 95 66 79
◆ EURODOLLAR
Reservations:
Tel. 167-018668 (toll-free)
Aeroporto Leonardo Da Vinci di Fiumicino
Tel. 65 95 35 47
or 65 01 00 84
Fax 65 01 03 73

◆ EUROPCAR
Via Fiume Giallo, 196
Tel. 52 08 11
Fax 520 23 17
Reservations:
Tel. 70 39 97 00
◆ MAGGIORE-BUDGET
Reservations:
Tel. 1478-67067
Information:
Tel. 229 15 30

PUBLIC TRANSPORT
A.T.A.C. AZIENDA TRANVIE E AUTOBUS DEL COMUNE DI ROMA
Via Volturno, 65
Tel. 46951
Fax 46 95 20 87
Information:
Tel. 46 95 44 44
Open weekdays 8am–8pm, Sat. 8am–1.30pm

TAXIS
COSMOS RADIO TAXI
Tel. 88177
SOCIETÀ LA CAPITALE
Tel. 4994
SOCIETÀ COOPERATIVA AUTORADIOTAXI ROMA
Tel. 3570
TEVERE
Tel. 4157
PRONTO TAXI
Tel. 6645

ACCOMMODATION

ALDROVANDI PALACE*****
Via U. Aldrovandi, 15
Tel. 322 39 93
Fax 322 14 35
In the heart of the Parioli, this elegant palazzo built in the late 1800's has a splendid view of the Villa Borghese and a large park. A traditional hotel with conference facilities. Excellent restaurant, "Relais la Piscine". Garden, air conditioning, conference room.
�► 🔼 ◆ 🅿 ⌄ ⊗ ▭ 🗔

AMALIA**
Via Germanico, 66/5
Tel. 39 72 33 54
Fax 39 72 33 65
Good value for money in this small, family-run hotel housed in a late-19th-century building.
◆ ⊗ ▭

ARCANGELO***
Via Boezio, 15
Tel. 687 41 43
Fax 689 30 50
Situated in the Prati neighbourhood, this

charming hotel boasts beautiful interiors and friendly service. Air conditioning.
🅿 ⊗ ▭ 🗔

ARTDECO****
Via Palestro, 19
Tel. 445 75 88
Fax 444 14 83
The attractive terrace garden is just one of the many features which make for a pleasant stay in this newly renovated hotel (both inside and out). Air conditioning, conference room.
◆ ⊗ ▭ 🗔

ATLANTE GARDEN****
Via Crescenzio, 78/A
Tel. 687 23 61
Fax 687 23 15
Elegant furnishings, with areas reserved for non-smokers. Offers every comfort. Air conditioning, disabled access.
◆ 🅿 ▭ 🗔

ATLANTE STAR****
Via Vitelleschi, 34
Tel. 687 32 33
Fax 687 23 00
Situated right in front of the basilica of St Peter's, this hotel is notable for its sober elegance. The roof garden restaurant, "Les Etoiles" serves superb food. Garden, air conditioning, conference room, solarium, disabled access.
🔼 ◆ 🅿 ⊗ ▭ 🗔

BERNINI BRISTOL*****
Piazza Bernini, 23
Tel. 488 30 51
Fax 482 42 66
Though recently rebuilt, this hotel maintains traditional hospitality and elegance. Right in the center, close to Via Veneto – the heart of first-class nightlife. Some rooms have balconies. Excellent food in the "Il Corallo" restaurant. Air conditioning, conference room, disabled access.
🅲 🔼 ◆ ⊗ ▭ 🗔

BRUNA**
Via Marghera, 13
Tel. 444 08 34
Fax 495 73 96
Well-managed, family-

run hotel boasting a charming breakfast-room with panoramic views.
✗ ▢

CANADA***
Via Vicenza, 58
Tel. 445 7 70
Fax 445 07 49
Elegant decor and charming service mark out this hotel that has been run by the same family for many years.
🚗 ✗ ▢ ▢

CAVALIERI HILTON*****
Via Cadiolo, 101
Tel. 35091
Fax 35 09 22 41
Large, modern, luxury hotel, recently reconstructed. Two restaurants are available for the guests, "Giardino dell'Uliveto" and "La Pergola". Garden, air conditioning, conference room, tennis, gym, solarium, sauna, disabled access.
⛷ 🚗 P ⏚ ▢ ▢

COLONNA PALACE****
Piazza di Montecitorio, 12
Tel. 678 13 41
Fax 679 44 96
Situated in front of the Parliament, this hotel offers maximum comfort in an elegant period building. Disabled access.
⛷ 🚗 ✗ ▢ ▢

COROT***
Via Marghera, 15/17
Tel. 44 70 09 00
Fax 44 70 09 05
A few steps from Termini station, this hotel caters for your every need. Air conditioning.
🚗 ▢ ▢

DE LA VILLE INTERCONTINENTAL ****
Via Sistina, 69
Tel. 67331
Fax 678 42 13
Art Nouveau style palazzo situated in one of the city's most interesting streets. Elegant hotel with neoclassical fittings. Excellent restaurant, "La Piazzetta de la Ville". Garden, air room, solarium.
C 🚗 ✗ ▢ ▢

DELLE NAZIONI****
Via Poli, 7
Tel. 679 24 41
Fax 678 24 00
Located in a renovated ancient patrician palazzo, this hotel has large and elegant salons and stylish, comfortable bedrooms. The independently-run "Le Grondici" restaurant is charming. Air conditioning, conference room, disabled access.
🚗 ✗ ▢ ▢

D'INGHILTERRA****
Via Bocca di Leone, 14
Tel. 69 92 13 66
Fax 69 92 22 43
Originally the guest-quarters of the Torlonia princes, this palatial hotel has retained its distinctive atmosphere and antique furnishings. Air conditioning.
🚗 ✗ ▢ ▢

DOMUS AVENTINA***
Via di S. Prisca, 11/B
Tel. 574 61 35
Fax 57 30 00 48
This building dates from the 16th century and the bedrooms face onto a garden which is almost as old. Splendid interiors including a trompe l'oeil in the reception area. Air conditioning.
⛷ 🚗 ✗ ▢ ▢

EDEN*****
Via Ludovisi, 49
Tel. 47 81 21
Fax 482 15 84
This late-19th-century building has been modernized with style. Many rooms have a
splendid view of imperial Rome, and the excellent "Terrazza" restaurant also offers a striking vista. Air conditioning, gym, sauna.
⛷ ✗ ▢ ▢

EXCELSIOR*****
Via Vittorio Veneto, 125
Tel. 4708
Fax 482 62 05
Elegant hotel with period furnishings whose prestige is inextricably linked with the legendary fascination of Via Veneto. The hotel is home to the restaurants

"La Cupola" and the "Gran Caffè Doney" which faces onto the famous street. Air conditioning, conference room.
C ⛷ 🚗 P ▢ ▢

FARNESE****
Via A. Farnese, 30
Tel. 321 25 53
Fax 321 51 29
The stately elegance of this hotel has been enhanced by the recent renovation. Located in an early-20th-century palazzo, it has period furnishings and attractive tapestries in the bedrooms. Air conditioning.
🚗 ✗ ▢ ▢

LE GRAND HOTEL*****
Via V. E. Orlando, 3
Tel. 4709
Fax 474 73 07
Lavish interiors characterize this imposing hotel. Very well equipped for conferences. Air conditioning, conference room.
🚗 ✗ ▢ ▢

GRAND HOTEL PALACE****
Via Vittorio Veneto, 70
Tel. 47 87 19
Fax 47 87 18 00
The Art Deco hall offers a fitting introduction to this stylish hotel. Situated in the most famous street in Rome, it is housed within a renovated period palazzo. Comfortable and well equipped. Air conditioning, conference room, solarium, sauna.
C 🚗 ⏚ I ▢ ▢

HASSLER*****
Piazza Trinità dei Monti, 6
Tel. 678 26 51
Fax 678 99 91
This hotel, in a 20th-century building, unites period fittings with modern comfort. Fantastic panoramic view, especially from the roof restaurant. Garden, air conditioning, conference room, solarium, disabled access.
⛷ 🚗 ✗ ▢ ▢

HELIOS***
Via Sacco Pastore, 13
Tel. 860 39 82
Fax 860 43 55
Recently renovated, this hotel has a pleasant roof garden in summer. Air conditioning, conference room.
🚗 ▢ ▢

JOLLY LEONARDO DA VINCI****
Via dei Gracchi, 324
Tel. 32499
Fax 361 01 38
Particularly suitable for conferences and business meetings, this hotel boasts large salons and well-equipped bedrooms. Air conditioning, conference room,

DIALING CODE 06

disabled access.
🚗 🍽 📺📶

JOLLY MIDAS**
Via Aurelia, 800
Tel. 66396
Fax 66 41 84 75
*Located near the ring
road, this hotel offers its
guests particularly good
sports facilities, and a
free shuttle service into
town. Garden, air
conditioning,
conference room,
tennis, disabled
access.*
🅿🚗🍽📺📶

**JOLLY VITTORIO
VENETO****
Corso d'Italia, 1
Tel. 8495
Fax 884 11 04
*Enjoying an
inspirational view of the
Villa Borghese, this
hotel offers excellent
facilities and good
service. Air
conditioning,
conference room,
disabled access.*
🍸🚗📺📶

LORD BYRON***
Via G. de Notaris, 5
Tel. 322 45 41
Fax 322 04 05
*A small hotel
distinguished by careful
service and a discreet
atmosphere. The
restaurant "Relais le
Jardin" is well worth
a visit. Garden,
air conditioning,
conference room.*
🍸🚗🍽📺📶

MAJESTIC**
Via Vittorio Veneto, 50
Tel. 48 68 41
Fax 488 09 84
*Housed in a splendid,
elegantly refurbished
fin-de-siècle palazzo,
this palatial hotel is
often chosen by the
rich and famous. The
"La Veranda" restaurant
offers a range of
carefully prepared
dishes. Air conditioning.*
🍸🅿📺📶

**MASSIMO
D'AZEGLIO****
Via Cavour, 18

Tel. 487 02 70
Fax 482 73 86
*Originally a restaurant,
today this is also an
atmospheric and
comfortable hotel.
Air conditioning,
conference room.*
🍸🚗🍽📺📶

MEDITERRANEO**
Via Cavour, 15
Tel. 488 40 51
Fax 474 41 05
*With panoramic views
from the top floor, a
good restaurant (the
"21"), and classically
elegant furnishings,
this hotel offers a range
of good facilities.
Air conditioning,
conference room.*
🍸🚗🍽📺📶

MIAMI*
Via Nazionale, 230
Tel. 481 71 80
Fax 48 45 62
*You are guaranteed a
warm welcome in the
elegant Miami, thanks
to the attention to
detail paid by the
knowledgeable family
who manage it. Air
conditioning, disabled
access.*
🚗📺📶

MONDIAL**
Via Torino, 127
Tel. 47 28 61
Fax 482 48 22
*A comfortable hotel
in a renovated
19th-century building.
Air conditioning,
conference room.*
🚗🅿🍽📺📶

MONTREAL**
Via Carlo
Alberto, 4
Tel.
446 55 22
Fax
445 77 97
*Situated very
near Termini
station, this
recently
renovated hotel
has attractively
furnished bedrooms.*
🚗🍽📺📶

MOZART*
Via dei Greci, 23/B
Tel. 69 94 00 41
Fax 678 42 71
*Built at the start of the
century, this palazzo
now houses an
attractive hotel,
equipped with a*

welcoming taverna.
Air conditioning.
🍸🚗🍽📺📶

NAPOLEON**
Piazza Vittorio
Emanuele, 105
Tel. 446 72 64
Fax 446 72 82
*This hotel has a historic
bar (the "Trafalgar
Bar"), and offers first-
class hospitality.
Air conditioning,
conference room,
solarium.*
🚗🍽📺📶

PICCADILLY*
Via Magna Grecia, 122
Tel. 70 47 48 58
Fax 70 47 66 86
*Attractive panoramic
views of the city are
enjoyed by this
comfortable modern
hotel. Air conditioning.*
🍸🅿🍽📺📶

PRESIDENT**
Via Emanuele
Filiberto, 173
Tel. 77 01 21
Fax 700 87 40
*In the heart of San
Giovanni, the
President's rooms are
modern, comfortable
and stylish. The hotel
restaurant offers
traditional Roman
cuisine. Air conditioning,
conference room,
disabled access.*
🚗📺📶

RICHMOND*
Largo C. Ricci, 36
Tel. 69 94 12 56
Fax 69 94 14 54
*A stunning
view of
the Forti
Imperiali can
be enjoyed
from the roof
garden in this
fine building.
Good security
system. Air
conditioning,
conference
room,
disabled access.*
🚗📺📶

RIVOLI**
Via Taramelli, 7
Tel. 322 40 42
Fax 322 73 73
*Situated close to the
Villa Borghese, this
attractive hotel is
endowed with every
modern comfort.
Air conditioning,*

conference room.
🅿🍽📺📶

SANTA COSTANZA*
Viale XXI Aprile, 4
Tel. 860 06 02
Fax 860 27 86
*The hotel's bar faces
a lovely garden, as
peaceful as the rest
of the complex. A stylish
hotel that maintains
a classic tone.
Air conditioning,
conference room.*
🚗📺📶

**TEATRO DI
POMPEO***
Largo del Pallaro, 8
Tel. 68 30 01 70
Fax 68 80 55 31
*This small but charming
hotel gets its name
from the ruins of the
ancient Roman theater
upon which it is built.
It maintains elements
of Roman classicism
in some of its fittings.
Stunning dining room.
Air conditioning,
disabled access.*
🚗🍽📺📶

VENETO*
Via Piemonte, 63
Tel. 482 43 46
Fax 481 45 83
*The tastefully furnished
bedrooms are very
comfortable. The hotel
boasts an excellent
central location and
a lovely roof garden
restaurant. Air
conditioning.*
🚗🍽📺📶

VENEZIA*
Via Varese, 18
Tel. 445 71 01
*Family-run hotel in a
19th-century palazzo
furnished with period
fittings. Lovely reception
rooms. Wonderful
service, especially
at breakfast. Air
conditioning.*
🚗🍽📺📶

VILLA BORGHESE*
Via Pinciana, 31
Tel. 854 96 48
Fax 841 41 00
*Facing the park of the
Villa Borghese, this
comfortable hotel
enjoys an enviable
position and offers
a warm, discreet
atmosphere with
touches of Art Nouveau
style. Garden.*
🍸🚗🍽📺📶

VILLA DEL PARCO***
Via Nomentana, 110
Tel. 44 23 77 73
Fax 44 23 75 72
Perfect English style for this Art Nouveau gem, from the furnishings to the breakfast served in the small garden. Air conditioning, disabled access.

VILLA FLORENCE***
Via Nomentana, 28
Tel. 440 30 36
Fax 440 27 09
Renovated Art Nouveau villa. The garden contains archeological finds from Roman times. Air conditioning, solarium, disabled access.

RESTAURANTS

AGATA E ROMEO
Via Carlo Alberto, 45
Tel. 446 61 15
Fax 446 58 42
Closed Sun. and various public holidays.
Regional cuisine served without frills, and accompanied by an extensive wine list.

AGUSTARELLO A TESTACCIO
Via G. Branca, 98
Tel. 574 65 85
Closed Sun., public holidays and part of Aug.
Run by the Commentucci family, this restaurant has been serving traditional Italian food since 1957. Offal dishes a specialty.

AL MORO
Vicolo delle Bollette, 13
Tel. 69 94 07 36
Closed Sun. and throughout Aug.
Friendly service and traditional Roman cooking. Fish and mushroom specialties and a good selection of international wines.

★ DO NOT MISS ★
EATING IN THE GHETTO
The cuisine of the Roman ghetto must definitely be sampled. There are delicious fried specialties, from salted cod fillets (*baccalà*) to the unexpected taste of fried sage in fritter dough or *carciofi alla guidea* (artichokes with mint). Excellent, especially in the Portico d'Ottavia area.

ALBERTO CIARLA
Piazza S. Cosimato, 40
Tel. 581 86 68
Fax 588 43 77
Closed Sun., New Year–Jan. 6 and part of Aug.
Family-run seafood restaurant. Great wines and innovative cuisine.

BACCO
Via dell'Arco del Monte, 94/95
Tel. and fax 68 80 53 49
Closed Sun. evenings, Mon. and Christmas–New Year; in summer closed Sun. and Mon. and throughout Aug.
Housed in an old palazzo, this restaurant serves typical dishes from Puglia. Good selection of wines.

CAMPONESCHI
Piazza Farnese, 50
Tel. 687 49 27
Fax 686 52 44
Closed lunchtimes, Sun. and part of Aug.
In the luxurious setting of Piazza Farnese with its twin fountains, this first-class eating-house guarantees great service. The cuisine on offer is traditional regional food, imaginatively and carefully prepared.

CECILIA METELLA
Via Appia Antica, 125
Tel. 511 02 13
Thirty-year-old eatery run by the Graziani brothers, who offer traditional fish and meat dishes.

Very spacious both inside and in the delightful garden.

CEPPO
Via Panama, 2
Tel. 841 96 96
Closed Mon. and part of Aug.
Attentive service and good food offered by the Milozzi sisters in a warm atmosphere.

CESARINA
Via Piemonte, 100
Tel. 488 08 28
Closed Mon.
A good-quality traditional eatery serving cuisine from Romagna.

CHARLY'S SAUCIER
Via di S. Giovanni in Laterano, 270
Tel. 70 49 56 66
Closed Sun. and part of Aug.
A reserved, peaceful atmosphere with good, classic French cooking.

CHECCO ER CARETTIERE
Via Benedetta, 10
Tel. 580 09 85
Closed Sun. evenings, Mon. and part of Aug.
Gastronomic specialties in the tradition of the Trastevere area of Rome. Good atmosphere.

CHECCHINO DAL 1887
Via Monte Testaccio, 30
Tel. 574 63 18
Fax 574 38 16
Closed Sun. evenings, Mon. and Christmas–New Year; in summer closed Sun. and Mon. all day and Aug.
Built in vaults under Monte dei Cocci, this restaurant has a unique setting on the edge of Monte

Testaccio. The Mariani family, with over a century of experience, provides impeccable service, excellent hearty food and an interesting, well-selected wine list.

CORIOLANO
Via Ancona, 14
Tel. 44 24 98 63
Closed Sun. and throughout Aug.
For almost fifty years Coriolano Mastrantonio has been running this elegant restaurant furnished with period pieces. His first-class trattoria offers creative Italian dishes. Specialties: fish and truffle dishes.

EL TOULÀ
Via della Lupa, 29/B
Tel. 687 37 50
Fax 687 11 15
Closed Sat. lunchtimes, Sun., Mon. and throughout Aug.
Set in a small Art Nouveau palazzo, this long-standing Roman eatery offers traditional food, a refined atmosphere and impeccable service.

ENOTECA CAPRANICA
Piazza Capranica, 99/100
Tel. 69 94 09 92
Fax 69 94 09 89
Closed Sat. lunchtimes and Sun. and throughout Aug.
Located on the site of what was one of the oldest wine cellars in Rome, this "enoteca" offers traditional dishes.

FELICE
Via Mastro Giorgio, 29
Tel. 574 68 00
Closed Sun. and part of Aug.

Typical Italian restaurant serving simple, traditional, popular Roman cuisine. Authentic flavors and huge portions. Very popular with the locals. Book in advance.

GENSOLA

Piazza della Gensola, 15
Tel. 581 63 12
One of Rome's few historic "osterie" (its origins are said to date back to the 8th century), in the Trastevere district. Gensola has, for the last decade or so, been serving up the tasty specialties of

Sicily: eggplant predominates, in many different guises, but there are also some wonderful pasta dishes and an exquisite fish roulade.

GEORGE'S

Via Marche, 7
Tel. 42 08 45 75
Fax 42 01 00 32
Closed Sun. and part of Aug.
This elegant restaurant offers authentic Italian cuisine with the occasional French flourish. Attractive 19th-century building with lovely summer garden. Has the atmosphere of a private club.

GIRARROSTO TOSCANO

Via Campania, 29
Tel. 482 18 99
Closed Wed.
A rustic ambience in the most traditional Tuscan restaurant in the city. Straightforward dishes

---

★ DO NOT MISS ★
MASSENZIO

This cinematic event has two screens with a total seating capacity of 2500. New releases, repertory, retrospectives and animation are all shown in the open air, near the Basilica of Massenzio. The *Schermo Grande* (large screen) has a backdrop of the apse of the church of *San Giovanni e San Paolo*, while the *Schermo Piccolo* (small screen) is grafted onto the surreal landscape of the Antiquarium. Art within art, then, for movies under the stars.

INFORMATION

Comune di Roma, Assessorato alla Cultura, Cooperativa Massenzio
Via C.B. Piazza, 8
Tel. 44 23 80 02
Runs during July and August.

---

created from the freshest local produce. Very courteous service and splendid desserts.

HARRY'S BAR

Via Vittorio Veneto, 150
Tel. 48 46 43
Fax 488 31 17
Closed Sun. and part of Aug.
A good range of traditional and international cuisine in this popular eatery.

IL DITO E LA LUNA

Via dei Sabelli, 51
Tel. 494 07 26
Open evenings only.
Closed Sun., part of Aug. and the last week in Dec.
This recently opened "osteria" has already earned itself a very good reputation. Traditional Sicilian-influenced dishes include specialties such as "caponata di melanzane". Food is carefully prepared and beautifully presented.

ORTICA

Via Flaminia Vecchia, 573
Tel. 333 87 09
Closed Sun. and part of Aug.

Friendly restaurant in a pleasant setting serving good-quality Campanian cuisine.

PAPA GIOVANNI

Via dei Sediari, 4
Tel. 68 80 48 07
Fax 686 53 08
Closed Sun., Christmas; New Year and Ferragosto (Aug. 15).
A family-run concern with a warm atmosphere, traditional Roman cuisine, and a great selection of wines. Zucchini dishes a specialty.

PEPPONE

Via Emilia, 60
Tel. 48 39 76
Closed Sun. and throughout Aug.
This restaurant is run by the Tozzi family, who started here over a century ago. Traditional local fare.

PORTO DI RIPETTA

Via di Ripetta, 250
Tel. 361 23 76
Fax 322 70 89
Closed Sun. and part of Aug.
This family-run eatery offers a good selection of wines. Seafood dishes

---

are a house specialty. It is also well situated, being very near to the Piazza del Popolo.

ROSETTA

Via della Rosetta, 8
Tel. 686 10 02
Fax 687 28 52
Closed Sat. lunchtimes, Sun. and part of Aug.
Very near the Pantheon, Rosetta is famous for its fish (reputed to be the best in Rome) and for its quality wine list.

SABATINI

Piazza di S. Maria in Trastevere, 13
Tel. 581 20 26
Fax 589 83 86
Closed Wed., Christmas and part of Aug.
Traditional cuisine, antique furnishings, and a typical Italian atmosphere. Tables outside.

SAN LUIGI

Via Mocenigo, 10
Tel. 39 72 07 04
Fax 39 72 24 21
Closed Sun. and part of Aug.
Traditional food with an innovative edge. Good service in a refined atmosphere.

SANS SOUCI

Via Sicilia, 20
Tel. 482 18 14
Fax 482 17 71
Closed Mon. and part of Aug.
A chic restaurant with period pictures hanging on the walls. The furnishings are exquisite. Bruno Borghesi has long been the chef here, creating splendid French-inspired dishes.

SCOGLIO DI FRISIO
Via Merulana, 256
Tel. 487 27 65
Closed Sat. lunchtimes
and Sun.
*Authentic Neapolitan
cuisine with particular
emphasis on fish
specialties.*

**TABERNA DE'
GRACCHI**
Via dei Gracchi, 268
Tel. 321 31 26
Closed Sun., and
Mon. lunchtime
*Traditional regional
cuisine, with modern
innovative touches.
Air conditioning.*

CULTURE

CIVIC BUILDINGS

◆ AULA OTTAGONA
Via Romita
Tel. 487 06 90
Closed Mon.
Open 10am–7pm
◆ PALAZZO MASSIMO
Largo di Villa
Peretti, 1
Tel. 48 90 35 00
Closed Mon.
Open 9am–2pm
◆ PALAZZO ALTEMPS
Via di S. Apollinare, 8
Tel. 683 37 59
Closed Mon.
Open 9am–1pm

RELIGIOUS
BUILDINGS

◆ CATACOMBE
DI S. SEBASTIANO
Via Appia Antica, 136
Tel. 788 70 35
Closed Thur.
Open 8.30am–noon,
2.30–5.30pm (summer);
8.30am–noon,
2.30–5pm (winter).

MUSEUMS

◆ GALLERIA DORIA
PAMPHILIJ
Piazza Collegio
Romano, 2
Tel. 679 73 23
Closed Wed. and
Thur.
Open 10am–1pm
◆ GALLERIA NAZIONALE
D'ARTE ANTICA
(NATIONAL GALLERY
OF ANCIENT ART)
c/o Palazzo Barberini
Via Quattro Fontane, 13
Tel. 482 41 84
Closed Mon.
Open 9am–7pm;
Sun. 9am–1pm
◆ GALLERIA NAZIONALE
D'ARTE MODERNA

(NATIONAL GALLERY
OF MODERN ART)
Viale delle Belle Arti, 131
Tel. 322 41 52
or 322 41 53
Closed Mon.
Open Tue.–Sat.
9am—7pm;
Sun. 9am–1pm
◆ MUSEI CAPITOLINI
Museo Capitolino
and Palazzo dei
Conservatori
Piazza del
Campidoglio, 6
Tel. 67 10 20 71
Closed Mon.
Open Tue.–Sat.
9am—7pm;
Sun 9am–1.45pm
◆ MUSEO DELL'
ALTO MEDIOEVO MUSEUM
OF THE LATE MIDDLE
AGES)
Viale Lincoln, 3
Tel. 592 58 06
Open Mon.–Sat.
9am–2pm; Sun.
9am–1pm
◆ MUSEO DI PALAZZO
VENEZIA
Via del Plebiscito, 118
Tel. 679 88 65
Open Tue.–Sat.
9am–2pm; Sun.
9am–1pm
◆ MUSEO E GALLERIA
BORGHESE
Villa Borghese
Piazza Scipione
Borghese, 5
Tel. 854 85 77
Closed Mon.
Open 9am–7pm;
Sun 9am–1pm
◆ CASTEL SANT'ANGELO
Lungotevere Castello, 1
Tel. 687 50 36
Closed second and
fourth Tue. of each
month.
Open Mon.–Sat.
9am–2pm;
Sun. 9am–1pm
◆ MUSEO NAZIONALE
ETRUSCO DI VILLA GIULIA
(ETRUSCAN MUSEUM
OF VILLA GIULIA)
Piazzale di Villa
Giulia, 9
Tel. 322 65 71
or 320 17 06
Closed Mon.
Open 9am–7pm;
Sun. 9am–1pm
◆ MUSEO NAZIONALE
PREISTORICO
ED ETNOGRAFICO
LUIGI PIGORINI (NATIONAL
MUSEUM
OF PREHISTORY AND
ETHNOGRAPHY)
Piazza Marconi, 14
Tel. 549521
Closed Mon.
Open Tue.–Fri.

9am–2pm;
Sat. 9am–7pm;
Sun. 9am–1pm
◆ MUSEO
NAZIONALE
ROMANO
(NATIONAL
MUSEUM OF
ROME)
Via Enrico De
Nicola, 79
Tel. 488 22 98,
488 08 56 or
488 23 64
Closed Mon.
Open 9am–2pm
◆ MUSEI VATICANI
CAPPELLA SISTINA
(VATICAN MUSEUMS
SISTINE CHAPEL)
Città del Vaticano
Viale Vaticano
Tel. 69 88 33 33
Open Nov.–Mar. and
June 15–Aug. 31
8.45am–2pm
(Mon.–Sat. and last
Sun. of each month);
April–June 14 and
Sep.–Oct.,
8.45am–4pm
(Mon.–Fri.);
Sat. and last Sun.
of each month,
8.45am–1pm
Closed Sun.

OTHER
MONUMENTS

◆ AREA
ARCHEOLOGICA
DEL FORO
ROMANO E
DEL PALATINO
(ROMAN FORUM)
Piazza Santa Maria
Nova, 53
Tel. 69 90 11 00

For all museums
and cultural
institutions not
listed here,
contact:

ENTE PROVINCIALE
PER IL TURISMO
Via Parigi, 5
Tel. 48 89 92 55
or 48 89 92 53

★ **DO NOT MISS** ★
TEVEREXPÒ
An exhibitors' market of crafts and other wares
with shows and concerts along the banks of the
river Tevere. *Teverexpò* is the most distinctive
and varied event held during the abundant
Roman summer.
INFORMATION
Publiaci srl
Corso V. Emanuele II, 326
Tel. 686 90 68
Fax 687 59 47
Takes place during the second half of June.

DIALING CODE 081

PRACTICAL INFORMATION

POSTAL CODE
80100

DIALING CODE
081

TOURIST INFORMATION
◆ EPT
Piazza dei Martiri, 58
Tel. 40 53 11
Fax 40 19 61
◆ UFFICIO INFORMAZIONI
STAZIONE CENTRALE
Tel. 26 87 79
◆ AA
Ufficio Information
Piazza del
Gesù Nuovo, 78
Tel. 552 33 28

EMBASSIES AND CONSULATES
US
Piazza della Repubblica
Tel. 583 81 11
UK
Via Crispi, 122
Tel. 663 511

MAIN POST OFFICE
Agenzia P.I. Napoli
succursale 1
Piazza Rodinò
Tel. 41 72 66
or 40 12 96
Open 8.30am–1.30pm

EMERGENCIES

AMBULANCE SERVICE
ITALIAN RED CROSS
Tel. 752 82 82

MEDICAL SERVICES
Chiaia, Posillipo and
S. Ferdinando districts
Tel. 761 34 66
Bagnoli and Fuorigrotta
districts
Tel. 768 64 23
Pianura and Soccavo
districts
Tel. 715 06 70
or 715 06 71
Arenella and Vomero
districts
Tel. 578 07 60
or 747 58 97
Marianella, Piscinola
and Chiaiano
Tel. 70 21 11 16
S. Carlo Arena and
Stella districts

Tel. 751 75 10
Miano, S. Pietro a
Patierno and
Secondigliano districts
Tel. 235 25 32
or 235 27 27
Avvocata, Mercato,
Montecalvaro, Pendino,
Ponte and S. Giuseppe
districts
Tel. 563 11 11
Barra, Ponticelli and
S. Giovanni a Teduccio
districts
Tel. 596 98 18
Poggio Reale,
S. Lorenzo and Vicaria
districts
Tel. 779 69 37
Emergency psychiatric
help
Tel. 743 43 43
Anti-poison center
Ospedale Cardarelli
Tel. 545 33 33

POLICE
Central headquarters
Tel. 794 11 11
Servizio Arcobaleno
Emergency intervention
for juvenile crime
Tel. 580 19 38
Stolen car service
Tel. 794 14 35
Highway patrol
Tel. 751 59 02
or 751 59 03
Emergency intervention
Tel. 751 59 04
or 751 59 05

FIRE SERVICE
Tel. 115

TRANSPORT

AIR
AIRPORT: AEROPORTO
NAPOLI CAPODICHINO
4 miles from the city
Information:
Tel. 789 62 59
or 789 62 45
◆ ALITALIA
Via Medina, 41
Tel. 542 53 33

RAIL
STAZIONE FS
NAPOLI CENTRALE
Piazza Garibaldi
MERGELLINA
Piazza Piedigrotta
CAMPI FLEGREI
Piazzale Tecchio
Tel. 554 31 88

CAR
ACI-AUTOMOBILE
CLUB NAPOLI
Piazzale Tecchio,
49/D
Tel. 239 45 11
Breakdown services:
Via Briganti, 522
Tel. 780 62 25
Via Gemito, 27
Tel. 579 16 27
Breakdown services:
Tel. 116

CAR RENTAL
◆ AVIS
Viale U. Maddalena,
196
Tel. 751 60 52
or 780 77 63
Fax 751 60 51
Reservations
Tel. 41999
Information:
Tel. 41998
Aeroporto
Capodichino
Tel. and fax 780 57 90
◆ EURODOLLAR
Via Partenope, 13
Tel. 764 63 64
Aeroporto
Capodichino
Tel. 780 29 63
or 167-01 86 68
(toll-free)
Fax 751 20 46
◆ EUROPCAR
Viale Ruffo Calabria
Tel. 780 47 80
or 780 56 43
◆ HERTZ
Piazza Garibaldi, 93
Tel. 554 86 57
or 20 62 28
Aeroporto
Capodichino
Tel. 599 09 24
◆ MAGGIORE-BUDGET
Viale Ruffo Calabria
Tel. 599 12 33
or 780 30 11
Stazione FS
Centrale
Tel. 26 53 81
or 28 78 58

PUBLIC TRANSPORT
A.N.M. AZIENDA
NAPOLETANA MOBILITÀ
Via G.B. Marino, 1
Tel. 763 11 11
Fax 763 20 70
Servizio Utenti
Tel. 763 21 77

TAXIS
AUTORADIO TAXI
Via Angelini, 20/c
Tel. 556 44 44
AUTORADIOTAXI
PARTENOPE
Tel. 560 66 66

HOTELS

BRITANNIQUE**
Corso V. Emanuele, 133
Tel. 761 41 45
Fax 66 04 57
*Bedrooms in this
attractive hotel have
beautiful views across
the bay. Lovely garden
reserved for guests.
Air conditioning,
conference room,
solarium.*
🌙 🚗 🅿 🛍 ⛐ 🖵

CONTINENTAL**
Via Partenope, 44
Tel. 764 46 36
Fax 764 46 61
*In a spectacular position
with panoramic views,
this hotel has very
comfortable rooms,
plus impressive
congressional facilities.
Air conditioning,
conference room,
solarium, disabled
access.*
🌙 🚗 🅿 🖂 ⛐
⛐ 🖵

EXCELSIOR**
Via Partenope, 48
Tel. 764 01 11
Fax 764 97 43
*This luxury hotel
offers magnificent
views of the Castel
dell'Ovo and the
island of Capri.
Empire-style public
rooms, charming
bedrooms and
beautiful suites.
The "Casanova
Grill" restaurant
serves traditional
Mediterranean cuisine.*

Air conditioning,
conference room,
solarium.

G.H. PANKER'S★★★★
Corso V. Emanuele, 135
Tel. 761 24 74
Fax 66 35 27
Opened in 1870,
this charming
hotel retains
a traditional
atmosphere.
Comfortable,
stylish
bedrooms
with views
toward Capri.
Elegant public
rooms furnished
with antiques.
The "Bellevue"
restaurant is
well worth a visit.
Air conditioning,
conference room,
disabled access.

HOLIDAY INN★★★★
Centro Direzionale Isola
E6
Tel. 225 01 11
Fax 562 80 74
A modern hotel with
impressive facilities and
business center.
Air conditioning,
conference room, gym,
sauna, disabled access.

**JOLLY
AMBASSADOR'S★★★★**
Via Medina, 70
Tel. 41 60 00
Fax 551 80 10
An imposing 1950's
building. Ask for a room
above the 16th floor for
splendid views of the
city. Roof garden.
Air conditioning,
conference room.

MAJESTIC★★★★
Largo Vasto a Chiaia,
68
Tel. and fax 41 65 00
Right in the city center,
the Majestic has a good
restaurant, "Magic Grill",
which offers regional
and international dishes.
Air conditioning,
conference room.

MIRAMARE★★★★
Via N. Sauro, 24
Tel. 764 75 89
Fax 764 07 75
A small hotel in an early
20th-century palazzo.

Its numerous terraces
have panoramic views.
Impeccable service.
Air conditioning,
conference room,
solarium.

PALACE★★★
Piazza
Garibaldi, 9
Tel. 26 70 44
Fax 26 43 06
In an enviable
position in the
heart of the city,
this is a traditional
old-style hotel.
Air conditioning,
conference room.

PARADISO★★★★
Via Catullo, 11
Tel. 761 41 61
Fax 761 34 49
Situated on a hillside,
away from the hustle
and bustle of the city.
The bedrooms, recently
redecorated in modern
style, look out toward
Vesuvius. Attractive
terrace-garden.
Air conditioning,
conference room,
solarium.

PRATI★★★
Via C. Rosaroll, 4
Tel. 26 88 98
Fax 554 18 02
Serene and
comfortable, Prati is
situated in the historic
center. The pleasant
restaurant has a
terrace.

REX★★★
Via Palepoli, 12
Tel. 764 93 89

Fax 764 92 27
Classic city furnishings
with a good level of
comfort. Air
conditioning.

SPLENDID★★★
Via A. Manzoni, 96
Tel. 714 56 30
Fax 714 64 31
A modern complex at
the exit to the gates of
the city center, in a
residential area. It has a
good restaurant and
business facilities.
Garden, air
conditioning,
conference room,
solarium, disco,
disabled access.

**VILLA
CAPODIMONTE★★★★**
Via Moiariello, 66
Tel. 45 90 00
Fax 29 93 44
Elegant, comfortable
hotel with impressive
facilities, in a unique
position on
Capodimonte hill.
Garden, air
conditioning,
conference room,
tennis, solarium,
disabled access.

In Agnano Terme:
SAN GERMANO★★★★
Via Beccadelli, 41
Tel. 570 54 22
Fax 570 15 46
In an ideal position
deep in the green
basin of Agnano, this
hotel offers high-class
conference facilities,
good amenities and
excellent service.
Air conditioning,

conference room,
tennis, solarium.

DELLE TERME★★★
Via Agnano Astroni
Tel. 570 17 33
Fax 762 64 41
Located in the center
of a park, this hotel
prides itself on its
comfortable and
elegant rooms.
A lovely restaurant
on the top floor
enjoys panoramic views.
Garden,
air conditioning,
conference room,
solarium, sauna,
disabled access.

YOUTH HOSTEL

A.I.G. MERGELLINA
Salita della Grotta a
Piedigrotta, 23
Information:
Tel. 761 23 46

RESTAURANTS

A' FENESTELLA
Calata Ponticello a
Marechiaro, 25
Tel. 769 00 20
Fax 575 06 86
Open evenings only
during Aug.
Closed Wed. lunchtime
and Sun. evenings.
Facing onto the bay,
projecting out over the
sea with an inspiring
panoramic view,
A' Fenestella boasts
an elegant decor,
delicious food, and
excellent service.

AMICI MIEI
Via Monte di Dio, 77/78
Tel. 764 60 63
Closed Sun. evenings;
Mon. and throughout
Aug.
This family-run eatery
offering good value
for money has gained
a regular clientele.
Regional food,
wonderful desserts.

BERSAGLIERA
Borgo Marinaro, 10/11
Tel. 764 60 16
Closed Tue. and some
public holidays.
*A restaurant with a
long tradition: it has
been open since 1919.
Serves the many
tasty dishes which
have made Neapolitan
cooking world famous.*

LA CANTINELLA
Via Cuma, 42
Tel. 764 86 84
Fax 764 87 69
Closed Sun. and part
of Aug.
*Renowned as one of
the best restaurants in
Naples. Excellent food,
with particularly enticing
pasta dishes and a
famous risotto.
Attentive service and
an impressive selection
of wines.*
🖃

CIRO A SANTA BRIGIDA
Via S. Brigida, 71/73
Tel. 552 40 72
Closed Sun. and part
of Aug.
*Family-run restaurant
serving traditional
Neapolitan fare in
generous portions.
Good regional wines.*
🖃

DA TONINO
Via S. Teresa a Chiaia,
47
Tel. 42 15 33
Open lunchtimes only;
closed Sun. and part
of Aug.
*A traditional "osteria",
among the oldest
serving Neapolitan
"Cucina Povera"
(peasant cooking).*

DON SALVATORE
Via Mergellina, 5
Tel. 68 18 17
Fax 66 12 41
Closed Wed.
*Located in an old boat-
house, this attractive
restaurant offers
traditional dishes with a
modern slant. Local fish
is always on the menu.
Impressive wine list.*

ENOTECA GRA.PA.L.
Via Toledo, 16
Tel. 552 21 14
Closed Sun. and Mon.;
Christmas–Jan. 6.
*An extremely well-
researched wine list,
with bottles dating
back to 1840 and a
welcoming atmosphere
within a lovely 17th-
century villa.*

FAZENDA
Via Marechiaro, 58/A
Tel. 575 74 20
Closed Mon.; Sun.
evenings and Mon.
lunchtime June–Aug.,
and part of Aug.
*Traditional local cuisine
with the focus on fish
dishes; a stunning
panoramic view of the
gulf of Naples.*
🖃

GALLO NERO
Via T. Tasso, 466
Tel. 64 30 12
Closed Sun. evenings,
Mon., Christmas–Jan. 6
and throughout Aug.
*Housed in an attractive
early 20th-century villa,
this restaurant has a
splendid terrace with
a view of the sea.
Discreet and elegant.*
🖃

GIRULÀ
Via Vetriera a Chiaia, 7/A

Tel. and fax 42 55 11
Closed Sun. and
throughout Aug.
*A well-known restaurant
serving traditional
Neapolitan cuisine.
Sometimes puts on
cabarets and operettas.*
🖃

GIUSEPPONE A MARE
Via F. Russo, 13
Tel. 575 60 02
Fax 764 01 95
Closed Mon.;
Christmas–New Year
and part of Aug.
*This traditionally
Neapolitan rustic
eatery has a convivial
atmosphere and
attentive, cordial
service. Good fish.*
🖃

GROTTINO
Piazzetta del Leone, 7
Tel. 66 46 08
Closed Mon.
*The cuisine is traditional
Neapolitan, with a wide
selection of pizzas.
Situated in a good
position in Mergellina.
Great value for money.*
🖃

AL POETA
Piazza di S. Giacomo,
133
Tel. and fax 575 69 36
Closed Mon. and part
of Aug.
*Located on the Posillipo
hill, this seafood
restaurant is usually full
of locals. Book ahead
if you want to eat
outdoors. Wide choice
of regional wines.*
🖃

POSTO ACCANTO
Via N. Sauro, 2
Tel. 764 86 00
Closed Sun. evenings

*The name ("next door")
came from being next to
Rosolino, owned by the
same person. Pizza and
Neapolitan dishes are
served accompanied by
an ample selection of
wines.*
🖃

★LA SACRESTIA
Via Orazio, 116
Tel. 66 41 86
Closed Mon. and part
of Aug.
*This restaurant is
famed for its excellent
traditional food, elegant
surroundings and
panoramic views. Save
a space for the splendid
desserts. Flower-filled
garden terrace.*
🖃

SALVATORE ALLA RIVIERA
Riviera Chiaia, 91
Tel. 68 04 90
Closed Tue.
*Traditional regional
and local cooking;
also a pizzeria.*
🖃

SAN CARLO
Via Cesario Console
18/19
Tel. 764 97 57
Fax 245 11 66
Closed Sun. and part
of Aug.
*Located in a historic
building in the city
center, San Carlo is
distinguished by
English-style wood
fittings emblazoned with
Bourbon coats-of-arms.
Classic regional menu,
with fish specialties.*
🖃

SBRESCIA
Rampe S. Antonio a
Posillipo, 109
Tel. 66 91 40
Closed Mon.
*Run by the same family
for many generations,
the quality of the fish
(kept live in tanks) is
guaranteed here.
A typically Neapolitan
place to eat.*
🖃

TAVERNA DELL'ARTE
Rampe di S. Giovanni
Maggiore, 1/A
Tel. 552 75 58
Closed Sun. and part
of Aug.
*Booking is essential if
you want to taste the
authentic flavors of
Neapolitan cuisine in
this small eatery.
Excellent desserts and
house liqueurs.*

TRIANON
Via P. Colletta, 46
Tel. 553 94 26
Closed Sun.
*The most popular
pizzeria in Naples,
offering every kind of
topping imaginable.
Original 1930's decor.
Friendly, lively place to
eat.*

UMBERTO
Via Alabardieri, 30
Tel. 41 85 55
Closed Mon, and
throughout Aug.
*Situated right in the
city center, this long-
established restaurant
serves excellent pizzas
and authentic regional
dishes.*
▭

VADINCHENIA
Via Pontano, 21
Tel. 66 02 65
Open evenings only.
Closed Sun.; Aug.
*A modern, minimalist
decor provides the
setting for traditional
Campanian cuisine
reinterpreted with a
modern touch. Seafood
dominates the menu.
Interesting wine list.*

CULTURE

CIVIC BUILDINGS
◆ BIBLIOTECA MUSICALE
CONSERVATORIO
S. PIETRO A MAIELLA
Via S. Pietro a Maiella
Tel. 45 92 55
◆ CASTEL SANT'ELMO
Largo S. Martino
Tel. 578 40 30
Closed Mon.
Open Tue.–Sun.
9am–8pm
◆ PALAZZO REALE
Piazza del Plebiscito
Tel. 41 38 88
Open 9am–1.30pm;
public holidays
9am–1pm
◆ APPARTAMENTO
STORICO DEL PALAZZO
REALE

Closed Mon
Open 9am–2pm; public
holidays 9am–1pm
◆ PARCO DEL
PALAZZO REALE
Open 9am–sunset

RELIGIOUS BUILDINGS
◆ BATTISTERO DI
S. RESTITUTA (BAPTISTRY
OF S. RESTITUTA)
Closed Tue.
Open 9am–noon,
4–6pm; public holidays
9am–noon
◆ CASTELCAPUANO
CAPPELLA DELLA
Palazzo di Giustizia
Open at 8am for mass;
other times to be
arranged with Signor
Guglielmo Del Piano.
Tel. 554 54 49
◆ CATACOMBE
DI S. GENNARO
(CATACOMBS)
Via Capodimonte
Tel. 881 21 32
Guided tours Fri., Sat.
and Sun. at 9.30am,
10.15am, 11am and
11.45am
CAPPELLA DI
S. GENNARO
Open 9am–noon
◆ DUOMO (CATHEDRAL)
Via Duomo
Tel. 44 90 97
Open 9am–noon,
4–6pm (summer);
4–7pm (winter).
◆ MONTEOLIVETO
(S. ANNA DEI
LOMBARDI)
Via Monteoliveto
Closed Sun.
Open 9am–noon
◆ PIO MONTE DELLA
MISERICORDIA
CHIESA E PINACOTECA
Via Tribunale, 253
Tel. 44 69 44
or 44 55 17
Closed Sun.
Open 9am–4pm
◆ CHURCH OF S. CLARA
AND CLOISTER OF THE
POOR CLARES
Via Benedetto Croce
Tel. 552 62 09
Cloister Open
8.30am–12.30pm,
4–6.30pm
◆ S. LORENZO
MAGGIORE E SCAVI
ARCHEOLOGICI
Piazza S. Gaetano
Tel. 29 05 80
◆ S. MARIA DELLA
SANITÀ CATACOMBS OF
S. GAUDIOSO
Piazza Sanità, 124
Tel. 544 13 05
Catacombs open Sun.,
9.45am, 11.45am;
guided tours by previous

arrangement.
◆ S. MARIA
DONNAREGINA
vico Donnaregina
Open Mon.–Fri., 9am–
1pm; or contact the
secretary of the Scuola
di Perfezionamento
Restauro Monumenti
to arrange visits.
Tel. 29 91 01
◆ SS. SEVERINO
E SOSSIO
c/o Ss. Filippo e Giacomo
Tel. 551 66 66
Open Sun., 9am–noon

MUSEUMS
◆ MUSEO
ARCHEOLOGICO
NAZIONALE (NATIONAL
ARCHEOLOGY MUSEUM)
Piazza Museo
Tel. 44 01 66
Closed Mon.
Open 9am–2pm; public
holidays 9am–1pm
◆ MUSEO CAPPELLA
DI S. SEVERO
Via Francesco De
Sanctis, 19
Tel. 551 84 70
Open Jan.–Dec. 7:
Wed.–Sat. and Mon.,
10am–5pm; Tue. and
Sun. 10am–1.30pm;
Dec. 8–Jan. 6: 10am–
7pm
◆ MUSEO CIVICO
(CITY MUSEUM)
Piazza Municipio
Castel Nuovo
Tel. 795 11 11
Closed Sun.
Open Mon.–Fri. 9am–
2pm; Sat. 9am–1.30pm
◆ MUSEO CIVICO
FILANGIERI
PALAZZO COMO
Via Duomo, 288
Tel. 20 31 75
or 20 32 11
Closed Mon.
Open 9am–1.30pm
◆ MUSEO E GALLERIE
NAZIONALI DI
CAPODIMONTE
PARCO DI CAPODIMONTE
Via Miano, 2
Tel. 744 13 07
Closed Mon.

Open Tue.–Sat.
10am–6pm;
Sun. 9am–2pm
◆ MUSEO NAZIONALE
DELLA CERAMICA
DUCA DI MARTINA
(NATIONAL CERAMICS
MUSEUM)
Villa Floridiana
Via Cimarosa, 77
Tel. 578 84 18
Closed Mon.
Open 9am–2pm; public
holidays 9am–1pm
◆ MUSEO NAZIONALE
DI S. MARTINO
MUSEO E GIARDINI
Largo S. Martino, 5
Tel. 578 17 69
Closed Mon.
Open 8am–1.30pm;
public holidays
9am–1pm

For all monuments
and cultural
institutions not listed
here, contact:
EPT
Piazza dei Martiri, 58
Tel. 40 53 11
Fax 40 19 61

DIALING CODE 080

PRACTICAL INFORMATION

POSTAL CODE
70100

DIALING CODE
080

TOURIST INFORMATION
◆ AZIENDA AUTONOMA DI SOGGIORNO E TURISMO
Corso Vittorio. Emanuele II, 68
Tel. 521 19 95
or 523 51 86
◆ EPT
Piazza Moro, 33
Tel. 524 22 44

MAIN POST OFFICE
Agenzia P.I. Bari Succursale 1
Via dell'Arca, 11
Tel. 523 29 79
Open 8.30am–1.30pm

EMERGENCIES

AMBULANCE SERVICE
Italian Red Cross
Tel. 553 98 88
Serbari
Tel. 504 40 40

MEDICAL SERVICES
Bari
Tel. 5242389
Iapigia and Torre a Mare
Tel. 553 10 50
Carbonara, Ceglie and Loseto
Tel. 565 01 25
Palese and Santo Spirito
Tel. 530 00 67

POLICE
Central headquarters
Tel. 529 11 11
Highway patrol
Tel. 534 96 80

FIRE SERVICE
Tel. 115

TRANSPORT

AIR
AIRPORT: AEROPORTO DI BARI PALESE
6 miles from the city
Tel. 538 23 70
Information
Tel. 583 52 30
◆ ALITALIA
Via Calefati, 37/41
Tel. 524 44 40

RAIL
STAZIONE FS
Piazza Moro
Tel. 521 68 01
Travel information:
Tel. 1478-88088

CAR
ACI-AUTOMOBILE CLUB BARI
Via O. Serena, 26
Member and tourist office:
Tel. 553 17 17
Emergency service:
Via O. Serena, 16
Tel. 558 00 58
Emergency service:
Tel. 116

CAR RENTAL
◆ AVIS
Via S. Matarrese, 4/F
Tel. 561 41 99
Via Zuppetta, 5/A
Tel. 52 471 54
Aeroporto Palese
Tel. 531 61 68
◆ EURODOLLAR
Aeroporto Palese
Tel. 531 61 76,
or 538 36 15
Fax 537 10 51
Toll-free:
167-01 86 68
◆ EUROPCAR
Strada Provinciale Aeroporto
Tel. 531 61 44
◆ HERTZ
Via Aeroporto Civile, 1
Tel. 531 61 71
◆ MAGGIORE-BUDGET
Via Pordenone, 21
Tel. 531 61 80
Via Amendola, 106/A
Tel. 558 08 17
Reservations:
1478-67067

PUBLIC TRANSPORT
A.M.T.A.B. (AZIENDA MUNICIPALIZZATA TRASPORTI AUTOFILOVIARI DI BARI)
Viale de Blasio
Tel. 531 13 98
or 539 31 11
Ticket office:
Via de Cesare, 5
Tel. 523 26 33

TAXIS
TAXI RADIO TAX
Tel. 554 33 33

HOTELS

7 MARI***
Via Verdi, 60
Tel. 534 15 00
Fax 534 44 82
This elegant seafront hotel is equipped with its own private beach and is very near the Fiera. Annexed to the restaurant "Il Corsaro". Air conditioning, conference room, private beach.

BOSTON***
Via Piccinni, 155
Tel. 521 66 33
Fax 524 68 02
Immaculate service makes a stay in this typical town hotel most agreeable. Situated in the center, it has a simple, warm atmosphere. Air conditioning, conference room.

G.A. VILLA ROMANAZZI CARDUCCI****
Via Capruzzi, 326
Tel. 542 74 00
Fax 556 02 97
A splendid 19th-century villa with modernized fittings and interior. It is situated in a park with a swimming pool, and is particularly well equipped. Garden,

air conditioning, conference room, gym, sauna, disabled access.

JOLLY****
Via G. Petroni, 15
Tel. 556 43 66
Fax 556 52 19
A hotel in the classic tradition, charming and welcoming. Has a pleasant restaurant, "La Tiella". Air conditioning, conference room, disabled access.

MAJESTY****
Via Gentile, 97/B
Tel. 549 10 99
Fax 549 23 97
Recently renovated. A comfortable stay is guaranteed here. Garden, air conditioning, conference room, tennis.

ORCHIDEA**
Via Giulio Petroni, 11/2
Tel. 542 19 37
Fax 542 69 43
A traditional family-run hotel, offering a warm welcome.

PALACE HOTEL****
Via Lombardi, 13
Tel. 521 65 51
Fax 521 14 99
An elegant, multi-functional complex in which ancient and modern combine beautifully. The top floor has a magnificent view and a famous restaurant, the "Murat", which offers first-class regional cuisine. Air conditioning, conference room.

RONDÒ RESIDENCE HOTEL***
Corso Alcide De Gasperi, 308/E

Tel. 502 34 44
Fax 502 34 95
A special blend of hotel and self-catering apartments whose rooms all have cooking facilities. This modern and comfortable hotel is situated away from the center and enjoys a peaceful atmosphere. Garden, air conditioning, conference room, sauna.
🚗 P □

SHERATON NICOLAUS**
Via Cardinale A. Ciasca, 9
Tel. 504 26 26
Fax 504 20 58
Hidden in the greenery of an attractive park, the comfortable Sheraton Nicolaus boasts two renowned

restaurants: "Le Stagioni" and "Le Pleiadi", both serving regional specialties as well as international cuisine. Air conditioning, conference room, gym, solarium, sauna.
P 🛏 ✄ □ □

VICTOR**
Via Nicolai, 69/71
Tel. and fax 521 66 00
Right in the city center, this elegant hotel has excellent modern amenities. Air conditioning, conference room.
🚗 □ □

WINDSOR*
Via Parallela Amoruso, 62/7
Tel. 561 00 11
Fax 551 00 11
Situated away from the noise and bustle of the town, this modern hotel has fittings that complement the stylish interior. Air conditioning, conference room.
🚗 P ✄ □ □

YOUTH HOSTELS

OSTELLO DEL LEVANTE
Lungomare Colombo, Palese Macchie
Tel. 530 02 82

CAMPING AND TOURIST VILLAGES

CAMPING SEA WORLD
Via Adriatica, 78
S. Giorgio
Tel. 549 11 75
or 549 12 02

RESTAURANTS

AI 2 GHIOTTONI
Via Putignani, 11
Tel. 523 22 40
Closed Sun. and part of Aug.
Tasty regional cookery is accompanied here by an excellent selection of wines.

NUOVA VECCHIA BARI
Via Dante, 47
Tel. 521 64 96
Closed Fri. and Sun. evenings and part of Aug.
The service is excellent in this traditional regional restaurant located in the vaults of an old oil depository.

PICCINNI
Via Piccinni, 28
Tel. 521 12 27
Closed Sun. and part of Aug.
Offers classic, well-presented cuisine. Vast choice of wines.

PIGNATA
Corso Vittorio Emanuele, 173
Tel. 523 24 81
Fax 524 75 90
Closed Mon. and throughout Aug.
Traditional Puglian cuisine is stylishly reinterpreted here, with excellent results.
□

SORSO PREFERITO
Via De Niccolò, 46
Tel. 523 57 47
Closed Sun.
Situated right on the seafront, this restaurant offers good food at a reasonable price.

TERRANIMA
Via Putignani, 213/215
Tel. 521 97 25
Closed Sun. and throughout Aug.
A characteristic atmosphere in which to sample traditional local dishes.

In Carbonara di Bari:
TABERNA
Via Ospedale di Venere, 6
Tel. 565 05 57
Closed Mon. and throughout Aug.
This restaurant, with four rooms, is very spacious and situated on two levels. Regional cuisine.
□

In Torre a Mare:
NICOLA
Via Principe di Piemonte, 3
Tel. 543 00 43
Closed Sun. evenings and Mon., and from mid-Dec. to mid-Jan.
This little restaurant has a long tradition as a family-run business. Good views of the "porticciolo" and a lovely terrace.
□

CULTURE

CIVIC BUILDINGS
◆ ACQUARIO PROVINCIALE (AQUARIUM)
Molo Pizzoli
Tel. 521 12 00

Closed Sun.
Open 9am–12.30pm
◆ CASTELLO E GIPSOTECA PROVINCIALE (CASTLE AND PLASTER GALLERY)
Piazza Federico II di Svevia
Tel. 521 43 61
Open 9am–1pm, 3.30pm–7pm
◆ PINACOTECA PROVINCIALE/PALAZZO DELLA PROVINCIA (PICTURE GALLERY)
Via Spalato, 19
Closed Sun. afternoons and Mon.
Open 9am–1pm, 4–7pm

MUSEUMS
◆ MUSEO ARCHEOLOGICO (ARCHEOLOGICAL MUSEUM)
Piazza Umberto I
Tel. 521 15 59, or 521 15 76
Visits only on request.
◆ MUSEO CIVICO STORICO
Via Boccapianola
For more information contact: Assessorato alla Cultura del Comune
Tel. 577 23 38
◆ MUSEO DELLA BASILICA DI S. NICOLA
Largo Abate Elia
Tel. 521 12 69
Open Wed. 10am–noon; Fri. 10am–noon, 5–7pm
◆ MUSEO DIOCESANO
c/o Palazzo Arvescovile
Piazza Odegitria
Tel. 521 27 25
Open Mon. and Sat. 10am–noon

For information on all monuments and cultural institutions not listed here contact:

AZIENDA AUTONOMA DI SOGGIORNO E TURISMO Corso Vittorio. Emanuele II, 68
Tel. 521 99 51 or 523 51 86

★ **DO NOT MISS** ★
FIERA DEL LEVANTE ("EASTERN FAIR")
The most important market display of crafts and other wares held in the south. You can find every sort of product here and learn a great deal about the traditions and crafts of southern Italy. Takes place in mid-September.
INFORMATION
Ente Autonomo Fiera del Levante Lungomare Starita Bari
Tel. 536 64 75
Fax 536 64 88

DIALING CODE 091

PRACTICAL INFORMATION

POSTAL CODE
90100

DIALING CODE
091

TOURIST INFORMATION
◆ AAPT
Piazza Castelnuovo, 34/35
Tel. 58 38 47
Fax 58 27 88
◆ AA
Salita Belmonte
Tel. 54 01 22
◆ INFORMATION OFFICE
Piazza Cavalieri del Santo Sepolcro
Tel. 616 13 61

MAIN POST OFFICE
Agenzia P.I. Bari
Succursale 1
Via Aquileia, 7
Tel. 20 58 45,
or 20 61 42
Open 8.30am–1.30pm

EMERGENCIES

AMBULANCE SERVICE
Croce Azzurra
Tel. 48 56 07
Croce delle Stelle
Tel. 59 99 24
or 59 62 36
Croce Sana
Tel. 48 46 11
Croce Siciliana
Tel. 621 28 88
Croce S. Caterina
Tel. 652 13 97

MEDICAL SERVICES
Via Massimo d'Azeglio
Tel. 780 81 97
◆ Tribunali, Castellamare, S. Rosalia
Montegrappa, Palazzo Reale Monte di Pietà, Politeama districts
Piazza Marmi
Tel. 58 53 57

◆ Cuba Calatafimi, Zisa, Villatasca
Mezzomonreale, Altarello, Boccadifalco districts
Via C. Onorato
Tel. 21 95 02
◆ Noce Malaspina, Palagonia, CEP uditore, Passo di Rigano, Borgonuovo, Cruillas, Tommaso Natale
Sferracavallo districts
Via Roccazzo (Casa del Sole)
Tel. 673 06 67

◆ Libertà, Montepellegrino, Arenella Vergine Maria, Resuttana, Partanna, Mondello, Pallavicino
S. Lorenzo districts
Via M. d'Azeglio
Tel. 780 81 97
◆ Oreto, Stazione, Settecannoli Brancaccio, Ciaculli, Villagrazia
Falsomiele, Villabate districts
Via Sperone, 4
Tel. 39 72 50,
39 74 37

POLICE
Central headquarters
Tel. 21 01 11
Highway patrol
Tel. 656 95 11
or 656 97 21

FIRE SERVICE
Tel. 115

TRANSPORT

AIR
AIRPORT: AEROPORTO CIVILE PUNTA-RAISI
19 miles from the city center
Tel. 59 14 14
◆ ALITALIA
Via Mazzini, 59
Tel. 601 93 33

RAIL
STAZIONE FS CENTRALE
Piazza Giulio Cesare
Tel. 616 18 06

CAR
ACI-AUTOMOBILE CLUB PALERMO
Via delle Alpi, 6
Tel. 30 04 68
Emergencies
Via Strasburgo, 277
Tel. 688 62 97
or 116

CAR RENTAL
◆ AVIS
Aeroporto Punta Raisi
Tel. 59 16 54
◆ EURODOLLAR
Via Alfredo Casella, 66
Tel. 682 35 57
Fax 667 11 56
Aeroporto Punta Raisi
Tel. 651 13 93
or 167-018668 (toll-free)
Fax 651 43 64
◆ EUROPCAR
Stazione FS Centrale
Piazza G. Cesare
Tel. 616 50 50
◆ HERTZ
Via Messina, 7/E
Tel. 33 16 68
or 32 34 39
◆ MAGGIORE-BUDGET
Viale de Gasperi, 179
Tel. 51 73 05
Reservations:
Tel. 1478-67067

PUBLIC TRANSPORT
A.M.A.T. AZIENDA MUNICIPALIZZATA AUTOTRASPORTI PALERMO
Via Roccazzo, 77
Tel. 35 01 11
Fax 22 45 63
Ticket office:
Via Alfonso Borrelli, 16
Tel. 32 13 33
Fax 611 00 62

TAXIS
RADIOTAXI COOPERATIVA TRINACRIA
Tel. 22 54 55

HOTELS

ASTORIA PALACE****
Via Monte Pellegrino, 62
Tel. 637 18 20
Fax 637 21 78
A comfortable hotel with a good restaurant, the "Cedro", which serves typical regional cuisine. Air conditioning, conference room, disabled access.
⛄ P ✂ ⌂ ☐

BEL TRE***
Via Ruffo di Calabria, 20
Tel. and fax 22 35 60
Built on hills, the Bel Tre's unique structure (on different levels) allows each room to have its own balcony with a splendid view of the sea. Garden, air conditioning, conference room, disabled access.
⛄ P ✂ ⌂

EXCELSIOR PALACE****
Via Marchese Ugo, 3
Tel. 625 61 76
Fax 34 21 39
Period furnishings and comfort characterize this hotel, situated in the environs of the Villa Gonzaga. Conference room, disabled access.
P ✂ ⌂ ☐

EUROPA***
Via Agrigento, 3
Tel. 625 63 23
Fax 625 63 23
Classic town style, comfortable and convenient, a few steps from Piazza Politeana. Air conditioning.
✂ ⌂ ☐

FORTE AGIP****
Viale Regione Siciliana, 2620
Tel. 55 20 33
Fax 40 81 98
A modern hotel. Better for those who have their own means of transport. Air conditioning, conference room.
P ✂ ⌂ ☐

GRANDE ALBERGO E DELLE PALME****
Via Roma, 398
Tel. 58 39 33
Fax 33 15 45
Traditional elegance blended with modern amenities. Air conditioning, conference room, disabled access.
🚗 ✂ ⌂ ☐

JOLLY DEL FORO ITALICO****
Foro Italico, 22
Tel. 616 50 90
Fax 616 14 41
Located in the peaceful gardens of the Villa Giulia. Air conditioning, conference room.
⛄ P ☐ ⌂ ☐

MEDITERRANEO***
Via Rolono Pilo, 43

Tel. 58 11 33
Fax 58 69 74
*This charming hotel
boasts a central
position near the
archeological museum
(Museo Archeologico).
Air conditioning,
conference room.*
🚗 🎿 ▭ ▢

**POLITEAMA
PALACE******
Piazza Ruggero
Settimo, 15
Tel. 32 27 77
Fax 611 15 89
*Modern, comfortable
and well located,
near the Politeama
theater. Air conditioning,
conference room .*
🚗 🎿 ▭ ▢

PONTE***
Via Crispi, 99
Tel. 58 37 44
Fax 58 18 45
*Recently renovated
and refurbished.
Situated in a good
position in the port
area. Air conditioning.*
🚗 🎿 ▭ ▢

PRESIDENT****
Via Crispi, 230
Tel. 58 07 33
Fax 611 15 88
*Facing onto the port,
this is an intimate
and exclusive hotel.
The charming roof
terrace restaurant
has a view over the
port. Air conditioning,
conference room,
disabled access.*
🎿 P 🎿 ▭ ▢

**SAN PAOLO
PALACE*****
Via Messina Marine, 91
Tel. 62 11 12
Fax 621 53 00
*The panoramic view
from the elevator
attached to the
building's exterior, the
hotel's spectacular
position (right on the
seafront), the swimming
pool on the top floor
and the two restaurants
all contribute to a
pampered stay.
Air conditioning,
conference room, tennis
court, gym, sauna,
disabled access.*
🎿 🚗 🎿 ▭ ▢

VILLA ARCHIRAFI**
Via Lincoln, 30
Tel. 616 88 27
Fax 616 86 31

★ **DO NOT MISS** ★
**FIERA CAMPIONARIA INTERNAZIONALE
("INTERNATIONAL EXHIBITION FAIR")**
Displays include a crafts market and more.
Takes place during the second half of May.
INFORMATION
Ente Autonomo Fiera del Mediterraneo
Piazza General Cascino, 177
Palermo
Tel. 620 91 47   Fax 620 91 70

*A villa built in the early
20th century in a
particularly tranquil
area (nearby is the
interesting botanic
garden or "Orto
Botanico"), is the setting
for this simple yet
pleasant hotel. Garden,
disabled access.*
🏠 P ▭ ▢

**VILLA IGIEA
GRAND HOTEL*******
Salita Belmonte, 43
Tel. 54 37 44
Fax 54 76 54
*A warm welcome
awaits you in the
ample and light-filled
surroundings of this
19th-century patrician
villa. Garden,
air conditioning,
conference room,
tennis, disabled
access.*
🎿 P ⛵ ▭ ▢

CAMPSITES

**CAMPEGGIO
DEGLI ULIVI**
Via Pegaso, 25
90148 Sferracavallo
(Palermo)
Tel. 53 30 21
Open all year

RESTAURANTS

AL GENIO
Piazza S. Carlo, 9
Tel. 616 66 42
Closed Sun. evening,
Mon. and part of Aug.
*A few steps from the
Fontana del Genio,
in a 17th-century
building. Here classic
Sicilian cuisine can be
sampled – seasonal
vegetables, fish
(anchovies, cuttlefish),
sausages. First-class
trattoria. Garden.*

**L'APPRODO
RISTORANTE RENATO**
Via Messina Marine, 224
Tel. 630 28 81
Closed Sun. and
part of Aug.
*Especially welcoming,
this eatery is right on
the seafront. The
cuisine is Sicilian but
with the occasional
experimental touch.
Has an attractive neo-
medieval cellar with
wines from all over
the world and a vast
assortment of extra-
virgin olive oils.
Air conditioning.*
🎿 ▭

LA BRICIOLA
Via Castriota, 3
Tel. 32 06 97
Closed Sun. and
throughout Aug.
*The atmosphere and
decor recall Palermo at
the start of this century;
the chef offers his own
variations on the Sicilian
classics.*
▭

BYE BYE BLUES
Via del Garofalo, 23
Tel. 684 14 15
Open evenings only.
Closed Mon. and part
of Nov.
*A very un-Sicilian
name for a restaurant
whose objective is to
mix international and
Sicilian cuisine. The
menu is diverse and
follows the seasons
in its offerings of
vegetables, meat and
fish. An interesting
cellar includes
prestigious Sicilian
wines.*

CAPRICCI DI SICILIA
Via Istituto Pignatelli, 6

Piazza Sturzo
Tel. 32 77 77
Closed Mon. and
part of Aug.
*An extremely central
location (almost on
Piazza Politeama),
and a good reputation.
Try the traditional
cuisine from Palermo
(such as starters of
fried cheese), and
indulge in some modern
reinterpretations of
classic Sicilian dishes,
like "pasta con le sarde"
(pasta with sardines).
Garden.*
▭

★**CHARLESTON**
Piazzale Ungheria, 30
Tel. 32 13 66
Fax 32 13 47
Closed Sun.
*Decorated in Art
Nouveau style, this
restaurant offers both
classic Italian and
excellent Sicilian
cuisine. One of the
best addresses in the
city. Air conditioning.*
▭

DA ROSARIO
Via Giacomo
Cusmano, 25
Tel. 611 23 30
or 32 29 92
Closed Sun. and
throughout Aug.
*A trattoria respectful
of tradition, serving
interesting seafood
dishes. Choose from the
impressive list of
excellent desserts,
from the oven-cooked
"cassata" to the
"cannoli". Even the
liqueurs are homemade.*
▭

I GRILLI
Largo Cavalieri
di Malta, 2
Tel. 33 41 30
Open evenings only.
Closed Mon. and
from July–Sep.

541

DIALING CODE 091

A restaurant-bar in the historic center, on the first floor of a lovely patrician palazzo. A well-researched Sicilian menu and excellent service. An interesting cellar, with wines from the island.

OSTERIA FRATELLI LO BIANCO
Via Emerico Amari, 104
Tel. 58 58 16
Closed Sun. and part of Aug.
In a "strategic" position, near the entrance to the port and Piazza Politeama, this "osteria" (inn), popularly known as "il tavernone", boasts a warm welcome and friendly service. The dishes are traditional, and described to diners by the owner himself.

PARADISO
Via Serradifalco, 23
No telephone
Open lunchtimes only.
Closed Sun.and part of Aug.

A traditional restaurant which resists modernity in all its forms: not always a bad thing, especially if, like this trattoria, such resistance signifies being supplied with fresh fish by the same fisherman for over thirty years. Air conditioning.

IL RISTORANTINO
Piazzale De Gasperi, 19
Tel. 51 28 61
Fax 670 29 99
Closed Mon. and throughout Aug.
Authentic cuisine in a charming restaurant away from the hustle and bustle of the city center. Simple fare, dedicated mostly to fish dishes. The desserts and wine list should not be overlooked. Garden, air conditioning.

SANT'ANDREA
Piazza Sant'Andrea, 4
Tel. 33 49 99
Closed Tue. and throughout Jan.
A newly established restaurant serving simple, authentic Mediterranean dishes. Air conditioning.

SCUDERIA
Viale del Fonte, 9
Tel. 52 03 23
Fax 52 04 67
Closed Sun. evenings and part of Aug.
Sicilian and classic Italian cuisine served in a friendly atmosphere. As well as the large dining room, you can also have your meal out on the terrace or in the garden. Air conditioning.

VILLA FLORA
Piazzetta Villa dei Colli, 3
Tel. 668 69 16
Closed Tue. and throughout Aug.
This restaurant is housed within an elegant 18th-century villa; have lunch outside on the attractive terrace and enjoy the splendid panorama. Air conditioning.

CULTURE

CIVIC BUILDINGS
◆ CUBA
Corso Calatafimi, 100
Tel. 59 02 99
Visits by request at Tuköry barracks
Open 9am–1pm (public holidays on the first and third Sun. of each month).
Open Wed. and Thur. 9am–1pm, 3–5pm
◆ ORTO BOTANICO (BOTANICAL GARDENS)
Via Lincoln, 2/B
Tel. 616 14 93
Winter: open 9am–5pm, Sat. and Sun. 9am–1pm
Summer: open 9am–6pm, Sat. and Sun. 9am–1pm
◆ TEATRO MASSIMO
Piazza Verdi
Tel. 605 31 11
◆ TEATRO POLITEAMA
Piazza Politema, on the corner with V. Turati
Tel. 605 33 21
◆ ZISA
Piazza Guglielmo il Buomo
Tel. 652 02 69
Open 9.30am–1.30pm; Tue. and Fri. 9.30am–1.30pm, 3–5.30pm; Sun. 9.30am–12.30pm

RELIGIOUS BUILDINGS
◆ CAPPELLA PALATINA
PALAZZO DEI NORMANNI
Tel. 651 96 02
Open 9am–noon, 3–5pm; Sat. 9am–noon; Sun. 9–10am, 12–1pm

MUSEUMS
◆ CIVICA GALLERIA D'ARTE MODERNA E. RESTIVO (MUNICIPAL GALLERY OF MODERN ART)
Via Turati, 10
Tel. 58 89 51
Open 9am–1pm; Wed. 9am–1pm, 3–6pm
◆ GALLERIA REGIONALE DELLA SICILIA PALAZZO ABATELLIS (REGIONAL GALLERY OF SICILY)
Via Alloro, 4
Tel. 616 43 17
Open 9am–1.30pm; Tue.–Fri. 9am–1.30pm, 3–7pm; Sun. 9am–12.30pm
◆ MUSEO DIOCESANO
Via Bonello
Tel. 607 71 11
◆ MUSEO ETNOGRAFICO SICILIANO G. PITRE (MUSEUM OF SICILIAN ETHNOGRAPHY)

Palazzina Cinese
Tel. 671 10 60
Closed Fri.
Open 9am–1pm; Wed. 9am–1pm, 3.30–5.30pm
◆ MUSEO INTERNAZIONALE DELLE MARIONETTE (INTERNATIONAL MUSEUM OF PUPPETS)
Via Butera, 1
Tel. 32 80 60
Open 9am–1pm, 4–7pm;
Sat. 9am–1pm
Closed Sun.
◆ MUSEO REGIONALE ARCHEOLOGICO (REGIONAL MUSEUM OF ARCHEOLOGY)
Piazza Olivella
Tel. 662 02 20
Open 9am–1.30pm; Tue., Wed. and Fri. 9am–1.30pm, 3–6.30pm
◆ TESORO DELLA CATTEDRALE (CATHEDRAL TREASURES)
Corso V. Emanuele
Tel. 33 43 73
Open 9.30am–noon, 4–5.45pm.
Closed Sun.

For information on all monuments and cultural institutions not listed here, contact:
AAPT
Piazza Castelnuovo, 34/35
Tel. 58 38 47
Fax 58 27 88

★ **DO NOT MISS** ★
PALERMO IN SCENA
An important event incorporating theater, dance and music. Great international names alternate with the island's own festival (the small festival of the patron saint of Palermo, Saint Rosalia), with processions, floats and spectacles of every kind. Classic, modern, and experimental drama all share the stage here.
INFORMATION:
Comune di Palermo, Assessorato alla Cultura
Tel. 740 11 11
Takes place during July and August.

PRACTICAL INFORMATION

POSTAL CODE
09100

DIALING CODE
070

TOURIST INFORMATION
◆ EPT
Piazza Deffenu, 9
Tel. 65 48 11
Fax 66 32 07
◆ UFFICO INFORMAZIONI
AEROPORTO ELMAS
Tel. 24 02 00
◆ AA
Via Mameli, 97
Tel. 66 41 95
Fax 65 82 00
◆ UFFICO INFORMATION
Piazza Matteotti
Tel. 66 92 55
◆ ET
Via Mameli, 97
Tel. 60231
Fax 66 46 36

MAIN POST OFFICE
Agenzia P.I. Cagliari
Succursale 1
Via Fara, 9/11
Tel. 66 31 74
Open 8.30am–1.30pm

EMERGENCIES

AMBULANCE SERVICE
Red Cross
Tel. 27 23 45

MEDICAL SERVICES
S. Giovanni di Dio
Tel. 6091
Ospedale Marino
Tel. 37 02 23
Ospedale Brotzu
Tel. 54 32 66
Ospedale SS. Trinità
Tel. 28 19 25

POLICE
Emergency intervention
Tel. 44444

★ DO NOT MISS ★
LA NOTTE DEI POETI
(THE NIGHT OF POETS)
Linked to Cagliari by a reliable bus service.
Nora hosts a dance, music and theater show
in the spectacular setting of its Roman theater.
Traditionally every year sees classic and
modern pieces performed by international
stars of the stage.
INFORMATION
Codac
Via dei Passeri, 9 Cagliari
Tel. 30 70 25
Fax 30 27 31
Runs from mid-July to mid-August.

Highway patrol
Tel. 66 66 66

FIRE SERVICE
Tel. 115

TRANSPORT

AIR
AIRPORT:
AEROPORTO ELMAS
4 miles northwest
of the town
Information:
Tel. 24 01 19
◆ ALITALIA
Via Caprera, 14
Tel. 60107

RAIL
STAZIONE FS
Piazza Matteotti
Tel. 65 62 93
STAZIONE FERROVIE
DELLA SARDEGNA
Piazza Repubblica
Tel. 49 13 04

CAR
ACI-AUTOMOBILE CLUB
D'ITALIA
Via S. Simone, 60
Tel. 28 30 00
Breakdown
services:
Tel. 54 11 60

Viale Marconi, 229
Tel. 49 56 69
or 49 58 77
Breakdown services:
Tel. 116

CAR RENTAL
◆ AVIS
Rail station
Tel. 66 81 28
Aeroporto
Elmas
Tel.
24 00 81
◆ HERTZ
Aeroporto
Elmas
Tel. 24 00 37
◆ EUROPCAR
Aeroporto Elmas
Tel. 24 01 26
◆ MAGGIORE-
BUDGET
Viale Monastir, 116
Tel. 27 36 92
Aeroporto Elmas
Tel. 24 00 69

PUBLIC TRANSPORT
A.C.T. AZIENDA
CONSORZIALE
TRASPORTI
Via Lunigiana, 29
Tel. 20081

TAXIS
RADIO TAXI 4 MORI
Tel. 40 01 01
RADIOTAXI FORZA
CAGLIARI
Tel. 65 70 70

HOTELS

FORTE AGIP*
Circonvallazione
Nuova, 626
Tel. 52 13 73
Fax 50 22 22
*Situated out of the
city center on
Route 131, this is
a classic first-class
motel. Air conditioning,
conference room,
disabled access.*
P � ⊡ ☐

ITALIA***
Via Sardegna, 31
Tel. 66 04 10
Fax 65 02 40
*This hotel is equipped
with every modern
convenience.
Air conditioning,
conference room.*
✳ ⊡ ☐

MEDITERRANEO**
Lungomare Colombo,
46
Tel. 30 12 71
Fax 30 12 74
*The hotel's lovely
garden of exotic plants
and its good location
near to the Santuario
di Bonaria make for
an exclusive stay here.
Air conditioning,
conference room,
disabled access.*
⋇ P ⊡ ☐

PANORAMA**
Viale Diaz, 231
Tel. 30 76 91
Fax 30 54 13
*In the vicinity of the
Fiera Campionaria,
this hotel is convenient
for business guests.
Air conditioning,
conference room,
disabled access.*
P ✳ ⌒ ⊡ ☐

**REGINA
MARGHERITA****
Viale Regina
Margherita, 44
Tel. 67 03 42
Fax 66 83 25
*This charming,
comfortable hotel
boasts good facilities.
Air conditioning,
disabled access.*
C P ✳ ⌒ ⊡ ☐

CAMPING AND TOURIST VILLAGES

**CAMPING
TONNARA**
Calasapone district,
in the network of streets

DIALING CODE 070

between San Antioco
and Distretto di Iglesias.
Tel. 80 90 58
Fax 0781-80 90 36

RESTAURANTS

AL PORTO
Via Sardegna, 44
Tel. 663131
Closed Mon. and
part of Jan.
*Elegantly decorated,
serving classic
Sardinian gastronomy
with the emphasis
on fish dishes.
Air conditioning.*

ANTICA HOSTARIA
Via Cavour, 60
Tel. 665870
Closed Sun. and
part of Aug.
*This small elegant
restaurant offers a
wide variety of regional
dishes, as well as some
interesting innovations.
Air conditioning.*

BASILIO
Via Satta, 112/A
Tel. 48 03 30
Closed Sun. and
part of Aug.
*A menu well balanced
between classic Italian
dishes and traditional
Sardinian fare, from
donkey meat to fish
kebabs. The excellent
desserts are not to be
missed. An interesting
selection of Sardinian
wines. Garden.*

BUONGUSTAIO
Via della Concezione, 7
Tel. 66 81 24
Closed Mon. evenings,
Tue. and throughout
Aug.
*Near the port, this
restaurant offers
Sardinian cuisine in a
convivial atmosphere.
Fish dishes a specialty.*

CORSARO
Viale Regina

Margherita, 28
Tel. 66 43 18
Fax 65 34 39
Closed Sun. and
throughout Aug.
*One of the most
renowned
restaurants in
all the island.
Typical
Sardinian
cuisine, with
fish specialties.
Air conditioning.*

CRACKERS
Corso Vittorio
Emanuele, 195
Tel. 65 39 12
Closed Wed. and
part of Nov. and Feb.
*This interesting trattoria
presents, along with
fish dishes, a fusion
of traditional Sardinian
and Piedmontese
gastronomy; thus
risotto is married
with "malloreddu", a
Sardinian grilled beef.*

FLORA
Via Sassari, 45
Tel. 664735
Closed Sun. and
part of Aug.
*Fish and meat dishes
created from the
freshest ingredients.
Food is based on
traditional recipes with
innovative modern
touches. Garden.*

ITALIA
Via Sardegna, 30
Tel. 65 79 87
Closed Sun. and
part of Aug.
*A restaurant with
modern furnishings; the
glass cases where the
fish is displayed, leave
one in no doubt of its
quality. Air conditioning.*

LANTERNA
Via Cugia, 7
Tel. 30 82 07
Closed Tue., and
part of Aug.

*Near the
Palazzo di
Giustizia,
Lanterna offers
traditional
Sardinian
dishes of
both meat
and fish. Air
conditioning.*

LILLICU
Via Sardegna, 78
Tel. 65 29 70
Closed Sun. and
part of Aug.
*Traditional cuisine from
Cagliari. Excellent
'burrida'
and crayfish. The
lamb dishes are also
particularly good.*

SAINT REMY
Via Torino, 16
Tel. 65 73 77
Closed Sun. and Sep.
*An inspired interior,
decorated as a 16th-
century pharmacy-
apothecary. The
atmosphere is intimate;
the cuisine offers the
very best of the
island's specialties.
Air conditioning.*

SAN CRISPINO
Corso Vittorio
Emanuele, 190
Tel. 65 18 53
Closed Mon., part of
July and throughout
Aug.
*Delicious Sardinian
cuisine from which the
tradition of the "bottarga",
of fresh cheeses, meats,
herbs and spices,
emerges and triumphs.
Good choice of
Sardinian wines.*

MUSEUMS AND GALLERIES
◆ CITTADELLA DEI MUSEI
Piazza Arsenale

◆ MUSEO ARCHEOLOGICO
NAZIONALE
(ARCHEOLOGICAL
MUSEUM)
Tel. 65 59 11
Closed Mon.
Open 9am– 2pm
◆ MUSEO SIAMESE
CARDU
Information
Tel. 60231
◆ PINACOTECA
NAZIONALE (NATIONAL
PICTURE GALLERY)
Tel. 67 01 57
Closed Mon. am
Open 8.30am–1.30pm,
2.30–7.30pm
◆ RACCOLTA DI
CERE ANATOMICHE
(COLLECTION OF
ANATOMICAL WAXWORKS)
Tel. 66 47 83
Closed Sun. Open
4–7pm Tue. and Thur.,
other days on request.
◆ GALLERIA COMUNALE
D'ARTE MODERNA
(MODERN ART GALLERY)
Viale Regina Elena
Tel. 49 07 27

★ DO NOT MISS ★
JAZZ IN SANT'ANNA ARRESI
A large music event, this traditional festival
plays host to the international greats of jazz,
from Wynton Marsalis to Chick Corea, and
also showcases the best Italian jazz bands.
The festival takes place in mid-August.
INFORMATION
Associazione Culturale *Punta Glara*
Piazza Martiri, 5 Sant'Anna Arresi
Tel. and fax 0781-96 70 18

On Mon. gallery is
open to educational
groups only
Open 9am–1pm,
4–7pm (winter);
9am–1pm, 5–8pm
(summer).
◆ MUSEO SARDO
DI ANTROPOLOGIA
ED ETNOLOGIA
Via Porcell, 2
Open 9am–1pm
◆ MUSEO DI BONARIA
c/o Santuario di Nostra
Signora di Bonaria
Tel. 30 17 47
Visits by appointment.

For information on
monuments and
cultural institutions not
listed here contact:
EPT
Piazza Deffenu, 9
Tel. 65 48 11
Fax 66 32 07

APPENDICES

◆ BIBLIOGRAPHY

ESSENTIAL ◆ READING ◆

◆ ACTON (H.) & CHANEY (E.): *Florence: A Traveller's Companion*, London, 1986

◆ BURCKHARDT (J.): *The Civilization of the Renaissance in Italy*, London, 1965

◆ GUNN (P.): *Naples, a palimpsest*, London, Chapman & Hill, 1961

◆ HAY (D.): *The Age of the Renaissance*, London, 1967

◆ HAY (D.): *The Italian Renaissance and its Historical Background*, Cambridge, 1961

◆ KING (F.): *Florence: A Literary Companion*, London, 1991

◆ LORENZETTI (G.): *Venice and Its Lagoon*, Rome, 1961

◆MASSON (G.): *Companion Guide to Rome*, London, 1965

◆MORRIS (J.):*Venice*, London, 1960; also *The Venetian Empire*, London, 1980

◆ NORWICH (J.J.): *The History of Venice*, London, 1988

◆ NORWICH (J.J.): *The Italian World*, ed., London, 1983

◆ STORTI (A.): *Rome, A Practical Guide*, Venice, 1980

◆ VARRIANO (J.): *Rome, A Literary Companion* London, 1991

GENERAL ◆ READING ◆

◆ ANDREWS (I.): *Pompeii*, Cambridge University Press, Cambridge, 1978

◆ BARZINI (L.): *The Italians*, Hamish Hamilton, 1964

◆ BARZINI (L.): *From Caesar to the Mafia - Sketches of Italian Life*, Hamish Hamilton, London, 1971

◆ BENTLEY (J.): *Rome: Architecture, History, Art*, London, 1991

◆ BORSOOK (E.): *Companion Guide to Florence*, London, 1966

◆ DAVID (E.): *Italian Food*, Macdonald, London, 1954

◆ ETIENNE (R.): *Pompeii, the day a city died*, Thames & Hudson, London, 1992

◆ FACAROS (D.) & PAULS (M.): *The Bay of Naples and the Amalfi Coast*, Cadogan, London, c. 1994

◆ GRANT (M.): *Cities of Vesuvius, Pompeii and Herculaneum*, Penguin Books, Harmondsworth, 1976

◆ HAUSER (E.D.): *Italy, A Cultural Guide*, New York, 1981

◆ Hutton (E.): *Rome*, London, 1950

◆ HUTTON (E.): *Naples and Campania Revisited*, London, 1958

◆ HUTTON (E.): *Florence, Assisi, and Umbria Revisited, Venice and Venetia, Siena and Southern Tuscany*, Hollis & Carter, 1958

◆ KAUFFMANN (G.): *Florence, Art Treasures and Buildings*, London, 1971

◆ KEATES (J.): *Italian Journeys*, Picador, 1991

◆ McCARTHY (M.): *The Stones of Florence and Venice Observed*, Penguin, 1986

◆ MULFORD (W.): *The Bay of Naples*, Reality Studios, London, c. 1992

◆ NEWBY (E.): *Love and War in the Appennines*, Picador, 1983

◆ NICHOLS (P.): *Italia, Italia*, Macmillan, 1973

◆ PARTNER (P.):*The Lands of St. Peter*, London, 1972

◆ PEREIRA (A.): *Rome*, London, 1990 *Pompeii, Naples and Southern Italy*, Batsford, London, 1977

◆ PICHEY (M.): *Naples and Campania*, A. & C. Black, London, 1994

◆ SEWARD (D.): *Naples, A Traveller's Companion*, Constable, London, 1984

◆ SHARP (M.): *A Guide to the Churches of Rome*, Philadelphia, 1966

◆ HISTORY ◆

◆ ACTON (H.): *The Bourbons of Naples*, Methuen, 1956

◆ BAKER (G.B.): *Twelve Centuries of Rome, 753 BC–AD 476*, London, 1936

◆ BALSDON (J.P.V.D.): *Julius Caesar and Rome*, Harmondsworth, 1967

◆ BENTLEY (J.H.): *Politics and Culture in Renaissance Naples*, Princeton University Press, Princeton, N.J., 1987

◆ BLUNT (A.): *Guide to Baroque Rome*, London, 1982

◆ BRENTANO (R.): *Rome before Avignon, a Social History of 13th-Century Rome*, London, 1991

◆ BROWN (H.): *Studies in the History of Venice, 2 vols*, London, 1907

◆ BRUCKER (G.A.): *Florence: 1138–1737*, London, 1984

◆ CALABRIA (A.): *The Cost of Empire – Finances of the Kingdom of Naples in the Time of Spanish Rule*, Cambridge University Press, Cambridge, 1991

◆ CARY (M.): *History of Rome down to the Reign of Constantine*, London and New York, 1935

◆ CHAMBERS (D.S.): *The Imperial Age of Venice, 1380-1580*, London 1970

◆ CLARK (A.): *Studies in Eighteenth Century's Roman Baroque*, London, 1982

◆ FINLAY (R.): *Politics in Renaissance Venice*, New Brunswick, 1980

◆ FRANK (T.): *Roman Buildings of the Republic*, Rome, 1924

◆ FRIEDMAN (J.): *Inside Rome*, London, 1993

◆ GIBBON (E.): *The Decline and Fall of the Roman Empire* (many editions)

◆ GINSBORG (P.): *A History of Contemporary Italy: Society and Politics 1943–88*, Penguin, 1990

◆ GRANT (M.): *The Roman Emperors, 31 BC–476 AD*, London

◆ HALE (J.R.): *Florence and the Medici*, London, 1977

◆ HALE (J.R.): *Ed., Renaissance Venice*, London, 1973

◆ HAZLITT (W.C.): *History of the Origin and Rise of the Venetian Republic, 2 vols*, London, 1900

◆ HIBBERT (C.): *Benito Mussolini*, Penguin, 1965

◆ JOLL (J.): *Gramsci*, Fontana, 1977

◆ KOGAN (N.): *A Political History of Post-War Italy*, Pall Mall Press, London, 1966

◆ KOGAN (N.): *The Government of Italy*, Thomas Y. Crowell, New York, 1982

◆ KOSTOF (S.): *The Third Rome, 1870-1950*, Berkeley, 1973

◆ KRAUTHEIMER (R.): *Rome, Profile of a City, 312–1308*, Princeton, 1980

◆ Kreutz (B.M.): *Before the Normans – Southern Italy in the Ninth and Tenth Centuries*, University of Pennsylvania Press, Philadelphia, 1991

◆ LANE (F.C.): *Venice,* a Maritime Republic, Baltimore, 1966

◆ LANE (F.C.): *Venice and History*, Baltimore, 1966

◆ LEWIS (N.) & REINHOLD (M.): *Roman Civilization: Vol.1, The Republic*, New York, 1952

◆ LEWIS (N.) & REINHOLD (M.): *Roman Civilization: Vol. 2, The Empire*, New York, 1955

◆ LLEWELLYN (P.): *Rome in the Dark Ages*, New York, 1971

◆ LONGWORTH (P.): *The Rise and Fall of Venice*, London, 1974

◆ MARTINELLI (G): ed., *The World of Renaissance Florence*, London, 1968

◆ MASSON (G): *Frederick II of Hohenstaufen*, London, 1957

◆ McNEIL (W.H.): *Venice, the Hinge of Europe 1081–1797*, University of Chicago, 1974

◆ MOMMSEN (T.): *The History of Rome* (many editions)

◆ MURRAY (P.): *Architecture of the Italian Renaissance*, London, 1960

◆ PARKER (J.H.): *The Archaelogy of Rome*, Oxford and London, 1974

◆ POPE-HENNESSY (J.): *Italian High Renaissance and Baroque Sculpture*, Vol. III, 3rd ed., Oxford, 1985

◆ PORTOGHESI (P.): *Rome of the Renaissance*, London, 1972

◆ PORTOGHESI (P.): *Baroque Rome*, London, 1970

◆ PROCACCI (G.): *History of the Italian People*, Penguin, 1973

◆ RUBINSTEIN (N.): *The Government of Florence under the Medici*, Oxford, 1966

◆ SCHEVIL (F.): *Medieval and Renaissance Florence*, London, 1961

◆ SISMONDI (J.C.L. DE): *A History of the Italian Republics*, London, 1907

◆ *The Vatican Collections, The Papacy and Art*, New York, Chicago and San Francisco, 1983

◆ TREVELYAN (R.): *Rome '44, the Battle for the Eternal City*, London, 1981

◆ VILLARI (R.): *The Revolt*

of Naples, trans. Newell (J.) & Marino (J.A.), Polity Press, Cambridge, 1993
◆ WALEY (D.): *The Papal State in the Thirteenth Century*, London, 1969
◆ WILKINSON (L.P.): *The Roman Experience*, London, 1975

ART AND ◆ ARCHITECTURE ◆

◆ ACKERMANN (J.S.): *The Architecture of Michelangelo*, London, 1961
◆ ANTHONY (F.W.): *Early Florentine Architecture and Decoration*, Cambridge, 1927
◆ BATTISTI (E.): *Brunelleschi, The Complete Work*, London, 1981
◆ BLUNT (A.): *Neapolitan Baroque and Rococo Architecture*, Zwemmer, London, 1975
◆ MCANDREW (J.): *Venetian Architecture of the Early Renaissance* M.I.T., Cambridge, Mass., 1980
◆ MARE (A.), SUKUXTER (I.P.J.) & TEMPLE (S.): *Around Midnight: Florence on Decadence*, Harvard Press, 1989
◆ MURRAY (P.): *The Architecture of the Italian Renaissance*, London, 1969
◆ PARSLOW (C.C.): *Rediscovering Antiquity, Karl Weber and the Excavation of Herculaneum, Pompeii and Stabiae*, Cambridge University Press, Cambridge, 1994
◆ RICHARDSON JNR (L.): *Pompeii, An Architectural History*, Johns Hopkins University Press, Baltimore, 1988
◆ ROSS (J.): *Florentine Palaces*, London, 1905
◆ RUSKIN (J.): *The Stones of Venice, 3 Vols.*, London, 1851–53
◆ RUSKIN (J.): *St. Mark's Rest*, London, 1877
◆ SALVADORI (A.): *Architect's Guide to Venice*, Canal Libri, Venice, 1990
◆ VASARI (G.): *Lives of the Painters, Sculptors and Architects*, London, 1927
◆ WITTKOWER (R.): *Art and Architecture of Italy, 1600–1750*, London, 1991

PAINTING AND ◆ SCULPTURE ◆

◆ ANTAL (F): *Florentine*
Painting and its Social Background, London, 1948
◆ ARGAN (G.C.): *Botticelli*, Geneva, 1989
◆ BATTISTI (E.): *Giotto*, Geneva, 1990
◆ BAXANDALL (M.): *Painting and Experience in 15th-Century Italy*, Oxford, 1975
◆ BERENSON (R.): *The Italian Painters of the Renaissance*, Oxford, 1957–68
◆ BORSOOK (E.): *The Mural Painters of Tuscany*, London, 1960
◆ CLARK (K.): *Florentine Painting: 15th Century*, London, 1945
◆ *Frescoes from Florence*, Hayward Gallery, London, 1969
◆ LAIDLAW (A.): *The First Style in Pompeii, Painting and Architecture*, Bretschneider, Rome, 1985
◆ LEVEY (M.): *Painting in 18th-Century Venice*, University of London, 1959
◆ MORGAN (C.H.): *The Life of Michelangelo*, New York, London, 1961
◆ NAPIER (Lord): *Notes on Modern Painting at Naples*, London, 1855
◆ OFFNER (R.): *A Critical and Historical Corpus of Florentine Paintings*, New York, 1947
◆ *Pompeii AD79, Treasures from the National Archeological Museum, Naples, and the Pompeii Antiquarium*, Museum of Fine Arts, Boston, 1978
◆ POPE-HENESSY (J.): *Italian Renaissance Sculpture*, London, 1958
◆ POWELL (C.): *Turner in the South: Rome, Naples, Florence*, Yale University Press, New Haven, Conn., 1987
◆ ROSSI (M.): *The Uffizi and Pitti Galleries*, London, 1964
◆ SCHULTZ (J.): *Venetian Painted Ceilings of the Renaissance*, University of California, Berkeley
◆ *The Genius of Venice (1500–1600)*, (catalogue of the exhibition), Royal Academy of Arts, London, 1983
◆ *Tiziano* (catalogue of the exhibition), Marsilio, Venice, 1990
◆ WHITEFIELD (C.) & MORTIMER (J.): *Painting in Naples 1606–1705, from Caravaggio to Giordano*, Catalogue, Royal

Academy of Arts, London, 1982

LANGUAGE AND ◆ LITERATURE ◆

◆ ALIGHIERI (Dante): *Italiano Antico e Nuovo*, Milan, 1988
◆ BOCCACCIO (G): *The Decameron*, London, 1741, and many later translations
◆ BYRON (LORD): *Childe Harold*, London 1812–17 (many editions)
◆ BYRON (Lord): *Beppo, A Venetian Story*, London
◆ CALVINO (I.): *Invisible Cities, If Upon a Winter's Night a Traveller*, Picador
◆ CRAVEN (R.K.): *A Tour through the Southern Provinces of the Kingdom of Naples*, London, 1821
◆ DICKENS (C.): *Pictures from Italy*, London, 1846
◆ FORSTER (E.M.): *A Room with a View*, London, 1908
◆ GOETHE (J.W. VON): *Italian Journey* (tr. W.H. Auden and E. Mayer), London and New York, 1968
◆ GRANT (M.): *Latin Literature, an Anthology*, Harmondsworth, 1978 ed., *Roman Readings*, Harmondsworth, 1958
◆ GRAVES (R.): *I Claudius*, London, 1934
◆ HEMINGWAY (E.): *Across the River and into the Trees*, Cape, London, 1952
◆ HOFFMANNSTHAL (H. VON): *Andreas*, 1930
◆ KEATS (J.): *The Letters of John Keats*, ed., Forman (M.B.), Oxford University Press, London, 1931
◆ LAWRENCE (D.H.): *Etruscan Places*, Olive Press
◆ LIVY: *History of Rome* (many translations)
◆ MANN (T.): *Death in Venice*
◆ MELVILLE (H.): *At the Hostelry and Naples in the Time of Bomba*, ed., Poole (G.) Instituto Universario Orientale, Naples, 1989
◆ MILTON (J.): *The Works of John Milton*, Vol. VIII, Columbia University Press, New York, 1933
◆ MONTAIGNE (M. DE): *The Journal of Montaigne's Travels in Italy*, London, 1903
◆ MORTON (H.V.): *A Traveller in Southern Italy*,

Methuen & Co. Ltd., London, 1969
◆ NIGHTINGALE (F.): *Florence Nightingale in Rome. Letters Written in the Winter of 1847–48*, Philadelphia, 1981
◆ PETRACH (F.): *Canzoniere and Other Works*, Oxford, 1985
◆ RUSKIN (J.): *Mornings in Florence*, London, 1876
◆ SANDYS (G.): *A Relation of a Journey Begun AD 1610*, Alfred Knopf, New York, 1986
◆ SHAKESPEARE (W.): *Julius Caesar*
◆ SHAKESPEARE (W.): *The Merchant of Venice*
◆ SHELLEY (P. B.): *Collected Works*
◆ STENDHAL: *A Roman Journal* (tr. H. Chevalier), London, 1959
◆ STENDHAL: *Rome, Naples, Florence* (tr. R.N. Coe), London, 1959
◆ SUETONIUS: *The Twelve Caesars* (tr. R. Graves), Harmondsworth, 1957
◆ TACITUS: *The Histories, The Annals* (several translations)
◆ TWAIN (M.): *Innocents Abroad*, Hartford, Connecticut, 1869
◆ WHITFIELD (H.): *Petrarch and the Renaissance*, Oxford, 1943
◆ WILDE (O.): *A Florentine Tragedy*, London, 1895
◆ ZOLA (E.): *Rome* (tr. E.A. Vitzetelly), New York, 1896

◆ FILMOGRAPHY ◆

◆ *The Belly of an Architect*, GREENAWAY P., 1987
◆ *Ben Hur*, WYLER W., 1959
◆ *Cleopatra*, MANKIEWICZ J.L., 1963
◆ *La Dolce Vita*, FELLINI F., 1960
◆ *The Fall of the Roman Empire*, BRANSTON S., 1964
◆ *Fellini Roma*, FELLINI F., 1971
◆ *Fellini-Satyricon*, FELLINI F., 1969
◆ *Julius Caesar*, MANKIEWICZ J.L., 1953
◆ *Nights of Cabiria*, F. FELLINI, 1957
◆ *Roman Holiday*, WYLER W., 1953
◆ *Roman Spring of Mrs Stone*, QUINTERO J., 1961
◆ *Rome, Città aperta*, ROSSELLINI F., 1945
◆ *Three Coins in a Fountain*, NEGULESCO J., 1954

◆ LIST OF ILLUSTRATIONS

◆ List of illustrations

482 Painting from the Tomb of Ureo, 3rd century BC, Tuvixeddu necropolis.
Eleonora of Arborea, Castello di Sanluri, © Archivio fotografico TCI.
482–483 Cagliari, from *Theatrum Orbis Terrarum*, 1570, Biblioteca Estense, Modena, © Realy Easy Star/T. Spagone.
483 The Savoy royal family arrives at Cagliari, 1799, watercolor painted by Vittorio Emanuele I, Civica Raccolta Stampe A. Bertarelli, Milan.
The port, © Realy Easy Star/S. Zanardi
484 Cupola of the Duomo, © Il Dagherrotipo/G. Rinaldi.
485 Tower of the Elephant, detail, © Marka/A. Quattrocchi.
Bastione di Saint-Rémy from the terrazza Umberto I, © Il Dagherrotipo/R. D'Errico.
486 Bracelet with winged scarab, palms and lotus flowers, from Tharros, 7–6th centuries BC, Museo Archeologico Nazionale, Cagliari, © Archivio fotografico TCI.
Tribal chief, from Uta, Nuraghic bronze, Museo Archeologico Nazionale, Cagliari, © Scala.
Glass jewel, Phoenician art, Museo Archeologico Nazionale, Cagliari, © Marka/A. Quattrocchi.
Crucifixion, A. Mainas, Pinacoteca Nazionale, Cagliari.
487 Castello from the Porta dei Leoni, © Marka/A. Quattrocchi.
The Stampace district, © idem.
Statue of Carlo Felice, at the entrance of highway 131, © idem.
488 Entrance to the Grotta della Vipera, 1st century AD, © Marka/A. Quattrocchi.
Flamingo, watercolor lithograph, 19th century, Civica Raccolta Stampe A. Bertarelli, Milan.
488–489 Flamingos, Cagliari, © Marka/C. Dogliani.
489 Church of San Salvatore, © Realy Easy Star/R. Barni.
Sanctuary and Basilica of Bonaria, © Il Dagherrotipo/R. D'Errico.
Roman Amphitheater,

© Marka/A. Quattrocchi.
492 Peony, (paeonia mascula), symbol of Sardinia, © Panda Photo/L. Cinaciotto.
Cagliari, festival of Sant' Efisio, © Il Dagherrotipo/G. Rinaldi.
Idem, © Il Dagherrotipo/R. D'Errico.
Excavations at Nora, © Marka/J. Huber.
493 Costa del Sud, © Il Dagherrotipo/G. Rinaldi.
Tophet ofi Sant'Antioco, © Archivio fotografico TCI/F. Radino.
Barumini, Su Nuraxi, © Il Dagherrotipo/M. Ravasini.
Giara di Gesturi, horses, © Realy Easy Star/G. Corte.
494 Mask of Silenus, from Tharros, terracotta, 5–4th centuries BC, Museo Archeologico Nazionale, Cagliari.
Head of a woman, from Tharros, terracotta, 6th century BC, idem.
Bosa, tanneries along the the banks of the Temo, © Marka/A. Quattrochi.
Bosa, high relief, featuring saints, Church of San Pietro, © idem.
495 Alghero, bell-tower of the church of San Francesco, © Marka/M. Capovilla.
A myrtle branch, © Panda Photo/A. Pedretti.
Santu Antine nurhags, © Il Dagherrotipo/G. Rinaldi.
496 Santissima Trinità di Saccargia, © Realy Easy Star/Piga & Catalano.
Costa Smeralda, © Marka/J. Huber.
Garibaldi at Caprera, Mantegazza, oil on canvas, 1885, Museo del Risorgimento, Milan.

◆ INDEX

Page numbers in bold refer to the
Practical information section.

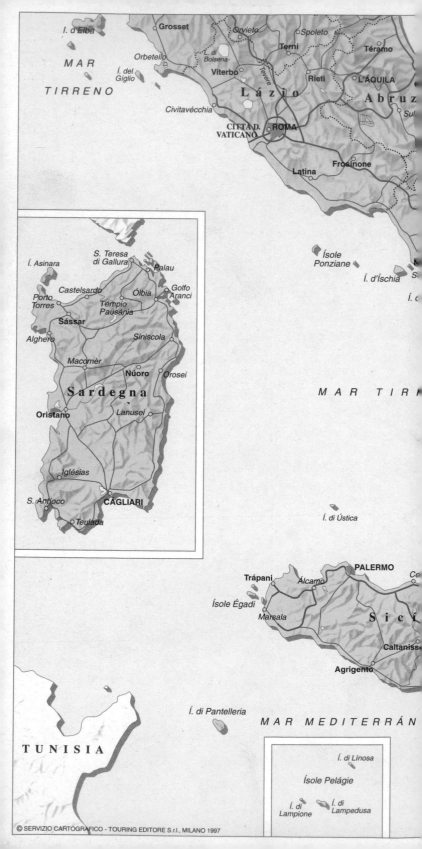

MAR TIRRENO

I. d'Elba

Grosset

Orbetello

Orvieto

Spoleto

Terni

Téramo

I. del Giglio

L. di Bolsena

Viterbo

Tevere

Rieti

L'ÁQUILA

Civitavécchia

Lázio

Abruz

Sul

CITTA D. VATICANO

ROMA

Latina

Frosinone

Ísole Ponziane

I. d'Íschia

I. c

S

S. Teresa di Gallura

Palau

Castelsardo

Ólbia

Golfo Aranci

Porto Torres

Témpio Pausánia

I. Asinara

Sássar

Siniscola

Alghero

Macomèr

Núoro

Crosei

Sardegna

Lanusei

Oristano

Iglésias

S. Antioco

CÁGLIARI

Teulada

MAR TIRI

I. di Ústica

PALERMO

Ce

Trápani

Álcamo

Ísole Égadi

Marsala

Sicí

Caltaníss

Agrigento

I. di Pantelleria

MAR MEDITERRÁN

TUNISIA

I. di Linosa

Ísole Pelágie

I. di Lampione

I. di Lampedusa

© SERVIZIO CARTOGRAFICO - TOURING EDITORE S.r.l., MILANO 1997